The Effective Teaching of Language Arts

SIXTH EDITION

Donna E. Norton
Texas A & M University

PEARSON

Merrill
Prentice Hall

Upper Saddle River, New Jersey
Columbus, Ohio

Library of Congress Cataloging-in-Publication Data

Norton, Donna E.
    The effective teaching of language arts / Donna E. Norton.—6th ed.
        p. cm.
    Includes bibliographical references and index.
    ISBN 0-13-111730-0
        1. Language arts (Elementary) I. Title.

LB1576.N84 2004
372.6—dc21   2002193106

Vice President and Executive Publisher: Jeffery W. Johnston
Senior Editor: Linda Ashe Montgomery
Production Editor: Mary M. Irvin
Design Coordinator: Diane C. Lorenzo
Production Coordination: Amy Gehl, Carlisle Publishers Services
Cover Designer: Ali Mohrman
Cover Image: Getty One
Production Manager: Pamela D. Bennett
Director of Marketing: Ann Castel Davis
Marketing Manager: Darcy Betts Prybella
Marketing Coordinator: Tyra Poole
Photo Coordinator: Kathy Kirtland

Photo Credits: Karen Mancinelli/Pearson Learning, pp. 2, 421; Barbara Schwartz/Merrill, pp. 9, 12, 70, 116, 173, 214, 232, 235, 341, 360, 415, 456; Tom Watson/Merrill, pp. 11, 15; Anthony Magnacca/Merrill, pp. 22, 166, 175, 328, 546, 567; Anne Vega/Merrill, pp. 26, 29, 41, 72, 125, 226, 276, 302, 307, 318, 380, 484, 494, 498, 504; Dan Floss/Merrill, p. 60; Todd Yarrington/Merrill, pp. 90, 93, 459; Scott Cunningham/Merrill, pp. 121, 241, 257, 293, 355, 385, 394, 462, 551, 552; Susan Woog Wagner/PH Merrill, p. 131; Pearson Learning, p. 144; Linda Peterson/Merrill, pp. 168, 217, 412, 443; Houghton Mifflin Company, p. 194; Silver Burdett Ginn, p. 330; Jean Greenwald/Merrill, p. 471.

This book was set in New Caledonia by Carlisle Communications, Ltd., and was printed and bound by Courier Kendallville, Inc. The cover was printed by the Lehigh Press, Inc.

Pearson Education Ltd.
Pearson Education Singapore Pte. Ltd.
Pearson Education Canada, Ltd.
Pearson Education—Japan

Pearson Education Australia Pty. Limited
Pearson Education North Asia Ltd.
Pearson Educación de Mexico, S.A. de C.V.
Pearson Education Malaysia Pte. Ltd.

10 9 8 7 6 5 4 3 2 1
ISBN 0-13-111730-0

Preface

Effective teaching of language arts requires commitment to excellence on the part of class-room teachers. The language arts include speaking, listening, reading, and writing. Excellence cannot be attained without thorough knowledge of the language arts and understanding of methods that develop language arts abilities in children.

Because teachers are accountable to the children they teach, to the administrators of the school, and to the parents, they must have knowledge about their students. Diagnostic procedures are suggested for evaluating children's strengths, weaknesses, and interests. This test includes numerous formal and informal assessment strategies that will improve the teaching of the language arts.

Diagnosis is worthless, however, without research-based knowledge about learning environments, motivation, objectives, instructional procedures, grouping, and teacher effectiveness. Because effective teaching is built on a solid knowledge base, the latest research citations have been added to this edition. In addition, examples of lesson plans, instructional/thematic units, and learning centers demonstrate how theory can inform classroom practice. The successful use of these ideas with children is indicated by the inclusion of examples of children's oral and written responses.

For preservice teachers needing experience planning lessons, evaluating language arts abilities, or teaching a lesson, activities designed to help students apply these abilities are included throughout each chapter and at the conclusion of each chapter. All of the "For Your Development" activities have been used with college language arts classes or as inservice presentations with experienced teachers. The professor and the students may choose as many of these activities as they wish in order to develop the objectives of the chapter and to explore effective teaching strategies.

Each chapter in this text contains features geared to the development of effective language arts instruction. At the beginning of each chapter, chapter objectives are listed to provide an overview of content, preview the materials to be covered, and stress the major concepts to be mastered.

The chapters on tools for writing—grammar and mechanics, handwriting, and spelling—have been maintained and updated. There is currently an increased interest in improving children's abilities in all of these areas.

Changes to This Edition

This new edition of *The Effective Teaching of Language Arts* includes the following:

1. A "Best Practices" table has been added to Chapter 1, which lists the chapters in the book that deal with the instructional strategies developed around these best practices for teaching based on recent research.

2. A significant amount of new children's literature titles have been added throughout the book, including a variety of new uses and activities with which to use these latest works.
3. Chapter 5 goes into detail regarding the recent research on "best practices" for teaching, as well as reviewing approaches that increase phonemic awareness and phonics and vocabulary understanding. Assessing students' reading abilities is also covered.
4. Chapter 8 offers a new section on the authentication of literature, including projects and activities for use with students to help them learn this valuable skill.
5. A new section on using literature models of effective sentences and paragraphs for teaching is included in Chapter 10.
6. Chapter 11 offers the latest on handwriting research, including a list of guidelines for effective handwriting instruction and new lesson plan ideas.
7. The newest titles in multicultural literature have been incorporated into Chapter 12, as well as the latest research on teaching English as a second language. An updated and greatly expanded section on multicultural education has been added as well, including new lesson plans geared toward integrating Latino, African American and other cultures into teaching. Developing a multicultural storytelling festival for the classroom is also detailed.

The goal of this text is to provide support, motivation, and knowledge for the classroom teacher who is responsible for the effective teaching of all children. This goal can be achieved if we can instill in teachers a commitment to excellence.

Discover the Companion Website Accompanying This Book

The Prentice Hall Companion Website: A Virtual Learning Environment

Technology is a constantly growing and changing aspect of our field that is creating a need for content and resources. To address this emerging need, Prentice Hall has developed an online learning environment for students and professors alike—Companion Websites—to support our textbooks.

In creating a Companion Website, our goal is to build on and enhance what the textbook already offers. For this reason, the content for each user-friendly website is organized by topic and provides the professor and student with a variety of meaningful resources. Common features of a Companion Website include:

For the Professor—

Every Companion Website integrates **Syllabus Manager™,** an online syllabus creation and management utility.

- **Syllabus Manager™** provides you, the instructor, with an easy, step-by-step process to create and revise syllabi, with direct links into the Companion Website and other online content without having to learn HTML.
- Students may logon to your syllabus during any study session. All they need to know is the web address for the Companion Website and the password you've assigned to your syllabus.

- After you have created a syllabus using **Syllabus Manager™,** students may enter the syllabus for their course section from any point in the Companion Website.
- Clicking on a date, the student is shown the list of activities for the assignment. The activities for each assignment are linked directly to actual content, saving time for students.
- Adding assignments consists of clicking on the desired due date, then filling in the details of the assignment—name of the assignment, instructions, and whether or not it is a one-time or repeating assignment.
- In addition, links to other activities can be created easily. If the activity is online, a URL can be entered in the space provided, and it will be linked automatically in the final syllabus.
- Your completed syllabus is hosted on our servers, allowing convenient updates from any computer on the Internet. Changes you make to your syllabus are immediately available to your students at their next logon.

For the Student—

- **Topic Overviews**—Outline key concepts in topic areas.
- **Strategies**—These websites provide suggestions and information on how to implement instructional strategies and activities for each topic. The Assessment topic also contains Practice Case Studies as well.
- **Web Links**—A wide range of websites that allow the students to access current information on everything from rationales for specific types of instruction, to research on related topics, to compilations of useful articles, and more.
- **Electronic Bluebook**—Send homework or essays directly to your instructor's email with this paperless form.
- **Message Board**—Virtual bulletin board to post or respond to questions or comments from a national audience.
- **Chat**—Real-time chat with anyone who is using the text anywhere in the country— ideal for discussion and study groups, class projects, etc.

To take advantage of these and other resources, please visit *The Effective Teaching of Language Arts,* Sixth Edition, Companion Website at

www.prenhall.com/norton

Acknowledgments

I would like to extend my thanks to the following reviewers of this edition: Alan F. Cook, University of Illinois at Springfield; Thomas Devine, University of Massachusetts, Lowell; Marsha Savage, Santa Clara University; and Lana Smith, University of Memphis. My thanks to the Merrill/Prentice Hall editors who produced this text: Linda Montgomery, Mary Irvin, and Amy Gehl and the production services staff.

Contents

PART II   *Developing the Language Arts*   59

Note: Every effort has been made to provide accurate and current Internet information in this book. However, the Internet and information posted on it are constantly changing, so it is inevitable that some of the Internet addresses listed in this textbook will change.

Special Features

For Your Plan Book: Unit and Lesson Plans

About the Author

Following the completion of her doctorate at the University of Wisconsin, Madison, Donna E. Norton joined the College of Education faculty at Texas A & M University where she teaches courses in children's literature, language arts, and reading. Dr. Norton is the 1992 recipient of the Virginia Hamilton Essay Award. She is listed in *Who's Who of American Women, Who's Who in America,* and *Who's Who in the World.*

Dr. Norton is the author of four books in addition to this volume—*Through the Eyes of a Child: An Introduction to Children's Literature,* 6th ed., *Language Arts Activities for Children,* 5th ed., *The Impact of Literature-Based Reading,* and *Multicultural Children's Literature . . . Through the Eyes of Many Children.* She is on the editorial board of several journals and is a frequent contributor to journals and presenter at professional conferences. The focus of her current research is multicultural literature, comparative literature and reading, and literature-based reading programs. The multicultural research includes a longitudinal study of multicultural literature in classroom settings. This research is supported by grants from the Meadows Foundation and the Texas A & M Research Association. In conjunction with the research in comparative education, she developed a graduate course that enables students to study children's literature and reading instruction in England and Scotland and is evaluating educational programs in several Asian and European countries. She is currently involved in research and storytelling.

Prior to her college teaching experience, Dr. Norton was an elementary teacher in River Falls, Wisconsin and in Madison, Wisconsin. She was a Language Arts/Reading Consultant for federally funded kindergarten through adult basic education programs. In this capacity she developed, provided in-service instruction, and evaluated kindergarten programs, summer reading and library programs, remedial reading programs, learning disability programs for middle school children, elementary and secondary literature programs for the gifted, and diagnostic and intervention programs for adults with reading disabilities. Dr. Norton's continuing concern for literature programs results in frequent consultations with educators from various disciplines, librarians, and school administrators and teachers.

Part I

Language as the Key to Communication

Introduction to the Language Arts

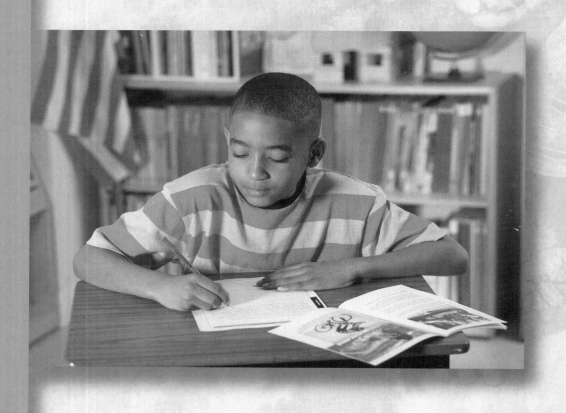

After completing this introductory chapter, you will be able to:

1. Describe the contents and importance of the language arts curriculum.
2. Identify "best practices" for teaching the language arts and describe how best practices will be developed throughout this text.
3. Describe the format of this textbook.
4. Identify current issues that affect language arts instruction.
5. Evaluate elementary language arts textbooks based on national guidelines for judging and selecting these textbooks.

*L*anguage is the most important form of human communication. Language communication includes speaking, writing, listening, and reading and, as such, it is the most important and the most exciting part of the elementary curriculum. Its importance is reflected in estimates that the average person listens to the equivalent of a book each day, talks the equivalent of a book each week, reads the equivalent of a book each month, and writes the equivalent of a book each year. It is your responsibility as a language arts teacher to promote the ability to communicate effectively. The purpose of this textbook is to provide you with effective methods for developing language arts skills in all children.

The Language Arts Curriculum

A brief overview of the language arts curriculum reinforces the suggestion that the language arts are both important and exciting. In an elementary school where learning is taking place, the teachers use language arts in all areas of the curriculum. Exciting learning experiences are developed in all areas as teachers integrate the various language arts and the content areas. Thematic units are frequently one way in which teachers integrate both the language arts and the content areas. Consequently, this text will include numerous units within each chapter that show how integration across the curriculum may be accomplished.

Literature is a dynamic part of effective language arts classrooms. Books are everywhere. Effective teachers read to the students and allow them many opportunities to read for enjoyment and to discuss the books they read with other children. The teachers model behavior and help children through the decision-making process as they approach various literary elements in literature. A classroom where literature is important should contain a colorful library corner with attractive and comfortable places for children to read. Children should share their books through creative oral, written, and art ideas. Consequently, literature provides an excellent means for both integrating the curriculum and developing thematic units.

Most important, teachers should read and tell stories to the students so that the students know storytelling is a wonderful experience. Use literature to stimulate research and interest in social studies and science subjects. A class studying the westward expansion of the United States, for example, can add to its knowledge of frontier life by reading the "Little House" books by Laura Ingalls Wilder. A class studying science can learn more about a famous scientist by reading a biography or autobiography. In this environment, teachers evaluate the interests of the students in literature and their ability to read and then use this information to help the children find books to read and enjoy.

3

Because oral language is a vital form of human communication, effective teachers provide many opportunities for oral language development and do not assume that oral language skills cannot be improved. Good oral questioning strategies focus on an initial question, extend information and understanding, clarify facts, and raise the comprehension levels of children. Exciting discussions take place in all subject areas when teachers use oral questioning strategies that encourage children to develop their individual thought processes. Discussions are also extended through such techniques as buzz sessions, round table and panel discussions, and debates.

Original drama is an extremely exciting method for developing creative thinking and oral language skills. In a stimulating elementary school, children are presenting puppet plays, doing improvisations, using creative play activities, pantomiming characters and objects, role-playing experiences, and doing choral poetry reading. Children in such an environment are involved in all aspects of oral language, and the teachers increase the participation of students in oral language as they evaluate and improve it.

The teachers in this environment recognize that effective oral language instruction requires an audience, and that this audience needs to refine its listening skills. Research shows that listening skills can be improved through instruction, although both evaluation and instruction are complicated. Listening includes hearing; auditory discrimination; literal, interpretational, critical, and evaluational comprehension; and appreciation. Effective language arts teachers recognize the importance of each aspect of listening. They use audiometers to screen children suspected of hearing loss; auditory discrimination tests to identify students who have problems with auditory perception; informal tests to identify children who have problems with achievement due to inattentive listening; and listening comprehension tests to evaluate the ability of students to restate, interpret, and critically evaluate what they hear.

Teachers use the information obtained through evaluation to provide exciting and effective learning activities. To develop auditory awareness, have young children listen to and describe sounds they hear in their environment. Have them listen to music, rhymes, and limericks to become aware of the lovely sounds in our language. To improve auditory discrimination, have them listen to and describe likenesses and differences in sounds, words, and rhymes. Many of these discrimination activities can take the format of games. To develop attentive listening skills, help children set purposes for listening, provide opportunities for children to give as well as follow directions, and provide instruction that requires children to listen for specific purposes. Many stimulating methods can help children develop listening comprehension. In one class, children might listen to a taped conversation between two famous people for the purpose of identifying the individuals. Another class might listen to the beginning of a story and then predict its outcome. Students can listen to commercials and critically evaluate the propaganda techniques or develop appreciative listening skills by listening to poetry, music, or literature for pure enjoyment.

Teachers in an effective language arts curriculum provide many opportunities for children to develop their writing skills. Such teachers should keep folders of each child's writing so that the student and teacher can evaluate growth in writing. The environment is critical when developing writing skills. Stimulate, react to ideas, confer with the writer, listen to and read the writing, and provide opportunities for sharing writing, rather than merely assign projects and provide group instruction. Stimulation is essential. Before children write poetry, let them go out into a field or the woods to experience nature; before they write a creative story, let them listen to music or discuss a thought-provoking item or picture. Have the children in this environment experience the development of a composition by identifying their audience and purpose, deciding on the subject, and organizing their ideas. Also have them write a great deal—biographies, classroom newspapers, and creative stories.

Effective language arts curriculums also include the more mechanical aspects of written and oral language. Young children experience readiness activities for handwriting. First-grade children are usually instructed in manuscript printing. About third grade, children receive instruction in switching from manuscript to cursive writing. Numerous writing activities in the classroom offer opportunities to use and improve handwriting skills. Because the study of modern grammar stresses that children should understand their language, effective language arts teachers use activities such as sentence-pattern exploration, sentence combining, sentence expansion, and sentence transformation to allow children to explore language and discover how it works. Children also examine appropriate levels of usage. They learn that different levels of usage are appropriate for different audiences and purposes. Instruction is flexible and increases the levels of usage available to the children. Effective teachers assess spelling levels and provide instruction at the appropriate level for each child.

Language arts instruction that utilizes the various media can be highly motivating for many children. Multimedia studies include television and other media as integral parts of the curriculum. Creative teachers use television to motivate reading, to develop discussion skills, and to develop critical thinking. Commercial films and filmstrips can add visual interpretations to books, stimulate creative writing, and stimulate oral expression. A visit to an effective language arts class might find the students actively involved in making their own film, providing a musical background for it, and showing the finished product to an appreciative audience. Another class might be developing critical evaluation skills by studying propaganda techniques used in newspaper, television, and radio commercials. The students can distinguish fact from opinion in newspapers or write their own newspaper ads, news stories, or special features. A class-produced newspaper, television show, radio program, or film is an exciting culminating activity for a study of media. Computers may be used to increase writing efficiency or to develop desktop publishing products. CD-ROMs expose students to new environments in the classroom.

The subjects covered in the language arts curriculum are obviously important. Effective language arts teachers must be able to provide instruction in each of these subject areas—oral language, literature, reading, listening, written composition, handwriting, grammar, usage, media, and using references—to a wide variety of children. There is also a need to integrate the language arts across the curriculum. This text is designed to prepare prospective teachers for this exciting work.

"Best Practices" for Teaching the Language Arts

There is currently considerable interest in developing language arts and literacy instruction based on research. Educators use terms such as *research-based education* and *best practices* for teaching. This edition of *The Effective Teaching of Language Arts* includes the best practices that have been identified through careful research.

As you read and study each of the chapters you will find references to such sources as *Handbook of Research on Teaching the English Language Arts*, second edition (Flood, Jensen, Lapp, & Squire, 2002), *Schools That Work: Where All Children Read and Write*, second edition (Allington & Cunningham, 2002), *An Educators' Guide to School Reform* (American Institutes for Research, 1999), *Misreading Reading: The Bad Science That Hurts Children* (Cole, 2000), *Classrooms That Work: They Can All Read and Write*, third edition (Cunningham & Allington, 2003), "Examining Evidence: New IRA Position Statement on Evidence-Based Reading Instruction" (2002), *Report of the National Reading Panel* (2000), and *Literacy at the Crossroads* (Routman, 1996).

Table 1–1 identifies many of these best practices and lists the chapters in which you can locate instructional strategies that are developed around these best practices. As you analyze

Table 1–1   Best practices and locations within the language arts book

Best Practices	Language Arts Chapters
1. Read aloud to students	Listening; Literature and the Language Arts; Composition: Expressive, Imaginative, and Expository Writing; Multicultural Education: Working with Children Whose First Language Is Not English
2. Provide time for independent reading	Literature and the Language Arts; Library and Reference Skills
3. Allow children to make choices	Reading and the Language Arts; Literature and the Language Arts; Library and Reference Skills
4. Expose children to a wide range of materials	Language and Cognitive Development; Oral Language Development; Listening; Literature and the Language Arts; Composition: The Writing Process; Composition: Expressive, Imaginative, and Expository Writing; Multicultural Education: Working with Children Whose First Language Is Not English; Library and Reference Skills
5. Use modeling in teaching	Oral Language Development; Literature and the Language Arts; Reading and the Language Arts; Composition: The Writing Process; Composition: Expressive, Imaginative, and Expository Writing; Handwriting
6. Emphasize comprehension during instruction	Oral Language Development; Listening; Reading and the Language Arts; Literature and the Language Arts
7. Activate prior knowledge	Oral Language Development; Listening; Reading and the Language Arts; Literature and the Language Arts; Composition: The Writing Process
8. Make predictions	Language and Cognitive Development; Listening; Reading and the Language Arts
9. Provide after-reading applications	Literature and the Language Arts; Composition: Expressive, Imaginative, and Expository Writing
10. Expand students' vocabularies	Literature and the Language Arts; Composition: Expressive, Imaginative, and Expository Writing
11. Provide guided instruction	Oral Language Development; Literature and the Language Arts; Composition: The Writing Process; Grammar, Usage, and the Mechanics of Language; Handwriting
12. Use graphic and semantic organizers	Listening; Composition: The Writing Process; Composition: Expressive, Imaginative, and Expository Writing; Multicultural Education: Working with Children Whose First Language Is Not English
13. Provide instruction in phonemic awareness	Listening; Reading and the Language Arts; Spelling
14. Follow questioning strategies with immediate feedback	Reading and the Language Arts
15. Use story structures	Listening; Literature and the Language Arts; Composition: Expressive, Imaginative, and Expository Writing
16. Teach summarizing	Language and Cognitive Development; Composition: Expressive, Imaginative, and Expository Writing
17. Teach integration of ideas and generalizations	Listening; Reading and the Language Arts; Literature and the Language Arts; Composition: Expressive, Imaginative, and Expository Writing; Library and Reference Skills
18. Develop balanced programs	Literature and the Language Arts; Composition: The Writing Process; Composition: Expressive, Imaginative, and Expository Writing; Multicultural Education: Working with Children Whose First Language Is Not English
19. Improve phonemic awareness	Listening; Reading and the Language Arts; Spelling
20. Teach vocabulary both directly and indirectly	Language and Cognitive Development; Reading and the Language Arts

Best Practices	Language Arts Chapters
21. Relate new vocabulary to previous experience (schema)	Language and Cognitive Development; Reading and the Language Arts
22. Expand word knowledge into multiple meanings	Language and Cognitive Development
23. Develop vocabulary webs	Language and Cognitive Development; Reading and the Language Arts
24. Teach contextual clues	Reading and the Language Arts
25. Encourage discussions	Oral Language Development; Literature and the Language Arts; Composition: The Writing Process; Composition: Expressive, Imaginative, and Expository Writing
26. Use writing associated with reading	Composition: The Writing Process; Composition: Expressive, Imaginative, and Expository Writing
27. Teach skills in context of meaningful literature	Oral Language Development; Literature and the Language Arts; Composition: The Writing Process; Composition: Expressive, Imaginative, and Expository Writing; Grammar, Usage, and the Mechanics of Language; Library and Reference Skills
28. Motivate students	Oral Language Development; Listening; Literature and the Language Arts; Composition: Expressive, Imaginative, and Expository Writing
29. Build foundations for word attack strategies	Spelling; Grammar, Usage, and the Mechanics of Language
30. Expand vocabulary through concept books	Language and Cognitive Development
31. Use drama to help understanding of language	Oral Language Development
32. Use journal writing learning logs	Composition: Expressive, Imaginative, and Expository Writing
33. Use thematic units to expand understanding	Listening; Reading and the Language Arts; Literature and the Language Arts; Composition: Expressive, Imaginative, and Expository Writing; Multicultural Education: Working with Children Whose First Language Is Not English; Handwriting
34. Use interactive and cooperative classroom study	Oral Language Development; Composition: The Writing Process; Multicultural Education: Working with Children Whose First Language Is Not English
35. Use questioning, thinking, and problem solving	Listening; Reading and the Language Arts; Composition: Expressive, Imaginative, and Expository Writing
36. Have students conduct inquiry about cultural groups	Composition: Expressive, Imaginative, and Expository Writing; Handwriting; Multicultural Education: Working with Children Whose First Language Is Not English
37. Emphasize process writing: pre-writing, composing, and revising	Composition: The Writing Process
38. Use feedback and interact with peers during total writing process	Composition: The Writing Process; Composition: Expressive, Imaginative, and Expository Writing
39. Use in-depth study of topics	Reading and the Language Arts; Composition: Expressive, Imaginative, and Expository Writing; Multicultural Education: Working with Children Whose First Language Is Not English
40. Use activities that engage students in inquiry and problem solving	Listening; Literature and the Language Arts; Composition: Expressive, Imaginative, and Expository Writing; Library and Reference Skills
41. Use requisites of good scholarly writing: accuracy of facts, soundness of reasoning, clear explanation, and lucid prose	Composition: The Writing Process; Composition: Expressive, Imaginative, and Expository Writing

the content of the table, notice that many of these best practices are reinforced in different ways through several chapters. Why do you believe that this reinforcement is essential if children are to master these language arts strategies?

This Text

This text includes several features to help preservice and in-service teachers become effective language arts teachers. Look at each feature to see how it can improve your understanding of and instruction ability in the language arts.

Chapter Objectives

Each chapter includes a list of objectives. This list provides an overview of the chapter as well as a means of evaluating your learning after you have completed the chapter.

Diagnostic Procedures

Assessment is considered fundamental to the improvement of education. Effective language arts teaching combines children in small groups, large groups, or individually, according to each child's strengths and weaknesses. For this reason, many chapters describe both formal and informal diagnostic procedures for assessing children's abilities.

Informal assessment techniques are especially valuable in language arts. Because many of the standardized tests given in elementary schools do not adequately assess language arts skills, teachers cannot use the information gained from these tests to improve instruction. Assessment of oral language is an example. Group-administered, standardized tests do not have oral language components. If oral language is a vital part of language arts instruction, then assessment techniques must allow for observation and evaluation of each child's total language apparatus under many different circumstances.

This text includes checklists for immediate use by teachers. Examples include an interest inventory for literature; an individual student profile to accompany oral language evaluation; an auditory inventory; a listening comprehension inventory; a handwriting analysis checklist; a writing evaluation checklist; a usage, punctuation, and capitalization inventory; an interest inventory for literature; and a library reference skills checklist. Teachers must avoid repeating skills a child has already mastered. Spelling is one example. Without assessment of spelling levels, a child may be receiving instruction on words he or she already knows, which is boring for the child and a waste of valuable instructional time. It is equally wasteful to provide spelling instruction at a level so difficult that it frustrates the child. Diagnostic procedures include an emphasis on the portfolios that are especially helpful when assessing literature-based instruction.

"For Your Development" and "For Your Plan Book" Features

People learn and retain knowledge by becoming actively involved in their own education. This is particularly true in an educational methods course such as language arts. To understand assessment techniques thoroughly, you must use them with children or adults. Likewise, to develop skills in teaching various language arts subjects, you must design lessons and teach them, either to children or to peers. Each chapter includes activities identified as "For Your Development" so that you can immediately apply a language arts assessment or instructional technique. Chapters 3 through 13 also include field-tested, exemplary lesson or unit plans for you to try. The "For Your Plan Book" features are listed in a separate table of contents to help you locate them quickly.

Research

Teachers of language arts are fortunate in that a great deal of research has been done in most areas of the language arts. This is important because sound instructional practices are based on research. This text includes reviews of research that provide rationales for suggestions concerning diagnosis and instruction. This research may also be used for further study in that area of language arts. Research findings have changed some of the instructional emphases in language arts and have explored the most effective roles for teachers. As indicated in Table 1–1, research into best practices for teaching the language arts is an important component of this text.

Hoffman (1991) expresses concern, however, that the knowledge gained from research is not applied in many classrooms: "Although our knowledge of the language arts has grown enormously through research, the day-to-day teaching of literacy in schools has remained remarkably unchanged over the decades. In fact, the insights gained from research regarding effective practices appear to be grossly at odds with the 'typical' instruction offered on a day-to-day basis in classrooms across the country. How do we explain the ever-widening gap between knowledge and practice? Why aren't teachers using what researchers have found to be effective in instruction? Where has the system broken down?" (p. 61). Hoffman maintains that illiteracy could be eradicated in the next century if only we could find a way to bridge the gap between research and practice. Such an effort would require the combined efforts of researchers, teacher educators, administrators, and businesspeople.

Effective language arts teachers understand the individual needs of children.

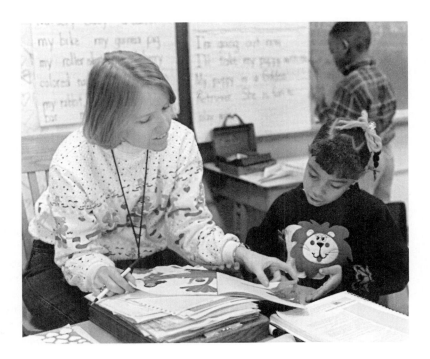

Developmental Instruction

After diagnosis, the next step is to provide the most effective language arts instruction for each child. This instruction encompasses the learning environment, motivation, objectives, instructional procedures, and teacher effectiveness. None of these elements can be ignored in an effective language arts classroom. Notice these essential elements as students proceed from a motivation for writing, to consideration of a topic, to a tentative approach for writing, to gathering materials, to organizing ideas and materials, to writing first drafts, to reviewing and rereading drafts, to revising and making changes in the content, to proofing and editing, and to sharing the works with the intended audiences. Such various prewriting, writing, and postwriting activities encourage interactions between students and between students and teachers. This text explores instructional interactions in a chapter on the writing process and a chapter on developing expressive, imaginative, and expository writers.

Researchers such as Roehler and Duffy (1984) and Gordon (1985) developed instructional approaches that place teachers in active learning roles with students and that show students how teachers approach thought processing before the students are expected to perform similar tasks. Effective modeling approaches proceed from identifying skill requirements, to providing examples showing that skill, to identifying why the skill is important to students, to identifying text samples, to developing questions, to considering the answers to the questions, to citing the evidence that supports the answers, and to thinking through the reasoning process used to acquire the answers. As modeling progresses, the approach proceeds from total teacher modeling, to gradual student interaction, to total student responses. Several chapters demonstrate modeling, including those on literature, oral language, and grammar.

Integrated Approach and Thematic Units

This book includes examples of lesson plans, instructional units, and learning centers to help you visualize instructional procedures and to give you ideas for developing similar lessons. Many of these lesson plans focus on how you can integrate the language arts. Lesson plans include activities such as language experience chart stories, expressive writing, vocabulary webs, manuscript writing, sentence transformations, usage, and modeling of various literary elements and cohesive devices. There are examples of thematic units that stress language arts across the curriculum. For example, there is a folktale unit that emphasizes the authentication of folktales and also the use of folktales in social studies and geography curricula. The series of folktale lessons may easily be expanded into a total thematic unit that emphasizes the development of cultural understanding as well as other language arts. Additional examples of units include a puppetry project that integrates oral language, listening, writing, and art. Units emphasizing a composition approach to biography and a literary approach to biography emphasize written composition, literary criticism, and reading. An advertising unit for critical evaluation of propaganda techniques emphasizes critical listening and thinking skills, writing, listening, and oral language. Learning centers include a listening learning center and a newspaper learning center. These lesson plans, units, and learning centers have been used effectively with children.

Where feasible, examples of products from a lesson are included. The examples, many of which are in creative poetic writing, range from first grade through middle school and illustrate the results of instruction.

Developmental instruction is not accomplished in isolation. Any language arts topic requires interaction and integration of numerous areas. For example, a series of language arts lessons based on folktales may require development of critical and appreciative listening, analysis of literary elements, comparison of folklore types, creation of a play or oral storytelling based on folktales, and creative writing that follows similar forms. Consequently, such lessons require integration of listening, literature, reading, oral language, writing, and social studies. In addition, a film or filmstrip may supplement folklore references selected from the school media center. Integration of such language arts subjects and various content areas is emphasized throughout the text.

The Literature Connection

The role of primary literature sources in the language arts and reading curriculum is receiving renewed interest. There are two types of considerations. First are those for using literature to motivate students to read and to appreciate literature. Second are those for instructional approaches to encourage understanding of various genres, story structures, literature elements, and reading improvement. Because literature is frequently used as a major focus in developing an integrated curriculum and thematic units, a chapter on literature appears early in the text.

Two chapters within this text emphasize the roles of pleasure and understanding. The literature chapter focuses on selection of literature from various genres, identification of students' interests as they relate to literature, stimulation of interest and appreciation of literature, and methodologies that help students understand particular genres and literary elements within books. The reading chapter emphasizes additional methodologies that you may use in the reading program. To help you increase the use of primary sources within all

Effective language arts teachers use literature to motivate children to read and to foster an appreciation of literature.

areas of language arts, chapters on oral language, listening, writing, and multicultural education include strong literature components.

Mainstreaming and the Language Arts

The current focus in education is to include students with learning disabilities in regular classroom settings. Research with children who have special needs has identified specific characteristics of the children and teaching strategies that improve learning experiences for children with those characteristics. Consequently, many of the chapters in this text conclude with charts that identify these specific characteristics and various strategies you may choose to use to improve the language arts instruction of children with special needs.

Children Whose First Language Is Not English and Multicultural Education

Many children in our schools do not speak and read the language of the classroom and the teacher, and as a result, these children are frequently unsuccessful in our schools. The chapter on these children stresses research that classroom teachers can use to improve instruction, techniques effective for diagnosing language arts needs of these children, and factors influencing performance. It describes programs that have been successful with speakers of black English and with Mexican-American children. It also places special stress on evaluation of literature for and about linguistically different children.

Summaries

A summary at the end of each chapter reviews the most important information presented in the chapter. As with the chapter objectives, you can read all the summaries before you read

Many different languages and cultures are represented in today's classrooms, and effective teachers adapt teaching techniques to meet the needs of all students.

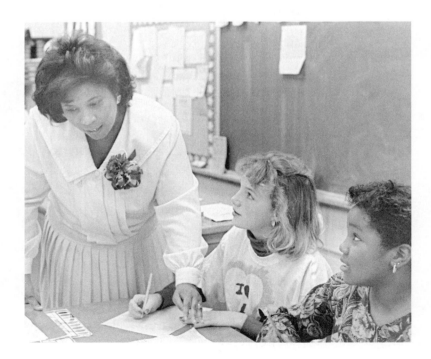

the text to obtain a quick overview of the information covered. You should also read the summary after completing each chapter to help you understand the important concepts.

For Your Development

Preview this language arts text. Read the objectives at the beginning of each chapter and the summaries at the end of each chapter. Locate the sections containing diagnostic procedures; briefly glance over the informal checklists. Read the "For Your Development" activities; they provide another overall view of the information covered in the text. Look for research pertaining to a language arts subject. Find a lesson plan, unit, or learning center that illustrates developmental instruction. In class, or with a group of teachers, discuss the scope and importance of the subject matter covered in the language arts.

Current Issues and Concerns

Many of the issues that surround education in general and language arts instruction in particular can be classified under either control of our profession from the outside or improvement of our profession from within. College students, college professors, and classroom teachers are affected by these influences.

Control from Outside

Control of the profession from the outside includes legislative mandates, public opinion responses to studies on education, and censorship attempts by various interest groups. For example, states such as Texas have mandated language arts objectives to be taught and assessed. Texas law includes detailed objectives for language arts teaching and assessment. Many states across the country either have similar mandates or are in the process of developing or considering such mandates. State-mandated achievement tests are receiving considerable attention in professional journals and in newspapers. Articles such as "High-Stakes Testing in Reading: Today in Texas, Tomorrow?" (Hoffman, Assaf, & Paris, 2001) discuss the implications of and the often detrimental consequences associated with state-wide testing.

Responses of school districts to these mandates have been both positive and negative. Negative responses include minimal individualization and teaching to the assessment instruments. In schools where such practices are common, teachers lose control over curricular development. In contrast, positive responses include using the mandates to identify knowledge areas that should be improved through varied types of instruction. This positive response views mandates as minimal requirements. Within this attitude, educators search for ways to improve instruction based on sound theory and practice. Methodologies are included throughout this text that show teachers how to both improve language arts instruction and meet legislative mandates.

Public responses to national studies, evaluative reports, and critical statements affect language arts instruction at all levels of education and cause local school districts and colleges of education to evaluate their programs. Results of national testing of students generate a variety of responses. For example, articles in local newspapers frequently list the achievement test scores of schools within a district and label them according to their achievement levels. These articles may report comparisons between achievement levels from one year to the next. Other articles such as "The Elderly Man and the Sea? Test Sanitizes Literary Texts"

(Kleinfield, 2002) question the content of tests in which the test developers may be altering the content of passages written by well-known authors.

Public responses to news coverage about national studies frequently focus on various recommendations for national standards. Heated debates may arise over the content of these standards. For example, Leo (1995) in an article in *U.S. News & World Report* discusses the National History Standards and the possible influence of these standards on textbooks if the standards are approved by a public body.

As might be expected, considerable disagreement surrounds the establishment of national standards. Some groups are concerned with measurement associated with the standards. Questions arise: Do standardized achievement tests and minimal competency levels for exams place too much pressure on teachers to teach toward the text? Will national standards help or hinder the problems facing the American education system? Are national standards an oversimplification of conditions that need to be addressed to improve schools?

The development of critical thinking and problem solving is related to debates on national standards. Educators and researchers often recommend reading and writing assignments that allow students to use critical thinking and problem-solving abilities. Unfortunately, studies show that even college students are not required to do many higher level writing assignments. In an analysis of the writing assignments of elementary education majors, Pearce (1990) found only a very small percentage of assignments in which students were required to "synthesize, analyze, or explore course concepts in a coherent and systematic way" (p. 65).

Language arts educators and researchers are not alone in requesting more opportunities for developing critical thinking abilities. For example, O'Reilly (1991) argues for the in-depth study of history and other social studies areas that promote critical thinking. In writing about the lack of science literacy among young people, Steen (1991) decries passive learning through memorization and emphasizes the need to develop critical thinking skills by encouraging students to explore, use, revise, test, modify, and finally accept through a process of active investigation, argument, and participation. Steen also maintains that "students must be encouraged to make connections—whether to social, historical, or personal contexts, to scientific and social phenomena, or to elegant argument and compelling logic" (p. 12). Notice how Steen's recommendations cross the language arts curriculum and require speaking, listening, reading, and writing.

A third type of control from outside forces includes organized group efforts to censor children's literature and school textbooks. Certain groups believe that some books are capable of subverting children's religious, social, or political beliefs and that teachers should not be allowed to use such materials in the classroom. According to a survey by People for the American Way, censorship attempts "increased by 20 percent during the 1986–87 school year and by 68 percent in the last five years" (Wiessler, 1987, p. 1). A report by Dronka (1987) indicates that organized groups are increasing their sponsorships of censorship. According to Dronka, 17 percent of the censorship incidents in 1982–83 were linked to organizations. By 1985–86, 43 percent were associated with organized group efforts. Currently, considerable controversy exists over trade book and textbook censorship. As schools increase their use of primary sources of literature and literature anthologies containing uncut material, selections are subject to increased scrutiny by various groups. According to Russ (1991), literature-based programs in general have come under attack by special-interest groups. For example, O'Neal (1990) describes challenges to such books as Mary Rayner's *Mr. and Mrs. Pig's Evening Out,* Rumer Godden's *The Battle of the Villa Fiotita,* and Katherine Patterson's *The Bridge to Terabithia* and *The Great Gilly Hopkins.* Hicks (1991) reports challenges to Frank Baum's *The Wizard of Oz* and to other books that describe witches. Gregory (1991) answers a criticism that a book of nursery rhymes, Wallace Tripp's *Granfa Grig Had a Pig and Other Rhymes Without Reason from Mother Goose,*

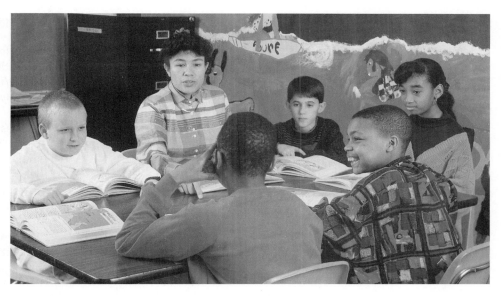

Assessing for comprehension has often in the past been confused with teaching for reading comprehension.

should be censored because the book includes comic illustrations of devils. Meade (1990) describes controversy in a California community as parents debate the content of a literature anthology: "Depending on your point of view, [the anthology] is either a treasure-trove of children's literature or a passport to perdition" (p. 38).

By identifying the most frequently challenged books of 2001 (American Library Association, http://www.ala.org/bbooks/challeng.html#mfcb) we can evaluate the types of books that are currently being challenged. According to the American Library Association the following books were the most frequently challenged in 2001:

1. "Harry Potter" series by J. K. Rowling: focus on wizardry and magic
2. *Of Mice and Men* by John Steinbeck: focus on offensive language
3. *The Chocolate War* by Robert Cormier: focus on offensive language
4. *I Know Why the Caged Bird Sings* by Maya Angelou: focus on sexual content, racism, offensive language, and violence
5. *Summer of My German Soldier* by Bette Greene: focus on racism, offensive language, and sexually explicit content
6. *The Catcher in the Rye* by J. D. Salinger: focus on offensive language
7. "Alice" series by Phyllis Reynolds Naylor: focus on sexually explicit and offensive language
8. *Go Ask Alice* by anonymous: Focus on sexually explicit, offensive language, and drug use
9. *Fallen Angels* by Walter Dean Myers: focus on offensive language
10. *Blood and Chocolate* by Annette Curtis Klause: focus on sexually explicit content

The most frequently challenged authors in 2001 were J. K. Rowling, Robert Cormier, John Steinbeck, Judy Blume, Maya Angelou, Robie Harris, Gary Paulsen, Walter Dean Myers, Phyllis Reynolds Naylor, and Bette Greene.

Issues such as the political correctness of specific language and certain subjects and points of view also add a measure of censorship and control. Political correctness is not only an issue in the United States, but is also common in other parts of the world. For example, Lodge (1994) writing from London in *The Sunday Times Books* focuses on the history of the term and the impact of the phenomenon.

Various organizations have provided guidelines and suggestions for responding to censorship attempts. For example, the International Reading Association's Delegates Assembly passed the following resolution on textbook and reading program censorship:

1. The Association should commend those state, provincial, and local bodies that consistently support teachers' professional judgment even when "self-appointed censors" try to restrict students' freedom to read.
2. The Association should condemn attempts by those with narrow interests who try to deprive students of quality reading programs.
3. The Association should condemn efforts to prevent or disrupt objective discussions on issues related to reading materials and school reading programs (Russ, 1991, p. 1).

Improvement from Within

The forces concerned with improving our profession from within include resolutions by professional societies, studies conducted by respected language arts authorities, and studies and recommendations by university groups. Issues related to both control and improvement of the curriculum are found in the resolutions adopted by the National Council of Teachers of English (NCTE).

The NCTE resolutions geared toward instructional improvement emphasize integration of accounts of racial and ethnic minorities and their contributions to American history and literature; recommend discontinuance of isolated grammar and usage exercises not supported by theory and research; and endorse inclusion of meaningful listening, speaking, reading, and writing activities at all levels of language arts instruction.

As more school districts use literature across the curriculum, the quality of the literature available to teachers and students becomes an even greater issue. Teachers, librarians, and students face problems of selecting literature from the thousands of books that are published each year. Nilsen (1991) argues that "good books are still being published. It's just harder to find the wheat because there's now twice as much chaff" (p. 181). Because of the proliferation of mediocre literature, Nilsen reinforces the need to teach individuals how to evaluate literature carefully and how to use the variety of excellent books available.

This concern for quality of literature is an issue not only for language arts teachers but for other teachers as well. According to Millhouser (1991), adults use science to explore and explain the unknown and good books are children's first step toward this lifelong process. Unfortunately, she concludes that there is currently a trend to flood the market with children's books "no matter what the quality" (p. 47). This question of poor-quality science books is addressed in an analysis of the qualifications of authors who write science trade books for children (Broadway & Howland, 1991). Findings indicated that only 19 percent of the authors of science books for children selected topics on the basis of their own expertise or experience. As stated by Broadway and Howland "the findings suggest an insufficient concern about the qualifications and authority of those who write science and technology books for children and adolescents. Perhaps too many publishers and authors may believe that writing ability and interest qualify authors to write science books for children, regardless of credentials in a particular subject" (p. 38). They recommend that teachers and students be taught how to evaluate and select nonfiction and to be concerned with the accuracy of the author's documentation. They conclude: "We must insist that publishers require authors to demonstrate their authority in the subject areas in which they write. Certainly, education, experience, and interest in a topic are three manifestations of authority. Well-documented research is another barometer of authority that is needed in children's books. As long as we accept and purchase the hundreds of only fair-to-good books that are issued each year, publishers and authors will have less incentive to produce more excellent informational books for young people" (p. 38).

With reference to the social studies curriculum, Lee (1991) argues that teachers in early childhood education use too many outdated materials that teach children outdated concepts. She maintains that concepts such as milkmen delivering milk to the door should be placed in a historical context; they should not be used to suggest contemporary lifestyles. Again, this concern indicates that teachers must carefully evaluate the books that will be used in the various curricula areas.

Other researchers are exploring issues related to improving textbook writing and illustrating. For example, Beck et al. (1991) report that texts that have been revised to include findings from cognitive theory and research are better understood by fourth- and fifth-grade students than the original texts. Graves et al. (1991) point out the need to consider both the development of cognitive abilities and positive attitudes among readers; consequently, they explore the need for texts to be vivid, lively, and interesting as well as to reinforce cognitive theory. Purnell and Solman (1991) found that quality illustrations increase comprehension in geography. Writing style, textbook design, and graphics are currently receiving a lot of attention and are pointing up the need for high-quality classroom materials.

Textbooks also receive the attention of textbook adoption committees at both the state and local levels. These adoption committees have a great deal of powerful influence, especially in states that have statewide adoption. A survey of all of the state-level textbook adoption committee members in 13 states that rely on state-level adoption procedures reveals the four most important unresolved reading issues that influence the committee members. According to the results of the survey, Reutzel, Sudweeks, and Hollingsworth (1994) report that these unresolved issues include assessment of students' reading progress, whole-language versus basal approaches, use of ability grouping for reading instruction, and use of trade books in place of basals.

Judging and Selecting Elementary Language Arts Textbooks

The Committee on Elementary Language Arts Textbooks of the National Council of Teachers of English (1991) has published a list of guidelines for you to use when judging and selecting elementary language arts textbooks (see Figure 1–1). Notice how these guidelines reflect all areas of the language arts, including reading, writing, speaking, and listening. Also, think about how you might incorporate some of the guidelines into your total language arts curriculum, whatever methods and materials you may be using now.

For Your Development

With a group of your peers, use the evaluation criteria for elementary language arts textbooks (Figure 1–1) to evaluate a selection of textbooks. Share your findings and your recommendations with your class. Check websites to discover what various sources are recommending for textbooks. To discover how a conservative organization evaluates textbooks, check "Mel Gablers' Textbook Analysis" (http://www.textbookreviews.org/).

1. Language arts textbooks should center on children's language. Lessons should help teachers focus on students' real purposes for communication. Textbooks should supplement and enrich students' active use of language through listening, speaking, reading, and writing.

2. Language arts textbooks should emphasize activities that focus on social uses of language. The lessons should help students value their own speaking and writing efforts and help them learn to develop clear and appropriate communication.

3. Language arts textbooks should reflect the integrated nature of listening, speaking, writing, and reading. Lessons should include provocative literature and language activities.

4. Language arts textbooks should recognize broad patterns of developmental language growth. Students should learn to use their knowledge, skills, strategies, and awareness with increasingly complex samples of language and in more sophisticated contexts.

5. Language arts textbooks should help teachers assess students' use of language. Textbooks should guide teachers in developing assessment procedures for the major goals in the language arts curriculum and should provide help in interpreting observations of students' daily use of language for a variety of purposes.

6. Language arts textbooks should stimulate children's and teachers' thinking. Textbooks need to promote inquiry about language: its purposes, its origins, its growth, and change.

7. Language arts textbooks should be equity balanced. Textbooks should help students become aware of the cultural aspects of their own language and help them achieve a sensitivity toward and understanding of the cultural aspects of the language of others.

8. Language arts textbooks should reflect the centrality of listening, speaking, writing, and reading for learning in all subject areas. Examples and suggested activities in the textbooks need to be selected from a variety of subject areas.

FIGURE 1–1   Evaluation Criteria for Elementary Language Arts Textbooks
Adapted from: Guidelines for Judging and Selecting Elementary Language Arts Textbooks, Language Arts Vol. 68(3), pp. 253–54.

SUMMARY

Effective teaching of language arts includes assessment of all areas of the language arts. The language arts curriculum includes instruction that fosters development of oral language, listening, handwriting, creative writing, written composition, grammar, usage, and spelling. This curriculum also allows children to develop an appreciation for literature and other media. Literature is frequently the focus for the development of thematic units within the curriculum. Effective teaching of language arts includes using the best practices that have been identified by studies in the various components of the language arts.

Language arts classrooms must accommodate children who demonstrate various needs and ability levels. In addition to serving children who acquire the various language arts skills without undue difficulties, the classrooms must serve children who require slower paced instruction and those who demonstrate various learning disabilities.

Control of the profession from the outside includes legislative mandates, public opinion responses to studies on education, and censorship attempts by various interest groups. The forces concerned with improving our profession from within include professional societies and university groups.

In judging and selecting elementary language arts textbooks, national guidelines reflecting all areas of the language arts curriculum are now available to assist teachers.

BIBLIOGRAPHY

Allington, Richard; and Cunningham, Patricia M. *Schools That Work: Where All Children Read and Write,* 2nd ed. Boston: Allyn & Bacon, 2002.

American Institutes for Research. *An Educators' Guide to School Reform.* Arlington, Va.: Educational Research Service, 1999.

Beck, I.; McKeown, M.; Sinatra, G.; and Loxterman, J. "Revising Social Studies Texts from a Text-Processing Perspective: Evidence of Improved Comprehension." *Reading Research Quarterly* 26 (1991): 251–76.

Broadway, M.; and Howland, M. "Science Books for Young People: Who Writes Them?" *School Library Journal* 37 (1991): 35–38.

Cole, Gerald. *Misreading Reading: The Bad Science That Hurts Children.* Portsmouth, N.H.: Heinemann, 2000.

Committee on Elementary Language Arts Textbooks. "Guidelines for Judging and Selecting Elementary Language Arts Textbooks." *Language Arts* 68 (1991): 253–54.

Cunningham, Patricia M.; and Allington, Richard L. *Classrooms That Work: They Can All Read and Write,* 3rd ed. Boston: Allyn & Bacon, 2003.

Dronka, Pamela. "Forums for Curriculum Critics Settle Some Disputes: Clash Persists on Students' Thinking about Controversy." *Update* (March 1987): 1, 6, 7.

"Examining Evidence: New IRA Position Statement on Evidence-Based Reading Instruction." *Reading Today* 20 (August/September 2002): 1, 4.

Flood, James; Jensen, Julie; Lapp, Diana; and Squire, James. *Handbook of Research on Teaching the English Language Arts,* 2nd ed. Mahwah, NJ: Lawrence Erlbaum, 2002.

Gordon, Christine J. "Modeling Inference Awareness across the Curriculum." *Journal of Reading* 28 (February 1985): 444–47.

Graves, M.; Prenn, M.; Earle, J.; Thompson, M.; and Slater, W. "Improving Instructional Text: Some Lessons Learned." *Reading Research Quarterly* 26 (1991): 110–12.

Gregory, Helen. "A Tale of Granfa Grig." *School Library Journal* 37 (1991): 32.

Hicks, R. "The Devil in the Library." *School Library Journal* 37 (1991): 53.

Hoffman, J. "Research Directions: Literacy in the 21st Century: Who Can Prevent It?" *Language Arts* 68 (1991): 60–66.

Hoffman, James V.; Assaf, Lori Czop; and Paris, Scott G. "High-Stakes Testing in Reading: Today in Texas, Tomorrow?" *The Reading Teacher* 54 (February 2001): 482–92.

Kleinfield, N. R. "The Elderly Man and the Sea? Test Sanitizes Literary Texts." *The New York Times* (June 2, 2002): 1, 30.

Lee, M. "The Milkman Doesn't Come to My Door: Teaching About Family Service Providers." *Social Education* 55 (1991): 307–10.

Leo, John. "Historical Standards Are Bunk." *U.S. News & World Report* 118 (February 6, 1995): 23.

Lodge, David. "Mind Your Language." London, England: *The Sunday Times Books* (October 16, 1994): 1–2.

Meade, J. "A War of Words." *Teacher Magazine* (November–December 1990): 36–45.

Millhouser, F. "Beautiful Science: Books That Cash in on Children's Curiosity." *School Library Journal* 37 (1991): 47–48.

National Reading Panel. *Report of the National Reading Panel.* Washington, D.C.: U.S. Department of Health and Human Services, 2000.

NCTE Committee on Elementary Language Arts Textbooks. *Guidelines for Judging and Selecting Elementary Language Arts Textbooks.* Urbana, Ill.: National Council of Teachers of English, 1991.

Nilsen, A. "Speaking Loudly for Good Books: Promoting the Wheat and Winnowing the Chaff." *School Library Journal* 37 (1991): 180–83.

O'Neal, S. "Leadership in the Language Arts: Controversial Books in the Classroom." *Language Arts* 67 (1990): 771–75.

O'Reilly, K. "The Commission Report and Critical Thinking: A Defense." *Social Education* 55 (1991): 298.

Pearce, D. "An Examination of the Writing Required in an Elementary Education Degree Program." *Action in Teacher Education* 12 (1990): 61–67.

Purnell, K.; and Solman, R. "The Influence of Technical Illustrations on Students' Comprehension in Geography." *Reading Research Quarterly* 26 (1991): 277–99.

Reutzel, D. Ray; Sudweeks, Richard; and Hollingsworth, Paul M. "Issues in Reading Instruction: The Views and Information Sources of State-Level Textbook Adoption Committee Members." *Reading Research and Instruction* 34 (1994): 149–71.

Roehler, Laura; and Duffy, G. "Direct Explanation of Comprehension Processes." In *Comprehension Instruction,* edited by Gerald G. Duffy, Laura R. Roehler, and Jana Mason. New York: Longman, 1984, pp. 265–80.

Routman, Regie. *Literacy at the Crossroads.* Portsmouth, N.H.: Heinemann, 1996.

Russ, W. "Controversy Continues over Reading Textbook Censorship." *Reading Today* 8 (1991): 1, 5.

Steen, L. "Reaching for Science Literacy." *Change* 23 (1991): 11–19.

Wiessler, Judy. "Book Censorship Attempts Are Soaring, Group's Survey Says." *Houston Chronicle* (August 28, 1987): 1–8.

Language and Cognitive Development

After completing this chapter on language and cognitive development, you will be able to:

1. Describe a genetic theory of language acquisition and analyze instructional outcomes according to this view.

2. Describe a sociocultural theory of language acquisition and evaluate the impact of sociocultural research on language acquisition.

3. Relate a child-development-oriented philosophy to an instructional program.

4. Describe the sequence of language development in preschool and early-elementary-age children.

5. Understand that all children go through approximately the same stages of language development but the rate of development varies from child to child; relate this understanding to instructional practice.

6. Describe some implications for language study developed from linguistic investigations.

7. Understand the importance of cognitive development and describe some instructional activities that stimulate cognitive development.

8. Understand the importance of personality and social development and describe some instructional activities that stimulate personality and social development.

*I*f someone asks you to name the most important means of communication, what would you answer? Most of you would probably respond, "Language." Language is the key to human communication. We can use written language to convey information or to read the vast accumulation of knowledge available to us.

The spoken and written language that separates us from the animal kingdom is made up of sounds and symbols that are grouped into words. Although words are the fundamental units of language, they must be placed within the structure of a sentence to convey complete meaning. For example, if you see the word *wind*, can you even pronounce the word correctly without knowing the sentence context in which it is to be placed? This isolated word may refer to a breeze, as in the sentence "The wind blew the kite up into the sky." In contrast, the same word may refer to an action, as in "You must wind the clock." The identical spellings have two pronunciations and two meanings. They are different parts of speech, depending on the surrounding sentence. Every language has sounds, or *phonemes,* that combine to form words. The words are put into certain sequences to comprise grammatical forms that are structured within the language (syntax).

Strickland and Feeley (2003) emphasize the importance of knowledge about language development: "We believe that teachers' knowledge about language learning is a major source of empowerment. It enables them to take control over methods and materials and to make informed curricular decisions. . . . It is our belief that a better understanding of children as language learners will lead to improved classroom instructional practices" (p. 339).

Theories of Language Acquisition

How do children acquire language? This question has fascinated people since the early days of recorded history. According to Herodotus, as early as 600 B.C. Egyptian King Psammetichus I tried to answer this question by having two children raised in a speechless environment. Although modern experimenters dispute both the scientific and ethical status of such research, they are still trying to answer the same question.

The last seventy years have produced many changes in language study. Early studies often took the form of diary investigations, in which investigators listened to young children and recorded their language as the children progressed through the various stages of language development. The 1930s and 1940s produced a movement calling for scientific rigor in research. During this time, researchers considered earlier studies by parents suspect, because they assumed that parents would show bias in their recordings. The concern for rigorous scientific experimentation led to language studies with large groups of children. These studies described properties of children's speech, such as the average length of utterance, parts of speech used, and number of different words spoken by a child during a specific period of time. Madorah Smith (1933) was one of the earliest researchers to conclude that the language of children is systematic and governed by rules.

In the 1950s language researchers began to investigate what children know about language. They stressed systematic study of fewer children over longer periods of time. The studies, summarized by Ervin-Tripp (1966), concluded that children learn an underlying linguistic system rather than all of the sounds or words in the language. These studies also implied that children's language is systematic and rule governed.

In the late 1950s and the 1960s, researchers sought to describe rule systems that could account for children's use of sentences. Language investigators developed theories about how children acquire language. Researchers such as Lawton (1968) from England and Poole (1976) from Australia investigated the linguistic strategies of working-class and middle-class subjects and added to the increasing body of research in language development.

As researchers began to use computer analysis and electronic recording to investigate language systematically in the 1970s and 1980s, their investigations became more sophisticated. These researchers also considered the social context in which children develop language.

As research methods have changed over time, theories about language acquisition have also changed. According to Menyuk (1991), "one of the more dramatic changes occurred some 30 years ago. This was the advent of transformational or, more accurately, generative grammar. Previously language theories were influenced by behaviorists' theories of learning. Language was described as a set of learned habits and was acquired . . . through stimulus, response, and reward conditions. Generative theories hold that language knowledge is represented in the mind as a system of rules, and that language is acquired by an active learner" (p. 24).

Menyuk (1991) maintains that only the influences of this generative theory in its various forms are now considered relevant for understanding language acquisition. She states: "The aspects of current linguistic theory most germane to the teaching of the language arts are theoretical positions now held about the nature of language knowledge and its acquisition, about the process of language acquisition and application of linguistic knowledge in learning, and about how differing sociocultural experiences can affect what the child knows when entering school. These aspects are studied by linguists, psycholinguists and sociolinguists" (p. 24).

We now briefly examine the various theories of language acquisition. Not only will we see how theories have changed over time, we will also see how theories influence instruction in the language arts.

Genetic Theory

Some researchers believe that children possess innate, or instinctive, language ability. According to this theory, language learning is largely instinctive rather than imitative. All children are thus believed to be born with the ability to use language; they start with a language of their own and amend their language to conform to adult language.

Researchers such as Carol Chomsky (1969) argue that imitation theories of language acquisition do not explain how children create sentences they have never heard. Chomsky found sentence structures that school-age children consistently misinterpreted prior to a certain stage in development. Language acquisition studies reinforce this viewpoint. For example, a study by Menyuk (1963) found that preschool children develop a grammar that differs from the adult model. Ervin-Tripp (1964) provides additional insights into the role of imitation and innate ability. She asked children to repeat sentences such as "Mr. Miller will try." Young children who were speaking at the two-word level responded with "Miller try" rather than the longer adult sentence. Ervin-Tripp concluded that children imitate only the language structures that already appear in their speech.

A rule-learning theory began to emerge as researchers investigated children's grammatical structures. Researchers such as Slobin and Welsh (1973) and Cazden (1972) added to the knowledge about syntactic development in children. Slobin and Welsh asked two- and three-year-old children to repeat sentences. They found that children repeat sentences according to their own levels of grammatical development. Likewise, Cazden concluded that the language of children is rule governed. Consequently, children process language data around them, draw rules that they test, and revise rules based on feedback they receive. In this way, children's speech gradually approaches adult speech.

Sociocultural Theory

Early learning opportunities provided by parents and other adults in the sociocultural context of the home and the community may establish much of what is learned. The sociocultural theory stresses the interactive reality of language acquisition. Although many researchers in the 1960s and 1970s concluded that language is an innate capability triggered by the presence of language in the environment, other researchers in both America and England (Wells, 1979, 1981) considered the importance of the social environment in which language is acquired and the interaction that takes place between children and adults. Bruner (1978) describes a sociocultural viewpoint of language acquisition: Language is "encountered in a highly orderly interaction with the mother, who takes a crucial role in arranging the linguistic encounters of the child. What has emerged is a theory of mother–infant interaction in language acquisition—called the fine tuning theory—that sees language mastery as involving the mother as much as it does the child" (p. 44).

Support for a social context for language acquisition frequently relies on cases in which children do not interact with adults. For example, Moskowitz (1978) describes a boy with normal hearing who was raised by deaf parents. Although the child listened to television daily, by the age of three he could neither speak nor understand English. He was, however, fluent in sign language. Moskowitz concludes, "It appears that in order to learn a language a child must also be able to interact with real people in that language" (p. 94).

Snow (1977) and Lindfors (1987) suggest that adults play an important role in the socialization process. Snow studied the interactions between infants and their mothers. She found that mothers adjust their speech to meet the conversational skills of their children. Likewise, Lindfors found that adults adjust their language to fit the oral language skills of

Research supports the positive role parents can play in reading and language development.

their children. Consequently, early conversations include shorter sentences characterized by considerable contextual support, repetitions, and exaggerated intonational patterns. The goal of these early conversations is apparently a meaningful exchange of language.

Conversational skills apparently develop quite early in infants. Shugar (1978) found that the interchange of conversation occurs before very young children are able to speak in two-word utterances. She maintains that the initial burden for oral interaction rests on the adults, who identify the children's meanings and build conversations based on those meanings. During these interactions, socialization also occurs. In a study of children between thirteen and twenty months old, Tamis-LeMonda and Bornstein (1994) found that mothers' language was highly related to toddlers' language.

Language acquisition research has changed since the 1960s. A study by Shatz and Ebeling (1991) reflects this change in emphasis. These researchers focused on the conversations of six children from age two to two years, six months as they interacted with parents and siblings at home. Revisions in the speech of these children usually involved grammatical changes. Shatz and Ebeling concluded that the spontaneously initiated speech of these children "adds support to the arguments and evidence presented by researchers over the years that children work actively at language learning during the third year of life" (p. 307). In another recent study, Akhtar, Dunham, and Dunham (1991) examined how mothers use language to direct their young children's attention. They found that mothers who followed their children's attention during their conversations, rather than trying to change the focus of this attention, had beneficial effects on their children's subsequent vocabulary development. In still another study, Sorsby and Martlew (1991) analyzed mothers' conversations with their four-year-old children while picture-book reading and modeling with clay. They found that the mothers' conversations were on a higher level of abstraction and the accuracy of the children's responses was superior during the reading activity.

Some researchers focus attention on children's language interactions during play. For example, Pellegrini et al. (1991) studied the influence of specific types of language used during play on early literacy. They used audiotapes and behavior notes to collect language samples from which they obtained "symbolic play scores." They found that these scores could be used to predict the emergence of children's writing.

A longitudinal study of children from kindergarten through third grade conducted by Walker et al. (1994) found that the environment and early language experiences are so important that many children from lower socioeconomic environments who may have fewer early language experiences demonstrate differences in language ability. They conclude, "The constraints placed on their language development in the context of early parenting may compromise growth in both early language and intelligence as well as later success in terms of reading and spelling achievement in particular. . . . The results demonstrated that the earlier differences were predictive of children's language and reading-related achievement seven years beyond the initial measure" (p. 617).

Research findings from investigations of the interactive nature of language are frequently used to support efforts to improve parent–child interactions and to increase play opportunities in early childhood education. Strickland and Morrow (1990) emphasize the importance of developing a positive verbal interaction between parent and child during story readings. They then describe how such an environment can be created in the home. Likewise, Smith (1990) provides guidelines to help parents effectively interact with their children for the purpose of reading development. Morrow and Rand (1991) describe the need to recognize the importance of play when designing early childhood classroom environments that promote literacy. They, too, emphasize adult interactions with children during these play experiences: "Preschool and kindergarten children are likely to engage in more voluntary literacy behaviors during free-play periods when literacy materials are introduced and teachers guide children to use these materials" (p. 399).

Vygotsky's (1981, 1987) sociohistorical theory of development is receiving renewed interest as educators consider the ways in which it applies to education. Vygotsky's sociohistorical psychology focuses on the social origins and cultural bases of individual development. He believes that higher psychological processes develop in children through enculturation into the practices of society. In his various writings, Vygotsky emphasizes the social context of thinking and discusses the cooperation between children and adults that is central to the educational process. He maintains that "knowledge is transferred to the child in a definite system" (1987, p. 169) within our social activities and cultural practices. How important are Vygotsky's theories today? Schallert and Martin (2003) state: "Much of the most exciting work in current educational research involves a focus on how language participates in and mediates learning, a view that is often framed in Vygotsky's sociocultural theory of human development" (p. 39).

For Your Development

To discover additional information about Vygotsky's sociohistorical theory and its application to education read one of the articles in Luis C. Moll's edited text, *Vygotsky and Education: Instructional Implications and Applications of Sociohistorical Psychology* (1990). For example, you might read "A Vygotskian Interpretation of Reading Recovery," "Vygotsky in a Whole-Language Perspective," "The Development of Scientific Concepts and Discourse," "Learning to Read and Write in an Inner-City Setting," or "Writing as a Social Process." Discuss the implications of the article with your language arts class.

Child Development Theory

If you are aware of the teachings of Piaget, you are already familiar with the concept that interaction with the physical and social environment is critical to both intellectual and language development in children. Piaget related intellectual development to several stages of child development. Raven and Salzer (1971) developed some of the instructional implications of Piaget's theory. According to Raven and Salzer, during the sensorimotor period, from birth to about two years, children should manipulate objects and materials to enable them to develop images and to stimulate cognitive growth.

The second stage, the preconceptual period, is divided into two developmental phases. During the first phase, from two to four years, it is important to provide many varied concrete experiences. Sensory and motor activities are necessary for developing concepts and complex thinking, which are necessary for the development of advanced language art skills. The second phase, or preoperational period, is the intuitive phase from ages four through seven years. During this time, activity-oriented curricula are desirable. Children should have chances to manipulate objects such as books and explore such skills as language and reading. This theory suggests that children in this stage should not be taught in a program that demands the mental gymnastics necessary for reading or spelling programs based on rules of grapheme–phoneme relationships.

During the third stage, the concrete-operational period from ages seven to eleven years, children have the ability to reason, but they can reason adequately only about direct experiences, not about abstractions. Because children are able to reason about what they read only if it relates closely to direct experience, the environment should enrich that direct experience. During the concrete-operational stage, students should have opportunities to combine sentence and word elements and to associate the elements in different ways. They should be encouraged to transform the word elements and observe the differences produced. Questioning techniques developed from the child's own experience should be used.

During the final stage hypothesized by Piaget, the formal-operational period that begins at eleven or twelve years of age, children have the ability to control formal logic. They can begin to deal with propositions and hypotheses that are not related to direct experience. During this period, instructional procedures should be structured so that students may analyze various logical relationships. Oral discussion, listening, and writing experiences allow children opportunities to deal with logic.

Educational strategies formulated from Piaget's beliefs include close observation of children, numerous opportunities for children to manipulate things in the environment and to work individually at tasks of their own choosing, and encouragement of oral language development through such activities as arguing and debating. Strickland and Feeley (2003) emphasize that the theories of both Piaget and Vygotsky have implications for the classroom. They state: "Teachers should avoid confusing children by presenting them with abstract ideas in adult language before they have the background of concrete experiences to act as a framework for understanding. . . . Interactive language between child and adult is a significant part of every stage in the child's language development" (p. 343).

Language Development

Linguists have provided increasing knowledge about language development by asking questions: What features of phonological (sound), grammatical, and semantic (meaning) development seem to be universal? Why is one linguistic skill acquired before another? What is the nature of the child's linguistic ability during various stages of development? There appears to be more agreement about the sequence of language development than about language acquisition.

During the preverbal period, children learn to exert increasing control over vocal production.

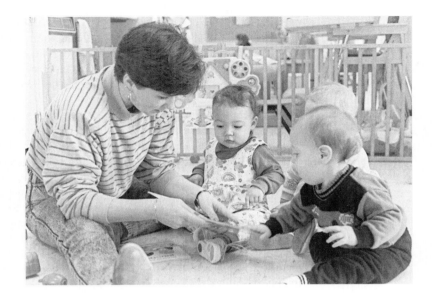

Early Development

The first few years of life produce dramatic changes in language ability. An infant begins communicating by crying, then progresses to cooing and babbling. Linguists have used several different terms to label the speech produced by children during the first year of life. *Infant vocalization, preverbal period,* and *prelinguistic vocalization* have been used to describe the early speech of babies. Researchers interested in this stage of language development have listened to young children and analyzed what they have heard. In this early stage, infants show increasing control over vocal production. Fry (1966) describes this babbling stage:

> During the babbling stage, the child is doing two important things: he is trying out mechanisms that will be needed for speech, combining phonation with articulation and no doubt gaining a certain control of the respiratory system, and he is establishing the circuits by which motor activity and auditory impressions are firmly linked together. He is learning the acoustic effect of making certain movements and finding out how to repeat a movement, how to do it again and again to get more or less the same acoustic results. In one sense he is learning a trick, and the experience lasts him, so to speak, for the rest of his life. (p. 190)

During the first few years of life, children move from vocalizing to meaningful language use. Woodward, Markman, and Fitzsimmons (1994) found that children as young as thirteen months showed comprehension of new words after limited exposure and could learn a new object label quickly. When children produce and comprehend meaningful sentences they have never heard before, we say that they have learned the language. Linguists have studied the early speech of children in many different countries and have concluded that children throughout the world have the innate capacity to make the various speech sounds. The linguists believe that some of these universal sounds are encouraged by the specific language heard, and that others disappear from early language because they are not part of the child's environment. Consequently, each child learns a particular grammar, language, and phonological system. Linguists refer to this process as *internalizing*.

Language development is very rapid in most children, who usually speak their first word at about one year of age. As you know, this is an important occasion; your parents can probably remember your first word and when you said it. Early words probably mean more than the single word implies. For example, the child who says "mama" may mean "Mama come here," "Where is mama?" or "Mama pick me up." Linguists use the term *holophrastic* to describe this speech.

At about eighteen months, children usually begin putting two words together. According to Braine (1978), the number of different two-word combinations increases slowly, then shows a sudden upsurge around the age of twenty-three or twenty-four months. Braine recorded the speech of three children from the ages of eighteen months. The cumulative number of different two-word combinations for one child in successive months was 14, 24, 54, 89, 350, 1,400, 2,500+. Obviously, this is a rapid expansion of speech in such a short time.

The time when children put two words together for speech is also considered important by linguists. At this time a child's active grammar can be investigated. For example, Peterson and Dodsworth (1991) conducted a longitudinal study of the cohesive links used by children from age two to three years, six months. They found that young children do use cohesive devices and these cohesive devices increase with age. They conclude, "On average, the children linked successive utterances with approximately two cohesive ties and there is an increase in such linkage with age. Normal adults link their sentences with between three and four cohesive ties on average, so these children still have room for considerable improvement" (p. 409). Speech usually becomes more complex by age three, when most children have added adverbs, pronouns, prepositions, and more adjectives to their vocabularies. Children also enjoy playing with the sounds of words at this stage of language development. By age four, they produce grammatically correct sentences. This stage is a questing one, during which language is used to ask *why* and *how.*

Brown (1973) conducted one of the most extensive longitudinal studies of early language acquisition. In this study, the speech of three children was recorded over a five-year period. Brown found that during approximately the first two years of life speech could be described as telegraphic. During this stage, speech was made up of content words belonging to the large open classes called nouns, verbs, and adjectives. The speech in this telegraphic period did not utilize function words such as prepositions, articles, auxiliary verbs, or pronouns. When children say such phrases as "pretty flower" or "allgone milk," they are using telegraphic speech.

Brown's research (1973) also provides valuable insight into the next stage of language acquisition. During this second stage, children acquire the ability to use grammatical morphemes, which are the smallest significant units of syntax. These units may be whole words, as in *came* to show the past tense of *come,* or only parts of words, as in *s* added to a word to form the plural (for example, *balls*) or possessive (for example, *baby's*).

In *A First Language/The Early Stages,* Brown (1973) analyzes the results of his longitudinal study and combines them with other early language studies to determine the order in which children acquire fourteen of the grammatical morphemes. This order is apparently consistent for most children. Table 2–1 shows this order of language acquisition and provides an example of each grammatical morpheme.

All children appear to go through the same stages of language development, although the rate of development varies from child to child. Even Brown's study (1973) showed great variance among the three children he studied. For example, one child successfully used six grammatical morphemes by the age of two years, three months, while a second child did not master them until the age of three years, six months. The third child was four years old before reaching an equivalent stage in language development.

Table 2–1 The order of grammatical morphemes acquired in early stages of language

Grammatical Morpheme	Example
1. Present progressive *-ing*	Jimmy eating
2. and 3. *in, on*	toy in box
	Sally sit on bed
4. Plural *-s*	tables
5. Past irregular	came, went
6. Possessive	Sandy's chair
7. Uncontractible copula (linking verb)	am, is, are, be
8. Articles	the, a
9. Past regular *-ed*	Billy walked home
10. Third person regular *-s*	He plays
11. Third person irregular *-s*	He does
12. Uncontractible auxiliary *is*	This is going fast
13. Contractible copula (linking verb) = *s*	Billy's sleepy
14. Contractible auxiliary	He's flying

Source: Roger Brown, *A First Language/The Early Stages* (Cambridge, Mass.: Harvard University Press, 1973). Copyright © 1973 by the President and Fellows of Harvard College. Reprinted with permission.

Research considers metalinguistic awareness—the ability to think about language, to manipulate structural features of language, and to focus on the forms of language. Metalinguistic skills include the ability to segment sentences into words and words into syllables and phonemes. Metalinguistic ability seems to develop at an early age. For example, Chaney (1992) found that children as young as three years are rapidly developing a mental framework for analyzing language structure separately from language meaning.

The children in any one nursery school, kindergarten, or elementary class are in various stages of language development. Because language is such a vital aspect of education and is basic to the skills of oral communication, listening, writing, and reading, teachers must understand the process of language development. Such knowledge is essential to diagnose oral language skills or to create an educational environment that will foster development of all the communication skills.

Development in the Elementary Grades

The most extensive study of language development in school-age children is a longitudinal study conducted by Loban (1976). Loban examined the language development of more than 200 children from the ages of five to eighteen years. This study has numerous implications for language arts teachers, because Loban investigated stages of language development, identified differences between students who ranked high in language proficiency and those who ranked low, and stressed the use of taped oral language samples rather than published language tests.

What were the differences between children who ranked high in language proficiency and those who ranked low? First, students who demonstrated high language proficiency excelled in the control of expressed ideas. Both speech and writing showed unity and planning. They spoke freely, fluently, and easily; used a rich variety of vocabulary; and adjusted the pace of their words to their listeners. The high-proficiency group also used more words in each oral sentence. The difference in language development was dramatic: The higher group had reached a level of oral proficiency in first grade that the lower group did not attain until the sixth grade. The lower group's oral communication was characterized by rambling and un-purposeful dialogue that showed a meager vocabulary.

In addition, in the area of writing, the high group was more fluent, used more words per sentence, showed a richer vocabulary, and was superior in using connectors such as *meanwhile* and *unless* in writing. This group also used more subordination in combining thoughts into complex forms. The high group again showed greater proficiency at a much younger age than did their peers; the fourth-grade level of proficiency shown by the high group was not shown by the low group until the tenth grade. Moreover, the students who were superior with oral language also ranked highest on listening. They were both atten-tive and creative listeners. Children who were superior in oral language in kindergarten and first grade also excelled in both reading and writing in the sixth grade. In a more re-cent review of the implications of language research, Loban (1986) concluded, "The awe-some importance of oral language as a base for success with literacy is crystal clear" (p. 612). Consequently, children need oral language instruction to help them organize ideas and illustrate complex generalizations. Oral discussion should be a vital part of the elementary school program.

Power over language increases through successive control over forms of language, in-cluding the ability to handle pronouns, to use appropriate verb tenses, and to use connec-tors. There is also steady growth in the average number of words per sentence and the average number of dependent clauses per sentence. Consequently, although language de-velopment is well advanced by the time children enter school, it is far from complete. Clay (1991) states, "Perhaps because children seem to have well-formed response systems for comprehending and producing language prior to entering school, the continuing develop-ment of oral language during schooling is not often seen by teachers to be important. In fact, individual differences in oral language achievement vary greatly. While teachers see oral lan-guage as central to writing and reading acquisition, they often do not recognize the need to foster further development" (p. 41).

Carol Chomsky (1969) emphasizes the expanding acquisition of syntax in children ages five through ten years. Chomsky found that children in this age group are still ac-quiring syntactic structures. Language learning does not cease, nor is it limited to an ex-pansion of previously acquired structures. Likewise, McGhee-Bidlack (1991) analyzed the ability to define nouns in students ages ten, fourteen, and eighteen years. She found that there are significant differences in the way concrete and abstract nouns are defined: "All three age groups defined concrete nouns mainly by class and characteristic re-sponses. But it was not until age 18 that abstract nouns were defined by class and char-acteristic responses. The development of abstract noun definitions follows the development of concrete noun definitions. The ability to define is dependent upon knowledge of the meaning of the word but it is also dependent upon implicit or explicit knowledge of the definitional form. The ability to define abstract nouns is a late devel-oping metalinguistic skill" (p. 417).

Although the rate of language development differs, Table 2–2 may help you visualize the language acquisition stages common to many children at specific age levels. This table was compiled from studies by Brown (1973) and Loban (1976) and a report by Bartel (1995).

Table 2–2 A general overview of language development

Age	General Language Characteristics
3 months	Young children start with all possible language sounds and gradually eliminate the sounds that are not used around them.
1 year	Many children are speaking single words (for example, *mama*). Infants use single words to express entire sentences. Complex meanings may underlie single words.
18 months	Many children are using two- or three-word phrases (for example, "see baby"). Children are developing their own language rule systems. Children may have a vocabulary of about 300 words.
2–3 years	Children use such grammatical morphemes as plural suffix /*s*/, auxiliary verb *is* past irregular. They use simple and compound sentences. They also understand tense and numerical concepts such as "many" and "few." They have a vocabulary of about 900 words.
3–4 years	The verb past tense appears, but children may overgeneralize the *ed* and *s* markers. Negative transformation appears. Children understand numerical concepts such as *one, two,* and *three.* Speech becomes more complex, with more adjectives, adverbs, pronouns, and prepositions. Vocabulary is about 1,500 words.
4–5 years	Language is more abstract and children master most basic rules of language. Children produce grammatically correct sentences. Vocabularies include approximately 2,500 words.
5–6 years	Most children use complex sentences quite frequently. They use correct pronouns and verbs in the present and past tense. The average number of words per oral sentence is 6.8. Children understand approximately 6,000 words.
6–7 years	Children are speaking in complex sentences that use adjectival clauses. Conditional clauses beginning with *if* begin to appear. Language becomes more symbolic. Children begin to read and write and understand concepts of time and seasons. The average sentence length is 7.5 words.
7–8 years	Children use relative pronouns as objects in subordinate adjectival clauses. ("I have a cat, which I feed every day.") Subordinate clauses beginning with *when, if,* and *because* appear frequently. The average number of words per oral sentence is 7.6.
8–10 years	Children begin to relate concepts to general ideas through use of such connectors as *meanwhile* and *unless.* Fifty percent of the children correctly use the subordinating connector *although.* Present participle active and perfect participate appear. The average number of words in an oral sentence is 9.0.
10–12 years	Children use complex sentences with subordinate clauses of concession introduced by *nevertheless* and *in spite of.* The auxiliary verbs *might, could,* and *should* appear frequently. Children have difficulties distinguishing among past, past perfect, and present perfect tenses. The average number of words in an oral sentence is 9.5.

Listen to the oral language of several preschool children or elementary-age children. How does their oral language development compare to that found by Brown or Loban? Write some specific examples of speech found at a certain age level and share your findings with your classmates.

Linguistics

Linguists observe and record people to discover how language functions and how it evolves. They use their data to draw conclusions and formulate generalizations about the nature of language. For communication to take place, both speakers and listeners must use the same code system. Linguists refer to several code signals, including phonology, morphology, syntax, and semantics.

Phonology is the sound system within a language. Each language has a set of sounds that provides meaningful differences within that language. The smallest distinctive unit of sound within the language is a *phoneme*. A phoneme is the minimal linguistic unit, and replacement of a phoneme can result in a meaning difference. For example, in the words *c/a/t* and *m/a/t*, the /c/ and /m/ sounds are distinct phonemes. There are forty-four sounds in the English language that communicate such meaning. The written representations of the sounds are called *graphemes*. Because there are only twenty-six graphemes in English, some children have trouble relating the correct phoneme to the grapheme, especially in reading and spelling.

In an effort to limit the sound/symbol inconsistencies, some instructional systems present only consistent spellings in beginning materials. These materials present sentences such as "The cat sat on a bat." Another attempt to overcome inconsistencies is the *i/t/a* alphabet developed by Sir James Pitman. This alphabet has forty-four graphemes, one for each phoneme. Children learn to read and spell in this alphabet and then go through a transitional period in which they learn standard English spelling (Fink & Keiserman, 1969). Figure 2–1 illustrates the *i/t/a* alphabet.

The second code signal studied by linguists is *morphology,* or word structure. The smallest meaning-bearing units are called *morphemes*. Thus, *girl* is a morpheme, and it is also the smallest meaningful unit; if any of the graphemes are removed, the combination of letters does not mean *girl*. Because *girl* can also stand alone in meaning, it is called a *free morpheme*. If we add an *s* to *girl* to form *girls*, we have two small units of meaning. We still have the meaning *girl,* but the *s* has added the meaning of plurality. Because *s* cannot stand alone and still mean plurality, it is called a *bound morpheme*. Prefixes and suffixes have meanings, and also change the meaning of root words when they are added to the root.

The study of word changes attributable to bound morphemes helps children understand meaning and develop vocabulary. For example, consider the list of free and bound morphemes below. What happens to the meaning of the words when the prefix *un* is added?

Bound Morpheme	Free Morpheme
un	happy
un	done
un	desirable
un	domesticated

FIGURE 2–1   The *i/t/a* Alphabet
Source: Reprinted with the permission of Pitman Learning, 6 David Drive, Belmont, CA 94002.

æ face	**b** bed	**c** cat	**d** dog	**ɶ** key
f feet	**g** leg	**h** hat	**ie** fly	**j** jug	**k** key
l letter	**m** man	**n** nest	**œ** over	**p** pen	**ɾ** girl
r red	**s** spoon	**t** tree	**ue** use	**v** voice	**w** window
y yes	**z** zebra	**ʒ** daisy	**wh** when	**ꞔh** chair
th three	**ŧh** the	**ʃh** shop	**ʒ** television	**ŋ** ring
ɑ father	**ʼau** ball	**a** cap	**e** egg	**i** milk	**o** box
u up	**ω** book	**ꞷ** spoon	**ou** out	**oi** oil

A third code signal is *syntax,* or how words are put together in meaningful order to form sentences. The study of syntax in school may be referred to as *grammar.* Grammar is either structural grammar, which looks at the grammatical structure of a sentence, or, more recently, transformational grammar, which looks at how meaning is communicated in sentences. According to many linguists, instruction should emphasize the systematic building of sentences according to certain patterns rather than the diagramming of sentences. Sentence building should also stress the functions of words in sentences rather than rigid categorizations. Consequently, the term *usage* is often preferred to *grammar.*

The final code signal usually studied by linguists is *semantics,* or the study of meaning, and is probably the most important code signal.

Through the study of code signals, we can make several conclusions about linguistic development in children. Even though well advanced by the time children enter school, language development is not complete. Growth is found in all areas including phonology, morphology, syntax, and semantics. There are probably close corollaries between cognitive growth and linguistic development.

Cognitive Development

How important is an understanding of cognitive development? According to Morrow (1989), "Researchers investigating early childhood literacy development are bringing about changes in theory and practice. Generally, they base learning and instructional strategies on what is known about cognitive development" (p. 11). In an article describing research on reading comprehension, Dole et al. (1991) emphasize important understandings about comprehension and instruction that have been gained from cognitive research: "In a cognitively based view of comprehension instruction, the teacher becomes a mediator who helps students construct understandings about: (a) the content of the text itself; (b) strategies that aid in interpreting the text; and (c) the nature of the reading process itself. Elements of this perspective are seen in virtually all comprehension instruction research. Taken as a whole, such instruction can be described as consisting of four kinds of instructional actions: planning, selecting academic work, providing information, and restructuring student understandings" (p. 252).

Cognitive psychologists study not only how information is presented to students but also how learners process the information. Within cognitive psychology, learning is considered a process in which learners actively participate in the teacher–learner act. Educational approaches include teaching students how to think, how to learn, how to remember, and how to motivate themselves. Weinstein and Mayer (1986) identify the following learning strategies under cognitive processes: (a) rehearsal strategies, such as repeating names in an ordered list and underlining pertinent information; (b) elaborative strategies, such as forming mental images, paraphrasing, and creating analogies; (c) organizational strategies, such as grouping, categorizing, and creating diagrams; (d) comprehension monitoring strategies, such as self-questioning and using guide questions to structure reading behavior; and (e) affective strategies, such as reducing external distractions by studying in a quiet place. Terminology frequently associated with cognitive processing includes *schema* (an individual's conceptual system or structure for understanding something), *metacognition* (an individual's knowledge of the functions of his or her own mind and conscious efforts to monitor or control those functions), and *semantic maps* or *webs* (diagrams that help individuals visualize the relationships of words or concepts to one another). The "Essentials of English" adopted by the National Council of Teachers of English (1983) emphasizes stimulating cognitive development. Child development authorities Mussen, Conger, and Kagan (1989) emphasize developing cognitive processes necessary for perception. They identify the following essential processes:

1. *Perception*—the identifications, organization, and interpretation of information
2. *Memory*—the storage and retrieval of perceived information
3. *Reasoning*—the use of knowledge to make inferences and draw conclusions
4. *Reflection*—the evaluation of the quality of ideas and solutions
5. *Insight*—the recognition of new relationships between two or more segments of knowledge.

What instructional strategies are recommended for developing cognitive processes? Interestingly, silence can be an important strategy. Allowing time to think about a discussion, to formulate questions, and to answer questions increases the cognitive level of both responses and questions. Tobin (1987) reviewed research that extended the average one-second wait time in discussions to between three and five seconds. He reported that such extensions cause teachers to repeat fewer questions, to ask higher level questions, and to ask more probing questions. Positive changes in student behavior included more responses, longer responses, increases in the cognitive levels of responses, greater initiation of discussions, more student-to-student interaction, decreases in confusion, and higher achievement. Tobin concludes "silence provides teachers with time to think and to formulate and use higher quality discourse that then influences the thinking and responding of students" (p. 87).

George Maxim (1997) emphasizes cognitive development that includes two major areas: physical knowledge and logicomathematical ability. Physical knowledge is gained through observing properties of objects within the child's experience. The child learns about the physical environment through observation and experimentation. Logicomathematical ability includes the ability to classify or group objects on some common criterion; to arrange objects according to size, quality, or quantity and then compare likenesses and differences among objects in the same category and order them according to relative differences; to understand spatial relations in terms of direction, distance, and perspective; to understand temporal relations that allow perception of time sequences; and to conceptualize properties of objects.

Dole et al. (1991) identify effective instructional actions related to cognitive development. First, teachers modify the instructional plan to accommodate students and to allow teachers to respond to students' emerging understandings. Second, teachers select academic work that provides appropriate experiences; that allows students to conclude that comprehension requires making predictions, asking questions, summarizing, and clarifying parts of the text; that focuses students' attention on the reasoning processes expert readers use when they read; and that allows students to apply the cognitive strategies that teachers model. Third, teachers provide students with information about the usefulness of what is being taught. Through modeling, they provide explicit, unambiguous information that allows students to understand the teachers' reasoning processes when approaching a task, solving a problem, and answering questions. Fourth, as the lessons progress, teachers obtain feedback from students so as to assess their understanding. On the basis of this informal assessment, "effective teachers spontaneously create instructional scaffolding—cuing, prompting, analogies, metaphors, questioning, elaborations, and remodeling—to provide students with the necessary information that will help them restructure their understandings" (p. 255). Gradually, teachers move from instruction in which they provide the scaffolding, to instruction in which students assume increasing responsibility. This instruction takes time, however. Brown, Dole, and Trathen (1990) report that it took four weeks of instruction using a variety of instructional activities before fifth-grade students could transfer a prior knowledge prereading strategy to independently read selections.

The literature provides numerous suggestions for ways to develop students' cognitive abilities. Myers (1983) suggests activities that encourage students to organize information into meaningful wholes. Myers also recommends semantic mapping strategies to help students visualize concepts and relationships. A similar approach for concept and vocabulary development is recommended by Johnson and Pearson (1984). Squire (1982) focuses instruction on language tasks that encourage analyzing, reporting, persuading, interpreting, reflecting, imagining, and inventing. Fitzpatrick (1994) recommends higher order questions that require critical thinking. Schmitt (1990) develops a questionnaire that measures students' awareness of the strategies they use. Flynn (1989) helps students analyze, synthesize, and evaluate ideas through cooperative problem solving. Stahl and Kapinus (1991) teach students to predict word meanings in content areas. Wade (1990) uses think-alouds to assess comprehension. Hadaway, Vardell, and Young (2001) stress the scaffolding of oral language development through oral poetry reading. Norton (2003) recommends literature-related oral activities to develop skills in observing, comparing, classifying, hypothesizing, organizing, summarizing, applying, and criticizing.

Scientist and author Chet Raymo (1992) highlights the role of children's books in developing a scientific imagination. He states, "Creative science depends crucially upon habits of mind that are most readily acquired by children: curiosity; voracious observation; sensitivity to rules and variations within the rules; and fantasy. Children's books that instill these habits of mind sustain science" (p. 561).

The development of these important cognitive operations is stressed throughout this text. Oral language activities as well as other language arts activities are especially beneficial for developing cognitive skills. Teachers may also base activities that encourage the development of these operations on the various content areas. Literature, history, geography, art, math, and science provide excellent sources. Oral language activities frequently precede or accompany written composition, listening, reading, and literature activities.

Basic Operations Associated with Thinking

As teachers use more literature-based instruction within their classrooms, they may easily use books to help focus students' attention on the basic operations associated with thinking. We now recommend some language arts activities that focus attention on observing, comparing, classifying, hypothesizing, organizing, summarizing, applying, and criticizing. Specific books to enhance these activities are mentioned.

Observing.   Language arts teachers have many opportunities to develop observational skills. Teachers of young children may focus children's observations on concrete objects in the school, home, or neighborhood. Young children can describe the color, size, shape, and use of objects in their environment.

Colorful illustrations in picture books enhance observational skills as children identify objects and describe the content. Number and alphabet books are particularly good sources. For example, students can search for and describe the objects that illustrate each number in Suse MacDonald's *Look Whooo's Counting* (2000). Maggie Smith's *Counting our Way to Maine* (1995) encourages children to observe and count up to twenty objects in the illustrations. Suse MacDonald's *Alphabatics* (1986) entices viewers to follow the illustrations and to describe the changes in each letter of the alphabet as the letter is transformed into an object that represents the letter. In addition to visual observations, children may observe, experience, and describe sensations related to the senses. In Grace Lin's *Kite Flying* (2002), they can observe how to make a dragon kite.

Older students can search for literary, art, or historical objects in Mitsumasa Anno's *Anno's U.S.A.* (1983). They may observe and describe the various stories and geographical locations that inspire the boy's dream in David Wiesner's wordless book, *Free Fall* (1988). Anthony Browne's *Willy's Pictures* (2000) provides an observational task in which readers are asked to identify the artistic works that inspired Browne's illustrations. The book concludes with copies of the original paintings. This book encourages both careful observation and comparisons among Browne's paintings and the original art. Roxie Munro's *Mazescapes* (2001) challenges readers to follow a series of mazes through cityscapes and over country roads. The opening shows a hand carrying the book to a car, which infers that the book might be used to provide entertainment during a car trip. Ed Emberley's *The Wing on a Flea: A Book About Shapes* (2001) encourages readers to observe, locate, and describe the locations of geometric forms such as triangles, rectangles, and circles. Emberley's book could also be used to motivate students to create their own pictures using these shapes or to search their environments for similar shapes. Both observation and knowledge of geography are enhanced as students use clues from illustrations to identify various locations in Edith Baer's *This Is the Way We Go to School: A Book About Children Around the World* (1990). Students may check the accuracy of their observations on a world map located at the back of the book.

Word association activities enhance observational skills, vocabulary development, and writing capabilities. These activities are appropriate for any age level, but you should change them to meet the developing language capabilities of children. Younger children may consider words that create strong emotions. You may ask, "What causes you to feel angry? How do you show your anger? How do other people or even animals display anger?" Similar discussions and observations may invoke students into thinking about feelings of love, happiness, and fear.

A verbal observation activity for older children may follow the format developed by Catherine Daughtery, a headmistress of a primary school in Scotland. In an effort to help children visualize and describe emotional experiences, she tells them a short story. For example, to enhance observations about misery, she tells children a story about a puppy lost in the snow after it is taken from its mother. She asks the children to describe orally their visual pictures. Next, they list words, mainly verbs and adjectives, that convey the emotional message of the story. Finally, each child provides one sentence, with carefully selected words, that describes a visual picture. This activity can expand as children first observe and then describe people in the environment, on film, or in pictures.

Daughtery maintains that oral language development is very important if children are to develop observational skills and imagination and use them in oral and written compositions. She states: "Broadly speaking, we must begin by training the children's observation of things which are to them commonplace and very often not worthy of notice. We must then explore the way in which they tell or write the results of their observations. Initially, these will be 'flat' matter-of-fact observations with no attendant aids from emotive language or imagery. The use of emotive language and imagery is not essentially instinctive unless to a particular gifted child, so a great deal of groundwork, including vocabulary building, must be done. The bulk of this work should be, in the initial stages, oral. Free expression and expansion of thought are inhibited by the superfluous process of recording at this level" (personal communication, June 20, 1983).

Comparing.   Readers can compare how a location might appear at different time periods in Jeannie Baker's *Where the Forest Meets the Sea* (1987). The story is set in the tropical rain forest between the Daintree River and Bloomfield in North Queensland, Australia, near the Great Barrier Reef. The collage illustrations show a contemporary boy and his father visiting the location and imagining what it might have looked like 100 million years ago. Careful observation reveals extinct and rare animals living in the forest and aboriginal children playing there. In the final illustration, the boy is visualizing what the same location might look like if the trappings of modern culture were to impinge.

Changes over time periods may be compared using John Goodall's *The Story of a Main Street* (1987), Renata Von Tscharner and Ronald Fleming's *New Providence: A Changing City Scape* (1987), and Mary Blocksma's *Ticket to the Twenties: A Time Traveler's Guide* (1993). Goodall's illustrations portray the same English town from medieval through contemporary times. Students can compare buildings, transportation, clothing, and hairstyles. Von Tscharner and Fleming's text and illustrations follow a small town from 1910 through 1987. Geography teachers find this book exciting because students can search for changes in land use, transportation, and culture. Blocksma's text provides a history of social life and customs and encourages students to describe characteristics of the 1920s. They may also conduct research into other time periods and compare these time periods. Anne Millard's *A Street Through Time: A 12,000-Year Walk Through History* (1998) includes detailed illustrations that depict the same street from the "Stone Age" to "Modern Times." Information books for older readers such as James Cross Giblin's *The Century That Was: Reflections on the Last One Hundred Years* (2000) presents essays about important happenings in history such as "Great Strides: Women in the Twentieth Century," "The Changing Concept of Civil Rights in America," and "A Hundred Years of Wheels and Wings."

Some books emphasize changes that result from natural disasters. For example, students can use Carole Vogel and Kathryn Goldner's *The Great Yellowstone Fire* (1990) to compare the Yellowstone Park before and after the fire. Or they can use Patricia Lauber's *Volcano: The Eruption and Healing of Mount St. Helens* (1986) to compare the area before, during, and after the volcanic eruption.

Books that focus on sequential development may be very creative and require considerable comparisons as readers explore the relationships in books such as Richard McGuire's *Night Becomes Day* (1994). Children can discuss the associations in the book during such changes as when trees become logs, logs become paper, and newspapers become trash. Other associations proceed from streets to highways to cities. After reading this book children may create their own chains of associations.

Older students may compare plots and characterizations in stories that have similar conflicts. For example, in Marion Bauer's *On My Honor* (1986), person-versus-self conflict results when a boy disobeys his father and swims in a river, resulting in the drowning of his best friend. In Paula Fox's *One-Eyed Cat* (1984), personal conflict results when a boy disobeys his father and shoots an air rifle, wounding a cat. Students can compare the plot development in the two stories, the ways in which conflict is portrayed, and how each character overcomes conflict. They can also compare their personal responses to the conflicts of the characters.

Different artists' and authors' renditions of the same story or of similar stories provide numerous opportunities for comparisons and critical evaluations. Multicultural components come into play with different versions of "Little Red Riding Hood." Four excellent choices would be the Brothers Grimm's *Little Red Riding Hood* (1983), James Marshall's *Red Riding Hood* (1987), Charles Perrault's *Little Red Riding Hood* (1983), and Ed Young's *Lon Po Po: A Red-Riding Hood Story from China* (1989). Several adaptations of folktales are available in which the authors write the stories from the point of view of one of the other characters. For example, students may compare the plot, conflict, and characters in the original folktale of "The Three Little Pigs" with the same elements in Eugene Trivizas's *The Three Little Wolves and the Big Bad Pig* (1993) and in Jon Scieszka's *The True Story of the 3 Little Pigs!* (1989).

Comparing the quality of coverage in two books about the same subject is also excellent for developing critical abilities. For example, older students may compare the quantity and the quality of the content in Alexander Sturgis's *Introducing Rembrandt* (1994) with Gary Schwartz's *First Impressions: Rembrandt* (1992). Interesting comparisons can also be made between original novels and movie or television adaptations. For example, students can make interesting comparisons between the various "Harry Potter" books by J. K. Rowling such as *Harry Potter and the Sorcerer's Stone* (1998) and *Harry Potter and the Chamber of Secrets* (1999) and the film versions. Additional comparisons can be made between Tolkien's "Lord of the Rings" trilogy and the movie versions of the books: *The Fellowship of the Ring* (1965), *The Two Towers* (1965), and *The Return of the King* (1965). Comparisons among responses to and illustrations associated with *The Wizard of Oz* can be made using Peter Glassman's *Oz: The Hundredth Anniversary Celebration* (2000). Various artists such as Maurice Sendak, Trina Schart Hyman, and Paul O. Zelinsky have contributed to the volume. Students can consider the changes that were made, the reasons for the changes, and their personal responses to the different versions.

Comparisons between two points of view may be made using Dorothea P. Seeber's *A Pup Just for Me: A Boy Just for Me* (2000). There are two stories in the book. One is told from the point of view of a boy who wants a puppy and the other from a puppy who wants a kind, loving master. Older students may compare points of view in Paul Fleischman's *Bull Run* (1993) in which the story of the first battle of the Civil War is told from the viewpoint of various people involved in the war. Eight of these people express the Northern point of view and eight express the Southern point of view. Helping students identify and understand point of view, according to middle-school principal Marie Petrie, is one of the most important comprehension skills that need to be taught (personal communication, October 2001).

Classifying.   Children may describe and classify concrete objects in the environment according to shape, color, size, and use. Concept books that emphasize alphabetical order, colors, numbers, sizes, and shapes enhance classifying activities. For example, Arnold Lobel's

Classifying activities stimulate cognitive development in children.

On Market Street (1981), an alphabetical trip through a market street of an earlier time, encourages children to add to various objects categorized in groups, such as apples, books, clocks, instruments, and toys. Tana Hoban uses colors to classify objects in *Of Colors and Things* (1989). Her numerous concept books on colors and shapes provide excellent sources for the classification activities of young children.

Picture books stimulate numerous discussions and applications related to classifying. Students can add their own sounds to those described in Rebecca Emberley's *City Sounds* (1989). Lloyd Moss's *Zin! Zin! Zin! A Violin* (1995) may be used to encourage students to classify and compare various sounds made by instruments of the orchestra. Ann Jonas's *Aardvarks, Disembark!* (1990) may stimulate a classification scheme for endangered and extinct animals. Jonas's book may be compared with Patricia Mullins's *V for Vanishing: An Alphabet of Endangered Animals* (1994) to encourage additional classifications and comparisons.

Hypothesizing.   Literature selections can encourage children to hypothesize about the language an author might use, about the plot from clues in the title, and about how the plot will develop. In *Joseph Had a Little Overcoat* (1999), Simms Taback uses cutouts in illustrations to provide clues about the next, always smaller, item that he makes out of the material that was once his old and worn jacket. Rhyming patterns in books for younger children provide powerful language cues. Read such books as Jack Prelutsky's *Beneath a Blue Umbrella* (1990) and ask children to complete a missing word in these humorous rhyming poems. Debra and Sal Barracca's *The Adventures of Taxi Dog* (1990) encourages children to fill in rhyming words in a story about Maxie as he accompanies the driver around New York City. Let older children listen for and complete the rhyming elements in "The King of Cats" in Nancy Willard's *A Visit to William Blake's Inn* (1981). In addition, the poems in Jack Prelutsky's *The Random House Book of Poetry for Children* (1983) provide a rich source for rhyming activities.

Stories that use repetition of language or plot stimulate children to hypothesize about what will happen next. While listening to Mem Fox's *Hattie and the Fox* (1987), children can hypothesize about the language to be used and changes in the story. In a similar approach, students can provide the next lines in Michael Rosen's *We're Going on a Bear Hunt* (1989). This cumulative tale adds a new incident with each telling until the story is complete. Verna Aardema's *Why Mosquitoes Buzz in People's Ears* (1975), Janet Stevens's *The House That Jack Built* (1985), the "Gingerbread Boy," "Henny Penny," and "The Fat Cat" are other good examples of cumulative tales that encourage children to hypothesize and join in with appropriate words.

Descriptive and imaginative book titles, such as Judith Viorst's *Alexander and the Terrible, Horrible, No Good, Very Bad Day* (1972), James Stevenson's *The Wish Card Ran Out!* (1981), Kit Pearson's *A Handful of Time* (1989), and Geraldine McCaughrean's *A Pack of Lies* (1988), encourage hypothesizing about story content. Chapter titles also can be used for this purpose.

Stories that speculate about "what if" or that provide opportunities to decide on conclusions are excellent for hypothesizing. Ian McEwan's *The Daydreamer* (1994) provides such an opportunity for readers as they vicariously accompany ten-year-old Peter on a series of fantasy adventures. What would happen if he used vanishing cream? How would it feel to switch bodies with a cat or a baby? Nina Jaffe and Steve Zeitlin's *While Standing on One Foot: Puzzle Stories and Wisdom Tales from the Jewish Tradition* (1993) is written in the form of an intellectual puzzle. Each story is written in two parts. The first part develops the conflict or problem. A question follows that is designed to challenge children into thinking about a possible solution and to match the wisdom of the storyteller. The second part of the story resolves the conflict. Now readers may compare their responses with the actual one in the story.

Organizing.   Stories that chronicle the cycle of a day are meaningful to younger children. Jonathan London's *Like Butter on Pancakes* (1995) begins early with "spoons sleep nestled in the kitchen drawers" (unnumbered) and concludes with night as "Mama sings in your dark blue room" (unnumbered). Picture books that develop stories using seasonal changes, such as Donald Hall's *Ox-Cart Man* (1979), can help children understand the time sequence in which events take place. Susi Gregg Fowler's *When Summer Ends* (1989) portrays a young child as she thinks about all the good experiences she has had through the various seasons of the year. Carolyn Lesser's *What a Wonderful Day to Be a Cow* (1995) is a concept book that presents the sequence associated with the twelve months on a farm.

Informational books for older students often follow a chronological order. Judith St. George's *The White House: Cornerstone of a Nation* (1990) discusses the changes and events that have occurred during the last two centuries. It begins in 1791 and progresses into the late 1900s. In Kathryn Lasky's *Sugaring Time* (1983), photographs and text describe the procedures used to collect sap from maple trees and process it into syrup.

Stories that stress scientific time sequences help children understand organizational plans in nature. Douglas Henderson's *Dinosaur Tree* (1994) is the life story of a tree beginning in a Triassic forest 225 million years ago and extending through time until the tree is 500 years old and beginning to fossilize. The illustrations and text include details about the dinosaurs that lived during this period in what is now the Painted Desert in Arizona. Scientific time lines are also important when understanding inventions and the consequences of those inventions. Richard Platt's *The Smithsonian Visual Timeline of Inventions* (1994) includes inventions organized into five categories: world events, travel and conquest, agriculture and industry, daily life and health, and measurement and communication. The time line begins in 600,000 B.C. and proceeds to the present.

Stories with strong sequential plots help younger children analyze plot structures. Flannel board presentations may be used to identify logical organization in these stories:

1. "The Three Little Pigs"—progressing from flimsiest to strongest building materials
2. "The Little Red Hen"—following chronological order in the steps for preparing bread
3. "The Three Billy Goats Gruff"—proceeding according to size from smallest to largest.

Summarizing. Children should be given many opportunities to summarize the stories they hear or read, the content covered in course work, and the points made by visiting speakers. Summaries of a given story may vary. Some children may summarize the most exciting part; others, the funniest part; still others, the actions of the main character. Summarizing can easily relate to the most important knowledge gained from an informational book such as Laurie Coulter's *Secrets in Stone: All About Maya Hieroglyphs* (2001).

Applying. Books that encourage children to observe, gather data, experiment, compare, and formulate hypotheses are excellent for cognitive development. For example, after students have been involved with an in-depth study of Native American cultures they might search for and evaluate the settings, values, and beliefs developed in Louise Erdrich's *The Birchbark House* (1999), an Ojibwa story set on an island in Lake Superior in 1847. After completing a study of India they might analyze the way the author develops the Hindu culture in Gloria Whelan's *Homeless Bird* (2000). This book, set in modern India, is worthy of an in-depth analysis of both the author's development of cultural authenticity and literary style. As part of a study of World War II and the Holocaust, students could evaluate the author's effectiveness in using parallel voices to express two points of view in Miriam Bat-Ami's *Two Suns in the Sky* (1999). The story chronicles both the problems of Jewish refugees in America during World War II and the responses to the refugees by Americans living near the refugee shelters. One point of view belongs to Chris, a teenage girl who lives near a refugee camp in Oswego, New York. The second point of view belongs to Adam, a Jewish youth whose family first escaped from Yugoslavia and then from hiding in Italy. (In-depth analyses of all of these books are developed in Norton's *Through the Eyes of a Child: An Introduction to Children's Literature,* sixth edition, 2003.)

Books encourage students to develop hobbies and those hobbies may even lead to careers. Jon Cech's *Jacques-Henri Lartigue: Boy With a Camera* (1994) presents the photographs of a photographer who started taking pictures in his childhood. Sylvia Wolf's *Focus: Five Women Photographers* (1994) presents information about and examples of the works of photographers Margaret Bourke-White, Julia Margaret Cameron, Flor Garduno, Sandy Skoglund, and Lorna Simpson. *Restless Spirit: The Life and Work of Dorothea Lange* by Elizabeth Partridge (1998) is a biography that presents both the photographer's life and many of her works. Numerous other books focus on the work of specific professions. For example, Nic Bishop's *Digging for Bird-Dinosaurs: An Expedition to Madagascar* (2000) follows the experiences of a team of paleontologists as they search for fossils. Sy Montgomery's *The Snake Scientist* (1999) discusses the work of Bob Mason as he studies the red-sided garter snakes at the Narcisse Wildlife Management area in Manitoba, Canada.

Books that provide detailed descriptions of experiments that may be replicated at school or home are excellent sources for applying knowledge and gaining information. Steve Parker's *How the Body Works* (1994) includes detailed experiments that are illustrated through photographs. Discussions and interactions are enhanced because many of the experiments suggest adult supervision.

Criticizing. Developing students' critical evaluation skills may be one of the most important cognitive skills. Students should have many opportunities to critically evaluate an author's ability to create both believable and enjoyable texts. For example, how does Jack Gantos in *Joey Pigza Loses Control* (2000) develop both a humorous story and one that reflects the problems and characteristics of a hyperactive boy? How do authors such as Beverly Cleary (*Ramona Quimby, Age 8* and *Ramona the Pest*) and Betsy Byars (*Bingo Brown and the Language of Love* and *The Cybil War*) develop humorous texts?

Nonfiction information books provide many opportunities for readers to critically evaluate how the information is presented and the effectiveness and authenticity of the information. For example, readers can evaluate the author's ability to show how the Nazi government tried to turn the 1936 Olympic games held in Berlin into a propaganda tool for their cause. In *The Nazi Olympics: Berlin 1936* (2000), Susan D. Bachrach provides background information, a discussion using titles such as "The Nazification of German Sport," a review of "The Boycott Debate," and a summary of "The Nazi Olympics." The text also provides many opportunities for debate as students consider the negative or positive aspects of incorporating politics into sports. This topic interests older students because they can also research the role of politics in sports today.

Semantic Mapping and Vocabulary Development

Semantic mapping and webbing, a method for graphically and visually displaying relationships between various ideas and concepts, emphasizes cognitive processes and encourages problem solving. Semantic mapping encourages higher thought processes, stimulates ideas, and promotes discussion between students and teachers. Semantic mapping procedures promote vocabulary development (Johnson & Pearson, 1984; Toms-Bronowski, 1983); enhance literary discussions that highlight plot, setting, characterization, and theme (Norton, 2003); improve reading comprehension (McNamara & Norton, 1987; Prater & Terry, 1985); enhance development of instructional units (Norton, 1982); stimulate the composition process (Cunningham & Allington, 2003; Myers & Gray, 1983); encourage interaction and understanding in various content areas (Heimlich & Pittelman, 1986); provide ways of assessing understanding of literature (Norton, 1991); stimulate the identification of background knowledge (Norton, 1991); and encourage the integration of reading, literature, writing, listening, and oral discussion within the language arts curriculum (McNamara & Norton, 1987).

Each of the objectives for the semantic mapping strategy uses slightly different procedures. An in-depth approach to each procedure is provided as it is developed within the appropriate chapters of this text. General procedures, however, usually begin with brainstorming activities in which teachers encourage students to verbalize associations or ideas while the teachers map the ideas on the chalkboard. The content of an initial map varies according to teaching and learning objectives and the subject matter being visualized. Semantic mapping may be an introductory activity to organize and extend previous knowledge or to explore various possibilities, a discussion activity to visualize relationships and promote understanding of content, or a follow-up activity to reinforce learning or even to test understandings. Semantic mapping strategies may help children identify words with similar meanings, expand vocabulary, understand multiple meanings for words, develop concepts, and perceive relationships between words and between ideas. The activities we describe in this section can be stimulated through brainstorming and group or class discussion.

Similar Meanings and Semantic Precision.   Numerous words, such as *said* and *went,* are overused in speaking and writing. Helping children use words precisely will improve both their speaking and writing and stimulate their cognitive development. A fourth-grade teacher developed the following procedures using the word *went*. First, the teacher wrote and then read several sentences on the chalkboard. For example:

Jackie <u>went</u> *to the park to find a lost football.*

Mike <u>went</u> *to the store to spend his birthday money.*

Sharon <u>went</u> *to school to take a spelling test.*

Terry <u>went</u> *to the park to play in the championship soccer game.*

Next, the class identified the word *went* and discussed how well the word expressed the feelings and actions of the subjects. To illustrate different meanings, the teacher asked the students to dramatize each sentence. The students also dictated additional sentences in which *went* could be used but might not be appropriate. The teacher then led a brainstorming activity, encouraging the children to identify numerous words that could be used in place of *went*. The following is a partial list:

ran	jogged	hurried	strutted
marched	danced	pranced	promenaded
raced	flounced	dawdled	sauntered
ambled	swaggered	rambled	crawled
glided	drifted	skipped	bounced
wandered	staggered	bounded	meandered
strolled	dashed	trotted	hopped
hastened	shuffled	scampered	capered
lurched	stumbled	wobbled	tottered
swayed	moseyed	struggled	limped

In an effort to categorize meanings for *went,* the teacher and class identified happy meanings, tired meanings, slow meanings, fast meanings, proud meanings, frightened meanings, and sad meanings. Then they used the meanings as subheadings in a web around the word *went* (see Figure 2–2).

Finally, the class considered the words on the list and placed them around the appropriate meaning or meanings. The children identified additional words as they considered each classification. They also discussed the relationships between words that had several meanings. Figure 2–3 represents a partial web developed by the class.

Multiple Meanings and Different Parts of Speech.   Even simple words may become difficult for children to understand if they are used in unfamiliar contexts or as previously unused parts of speech. Three meanings for the word *act* are illustrated in Figure 2–4, which was developed in an upper elementary social studies class.

FIGURE 2–2   First Step in a Web Designed to Categorize Meanings of *Went*

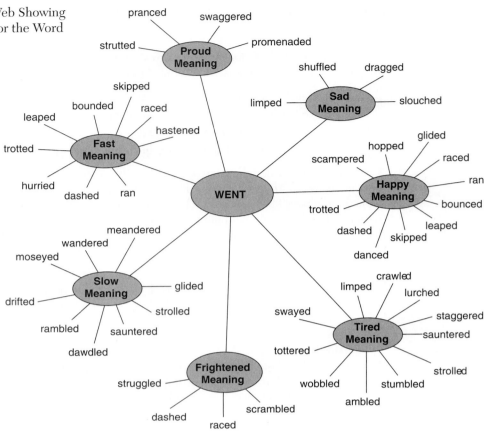

FIGURE 2–3 A Web Showing Various Meanings for the Word *Went*

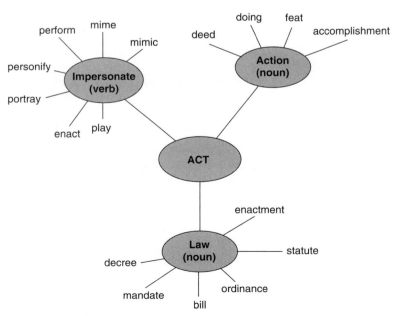

FIGURE 2–4 A Map Illustrating Three Meanings for the Word *Act*

Semantic Maps Representing Concepts. Johnson and Pearson (1984) recommend developing semantic maps to illustrate class and property links that "capture the character of our intuitive notions about the similarities and differences among concepts" (p. 29). Figure 2–5 illustrates the concepts related to two types of horses: riding horses and work horses.

Semantic Maps and Story Comprehension. Semantic maps help children understand stories and see relationships between various character traits, settings, and plots. Semantic maps are developed throughout this text.

Semantic Maps and Vocabulary Development. Webbing can relate to the vocabulary of a single book or it can suggest related words in a unit or theme approach. A web can be drawn as a prereading vocabulary activity or it can be used in a follow-up approach. Students can exhibit prior knowledge about vocabulary on the web before they read and then add to and even change the web after they have read a book. For example, to accompany Katherine Paterson's *The Tale of the Mandarin Ducks* (1990), the teacher could draw a web on the board with *The Tale of the Mandarin Ducks* in the center. Words that have special relevance to the story would be placed on the branches of the web. In this case, the words might in-

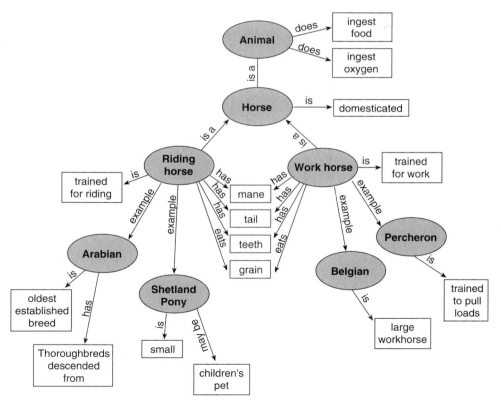

Figure 2–5 A map representing the concepts related to two types of horses: riding horses and work horses

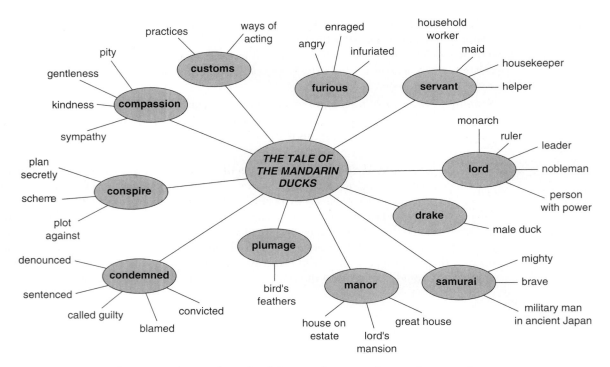

FIGURE 2–6   A Web to Accompany *The Tale of the Mandarin Ducks.* On the Branches
Are Words that Are Particularly Meaningful for the Story

clude *servant, lord, drake, samurai, manor, condemned, conspire, compassion,* and *customs.*
The web shown in Figure 2–6 was developed with a group of middle elementary students.

A similar approach may be used when identifying important words in a unit. For example,
in completing a unit on friendship, students could identify important characteristics associated
with friendship. They could then brainstorm additional words relating to those characteristics.

Connections Between Language and Social Development

Language development and social development are closely related. Gallagher (1993) and
Daiute and Griffin (1993) relate language skill and the development of social competence.
Gallagher emphasizes that the roles peers play in the development of language by providing opportunities for establishing and practicing language skills, role modeling, and feedback are being increasingly cited. She states, "the ability of school-age children to adjust
their messages in light of their listener's needs, to initiate conversation successfully, to ask
appropriate questions, to contribute substantively to ongoing conversations, to communicate intentions clearly, to address all participants when joining a group, and to present comments positively more often than negatively have been found to relate to measures of peer
acceptance and sociometric status" (p. 199).

Gallagher (1993) reviews peer aspects of developing social competence of school-age
children and concludes that language facility is important when developing social competence. For example, at the preschool and early elementary levels, children externalize their

understanding of friendship. They have a tendency to confuse feelings and behaviors and to deal with interpersonal conflict in physical terms. Fantasy play, their most valued form of play, requires clear communication skills. Children with limited language skills are susceptible to misinterpretations because their verbal behaviors may be misleading. They rely heavily on interpretations of intentions and feelings that reflect their own perspective. During this developmental period, when self-presentation and peer group inclusion are highly valued, language skill differences could become the focus of negative peer attention.

Daiute and Griffin (1993) emphasize the importance of social interaction in classrooms that develop language abilities. They state: "Classrooms that are rich in social interaction engage children in the use of discourse styles that move beyond their home discourse and beyond traditional school discourse. A major element of classrooms where children can truly make sense of the curriculum is peer interaction, which links culture and development since it involves children in interpreting academic material in their own ways" (p. 98). Developing rewarding friendships are important themes for children as found in Miriam Cohen's *Best Friends* (1971) or interracial friendships may be emphasized as in Carole Lexa Schaefer's *Snow Pumpkin* (2000).

Socialization occurs when children learn the ways of their groups so that they can function acceptably within those groups. Acceptable relationships require an understanding of the feelings and viewpoints of others. Consequently, socialization is a very important part of child development. Three processes are influential in the socialization of children. First, reward or punishment by parents and other adults reinforces socially acceptable attitudes and behaviors and discourages socially unacceptable ones. Second, observation of others teaches children the responses, behaviors, and beliefs considered appropriate within their culture. Children learn how to act and what to believe by imitating adults and peers. Third, through identification, children develop emotional ties with models. Children's thoughts, feelings, and actions become similar to those of people they believe are like them.

Books and literature-related discussions can aid in the development of socialization by encouraging children to become sensitive to the feelings of others. Developing rewarding friendships may be one of the most important social relationships for many children. The importance of discovering a friend with similar interests and helping a friend are both important themes in Patricia Lee Gauch's *Tanya and Emily in a Dance for Two* (1994). The importance of friendship and developing pride in one's work are themes developed in Roni Schotter's *A Fruit & Vegetable Man* (1993) in which friends help an elderly man keep his market open when he becomes ill. Overcoming sibling rivalry is another aspect of socialization. Jeers and taunts of an older brother emphasize the rivalry between a young girl and her older brother in Patricia Polacco's *My Rotten Redheaded Older Brother* (1994). In a satisfying ending, the older brother provides support when she needs him. Overcoming sibling rivalry is also the focus of P. J. Petersen's *The Amazing Magic Show* (1994) as two brothers make discoveries about themselves and their relationships during a series of humorous episodes connected with the arrival of a magic show in their town. What happens to people when they want to be different from those around them is the subject of Toni Morrison's *The Big Box* (1999). The story, told in poetic form, provides an interesting discussion as children are placed in a box because they cannot handle their freedom and act differently than their teachers and parents desire. A tender story about accepting others is developed by Cari Best in *Goose's Story* (2002), in which a girl interacts with a goose that is missing a foot.

Developing an understanding of the responsibilities associated with, and the requirements for, parenting and family unity are important socialization processes for older students. Anne Fine's *Flour Babies* (1994) is one of the most humorous and thought-provoking books for older readers. This story follows a class as each student takes part in a three-week experiment that requires them to care for a six-pound bag of flour that represents a baby. It is Simon who becomes attached to his baby as he tries to discover why his father left him when he was a young child. In a story set in the Middle Ages, Karen Cushman's heroine in *Catherine, Called Birdy* (1994) faces numerous social and personal problems as her rebellious nature makes it difficult for her to adjust to the requirements of being the daughter of an impoverished knight. Contemporary readers may have thought-provoking discussions as they try to envision Catherine's conflicts as she records her experiences in her diary in 1290. Both the discussions and the text increase language and social development.

SUMMARY

Language is the basis of human communication. In fact, language is uniquely human, and it is the only form of communication that allows its users to devise theories about the language system itself. This chapter discusses several theories of language acquisition. The genetic theory states that language is not learned through imitation but is innate, or instinctive. Proponents of this theory believe all children are born with the ability to use language. They begin with a language of their own and amend it to conform to adult language. Linguists give three reasons to support the theory that language ability is biologically inherited: (1) There are many features common to all languages; (2) word patterns that children construct are not imitations of adult speech; and (3) the sequence of language development in children is orderly and systematic, related to the physical and motor aspects of development.

Although scholars disagree about theories of language acquisition, most agree about the sequence of events in language development. Research concludes that all children appear to go through approximately the same stages of language development, although the rate of development varies from child to child. Longitudinal studies by Brown and Loban provide educators with extensive knowledge about language development. Although language development is advanced by the time most children enter school, it is far from complete; thus, teachers should adjust their expectations in written and oral composition as well as in reading comprehension to the level of language development of each child.

This chapter also reviews a linguistic analysis of language and discusses some of its implications for instruction. Linguists investigate the code signals of language, including phonology (the sound system), morphology (meaning in relation to speech sounds), syntax (how words are put together to form sentences), and semantics (meaning).

Learning environments must stimulate cognitive development in children. Therefore, teachers should provide stimulating activities for students. Activities that encourage children to observe, compare, classify, hypothesize, organize, summarize, apply, and criticize what they have learned are important. Semantic mapping and webbing strategies emphasize cognitive processes and encourage problem solving.

ADDITIONAL LANGUAGE AND COGNITIVE DEVELOPMENT ACTIVITIES

1. Look at several different instructional materials used to develop language or reading skills with children. Do the materials fragment the instruction of the linguistic code into phonology, morphology, syntax, and semantics, or do they stress the interrelationship between the linguistic signals? Find some examples of each approach and share them with your class.

2. Visit several nursery school or kindergarten classrooms. Observe the environments and the instructional activities. Can you identify a theory of language acquisition supported by the instructional activities for each classroom?

3. Interview a professor of early childhood development, educational psychology, or special education. What is the professor's view on language acquisition? What type of learning environment and instructional activities does the professor recommend? Share the results of your interview with your language arts class. Do all of the professors agree on a theory of language acquisition and learning environments? Can you provide any reasons for differences of opinion?

4. Tape-record a conversation between a very young child and his or her parents. How does the parent adjust his or her language to the conversational skills of the child? How is meaning achieved?

5. Read a recent journal article or chapter in a text emphasizing language acquisition or development. What is the major emphasis of the author? What theory of language acquisition does the author support? What evidence does the author include? What implications for instruction are included or implied?

6. Read an article on cognitive development and identify an instructional application important in the language arts.

7. Select one of the cognitive operations discussed in the chapter. Develop a lesson plan to help children observe, compare, classify, hypothesize, organize, summarize, apply, or criticize.

8. Plan a lesson to encourage vocabulary development. With a group of children or your peers, develop a semantic map that identifies words with similar meanings, expands a precise vocabulary, or increases understanding of multiple meanings.

BIBLIOGRAPHY

Akhtar, N.; Dunham, F.; and Dunham, P. "Directive Interactions and Early Vocabulary Development: The Role of Joint 1 Attentional Focus." *Journal of Child Language* 18 (1991): 41–49.

Bartel, Nettie. "Assessing and Remediating Problems in Language Development." In *Teaching Children with Learning and Behavior Problems*, 3rd ed., edited by Donald Hammill and Nettie Bartel. Boston: Allyn & Bacon, 1995.

Braine, Martin D. S. "The Ontogeny of English Phrase Structure: The First Phase." In *Readings in Language Development*, edited by Lois Bloom. New York: John Wiley & Sons, 1978.

Brown, K. B.; Dole, J. A.; and Trathen, W. "A Comparison of Alternative Approaches to Prereading Instruction." Paper presented at the meeting of the National Reading Conference, Miami, 1990.

Brown, Roger. *A First Language/The Early Stages.* Cambridge, Mass.: Harvard University Press, 1973.

Bruner, Jerome. "Learning the Mother Tongue." *Human Nature* 1 (September 1978): 42–49.

Cazden, Courtney B. *Child Language and Education.* New York: Holt, Rinehart & Winston, 1972.

Chaney, Carolyn. "Language Development, Metalinguistic Skills, and Print Awareness in 3-Year-Old Children." *Applied Psycholinguistics* 13 (1992): 485–514.

Chomsky, Carol. *The Acquisition of Syntax in Children from 5 to 10.* Research Monograph 52. Cambridge, Mass.: The MIT Press, 1969.

Clay, Marie M. "Child Development." In *Handbook of Research on Teaching the English Language Arts,* edited by James Flood, Julie M. Jensen, Diane Lapp, and James R. Squire. New York: Macmillan, 1991.

Cunningham, P.; and Allington, R. *Classrooms That Work: They Can All Read and Write.* Boston: Allyn & Bacon, 2003.

Daiute, Colette; and Griffin, Terri M. "The Social Construction of Written Narratives." *New Directions for Child Development* 61 (1993): 97–120.

Dole, J.; Duffy, G.; Roehler, L.; and Pearson, P. "Moving from Old to the New: Research on Reading Comprehension Instruction." *Review of Educational Research* 61 (1991): 239–64.

Ervin-Tripp, Susan. "Imitation and Structured Change in Children's Language." In *New Directions in the Study of Language,* edited by E. H. Lenneberg. Cambridge, Mass.: The MIT Press, 1964.

Ervin-Tripp, Susan. "Language Development." In *Review of Child Development Research,* edited by L. Hoffman and M. Hoffman. New York: Russell Sage Foundation, 1966.

Fink, Rychard; and Keiserman, Patricia. *i/t/a. Teacher Training Workbook and Guide.* New York: Initial Teaching Alphabet Publications, 1969.

Fitzpatrick, Karen. "Improving Reading Comprehension Using Critical Thinking Strategies." *Reading Improvement* 31 (Fall 1994): 142–144.

Flynn, L. "Developing Critical Reading Skills through Cooperative Problem Solving." *The Reading Teacher* 42 (1989): 664–68.

Fry, Denis B. "The Development of the Phonological System in the Normal and the Deaf Child." In *The Genesis of Language: A Psycholinguistic Approach,* edited by Frank Smith and George A. Miller. Cambridge, Mass.: The MIT Press, 1966.

Gallagher, Tanya M. "Language Skill and Development of Social Competence in School-Age Children." *Language, Speech, and Hearing Services in Schools* 24 (October 1993): 199–205.

Hadaway, Nancy L.; Vardell, Sylvia M.; and Young, Terrell. "Scaffolding Oral Language Development through Poetry for Students Learning English." *The Reading Teacher* 54 (May 2001): 796–806.

Heimlich, Joan E.; and Pittelman, Susan D. *Semantic Mapping: Classroom Applications.* Newark, Del.: International Reading Association, 1986.

Johnson, Dale D.; and Pearson, P. David. *Teaching Reading Vocabulary,* 2nd ed. New York: Holt, Rinehart & Winston, 1984.

Lawton, Denis. *Social Class, Language, and Education.* New York: Schocken Books, 1968.

Lindfors, Judith W. *Children's Language and Learning,* 2nd ed. Englewood Cliffs, N.J.: Prentice Hall, 1987.

Loban, Walter. *Language Development: Kindergarten Through Grade Twelve.* Urbana, Ill.: National Council of Teachers of English, 1976.

Loban, Walter. "Research Currents: The Somewhat Stingy Story of Research into Children's Language." *Language Arts* 63 (October 1986): 608–16.

Maxim, George. *The Very Young: Guiding Children from Infancy Through the Early Years.* Upper Saddle River, NJ: Merrill/Prentice Hall, 1997.

McGhee-Bidlack, B. "The Development of Noun Definitions: A Metalinguistic Analysis." *Journal of Child Language* 18 (1991): 417–34.

McNamara, James; and Norton, Donna E. *An Evaluation of the Multiethnic Reading/Language Arts Program for Low Achieving Elementary and Junior High School Students, Final Report.* College Station, Tex.: Texas A&M University, 1987.

Menyuk, Paula. "Linguistics and Teaching the Language Arts." In *Handbook of Research on Teaching the English Language Arts,* edited by James Flood, Julie M. Jensen, Diane Lapp, and James R. Squire. New York: Macmillan, 1991, pp. 24–29.

Menyuk, Paula. "Syntactic Structures in the Language of Children." *Child Development* 34 (June 1963): 407–22.

Moll, Luis C. *Vygotsky and Education: Instructional Implications and Applications of Sociohistorical Psychology.* New York: Cambridge University Press, 1990.

Morrow, L. *Literacy Development in the Early Years.* Englewood Cliffs, N.J.: Prentice Hall, 1989.

Morrow, L.; and Rand, M. "Promoting Literacy during Play by Designing Early Childhood Classroom Environments." *The Reading Teacher* 44 (1991): 396–402.

Moskowitz, Breyne Arlene. "The Acquisition of Language." *Scientific American* (November 1978): 92–108.

Mussen, Paul Henry; Conger, John Janeway; and Kagan, Jerome. *Child Development and Personality,* 6th ed. New York: Harper & Row, 1989.

Myers, Miles. "Approaches to the Teaching of Composition." In *Theory and Practice in the Teaching of Composition: Processing, Distancing and Modeling,* edited by Miles Myers and James Gray. Urbana, Ill.: National Council of Teachers of English, 1983, pp. 3–43.

Myers, Miles; and Gray, James. *Theory and Practice in the Teaching of Composition: Processing, Distancing, and Modeling.* Urbana, Ill.: National Council of Teachers of English, 1983.

National Council of Teachers of English. "Forum: Essentials of English." *Language Arts* 60 (February 1983): 244–48.

Norton, D. "Developing Higher Cognitive Skills through Children's Literature." Address presented at Clemson University Reading Conference, Clemson, South Carolina, 1991.

Norton, Donna E. *Through the Eyes of a Child: An Introduction to Children's Literature,* 6th ed. Upper Saddle River, N.J.: Merrill/Prentice Hall, 2003.

Norton, Donna E. "Using a Webbing Process to Develop Children's Literature Units." *Language Arts* 59 (April 1982): 348–56.

Pellegrini, A. D.; Galda, L.; Dresden, J.; and Cox, S. "A Longitudinal Study of the Predictive Relations among Symbolic Play, Linguistic Verbs, and Early Literacy." *Research in the Teaching of English* 25 (1991): 219–35.

Peterson, C.; and Dodsworth, P. "A Longitudinal Analysis of Young Children's Cohesion and Noun Specification in Narratives." *Journal of Child Language* 18 (1991): 397–415.

Poole, Millicent E. *Social Class and Language Utilization at the Tertiary Level.* St. Lucia: University of Queensland Press, 1976.

Prater, D. C.; and Terry, C. A. *The Effects of a Composing Model on Fifth Grade Students' Reading Comprehension.* Paper presented at the American Educational Research Association, 1985 (ERIC Document Reproduction Service No. ED 254 825).

Raven, Ronald J.; and Salzer, Richard T. "Piaget and Reading Instruction." *Reading Teacher* 24 (April 1971): 630–39.

Raymo, Chet. "Dr. Seuss and Dr. Einstein: Children's Books and Scientific Imagination." *The Horn Book* 68 (September/October 1992): 560–567.

Schallert, Diane Lemonnier; and Martin, Debra Bayles. "A Psychological Analysis of What Teachers and Students Do in the Language Arts Classroom." In *Handbook on Research on Teaching the English Language Arts*, 2nd ed., edited by James Flood, Diane Lapp, James R. Squire, and Julie M. Jensen. Mahwah, NJ: Lawrence Erlbaum, 2003, pp. 31–45.

Schmitt, M. "A Questionnaire to Measure Children's Awareness of Strategic Reading Processes." *The Reading Teacher* 43 (1990): 454–61.

Shatz, M.; and Ebeling, K. "Patterns of Language Learning-Related Behaviors: Evidence for Self-Help in Acquiring Grammar." *Journal of Child Language* 18 (1991): 295–313.

Shugar, G. W. "Text Analysis as an Approach to the Study of Early Linguistic Operations." In *The Development of Communication*, edited by Catherine Snow and N. Waterson. Chichester, England: John Wiley, 1978.

Slobin, Dan I.; and Welsh, Charles A. "Elicited Imitation as a Research Tool in Developmental Psycholinguistics." In *Studies of Child Language Development*, edited by Charles A. Ferguson and Daniel I. Slobin. New York: Holt, Rinehart & Winston, 1973.

Smith, C. "Involving Parents in Reading Development." *The Reading Teacher* 43 (1990).

Smith, Madorah. "Grammatical Errors in the Speech of Preschool Children." *Child Development* 4 (1933): 182–90.

Snow, Catherine E. "The Development of Conversation between Mothers and Babies." *Journal of Child Language* 4 (February 1977): 1–22.

Sorsby, A.; and Martlew, M. "Representational Demands in Mothers' Talk to Preschool Children in Two Contexts: Picture Book Reading and a Modelling Task." *Journal of Child Language* 18 (1991): 373–95.

Squire, James R. "The Collision of the Basics Movement with Current Research in Writing and Language." In *The English Curriculum Under Fire: What Are the Real Basics?*, edited by George Hillocks, Jr. Urbana, Ill.: National Council of Teachers of English, 1982, pp. 29–37.

Stahl, S.; and Kapinus, B. "Possible Sentences: Predicting Word Meanings to Teach Content Area Vocabulary." *The Reading Teacher* 45 (1991): 36–43.

Strickland, D. S.; and Feeley, Joan T. "Development in the Elementary School Years." In *Handbook of Research: Teaching the English Language Arts*, 2nd ed., edited by James Flood, Diane Lapp, James R. Squire, and Julie M. Jensen. Mahwah, NJ: Lawrence Erlbaum, 2003, pp. 339–56.

Strickland, D.; and Morrow, L. "Family Literacy: Sharing Good Books." *The Reading Teacher* 43 (1990): 518–19.

Tamis-LeMonda, Catherine S.; and Bornstein, Marc H. "Specificity in Mother-Toddler Language-Play Relations Across the Second Year." *Developmental Psychology* 30 (March 1994): 283–92.

Tobin, Kenneth. "The Role of Wait Time in Higher Cognitive Level Learning." *Review of Educational Research* 57 (Spring 1987): 69–95.

Toms-Bronowski, S. "An Investigation of the Effectiveness of Selected Vocabulary Teaching Strategies with Intermediate Grade Level Students." *Dissertation Abstracts International* 1983, 44, 1405 A (University Microfilms No. 83–16, 238).

Vygotsky, Lev Semenovich. *Mind in Society.* Cambridge, Mass.: Harvard University Press, 1981.

Vygotsky, Lev Semenovich. "Thinking and Speech." In *L. S. Vygotsky, Collected Works, Vol. 1*, edited by R. Rieber and A. Carton. New York: Plenum, 1987, pp. 39–285.

Wade, S. "Using Think-Alouds to Assess Comprehension." *The Reading Teacher* 43 (1990): 442–51.

Walker, Dale; Greenwood, Charles; Hart, Betty; and Carta, Judith. "Prediction of School Outcomes Based on Early Language Production and Socioeconomic Factors." *Child Development* 65 (April 1994): 606–621.

Weinstein, Claire E.; and Mayer, Richard E. "The Teaching of Learning Strategies." In *Handbook of Research and Teaching*, 3rd ed., edited by Merlin C. Wittrock. Upper Saddle River, N.J.: Merrill/Prentice Hall, 1986, pp. 315–27.

Wells, Gordon. "Describing Children's Linguistic Development at Home and at School." *British Educational Research Journal* 5 (1979): 75–98.

Wells, Gordon, ed. *Learning through Interaction: The Study of Language Development.* London: Cambridge University Press, 1981.

Woodward, Amanda L.; Markman, Ellen M.; and Fitzsimmons, Colleen M. "Rapid Word Learning in 13- and 18-Month-Olds." *Developmental Psychology* 30 (July 1994): 553–66.

CHILDREN'S LITERATURE REFERENCES

Aardema, Verna. *Why Mosquitoes Buzz in People's Ears.* New York: Dial Press, 1975.

Anno, Mitsumasa. *Anno's U.S.A.* New York: Philomel, 1983.

Baer, Edith. *This Is the Way We Go to School: A Book About Children Around the World.* Illustrated by Steve Bjorkman. New York: Scholastic, 1990.

Bachrach, Susan D. *The Nazi Olympics: Berlin 1936.* Boston: Little, Brown, 2000.

Baker, Jeannie. *Where the Forest Meets the Sea.* New York: Greenwillow, 1987.

Barracca, Debra; and Barracca, Sal. *The Adventures of Taxi Dog.* Illustrated by Mark Buehner. New York: Dial Press, 1990.

Bat-Ami, Miriam. *Two Suns in the Sky.* Chicago: Front Street, 1999.

Bauer, Marion. *On My Honor.* New York: Houghton Mifflin, 1986.

Best, Cari. *Goose's Story.* Illustrated by Holly Meade. New York: Farrar, Straus & Giroux, 2002.

Bishop, Nic. *Digging for Bird-Dinosaurs: An Expedition to Madagascar.* Boston: Houghton Mifflin, 2000.

Blocksma, Mary. *Ticket to the Twenties: A Time Traveler's Guide.* Illustrated by Susan Dennen. Boston: Little, Brown, 1993.

Browne, Anthony. *Willy's Pictures.* Cambridge, Mass: Candlewick, 2000.

Byars, Besty. *Bingo Brown and the Language of Love.* New York: Viking, 1989.

———. *The Cybil War.* Illustrated by Gail Owens. New York: Viking, 1981.

Cech, Jon. *Jacques-Henri Lartigue: Boy with a Camera.* New York: Four Winds, 1994.

Cleary, Beverly. *Ramona the Pest.* Illustrated by Louis Darling. New York: Morrow, 1968.

———. *Ramana Quimby, Age 8.* Illustrated by Alan Tiegreen. New York: Morrow, 1981.

Cohen, Miriam. *Best Friends.* New York: Macmillan, 1971.

Coulter, Laurie. *Secrets in Stone: All About Maya Hieroglyphs.* Illustrated by Sarah Jane English. Boston: Little, Brown, 2001.

Cushman, Karen. *Catherine, Called Birdy.* New York: Carion, 1994.

Emberley, Ed. *The Wing on a Flea: A Book About Shapes.* Boston: Little, Brown, 2001.

Emberley, Rebecca. *City Sounds.* Boston: Little, Brown, 1989.

Erdrich, Louise. *The Birchbark House.* New York: Hyperion, 1999.

Fine, Anne. *Flour Babies.* Boston: Little, Brown, 1994.

Fleischman, Paul. *Bull Run.* New York: HarperCollins, 1993.

Fowler, Susi Gregg. *When Summer Ends.* Illustrated by Marisabina Russo. New York: Greenwillow, 1989.

Fox, Mem. *Hattie and the Fox.* Illustrated by Patricia Mullins. New York: Bradbury, 1987.

Fox, Paula. *One-Eyed Cat.* Scarsdale, N.Y.: Bradbury Press, 1984.

Gantos, Jack. *Joey Pigza Loses Control.* New York: Farrar, Straus & Giroux, 2000.

Gauch, Patricia Lee. *Tanya and Emily in a Dance for Two.* Illustrated by Satomi Ichikawa. New York: Putnam, 1994.

Giblin, James Cross, edited by. *The Century That Was: Reflections on the Last One Hundred Years.* New York: Atheneum, 2000.

Glassman, Peter, edited by. *Oz: The Hundredth Anniversary Celebration.* New York: HarperCollins, 2000.

Goodall, John. *The Story of a Main Street.* New York: Macmillan, 1987.

Grimm, Brothers. *Little Red Riding Hood.* Retold by Trina Schart Hyman. New York: Holiday, 1983.

————. *Red Riding Hood.* Retold by James Marshall. New York: Dial Press, 1987.

Hall, Donald. *Ox-Cart Man.* New York: Viking Press, 1979.

Henderson, Douglas. *Dinosaur Tree.* New York: Bradbury, 1994.

Hoban, Tana. *Of Colors and Things.* New York: Greenwillow, 1989.

Jaffe, Nina; and Zeitlin, Steve. *While Standing on One Foot: Puzzle Stories and Wisdom Tales from the Jewish Tradition.* Illustrated by John Segal. New York: Holt, 1993.

Jonas, Ann. *Aardvarks, Disembark!* New York: Greenwillow, 1990.

Lasky, Kathryn. *Sugaring Time.* Photographs by Christopher G. Knight. New York: Macmillan, 1983.

Lauber, Patricia. *Volcano: The Eruption and Healing of Mount St. Helens.* New York: Bradbury, 1986.

Lesser, Carolyn. *What a Wonderful Day to Be a Cow.* Illustrated by Melissa Bay Mathis. New York: Knopf, 1995.

Lin, Grace. *Kite Flying.* New York: Knopf, 2002.

Lobel, Arnold. *On Market Street.* Illustrated by Anita Lobel. New York: Greenwillow, 1981.

London, Jonathan. *Like Butter on Pancakes.* Illustrated by G. Brian Karas. New York: Viking, 1995.

MacDonald, Suse. *Alphabatics.* New York: Bradbury Press, 1986.

MacDonald, Suse. *Look Whooo's Counting.* New York: Scholastic, 2000.

McCaughrean, Geraldine. *A Pack of Lies.* New York: Oxford University Press, 1988.

McEwan, Ian. *The Daydreamer.* Illustrated by Anthony Browne. New York: HarperCollins, 1994.

McGuire, Richard. *Night Becomes Day.* New York: Viking, 1994.

Millard, Anne. *A Street Through Time: A 12,000-Year Walk Through History.* Illustrated by Steve Noon. New York: Dorling Kindersley, 1998.

Montgomery, Sy. *The Snake Scientist.* Photographs by Nic Bishop. Boston: Houghton Mifflin, 1999.

Morrison, Toni. *The Big Box.* Illustrated by Giselle Potter. New York: Hyperion, 1999.

Moss, Lloyd. *Zin! Zin! Zin! A Violin.* Illustrated by Marjorie Priceman. New York: Simon & Schuster, 1995.

Mullins, Patricia. *V for Vanishing: An Alphabet of Endangered Animals.* New York: HarperCollins, 1994.

Munro, Roxie. *Mazescapes.* New York: SeaStar, 2001.

Parker, Steve. *How the Body Works.* New York: Reader's Digest, distributed by Random House, 1994.

Partridge, Elizabeth. *Restless Spirit: The Life and Work of Dorothea Lange.* New York: Viking, 1998.

Paterson, Katherine. *The Tale of the Mandarin Ducks.* Illustrated by Leo and Diane Dillon. New York: Lodestar, 1990.

Pearson, Kit. *A Handful of Time.* New York: Viking, 1989.

Perrault, Charles. *Little Red Riding Hood.* Illustrated by Sarah Moon. Mankato, Minn.: Creative Education, 1983.

Petersen. P. J. *The Amazing Magic Show.* Illustrated by Renee Williams-Andriani. New York: Simon & Schuster, 1994.

Platt, Richard. *The Smithsonian Visual Timeline of Inventions.* New York: Dorling Kindersley, 1994.

Polacco, Patricia. *My Rotten Redheaded Older Brother.* New York: Simon & Schuster, 1994.

Prelutsky, Jack. *Beneath a Blue Umbrella.* Illustrated by Garth Williams. New York: Greenwillow, 1990.

———, edited by. *The Random House Book of Poetry for Children.* New York: Random House, 1983.

Rosen, Michael. *We're Going on a Bear Hunt.* Illustrated by Helen Oxenbury. New York: Macmillan, 1989.

Rowling, J. K. *Harry Potter and the Chamber of Secrets.* New York: Scholastic, 1999.

———. *Harry Potter and the Sorcerer's Stone.* New York: Scholastic, 1998.

St. George, Judith. *The White House: Cornerstone of a Nation.* New York: Putnam, 1990.

Schaefer, Carole Lexa. *Snow Pumpkin.* Illustrated by Pierre Morgan. New York: Crown, 2000.

Schotter, Roni. *A Fruit & Vegetable Man.* Illustrated by Jeanette Winter. Boston: Little, Brown, 1993.

Schwartz, Gary. *First Impressions: Rembrandt.* New York: Abrams, 1992.

Scieszka, Jon. *The True Story of the 3 Little Pigs!* Illustrated by Lane Smith. New York: Viking, 1989.

Seeber, Dorothea P. *A Pup Just for Me: A Boy Just for Me.* Illustrated by Ed Young. New York: Philomel, 2000.

Smith, Maggie. *Counting Our Way to Maine.* New York: Orchard, 1995.

Stevens, Janet. *The House That Jack Built.* New York: Holiday, 1985.

Stevenson, James. *The Wish Card Ran Out!* New York: Greenwillow, 1981.

Sturgis, Alexander. *Introducing Rembrandt.* Boston: Little, Brown, 1994.

Taback, Simms. *Joseph Had a Little Overcoat.* New York: Viking, 1999.

Tolkien, J. R. R. *The Fellowship of the Ring.* New York: Random House, 1965.

————. *The Return of the King.* New York: Random House, 1965.

————. *The Two Towers.* New York: Random House, 1965.

Trivizas, Eugene. *The Three Little Wolves and the Big Bad Pig.* Illustrated by Helen Oxenbury. New York: Macmillan, 1993.

Viorst, Judith. *Alexander and the Terrible, Horrible, No Good, Very Bad Day.* New York: Atheneum, 1972.

Vogel, Carole; and Goldner, Kathryn. *The Great Yellowstone Fire.* San Francisco: Sierra Club, 1990.

Von Tscharner, Renata; and Fleming, Ronald. *New Providence: A Changing City Scape.* Illustrated by Denis Orloff. San Diego: Harcourt Brace Jovanovich, 1987.

Whelan, Gloria. *Homeless Bird.* New York: HarperCollins, 2000.

Wiesner, David. *Free Fall.* New York: Lothrop, 1988.

Willard, Nancy. *A Visit to William Blake's Inn.* San Diego: Harcourt Brace Jovanovich, 1981.

Wolf, Sylvia. *Focus: Five Women Photographers.* Morton Grove, Ill.: Whitman, 1994.

Young, Ed, retold by. *Lon Po Po: A Red-Riding Hood Story from China.* New York: Philomel, 1989.

Part II

Developing the Language Arts

Oral Language Development

After completing this chapter on oral language development, you will be able to:

1. State the objectives of oral language instruction.
2. Design a stimulus for eliciting an oral language sample.
3. Evaluate a child's oral language after administering several informal tests.
4. Describe several instructional practices that help to build an environment in which oral language flourishes.
5. Describe how oral communication skills may be developed through conversation, storytelling, and oral discussion.
6. Describe and demonstrate the sequential development of questioning strategies designed to develop students' higher level thought processes.
7. Demonstrate the use of pantomime as a basic dramatic technique.
8. Describe the five steps to guide children in dramatization.
9. Develop a puppetry activity.
10. Describe and demonstrate the major types of choral speaking arrangements.
11. Describe the use of oral reading and reader's theater.

*W*hat do we know about effective teaching of oral language from either researchers in the area of literacy or from teacher practitioners who develop their own effective strategies? The 2002 "Reading Hall of Fame" at the International Reading Association provides several suggestions that support oral language activities through research results. For example, Jewel's research (2002) emphasizes the importance of language development for preschool and kindergarten students. She stresses that oral vocabulary development is very important because children are behind in vocabulary. Barr (2002) emphasizes that oral reading by the teachers is important because reading aloud shows children the language. Barr also reports that drama is effective; when teachers use drama, students' writing becomes more detailed and imaginative. Each one of these researchers used the term *extremely important* when discussing these findings.

Just as several members of the Reading Hall of Fame stress the importance of vocabulary development, so does the National Reading Panel (2000). Its report states, "Vocabulary is critically important in oral reading instruction. There are two types of vocabulary—oral and print. A reader who encounters a strange work in print can decode the word to speech. If it is in the reader's oral vocabulary, the reader will be able to understand it. If the word is not in the reader's oral vocabulary, the reader will have to determine the meaning by other means, if possible. Consequently, the larger the reader's vocabulary (either oral or print), the easier it is to make sense of the text" (p. 13).

Teachers in the field also emphasize characteristics of an ideal classroom. Notice how many of these ideal characteristics relate to oral language. In an article titled "Characteristics of an Ideal Reading Classroom," (1999) several readers share their suggestions. The following strategies are discussed in this chapter: classroom conversations that encourage students to develop oral literacy and to expand their vocabularies, wordless books, scanning of illustrations and illustrator studies, questioning, puppet theaters that allow children to perform their favorite stories, choral speaking, and reader's theater stage.

Objectives of Instruction

Educators emphasize the importance of both providing many opportunities for language interactions and developing a rich environment for oral language. The "Essentials of English" adopted by the National Council of Teachers of English (1983) provides excellent objectives in the areas of speaking and creative thinking. Both areas are closely related to the development of effective oral communication. For speaking, students should learn

to speak clearly and expressively about their ideas and concerns.

to adapt words and strategies according to varying situations and audiences, from one-to-one conversations to formal, large-group settings.

to participate productively and harmoniously in both small and large groups.

to present arguments in orderly and convincing ways.

to interpret and assess various kinds of communication, including intonation, pause, gesture, and body language that accompany speaking. (p. 246)[1]

In a rapidly expanding knowledge base, knowing how to think creatively, logically, and critically is essential. The ability to analyze, classify, compare, formulate hypotheses, make inferences, and draw conclusions is crucial for all adults. Early and continuous stimulation is necessary, however, if these important cognitive skills are to develop. Notice how many of them can be enriched through oral language. The National Council of Teachers makes the following recommendations:

In the area of creative thinking, students should learn

that originality derives from the uniqueness of the individual's perception, not necessarily from an innate talent.

that inventiveness involves seeing new relationships.

that creative thinking derives from their ability not only to look, but to see; not only to hear, but to listen; not only to imitate, but to innovate; not only to observe, but to experience the excitement of fresh perception.

In the area of logical thinking, students should learn

to create hypotheses and predict outcomes.

to test the validity of an assertion by examining the evidence.

to understand logical relationships.

to construct logical sequences and understand the conclusions to which they lead.

to detect fallacies in reasoning.

to recognize that "how to think" is different from "what to think."

In the area of critical thinking, students should learn

to ask questions in order to discover meaning.

to differentiate between subjective and objective viewpoints; to discriminate between opinion and fact.

---

[1] From the National Council of Teachers of English, "Forum: Essentials of English," *Language Arts* 60 (February 1983):244–48. Copyright © 1983 by the National Council of Teachers of English. Reprinted by permission of the publisher and author.

to evaluate the intentions and messages of speakers and writers, especially attempts to manipulate the language in order to deceive.

to make judgments based on criteria that can be supported and explained. (p. 247)[2]

Assessment of Oral Language

Much of the assessment connected with oral language development relies on informal techniques for eliciting and evaluating language. Goodman (1985) states that assessment is an ongoing activity and that "informal, naturalistic observation is the most effective way to learn about children's language and their ways of learning" (p. 8). According to Goodman, teachers should evaluate the ability to adjust language to meet the demands of new situations and settings. Consequently, during evaluation, teachers should observe children using language to explore concepts in a variety of areas—art, social studies, math, and physical education, for example.

Results of research indicate the importance of adding oral interview techniques to paper-and-pencil tests when analyzing students' understanding of a topic. For example, Valencia et al. (1991) used both interview techniques and paper-and-pencil tests to assess students' topical knowledge. They found that interview techniques pointed up individual differences more dramatically than recognition tests. They concluded: "If one's goal is to obtain a fairly complete picture of a person's topical knowledge, then both interview and recognition measures seem appropriate. If the goal is to assess only a specific body of information, then a recognition measure might suffice. And if the goal is to open a broader window on a student's knowledge, then an interview seems preferable" (p. 204). Oral interviews are possible within any content area and add considerable information about each student's language and knowledge.

Language Experience Stories

A dictated story or language experience may be used to evaluate language informally. This approach may be as simple as asking a child to draw or paint a picture and tell the story to a teacher or an aide, who writes down the story as it is dictated. The completed story provides the teacher with information about both language and thought processes of the child. (See the "For Your Development" activity at the end of this section on oral language assessment for an appropriate chart.)

A more structured language experience approach for evaluating language is recommended by Dixon (1977). She states: "The ease with which the language experience stories can be obtained and their reflection of the uniqueness of each child, make their use as informal diagnostic–evaluative tools worth further consideration" (p. 501). Dixon distinguishes among three types of information that can be obtained from the language experience. First is observable behavior, which includes watching as words are written, pacing dictation, pausing at the end of a phrase or sentence, providing an appropriate title, and attempting to read back the story. Second is global language usage, which includes dictating complete sentences and using a variety of words. Third is refined language usage, which includes counting the number of adjectives, adverbs, prepositional phrases, and embedded sentences.

Dixon (1977) uses a puppet from the Peabody Language Development Kit to motivate the language experience story. She allows a child to feel and manipulate the puppet while discussing it. She asks questions such as "What does it look like? How does it feel? What color is it? What do you think it is?" Then, she asks the child to tell a story about the puppet

---

[2] Ibid.

and writes a two-minute sample. Following the dictation, she gives the child an opportunity to "read" the story with her and scores the language sample according to the checklist shown in Figure 3–1.

Dixon (1977) suggests that a weighted score is the most desirable because it allows equal value within categories of the checklist. She believes that a low score in the first category may imply a need for more language enrichment activities and exposure to stories before normal reading instruction because a child who does not watch or pace dictation while words are being written may not be aware that the words being written are the same as those being spoken. A low score in the second category may indicate that language enrichment and development activities should be a large part of the instructional program. A low score in the final category may imply a need for vocabulary development and language refinement activities as part of the language arts program.

I. Observable Behaviors:			
1. Watches when words are written down	(usually)	(sometimes)	(seldom)
2. Paces dictation	(usually)	(sometimes)	(seldom)
3. Pauses at end of phrase or sentence	(usually)	(sometimes)	(seldom)
4. Appropriate title	(very)	(acceptable)	(poor)
5. Attempts to read back	(most)	(some)	(none)
II. Global Language Usage:			
1. Complete sentences	(all)	(some)	(none)
2. Total words	(31+)	(16–30)	(0–15)
3. Total different words	(30+)	(15–29)	(0–14)
III. Refined Language Usage:			
1. Number of adjectives	(9+)	(4–8)	(0–3)
2. Number of adverbs	(3+)	(1–2)	(0)
3. Number of prepositional phrases	(4+)	(1–3)	(0)
4. Number of embedded sentences	(2+)	(1)	(0)
Total	____3×	____2×	____1×
Total points	____	____	____
Grand total ____			

FIGURE 3–1   Language Experience Checklist

Source: Carol N. Dixon, "Language Experience Stories as a Diagnostic Tool," *Language Arts* 54 (May 1977). Copyright © 1977 by the National Council of Teachers of English. Reprinted by permission of the publisher and the author.

Story Retelling

Story retelling is a means of evaluating the ability of a child to perceive and recall events. Story retelling may be effective because the organization, comprehension, and sentence structures of a student are not biased by prestructured teacher questions.

For this assessment, a teacher tells a short story individually to a student, asks the student to retell the story, and tape records the student's version. The story selected should have a plot simple enough for the age of the child but too long for memorization. Story retelling affords the following information:

1. *Comprehension*—Does the child comprehend the grammatical forms of the sentences and the meaning of the vocabulary? Children who do not understand sentence structures, words, or concepts may give the story a different but plausible ending.
2. *Organization and recall of information*—Does the child organize information and recall it in a logical manner? Are events left out, is the order confused, or is the task impossible to perform?
3. *Fluency*—Does the child express the story in fluent, connected sentences, using correct grammatical forms? If you understand the differences that age, experience, culture, and individual learning styles have on children's performance, you can use retelling to learn more about the children in their classroom and also learn which errors are typical of young children and which suggest more severe language disturbance.

Unaided Recall

Another evaluative measure is unaided recall of a story. You can use this technique to assess a child's oral ability to place materials in logical order; present main ideas, important details, and cause-and-effect relationships; analyze characters; defend a viewpoint; and use oral vocabulary and language structures. This approach differs from retelling because the child reads the selection rather than having it read to him or her.

The child first reads a selection that tells a complete story. *Reader's Digest Skill Builder* is a good tool for this activity, because it has short, interesting stories ranging in reading difficulty from first through eighth grade. The following is an example of a retelling activity for third-grade students. The three students in this example all have high reading ability.

First, each student reads a selection from a fifth-grade *Reader's Digest Skill Builder* entitled "Mustang's Last Stand." After the reading, each child tells the story individually. The unaided recall is taped. In addition, each child is asked, "Why did the author write this story for us to read?" and "How did the story make you feel?" After the taping, the unaided-recall stories are transcribed from the tape and analyzed for understanding of characters, logical outline of the story, grasp of main ideas and important details, and level of oral language development. To rate a child's ability to present the story with a logical organization, a list of characters and an outline of the story are developed and each student's number is placed by the list and outline if he or she recalls the item in its proper order. The format is as follows:

Mustang's Last Stand

Student Number	Characters
1 2 3	Mustangs—One was called ghost
1 2 3	Cowboys
1 2 3	Hunters
1 2	Man who wanted to save the mustangs

Outline

1		3	1. Mustangs were plentiful in the West in the 1800s.
1	2		2. Mustangs were trapped, broken for saddle horses, and used by farmers.
1	2	3	3. Some mustangs were too swift to be caught: ghosts.
1	2	3	4. Some mustangs when trapped jumped into the mud and suffocated.
	2		5. Ranchers disliked mustangs eating the grass they wanted for their cattle.
1	2	3	6. Many mustangs were killed from planes for sport.
1	2	3	7. Not many mustangs are left.
1			8. Some friends of mustangs have succeeded in a few states in getting laws passed to protect the mustangs. In other states, wild horses are still being killed.
1			9. In stories of the West, cowboys say thunderstorms are the rumbling hooves of mustangs running across pastures in heaven.

Why did the author write this story for us to read?

Student 1:   "The author wrote the story in order to tell us what is actually happening in the world to mustangs today. He wants us to help him get a law through all the states that will prohibit the killing of mustangs. If we don't, they'll become extinct. Our next generation won't know anything about mustangs."

Student 2:   "To make us think about horses. To think about stop killing them. They are starting to be extinct (sort of). He wants us to tell someone to do something about it."

Student 3:   "So we would know about the mustangs. There aren't many left."

How did the story make you feel?

Student 1:   "I felt sad about all of the mustangs who have been killed. There used to be millions, now there are only about 20,000."

Student 2:   "Sort of in between. I like cattle better than horses and horses are eating too much of the grass and there isn't enough for the cattle and then they would die off."

Student 3:   "Sad."

As you can see, even high-ability students demonstrate differences in abilities to develop an outline sequentially and to form opinions based on facts. Students 1 and 2 demonstrate the highest ability in retelling the story, formulating and supporting an opinion with facts, and level of oral vocabulary development. In contrast, student 3 misses several important details, misses the real purpose of the story, and does not substantiate opinions with facts; such skills can be improved with instruction. Many low-ability students find this task difficult, and cannot perform the activity without numerous structured questions.

Other Techniques

Puppets are excellent motivational devices, and you can use them in several different ways. First, a child who is reluctant to talk to an adult may speak without hesitation to a hand puppet. You can use a hand puppet to carry on a conversation with the child in order to collect a language sample and other information about the child. Puppets of familiar characters are good for this purpose. For prekindergarten language screening, you can use Winnie-the-Pooh puppets because children respond well to Pooh Bear. With first-grade children, a hand puppet of the elephant Dumbo is a great success. He has great big ears, which are ideal for listening to children's speech, and he has such a good memory that he can remember everything about the child. He is also a baby elephant, and needs to have many questions answered about the world around him!

A second way to use puppets for evaluation is to have a child manipulate the puppet and tell a story to you or to classmates. Evaluate the story according to some of the same criteria used for storytelling or language experiences.

One of the easiest ways to elicit a language sample is to show a child an interesting picture or series of pictures in a wordless book and encourage the child to tell you about the picture or to tell you a story suggested by the wordless book. Frame your introduction to the picture or book so that you provide the child with a language activity rather than a set of factual questions. Responses to certain questions may require only one or two words and therefore will not provide an accurate impression of the child's language. For example, use any of the illustrations in Chris Van Allsburg's *The Mysteries of Harris Burdick* (1984). Choose an illustration and read the accompanying title and the first line of a proposed story. Then, ask a child to tell you the story he or she believes could accompany the illustration, the title, and the sentence.

For Your Development

Use the following student profile when demonstrating the kinds of evaluative information that can be obtained from a dictated story. After you have looked at the profile, read the language experience story "Our Hunting Trip." Then, using the student profile, evaluate the language ability of this student. Finally, collect language samples from a student using two or three of the different methods described in this section. Evaluate the oral language information that you gain from the samples.

Student Profile to Accompany a Language Experience Evaluation

Name _____   Date _____

Grade _____   Motivation _____

Average number of words per sentence _____

	Yes	Sometimes	No
1. Dictates complete sentences	___	___	___
Example: _____			
2. Uses good sequential order	___	___	___
3. Demonstrates rich vocabulary	___	___	___
4. Indicates grasp of main idea	___	___	___
5. Is confident during the dictation experience	___	___	___
6. Indicates a background of experiences	___	___	___
7. Shows a consistency in noun–verb agreement in sentences	___	___	___
8. Uses pronouns correctly	___	___	___
9. Arranges words coherently	___	___	___
10. Includes all words needed for understanding	___	___	___

Continued

The following language experience story was dictated by a second-grade boy. Read the story and list some of the information you now have about his language ability:

Our Hunting Trip

Yesterday my friend Brian and I went hunting with my brother's pellet gun. I got two mallard ducks. They were sitting down in our pond. My dog Laddie was with me. He brought the ducks out of the pond. Laddie is my friend, I can really count on him. It was a happy day and it was my eighth birthday.

Classroom Environments That Promote Oral Language Development

The teachers who described their ideal classrooms at the beginning of this chapter (Barr, 2002; Jewel, 2002) emphasized rooms that were rich in oral language activities and numerous books that encouraged literacy. If oral language is to develop in the classroom, there must be ample opportunity for children to practice oral communication. Just as you cannot become an accomplished tennis player without practice and feedback, you cannot become an effective oral communicator without instruction and opportunity to develop communication skills. King (1985) emphasizes that "it is the obligation of the school to extend the opportunities for children to use language for an ever increasing range of purposes—especially to use it to learn" (p. 37).

According to Squire (1991), there is an emerging interest in oral language as it influences literacy across the curriculum. The development of a positive environment that encourages oral language is especially important for at-risk students. Squire states that the discovery that "at-risk children frequently lack opportunity in school or out of school to exchange ideas orally with others seems to be leading to a new emphasis in our classrooms" (p. 11). Brophy and Good (1986) found that young children with below-average ability benefit from active engagement. Menyuk's (1991) summary of research about language development concludes that "communication interaction between the child and more mature users of the language is vital for such growth" (p. 28). She maintains that children should be asked to actively think and talk about language. In a study of emergent literacy intervention in Head Start, Whitehurst et al. (1994) concluded: "Children from low-income families need frequent one-on-one language interactions with an adult to enhance their language skills. Group-based interactions may not be sufficient in the late preschool years, even if the groups are small and the forms of interaction are optimized " (p. 552).

Observations on communication between parents and their children often generates interesting suggestions for instructional environments. First, parents do not sequence or partition oral language (that is, phonics one day and syntax the next). Thus, classrooms should use more whole-language activities, including real projects that stress the use of oral language. Second, parents interact with learners. To meet this requirement, the classrooms should provide opportunities for interactions of teachers and students—in pairs, in small groups, and in large-group situations. Third, parents use language for nonlinguistic purposes—for instance, to correct ideas rather than language form. Classrooms, too, should examine children's ideas and ask for clarification, elaboration, and justification. Classrooms should provide an atmosphere in which children may explore and struggle with ideas. To achieve this objective, involve children in planning, decision making, and problem solving. Fourth, parents talk to children about things they can see or are actually attending to. Teachers should also notice what children are focusing on and supply language labels for what the children are actually doing. Finally, parents expect success and delight in progress. Teachers should also delight in children's progress in both language and thinking.

Research conducted with parents also shows that children's oral language ability improves if the parents receive instruction. For example, Whitehurst et al. (1988) found that children whose parents received instruction in how to do effective picture-book reading with their children scored higher on expressive language ability.

Some educators emphasize the quality of the physical environment. According to Morrow and Rand (1991), "the role of a classroom's physical environment in learning is typically overlooked. Most educators focus on pedagogy, content, and interpersonal dynamics, giving little formal consideration to the physical contexts in which teaching and learning occur" (p. 396). These educators present evidence that an environment for young children that encourages dramatic play and storytelling and that organizes space so that children can select reading and writing materials and produce creative art and written products enhances the development of oral language. Morrow and Rand's research also indicates the importance of adult guidance. They conclude: "Preschool and kindergarten children are likely to engage in more voluntary literacy behaviors during free-play periods when literacy materials are introduced and teachers guide children to use those materials" (p. 399).

Oral Language Activities

Pinnell and Jaggar (1991) state that the most effective techniques for promoting oral language development include small-group discussions and projects, informal conversations, storytelling, creative dramatics, and role-playing and improvisation. All of these activities also enhance the development of an oral vocabulary. In this section we consider the development of oral language through such activities as conversation, storytelling, oral discussion (including modeling), creative dramatics (including pantomime and puppetry), choral speaking and reading, and reader's theater. As you will see, speaking, listening, writing, and reading interact closely in many of these activities. Theme approaches are excellent; they develop serious explorations of content and encourage purposeful speaking, listening, reading, and writing.

Instructional units that develop various aspects of oral communication have always been extremely popular with both undergraduate and graduate students. One student titled her oral language unit "Life in the Himalayas—or how a group of intractable 4th- and 5th-graders can be made to clamber up the mountain, converse with the Sherpas, and tame the abominable snowman." You may wonder how she approached such a formidable project. She began by introducing various communication modes such as discussion, mime, oral story development, and creative dramatics. This student not only enjoyed teaching, but also helped children learn a great deal about oral language.

Conversation

In the early primary grades and especially in kindergarten, children spend much time developing oral conversation skills. Kindergarten teachers must frequently work hard toward developing the confidence of young children to the point where they feel at ease conversing with either teachers or fellow classmates. Children need opportunities to communicate their ideas to each other and to realize that they have information worth sharing

Conversations can help children realize that their ideas are worth sharing.

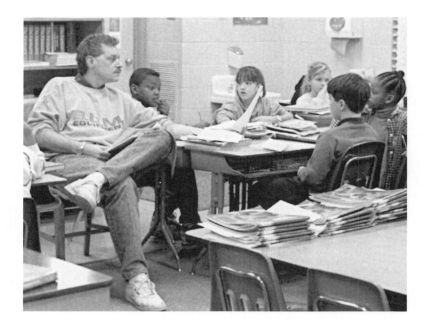

with someone else. Conversation is a more informal activity than discussion. It allows children to move more freely from one topic to another. Morrow and Rand (1991) found that even conversations during free-play periods are improved when literacy materials are introduced and teachers have guided children in the use of those materials. Show and tell and telephone conversations are two good activities for developing oral conversation skills.

Show and Tell.   This activity is almost a daily part of many kindergarten and first-grade classrooms. Teachers find that allowing children to talk about something familiar to them both stimulates conversation and builds confidence in speaking. Show and tell also provides a vital link between the home, where children may feel very confident, and the school, where they may be shy and reserved. Show and tell also provides listeners for the conversational experience. Children learn to ask appropriate questions and to respond to other children in a group. During a show and tell experience, children talk about an activity or show an object that they have brought to school. (A circular or semicircular arrangement, with children sitting in chairs or on the floor, allows more interaction than do rows.) The children voluntarily take turns talking about their objects or activities.

Teachers have a definite role during show and tell. When you first initiate show and tell, you may have to lead some of the conversation by asking questions that provide structure for the conversation and cues for the children to elaborate. Ask questions that provide models for appropriate questions, but encourage other children to ask questions, too. In addition, model attentive listening and prevent other children from interrupting the speakers. Finally, offer enthusiastic responses to all children.

One effective kindergarten teacher asked children to bring one of their favorite toys to class. She asked the children to join her in the conversation circle, and the children began to tell about their toys individually. One little girl showed her toys and said, "This is my panda." At that point, the child could not think of anything else to say, but the teacher carefully prompted her with remarks such as "Oh what a nice panda, we would like to know his name";

"Who gave you the panda?"; "Where does the panda sleep when he's at home?"; "What games does the panda play with you?"; and "Have you ever seen a real panda?"

Teachers may specialize show and tell and its resulting conversation by asking children to bring something they made, something they drew, something that illustrates a season of the year, and so forth. Having difficulty encouraging some of her kindergarten children to take part in show and tell, one student teacher asked them to bring a picture of their family and tell the rest of the class something special about the family. (The picture could be either a snapshot or a picture drawn by the child.) She was amazed when every child wanted to share. They held their pictures confidently and talked about something very precious to them. Another student teacher asked first-grade children to bring something small enough to fit in a paper sack. She asked the children not to tell anyone what was in their sacks. The children took turns describing the objects and allowing the other children to guess what was in the sack. This activity also assisted in vocabulary development, as the children (frequently encouraged by the teacher) discovered the importance of words indicating size, shape, color, and use.

After children are competent in conversation during show and tell, you may divide the group into smaller conversation circles and allow children to lead.

Telephone Conversations.   Play telephones in elementary classrooms provide opportunities for children to develop a specific type of conversation. With telephones, children learn about the importance of the quality of their speaking voices, to take turns during conversation, and to respond appropriately to another speaker. Through role-playing, they may learn how to use the telephone for reaching the fire or police departments. During role-playing, let one child assume the role of a person who needs assistance and another child assume the role of the person at the desired location. Children discover the necessity for giving exact directions or details, and learn procedures to use in real emergencies. Other role-playing with telephone conversations includes calling a grocery store to place an order, calling a friend to ask about his weekend trip, or calling Grandmother to wish her happy birthday.

Wordless Books

The illustrations in books encourage students to respond in a variety of ways. According to Cianciolo (1997), artists "can stimulate the reader to extract from the images new meanings about aspects of the human condition that the author or illustrator chooses to represent in the images created through carefully selected words or pictures" (p. 26). Books that encourage aesthetic responses and stimulate intellectual development are important in elementary classrooms. Wordless books—picture books in which the illustrations tell a story without words—provide excellent frameworks for various responses and for oral storytelling. Even young children can describe their responses to the characters and situations depicted. Strong story lines develop the ability to interpret sequential plot development. Detailed illustrations encourage observational capabilities and descriptive vocabularies. Emily Arnold McCully's *Four Hungry Kittens* (2001), *School* (1987), and *Picnic* (1984) have easily followed plots, familiar environments, and problem-solving situations. Mercer Mayer's humorous wordless books are especially appealing to primary children. The antics of a boy, a dog, and a frog stimulate oral interpretations in *A Boy, A Dog, and a Frog* (1967), *Frog, Where Are You?* (1969), *A Boy, a Dog, a Frog, and a Friend* (1971), and *Frog Goes to Dinner* (1974). The appealing characters and plot ideas in Peter Collington's *The Angel and the Soldier Boy* (1987) encourage children to respond to fantasy and to problem solving. Henrik Drescher's *The Yellow Umbrella* (1987) allows children to follow the plot line and predict what they think will happen.

A play telephone in the classroom motivates role-playing.

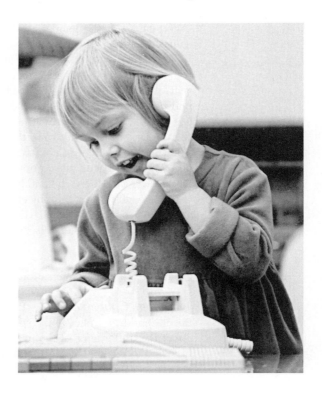

Wordless books are not just for very young children. Older children in the middle grades respond quite differently to books such as David Wiesner's *Free Fall* (1988) *Sector 7* (1999), and *Tuesday* (1991) than do very young ones. Younger children may interpret the illustrations more literally than older children. Older children frequently respond to and interpret the story according to their background knowledge of the various characters and settings developed through the illustrations. Eric Rohmann's *Time Flies* (1994) is another wordless book that may be interpreted at different levels. In this fantasy, a live bird flies into a museum display of dinosaurs. In a fantasy sequence, camarasaurus, crested parasaurolophus, albertosaurus, and pteranodons come to life and the bird encounters an earlier world and a quest for survival. In a happy ending, the dinosaurs return to their museum forms and the bird is saved. Mitsumasa Anno's rich details and intricate drawings in *Anno's Journey* (1978) encourage older children to journey through European countries and identify landmarks, sculptures, paintings, and well-known literary characters.

Because wordless books differ so greatly, you should consider the following questions when choosing books to promote oral language development:

1. Is there a sequentially organized plot that provides a framework for children who are just developing their own organizational skills?

2. Is the depth of detail appropriate for the children's age level? (Too much detail will overwhelm younger children, while not enough detail may bore older ones.)

3. Do the children have enough experiential background to understand and interpret the illustrations? Can they interpret the book or would adult interaction be necessary?

4. Is the size of the book appropriate for the purpose? (Larger books are necessary for group sharing.)

5. Is the subject one that will appeal to children? (Norton, 2003, p. 173)

The following lessons show how you can develop various responses with wordless books. The first lesson encourages children to make personal responses to several wordless books.

1. After looking at and talking about Peter Sis's *Dinosaur!* (2000), ask children to identify specific types of dinosaurs as the young boy takes his toy dinosaur into the tub only to be joined by many other dinosaurs. The dinosaurs are identified inside the front and back covers.

2. After looking at and talking about Wiesner's *Free Fall*, ask the students to describe their emotional responses to the book. Ask "What colors or techniques did the artist use to make you feel that way?" Ask the students to use their imaginations and put themselves into one of the pictures in *Free Fall*. How will they respond? How might experience with literature influence what they do in this situation? Ask the students to pretend they are having a dream that is influenced by what they were reading or doing before they went to bed. Ask them to describe their dream.

3. After looking at and talking about McCully's *School* ask the students to describe their feelings about the little mouse child and the mouse family. Ask them to assume the role of the mouse child. What feelings would they have when they looked at the new baby or watched their brothers and sisters go off to school? Ask "In your opinion are the little mouse child's feelings and actions believable?"

The next two lessons show how the same wordless book, in this case Emily Arnold McCully's *Picnic* (1984), may enhance oral language development in early-elementary and upper grades. *Picnic* has a sequentially developed plot. In the book, a mouse family prepares for a picnic, proceeds to the picnic grounds, unknowingly loses a child on the way, plays games, discovers the child is missing, and searches for the child. The detailed illustrations flash back and forth between the actions of the picnickers and the locations of the lost mouse child.

A lesson to encourage younger children to observe illustrations, describe actions, expand vocabulary, and create sequential narrative includes the following steps and discussions:

1. Ask the students to look carefully at the first double page. Ask them the following questions: Who is the story about? Look at each of the mice. How would you describe the mice? (Encourage expansion of descriptions to include color, size, emotions, and relationships within the family.)

2. Ask the students to look at the same pictures again. Ask them the following questions: What do you believe the mice are planning to do? Choose one of the characters and explain what you think the mouse is going to do. How will you know if you are right? What should we see on the next few pages?

3. Tell the students that all stories take place in some setting. Ask them: What is the setting on this first page? Look carefully at the picture. Describe the woods and the house. What setting do you expect for the remainder of the story? Why?

4. Continue an in-depth discussion of each double-page illustration focusing on descriptions of actions, characters, and setting.

5. Ask the students to retell the sequence of the story.

Older students may use the same book to enhance the development of language skills and to build an understanding of specific literary skills. The following lessons highlight setting, characterization, and point of view:

1. *Setting:* Discuss the importance of setting for developing geographic location and for identifying when the story takes place—past, present, or future. Have the students look at the illustrations and create descriptions that provide an accurate geographical location and that set the mood and time for the story. Have the students compare the settings in which the young mouse is lost and the settings in which the other mice are joyfully picnicking. Ask them to describe one setting so that the setting causes problems for the character (setting as antagonist) and to describe the other setting so that the setting enhances a happy, carefree mood. Ask the students to consider the importance of the words they use to describe each setting. Help them experiment with the impact of various descriptive adjectives, harsh verbs, and figurative language such as similes, metaphors, and other comparisons.

2. *Characterization:* Discuss the importance of characterization for developing characters who seem lifelike and who develop throughout the story. Share with the students that authors promote understanding of characters by describing appearance, feelings, actions, attitudes, strengths, and weaknesses. Have the students select one of the characters in the book and describe that character to provide a better understanding of the character. Expand this activity to teach or reinforce the ways in which authors reveal character. For example, have students create conversations through dialogue, such as between mother and father mouse before and after they discover the missing mouse child or between the mouse and mother before and after the incident to reveal family relationships and feelings. Have the students tell about the characters through oral narrative. Have them describe the thoughts of the characters. The inner thoughts of the lost mouse child should reveal both his fears and his self-determination, while the thoughts of brothers and sisters and of mother and father should reveal various attitudes toward the lost mouse. Finally, have the students describe actions revealing both the physical and emotional changes in the lost mouse or in the other mice toward the mouse.

3. *Point of view:* Discuss the importance of developing a story line from a specific point of view. Explore the impact of how a story might change if a different character tells the story. Have the students choose a character in the story and tell the story from that viewpoint. Examples include mother mouse, father mouse, the lost mouse, and any of the other children.

You may use this format with any wordless book that contains a story line and includes enough information to develop characterization, setting, and point of view. You can extend the activity to include the development of conflict and the exploration with various literary styles.

Enhancing Oral Language Through Aesthetic Scanning of Illustrations

Aesthetics refers to expressing personal reactions and emotions related to such fine arts as music, art, and literature. Activities that heighten aesthetic responses usually stress the development of enjoyment and help children to respond to the world around then. According to Hobbs and Rush (1997), "Aesthetic literacy refers to being able to 'read' or interpret another person's images in order to enjoy and appreciate them" (p. 3).

The idea of aesthetic responses to art, according to Manguel (2000), goes back to the sixteenth century, where "a painting, whether a portrait or a scene, whether religious or allegorical, historical or private, was meant to be read. This was an inherent and essential feature of the aesthetic act: the possibility, through a shared vocabulary, of communication between the viewpoint of the artist and the viewpoint of the audience" (p. 121).

Hobbs and Rush (1997) present the excitement that accompanies aesthetic responses: "Teaching children to make informed aesthetic responses by means of aesthetic scanning has all the excitement of a treasure hunt. The hunters are the children and their teacher. Their tools are a pair of sharp eyes. The treasures they seek to discover are the sensory, formal, expressive, and technical properties of works of art. Aesthetic scanning should occur at three times during the course of a comprehensive art lesson or unit: when children are viewing objects or images in preparation for art production, when they are examining their completed artworks, and when they are analyzing exemplary works of adult art (acting as art critics)" (p. 122).

In this discussion we consider how the teacher may use this approach with either illustrated books or works of art. There are so many beautifully illustrated books that a choice of materials is not difficult. It is also exciting to use the aesthetic scanning approach as students think and talk about the illustrations. Hewett and Rush (1987) identify two rules for this type of treasure hunt: (1) The aesthetic property must be in the artwork and observable by others and (2) the viewer must be able to identify and describe the property. Chart 3–1 presents examples of questions that adults may ask to encourage children to examine a work of art carefully and to volunteer information based on their own perceptions. These questions build in difficulty by beginning with easier questions and then progressing in the order of difficulty. The questions toward the end of the chart require higher levels of artistic knowledge and lead to better informed aesthetic responses. As children become experienced at looking at art and talking about aesthetic properties, teachers can expect longer and more detailed descriptions of the properties and can ask more open-ended questions. Teachers should encourage students to expand their responses by asking questions that clarify and elaborate on the responses.

You may use Jan Greenberg and Sandra Jordan's text *The Sculptor's Eye: Looking at Contemporary American Art* (1993) to provide guidance for developing discussions about art. The text begins with a discussion of contemporary American art, including steps in which viewers describe what they see by using sensory words that remind them of things that they touch, taste, see, hear, or smell. Next, it considers how artists use the elements of painting, including line, shape, texture, and color, and different styles, media, and methods. Other sections emphasize the meaning of various paintings; putting all of the elements together; and visual effects, including balance, visual rhythms that form patterns, emphasis, and space. The text is written to encourage interactions among readers and text. Thus, you may use it to develop aesthetic discussions with your students.

Lyn Ellen Lacy's *Art and Design in Children's Picture Books* (1986) provides in-depth suggestions for analyzing the visual elements in several Caldecott Medal book illustrations. After doing several group activities in which students observe and discuss the art, children enjoy developing their own observations and formulating questions that allow them to interact with art. Most libraries have the Caldecott Medal and Honor books, so it should not be difficult to obtain these illustrated books.

Chart 3-1   Focusing questions for aesthetic scanning

Question Type	Examples of Questions
Focusing on sensory properties of line, color, shape, and texture.	Look at the lines in this picture. Are they thin or wide, heavy or light, straight or curved? What feelings do you get from the lines? Identify the colors in the picture. What moods and feelings do you get from the colors? Why do you think the artist chose those colors? Look at the shapes in this picture. What do these shapes tell you about the subjects? What textures do you feel when you look at the picture? How do these textures match the subject or mood in the picture?
Focusing on formal properties such as balance, repetition, and contrast.	How has the artist brought balance into this picture? Is it successful? Why or why not? If there is repetition, how does it create rhythm in the picture? Look at the picture to identify any contrasts in colors or lines. What is the influence of such contrasts?
Expressing qualities used to express feelings such as mood, conflict, energy, and meaning.	Look at the picture carefully and describe the mood you feel. What in the picture gives you that mood? If you feel any conflict or energy, how has the artist expressed these feelings? What meaning do you receive when you look at the picture?
Technical properties such as media and techniques used by the artist.	Can you identify the type of media used by the artist? How do you think the media influences the picture? How would it change if the artist used a different media or a different technique such as collage?

Discussion

The goal of the discussion activities in this section is the development of higher level thought processes as well as the development of oral language; consequently, the time spent on these activities may be some of the most rewarding in the elementary classroom. It is through open discussion that children learn to express themselves clearly and convincingly, to share ideas, to appreciate others' opinions, and to cooperate in problem solving. The instructional environment should allow children to become involved in many different types of discussions. The activities we will highlight include teacher modeling, questioning strategies, and grouping techniques for discussion.

Teacher Modeling.   Researchers such as Roehler and Duffy (1984) and Gordon (1985) have developed approaches that allow teachers to interact with students and show them how to approach thought processing. According to Dole et al. (1991), modeling is one of the most effective ways of increasing students' higher thought processes and comprehension abilities. In a modeling approach, teachers explain the mental reasoning involved in performing various tasks. The goal is not to have students replicate the teacher's thinking, but to have teachers provide enough background so that learning takes place. Dole et al. identify three factors that improve the effectiveness of modeling. First, the information presented should be explicit. Second, the modeling should be flexible to allow teachers to adjust to cues. Third, the modeling should explain the reasoning employed to answer the questions. Without exploring the reasoning phase, many students have difficulty understanding how questions are answered.

Although modeling may be used with any subject, it is an excellent way to help students understand literature, especially in areas such as inferring characterization and understanding an author's use of figurative language. Making inferences about the characters through their actions, dialogues, and thoughts is difficult for many students. You can help students understand the often complex nature of inferences by modeling activities in which they analyze evidence from the text and speculate about the characters or other literary elements. The following steps are particularly useful in modeling understanding of various literary elements:

1. Identify the skill that you plan to teach and analyze the requirements for effective reasoning within that skill. Ask yourself "What do the students need to know to be successful? What types of cognitive processes are needed?" Decide how you will introduce the particular skill.
2. Make sure the students understand why this skill is important to them. Ask yourself "Why is this important to the students? How and when will they use the skill?"
3. Develop the model and the lesson. This includes identifying examples from the literature, stipulating questions that will be asked following the reading of each example, developing answers that typify the types of answers that students might give, identifying evidence from the text and other sources that supports the answer, and thinking through the reasoning used to reach the answer.
4. Introduce the subject and the literature selection. Review what the students know that is important to both the skill to be taught and to the literature selection. Provide any new information.
5. Teach the model. As part of the teaching, introduce the subject and the book and explain what the lesson will include. It is important that students understand terms such as *evidence* and *reasoning*. They should also understand that reasoning is a very personal part of the model. The students may draw on their background experience and knowledge as they explore their own reasoning processes. You then teach the model by completing the first series in which you read the example, ask the question, answer the question, provide the evidence, and explain how you reasoned out the answer. As part of the reasoning, be sure that students understand that you used your previous knowledge about the subject and any personal responses to the literature. After you have completely modeled the first example, make sure that students understand the process. If they do not, completely model another example. As soon as they understand the process, bring the students into the discussion as they answer questions, provide evidence, and explore their reasoning. Older students can take notes to use during the discussions.
6. Conclude the lesson by asking the students to summarize what they have learned and to consider what they would still like to know about the skill or the literature subject.

The following example shows how to develop and teach a modeling lesson using Patricia MacLachlan's 1986 Newbery Medal book, *Sarah, Plain and Tall*. This is an excellent source for modeling inferential reasoning because some of the characterizations are stated, whereas others are merely implied. Students frequently need considerable help in analyzing and understanding implied characterizations. Notice in this modeling activity the close relationship between listening and oral language.

For Your Plan Book

Lesson Plan

A Modeling Lesson Using *Sarah, Plain and Tall*

Requirements for Effective Inferential Reasoning

Effective inferential reasoning requires that readers go beyond the information an author provides in a book. Readers must use clues from the text to hypothesize about a character's emotions, beliefs, actions, hopes, and fears. Readers must also be aware that authors develop characters through dialogue, narration, a character's thoughts or the thoughts of others about the character, and the character's actions.

Introduction to Inferential Reasoning

Review characterization by asking students to identify how authors develop three-dimensional, believable characters. Share examples of each type of characterization as part of this review. Also explain to students that in this modeling activity they will listen to you ask a question, answer the question, provide evidence from the story that supports the answer, and share the reasoning process that you used to reach the answer. Tell them that after they have listened to you proceed through the sequence, they will use the same process to answer questions, identify evidence, and explore their own reasoning processes. As part of this introduction, discuss the meanings of the terms *evidence* and *reasoning*. Encourage the students to identify evidence about a character in literature and to share how they would use this evidence.

The Importance of Inferential Reasoning

Ask students to explain why it is important to be able to make inferences about characters in literature. Encourage them to discuss how understanding characterization makes a story more exciting, enjoyable, and believable. Also encourage them to think about when they could use inferences about characterization in their own writing.

An Introduction to the Story

There are two important settings in *Sarah, Plain and Tall*: (1) the pioneer setting in one of the prairie states and (2) the pioneer setting in Maine. To identify their understandings of these locations and time periods, ask students to pretend they are sitting on the front porch of a cabin in one of the prairie states in the 1800s, to look away from the cabin, and to describe what they see. Ask them to tell the colors they see. Then ask them to turn around and describe what they see through the open door of the cabin.

The Maine setting is also important to this story because Sarah's conflict results from love of a very different setting. Ask the students to pretend that they are sitting on the coast of Maine, to look out at the ocean, and to describe what they see. Ask them to turn toward the land and describe the setting. Ask them to discuss the differences between the prairie and the Maine coast and to consider whether these differences could cause conflicts for a character.

This discussion provides numerous opportunities for students to bring in their background knowledge. If it is necessary to provide additional background information, share and discuss pictures showing the two areas. Also, show the locations on a map.

The First Modeling Example

Read orally from the beginning of the book through the following line on page 5: "That was the worst thing about Caleb." Ask: "What was Anna's attitude toward her brother Caleb when he was a baby?" Answer: "I think Anna disliked her brother a great deal. We might even say she hated him." Provide the evidence: "Anna thinks that Caleb is homely, plain, and horrid smelling. Anna associates Caleb with her mother's death." Provide the reasoning that you used to reach the answer. For example, explain, "The words Anna uses, especially *horrid,* are often associated with things we do not like. I know from my own experiences that I would use those words about something I do not like. I know from the reference to the happy home that Anna loved her mother. When she says her mother's death was the worst thing about Caleb, I believe that she blamed him for the death." (Notice that you can encourage students to use both efferent and aesthetic responses as they describe their reasoning processes. Including both types of responses in the modeling lessons encourages students to respond with their own feelings and emotions.)

The Second Modeling Example

At this point, verify that the students understand the procedure. If they do not, continue by completely modeling another example. If the students understand the process, let them join the discussion by providing an answer, the evidence, and the reasoning. It is advisable to have the students jot down brief answers to the questions, evidence, and reasoning; these notes will enhance the quality of the discussion that follows each question.

The next logical discussion point occurs at the bottom of page 5. Read through the line "And Papa didn't sing." Ask: "What is Anna really telling us about her inner feelings?" The students will provide answers similar to this one: She believes that nothing can replace her lost mother and that the home will not be happy again. Ask the students to provide evidence; for example: The author tells us that the relatives could not fill the house; the days are compared to long, dark winter days; the author states that Papa did not sing. Ask the students to provide reasoning; for example: The author created a sad mood; we see a house filled with relatives that do not matter to Anna; I know what long, dark winter days are like; I can feel and visualize a house without singing; I think Anna is very unhappy and it may take her a long time to get over her loss; I wanted to cry when Anna described the setting and her feelings.

Continue this process, having the students discuss the many instances of implied characterization in the book. The letters written by Sarah to Mr. Wheaton (p. 9), to Anna (pp. 9–10), and to Caleb (p. 11) are especially good for inferring what the characters are like because students must infer what was in the letters written by Anna and Caleb. To help the students infer the contents of the letters, ask them to write the letters themselves.

Long stories, such as *Sarah, Plain and Tall,* lend themselves to discussions built around chapters. Students may read and discuss several chapters each day. After each session, however, ask the students to summarize what they know about Sarah, Anna, Caleb, and Papa. Ask: "What do you want to know about these characters?"

Additional Examples from the Remainder of the Book

Chapters 3 and 4: Read through page 17, "Caleb slipped his hand into mine as we stood on the porch, watching the road. He was afraid." Ask: "Why was Caleb afraid? What does this fear reveal about Caleb's character?" Students may answer: Caleb was afraid because Sarah was coming; Caleb was afraid he might disappoint Sarah and she would not stay; Caleb was afraid of the unknown; Caleb, a young child, was unsure of himself; Caleb really longed for a mother. Ask students to cite evidence; for example: The text tells that Caleb did his chores without talking; the text tells that Caleb stood for a long time holding his sister's hand and watching the road; the text tells that he asked many questions about what Anna thought about Sarah and he worried whether Sarah would like him. Ask the students to explore their reasoning; for example: Caleb longed for a mother during the first two chapters—his actions now show that he is afraid that Sarah will not like him or that she will not be nice; I know from my own experiences that I may be very quiet if I am afraid; I know from my own experiences that I

Continued

worry about unknown people and experiences; I know from my own experiences that I go to someone like an older sister if I am frightened; Caleb's actions let me know that he is close to his sister, that he wants a mother, and that he is afraid that his dreams will not come true; I think Caleb shows the needs of a little boy; I think that is how I would act if I were Caleb.

Continue following a similar approach with Chapters 3 and 4, stopping at the inference about Sarah's strong personality as reflected in her statement on page 19: "The cat will be good in the barn," said Papa. "For mice." Sarah smiled, "She will be good in the house too"; the inference about Anna's and Sarah's characterization in Anna's statement, "I wished we had a sea of our own" (p. 21); the characterization inferred by the flower-picking incident on page 23; the characterization of Papa inferred by the hair-cutting incident on page 25; and the inference about Sarah's conflicting emotions in the discussion of seals and singing on page 27.

Chapters 5 and 6: After the sheep incident on page 28, ask "What type of a person is Sarah? Do you believe that she will make a good mother for Caleb and for Anna? Why or why not?" Students may respond in the following ways: Sarah is a warm, tender person who likes animals and wants to protect Caleb and Anna from a sad experience; I think Sarah would make a good mother because she cares about people and about animals; I think Sarah would take good care of Caleb and Anna and bring laughter back into the house. Ask students to cite the evidence; for example: The text describes Sarah as naming the sheep after her favorite aunts, as smiling when she looks at and talks to the sheep, as crying when a lamb dies, as protecting the lamb from buzzards, and as not letting Caleb and Anna near the dead lamb. Previous descriptions in the text describe Sarah as caring for the children and being interested in what they do and feel. The students then explore their reasoning processes; for example: I think that Sarah's actions during the lamb incident indicate that she cares about animals; I know from my own experiences that I name things I like after favorite people; I know from my own experiences that if I like an animal I cry when it dies; I know from my own experiences that I want a mother who protects me and who demonstrates love; I like Sarah—I would like that kind of a person for my mother.

Continue reading Chapters 5 and 6, emphasizing the implications of the haystack incident and the comparison to sand dunes on page 32 and the inferences gained from Anna's dream described on page 37.

Chapters 7, 8, and 9: Stop after reading the description of a squall and the family's reactions to the storm on page 49. Ask "What do Sarah's actions and her statement, 'We have squalls in Maine too. Just like this. It will be all right, Jacob,' tell you about Sarah's character? What do you believe Sarah has decided to do?" Students may respond with the following statements: Sarah is finally satisfied with life on the prairie; she sees that storms in Maine and storms on the prairie are alike; she has changed her opinion about the importance of living near the sea and appears to be happy on the prairie; she may be saying that her life in the new family may sometimes be rough like a storm, but in the end everything will be fine; Sarah is a strong person who can live with hardships; I believe that Sarah has decided to stay on the prairie. Ask the students to cite the evidence; for example: The text tells us that she watched the storm for a long time and that she compared what she saw on the prairie to what she had experienced in Maine; this time Sarah touches Papa's shoulder and tells the family that everything is going to be all right; it sounds as if Sarah has finally made up her mind and that she will stay on the prairie even though it may sometimes be rough. Ask the students to discuss their reasoning; for example: I know from other chapters that Sarah was always making comparisons between Maine and the prairie—some of the comparisons showed a desire to return to Maine; this time, Sarah touches the family members and says that everything will be all right; I know from my own experiences that I may be silent for a long time when I am making important decisions; incidents in the book show that Sarah is a strong person who is willing to defend her beliefs and the people and things she loves; I feel that Sarah is now ready to love the family more than she loves her former home; I put myself in the place of Sarah as she watched the storm and finally touched the family—when I did that, I could feel the love within the family and I knew that if I were Sarah I would stay.

Continue reading the book, stopping to discuss the inference drawn from the reactions of the children when Sarah rides to town alone on page 52 and the inference drawn from Anna's comparison of Sarah's driving away in the wagon by herself to her mother's leaving in a pine box (p. 54).

For Your Development

Choose a skill that you can develop through modeling. Choose a book in which students must apply that skill. Identify the requirements for the skill, develop an example showing that skill, identify why it is important to students, identify the text samples, develop the questions, consider the answers, cite the evidence that supports the answers, and think through your own reasoning process used to acquire the answers. Present your modeling lesson to your language arts class. The following lesson plan may be used for this activity:

Modeling for _____

Requirements for understanding:

Example showing this skill:

Why is _____ important for students to understand and to use:

Text Examples:	Questions:	Answers:	Evidence Cited:	Reasoning Processes:

Questioning Strategies. Research findings indicate that many of the questions asked of students are at the simplest, literal level of comprehension; thus, they make the least demand on reasoning. Although there is certainly nothing wrong with asking literal questions, which demand comprehension prerequisite for higher levels of learning, this type of question should not dominate education.

In a classic study, Taba, Levine, and Elzey (1964) provide a framework for asking questions that will lead to higher reasoning abilities. In fact, they maintain that a teacher's way of asking questions is by far the single most influential teaching art. They believe that the teacher's questions define the mental operations that students perform and determine which points they explore and which modes of thought they learn. According to Taba, Levine, and Elzey, the steps in the cognitive operations are hierarchical; some operations represent a lower level of abstraction, and the mastery of a higher level task requires the ability to perform tasks at the lower level.

Taba et al. (1964) studied the questioning–response pattern of elementary-school social studies classes in the United States. They investigated whether the teacher questions and student responses focused the thought, extended the thought on the same cognitive level, or lifted the thought to a higher level. They concluded that only when students had first been involved at the lower levels of cognition could the discussion be lifted and continued at a higher level. The most important conclusion for teachers is that questions must be sequenced from

Table 3–1   Grouping and processing data

Ultimate Goal: Labeling Categories of Transportation	
Levels of Abstraction	**Example**
1. Data gathering— differentiating the specific properties of things, listing specific example	1. Listing, gathering, and describing various ways of travel. Look at concrete objects and discuss their properties (for example, cars, trucks, airplanes, sailboats, helicopters, submarines). Ask questions to help children discover properties of each item.
2. Data processing— grouping related items	2. Have children group items that are related. Ask questions and emphasize how these items are alike and how they are different. Help children discover that there are different ways to relate items, such as by color, shape, size, or use, and that sometimes one type of arrangement is more useful than another.
3. Abstracting— labeling each category that has been distinguished	3. Use questioning and discussion to lead to labeling: car, bus, truck—transportation that moves on land; sailboat, submarine—transportation that travels in the water; airplane, helicopter—transportation that travels in the air.

less to more abstract in order to get students to operate at higher thought levels. The researchers also found that teachers could be instructed in this sequential development.

Sequential development must progress from data gathering (the lowest level), to data processing, and, finally, to abstraction (the highest level). Tables 3–1 and 3–2 present the sequencing in grouping and processing data, interpreting data and making inferences, and applying previous knowledge to new situations. Each table includes examples of the steps as they might be used to develop thought processes with elementary children.

As seen in Table 3–1, the teacher's questions and class discussion allow the students time to explore the data thoroughly before they must provide abstract labels. The activity may be as complicated as the ability level of the children and subject matter. A kindergarten teacher may lead children through an activity in which they gather data, process and label objects according to shape, or label types of clothing, such as warm-weather clothing, cold-weather clothing, and rainy-weather clothing. A science class may progress through a similar sequence in order to categorize machines, plant families, or animal families.

In Table 3–2, the teacher encourages development of the ability to interpret data and to make inferences and generalizations. Students begin by assembling the data—the specifics on which a generalization will be based. They handle specific items cognitively before they develop the relationships and formulate generalizations. Table 3–2 follows a sequence that might be used to teach the generalization that when the letter *c* is followed by either *e*, *i*, or *y*, the *c* usually has the soft, or *s*, sound.

The sequence of development described in Table 3–2 is extremely useful in all subject areas. You may develop scientific principles through experimentation and formulation of a final generalization. Also, you may approach the meanings of prefixes, suffixes, and vocabulary words in this way.

Table 3–3 illustrates the steps used to help students apply previous knowledge to new situations (deduction). The activity is appropriate to use with children after they have read a literature selection. Have the children apply knowledge they have previously developed

Table 3–2 Interpreting data and making inferences

Ultimate Goal: Stating the *Ce, Ci,* and *Cy* Generalization	
Levels of Abstraction	**Example**
1. Data gathering—assembling, describing, and summarizing the data. What do we need to know before we make a decision?	1. Present sentences such as the following: "The *ceilings* in the house are eight feet high." "*Cider* is a drink made from apples." "A *cyclone* is a bad windstorm." Help students read the sentences. Ask for other words that have a beginning sound like *ceiling, cider,* and *cyclone.* Let the class provide other examples and place them under appropriate columns.

ce	*ci*	*cy*	*s*
cement	cinder	cycle	seam
cellar	city	cypress	(words that do not fit)

2. Data processing—relating aspects within the data. How is one item like another item? Is there any item that is different? Why does _____ happen?	2. Ask the students to look carefully at each word in the row and decide if there is anything similar about all the words in the first row, and so on. Ask the students to listen carefully as they say each word. Is there anything similar about their sounds?
3. Abstracting—forming generalizations and inferences	3. Help the students put together, in their words, a generalization incorporating the principles discovered. Ask "What generalization could we make about these letters?" When *c* has an *e, i,* or *y* after it, the *c* usually has the sound of *s.*

about the characteristics of a good plot and story (accomplished through inductive-thinking activities) to a new story, decide whether the story can be judged as excellent literature, and defend their decision.

The sequential questioning and discussion approach helps students formulate opinions and value judgments. For example, one social studies teacher used this technique to have children reach an opinion about the question "Should the government allow industrial expansion and other types of development in the Everglades? Why or why not?" The teacher first designed an activity in which the class identified the data required to reach an intelligent judgment. (This is an open-ended question, so there may be no "correct" answer.) The class listed, with the teacher's assistance, the questions they would have to answer before making a decision; for example: "What animals, plants, and people now live in the Everglades? Are any of the inhabitants endangered species? What conditions do the inhabitants need for survival? How would different kinds of development affect the Everglades (such as housing, airports, plastics industry, nuclear power plant)? How necessary is each kind of development to the economy?" The class investigated these questions, gathered their data, and discussed their findings.

Because students were expressing differences of opinion regarding the effects of development, the teacher next allowed the class to debate the issue. Some students supported ecology; some supported development. The class formed several teams for debate, so everyone had an opportunity to participate. Students who were not debating at a particular time

Table 3–3　Applying previous knowledge to new situations—deduction

Ultimate Goal: Making a Decision About Whether a New Literature Selection Should Be Judged Outstanding Literature	
Levels of Abstraction	**Example**
1. Data gathering—assembling related information and establishing the conditions under which to make predictions. What information do we need? What are the characteristics of the new example? What information do we already have that relates to the new situation?	1. Have the students gather information and examples about plot and character development, development of theme, the author's use of language, and development of an appropriate and realistic setting. Use questions and discussion to expand the base of critical data before you ask the students to make a judgment.
2. Data processing—relating the new situation to the previously stated generalization. How is the new situation like the one in the original generalization? How is it different? Does the generalization still apply?	2. Have the students compare their information about the story, plot, characterization, theme, language use, and setting with the set of criteria previously developed for evaluating literature. Do the criteria apply to the new story? If they do, why are they still applicable; if they are not, why are our criteria inappropriate?
3. Abstracting—applying the generalization. Supporting the prediction.	3. Let the children make a final decision as to whether they consider the new story an outstanding literature selection. Make them defend their decision with explanations.

acted as an audience for the others and were responsible for comparing the different points of view and substantiation of the views. The teacher encouraged the audience to ask questions. Discussion was lively because each child had previously investigated and discussed the pertinent data. When the teacher asked the final question, the students were able to provide answers demonstrating higher levels of thinking.

It is also important in the sequential questioning process to provide students with opportunities to ask appropriate questions. Students must assume the role of questioner for the teacher to be sure that they can carry on the cognitive operations independently. The teacher in the Everglades example allowed the children to ask many appropriate questions. You can plan activities with student questioning as the major goal. In these activities, present the group with the ultimate question, and have the students, individually or in groups, list pertinent questions. Obviously, some students will require considerable assistance, whereas others will be able to work independently.

For Your Development

Choose one of these sequential development areas: grouping and processing data, interpreting data and making inferences, or applying previous knowledge to new situations. You may use any part of the curriculum (science, social studies, literature, etc.) to design sequential activities that progress from data gathering to data processing to abstraction. Outline the activities you will use and provide examples of questions for each level.

If you are a student teacher or classroom teacher, use your activity with children and tape the activity for later evaluation. Listen to the tape and evaluate the effectiveness of your activities, your questions, and the children's interaction. Were the students able to progress from data gathering to processing to abstraction? Did any steps need to be improved? If you are not teaching children at this time, share the activities you have developed with your language arts class, and discuss the probable effectiveness of each activity.

Grouping Techniques. The second responsibility of teachers in effective oral discussion is to manage the environment so that discussion can take place. Some discussion activities may take place in a total classroom setting, whereas others may be more effective in smaller groups. Several discussion techniques may stimulate group interaction. During a brainstorming activity, have the children rapidly present as many ideas on a subject as they can think of; accept all ideas uncritically during the brainstorming experience. Also, let the students add to the ideas of others. Let a class secretary write down all the ideas as they are presented. The chalkboard or an overhead projector works well for this, because the class will need a copy of the ideas generated during the brainstorming. Brainstorming stimulates creative thought, and it can be the first step in a more detailed problem-solving or creative-writing activity—for example, thinking of all of the ways a class might raise money for a class trip or listing all words that can be used in place of *said.*

A discussion technique similar to brainstorming requires dividing the class into smaller groups, called *buzz groups.* During the buzz session, give the students limited time in which to generate a number of ideas or to solve a problem. You may wish to model brainstorming activities before using the small-group activity so that students will understand what they are to do in the buzz grouping.

An elementary class thought of all the ways you can prevent your dog from going under a fence during a five-minute buzz session. Another group used buzz sessions to solve such problems as "You have a poisonous spider in the terrarium and you want to get rid of the spider without killing the plants" and "Your mother put the paper boy's money on a high shelf in the kitchen. The paper boy came while she was out and you could not reach the money." The teacher gave the children a few minutes to think of as many solutions as they could and to talk about the pros and cons of each solution.

Two other discussion formats are effective in the classroom. A roundtable discussion includes a moderator and three to eight participants. The group deals with a problem or shares ideas informally. The moderator, who may also be a student, guides the group and assists it in summarizing conclusions. A roundtable discussion may also have an audience. You may divide the class into several small groups, or let one group participate in the discussion while the rest of the class listens. Activities that develop thinking and questioning strategies are prerequisites to effective roundtable discussions because skills in asking questions as well as in answering them are necessary for successful interaction in group discussions.

A more formal small-group discussion technique is panel discussion. During a panel discussion, make each member of the panel responsible for a particular aspect of the subject. Each member must be knowledgeable enough in the subject to present information and answer questions raised by the audience.

Many of the successful panel discussions used with upper elementary children may also use role-playing. For example, one science class pretended to be well-known scientists in the area of solar power and presented a panel discussion on the advantages and disadvantages of using solar energy. Classroom discussions can motivate interest, develop higher reasoning abilities, and provide opportunities for oral language development in children.

Cooperative Learning.   Cooperative learning is an instructional method that encourages small groups of students to work and learn together for both learning and social goals. The groups usually consist of two to six students who are from heterogeneous or mixed-ability learning groups. According to Saban (1994) cooperative learning is based on the following assumptions: (1) Cooperative learning overcomes student isolation in the classroom; (2) the grouping helps students become more accepting of individual differences and cultural diversity; (3) the approach may increase positive feelings toward peers and increase self-esteem of individual students; (4) students learn from each other; (5) students can be responsible for their own learning and motivated to learn; (6) teachers are not the only source of information; and (7) cooperative learning nourishes cooperation among students.

To make the cooperative learning experience successful, Saban (1994) maintains that students must be taught to work together productively. Consequently, learners need to know, accept, trust, and support each other. Saban states that students must be given reasons for their cooperative efforts and understand that there are benefits to the whole group. It is important that each individual in the group understands that he or she is responsible for learning the material because the group's success depends on each member in the group. In addition, the organization of the group needs to encourage face-to-face interaction by encouraging students to explain, elaborate, and relate their learning to previous learning.

To gain experience in cooperative learning groups, educators usually recommend that cooperative learning begin with a small group of two or three in which students practice simple or familiar tasks to gain experience before they work on more complex learning activities. Morrison (1995) maintains that students should be involved in a regular cycle of activities. For example, the teacher might present the lesson to the group, the students work to master the materials, the students explain their work and ideas to group members, and the students take a brief quiz to establish that they have all learned the material.

There are many types of learning activities that may be developed through cooperative learning. For example, Fitzpatrick (1994) recommends the following strategies to improve reading comprehension through cooperative learning groups: (1) Students discuss books and stories which they have read, and ask each other questions about the stories; (2) group members construct and discuss story maps that develop important components of the story; (3) students dramatize incidents from stories and books; (4) groups publish a classroom newspaper containing original stories composed by members of the group; and (5) members brainstorm vocabulary words related to a specific word or phrase that is of interest to them. As you read this short list of activities, notice that the activities integrate the language arts and provide opportunities for students to work together in cooperative learning groups.

When teachers are involved in cooperative learning experiences, they act as facilitators for the group process and channel and supervise the educational activities. There is disagreement, however, on the best approach to grading cooperative learning activities. Many educators stress the advisability of assigning both an individual and a group grade for cooperative learning. Others prefer only giving individual grades, while others maintain that group grades are the best approach for cooperative learning. Only your own experiences in a specific classroom and learning experience will help you make this grading decision.

Creative Dramatics

Probably no other areas of language arts stimulate children's imaginations and language abilities as much as do the various forms of drama. Children can explore real-life situations through role-playing; they can learn physical control and ways to express emotions confidently through pantomime; they can learn to interpret literature and to develop creative presentations through puppetry. Dramatic interactions provide reasons for children to use their oral language and develop crucial thought processes. Stewig and Nordberg (1995) emphasize the various values of drama including social and emotional growth, the encouragement of creativity, the opportunity to work in teams, the development of reasoning powers, the expansion of vocabulary, the opportunity to understand language features, and growth in spontaneous oral composition. Drama allows each child to develop the ability to use language independently and creatively.

Drama for younger children usually deals with imagined characters based on fantasy or on reality. Older children usually incorporate real-life situations into the content of drama activities. Such real-life situations often have a sense of struggle and excitement. Children seem to want to imagine themselves experimenting with courage and loyalty and solving difficult problems.

The drama curriculum should be a planned sequence of learning experiences. It should be geared to the developmental level, in which the children explore and apply the following concepts: (1) relaxation, concentration, and trust; (2) body movement; (3) use of the five senses; (4) imagination; (5) language, voice, and speech; and (6) characterization. Students should progress from these concepts related to the player, to playmaking and considerations of the audience. Siks (1983) suggests developing these concepts in varying time periods. For example, because children seem to learn player skills in short, concentrated experiences, you may devote fifteen minutes per day to exploring those concepts. However, when the children progress to playmaking, they need longer periods to explore the player, playmaker, and audience concepts. The longer periods might consist of several thirty-minute periods a week, or a one-hour period weekly.

Pantomime.   Pantomime is the creative drama in which actors play parts with gestures and actions without the use of words. Pantomime develops a sense of movement and helps children interpret situations. The following pantomime activities are from several undergraduate- and graduate-student experiences:

1. *The warm-up*—Even though the warm-up takes only a few minutes, it is essential to the rest of the session. If the students are not relaxed and comfortable, they will not get the most they can from the period. The warm-up also sets the mood, so that children know what to expect and what structure they must work within. Exercises that stretch and relax muscles are good.

2. *The glob*—This exercise is a warm-up for the mind. It's an imagination game in which a pretend glob is passed around a circle. Ask each individual to do something with the glob and to pass it on. This activity will stimulate the imagination when one child perceives the glob as hot, another cold, another sticky, and so forth. The activity also tells something about the abilities and inhibitions of the group.

3. *Ball tossing*—This exercise is similar in its level to the previous one. Students stand in a circle and throw a pretend ball around. They begin to watch their bodies as they throw and to see what movements they make when throwing a ball. They also begin working with focus, because they must watch the path of the pretend ball to know who will catch it. It's a good idea to change the size and weight of the pretend ball. You may begin by pretending to throw a volleyball, then a beach ball, then a bowling ball or football.

4. *Mirrors*—This is a great exercise for cooperation and concentration. Two students face each other with their legs crossed. One is the leader, and the other is to imitate the leader's movements as if he or she were a mirror image. They begin with large, slow movements. Later, if they are adept, they may add facial expressions to mimic also.

5. *Occupation and sport games*—There are many games to play with pantomime. One of the most enjoyable is to guess the occupation or sport being pantomimed. Each student performs a short pantomime activity and the others guess what it is. The first to guess in any pantomime activity performs the next one. Perhaps your biggest responsibility is to establish a trusting and open atmosphere. Be sure that the students do not laugh at or make fun of other students.

6. *People machine*—This is a common dramatic game. The students construct a working, interacting, and spontaneous machine. One person begins, and the others attach themselves wherever they see a possible position. Machine-like sounds help them to get into the activity and realize these positions. Usually students attempt an assembly-line machine, but it is best to encourage a conglomerate of interacting parts. For example, if the students choose a tractor, four students can be wheels, one the steering wheel, and others the body.

7. *Role-playing*—Role-playing works best with a more mature and experienced group. It is fascinating to watch, and the students learn from it. Start by giving the students a situation—something they can easily relate to. For example: The older daughter is setting the table, the younger daughter comes in and knocks a plate off the table and breaks it, and the mother blames the older. Explain the situation to each player, including the reasons for their actions. Tell the mother that she is tired from working all day; she thinks the younger daughter is too young to do much work; she feels the older daughter is often lazy and disobedient. Tell the older daughter that she feels she must do all the work while the younger daughter gets away with everything. Tell the younger daughter she is afraid of the mother because she is not in a good mood and does not want to take the blame.

8. *Imitation game*—This game is based on the game "telephone." Choose one child to perform a short pantomime with large motions. It should be something that all the students will be familiar with, such as getting ready for bed or making cookies. The other students can't watch when you watch the student for the first time. Then, the students come out one at a time; the first one watches, then must try to imitate the first student exactly. While the second student tries, the third one watches, and so forth. Each child gets only one chance to watch before he or she performs the pantomime, but after he or she performs the pantomime, the child may watch all the rest. This is an exercise in observation, but it is also fun to observe the mutations.

9. *Slow motion*—Any game in slow motion is good. The students learn how they use their bodies, and they must concentrate on what they are doing. They might all do a different sport simultaneously, or they can form pairs and guess what the other is performing.

10. *Actions and emotions*—Ask children to pretend to be a giant striding, a hobbled prisoner, someone pulling a sled, someone drinking something unpleasant. An individual pantomime game may be played by writing an emotion on paper, giving each child a different emotion, and having the child act out the emotion while the others guess. Include such emotions as anger, hunger, sadness, happiness, and gleefulness.

11. *Visiting the beach*—Ask students to lie comfortably on their backs. Tell them to clear their minds and concentrate on their breathing. Then tell them to react to what they hear, and take them to the beach through your voice. The students slowly "go to the beach," seeing things, hearing things, smelling things; the sun gets hot, the sun goes behind clouds, it becomes hot again, the students want to go for a swim. Suddenly rain clouds gather and your voice brings them quickly back to the cars. The students will react to your voice if it is sincere and descriptive. You can evaluate their in-

volvement by their movements. Does the breathing slow down in places? Does it quicken in others? Do the children squirm in the sand? Do they shade their eyes from the sun? Do they pretend to swim?

12. *Sense memory*—This exercise is only for an experienced and trusting group. It is a way to teach emotional expression, and it must be handled with skill. Ask the students to relax on the floor, preferably not close to anyone else. First, tell them to concentrate on their breathing, focusing their attention on themselves. Again, your voice leads them into their memories. Ask the students to recall a time when they felt extremely happy or maybe silly. This memory can be any emotion, but it is usually better to start with a happy feeling that is easy to remember. Later, you might ask for anger, loneliness, frustration, and so forth, but children must first learn to deal with the emotions and how to rid themselves of undesirable feelings after the exercise is completed. Ask them questions about the experience, such as "Where were you? Who else was there? What were you doing? What did it look like? Were there any sounds?" Guide them through the memory with your voice. Afterward, gather them into a group and talk about the experience. Don't ask them what the experience was, because it may be too personal to share; but if the children wish to talk about the experience, let them.

13. *Narration*—Narrate or read a story aloud, giving children time to pantomime each new act and to be each new character. Have the children pantomime all the roles, including the inanimate objects. Folktales such as "The Three Little Pigs" and "The Three Billy Goats Gruff" are appropriate for younger children. Children in the third and fourth grades enjoy pantomime scenes from "The Twelve Dancing Princesses" and the Jewish tale "Mazel and Shlimazel." Older children enjoy scenes from Greek and Norse mythology.

14. *Object game*—Write names of objects on separate pieces of paper. Have each student choose a paper and portray that object, allowing the rest of the class to guess the object. You might include a light bulb, an alarm clock, the sun rising, and the wind in a tree.

15. *Pantomime children's literature*—While listening to Carolyn Otto's *I Can Tell by Touching* (1994), have children act out text such as "I can feel my feet in my socks and my socks slipping in my shoes" (unnumbered) or "I feel the earth beneath me and the hot sun overhead" (unnumbered). They might also pantomime various musical instruments to accompany the reading of Lloyd Moss's *Zin! Zin! Zin! A Violin* (1995).

For Your Development

You will feel comfortable with the kind of movement and pantomime activities discussed in this section only if you actually try the activities. First, form a group of your peers and experiment with the activities. Take turns leading the activities. After you feel comfortable as part of this group, select several pantomime and movement activities and present them to a group of children.

Playmaking. Experiences that allow children to experiment with movement and to pantomime interpretations of characters and emotions provide foundations for other dramatic activities, whether acting in original plays or interpreting literature selections read by or to the

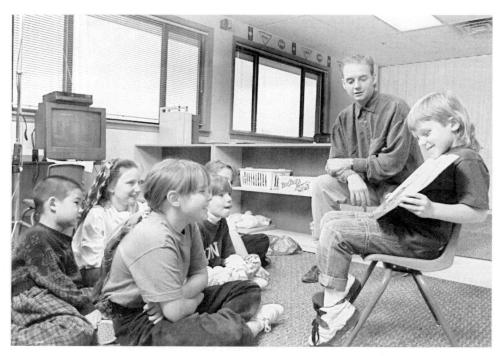

Retelling a story is often the beginning of creative dramatics.

children. During the process of acting out a role, the children develop new insights and are able to identify with the role. If children wish to share their performances with another group, they may use more elaborate settings, costumes, or masks to define the characters. Young children respond well when they are allowed to take on a character by dressing in appropriate costumes.

Both creative dramatics and improvisation are ways to develop creative thinking. To meet this goal, they must be open ended, develop divergent-thinking abilities, and result in creative products.

In improvisation, children develop dramatic experiences out of their own ideas, whereas in dramatization, they use the work and ideas of others to expand and develop their own ideas. Improvisation places on the teacher a guiding rather than a directing responsibility. As an example of improvisation, one group of third-grade children was motivated to act out a play after watching the television production *It's the Great Pumpkin, Charlie Brown* by Charles Schulz. The following day at school, the students were talking about what would happen if there really were a great pumpkin and it visited Linus in the pumpkin patch. The teacher allowed the children an opportunity to discuss what they felt would happen in those circumstances. There was enough difference of opinion that several groups were formed to further the discussion. These groups met and then presented their interpretations to the rest of the class.

Many ideas for dramatization come from story selections. Stories that are appropriate for dramatization meet these criteria:

1. The idea should have worth, and the story should be carefully written.
2. The story should involve conflict.
3. There should be action in the development of the plot, and it should be action that can be carried out satisfactorily.

4. The characters should seem real, whether they are human or animal.
5. The situations should call for interesting dialogue.

Numerous literature selections meet these criteria. For example, many of the folktales by the Brothers Grimm develop humorous conflict, easily identifiable characters, and plots that encourage dialogue. Stories such as *The Bremen Town Musicians* (1988) create interesting dialogue as the animals use their vocal talents to frighten the robbers. Stories that include twists also encourage children to try their own interpretations. Alix Berenzy's *A Frog Prince* (1989) provides such motivation as the frog rethinks his choice of a bride.

John Steptoe's *Mufaro's Beautiful Daughters: An African Tale* (1987) develops conflict between the selfish, spoiled daughter and the kind, considerate daughter. Janet Stevens's expanded version of the Aesop fable *The Tortoise and the Hare* (1984) stresses humorous action and dialogue among the various characters who try to help the tortoise or hinder the hare. Arthur Yorinks's *Hey, Al* (1986) involves conflict between a life with struggle and a life of endless leisure. Yorinks's book encourages expanded dialogue as students consider the consequences of each lifestyle.

Even after the story is selected teachers have a responsibility to give more guidance than they did in improvisation. In an earlier writing, Siks (1958) suggests five steps that teachers should follow in guiding children in story dramatization:

1. Motivate the children into a strong mood.
2. Present the story, poem, or idea from which the children are to create.
3. Guide the children in planning.
4. Guide the children in playing.
5. Guide the children in evaluating their own work.

One second-grade teacher used the story "Stone Soup" as a literature selection to motivate dramatization. To accomplish the first step in dramatization, motivating the children into a strong mood, the teacher placed a large soup kettle and a stone in the front of the classroom. As the children entered the classroom, they asked many questions. The teacher replied with a motivating question: "If you were hungry, could you get a meal out of a stone?"

To meet the second guiding step, the teacher told the story of "Stone Soup" to the class. While telling the story, she used as props the soup kettle, the stone, water, and the numerous soup ingredients the villagers were finally coaxed into bringing out from hiding. The class showed interest during the storytelling, and a desire to become involved in the presentation.

After hearing the story, the children talked about their favorite characters and scenes in the story. The teacher allowed them to improvise the actions of their favorite characters, such as a farmer hiding his barley from the soldiers, a hungry soldier marching into town, or a sly soldier stirring a stone into water to make soup. The class then discussed which characters should be in the play. They expanded the story with additional villagers that they felt should be in the play. They discussed how the mayor of the town, a baker, or a soldier might talk and act. They discussed a sequence of scenes, and decided they would use the soup kettle, the stone, and soup ingredients for props. The only costuming they considered necessary were single items for each person—an apron for a woman peasant, a badge for the mayor, a cardboard rifle for the soldier, a hat for the baker.

Next, the class acted out the story. The teacher added suggestions by becoming a character in the story. This was necessary at times to bring the story back to the discussed sequence. The children acted out the story several times so they could play different characters.

After acting out the story, the children, guided by the teacher, discussed and evaluated what had happened during the presentation. The teacher guided questions so that the class talked first about what was good about the play; for example, "How did the villagers show that they did not trust the soldiers? What did the baker do so you knew he was trying to hide the food? How did you know which actor was the leader of the soldiers?" After several questions, the children suggested ways they could improve the play another time.

Teachers play an important role in stimulating the drama experience. O'Neill (1989) identifies some of the tasks performed by an effective teacher. These tasks include encouraging student interaction and decision making, establishing the context for learning, taking risks with materials, working with a focus, tolerating ambiguity, devising fruitful encounters, and giving power to students.

Purves, Rogers, and Soter (1990) recommend that teachers enhance responses to literature by having students use their imaginations to role-play interesting and challenging situations from literature. In addition, they suggest that students perform poetry readings with various interpretations and feelings. Then, the students decide which interpretations they believe are the most effective. Segedy and Roosevelt (1986) recommend that teachers adapt a courtroom trial format in working with certain types of literature. This approach combines reading, writing, speaking, and listening as students analyze the characters and situations, develop courtroom proceedings, use the writing process to develop summations to the jury, link and express their ideas through oral debate, and interact with each other. Books such as Elizabeth George Speare's *The Witch of Blackbird Pond* (1958) provide an exciting context for developing trials.

As children move from player to playmaker and present dramas to others, they learn that the audience also has a purpose. Children need experiences being audience members as well as actors. In the role of audience children learn the responsibility of both listening and responding to peers with honest feedback about an activity. In this interactive process, which is extremely affective in nature, children gain respect and value for the efforts, imagination, and integrity of peers.

You should provide experiences for children to be audience members in both small and large groups. You can ask the audience to provide responses by asking the following questions: "What did you see that made you believe . . . ? How did you feel when . . . ? How did you know the players were in . . . ?"

One of the best ways for children to understand the role of the audience is for them to see excellent drama. When appropriate children's theater comes to your city, arrange trips, or have drama groups or puppeteers give presentations at your school. In addition to being marvelous opportunities for positive audience response, excellent presentations motivate child-produced drama.

For Your Development

Choose a literature selection you consider appropriate for dramatization. Does the selection contain the five criteria listed earlier for dramatizing a literature selection? Describe how you would develop the drama according to these five steps: (1) motivating the children, (2) presenting the story, (3) guiding the planning, (4) guiding the playing, and (5) guiding the evaluation.

If you are a student teacher or a classroom teacher, develop your drama activity with a group of children. If you are not teaching, share your drama activity with your language arts class or try to visit a class in which drama is part of the curriculum. Try to evaluate the teacher's use of Siks's five guiding steps.

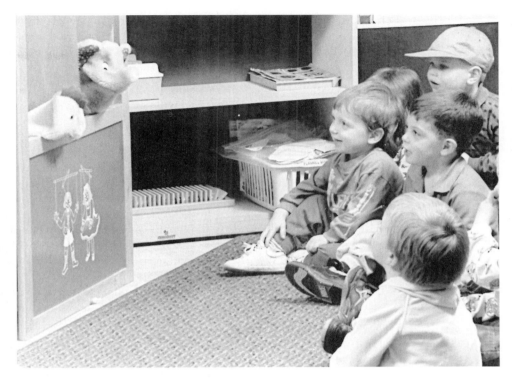

Puppets can encourage enthusiastic oral and written responses.

Puppetry.   What do you visualize when you hear "Punch and Judy" or "The Muppets"? Most of us associate these terms with a form of creative dramatics that has brought pleasure to both children and adults for many centuries. In Europe, puppet theaters are so elaborate that entire operas are performed by marionettes. The Japanese Bunraku puppets perform classical drama, and the puppeteers in Thailand perform in the temple courtyards. How many of you have observed children watching the Muppets on *Sesame Street* or the puppets in the Land of Make Believe on *Mr. Rogers's Neighborhood?* If you have watched children during a live puppet presentation, you know how responsive and attentive they become.

Young children need many experiences for developing their imaginations. Puppetry provides opportunities for children to develop communication skills. When children present a play, they are developing oral language and drama skills; when they write their own plays, they are developing creative writing skills; when they retell literature stories, they are developing interpretive and comprehension skills, as well as other reading skills; when they design sets and puppets, they are learning about art and the theater; and when they become the audience, they are developing appreciative listening skills.

Use puppets in prekindergarten and kindergarten programs for developing language skills. It is truly exciting to hear a young child who does not normally speak in the classroom respond to puppetry. Also use puppets in remedial reading and language classes to encourage reading and communication skills with older children.

INTRODUCING PUPPETS.   Children often respond to a puppet as if it were a real person or animal. Introduce children to puppetry by showing them a puppet play and presenting several puppets to them. Some puppets lend themselves better to certain types of drama.

Let children manipulate various types of puppets to discover the limitations and possibilities of each. Encourage children to explore some of the history of puppets; even young children can acquire information from pictures.

INITIAL PUPPET PROJECTS.   After you have introduced puppetry and the children have experimented with the puppets, begin a puppet project. Many puppets are simple enough for even young children to make. Good beginning projects include paper-plate puppets (Figure 3–2). Children can make the puppets by folding paper plates in the center, partially cutting eyes (so they stand up), and adding features. Children can manipulate these simple puppets to "talk" by folding and unfolding the paper plates. With unfolded paper plates, children can make an elephant by cutting out a round circle for the trunk, gluing on cardboard ears, and adding eyes. A puppeteer wearing a gray stocking on his or her hand can put the stocking through the circle in the plate to maneuver the hand as a trunk and communicate.

Another simple hand puppet is the paper-bag puppet (Figure 3–3). For this puppet, children draw features on a paper bag, allowing the mouth opening to fall on the fold of the bag. They can make features more lifelike by adding hair made from strips of paper, yarn, or felt. A scarecrow from *The Wizard of Oz* might even have real straw for the hair. Pieces of cloth add authenticity to the clothing.

Bring these first projects to life by having the puppeteers improvise short dialogues or present rhymes or riddles using the puppet. After the children share their puppets, have them gather in small groups and improvise short scenes with the puppets.

EXTENDING PUPPET PROJECTS.   The next step is to select a play to present. Children should begin developing puppetry plays by working with literature because literature provides a foundation of plot and character on which children can build. Learning prin-

FIGURE 3–2   Paper-Plate Puppets

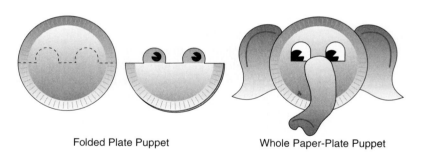

Folded Plate Puppet   Whole Paper-Plate Puppet

FIGURE 3–3   Paper-Bag Puppets

ciples of plot and character through the use of familiar stories also makes the transition to original work easier. These stories should have briskly moving actions, characters that are easily constructed as puppets, and not too many characters. In addition, it is helpful if the story has dialogue or speeches that children can convert easily into their own words. If sets are to be added to the puppet theater, the story should require only a few simple sets.

Many fairy tales and folktales meet the preceding criteria and offer enjoyable projects for kindergarten and early primary students. Some favorites are "Three Billy Goats Gruff," "The Three Bears," "Henny Penny," "Jack and the Beanstalk," "Bremen Town Musicians," "The Three Little Kittens," "Rumpelstiltskin," "Hansel and Gretel," "The Three Little Pigs," and Mother Goose verses. Also useful for puppetry are more contemporary stories such as *Winnie the Pooh* (1926, 1954) by A. A. Milne, *Where the Wild Things Are* (1963) by Maurice Sendak, and Rosemary Wells's *The Little Lame Prince* (1990).

Stories suitable for the intermediate grades include folktales and fairy tales as well as contemporary and historical fiction. Fairy tales such as "Aladdin and the Lamp" make excellent puppet productions. You also can use children's classics such as Robert Louis Stevenson's *Treasure Island* (1911), Howard Pyle's *The Merry Adventures of Robin Hood* (1883, 1946), and Rudyard Kipling's *Just So Stories* (1902, 1987). Charlotte, Wilbur, and the rest of the delightful characters from E. B. White's *Charlotte's Web* (1952) can come to life through puppetry. The Paul Bunyan and Mike Fink tall tales provide plenty of action. Children can dramatize the Revolutionary War period in connection with *Johnny Tremain* (1943) by Esther Forbes.

To give each child an opportunity to become involved in puppetry, perform several plays or have the children take turns performing various roles. As we have mentioned, children need experience both as actors and audience. Read the literature selections to the children or let the children read the selections themselves, depending on the reading ability of the group. Encourage the children to discuss the story freely in order to see how they might interpret it for puppet theater. This is a time for building imagination. As the plans of the children progress, you can refine them. Prepare an outline of the plot, characters, and scenes of the play, but keep in mind that improvisation and free interpretation are preferable to memorization.

HAND PUPPETS.   Because hand puppets are easy to manipulate, they become part of the puppeteer. Hand puppets are useful for dialogue because children can make many puppets appear to be speaking. Hand puppets also require less time and skill to make and perform with than do marionettes. Besides paper-plate puppets and paper-bag puppets, hand puppets include box puppets, sock puppets, cylinder puppets, molded-head puppets, and rod puppets.

Children can make a box puppet (Figure 3–4) by cutting the sides of a rectangular box so that it will fold or by lapping two boxes together so that the openings of the boxes face the puppeteer. Paint a face on the boxes so that the top half of the mouth is on the top box and the lower half of the mouth is on the lower box. Cut features from construction paper, cloth,

FIGURE 3–4   A Box Puppet

or other scraps to give a three-dimensional effect. A puppeteer manipulates the puppet by placing fingers in the top box and thumb in the lower box; the puppet "talks" when the mouth of the box opens and closes.

Make a sock puppet (Figure 3–5) by placing a stocking over your hand and manipulating the hand so the puppet moves and talks. The elephant's trunk is an example of this type of puppet. Make features for sock puppets by adding buttons or felt for eyes, yarn for hair, and so forth.

Construct a puppet from a cardboard cylinder by adding facial features to the front of the cylinder (Figure 3–6). This puppet will be more elaborate and lifelike if you form a papier-mâché head around the top of the cylinder. Paint on features for the face and add paper, yarn, or felt hair. Make clothing from felt or another material. Manipulate the puppet by placing your fingers inside the cylinder.

Make more lifelike puppets by molding the head around a clay form, a balloon, or a Styrofoam ball (Figure 3–7). Mold a clay ball or blow a balloon to the desired size. (If you use clay, grease it with vaseline.) Dip paper strips into wallpaper paste and place layers over the head mold. Form the desired features. When the head is dry, pop the balloon, or remove the clay by cutting the head in half. If you cut the head, papier-mâché the two halves together. Cut and sew a cloth costume that will go over the hand, and place the head on top of the costume. Manipulate the puppet by placing a finger inside the head and in each of the costume armholes.

Rod puppets (Figure 3–8) are easy to construct and manipulate. Draw pictures of animals, people, and so forth on stiff paper, or cut pictures from magazines, coloring books, or old storybooks, and tape or glue them to cardboard. Then, attach the drawn or pasted character to the top part of a dowel, straw, or tongue depressor. Maneuver the puppet by grasping the lower end of the rod and moving the puppet across the stage so the audience sees only the puppet.

FIGURE 3–5   A Sock Puppet

FIGURE 3–6   A Cylinder Puppet

FIGURE 3–7   A Molded-Head Puppet

FIGURE 3–8   A Rod Puppet

FIGURE 3–9   A Humanette
Puppet

HUMANETTE PUPPETS.   Humanette puppets (Figure 3–9) are large puppets that do not
need a puppet stage. For this puppet, draw a large cardboard shape of a person, animal, or
plant. Cut openings in the cardboard figure so the puppeteer's face is visible and the puppeteer can use his or her arms. The children themselves become the puppets.

PUPPET STAGES.   Puppet theaters (Figure 3–10) can be simple or elaborate. Make a stage
by cutting an opening in a very large box, such as a refrigerator box, and decorating it. Design

FIGURE 3–10   A Folding Puppet
Stage

an instant stage by turning a rectangular table on its side, or by placing the puppeteers behind a large desk. Turn an open doorway into a puppet theater by placing a length of material (with an appropriate opening cut out) across it. Construct a portable puppet theater out of lightweight wood framing covered with burlap. This puppet theater folds for easy storage.

PUPPET DRAMA.   Rehearse each puppet scene so the children can practice manipulating their puppets while speaking their parts. As indicated, improvising and interpreting a story freely work better than memorizing. Children will want to work with their puppets to develop character voices and to give the puppets life. When the children present a puppet drama to an audience, have the puppets exchange some dialogue with the audience. This involves the audience in the play and provides more opportunities for creative discussion. You can also add sound effects, lighting, and scenery to your puppet production. One student teacher even had the children write commercials, which different puppets presented between the acts of a formal puppet drama when they presented it for an audience! When children have learned some of the principles of puppet drama, have them create their own plays.

For Your Plan Book

Lesson Plan

A Puppet Project: Helping Freddie Frog

Grade level: Second

A teacher developed the following example of a creative writing and puppet project for a group of second-grade students. The objectives of this project were:

1. To use a puppet to motivate interest and response.
2. To help the children learn to work together—in composing their script, designing a cover for the puppet program, and designing scenery.
3. To reinforce creative abilities, including singing, drawing, oral expression, and drama.
4. To help the children put expression and emotion into their reading.
5. To give the children the experience of performing before the class.
6. To develop personal concern in the children for the problem of pollution, by writing a letter to their class, making posters, and by putting on the puppet show for others.

The teacher made the puppet Freddie Frog from a folded paper plate. He was green and had bulging eyes made from Ping-Pong balls. After the teacher introduced the puppet to the group, he delivered the following letter to each child:

Dear _____,

My name is Freddie Frog and I hopped over here today to ask you to help me out. You see, I am in two storybooks that have only pictures in them—no words. Can you imagine that? A book that you can't read?

I know how well you can write stories, so I wondered if you could write one of these stories. Please write sentences that tell what happens to me, and also draw pictures so that the other boys and girls in second grade can see what is happening.

First, I want you to look through the books very carefully. Then I will ask you questions to see if you will be able to write the story for me.

Well, what do you think? I hope you can help me. Imagine that! You can be the writer and illustrator of your very own book!

Thanks so much!

Your friend,
Freddie Frog

After looking through two picture books by Mercer Mayer, *A Boy, a Dog and a Frog* (1967) and *Frog, Where Are You?* (1969), the children wrote their stories, copied them into their booklets, and illustrated each page. After the children finished their booklets, Freddie Frog gave each child another letter. Freddie again requested help from the children. Many of his friends and relatives were sick from drinking the polluted water in their pond. Could the children put on a puppet show in which the forest animals would clean up the pond and save their water friends? Freddie Frog presented the following letter:

Hi _____,

I hopped over here today to see if you can help me. You see, I am very sad today because my wife, Fanny Frog, and my little son, Frankie Frog, are very sick. The water around our log and lily pads is polluted, so every time we take a drink of water, we get tummy aches.

And do you know what else? My friend Farley Fish can't even swim around in our stream without bumping into pop cans, bottles, and old tires. He is very thin now because he can't eat green plants without swallowing oil and acids in the water. Our other forest friends, Cubby Bear, Pudgy Porcupine, and Randy Raccoon, can't even play tag in the water because it is full of garbage.

So do you see how much I need your help? Our pond and stream need to be cleaned up so that everyone will be well again and so we can have fun swimming in clear, clean water. I thought that if you put on a puppet show for the rest of the second-grade boys and girls, they might help stop some of the litterbugs who throw paper and pop bottles on the ground and in the water. Maybe after seeing your puppet show, the children will tell everyone to be helpers, and we can save the lives of the many little fish, turtles, and frogs like me, who die because of the dirty water.

I know how well you can write stories and draw pictures, so I think you can put on a very good puppet show. You could make puppets of our forest friends and water friends, and act out a story about how they decide to go swimming and what happens when they see the stream full of trash. What will they do to solve the problem?

Thanks so much for helping Farley Fish, Fanny and Frankie Frog, and all our other forest friends!

Your friend,
Freddie Frog

After reading the letter and discussing the problem, the children listened to a story from *Ranger Rick* magazine, "How Rick's Rangers Came to Be." This story gave them additional ideas for their puppet show. The children chose specific characters and made up dialogue. The teacher recorded this conversation and typed a script from the tape.

The children made their own puppets out of paper plates. In addition, the children wrote letters about pollution to their classmates, including some of the letters in the puppet-show program that they distributed to the audience. They worked together in designing a cover for the program and a background mural for the puppet show. They also made pollution posters,

Continued

which they showed and explained to the audience after the puppet show. They incorporated music into the program with a rendition of "A Little Green Frog," making several changes in the song so the frog could sing: "He swallowed some water and he said, 'I'm sad, 'cause I'm a little sick frog swimming in the water. Glumph! Glumph! Glumph!'" The children presented their original puppet play, "The Bubbling Pond," to an appreciative audience and enjoyed positive experiences in creative writing, drawing, singing, and creative dramatics.

Choral Speaking and Reading.   Choral speaking is the interpretation of poetry or literature by two or more voices speaking as one. Choral speaking and reading allow children to respond to and enjoy rhymes and poetry in new ways. Children discover that speaking voices can be combined as effectively as singing voices in a choir. Young children who are not yet able to read can enjoy this activity by reciting memorized rhymes and verses. Older children can select anything suitable that is within their reading ability.

Choral speaking and reading synchronize the three language elements of listening, reading, and speaking. They help children develop interpretive skills, and heighten their appreciation of poetry and literature. Choral speaking can also improve children's speech. Teachers of remedial reading and learning disability classes find that choral reading provides repeated reading practice and develops a realization that reading can be fun. Because choral speaking is a group activity, it builds positive group attitudes and realization that some activities are better if they are performed cooperatively. This realization can be beneficial to shy children as well as aggressive ones. Kay (1991) also maintains that choral reading is an excellent approach for increasing children's interaction with literature both at school and at home. Eldredge (1990) found that using choral reading in which the teacher emphasizes correct phrasing, intonation, and pitch improves both comprehension and vocabulary.

Explore rhythm by allowing children to clap or beat out the rhythm of verses. Children may suggest ways to express rhythm, and should experience fast and slow rhythms as well as happy and sad ones.

During this initial phase, plan activities in which the children can sense the rhythm and tempo of music and poetry with their whole bodies. Have them react to different tempos played on the piano or on a record. Rhythm instruments, such as bongo drums or rhythm sticks, help children appreciate rhythm. Experiment with rhythm and tempo by accompanying a selection with a bongo or stick beat. The children realize how a slow tempo creates one meaning, a fast tempo another.

The second phase is understanding the color and quality of the voices available to a choral-speaking choir. Four terms describe the voice presentation of a selection: *inflection* is the rise or fall within a phrase; *pitch* is the highness or lowness of sound; *emphasis* is the verbal pointing of the most important word; and *intensity* is loudness or softness of the voices. While you and the children learn about voice color and quality, experiment with the facets of an effective choral chorus. Children learn to be sensitive to inflection, pitch, emphasis, and intensity by listening to and experimenting with simple but exciting materials.

Furthermore, children must understand the different ways in which choral arrangements can be expressed. Choral speaking is not merely the unison presentation of a poem. In fact, if that were the sole way of presentation, choral events would be extremely dull. It is of more value if children and teachers develop their own arrangements, rather than simply using those suggested by a text. To arrange choral presentations successfully, teachers and students need to know the various alternatives available. Five different types of presentation follow, with an example of each using a well-known Mother Goose rhyme.

REFRAIN ARRANGEMENT.   In this type of choral speaking, a teacher or child reads or recites the body of a poem, and the rest of the class responds in unison with the refrain, or chorus. Three poems with refrains are Maurice Sendak's "Pierre: A Cautionary Tale," Robert Louis Stevenson's "The Wind," and Jack Prelutsky's "The Yak." This example is based on the Mother Goose rhyme "A Jolly Old Pig."

Leader:	A jolly old pig once lived in a sty,
	And three little piggies had she,
	And she waddled about saying,
Group:	"Grumph! grumph! grumph!"
Leader:	While the little ones said,
Group:	"Wee! wee!"
Leader:	And she waddled about saying,
Group:	"Grumph! grumph! grumph!"
Leader:	While the little ones said,
Group:	"Wee! wee!"

LINE-A-CHILD OR LINE-A-GROUP ARRANGEMENT.   In this arrangement, one child or a group of children reads one line, another child or group reads the next line, a third child or group reads the third line, and so forth. Poems that can be used for line arrangements are Clyde Watson's "One, One," Carl Sandburg's "Arithmetic," and Eleanor Farjeon's "Geography." This example is "One, Two, Buckle My Shoe":

Group A:	One, two, buckle my shoe;
Group B:	Three, four, shut the door;
Group C:	Five, six, pick up sticks;
Group D:	Seven, eight, lay them straight;
Group E:	Nine, ten, a good fat hen.

ANTIPHONAL ARRANGEMENT.   This choral speaking arrangement, also called dialogue arrangement, involves alternate speaking by two groups. You may balance boys' voices against girls' voices, high voices against low voices, and so forth. Poems in which one line asks a question and the next answers it work well for dialogue arrangements. Christina Rossetti's "Who Has Seen the Wind?," A. A. Milne's "Puppy and I," and Rose Pyleman's "Wishes" are dialogue poems. One you may want to try is the Mother Goose rhyme "Pussy-Cat, Pussy-Cat":

Group A:	Pussy-cat, Pussy-cat, where have you been?
Group B:	I've been to London to visit the Queen.
Group A:	Pussy-cat, Pussy-cat, what did you there?
Group B:	I frightened a little mouse under the chair.

CUMULATIVE ARRANGEMENT.   This arrangement, also called crescendo arrangement, is used when a poem builds to a climax. One group reads the first line, the first and second groups read the second line, and so forth, until the poem reaches its climax, at which time all the groups read together. Two examples of cumulative poems are Edward Lear's "The Owl and the Pussy-Cat" and James Tippett's "Trains." This example is "There Was a Crooked Man":

Group A:	There was a crooked man, and he went a crooked mile,
Groups A, B:	He found a crooked sixpence against a crooked stile;
Groups A, B, C:	He bought a crooked cat, which caught a crooked mouse,
Groups A, B, C, D:	And they all lived together in a little crooked house.

UNISON ARRANGEMENT.   In unison arrangement, an entire group or class presents a whole selection together. This kind of presentation can be difficult because it often produces a singsong effect. Sandburg's "Fog" and Hugo's "Good night" are suitable for unison arrangements. An example for you to try with a group is "A Big Black Cat," by second-grade authors:

Whole Group: A big black cat walks down the street, meow, meow, meow.
A big black cat with a long black tail, meow, meow, meow.
He growls.
He spats.
He arches his back.
The big black cat walks down the street, meow, meow, meow.

To stimulate poetry and literature interpretations, encourage older children to experiment with the effects of grouping their voices according to light, medium, and dark voices. Children discover that light voices can effectively interpret happy, whimsical, or delicate parts; medium voices can add to descriptive and narrative parts; while dark voices can interpret robust, tragic, and heavier material. The following example is one way in which Robert Louis Stevenson's "From a Railway Carriage" (1885) can be interpreted:

(Light)	Faster than fairies, faster than witches,
(Medium)	Bridges and houses, hedges and ditches;
(Dark)	And charging along like troops in a battle,
(Medium)	All through the meadows the horses and cattle;
	All of the sights of the hill and the plain
(Dark)	Fly as thick as driving rain;
(Light)	and ever again, in the wink of an eye,
	Painted stations whistle by.
(Medium)	Here is a child who clambers and scrambles,
(Dark)	All by himself and gathering brambles;
(Medium)	Here is a tramp who stands and gazes;
(Light)	And here is the green for stringing the daisies!
(Dark)	Here is a cart runaway in the road
	Lumping along with man and load;
(Light)	And here is a mill and there is a river;
(All)	Each a glimpse and gone forever!

General guidelines follow for choral speaking and reading:

1. When selecting materials for children who cannot read, choose poems or rhymes that are simple enough to memorize easily.
2. Choose material that will interest children. Young children like nonsense and active words, so you may find it advantageous to begin with a humorous poem. Remember that choral speaking should be fun.
3. Especially for younger children, select poems or rhymes that use refrains. These are easy for nonreaders to memorize and result in rapid participation from each member of the group.
4. Let the children help select and interpret poetry. Allow them to experiment with the rhythm and tempo of a poem, improvise the scenes of the selection, and try different voice combinations and various choral arrangements before they decide on the best structural arrangement.
5. Allow children to listen to each other as they try different interpretations within groups.

For Your Development

First, with a group of your peers, practice until you feel confident with the different approaches. Second, select several pieces of poetry, rhymes, or short literary selections that you think are appropriate for choral speaking. Third, instruct a group of children using choral speaking or present the choral speaking or reading activity to your peers.

READER'S THEATER.   Reader's theater differs from oral reading in that several readers take the parts of the characters in a story or play. Reader's theater is not a play with memorized lines, detailed actions, or elaborate stage sets. Instead, it is an oral interpretation of literature, a dramatic reading for an audience who imagines the setting and the action. Consequently, reader's theater includes oral language, listening, literature, and writing. The actors are motivated to read, think, enjoy literature, and express themselves orally. If they develop or adapt their own materials, they enhance creative writing. Working together fosters teamwork and pride in accomplishment. The audience benefits through improved listening skills, literary enjoyment, and motivation for reading literature. The literary selections provide language models for both performers and audience.

Children's literature provides many excellent sources for reader's theater. Folktales originally told through the oral tradition, picture books designed to be read orally to children, and poetry are good sources for younger elementary children. Realistic stories, plays, and narrative poems are good for older students. When selecting materials, the story should be suspenseful, with a well-designed plot. It should be imaginative, presenting characters in a series of events complicated by problems. The action should turn on a dramatic moment and the ending should be clear and satisfying. The characters should be compelling and understandable quickly through the dialogue. The text should have sufficient dialogue or passages that can be changed into dialogue. Although narrative lines should be brief, they may introduce characters and setting or enhance plot development. Finally, repetitive words and phrases should produce rhythm patterns enjoyed by children and should encourage audience participation.

Examples of literature appropriate for younger children include Margaret Mahy's *17 Kings and 42 Elephants* (1987), Mem Fox's *Hattie and the Fox* (1987), Dayal Kaur Khalsa's *I Want a Dog* (1987), and Eve Bunting's *Ghost's Hour, Spook's Hour* (1987). Phillis Gershator's storytelling style in her *Tukama Tootles the Flute: A Tale from the Antilles* (1994) includes chants and a melodic quality that appeals to children. Edward Lear's *The Pelican Chorus: And Other Nonsense* (1995) appeals to all ages. More experienced readers can interpret Bill Martin, Jr., and John Archambault's *Knots on a Counting Rope* (1987), William Hooks's *Moss Gown* (1987), folktales such as the Grimm's "Rumpelstiltskin," and myths such as "Cupid and Psyche." Sylvia Kamerman's *Plays of Black Americans: The Black Experience in America, Dramatized for Young People* (1994) includes a collection of plays about notable African Americans. Two choral readings highlight the achievements of Harriet Tubman and Crispus Attucks.

Before sharing an oral reading, readers must understand what they read. Because readers interpret the materials according to their experiences, they benefit from discussion prior to the oral presentation. Accelerated students usually enjoy in-depth study of a selection, and research allows them to build a background of knowledge about the theater and literary selections. During an instructional sequence, have the children discuss theater-related experiences. Emphasize similarities and differences between reader's theater and other types of theater. Next help the students select and analyze literature for their presentation.

For an oral reading, let the students choose a poem, short story, or portion of a story that both interests and excites them. Have the students read the selection silently and respond to the mood, style, and plot. Help the students prepare a brief introduction to attract the attention of the audience and provide background information to let the audience understand what it is about to hear. The introduction should set a proper mood for the oral reading. Finally, have the students rehearse both the introduction and the selection orally until they are familiar with it. The readers should appear animated in face, voice, and body.

Reader's theater allows an audience to enjoy many types of literature, and allows the participants to interpret creatively such diverse scripts as poetry, short stories, radio scripts, and essays. First, allow the children to explore different ways of presenting the literature. There is no one correct way to perform reader's theater. Use guidelines, but let the material shape the method. Second, help children learn to stimulate the audience intellectually and emotionally by breathing life into the literature. They will be able to do this when they understand the literature and become excited about it.

A simplified reader's theater involves three steps. First, read the selection silently. Each child does the first silent reading individually. Do the second reading orally in a group. Let the children choose parts, or designate which part each child will read. Children learn to compromise, because they are not always able to read their favorite parts. Children also learn to listen during this first oral reading. The third reading is also an oral reading, but this time the children act it out. The director, who may be the teacher, reads the title, the cast of characters, and descriptions of the setting or action. The players walk through the action as they read their parts. Add suggestions when a player has problems. There may be a fourth reading in front of an audience. Again, read the title, cast of characters, setting, and descriptions of actions. There may also be a short musical introduction and simple scenery, but avoid having the play become too elaborate. After several such readings, many children wish to write original plays or adaptations of literature.

The concept of a reader's theater may also lend itself to centers developed in the classroom. Ford and Opiz (2002) state that a reader's theater center encourages practice in reading orally as well as building "fluency, oral performance skills, and confidence" (p. 715). These educators suggest a routine in which a leader reads the story to be performed aloud, students read the story together, partners read the story together, each student is assigned a part, students practice individually, students practice together, and students share the story with the class.

Worthy and Broaddus (2002) emphasize the value of using reader's theater as a means to promote fluency among students. They recommend sources for reader's theater such as poetry, folktales, and informational books. This type of activity could be used to conclude a unit on poetry in which students perform their favorite poetry such as the humorous poetry of Jack Prelutsky or Shel Silverstein. Worthy and Broaddus emphasize that this type of reader's theater experience and class responses is "especially gratifying for the struggling readers, who are able to read smoothly because they have sufficient practice and teacher guidance. Average and high-achieving readers also benefit from fluency practice and the opportunity to make personal decisions about how a character might be portrayed or a poem interpreted. Some of the most confident and accurate readers . . . tend to read too quickly, and with little expression or attention to punctuation. Practicing to perform gives students a chance to refine their oral reading and emphasize the importance of phrasing and expression" (p. 339).

For Your Development

Choose a selection you feel would be appropriate for an oral reading or a reader's theater production. Try the oral reading or reader's theater activity with a group of children or a group of your peers and do the activity.

For Your Plan Book

Lesson Plan

An Oral Language Unit: Debate in the Upper Grades

The puppet project, "Helping Freddie Frog," developed earlier in this chapter, integrated oral language, listening, writing, literature, art, science, and social studies in a project designed for lower elementary students. The project can easily be expanded into a longer thematic unit that explores issues surrounding ecology. Educators have asked me to develop an oral language unit that is appropriate for older students. Consequently, this final unit in the oral language chapter develops a thematic unit that emphasizes debate and also integrates other areas of the language arts and school curriculum (Norton & Norton, 2003).

Objectives

1. To identify and defend a position through oral language.
2. To come to conclusions based on evidence found in literature and in other sources such as television and newspapers.
3. To role-play situations motivated by plots and conflicts in literature and in other materials.
4. To develop tolerance for others' viewpoints and feelings.
5. To develop and expand research skills.
6. To integrate oral language, listening, writing, literature, social studies, and history through a thematic unit based on debate.

Procedures

1. Read and discuss Avi's *Nothing But the Truth: A Documentary Novel* (1991), which was a Newbery Honor book in 1992. For your information, *Nothing But the Truth* is a fictional novel written in documentary format. At Harrison High School there is a faculty rule that requires students to stand at "respectful, silent attention" during the playing of the national anthem during homeroom. When ninth grader Philip Malloy hums and breaks this rule, English teacher Margaret Narwin sends him to the vice principal's office. After Philip is suspended from school, community members, school officials, and national media become involved in charges and countercharges regarding patriotism, respect, and freedom of speech. Margaret Narwin is then asked to leave her teaching position. This book presents different interpretations of the same incident and it encourages readers to discover for themselves who is telling the truth and nothing but the truth.

2. This unit is designed to help students take, defend, and support a position first through oral language and then through written language. It is also designed to help students define, for themselves and the class, the elements of truth. They gain insights into how emotions define and distort truth.

Continued

3. Introduce this unit and Avi's book so that students are interested in the topic and motivated to become involved in the activities. For example, "Have you ever had an experience in which one version of an incident differed from another version of the same incident? Have you and a teacher or parent ever interpreted an experience in two completely different ways? Have you ever argued about who is to blame for an incident involving another person? Have you ever listened to two news reports and received different interpretations of the same incident? Have you ever listened to two opposing lawyers as they argue the same case? When you read (or listen to) Avi's *Nothing But the Truth* you will have an opportunity to read different interpretations of the same incident, but the author never tells you who he believes is right and who he believes is wrong. It is up to you, the reader, to come to your own conclusions."

4. Because this book is written in a format that is different from most novels, it is important to discuss the novel's format with students before they read it. Explain that the author is trying to document various reactions to the same incident through the use of memos, letters, diary pages, discussions, phone and personal conversations, speeches, and telegrams. Ask the students what kind of information could be found in each of these documents and why the author would include each of these types of documents. Because the students will be the ones to decide who is telling the truth at the end of the novel, emphasize that they should pay particular attention to details. They will use information found in the documents to come to their own conclusions.

5. After students have read the novel, lead a discussion in which they consider what happened to each character as a consequence of the story. Have them decide which character changes the most and which character is most harmfully influenced by the conclusion of the actions. Have students debate the accuracy of the various interpretations and the emotional responses generated by the conflict.

6. This activity may be developed as an oral debate in which students, divided according to position, debate whether the English teacher or the student is telling the truth. This activity may also be developed as a mock trial in which students volunteer or are chosen to play different characters from the novel. Other students would be chosen for the positions of judge, Margaret Narwin's attorney, Philip Malloy's attorney, and the jury. It is the judge and jury who make the final decision, based on the evidence, of who is telling the truth. For example, a student in the role of Philip Malloy would take the stand and present his version of the truth. Students role-playing Philip's parents, his neighbor, and members of the school board or media who support his position would each take the stand and present their versions of the truth. After these characters made their statements, they would each be cross-examined by Margaret Narwin's attorney. Margaret Narwin would then take the stand and make a statement presenting her version of the truth. The coach and students who support her position would each take the stand and present their versions of the situation. After these characters made their statements they would be cross-examined by Philip Malloy's attorney.

7. Students may write their responses to the various documents included in the book and to what happened to the teacher and the boy.

8. After completing the activities around *Nothing But the Truth* ask students to summarize what they have learned about the power of and requirements for debate.

9. Continue this unit centered around debate by encouraging students to choose, research, and debate other topics that may be used for debate. Ask the students to identify subjects that are debated on television and radio news and in newspaper and magazine articles. The following topics lend themselves to this type of activity.

Conservation issues may be researched and debated using contemporary information and quotes from historical documents. For example, after reading a biography about Theodore Roosevelt, students will discover that Roosevelt was a leading naturalist and conservationist. Ask "Why did Roosevelt become a conservationist? What influence did his conservationist attitudes have on the United States? Do you believe that these conservationist attitudes are still important today? Why or why not?" After this discussion, read and discuss the following quote from Jean Fritz's biography, *Bully for You, Teddy Roosevelt!* (1991):

> At every opportunity, he tried to educate the public to the dangers of waste and pollution, and it is no wonder that he became known as the "Conservation President." During his time in the White House he established 150 national forests, the first fifty-five bird and game preserves, and five national parks. Under the National Monuments Act he set aside the first eighteen "national monuments," including Devil's Tower in Wyoming, the Grand Canyon, California's Muir Woods, Arizona's Petrified Forest, and Washington's Mount Olympus. Indeed, Theodore Roosevelt deserves much of the credit for teaching Americans to respect what nature has given them. When the National Wildlife Federation established a Conservation Hall of Fame in 1965, Theodore Roosevelt was given first place, John Muir came in second, John James Audubon fifth, and Henry David Thoreau sixth. (p. 112)

After considering this quote, ask the students to pretend that they are sitting on the committee for the 1964 Conservation Hall of Fame. Ask them to choose one of the people who had been considered for placement in the Hall of Fame. After students have chosen their candidate, ask them to do research on the contributions of the candidate and to present their arguments in the form of a debate. Who would the class select as number one and so forth? Why would they place that person in the position? Who are the current people that they would place in the Conservation Hall of Fame? Again, ask the students to present and argue the case for their nominees.

Students can also debate the role of a naturalist and a conservationist versus the role of an industrialist. Do the two positions need to be contrary to each other? Why or why not? Students can locate a current environmental issue and debate the issue as if one group were representing the ideals of Theodore Roosevelt and the other group representing the ideals of the opposing forces.

Mainstreaming

Many of the oral language activities developed in this chapter are excellent for children with disabilities who have been mainstreamed into the regular classroom. Table 3–4 identifies specific characteristics of children with learning disabilities that might interfere with oral language development and lists teaching techniques recommended by research studies and/or authorities who work with these children. Table 3–5 provides the same information and guidelines for children with mental disabilities.

Table 3–4 Mainstreaming and oral language development of children with learning disabilities

Characteristics of Children with Learning Disabilities	Teaching Techniques for Language Arts Instruction
1. Problems in language and thought development characterized by poor repetitive speech, or in comprehending or remembering spoken language (Bryan & Bryan, 1986; Lewis & Doorlag, 1998; Lyon & Watson, 1981; Ysseldyke & Algozzine, 1995).	Use praise, flexible verbal behavior, effective questioning strategies, and acceptance of students' feelings to encourage academic growth (Smith, 1980). Try creative dramatics (Taylor, 1980) and reader's theater (Worthy & Broaddus, 2002). Use the language experience approach to focus attention on the purpose of language. Try the neurological impress method, in which you sit slightly behind the child and read directly into his or her ear while the child either reads along or trails slightly in pronunciation (Cook, Nolan, & Zanotti, 1980). Use familiar and predictable books (Katims, 1994).
2. Inability to follow directions (Lewis & Doorlag, 1998).	Enhance the stimulus value of teaching materials; encourage children to rehearse academic tasks verbally; provide explicit, clear verbal directions (Hallahan & Kauffman, 1999).
3. Inability to understand abstract words, form abstractions, acquire and use information, or demonstrate competencies essential to problem solving and reasoning (Kavale, 1980; Lerner, 2000).	Provide instruction in multiple meanings of words, relate unknown words to meaningful experiences, and emphasize vocabulary development within all content areas (Wallace & McLoughlin, 1990). Use collaborative communications so learning becomes a social endeavor (Schmidt et al., 2002).
4. Deficits in phonological processing may cause students to experience difficulty using the sounds of language in processing oral and written information (Johnson, 1993; Spector, 1995).	Direct attention to the sounds in words such as memorizing nursery rhymes and playing with language (Spector, 1995).
5. Disability in comprehending information signaled by grammatical morphemes (Fay, Trupin, & Townes, 1981).	Emphasize the comprehension information carried by function words, word endings, and word stem changes (McClure, Kalk, & Keenan, 1980). Use pictures to help children build morphological generalizations (Lerner, 2000).
6. Deficiencies in cognitive processes, especially at the higher cognitive levels of imagery, verbal processing, and concept information (Cohen & Plaskon, 1980).	Use semantic mapping strategies to help children visualize concepts and relationships (Cohen & Plaskon, 1980; Johnson & Pearson, 1984; Myers, 1983; Norton, 2003). Develop cognitive processes through oral language activities accompanying children's literature: observing, comparing, classifying, hypothesizing, organizing, summarizing, applying, and criticizing (Norton, 2003).

Characteristics of Children with Learning Disabilities	Teaching Techniques for Language Arts Instruction
7. Lack of linguistic sophistication characterized by sentences that are shorter and simpler than sentences developed by age-level peers (Lerner, 2000).	Encourage sentence expansion using descriptive words and phrases; transformations of kernel sentences; and oral language activities such as role-playing, show and tell, puppetry, interviewing, and storytelling (Lerner, 2000). Use choral speaking (Eldredge, 1990).
8. Deficiencies in memory and the development of memory strategies (Bryan & Bryan, 1986).	Help children select and organize materials in logical order. Use repetition and frequent reviews. Organize materials to increase chunking of material into already existing memory units. Help children relate what they are learning to what they already know. Use mnemonic strategies and flannel boards to help remember cues. Teach rhymes, poems, and finger plays that encourage auditory memory (Lerner, 2000).

Table 3–5 Mainstreaming and oral language development of children with mental disabilities

Characteristics of Children with Mental Disabilities	Teaching Techniques for Language Arts Instruction
1. Below-average language ability when compared with age-level peer group (Gearheart, Weishahn, & Gearheart, 1995). Delayed cognitive functioning (Ysseldyke & Algozzine, 1995).	Emphasize cognitive processes, problem-solving tactics, and motivation to improve mental abilities. Use concrete examples (Ysseldyke & Algozzine, 1995). Provide many language experiences tied to meaningful situations (Gearheart et al., 1995).
2. Poor self-concept and low self-esteem due to past failures in academic and social situations (Gearheart et al., 1995).	Encourage children to discuss issues that are important to them (Hart, 1981). Praise students for small accomplishments and work well done (Gearheart et al., 1995).
3. Below-average ability to generalize commonalities between similar situations as well as generalize one set of conditions or rules to another similar situation (Gearheart et al., 1995).	Integrate mechanical and conceptual skills into the lessons whenever possible and point out how one principle may apply to other academic or social situations (Gearheart et al., 1995).

SUMMARY

Speech is a primary means of human communication. Linguists emphasize a need for classroom instruction to encourage oral language development and use of evaluation techniques based on actual language samples. Because most published tests do not assess oral language, you should use informal ways to evaluate it. Use language experience stories, story retelling, unaided recall of stories, puppetry, and wordless books to elicit language samples.

A positive classroom environment is critical to the development of oral language skills. Teachers must (1) have the knowledge necessary for eliciting oral language; (2) be able to evaluate each child's oral language; (3) use projects such as puppetry to provide an environment conducive to developing oral language; (4) provide opportunities for children to interact in pairs, small groups, and large groups; and (5) develop critical thinking and reasoning skills through activities that allow children to progress from the concrete to the abstract.

Several instructional approaches can improve oral language skills. Conversation, especially through show and tell and telephone activities, can promote self-confidence in children as speakers.

To develop discussion skills, use modeling strategies to accompany oral discussion of characterization in books. Second, emphasize the development of oral interchange through questioning strategies. Use questioning and discussion that progress from data gathering (the lowest level of abstraction) to data processing, and finally to abstraction. Use question and discussion techniques to help students group and process data, interpret data and make inferences, and apply previous knowledge to new situations. Third, manage the environment in such a way that children can participate in discussion groups. Use brainstorming, buzz groupings, roundtable discussions, and panel discussions.

Under the category of creative dramatics, develop students as players with such activities as movement and pantomime. Next, consider improvisation and dramatization. Your role in story dramatization includes motivating children; presenting the story; and guiding the children in planning, playing, and evaluating. Puppetry is an excellent means for children to utilize all of the communication skills. The activity should not end with making the puppet; rather, it should go on to include dramatic techniques. To use the method effectively, you must be familiar with the background of puppetry and know how to initiate the activity. Choral speaking and reader's theater synthesize three language elements—listening, reading, and speaking. Choral speaking arrangements include refrain, line-a-child, antiphonal, cumulative, and unison arrangements.

ADDITIONAL ORAL LANGUAGE ACTIVITIES

1. Identify a group of wordless books appropriate for younger children and another group appropriate for older children. Evaluate the books according to the criteria listed in the section on wordless books. Share one of the books with a child or your language arts class.
2. Plan an oral language activity that encourages children to use brainstorming, buzz sessions, roundtable discussion, or panel discussion.
3. Identify a story appropriate for reader's theater. With a group of your peers or a group of children, adapt the selection for an oral presentation and present it to an audience.

4. Develop a file of literature selections appropriate for choral speaking arrangements. Provide some recommendations for the types of choral arrangements.
5. Develop a file of literature selections appropriate for puppetry. Provide some recommendations for puppetry characters and types of puppetry construction.
6. Develop a dramatization activity based on reader's theater.

BIBLIOGRAPHY

Barr, Myra. "The Reader in the Writer." In *Reading Hall of Fame*. San Francisco: International Reading Association, 2002.

Brophy, J.; and Good, T. L. "Teacher Behavior and Student Achievement." In *Handbook on Research on Teaching,* edited by M. C. Wittrock. New York: Macmillan, 1986, pp. 328–75.

Bryan, Tanis H.; and Bryan, James H. *Understanding Learning Disabilities.* Sherman Oaks, Calif.: Alfred Publishing Co., 1986.

"Characteristics of an Ideal Reading Classroom." *The Reading Teacher* 52 (May 1999): 904–06.

Cianciolo, P. *Picture Books for Children,* 4th ed. Chicago: American Library Association, 1997.

Cohen, Sandra B.; and Plaskon, Stephen P. *Language Arts for the Mildly Handicapped.* Upper Saddle River, N.J.: Merrill/Prentice Hall, 1980.

Cook, Jimmie E.; Nolan, Gregory A.; and Zanotti, Robert J. "Treating Auditory Perception Problems: The NIM Helps." *Academic Therapy* 15 (March 1980): 476–81.

Dixon, Carol N. "Language Experience Stories as a Diagnostic Tool." *Language Arts* 54 (May 1977): 501–05.

Dole, J.; Duffy, G.; Roehler, L.; and Pearson, P. D. "Moving from the Old to the New: Research on Reading Comprehension Instruction." *Review of Educational Research* 61 (1991): 239–64.

Eldredge, J. L. "Increasing the Performance of Poor Readers in Third Grade with a Group-Assisted Strategy." *Journal of Educational Research* 84 (1990): 69–77.

Fay, Gayle; Trupin, Eric; and Townes, Brenda D. "The Young Disabled Reader: Acquisition Strategies and Association Deficits." *Journal of Learning Disabilities* 14 (January 1981): 32–35.

Fitzpatrick, Karen. "Improving Reading Comprehension Using Critical Thinking Strategies." *Reading Improvement* 31 (Fall 1994): 142–44.

Ford, Michael P.; and Opitz, Michael F. "Using Centers to Engage Children During Guided Reading Time: Intensifying Learning Experiences Away from the Teacher." *The Reading Teacher* 55 (May 2002): 710–17.

Gearheart, Bill R.; Weishahn, Mel; and Gearheart, Carol J. *The Exceptional Student in the Regular Classroom,* 6th ed. Upper Saddle River, N.J.: Merrill/Prentice Hall, 1995.

Goodman, Yetta M. "Kidwatching: Observing Children in the Classroom." In *Observing the Language Learner,* edited by Angela Jaggar and M. Trika Smith-Burke. Urbana, Ill.: National Council of Teachers of English, 1985, pp. 9–18.

Gordon, Christine J. "Modeling Inference Awareness across the Curriculum." *Journal of Reading* 28 (February 1985): 444–47.

Greenberg, Jan; and Jordan, Saundra, *The Sculptor's Eye: Looking at Contemporary American Art.* New York: Delacorte, 1993.

Hallahan, Daniel P.; and Kauffman, James M. *Introduction to Learning Disabilities: A Psycho-Behavioral Approach,* 2nd ed. Upper Saddle River, N.J.: Prentice Hall, 1999.

Hart, Verna. *Mainstreaming Children with Special Needs.* New York: Longman, 1981.

Hewett, Gloria J.; and Rush, Jean C. "Finding Buried Treasures: Aesthetic Scanning with Children." *Art Education* 40 (January 1987): 41–43.

Hobbs, Jack A.; and Rush, Jean C. *Teaching Children Art.* Upper Saddle River, N.J.: Prentice Hall, 1997.

Jewel, Connie. In *Reading Hall of Fame.* "The Importance of Preschool and Kindergarten Language Development in Reading Acquisition." San Francisco: International Reading Association, 2002.

Johnson, Dale D.; and Pearson, P. David. *Teaching Reading Vocabulary,* 2nd ed. New York: Holt, Rinehart & Winston, 1984.

Johnson, Doris. "Relationships Between Oral and Written Language." *School Psychology Review* 22 (1993): 595–609.

Katims, David. "Emergence of Literacy in Preschool Children with Disabilities." *Learning Disability Quarterly* 17 (Winter 1994): 58–69.

Kavale, Kenneth A. "A Comparison of Learning Disabled and Normal Children on the Boehm Test of Basic Concepts." *Journal of Learning Disabilities* 15 (March 1982): 160–61.

———. "The Reasoning Abilities of Normal and Learning Disabled Readers on Measures of Reading Comprehension." *Learning Disability Quarterly* 3 (Fall 1980): 34–45.

Kay, R. "Commentary: Singing the Praises of Choral Reading." *Reading Today* 8 (1991): 12.

King, Martha L. "Language and Language Learning for Child Watchers." In *Observing the Language Learner,* edited by Angela Jaggar and M. Trika Smith-Burke. Urbana, Ill.: National Council of Teachers of English, 1985, pp. 19–38.

Lacy, Lyn Ellen. *Art and Design in Children's Picture Books.* Chicago: American Library Association, 1986.

Lerner, Janet W. *Children with Learning Disabilities,* 8th ed. Boston: Houghton Mifflin, 2000.

Lewis, Rena; and Doorlag, Donald. *Teaching Special Students in the Mainstream,* 5th ed. Upper Saddle River, N.J.: Merrill/Prentice Hall, 1998.

Lyon, Reid; and Watson, Bill. "Empirically Derived Subgroups of Learning Disabled Readers: Diagnostic Characteristics." *Journal of Learning Disabilities* 14 (May 1981): 256–61.

Manguel, Alberto. *Reading Pictures.* New York: Random House, 2000.

The National Reading Panel. *Report of National Reading Panel.* Washington, D.C: National Institute of Child Health and Human Development, 2000.

McClure, Judith; Kalk, Michael; and Keenan, Verne. "Use of Grammatical Morphemes by Beginning Readers." *Journal of Learning Disabilities* 13 (May 1980): 34–49.

Menyuk, P. "Linguistics and Teaching the Language Arts." *Handbook of Research on Teaching the English Language Arts,* edited by J. Flood, J. Jensen, D. Lapp, and J. Squire. New York: Macmillan, 1991, pp. 24–29.

Morrison, George S. *Early Childhood Education Today.* Upper Saddle River, N.J.: Merrill/Prentice Hall, 1995.

Morrow, L.; and Rand M. "Promoting Literacy during Play by Designing Early Childhood Classroom Environments." *The Reading Teacher* 44 (1991): 396–402.

Myers, Miles. "Approaches to the Teaching of Composition." In *Theory and Practice in the Teaching of Composition: Processing, Distancing and Modeling,* edited by Miles Myers and James Gray. Urbana, Ill.: National Council of Teachers of English, 1983, pp. 3–43.

National Council of Teachers of English. "Forum: Essentials of English." *Language Arts* 60 (February 1983): 244–48.

National Reading Panel. Report of the National Reading Panel. Washington, DC: National Institute of Child Health and Human Development, 2000.

Norton, Donna E. *The Impact of Literature-Based Reading.* Upper Saddle River, N.J.: Merrill/Prentice Hall, 1996.

———. *Through the Eyes of a Child: An Introduction to Children's Literature,* 6th ed. Upper Saddle River, N.J.: Merrill/Prentice Hall, 2003.

———, and Norton, Saundra. *Language Arts Activities for Children,* 5th ed. Upper Saddle River, N.J.: Merrill/Prentice Hall, 2003.

O'Neill, C. "Dialogue and Drama: The Transformation of Events, Ideas, and Teachers." *Language Arts* 66 (1989): 528–40.

Pinnell, G.; and Jaggar, A. "Oral Language: Speaking and Listening." In *Handbook of Research on Teaching the English Language Arts,* edited by J. Flood, J. Jensen, D. Lapp, and J. Squire. New York: Macmillan, 1991, pp. 691–720.

Purves, A.; Rogers, T.; and Soter, A. *How Porcupines Make Love II: Teaching a Response-Centered Literature Curriculum.* New York: Longman, 1990.

Roehler, Laura; and Duffy, Gerald G. "Direct Explanation of Comprehension Processes." In *Comprehension Instruction,* edited by Gerald G. Duffy, Laura R. Roehler, and Jana Mason. New York: Longman, 1984, pp. 265–80.

Saban, Ahmet. "Cooperative Learning: A Critical Analysis of the Group Investigation Model." *Reading Improvement* 31 (Fall 1994): 186–92.

Schmidt, Patricia Ruggiano; Gillen, Susan; Zollo, Teresa Colabufo; and Stone, Rhaenel. "Literacy Learning and Scientific Inquiry: Children Respond." *The Reading Teacher* 55 (March 2002): 534–48.

Segedy, M.; and Roosevelt, C. "Adapting the Courtroom Trial Format to Literature." *Activities to Promote Critical Thinking: Classroom Practices in Teaching English.* Urbana, Ill.: National Council of Teachers of English, 1986, pp. 88–92.

Siks, Geraldine. *Creative Dramatics: An Art for Children.* New York: Harper Brothers, 1958.

———. *Drama with Children.* New York: Harper & Row, 1983.

Sloyer, Shirlee. *Reader's Theatre: Story Dramatization in the Classroom.* Urbana, Ill.: National Council of Teachers of English, 1982.

Smith, Christine C. "The Relationship between Teacher–Pupil Interaction and Progress of Pupils with Reading Disabilities." *Reading Improvement* 17 (Spring 1980): 53–65.

Spector, Janet. "Phonemic Awareness Training: Application of Principles of Direct Instruction." *Reading & Writing Quarterly: Overcoming Learning Difficulties* 11 (1995): 37–51.

Squire, J. "The History of the Profession." In *Handbook of Research on Teaching the English Language Arts,* edited by J. Flood, J. Jensen, D. Lapp, and J. Squire. New York: Macmillan, 1991, pp. 3–17.

Stewig, John; and Nordberg, Beverly. *Exploring Language Arts in the Elementary Classroom*. Belmont, Calif.: Wadsworth, 1995.

Taba, Hilda; Levine, Samuel; and Elzey, Freeman F. *Thinking in Elementary School Children: Cooperative Research Project Number 1574*. Washington, D.C.: Research Program of the Office of Education, U.S. Department of Health, Education, and Welfare, 1964.

Taylor, Gail Cohen. "Creative Dramatics for Handicapped Children." Language Arts, 57 (January 1980): 92–97.

Valencia, S.; Stallman, A.; Commeyras, M.; Pearson, P. D.; and Hartman, D. "Four Measures of Topical Knowledge: A Study of Construct Validity." *Reading Research Quarterly* 26 (1991): 204–33.

Wallace, Gerald; and McLoughlin, James A. *Learning Disabilities: Concepts and Characteristics*, 3rd ed. Upper Saddle River, N.J.: Merrill/Prentice Hall, 1990.

Whitehurst, C. J.; Falco, F. L.; Lonigan, C. G.; Fischel, J. E.; DeBaryshe, B. D.; Valdez-Menchaca, M. C.; and Calfield, M. "Accelerating Language Development through Picture Book Reading." *Developmental Psychology* 24 (1988): 552–59.

———; Epstein, J. N.; Angell, A. L.; Payne, A. C.; Crone, D. A.; and Fischel, J. E. "Outcomes of Emergent Literacy Intervention in Head Start." *Journal of Educational Psychology* 86 (1994): 542–55.

Worthy, Jo; and Broaddus, Karen. "Fluency Beyond the Primary Grades: From Group Performance to Silent, Independent Reading." *The Reading Teacher* 55 (December 2001/January 2002): 334–43.

Ysseldyke, James; and Algozzine, Bob. *Special Education: A Practical Approach for Teachers*, 3rd ed. Boston: Houghton Mifflin, 1995.

CHILDREN'S LITERATURE REFERENCES

Anno, Mitsumasa. *Anno's Journey*. New York: Philomel, 1978.

Avi. *Nothing But the Truth: A Documentary Novel*. New York: Orchard, 1991.

Berenzy, Alix. *A Frog Prince*. New York: Henry Holt, 1989.

Brown, Margaret Wise. *Four Fur Feet*. Illustrated by Woodleigh Marx Hubbard. New York: Hyperion, 1994.

Bunting, Eve. *Ghost's Hour, Spook's Hour*. Illustrated by Donald Clark. New York: Clarion, 1987.

Collington, Peter. *The Angel and the Soldier Boy*. New York: Alfred A. Knopf, 1987.

Drescher, Henrik. *The Yellow Umbrella*. New York: Bradbury, 1987.

Forbes, Esther. *Johnny Tremain*. Boston: Houghton Mifflin, 1943.

Fox, Mem. *Hattie and the Fox*. Illustrated by Patricia Mullins. New York: Bradbury, 1987.

Fritz, Jean. *Bully for You, Teddy Roosevelt!* New York: Putnam, 1991.

Gershator, Phillis, retold by. *Tukama Tootles the Flute: A Tale from the Antilles*. New York: Orchard, 1994.

Grimm, Brothers, retold by Josef Palecek. *The Bremen Town Musicians*. Saxonville, Mass.: Picture Book Studio, 1988.

Hooks, William H. *Moss Gown.* Illustrated by Donald Carrick. New York: Clarion, 1987.

Kamerman, Sylvia, edited by. *Plays of Black Americans: The Black Experience in America, Dramatized for Young People.* Plays Inc., 1994.

Khalsa, Dayal Kaur. *I Want a Dog.* New York: Potter, 1987.

Kipling, Rudyard. *Just So Stories.* New York: Macmillan, 1902; Viking, 1987.

Lear, Edward. *The Pelican Chorus: And Other Nonsense.* Illustrated by Fred Marcellino. New York: HarperCollins, 1995.

MacLachlan, Patricia. *Sarah, Plain and Tall.* New York: Harper & Row, 1985.

Mahy, Margaret. *17 Kings and 42 Elephants.* Illustrated by Patricia MacCarthy. New York: Dial Press, 1987.

Martin, Bill, Jr.; and Archambault, John. *Knots on a Counting Rope.* Illustrated by Ted Rand. New York: Holt, Rinehart & Winston, 1987.

Mayer, Mercer. *A Boy, a Dog, and a Frog.* New York: Dial Press, 1967.

———. *A Boy, a Dog, a Frog, and a Friend.* New York: Dial Press, 1971.

———. *Frog Goes to Dinner.* New York: Dial Press, 1974.

———. *Frog, Where Are You?* New York: Dial Press, 1969.

McCully, Emily Arnold. *Four Hungry Kittens.* New York: Dial Press, 2001.

———. *Picnic.* New York: Harper & Row, 1984.

———. *School.* New York: Harper & Row, 1987.

Milne, A. A. *Winnie the Pooh.* New York: Dutton, 1926, 1954.

Moss, Lloyd. *Zin! Zin! Zin! A Violin.* Illustrated by Marjorie Priceman. New York: Simon & Schuster, 1995.

Otto, Carolyn. *I Can Tell by Touching.* Illustrated by Nadine Bernard Westcott. New York: HarperCollins, 1994.

Pyle, Howard. *The Merry Adventures of Robin Hood.* New York: Charles Scribner's Sons, 1883, 1946.

Rohmann, Eric. *Time Flies.* New York: Crown, 1994.

Sendak, Maurice. *Where the Wild Things Are.* New York: Harper & Row, 1963.

Sis, Peter. *Dinosaur!* New York: Greenwillow, 2000.

Speare, Elizabeth George. *The Witch of Blackbird Pond.* Boston: Houghton Mifflin, 1958.

Steptoe, John. *Mufaro's Beautiful Daughters: An African Tale.* New York: Lothrop, Lee & Shepard, 1987.

Stevens, Janet. *The Tortoise and the Hare.* New York: Holiday, 1984.

Stevenson, Robert Louis. *Treasure Island.* New York: Charles Scribner's Sons, 1911.

Van Allsburg, Chris. *The Mysteries of Harris Burdick.* Boston: Houghton Mifflin, 1984.

Wells, Rosemary, adapted by. *The Little Lame Prince.* Based on a story by Dinah Maria Mulock Craik. New York: Dial Press, 1990.

White, E. B. *Charlotte's Web.* New York: Harper & Row, 1952.

Wiesner, David. *Free Fall.* New York: Lothrop, Lee & Shepard, 1988.

———. *Sector 7.* New York: Clarion, 1999.

———. *Tuesday.* New York: Clarion, 1991.

Yorinks, Arthur. *Hey, Al.* New York: Farrar, Straus & Giroux, 1986.

chapter

4 Listening

After completing this chapter on listening, you will be able to:

1. Develop a comprehensive definition of listening.
2. Appreciate the importance of motivation and child involvement to listening improvement and describe classroom conditions and teacher behaviors conducive to good listening.
3. Evaluate students' ability to select and to use effective listening strategies.
4. Understand the importance of auditory discrimination.
5. Understand the importance of attentive listening, demonstrate several ways to diagnose a child's listening ability, and plan a series of lessons for improving attentive listening.
6. Evaluate listening comprehension tests, diagnose a student's level of listening comprehension, and develop directed listening for a specific purpose.
7. Develop activities that increase appreciative listening.

*R*esearch indicates that elementary children spend more than 50 percent of their classroom time listening. Teachers expect children to listen 60 percent of the day, and half of that time is spent listening to the teacher. Authorities stress, however, that children do not automatically learn the varied skills necessary for comprehensive listening. In addition, in a society where children are bombarded by the mass media, instruction in critical listening is vital to minimize misconceptions, prejudices, and stereotypes. It has been estimated that by the time most students graduate from high school, they will have spent 11,000 hours in class and 15,000 hours watching television. In developing effective curriculums, teachers must understand the components of listening, how to assess listening abilities, and how to use instructional strategies that improve listening ability in children.

Pinnell and Jaggar (2003) discuss the importance of listening for children's success in school and conclude "One wonders why listening has been so neglected considering how much time students spend listening in school" (p. 885). They also conclude: "The importance of listening in school success is widely accepted, but listening is largely ignored in instruction. Research over the years has spanned from considering listening as an isolated activity to the more recent view that listening is intertwined with the child's overall communication development" (p. 886).

There is a strong relationship between the instructional strategies discussed in the previous chapter on oral language and those in this listening chapter. Listening, oral language, literature, and writing are all closely related. For example, one of the modeling activities described in Chapter 6 includes choosing an appropriate literature selection; listening to the story; writing short responses; and discussing answers, evidence, and reasoning. Responding to the story requires analyzing content and describing personal feelings and background knowledge. As we develop the strategies in this listening chapter, you will notice these close relationships.

Listening is a complex topic. In fact, even education authorities do not fully agree on a definition of listening. For example, various studies define listening as the ability to hear sounds (hearing), ability to distinguish differences in the sounds heard (auditory perception), ability to concentrate on what is heard (attentive listening), ability to comprehend and critically evaluate what is heard (listening comprehension), and ability to appreciate what is heard (appreciative listening). Obviously, all of these definitions are useful, but the teaching purposes, classroom environments, and assessment strategies associated with each one may differ. In this chapter we describe listening assessment and instruction encompassing hearing, auditory perception, attention and concentration, listening comprehension, and listening appreciation. Assessment focuses on informal strategies that teachers develop themselves.

The various listening categories imply that students listen for a variety of reasons. It follows that the ways in which students approach listening tasks should change depending on the listening situation and the purpose for listening. Educators who are interested in the process approaches to instruction and self-monitoring strategies emphasize a need to teach appropriate listening strategies.

Classroom Environments That Promote Listening

To teach some types of listening, visual and auditory distractions must be kept to a minimum. For example, a teacher of a group of open-classroom first graders found that he had to find a quiet and less visually distracting environment for both assessing and teaching the auditory discrimination skills that were recommended in his teacher's manual before the introduction of vowel sounds. This teacher used movable bookshelves and screens to create a small area in the classroom where there would be few distractions. Another teacher in an open classroom moved to the gym to present the rhythms and movements of a listening experience. For students with hearing loss, special seating arrangements may be required to put them close to the sound source.

In a review of research on developing listening abilities, Funk and Funk (1989) provide the following guidelines:

1. Teachers and students should state the purpose for listening. Students should be given specific purposes for each listening experience. They should approach listening differently depending on the purpose; for example, listening for a main idea, differentiating fact from opinion, or visualizing and responding to vivid language in a literature selection or to pleasing passages in music.
2. Teachers and students should set the stage for listening. This requires a classroom atmosphere conducive to listening for the intended purpose. Teachers may need to provide interesting lead-up activities.
3. Follow-up activities should be used to help achieve listening goals and encourage students to apply their new information and techniques. Art projects, writing assignments, library research, and choral arrangements are a few possibilities.
4. Teachers should use instructional techniques that promote and develop positive listening habits. The techniques should include many different types of listening experiences, for example, listening to and responding to stories, poetry, and music. Critical analysis can be fostered by having students listen to determine a speaker's intention or bias. Students should be involved in strategies that improve listening comprehension as well as reading comprehension.

In addition to these guidelines, teachers should select and develop listening materials at the appropriate levels of difficulty, appreciate why listening instruction is important and guide children toward this realization, avoid needless repetition, encourage children to expect meaning from what they hear, and help children transfer listening ability to new contexts.

Listening is an active rather than passive activity. You should encourage students to participate in improving their abilities by asking them to restate questions, directions, and explanations. You should also develop their abilities through a variety of activities in which they see the consequences of their listening, such as when they enjoy listening to a story, to a good television show, or to a musical selection. Can they see that they enjoy playing a game when they understand the directions? Can they see that they understand a subject better if they participate in the class discussion? Can they see that they may lose some freedom of choice if they are not able to evaluate critically and act on what they hear?

You can improve a student's listening skills through specific instruction. Also, you may teach listening as part of many content areas, such as reading, literature, music, social studies, and science. Help students develop their own effective listening goals. If students do not see the necessity for or benefits of improved listening, they will not be motivated toward better listening and will not reach the desired level of competence.

Some student teachers have been disappointed in lessons that require listening during various activities when they have not included their students in the initial planning. For example, one student teacher asked third graders to listen to a story record, then asked them specific questions about the content. She had not adequately prepared the class for the listening activity, and was disappointed in the results. She realized her problem and approached the next lesson quite differently. This time, she asked children to list the various listening activities they performed in a day. Then, they listened to several quite different activities, including specific oral directions for a worksheet, a short story for pleasure, and a short oral presentation on brushing their teeth. The class discussed the purposes for listening in each situation and the students included the consequences of good and poor listening for each activity. Finally, they set up guidelines for improving their own listening ability, including the following:

1. I will get ready for listening by getting rid of distractions.
2. I will know my purpose for listening.
3. I will concentrate on the listening activity.
4. I will expect to get meaning from the listening activity.
5. I will try to see in my mind what I hear.
6. If I am listening to a speaker, I will ask myself:
   a. Did I know the speaker's purpose for speaking?
   b. Did I know my purpose for listening?
   c. Did the speaker back up his or her ideas?
   d. Did I ask intelligent questions?
   e. Can I retell in my own words what the speaker said?

Guidelines developed by students are stronger instructional motivators than are those developed by teachers. The teacher in the preceding example learned that, through using their own guidelines, the students in the class could judge their own behavior based on their own recommendations.

Hearing

Hearing without distortion is a prerequisite to listening. The term *auditory acuity* is usually applied to hearing, and the lack of this acuity is deafness. In school settings, nurses and trained teachers usually administer hearing tests. However, teachers should also observe children informally for indications of hearing problems. If a child frequently asks for directions to be repeated, rubs his or her ears, or does not speak clearly, the child may have hearing loss and should be referred for further testing and, if necessary, diagnosis by a hearing specialist.

Children listen under such diverse circumstances and for such different purposes that it is impossible to evaluate listening ability through the administration of only one hearing test. You may evaluate listening informally in the course of many of the activities recommended in this chapter. The evaluation of listening requires live listening situations involving a wide range of activities. According to Johnson (1993), "Auditory receptive language is one of the most important areas to investigate, but is often the least assessed, in part because of the limited number of tests available, and in part because word meanings change over time in various contexts" (p. 598).

Auditory Perception

Auditory perception may also be a prerequisite for effective listening. Auditory perception tests evaluate such factors as (1) whether children recognize that different sounds have different meanings; (2) whether children are able to distinguish one sound from another (auditory discrimination); (3) whether children are able to blend sounds to form words (auditory blending); and (4) whether children are able to hear sounds, remember the sounds, and repeat them in the same sequence in which they hear them (auditory sequential memory). Children with auditory perception problems may have difficulty with reading or spelling approaches that rely heavily on sound and letter relationships. As shown later in examples, children are likely to enjoy auditory perception activities, which are often developed in the form of games.

Auditory Awareness

Auditory awareness is a fundamental skill that requires children to hear and discriminate among sounds in the classroom, the home, and the rest of their environment. An instructional activity might consist of listening to and identifying sounds in a barnyard, on a street, at an airport, and so forth. One kindergarten teacher handled such an activity successfully by having the class walk around inside and then outside the school building. The children stopped periodically to close their eyes and listen to the sounds around them. They discovered, among other things, the difference between kitchen and playground sounds. After several experiences with sound awareness, the teacher taped sounds from different locations. The children listened to the tapes, identified the sounds, and classified them according to their locations.

You also can develop auditory awareness through the use of a sound box. Place several objects that have a characteristic sound on a box or tray. You might select a bell for ringing, a ball for bouncing, water for pouring, an egg beater for mixing, and a whistle for blowing. Using a screen to hide the objects, sound each object. Have the students listen carefully and identify the various sounds. Children can also bring in objects from home with which to mystify their classmates.

Other auditory awareness activities include imitation of animal sounds or other imitation sound games in which students or teachers present sounds for students to copy. Rhythm instruments and the piano are good props for sound awareness activities. Children can identify the sounds of rhythm sticks, blocks, triangles, and tambourines. They can imitate a pattern of sounds with these instruments, or can move—rapidly or slowly, sadly or joyfully—according to the rhythm of the instruments.

Listening to music, rhymes, and limericks helps children become aware of the lovely sounds in language. Older children can also listen to old radio broadcasts, available on records and tapes, and try to identify and duplicate the sound effects.

Auditory Discrimination

The most commonly evaluated auditory perception ability within classrooms is auditory discrimination—the ability to hear differences in letter sounds, words, and nonsense syllables. For example, can children discriminate between *bit* and *bet*? Most reading readiness programs include considerable work in auditory discrimination.

Listening is an active, complex process.

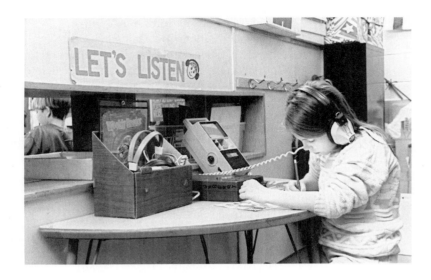

If auditory discrimination is a prerequisite skill for phonics, then, according to Harris and Sipay (1990), the most effective time to teach this skill is immediately before the corresponding discrimination is to be used in printed words. Thus, you must evaluate the sequence of the instructional program and also assess the ability of the children to perform the required tasks. Leslie and Allen (1999) found that teaching rhymes was one of the factors that predict success in an early literacy intervention program aimed at the improvement of reading for at-risk students.

Auditory discrimination can be measured by either standardized, norm-referenced tests or teacher-constructed informal approaches. The Wepman Auditory Discrimination Test (1973) is the best known standardized test of auditory discrimination. The test is designed to be used with children five through eight years old. The examiner reads two words to a child, who is positioned so that he or she cannot see the examiner's mouth. The child then states whether the words are alike or different. This individually administered test requires about five minutes for completion. Another type of auditory discrimination test for young children is part of the reading readiness test administered to many kindergarten and first-grade students.

Auditory Discrimination of Sounds, Words, and Rhymes.   Auditory discrimination of likenesses and differences in sounds, words, and rhymes requires finer auditory perception than does auditory awareness. Provide opportunities for children to decide whether two musical sounds are the same or different. For example, play two notes on the piano and have the students decide whether the notes are the same or different. Have them compare loudness and softness as well as high and low pitch.

Auditory discrimination activities can easily become games. Clap two patterns that are either alike or different, and have the children decide whether the two patterns were the same or different.

If you consider auditory discrimination a reading readiness skill, then include activities in which the children discriminate between likenesses and differences in words. Carefully pronounce two words, such as *red* and *roll,* and have the children indicate whether they are the same or different. Have the children form a circle and close their eyes to listen carefully to the two words. If the words are the same, as, for example, *pet* and *pet,* have them raise their hands; if the words are different (for example, *mother* and *father*), tell them not to raise their hands.

Rhyming elements in words, nursery rhymes, jingles, and stories provide many opportunities to develop auditory discrimination and an awareness of the pleasure to be gained from word sounds. Dr. Seuss books are especially good for this activity. Read *The Cat in the Hat* (1957), then reread it with the rhyming words deleted, to be supplied by the class. You also may utilize well-known nursery rhymes for this activity. For other rhyming activities, you can do the following:

1. Prepare two sentences in which the last words both rhyme. Read the sentences, omitting the final word, and ask the class to supply the missing rhyming word. (Several answers may be correct.)

   I just built a boat. I hope it will _____. (float)
   The big black cat wore a funny yellow _____. (hat)
   The robin built a nest. It was the very _____. (best)

2. Use a series of pictures that have several rhyming elements, such as *sack, bat, cat, track, hat, black*. Have the pictures in random order and ask the students to put the rhyming pictures together. You can use a flannel board or bulletin board for this activity.

3. Read a sentence and ask the class to supply as many words as they can that rhyme with the final word of the sentence.

   We all went to the store with *Bill. (will, pill, kill, mill, hill, fill, still, Jill, shrill)*
   On her head, Mary wore a red *cap. (lap, map, gap, strap, trap, tap, clap, flap)*
   The baker made a chocolate *cake. (lake, bake, rake, snake, fake, brake, shake)*

Many interesting poems for older children contain lovely rhyming elements. "The Table and the Chair" by Edward Lear (1846, 1871, 1946) describes the adventures of a table and a chair when they decide to take a walk. The poem has such rhyming combinations as *heat–feet, walk–talk, air–chair, table–able, down–town,* and *sound–round.* Another comical rhyming poem is "The Plaint of the Camel" by Charles Edward Carryl. In this poem, the poor camel complains in rhyme about his food, his housing, his workloads, and his shape. Some of the rhyming elements are *feed–seed, crunch–lunch, able–stable, enclosed–exposed, noodles–poodles, treated–heated,* and *lumpy–bumpy–jumpy.* Because many of the rhyming words in this poem contain long and short vowels, this poem may also be used for a listening activity connected with medial vowels. William Allingham's "A Swing Song" found in X. J. Kennedy and Dorothy M. Kennedy's *Talking Like the Rain: A Read-to-Me Book of Poems* (1992) includes *swing–sing–king–wing, high–fly–sky,* and *far–bar–star.* The following books contain rhyming elements or repeated phrases and are excellent for auditory discrimination:

Clare Beaton's *Mother Goose Remembers* (2000)

Arnold Lobel's *The Random House Book of Mother Goose* (1986)

Alan Marks's *Over the Hills and Far Away: A Book of Nursery Rhymes* (1994)

Jack Prelutsky's *Read-Aloud Rhymes for the Very Young* (1986)

Jane Yolen's *The Three Bears Rhyme Book* (1987)

Nadine Westcott's *Peanut Butter and Jelly: A Play Rhyme* (1987)

Reeve Lindbergh's *The Day the Goose Got Loose* (1990)

Auditory Discrimination of Beginning, Ending, and Middle Sounds.   Auditory discrimination of beginning and ending sounds is usually related to consonant sounds, whereas the auditory discrimination of middle sounds is usually associated with vowel sounds. Kindergarten and first-grade teachers often associate beginning sounds with the names of students in the class, or with common objects in the classroom. One successful first-grade teacher designed a sound board for her classroom. For example, if the letter *m* was being studied, children brought to school concrete examples of items beginning with the sound of *m*. Then, the class discussed and grouped these items on a bulletin board. Children also drew items to represent the sounds, such as mittens and monkeys.

Use listening activities in which children listen for and identify a beginning sound that is repeated frequently in a story, such as a writing-phonics review activity for second and third graders or an auditory discrimination activity for first graders. For a second/third-grade language arts class, review beginning consonant blends with the children and ask them to write stories that utilize a number of words containing the specific blend being reviewed. Have the second and third graders write these stories and then read them to the first graders. Have the first graders close their eyes, listen carefully, and raise their hands whenever they hear the specific sound in the story. The older children are motivated to write because they know they have an audience, and the first graders are interested in listening to stories written by children they know. Figure 4–1 shows an example of a *gr* story written by a third-grade girl.

Auditory discrimination also includes the ability to tell whether two words end with the same or different sounds. Rhyming activities require a child to listen to a group of sounds; now, ask children to discriminate between the ending consonants, which are usually harder

FIGURE 4–1 *Gr* Story Written by a Third-Grade Girl

to hear than rhyming sounds. Picture activities similar to those described for beginning sounds are appropriate. For example, show pictures of a mop, tub, cap, top, rug, and cup to the class. Ask the children to place all the pictures that end like *map* on a flannel board.

For another word-ending auditory discrimination activity, pronounce pairs of words and ask the children to tell whether the words end with the same sound or different sounds. Examples include these:

cot–cat	*dump–clap*	*trunk–scat*	*Sam–tan*
dad–tub	*mail–will*	*flag–snug*	*jump–wag*

Finally, auditory discrimination includes the ability to discriminate between medial sounds. This may be the most difficult auditory discrimination task for many students. Some programs demand that the child master this skill at the beginning of first grade, whereas other programs do not require it until second grade.

Examples of useful words for medial auditory discrimination include the following:

let–pen	*bug–bag*	*box–got*
lift–pig	*tap–cat*	*hug–but*
hot–rat	*plan–plane*	*read–red*

Auditory Memory.   Auditory memory activities include experiences in following and imitating sound, number, and sentence sequences. Auditory memory activities can be as simple as repeating a short, clapped rhythm pattern, or as difficult as repeating complex directions. For elementary children, many auditory memory activities can take the form of games. For example, play a rhythm on the piano or with rhythm sticks and have the class imitate the rhythm. Clap or rap rhythms, then have the class imitate them.

Children enjoy circle repetition games in which one child starts and each child has to repeat the same thing and add a new item. For example, the first child might say, "I'm going on a trip and I'm going to take an apple." The second child would say, "I'm going on a trip and I'm going to take an apple and a _____." This game may continue until it is impossible for anyone to remember the sequence of items. Adapt the game to have all items belong to a certain classification, such as food, toys, clothing; follow in alphabetical order, such as *apple, book, cat;* begin with the sound of *b,* such as *book, baby, bottle;* or contain the same vowel sound, such as *table, rake, pail, shape.*

Games of giving simple directions also provide practice in auditory memory. You or the children can present simple, two-part directions, such as "Jennifer, turn the light on and then go to your seat."

A trunk game also provides practice in following simple directions. For this activity, put a number of items, such as a ball, ruler, book, bat, picture, cap, game, toy, and glass, in a box or trunk. The leader names several items he or she would like from the box, and calls on another child to get the items. If the child responds correctly, he or she becomes the new leader and makes the next request.

Attention and Concentration

To reconstruct messages, listeners must be able to focus on speech sounds and select appropriate cues. Jane Simmons's *Quack, Daisy, Quack!* (2002) provides an interesting introduction to the importance of listening when Daisy and Pip find themselves in a noisy duck pond and cannot find Mama Duck. By focusing on the quacks of the young ducks, Mama Duck is able to locate the lost youngsters.

Research shows a strong correlation between attentive listening and achievement.

Some students are unable to follow verbal instructions adequately because they are easily distracted by competing noises. This is especially true of certain children with learning disabilities. Some children have difficulty concentrating on listening to various language elements in stories. Young children benefit from listening to books with repetitive language and joining in with the language. Margaret Wise Brown's *Four Fur Feet* (1994) contains rhythmic and repetitive language that appeals to young children and allows adults to determine if the children are concentrating well enough to join in with the language. The repetitive language in Judith Viorst's "Learning" found in X. J. Kennedy and Dorothy M. Kennedy's *Knock at a Star: A Child's Introduction to Poetry* (1999) appeals to many children. They can add their own lines about "I'm learning to. . . . "

Listening is an active process. It requires participation on the part of the listeners. Poor communication results when students do not pay attention or are thinking about their responses rather than concentrating on what a speaker is saying. Inattentive students may not ask questions when they need clarification. Readers can stop and reread, but most listening situations do not permit listeners to go back and review what they hear. In addition, listening usually takes place in a public setting; consequently, students may be distracted by noise, mannerisms of a speaker, or actions of other listeners.

Testing for ability to pay attention is complicated by the fact that students may attend to a speaker, yet not understand what is being said. Thus, poor communication can be caused by either inadequate attention or poor ability to process ideas.

Informal tests can be administered in many different classroom environments, whereas standardized listening tests are usually administered under controlled conditions. For this reason, the results of a standardized listening test may not indicate how a student attends in an actual classroom setting. Students may demonstrate completely different attentive-listening responses when tested in an isolated testing room instead of informally during a class activity.

To find out how well children attend during class activities, assess them in various settings and do not inform them that they are being tested. In designing an attentive-listening task for average achievers, make the level of difficulty about the same as the independent reading level. Note, however, that the listening ability of students with reading difficulties is usually greater than the reading ability.

Ability to follow oral directions explicitly demands attentive listening. You can give oral directions and see which students are able to complete the task, which ones cannot complete the task, and which ones ask you to repeat the directions. For example, a kindergarten teacher might say, "Take out your red crayon, your green crayon, and your brown crayon. Pick out your green crayon and show it to me." (Obviously, do not use this activity unless the children can already identify the colors.) An elementary teacher might say, "Put your spelling book and your arithmetic book on top of your desk. Place your spelling book on top of your arithmetic book so that I can see the spelling book when I walk around the room."

Although research has clearly defined the relationship between attention and achievement, it has not been as clear in identifying a methodology that effectively develops attentive listeners. Factors such as the following may cause inattentiveness: (1) poor motivation to hear a speaker's message, (2) too much teacher talk, (3) excessive distractions, and (4) lack of mental set for anticipating the messages of speakers. Eliminating these four factors should, obviously, improve attentive listening behavior. Review the teacher behaviors essential for developing effective listeners to see how closely these behaviors also relate to developing attentive listening. Involving students in setting instructional listening goals helps overcome some of the problems of poor motivation.

Developing a mental set for purposeful listening may be more difficult than eliminating outside distractions. If students are not able to form mental sets for anticipating messages, they will have difficulty preparing for the types of listening the messages demand. Students who listen to complicated directions with the same mental set they use for listening to a musical recording will have difficulty attending in situations requiring strict accuracy of comprehension.

You may use a number of methods to help students develop the attentive listening required for directions. The school day lends itself to this type of instruction because directions are an essential part of all content areas. Some teachers tape a series of directions that children must follow explicitly. Taping has two advantages. First, it discourages students from asking that directions be repeated before they are given completely. Second, taping reduces excessive teacher talk. A math teacher who is reviewing shapes might, for example, tape the following directions: "Draw a red triangle near the top of your paper. Draw a blue rectangle under the triangle. Draw a green square on the bottom of your paper." After the class has completed the directions, the teacher may replay the tape to let the students verify how well they followed the directions. You may design similar activities around any content directions and tailor them to the ability level of the students.

Games reinforce the teaching of attentive listening to directions. An example of such a game is "Listen, Start, and Stop." To play the game, children form a long line, leaving plenty of room for movement. The leader gives a clear direction, such as "hop on your right foot," "walk using small steps," and "pat your head." Students continue one action until the leader tells them to stop or blows a whistle. Children must stop immediately and turn toward the leader to wait for the next direction. Children who fail to follow directions or to stop immediately are eliminated from the game. The game "Simon Says" is another good listening game.

You should also evaluate a student's ability to give clear directions and to follow oral directions. Pretend that a classmate is a stranger who needs directions to a specific location (principal's office, gym, etc.) and have the remainder of the students prepare what they believe are explicit oral directions. Have a class member follow the directions to see if they are indeed adequate. Such an exercise evaluates both listening and oral directions.

Some additional activities follow for developing the ability to follow oral directions:

1. Have students write directions for a specific activity such as setting the table or washing a dog. Ask the students to read their directions without identifying the activity. Classmates must listen carefully and guess what the activity is as soon as they think they have enough clues.
2. Provide oral directions for making a simple object, such as a kite, and have the class make the object without telling them what it is.
3. Demonstrate the use of a camera, then ask a child to follow the exact directions to take a picture. This is especially good with instant cameras that provide an immediate picture.

Following directions may be more effective if students number the steps of the oral directions, then repeat the number of steps involved, and relate each step to its corresponding number. Helping students map out listening strategies and providing guideposts prior to listening instruction is called "applying advanced organizers." This strategy may be effective with all students, but it is especially appropriate for students with learning problems.

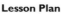

For Your Plan Book

Lesson Plan

An Attentive-Listening Unit

Objectives

1. After a motivational listening activity, the students will be able to realize the importance of attentive listening and develop their own guidelines for good listening.
2. The students will improve their listening skills through the use of listening games and other creative language arts activities.
3. The students will develop creative thinking through a variety of language arts activities, including oral communication, creative writing, and attentive-listening activities.

Procedure

Use the following procedures to implement the objectives of the unit. First, ask the fourth-grade students to keep track of the approximate time they spend in one day on the following ways of communicating: speaking, listening, writing, and reading. The next day have them discuss their findings. They will find that a great deal of time was spent in listening. Present several types of listening activities, such as following directions, listening to records, and listening to stories, in order to answer specific questions. Have the students list the requirements for each type of listening and develop their own guidelines for listening behavior. (They may find that they are not very attentive listeners.)

Listening games and exercises prove very motivating, and also serve as excellent warm-up drills and challenges to fill free time before a first class period, lunch, and so forth. Listening warm-ups cover three broad areas: (1) reception of sounds, (2) comprehension of listening and understanding the purposes for listening, and (3) reaction to the ideas expressed. The procedures are sequential in nature, starting from simple games and drills and progressing to more challenging activities. Listening games include the following:

1. *Telephone game:* The purpose of this game is to send a secret message around the room, to test a student's ability to listen attentively and to speak clearly. One student starts the

Continued

message, whispering it to the next student; the last person's response is matched with the beginning message.

2. *Recipe game:* The purpose of this game is to strengthen the ability of students to listen to and recite a sequential list of items. At first, students read recipes; later, they write their own.

3. *Direction game:* A student reads a task, and the remaining students test their ability to follow directions carefully. Students are not allowed to see the written directions.

4. *Morning sounds:* Students are assigned a specific time period and told to record all the sounds they hear during this period.

5. *Noise makers:* This activity uses a variety of sounds to test the aural perception abilities of students and their use of imagination. Students close their eyes and try to identify various noises. They use creative thinking to choose noises that will stump their classmates.

You may use many activities to stimulate creative thinking and listening, including role-playing, which you can motivate by large action pictures of events common to most of the students, or hypothetical situations, in which students listen to a taped discussion, then role-play their reactions. Let other students listen to the role-playing and discuss their reactions and the reasons for them. Have students write and tape many of the situations. Tapes of country sounds and city sounds provide opportunities to listen attentively, categorize the sounds, and specifically identify each sound. Let students listen to the beginning of a story and create an oral or written ending to the story. Finally, let students listen to television commercials and try to summarize what they hear. After the students listen to commercials, let them write their own commercials and present them to classmates, who, in turn, must listen attentively in order to summarize what they hear.

Following the completion of this listening unit, use the same types of listening experiences that you used to evaluate listening needs at the beginning of the unit. A majority of the students should improve in all types of listening. Informal observations should show that students require less repetition of directions and demonstrate greater accuracy in listening situations. In addition, speaking skills should improve.

Remember to involve students in setting their own goals. Remember also that listening improvement is a continuous activity that must be emphasized in all areas of the curriculum.

Listening Comprehension

Listening, or auditory, comprehension refers to the highly conscious seeking of meaning from a listening experience. Children may listen for factual or literal understanding, or they may reach the higher level of listening that allows them to think beyond listening. This level of listening involves such skills as classifying information, categorizing, indexing, comparing, defining, predicting, applying, seeing cause-and-effect relationships, critically evaluating, appreciating, and solving problems creatively. According to Johnson (1993), "studies of comprehension (semantics) should include an assessment of single words, sentences, question forms, and connected discourse" (p. 598). Johnson emphasizes that this assessment should include measures that detect ambiguity and multiple word meanings. Johnson recommends that auditory comprehension assessment use curriculum-based assessment in which teachers use the language of instruction in the classroom. This assessment should also include an assessment of figurative language.

Following a review of listening comprehension research, Pearson and Fielding (1982) draw the following conclusions about teaching listening comprehension:

1. Direct teaching of listening strategies appears to help children become more conscious of their listening habits than do more incidental approaches.
2. Listening training in the same skills typically taught during reading comprehension tends to improve listening comprehension (such as listening for a main idea, inference, sequence).
3. Active verbal responses on the part of students during and following listening enhance listening comprehension.
4. Listening to literature tends to improve listening comprehension.
5. Instruction directed toward writing or reading comprehension may also improve listening comprehension.

These conclusions suggest ways to improve listening comprehension. They are also useful for developing assessment strategies that are closely related to curricular objectives. Furthermore, the conclusions indicate that listening comprehension may enrich the content areas. Carefully selected activities teach or reinforce content and also enhance listening capabilities.

Assessing Listening Comprehension

Teachers frequently choose to include results from informal assessments of listening comprehension in the portfolios of students. One technique for measuring listening comprehension individually is to administer an informal inventory. The inventory may be ready-made, or it may be developed by the teacher.

Inventories that have been published usually have three forms, each of which includes paragraphs followed by comprehension questions for preprimary through eighth-grade levels. To test listening comprehension, read the paragraphs to the student. After each paragraph, ask the students to answer factual, vocabulary, and inference questions. The highest level, at which a child correctly answers 90 percent of the oral comprehension questions, is considered the independent level of listening comprehension. The level at which the student is able to answer 75 percent of the comprehension questions correctly is considered the instructional listening comprehension level.

One example of a listening comprehension inventory is the *Analytical Reading Inventory* by Woods and Moe (1995). This inventory has three forms, with paragraphs ranging in difficulty from primary through ninth grade. The paragraphs are followed by questions categorized according to main idea, facts, terminology, cause and effect, inferences, and conclusions. In addition to describing this inventory, Pikulski (1990) provides useful descriptions of two other informal reading inventories (IRIs): the *Basic Reading Inventory* (Johns, 1997) and the *Classroom Reading Inventory* (Silvaroli, 1999). Pikulski's chart allows teachers to compare the strengths and weaknesses of these inventories. If teachers choose to use ready-made reading inventories, they should analyze each and decide which one provides them with the most useful information. Such inventories enable teachers to analyze which types of questions are causing comprehension problems.

Comprehension Strategies

James Barton (1995) provides strategies for teaching listening that are also excellent with any content area. Barton states, "One key thing you can do to create a supportive classroom climate for discussions is to train yourself and your students to consistently apply listening strategies" (p. 347). Barton begins the teaching of listening strategies by teaching students to prepare mentally for the listening activity by encouraging them to consider the context of the discussion. For example, what do they already know about the topic? What is the setting? Who is involved in the activity? What are the purposes or goals for listening? Next, teach students to stay in communication when another person talks by actively signaling their listening involvement. They should use nonverbal behaviors when they listen such as eye contact, attentive facial expressions, and facing the person doing the speaking. Finally, students should have opportunities to be involved in activities for which they have a listening audience for their own ideas. Barton maintains that teachers need to model listening strategies so that they will not constantly interject their own thoughts, but will instead allow students to express their thoughts.

Main Ideas.   You can incorporate listening for main ideas into any content area. One successful method of instruction is to have children identify their purpose for listening. During this activity, read a short story or several paragraphs aloud and then ask the children to supply a good title for the selection. The best titles usually contain the main idea of the selection. For example, a social studies teacher might read the following paragraph:

> Mount Everest in Tibet is the highest spot on earth and is a challenge to mountain climbers. From 1922 until 1952 many climbers tried to reach the top of Everest but all failed to reach the dangerous summit. In 1953 a British expedition tried again to reach the summit. Inch by inch the group struggled over the ice-packed surface. The air was so thin and cold that the climbers finally had to put oxygen tanks on their backs in order to breathe at such heights. Finally, on May 29, 1953, two members of the group, Edmund Hillary and Tenzing Norkey, reached the summit. At last, Everest had been conquered.

After the oral presentation, ask students to offer their ideas for the best title. Write the suggested titles on the chalkboard and let the students discuss and defend their appropriateness and completeness. Use simpler paragraphs for early-elementary classes. For example, you might read Peggy Christian's *If You Find a Rock* (2000) and stop at the end of each page and ask children to supply the best title for each type of rock. The rocks discussed include skipping rocks, chalk rocks, resting rocks, a wishing rock, a splashing rock, sifting rocks, worry rocks, hiding rocks, crossing rocks, and fossil rocks. The last page reviews all of the rocks that have been discussed.

Two other methods are useful in helping students listen for the main idea:

1. Before you read several paragraphs, have students listen to oral subheadings. Ask them to turn the subheadings into questions to answer after listening to the selection. For example, a science subheading "The Shape of Molecules" could be changed to the question "What is the shape of molecules?" This procedure helps students develop a purpose for hearing specific information. To help children understand the importance of turning subheadings into questions, share with them Seymour Simon's *New Questions and Answers About Dinosaurs* (1990). Discuss the question headings such as "What Are Dinosaurs?" and "How Are Dinosaurs Different from Other Reptiles?" and how these questions focus their attention on the answers that follow.

2. Have children listen to a story. Stop periodically to have them summarize the main ideas of the selection up to that point. This is especially important when presenting information in various content areas. For example, while reading Debbie S. Miller's

Children need to learn to listen for important details that support main ideas.

A Woolly Mammoth Journey (2001), stop and ask students to summarize the main ideas about these ancient animals who lived more than 10,000 years ago. Older students learning about U.S. history could listen to Lynn Curlee's *Liberty* (2000) and summarize the main ideas as the story is shared. The book concludes with a time line on page 41. Students can compare this listing of main events with their own summaries.

Important Details. Students often have trouble differentiating between important and insignificant details. For example, one student listening to a description about Henry Ford's invention of the Model T could remember only that the car was black. Although this was an interesting detail, it was not one of the most significant details of the selection. Listening for important details is closely related to listening for main ideas because important details support the main ideas.

Children can listen for supporting information as well as for the main idea in paragraphs such as that describing the dangerous conquest of Mt. Everest. Science books provide excellent sources for such material. Books such as Pat Cummings and Linda Cummings's *Talking with Adventurers* (1998) provide numerous sources. This book is especially well written for this purpose because each section includes questions followed by important details. For example, the interview with archaeologist Zuris Zarins asks "What was the scariest thing that ever happened in your work?" (p. 84). The adventurer then discusses going into the desert without preparation and sufficient supplies, getting lost, and watching out for vipers. Interesting comparisons can be made because each of the eleven people are asked similar questions.

Briefly outlining an orally presented selection will also help students listen for both main ideas and supporting details. For example, a group of third graders listened to an introduction to the study of plants. The selection was called "Plants Are Important to People." The group first discussed the title and their purpose for listening to the selection. Next, the teacher asked for suggestions on how to turn the title into a question that would guide their selective listening. After writing the question on the chalkboard, the teacher read the selection to the class. Finally, the class developed an outline that answered their purpose question.

Why Are Plants Important to People?

A. *Plants give people oxygen to breathe.*
B. *Plants give people food to eat.*
C. *Plants like cotton give people clothes to wear.*
D. *Trees are plants that give people houses.*
E. *Plants decay and give people coal to burn.*

This activity helped the students define their purpose for listening and organize the presentation logically. Some other activities follow for helping children listen for important details:

1. Present a selection orally and have students classify the details according to whether they are important, helpful, or unnecessary.
2. Read a descriptive selection to your class. Find a selection that mentions such characteristics as size, color, texture, and number. Have the class listen carefully for descriptive details, then draw a picture that accurately represents the details. Wordless books such as Pat Hutchins's *Changes, Changes* (1971) and Tana Hoban's *Shapes, Shapes, Shapes* (1986) can provide source material for descriptive text developed by teachers. Informational books such as Margery Facklam's *And Then There Was One: The Mysteries of Extinction* (1990), Helen Roney Sattler's *Giraffes, the Sentinels of the Savannas* (1989), and Patricia Lauber's *Volcano: The Eruption and Healing of Mount St. Helens* (1986) provide detailed descriptions of science-related topics for older students.
3. Have students write detailed descriptions of characters in familiar stories. Have them read their descriptions to the class without naming the character. Let classmates try to identify the character and indicate which details were most helpful to them. Similar folktales from different cultures provide interesting sources for this activity. For example, have students describe the German Cinderella in a Brothers Grimm version, the French Cinderella in a Perrault version, and the Egyptian Cinderella in Shirley Climo's *The Egyptian Cinderella* (1989). In these examples, cultural information adds to the descriptions.
4. While one child reads a detailed description, have another draw the character described without knowing the identity of the character. Then, have the partners compare the picture with the original description.
5. Tape imaginary or real conversations between two famous people in history, two people with different occupations, or two school employees. Have students listen carefully for details that suggest the identities of the individuals.

Sequences.   Point out to your students that both speakers and writers use signal words to help organize selections. Have students listen to oral presentations in which signal words are used. For example, have students listen to the following oral presentation to discover the usefulness of signal words:

A moth that you see flying from plant to plant in the garden has not always been able to fly. In fact, there are four different stages in the life of that moth. The first stage in the life cycle of the moth is an egg. During the second stage the caterpillar hatches from the egg and starts to eat plants. After the caterpillar has been eating your garden plants for several weeks, he spins a cocoon of silk all around himself. During this third stage in the moth's cycle, he sleeps while his body actually changes. Finally, the cocoon breaks open and out flies the moth.

Which words in the preceding paragraph signal a sequence of events that actually took place? Help students discover the usefulness of the purpose statement "there are four different stages in the life of that moth" and that each cycle is identified with signal words—*first, second, third,* and *finally.*

Other useful sequential signal words and phrases are "to begin with," "at the same time," *before, after, previously,* "my next point," and "my final point." Signal words that emphasize a speaker's conclusion also deserve attention—"in conclusion," "in summation," *thus, consequently, therefore,* and *hence.*

Time lines are exceptionally appropriate devices to help students understand the sequences of orally presented selections. A group of fourth graders interested in the study of aviation developed the time line shown in Figure 4–2 after seeing and listening to several films and stories about aviation. Also, you can present this kind of time line before a listening activity as a visual advanced organizer for students who need more help than usual. They could compare their time line with the one presented in Harris's *Airplanes: A Fold-Out Book* (1995).

Other activities to help students listen for sequence include the following:

1. Cut up a story into paragraphs. Paste each paragraph on a piece of cardboard. Read the selection in proper sequence and have students place the mixed paragraphs into the right order.
2. Divide a sequentially developed paragraph into sentences. Paste the sentences on cardboard. Have students listen to the paragraph and place the sentences into proper sequence.
3. Comic strips work well for developing sequential skills. Have students listen while you read aloud a comic strip, then have them put individual panels into the right order.
4. A flannel board provides an excellent opportunity for children to listen to a story, hear its sequential organization, then retell the story in appropriate sequence.

Predicting Outcomes.   When children are asked to predict what happens next in a story or speech, they draw on their ability to understand sequential relationships. Predicting also

---

1783	—World's first recorded balloon flight—passengers included a rooster, a duck, and a sheep
1900	—Zeppelin was developed in Germany
1903	—Wright brothers flew at Kitty Hawk
1927	—Lindbergh flew the *Spirit of St. Louis* across the Atlantic from New York to Paris
1932	—Amelia Earhart became the first woman to fly across the Atlantic
1937	—Hindenburg burned and crashed
1945	—Fighter planes used in World War II could travel 450 miles per hour
1950	—American air force used mostly jets during Korean War
1970s	—Space travel
1980s	—Space shuttles

FIGURE 4–2   Aviation Time Line

requires children to listen carefully to the story so they can find out whether or not their predictions were accurate. One useful technique is to have students listen to the chapter titles of a book and predict what will be in each chapter.

For example, before reading *Runaway Slave—The Story of Harriet Tubman,* ask third-grade children to listen to the title of each chapter and write a brief prediction about what information they think will appear in the chapter. Writing involves each student in making predictions. After reading and discussing the title so everyone understands the time in which the book takes place, review the concept of slavery. After students write predictions about each chapter title, have the class discuss their predictions and give reasons for them. The chapter headings include the following: Who Was Harriet Tubman?; At Miss Susan's; Follow the North Star; Trouble; I'm Going to Leave You; Harriet Tubman, Conductor; Nighttime, Daytime; Go On—Or Die; A Sad Christmas; and The War Years. After each chapter, have the students review the accuracy of their predictions. This activity is also highly motivating because each child must listen carefully to see if his or her predictions are correct.

Other activities for predicting outcomes include these:

1. Present a selection such as Mildred Pitts Walter's *Brother to the Wind* (1985) or Arthur Yorinks's *Hey, Al* (1986) orally and stop at an interesting point in the story. Have students tell or write how they think the story will end.
2. Orally present short descriptions of stories such as Michael Bond's *A Bear Called Paddington* (1960), Pam Conrad's *Call Me Ahnighito* (1995), Nathan Zimelman's *Treed by a Pride of Irate Lions* (1990), E. B. White's *Charlotte's Web* (1952), Caroline Arnold's *Saving the Peregrine Falcon* (1985), Jean Fritz's *Make Way for Sam Houston* (1986), and Helen V. Griffith's *Grandaddy's Stars* (1995). Ask the children to predict whether the story will be fact or fantasy and to explain their decisions.
3. Films are also useful for predicting outcomes. Show a film until you reach an interesting point. Then, have students finish the story before they see the remainder of the film. You will note that many of the predicted endings may be as good or as logical as the actual endings.

Create a learning center for listening to find activities that will help develop listening for awareness, enjoyment, and specific purposes. The criteria for a listening learning center should include the following:

1. The activities should provide practice in developing one or more of the listening skills stated in the purpose.
2. The students should be able to work independently, either alone or in small groups. The listening material must be available on tape, and directions must be specific.
3. The activities should provide enough enjoyment to motivate the students without teacher assistance.
4. The activities should use a variety of skills and methods for responding.
5. The center should include activities geared to several ability levels.
6. The activities should be separate such that they can be completed in any sequence.
7. The activities should be related to other school subjects and to the listening needs of the individual child.

Prepare the students by discussing the purposes for the activities in the center. Teach the students how to use the equipment in the center, and teach at least one activity to the whole class before students use the center individually. Instruct the students to prepare themselves mentally to concentrate on listening, as athletes concentrate on their sports. Instruct the students on ways to get rid of distractions, to close their eyes, to form a picture in their minds, and to pretend they and the voice or sound are all alone in the room. Specific activities, all on tape, may include the following:

1. A descriptive paragraph—Have students draw the picture described, then listen again, and correct or add to their pictures in another color.
2. A story—Have students divide their paper into four squares and draw four pictures to show the sequence of story events.
3. The story and poem "The King's Breakfast"—Have students number in sequence printed sentences that describe the events in the story.
4. Mystery sounds (ball bouncing, blocks hitting together, water pouring, etc.)—Have students attempt to identify each sound.
5. Classmates' voices—Have students identify each voice.
6. Verbal descriptions of animals and their characteristics—Have the children listen to the tape and match the sounds to the appropriate picture.
7. Vivid verbal descriptions—Have students color a picture after listening to a description.
8. Poems that paint mental pictures, such as "Foul Shot," "Steam Shovel," and "Catalogue," which are all found in Stephen Dunning, Edward Lueders, and Hugh Smith's anthology *Reflections on a Gift of Watermelon Pickle . . . and Other Modern Verse* (1967)—Have the students draw the pictures they see in their minds.
9. Pictures of a city street, a farm, a zoo, and a seashore—Have the students view the pictures and list the sounds they would hear if they were in the location of one of the pictures.
10. A funny short story with dialogue between characters, such as Steven Kellogg's *Tallyho, Pinkerton!* (1982)—Have the children listen to the tape and draw the sequences in cartoon style.
11. Several short stories—Have the children write a title for each selection.

Be sure that all activities are carefully planned so that the students can understand the purpose, order, content, and vocabulary of the exercises. Also, be sure to tell the students what to listen for. The best listening activities demand extensive student involvement.

Integrating Listening and Geography

Asking students to listen to an oral reading of a book and to identify important details related to the geographical content of the book develops higher thinking skills and also integrates the study of geography and literature. Choosing a book such as Brian Floca's *Dinosaurs at the Ends of the Earth* (2000) allows older students to both listen for supporting details and to increase their knowledge of the five themes of geography.

The following categories identified by *GEO News Handbook* (1990) may be used for this activity:

1. *Location, including where and why*—Where does the story take place as far as city, country, continent, longitude, latitude, and so forth? Why does the story take place in this location?
2. *Place, including physical and human characteristics*—What are the physical features and characteristics? What are the characteristics of the people, including distinctive cultural traditions?

3. *Relationships with places, including cultural and physical interactions and how relationships develop*—How do human–environmental relationships develop and what are the consequences? What is the primary use of land? How have the people altered the environment?
4. *Movement, including people, ideas, and materials*—How are the movements of people, ideas, and materials influenced and accomplished? What are the consequences of such movements?
5. *Regions, including how they form and change*—What are the major languages? What are the vegetation regions? What are the country's political divisions?

Before reading the book to the class, the teacher should develop a chart that shows these themes. Each of the themes should be discussed so that students understand the purposes for listening to a book. Relate to students that geographers have developed a procedure that allows students to inquire about places on the earth and to analyze their relationships to the people who live there.

The chart shown in Table 4–1 provides a partial listing of information that could be discovered by listening to *Dinosaurs at the Ends of the Earth.* Before asking students to listen to this book, show and discuss the map of the Gobi Desert and the expedition track that the scientists used in their search for dinosaur fossils. It would also help understanding to read the author's "A Note on the Story."

Numerous other books are available that introduce geology and geography and that encourage students to develop insights into the changes in the earth, to understand the consequences of natural and human-produced disasters, and to understand the importance of developing cultural awareness. The following books may be used for this type of activity:

Jim Brandenburg's *Sand and Fog: Adventures in Southern Africa* (1994)

Jean Craighead George's *Everglades* (1995)

Rebecca Johnson's *Braving the Frozen Frontier: Women Working in Antarctica* (1997)

Anne Millard's *A Street Through Time: A 12,000-Year Walk Through History* (1998)

Lawrie Raskin and Debora Pearson's *My Sahara Adventure: 52 Days by Camel* (1998)

Literature-Related Activities

Literature provides excellent listening materials that encourage active verbal responses, develop understanding of story structure, foster literacy appreciation, and teach reading. Activities that involve children during a story experience also foster language development and cognitive development. Books such as Arthur Geisert's *Pigs from A to Z* (1986) encourage children to interact with the text during a listening experience. Listening activities are also important for improving comprehension. For example, according to Vosniadou, Pearson, and Rogers (1988), students can detect inconsistencies better when listening to a story than when reading a story. When the topic is familiar, even first graders can detect inconsistencies during a listening experience.

As we have mentioned, listening, oral language, literature, and writing are closely related. The quality of literature read aloud to and discussed by students affects their writing. Discussion helps some students improve their writing if the discussion focuses on the techniques used by the authors and if it encourages the students to use those techniques in their own writing. Discussions that highlight aspects of the narrative structure also improve writing. Asking students to identify and discuss story elements in legends and fables improves stu-

Table 4–1 Five themes of geography

Genre and Themes	Location Where/Why	Place Physical and Human Characteristics	Cultural and Physical Interaction/How Relationships Develop	Movement People/Ideas/ Materials	Regions/ How They Form and Change
Book/Story Brain Floca's *Dinosaurs at the Ends of the Earth*	Mongolia Central Asia, 1922 Expedition to find and study fossils Gobi Desert Longitude shown on map Map shows route of the expedition as it leaves Kalgan on April 21, 1922.	Travel is difficult where there are no roads. Afternoon temperatures on Gobi Desert reach 110 degrees. Flaming Cliffs, one of the richest sites for fossils ever found, is located there. Dedicated scientists. Text presents characteristics of protoceratops, psittacosaurus, velociraptor, and oviraptor.	Nomadic herdsmen interact with scientists. Scientists discover first dinosaur eggs ever found. Book has a time line of the history of life on earth beginning in the Precambian period and extending to present day. Excitement of discovery reveals scientific methods.	Camel caravans bring supplies across Gobi Desert and return with prepared fossils. Newspapers report scientific discovery of a dinosaur nest. Mongolia closes borders to Western scientists in 1930. Soviet, Polish, and Mongolian teams explore the Gobi Desert. Importance of knowledge from American Museum of Natural History.	Sand storms cause air to howl and gravel to whip through the air. The gorge was dated at 80 million years old. Dinosaur fossils lay buried and hidden for 80 million years.

dents' writing. In a study conducted with fifth graders, Dressel (1990) reports that students who listened to and discussed high-quality literature produced better writing samples than did students who listened to and discussed literature of lower quality. Dressel emphasizes not only the quality of the literature but the quality of the oral discussion as she describes the study: "First, to avoid the 'reading difficulty' problem, the literature was read aloud. Second, since poetic language requires the reader/listener to consider the work as a whole . . . the text was respected and presented intact. Finally, since research indicates that sensitizing children to story elements as well as to the authors' craft helps them gain metacognitive control over comprehension and writing, a carefully designed program was implemented to encourage the children to examine the literature from the author's perspective" (p. 399).

There is also a close relationship between the quality of the stories heard and the quality of children's retellings. In a study by Barrs (2002), for example, the richness of the original stories was reflected in the quality of the children's retellings and the quality of writing. Barrs found that reading aloud to children showed them the language and developed their ear for language.

Young children may become acquainted with story structure and language patterns by experiencing stories that have repetitive language patterns, such as "The Three Billy Goats Gruff," or repetitive or cumulative story events, such as "The Gingerbread Boy." Teachers frequently call such books predictable because the repetitive patterns encourage children to hypothesize about words that follow or events that happen next in the story. When using predictable books with children, present a series of activities during which children listen to a story and select the most useful phonemic, syntactic, and semantic information; predict the most probable language or happening; and confirm that their prediction was correct.

Sipe (2002) emphasizes the importance of children's expressive engagement while they listen to stories. He believes that understanding and encouraging young children's expressive engagement and responses during read-alouds is important because "Children who make such responses seem to view stories as invitations to participate or perform. Stories are understood not as fixed and rigid but as changeable texts, and the reader's role is not simply to understand but to actively control stories" (p. 479).

Sipe identifies the following five types of expressive engagements and then discusses ways that encourage that type of expressive engagement:

1. Spontaneously dramatizing the story while it is being read. While listening to books such as Maurice Sendak's *Where the Wild Things Are* (1963) children may dramatize the wild rumpus.
2. Talking back to the story characters suggests deep engagement with the story. While listening to Beatrix Potter's *The Tale of Peter Rabbit* (1902) they may caution Peter about how he might escape from Mr. McGregor.
3. Critiquing and controlling the story during which time children suggest changes in plots, characters, or settings. This engagement may be encouraged by teacher questions such as "What would you do?" while children listen to Paul Zelinsky's version of Grimm's *Rapunzel* (1997).
4. Inserting oneself into the story during which time children assume the role of story characters or place their friends in the roles. This engagement may be encouraged during listening to such books as Chris Raschka's *Yo! Yes?* (1993) as children consider how they would act.
5. Taking over the text and manipulating it for one's own purposes or treating the story as a means for his or her own creativity. This type of expression may be fostered while children listen to Jon Scieszka's *The True Story of the 3 Little Pigs* (1989). Many children think about how they might retell the text or retell other folktales using a different point of view.

It is interesting to apply Sipe's five examples of expressive engagements to one book. For example, when reading aloud *Tomás and the Library Lady* (1997) by Pat Mora the teacher will find many opportunities for children to respond to this story about a young son of a migrant worker family as they travel from Texas to Iowa. Listeners should be told that the story is based on the life story of Tomás Rivera who later became the chancellor of the University of California at Riverside. The following examples exemplify how teachers could encourage students to respond while listening: At the beginning of the story when Tomás is hot, tired, and missing his own bed in his house in Texas, the response might be a talking back engagement in which students tell Tomás about how he should behave, or the children might insert themselves into the story and consider how they would act if they were in a similar situation. When the two boys listen to Papa Grande tell stories they may be encouraged to be involved in dramatization of the story as Papa Grande uses lines such as "Once upon a time . . . on a windy night a man was riding a horse through a forest. The wind was howling, whoooooooooo, and the leaves were blowing, whish, whish. . . . All of a sudden something grabbed the man. He couldn't move. He was too scared to look around. All night long he wanted to ride away. But he couldn't" (unpaged). This example could also be used to encourage listeners to take over the text and tell the story in a way that expresses their own creativity.

Inserting oneself would be an excellent response when Tomás walks downtown and looks into the library and sees shelves filled with books. Children can assume the role of the story character and respond to how they would feel if they discovered such a large number of books for the first time. They can also insert themselves when the librarian greets Tomás and asks him what he would like to read. While Tomás responds with books about tigers and dinosaurs, listeners could agree or disagree with Tomás's choices. They could name their own choices for books to read.

Taking over the text and manipulating it to one's own purposes would be a response for many listeners when Tomás reads a book and visualizes the setting in which he sees dinosaurs and even rides on the back of a dinosaur. Listeners can imagine that they are in that situation and describe what they see when they read a book. This could also be a critiquing situation in which children change the plot, characters, and setting. When Papa Grande asks Tomás to read to him from the books that he brings home from the library, listeners might insert themselves by sharing what they read to parents or caregivers when they bring a book home. Papa Grande helps Tomás during the reading aloud by acting out the sounds of the animals in the stories.

Placing oneself into the book and taking over could accompany Tomás as he visualizes the settings and characters in the books. Finally, they can respond to Tomás and the librarian when Tomás tells her that it is time for him to return home. The librarian also gives Tomás a new book so that he and Papa Grande will have many new stories to tell. Listeners could use any of Sipe's responses as they dramatize the stories that they would like to prepare, talk back to Tomás and Papa Grande as they read stories and select them for telling, critique the story by adding what they think will happen after the family reaches their home, insert themselves in the story by telling what they would do in a similar situation, and take over the text and manipulate it to their own purposes as they consider how they might end the story of *Tomás and the Library Lady*. They could also respond to the author's note in which the author reveals that the story is motivated by the life of a migrant worker who valued education and had a strong love of reading. They might consider why the campus library at the University of California at Riverside is named after Tomás Rivera.

Levesque (1989) describes a five-part read-aloud strategy, ELVES, designed to develop listening comprehension through the following sequence of activities:

1. *Excite*—Focus the discussion on the listeners' experiences, the literary elements within the story, and predictions about the story.
2. *Listen*—Have the students listen to verify predictions and to comprehend other story elements.
3. *Visualize*—Have the listeners share their mental images.
4. *Extend*—Have the students gain new understandings by relating previous knowledge and new knowledge.
5. *Savor*—Have the students reflect on the story, verbalize their responses, and become involved with follow-up activities, such as writing or Reader's Theater.

For Your Plan Book

Using *Owl Moon* to Develop the ELVES Strategy

The following example shows how the ELVES strategy could be developed with Jane Yolen's *Owl Moon* (1987):

Excite: Begin the discussion by posing questions that encourage the students to relate their own experiences to various elements within the story. For example, ask: "Have you ever been out on a winter night when there is a full moon? What could you see and hear? Pretend you are in the woods. What would you see and hear? Why would you want to go out into the woods on a cold winter night?" Ask questions that encourage students to make predictions about the title and the cover illustration. For example, "What do you think the author means by the title, *Owl Moon?* When you look at the cover, describe your feelings. Why do you have those feelings? Pretend you are the child on the cover. What are your feelings? What do you think will happen to the man and the child as they explore the night in *Owl Moon?* What kind of a mood do you think will be developed in the story?"

Listen: Now, read the story and ask the students to listen to determine whether their earlier responses and predictions were correct. The students might use signals in particular places in the story to show that they were right or wrong. In addition to having an interesting plot, this story uses vivid language. Encourage students to listen for language that is especially vivid, such as "I could feel the cold, as if someone's icy hand was palm-down on my back" (p. 11, unnumbered). As you read, ask the students to try to visualize the story so they can describe the woodland setting and how the characters felt and reacted as they walked through the woods.

Visualize: Ask the students to describe their visual images. Pick out especially vivid sections and ask the students to close their eyes and describe what they see and feel as you read or reread these parts. For example, read: "We went into the woods. The shadows were the blackest things I have ever seen. They stained the white snow. My mouth felt furry, for the scarf over it was wet and warm. I didn't ask what kinds of things hide behind black trees in the middle of the night. When you go owling you have to be brave" (p. 13, unnumbered). Then, ask the students what they see and feel.

Extend: Lead a discussion in which students make connections between their previous knowledge and any new insights gained from listening to and experiencing this story. For example, ask: "How would the story change if the setting changed? Think about a story that might take place in the same location but in the daytime or in the summer. What would happen if the story were set at night in a town or city? Think about the point of view of the story. How would it change if the story were told through the point of view of the owl?"

Savor: Have students savor the story by describing additional thoughts and feelings about it. As a writing activity, they could write personal responses to the characters of the child, the father, or the owl, or to the vivid language in the book. They could write a story from the owl's point of view, or pretend they are exploring a different setting and searching for something from nature. For a comparative-literature activity, they could compare the stories, the winter settings, and the points of view in *Owl Moon,* Tejima's *Fox's Dream* (1987), and Jane Chelsea Aragon's *Winter Harvest* (1988). For oral language activities, they could develop a reader's theater production using *Owl Moon.* They could find poetry that explores winter settings and prepare the poems as choral reading arrangements. Various poems about winter in Jack Prelutsky's *The Random House Book of Poetry for Children* (1983) include A. A. Milne's

"The More It Snows," N. M. Bodecker's "When All the World Is Full of Snow," Robert Frost's "Stopping by Woods on a Snowy Evening," Walter de la Mare's "The Snowflake," Jack Prelutsky's "The Four Seasons," John Updike's "January," Charles G. D. Roberts's "Ice," Langston Hughes's "Winter Moon," Kay Starbird's "Wendy in Winter," and Karla Kuskin's "Winter Clothes."

Story Structure

Traditional tales with easily identifiable conflicts, characters, settings, and plot developments are excellent sources for helping children understand story structure and story elements. The nature of the oral tradition makes it imperative that listeners be brought quickly into the action and identify with the characters. Consequently, tales such as "The Little Red Hen," "Puss in Boots," "Jack the Giant Killer," "Three Billy Goats Gruff," and "The Fisherman and His Wife" allow children to be immersed into the major conflict within the first few sentences, understand the nature and importance of the building conflict, identify the characters and character traits, identify the setting, and recognize major features in plot development. For example, the conflict in Paul Galdone's *The Little Red Hen* (1973) is between laziness and industriousness. The first sentence introduces the animals who live together. The second sentence introduces the conflict; that is, the cat, dog, and mouse are lazy. Next, the industrious hen is introduced. The remainder of the story develops conflict between lazy and industrious animals. The conflict is quickly resolved when the hen eats her own baking.

Drawing semantic maps and webs for characters, settings, and plot helps children visualize the relationships between these important elements. Two examples developed around traditional tales illustrate a simpler and a more complex folktale. The first, "Three Billy Goats Gruff," introduces characters and plot in chronological order, proceeding from littlest to biggest. In Figure 4–3, notice how the map illustrates the close relationship between the characters and plot.

The second example, the Brothers Grimm tale of "The Fisherman and His Wife," is more complex and more appropriate for older children (see Figure 4–4). The characters change as the tasks change, the setting becomes more turbulent as the demands of the characters increase, and the plot relates directly to changes in characters and setting. Developing a map following a listening activity vividly illustrates these relationships.

Evaluating What Is Heard

The final category of listening comprehension usually mentioned by authorities is the ability to evaluate what is heard. This subject lends itself well to listening to television and radio presentations and to listening to and reading newspaper advertisements and editorials.

Critical Reading and Listening

Critical reading and listening demand careful evaluation. To determine what and whom to believe requires considerable judgment of the source. Critical reading and listening go beyond factual comprehension; they require weighing the validity of facts, identifying the real problem, making judgments, interpreting implied ideas, interpreting character traits, distinguishing fact from opinion, drawing conclusions, and determining the adequacy of a source of information.

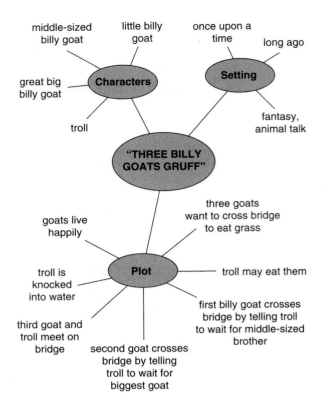

FIGURE 4–3 Semantic Web of "Three Billy Goats Gruff"

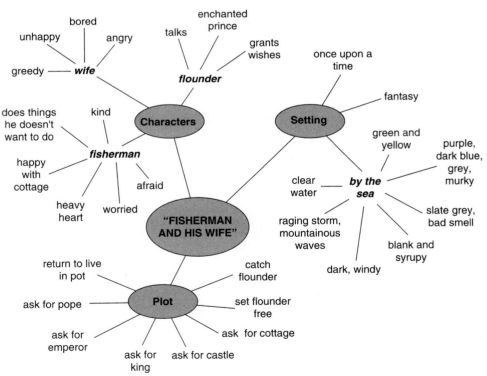

FIGURE 4–4 Semantic Map for a Book Report

142

Television, radio, and newspapers provide abundant material for teaching critical reading and listening skills. It is interesting to note that the latest "Texas Assessment of Knowledge and Skills" exam (Ferrell & Hipp, 2002) includes in the language arts portion reading pieces from magazine and newspaper articles as well as excerpts from novels and web pages. According to Arnold Cheyney (1984), students can learn many critical reading skills by carefully scrutinizing and questioning sources in newspapers. Cheyney provides a list of questions for teachers to put on charts for student referral when they read or discuss news items:

The Writer's Competency and Integrity

1. Is the writer an authority?
2. How does this writer know?
3. Does the writer make sense?

The Writer's Use of Sources and Evidence

4. What evidence is presented to document the assertions?
5. Is this fact or opinion?
6. Is anything missing?
7. What is the writer's purpose?
8. Does the writer have a hidden motive?

The Reader's Ability to Form, Revise, and Test Opinions

9. Are the premises valid?
10. Why are these facts important to me?
11. Do the conclusions necessarily follow?
12. What have others said about this topic?
13. Who stands to gain if I accept this without question?
14. Does my lack of knowledge keep me from accepting this?
15. Does my background make me intolerant of this point of view?
16. Is the information as true today as when it was written?
17. What more do I need to know before I come to my own conclusions?[1]

Fact versus Opinion.   To answer critical questions about news items, students need assignments that require them to read and listen to a variety of news sources. One of the first skills is ability to separate fact from opinion. You can begin to help students understand the difference by reading them several paragraphs written around either fact or opinion. For example, consider the following paragraphs:

1. The grizzly bear lives in Alaska, Canada, and in the northern part of the United States. A big grizzly may weigh up to 1,000 pounds. The grizzly has a large hump above his shoulders; this makes it recognizable even at a distance. The grizzly likes to eat fish, fruit, and honey.
2. The grizzly bear is a cruel killer and should be outlawed in all parts of the United States. This killer not only attacks cattle, it also attacks and injures tourists in the national

---

[1] From Cheyney, Arnold B. (1984). *Teaching reading skills through the newspaper* (2nd ed.). (Newark, DE: International Reading Association, 1984). Reprinted with permission of Arnold B. Cheyney and the International Reading Association. All rights reserved.

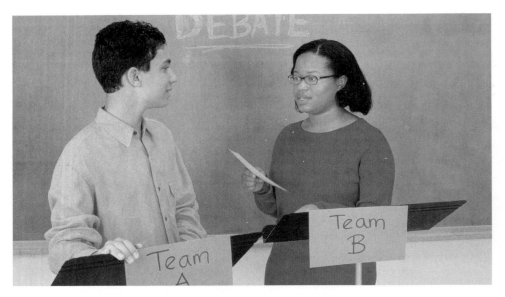

Functioning in this age of information requires learning to evaluate what is heard.

parks. The parks should be made safe for visitors, and they will not be safe for campers and hikers until this animal is removed.

3. The grizzly bear lived freely in the western part of the United States for hundreds of years. Humans have so infringed on the grizzly's hunting grounds that it now is found only in secluded areas of Alaska and Canada, and infrequently in the high country in the United States. The U.S. government must protect the grizzly and keep the tourists and ranchers out of the grizzly's territory. This powerful, beautiful animal deserves our best protection.

After reading paragraphs similar to these, ask students if they see any differences between the paragraphs. The conclusion should be that the first paragraph is based on facts and that the other two are based on opinions. The students should also note that the two opinion paragraphs are trying to sway opinion.

Next, have the students formulate their own definitions of fact and opinion. Their definitions might resemble the following:

Fact = Statements that can be checked and proven to be true are facts.

Opinion = Statements that tell what someone thinks or believes to be true but cannot be proven are opinions.

Allow the students to apply their knowledge of fact versus opinion and subsequently make judgments about new information. Have them search a newspaper for examples of factual writing and opinion writing. Make displays of the two kinds of writing and their characteristics. Students will find factual items in newspapers in the form of obituaries, birth notices, court announcements, and most news stories, although the last may also include opinion. They will find personal opinion writing in editorials, advertisements, letters to the editor, and advice columns. Students can reinforce their skills by writing factual and opinion paragraphs to share with the class, and classmates can then make judgments about the paragraphs.

News Coverage Comparisons.   Students can compare how television, radio, newspapers, and news magazines handle news. For stimulating discussions and learning experiences, assign children to report and analyze the various media presentations of an item reported in the news. For example, if your city has coverage on the three commercial television networks, a news channel, and an educational station, assign several students to watch the evening news on each channel. Have other students search newspapers for news stories, editorials, and editorial cartoons about the same subject. Have still other students listen to the news reports on the area radio stations. If possible, tape the television and radio segments for classroom listening and critical analysis. Have the students bring the newspaper items to the classroom for sharing and discussion. (Controversial news items that may result in editorial comment are especially interesting for this investigation. Comparisons among news coverage presented on commercial networks in the United States and coverage on the BBC, from British Broadcasting, is also interesting.)

The following day, have the students share their reports of the news presentations; discuss differences resulting from media requirements; discuss bias noted in the various media or between networks; compare editorial comment in a paper with its news coverage of the same topic; and discover words that might cause a biased reaction in readers or viewers. Have the students refer to Cheyney's list (1984) for evaluating the various news items. When they discuss media requirements, they should begin to see that television is primarily visual and presents brief coverage of a story. Radio relies entirely on words to develop images. Newspapers use both words and pictures and have room to discuss the who, what, when, where, why, and how of a story.

Advertising and Propaganda.   We are bombarded with advertising, visually and auditorily, during most of our waking hours. The morning newspaper often appears to be predominantly advertising; the same is true for many magazines. Radio and television sometimes seem to be one long series of commercials, interrupted occasionally by programming. Presumably, adults have acquired enough critical listening and reading skills to enable them to judge the value, worth, honesty, and acceptability of ads that try to persuade them to invest in a product or vote a certain way in an election. There is a great deal of concern, however, for preschool and school-age children, who may be unduly influenced by messages ads put forth. Although good commercials can raise the standards of civilization, bad commercials can distort reality and lead young people to think that what they see in television ads portrays real life, leading them to desire and expect the wrong things for the wrong reasons. Teachers should help students look closely at both the good and bad in advertising, so they can critically evaluate what they see and hear.

For Your Plan Book

Lesson Plan

An Instructional Unit on Advertising

Two undergraduate elementary education majors developed the following unit to promote intelligent decision making among today's young consumers. They designed the three-week unit for fourth-grade students, incorporating art, consumer education, language arts, math, reading, and social studies activities around the theme of advertising. Their ideas should stimulate your own thinking about teaching through the medium of advertising.

Continued

Idea One: American audiences are continually exposed to advertising.

1. Have the students view or listen to a one-hour program of their choice on television or radio. Have them record the time devoted to commercials and compare the total commercial time to total program time by constructing a bar graph.
2. Have each student tabulate the number of advertising billboards, posters, and signs he or she sees from Monday through Friday.

Idea Two: Advertising influences the purchases of the American public.

1. Facilitate discussion about the influences of advertising by comparing two products—one that is advertised a great deal and one that is not advertised. Include the following questions:
   a. Which product would you buy?
   b. Have you ever switched brands after seeing an advertisement that compared the old and new brands?
   c. What advertisements can you name that might influence your decision about buying food, clothing, toys, and so forth?
   d. How do you feel about an advertisement that influences your decision to vote, purchase a product, or contribute to a charity fund?

Idea Three: Advertising is a multimillion dollar business in America.

1. Have the students choose a facet of the advertising industry that interests them. Possible choices include annual expenditure on advertising, central locations of the advertising industry, or in-depth exploration of advertising spending for a particular type of product. Have the students present their findings orally.

Idea Four: Advertisements appear in many different types of media, including television, radio, newspapers, magazines, and billboards.

1. Utilize a guided discovery approach in a discussion of advertising media suitability. Topics include advertising cost, coverage, applicable regulations, use of jingles and catchy phrases, company logos, and visual appeal.
2. Let each student choose a product and decide whether the product is suitable for television or radio advertising. Have the student write a script to sell that product and tape an advertisement. The presentation should present characteristics suitable to television or radio.
3. Have the students use their imaginations to write an original classified advertisement to buy or sell an item or to gain employment.
4. Have each student compute the cost of placing his or her ad in a newspaper.

Idea Five: Professional advertising opens many career options for today's young people.

1. Present an expository lesson plan on a career in advertising. The lesson plan should cover such topics as jobs, training required for each job, related-interest fields, and salaries.
2. Have the students select a field in which they are interested or have special ability. Have each student research the chosen field and present a product representative of that field:
   a. *Drama:* dramatic presentation for selling a product.
   b. *Speech:* oral presentation of product, as on the radio with a microphone (disc jockey).
   c. *Art:* drawing, sketching, painting.

d. *Marketing:* design package of product or catchy presentation of product.

e. *Modeling:* modeling clothes.

f. *Journalism:* written script and layout.

g. *Photography:* pictures of product.

h. *Producing/directing:* producing skits or slide shows.

Idea Six: Some advertisements are designed to appeal to specific consumer groups.

1. Videotape television commercials that attempt to appeal to specific groups. Discuss and categorize the intended groups with the students.

2. Have each student choose one commercial that appeals to a specific group and write an adaptation of this commercial to appeal to another group, identifying the old and new groups.

Idea Seven: Television advertisements attempt to appeal to different audiences during different times of the day or week.

1. Conduct a guided discovery lesson on the influence that time of day or week has on the types of products advertised. Include such questions as these:

   a. Who is most likely to be watching television during the day?

   b. What products do you think would be advertised then?

   c. How many of you watch the cartoons on Saturday mornings?

   d. What kinds of consumers watch television on Saturday morning?

   e. What kinds of products are advertised then? Why?

Idea Eight: Advertisements are used by cities and states to attract tourists.

1. Tell the students that they have been chosen by the local Chamber of Commerce to write a description of their city in order to encourage people to visit. Tell them to make their city come alive with vivid verbs and descriptive adjectives.

Idea Nine: Professional advertisers attempt to appeal to the five senses: touch, taste, sight, smell, and hearing.

1. Instruct the students to choose, cut out, and categorize magazine advertisements into the above categories, underlining key words.

2. Have each student create one original product appealing to at least two of the senses and write an advertisement for the product.

Idea Ten: Much advertising is propaganda, the purpose of which is to influence the audience to buy something.

1. Have the students bring three newspaper or magazine ads and analyze each by answering the following questions:

   a. What product is being advertised?

   b. Has the advertiser used any tricks to attract you to the product and to make you think it is better or more popular than it actually is? Explain.

   c. Are any definite claims cited by the manufacturers? If so, what are they?

   d. Do you believe the ad? Why or why not?

2. Have the students orally present a sales pitch to their group, who will role-play the board of directors of an advertising firm. The salesperson will persuade the board of directors to sponsor the product. Visual aids are useful, and students should be as persuasive as possible.

Continued

Idea Eleven: Testimonial advertising quotes a favorable statement made about the product by a famous person.

1. Have students identify and describe in writing at least one testimonial advertisement seen during afternoon or evening television viewing.
2. Have students list famous persons who have endorsed a product or participated in a testimonial advertisement, relying on past viewing experience.

Idea Twelve: Transfer advertising pictures of a famous person or symbol with a product, although the person makes no statement about the product.

1. Have the students search magazines and view television advertisements at home to find examples of the transfer propaganda technique.
2. Ask the students to think of a famous person in history whom they admire. Then, have the students write a transfer advertisement with that person using a product of their choice.

Culminating Activities

1. Have the students advertise an upcoming school or community event. The event might be a book fair, carnival, Christmas program, band or choir presentation, or other type of assembly. The students should utilize as many forms of media as possible. Divide them into groups according to the medium each prefers. The advertisements should reflect the many forms and techniques studied during the unit.
2. Divide the students into several small groups. Have the groups take turns presenting several short skits with puppets. The groups not presenting a skit will present commercials between scenes and skits, so that each student will participate in both the commercials and puppet presentations. The commercials will be of the students' creation and should advertise imaginary products. The commercials, reviewed as a class effort, should reflect all of the advertising techniques learned in the unit.

Used with permission of Susan Watson and Sarah Wells, Texas A&M University.

For Your Plan Book

Lesson Plan

An Instructional Unit on Propaganda Techniques in Advertising

To develop powers of critical evaluation, begin by studying the various propaganda techniques frequently used to sway public opinion. A fourth-grade teacher used such a study to help children listen to and read advertisements more critically. This study was so successful that the students afterward did not believe anything in an ad unless they had investigated its claims and evaluated how authorities in a field would feel toward the advertisement.

The teacher introduced this particular study by asking a parent who worked for an advertising agency to visit the class and talk about advertising. The guest speaker discussed the purpose of advertising and the money spent on it. Then, he showed the students some of the ways ads try to influence opinion about their products. Children saw examples of ads that used snob appeal, testimonials, transfer, glittering generalities, plain folks, bandwagon, and name-calling techniques to sway public opinion. They discussed the various methods and asked numerous questions. This guest speaker gave a highly motivating introduction to advertising, which enabled students to see that companies spend millions of dollars trying to win prospective buyers.

Next, the students studied the various propaganda techniques presented by the guest speaker. They listed characteristics of each technique, found oral and written examples of them, and compiled Table 4–2. The students created several bulletin-board displays to illus-

Table 4–2 Characteristics and examples of propaganda techniques

Name	Characteristics	Example
1. Snob appeal	Makes us want a product because superior or wealthy people have it. Association with a small, exclusive group.	The jet set dine at _____, you should too. Drive a _____ like _____.
2. Name calling	Creates a feeling of dislike for a person or product by associating it with something disliked or undesirable. May appeal to hate and fear. Asks people to judge without first examining the evidence.	Congressman _____ associates with _____. The mayor has dishonest friends.
3. Glittering generalities	Uses broad general statements, whose exact meanings are not clear. Appeals to emotions of love, generosity, brotherhood. Words suggest ideals such as truth, freedom, and the American way.	Your wildest dreams of adventure will come true if you sail on the _____. Senator _____ will defend the American way.
4. Plain folks	Identifies the person or product with the average person. Politicians may try to win confidence by appearing to be like the good folks in your town.	For an honest used-car deal go to your friendly neighborhood _____ dealer. Senator _____ is a hometown boy who will vote for your interests.
5. Transfer	Creates a good or bad impression by associating a product or person with something respected or not respected. The feeling for the symbol is supposed to transfer to the new product or person.	_____ is as strong as Atlas.
6. Testimonial	A respected person, such as a movie star or athlete, recommends a product and suggests that you buy it because he or she uses it.	Lovely Lettie says, "I use Bright Hair shampoo because it leaves my hair silky and shiny."
7. Bandwagon	Follow the crowd and buy what everyone else is buying, or vote for the winner.	Everyone is rushing to _____ to buy the _____. If you want to belong to the "in" generation, drink _____.

trate the characteristics of the various propaganda techniques, with examples of newspaper and magazine advertisements and television and radio commercials. (They found that some advertising relied on more than one approach.) Next, the teacher taped commercials from television and radio. The students listened to them carefully and identified the different techniques and key words related to each selling approach.

Continued

After listening, identifying, and analyzing, the students chose a particular ad or commercial to research. They listed questions to answer before making an evaluative decision; for example, for a testimonial, the students tried to answer the following questions:

1. Who is the testimonial trying to persuade?
2. Who will benefit if I agree with the testimonial?
3. Who will be hurt if I agree with the testimonial?
4. Who is making the testimonial?
5. What is the credibility of this person in relation to the product or issue?
6. Who can make an honest appraisal of this product or issue?
7. What facts support the testimonial?
8. What facts disagree with the testimonial?

They asked similar questions for the remaining categories of advertising. The students presented their findings orally to the rest of the class and put their lists of answered questions next to the example of the advertisement or commercial on the bulletin board.

This advertising study concluded with an activity in which students divided into groups, wrote their own commercials, and presented them to the rest of the class. The class decided to write commercials on opposing issues, using the following four topics: (1) a commercial sponsored by an oil company that favored expansion and sale of oil and gasoline products, (2) an ecology commercial that opposed expanded use of oil and favored greater conservation of natural resources, (3) a commercial to sell big cars, and (4) a commercial to sell small cars. The students used any selling and propaganda techniques they wished, along with visual props, sound effects, and musical backgrounds. After each presentation, the remainder of the class identified the techniques in the commercial and discussed the truthfulness. (If the school has the equipment, videotape presentations and play them back as if they are commercials on a real television.)

For Your Development

1. Look for examples of the propaganda techniques described in this section. How could you use these examples to develop critical evaluation skills with children? What questions should you ask for each example?
2. Develop an instructional lesson or series of lessons for improving children's critical thinking, listening, and reading skills. Build your lessons around television, radio, and newspapers. State your objectives, motivation, instructional procedures, and reinforcement or enrichment activities.

Appreciation

Sometimes teachers become so engrossed in teaching specific skills that they forget that enjoyment is one of the main purposes of listening. Appreciative listening includes listening to poetry, music, stories, plays, and sounds in nature. In fact, the development of appreciative listening skills can establish lifelong pleasure while it motivates the utilization of other language arts skills. In a classic study, Durkin (1966) found that young children whose parents read to them at home were also high achievers in reading at school. This listening experience apparently illustrates to the child the benefits of learning to read enjoyable books.

Various taxonomies offer some guidelines for developing appreciative listening with literature. Barrett's (1972) taxonomy of comprehension, for example, stresses the development of appreciative skills. Although this taxonomy was developed in relation to reading, it also has application for listening. According to Barrett, appreciation includes a student's awareness of literary techniques, forms and styles of literature, and structures an author uses to stimulate emotional responses. Barrett identifies four tasks that fall under this appreciation component: (1) emotional response to plot or theme, (2) identification with characters and incidents, (3) reactions to the author's use of language, and (4) reactions to the author's use of imagery.

To apply the emotional response task to a listening situation, require students to listen to a selection and determine how the author developed the plot or theme to elicit certain responses in the listener. Why did the listener feel excitement, happiness, or sadness? Emotional response is an individual matter, so not all children will respond in the same way to the same selection. Encourage children to respond through pantomime or other creative dramatics and then discuss how and why a selection made them feel a certain emotion.

Also, have students record their favorite stories or poems and then let the listeners discover the qualities in the stories and poems that have emotional appeal. One creative fourth-grade teacher asked her students to interview their parents. The students asked their parents to identify selections from poetry or stories they remembered from their childhood. Then, the teacher presented the most popular selections orally. The fourth graders listened to the selections and discussed their universal appeal.

The task of identification with characters and incidents on the appreciation taxonomy requires students to become aware of literary techniques that prompt them to sympathize with, empathize with, or reject a character. Have students listen to a selection to discover how the author presents a character, then ask what descriptive words influenced how they felt about the characters. Did the author use terms such as *heroic, shiftless, lazy, beautiful,* and *strong*? How does the author have other people describe the character? Does the character tell you his or her inner feelings? How do other people in the story react to the character? How does the character overcome adversity?

For the third task, reaction to the author's use of language, students must pay attention to how the writer uses such devices as figures of speech, similes, and metaphors. Authors frequently use similes and metaphors to create new relationships between unrelated things. A simile is an expressed comparison of two different things or ideas; a metaphor is an implied comparison. For example, in *Secret of the Andes* (1952), Ann Nolan Clark uses a number of similes. Listen to two examples and visualize how you would respond to these descriptions: "The boy's thoughts were whirling like the foaming rapids on the far side of the valley" and "He bore the proud look of the giant condor circling a cliff nest on a mountain crest."

One of the strengths of Gloria Whelan's *Homeless Bird* (2000), a book written for upper-elementary and middle-school students, is her use of figurative language through similes, metaphors, and symbolism. This literary style is especially important in the references to birds and to the title of the book. Notice in the following quote how the heroine uses positive comparisons to describe her father's writing: "I watched as the spoken words were written down to become like caged birds, caught forever by my clever baap" (p. 2). In another place the author uses a comparison with caged animals to reveal the heroine's feelings of being trapped: "As I lay there in the strange house, I felt like a newly caged animal that rushes about looking for the open door that isn't there" (p. 24). This is an excellent book to read aloud and encourage older students to respond to the author's use of figurative language. They will even discover how figurative language may be related to the development of mood and theme in a book. Let students search for similar devices and share them with the class.

Besides similes and metaphors, authors often use sentence length and structure to denote pace. Authors may change language patterns to help create the action of the story. Short, staccato sentences impart a feeling of mounting excitement; long, lazy sentences produce a feeling of relaxation. Robert McCloskey (1957) uses this technique in *Time of Wonder:*

> [I]n the afternoon, when the tide is out, they build a castle out of the rocks and driftwood below the spot where they had belly-whopped and dog-paddled during the morning. . . . (p. 24)

> Suddenly the wind whips the water into sharp, choppy waves. It tears off the sharp tops and slashes them in ribbons of smoky spray. And the rain comes slamming down. The wind comes in stronger and stronger gusts. A branch snaps from a tree. (p. 44)

Read similar examples to children and see how their reactions change as sentence patterns vary.

One of the most common means for authors of books for young children to develop characterization is through personification. Personification is an excellent introduction to style for younger children because the texts that include personification of objects and animals often are reinforced through illustrations that also personify the subjects. For example, listening to Virginia Lee Burton's *The Little House* (1942) provides an enjoyable introduction to personification. As children listen to the text and view the illustrations, you may ask them to listen for answers to these questions: What pronoun is used when the author talks about the house? What actions can the house do that are similar to your actions? What feelings does the house express that are similar to your feelings? What causes the house to have each of these feelings? When have you had similar feelings? How do the illustrations help you understand the house's feelings and character?

Extend this understanding of personification by asking students to use pantomime or creative drama to enact the feelings expressed in the book. For example, have them listen to the text being read and pantomime the feelings expressed by the house. Have them create conversations that might occur between the house and her country or city neighbors. Have them tell the story from the point of view of one of the other objects found in the story.

Similar discussions may be used when listening to books in which toys are personified. Excellent books for this purpose include Anthony Browne's *Gorilla* (1983) and Margery Williams's *The Velveteen Rabbit* (1958). Books in which animals are personified include Alexandra Day's *Frank and Ernest on the Road* (1994), Diana Engel's *Josephina Hates Her Name* (1989), and Lillian Hoban's *Arthur's Great Valentine* (1989).

Older students can listen for the power of personification through such choices as Henry Wadsworth Longfellow's "Hiawatha" and Jamake Highwater's *Anpao: An American Indian Odyssey* (1977). These sources provide examples for listening to personification of nature.

The final appreciation-taxonomy task, reaction to the author's use of imagery, requires students to respond to an author's ability to paint word pictures. Can the students close their eyes and visualize the setting, a character, or a feeling? For example, when you listen to *Charlotte's Web*, can you visualize the barn that has such a peaceful feeling, as if nothing bad could ever happen again?

Sharing poetry with children is an excellent means for developing appreciative listening. Children's responses to Shel Silverstein's *Where the Sidewalk Ends* (1974) emphasize the importance of poetry. Poet José Garcia Villa (Cowen, 1983) maintains that children should be encouraged to enjoy poems for sound values, to hear the rhythm of language, and to be aware of the magic in a poetry line. While listening to poetry, children can sense and feel the meaning rather than explicitly state the meaning. Villa recommends that children listen to nursery rhymes and poems by Emily Dickinson, Robert Frost, e. e. cummings, Nathalia Crane, Lewis

Carroll, and Edward Lear. For older children, Villa recommends poems by John Donne, Gerard Manley Hopkins, Dylan Thomas, Wilfred Owen, Elinor Wylie, and Marianne Moore. Villa believes that these poets help children discover the magic in poetry. He stresses "the magic to be found in poetry rather than its meaning which is what most educational programs and texts emphasize. Only after the older student or budding poet considers the magical elements inherent in such techniques as the importance of a vivid first line; the musicality, tension, and movement of language; the intricacies of versification; the richness of metaphor; the necessity of economy; the element of surprise; and the implosive drama of the last line, will the neophyte begin to understand the power and magnificence of poetry" (p. 84).

Teachers who want to encourage children to expand the imaginative quality of their minds and appreciate the various elements in poetry may share poems emphasizing such elements as rhythm, rhyme, sound patterns, repetitions, and figurative language. For example, David McCord uses rhythm in "The Pickety Fence" (*Far and Few: Rhymes of the Never Was and Always Is,* 1952) to suggest the sounds a stick makes as a child walks by the fence. Likewise, Robert Louis Stevenson relies on rhythm to suggest the dash and rattle of a train as it crosses the countryside in "From a Railway Carriage" (*A Child's Garden of Verses,* 1885).

The auditory pleasure of rhyming words is heard in Zilpha Snyder's "Poem to Mud" (*Today Is Saturday,* 1969) and Edward Lear's "The Owl and the Pussy Cat" found in numerous texts including Jan Brett's illustrated version of *The Owl and the Pussycat* (1991). Alliteration, the repetition of initial consonants to create sound patterns, creates strong sound patterns in Jack Prelutsky's "The Yak" (*A Gopher in the Garden,* 1966). Repetition in poetry may emphasize words, phrases, lines, or verses. Lewis Carroll's repetitive patterns in "Beautiful Soup" (*Alice's Adventures in Wonderland,* 1886, 1984) seem to recreate the marvelous sounds of rich, hot soup ladled into a spoon and placed noisily into the mouth. Poets use figurative language to encourage their audiences to see things in new ways, to clarify, and to add vividness. Kaye Starbird's imagery in "The Wind" (*The Covered Bridge House and Other Poems,* 1979) depicts a wind that is sneaky, tricky, and full of life.

One of the most useful poetry texts for my own students when they are developing listening experiences with poetry is *Knock at a Star: A Child's Introduction to Poetry* (Kennedy & Kennedy, 1999). This anthology is divided into four sections. The first section, "What Do Poems Do?," includes poems that make you smile, tell stories, send messages, share feelings, help you understand people, and start you wondering. The second section, "What's Inside a Poem?," includes poems that create images, word music, beats that repeat, likenesses, and word play. The third section, "Special Kinds of Poetry," includes limericks, takeoffs, songs, show-and-spell poems, kinders-keepers poems, and haiku. The fourth section, "Do It Yourself," includes ideas for writing poems. The divisions in the text make it quite easy to find examples of poems to read orally that highlight various experiences with poetry. One class used this book to motivate their own collection of favorite poems for listening. They added additional poems to each of the categories listed in *Knock at a Star.* They presented their poems orally to the class and described their reasons for selecting the poetry.

Music and literature also offer excellent connections for developing appreciative listening. Many picture storybooks may be used to stimulate interest in music and to motivate musical interpretations. Lamme (1990) describes an elementary music classroom in which students are involved with musical performances and picture books with musical content. During a thematic study of musical instruments, the teacher read Karen Ackerman's *Song and Dance Man* (1988), a story about a grandfather who relives his vaudeville experiences for his grandchildren, as well as other nonfiction and fiction books on musical instruments. Adults and students played various musical instruments for the class. As part of the unit, the students created a musical instrument museum, researched different types of instruments, and created a class book about music and instruments.

Additional nonfictional and fictional books that stimulate an interest in music include Jill Krementz's *A Very Young Musician* (1991), Dee Lilligard's *An Introduction to Musical Instruments: Strings* (1988), Tomie de Paola's *Sing, Pierrot, Sing* (1983), Paul Fleischman's *Rondo in C* (1988), Bruce Koscielniak's *The Story of the Incredible Orchestra* (2000), Andrea Davis Pinkney's *Duke Ellington* (1998), and Deborah Hopkinson's *A Band of Angels* (1999).

Towel (2000) explores the ways that attitudes toward reading and motivation to learn can be increased through music and literature. She states, "Music is universal. Listening to music can soothe the soul, excite the emotions, and provide a sense of cultural identity" (p. 284). Towel uses music in the following ways:

1. Have children listen to and read picture books created from songs.
2. Have children listen to and read picture books written by musicians.
3. Use music to set the mood for various stories. Listen to music before reading a story and play it in the background while the story is read. For example, play baroque music while children listen to Yolen's *Owl Moon* (1987) and ask the children to visualize the story.
4. Combine the listening to poetry with listening to music.
5. Use rhythm instruments to provide sound effects and to enhance the beat of the stories or poems.

In 1991, the bicentennial of Mozart's birth, it was particularly appropriate for students to listen to works such as "The Magic Flute" and to read and discuss books about Mozart's life. For example, Mozart's youth is explored in Catherine Brighton's *Mozart: Scenes from the Childhood of the Great Composer* (1990), F. N. Monjo's *Letters to Horseface: Young Mozart's Travels in Italy* (1975), and Lisl Weil's *Wolferl: The First Six Years in the Life of Wolfgang Amadeus Mozart, 1756–1762* (1991). Information about his adult life and career is found in Julie Downing's *Mozart Tonight* (1991), Richard Tames's *Wolfgang Amadeus Mozart* (1991), and Wendy Thompson's *Wolfgang Amadeus Mozart* (1991). Elleman and LaBarbera (1991) recommend that students use the maps in Monjo's and Thompson's books to create their own maps, pinpoint important locations, and trace Mozart's travels.

Mainstreaming

Children with learning problems require more assistance in listening for a specific purpose than do children without learning problems. Ausubel (1960) stresses using advanced organizers in order to give students a sense of direction. (The use of advanced organizers is effective in listening for directions, as well as in listening for other specific information.) An advanced organizer for use with listening for directions might stress listening for key words in the directions, such as *first, second, third,* and *finally.* It helps students understand the purpose of the directions, the reason for each step, and the relation of each step to the set of directions.

One extremely useful technique is to ask students with learning problems to close their eyes and visualize themselves performing each step of a set of directions. You may want to try this activity with a pupil-motivated task, such as leaving the building when a fire alarm sounds. The purpose of an orderly, quick exit is easy to understand because the students are so vitally involved. Ask your students to close their eyes and visualize themselves doing each step of the following: "First, when you hear the fire bell, walk quickly to the classroom door. Second, form a line and turn to the right, walking close to the hall wall. Third, walk straight

Table 4–3 Mainstreaming and listening development for children with learning disabilities

Characteristics of Children with Learning Disabilities	Teaching Techniques for Language Arts Instruction
1. Difficulty attending to task-relevant information and hyperactivity impulsiveness, and distractibility (Bryan & Bryan, 1986; Hallahan & Kauffman, 1986; Lewis & Doorlag, 1998; Richards et al., 1995).	Use considerable positive reinforcement (O'Connor, Stuck, & Wyne, 1979). Help children attend by providing a private space for learning; maintain a structured, well-organized environment; help the children focus on the task; provide immediate reinforcement; give several short assignments rather than one long assignment; let the children reduce stress by standing; provide quiet opportunities during the school day; and help children experience success (Stoodt, 1981). Read to children (Mandel, O'Connor, & Smith, 1990). Tape texts or stories (Lewis & Doorlag, 1998). Use collaborative communication to stress social endeavors (Schmidt et al., 2002).
2. Auditory modality inferior to visual modality. Deficiencies in ability to blend words and difficulties in auditory closure related to problems in word analysis (Harber, 1979, 1980; Swanson, 1980).	Provide practice in analyzing syllables and short words into phonemes and then blending phonemes into syllables and words (Williams, 1980). Focus on the order of sounds and letters in words, multisensory presentation of stimuli, considerable repetition, and varied materials (Wallace & Kauffman, 1990).
3. Difficulties comprehending main ideas in listening materials (Wong, 1979, 1980) and understanding and following directions (Lewis & Doorlag, 1998).	Precede a listening experience with questions focusing on the purpose for listening (Wong, 1979, 1980). Teach children to set purposes for listening; give them training in critical thinking through texts such as social studies and propaganda materials (Spache, 1981).

ahead and go out the double doors in the front of the building. Finally, line up outside the building next to the flagpole so I can count to make sure you are all safe." Ask the children to describe what they see and hear. After they have described each step, have them try to visualize the whole sequence. Then, have them physically perform the activity, comparing their visualizations with what they actually do. After this activity, some children claim they could even hear the bell and smell smoke!

No group in school probably has as much to gain from knowing how to listen well as children who have problems keeping pace with the normal curriculum. If these children are treated as if their only difficulty in language arts is reading, and it is taken for granted that they can listen without further instruction, they undoubtedly suffer.

Many of the activities recommended in this chapter are good for children with special needs. To identify specific characteristics of children who might have difficulty during listening activities, see the charts that list possible characteristics of children with learning disabilities (Table 4–3) or in children with mental disabilities (Table 4–4). The techniques for language arts instruction are identified from research and authorities who work with mainstreamed children.

Table 4–4 Mainstreaming and listening development for children with mental disabilities

Characteristics of Children with Mental Disabilities	Teaching Techniques for Language Arts Instruction
1. Short attention span due to failure in past efforts, to inappropriate academic expectations, or to auditory or visual distractions in the classroom (Gearheart, Weishahn, & Gearheart, 1995).	Demonstrate consistency in classroom management techniques and model desired behaviors (Hart, 1981; Ysseldyke & Algozzine, 1995). It is easier to maintain attention and to recall things that are concrete rather than abstract, familiar rather than remote, and simple rather than complex. Use language and ideas that are as concrete, familiar, and simple as possible. Eliminate visual and auditory distractions that might decrease the ability of students to attend (Gearheart et al., 1995).
2. Below-average ability to generalize, conceptualize, and perform other cognitive-related tasks (Gearheart et al., 1995).	Provide instruction that encourages cognitive development and improvement of listening comprehension by encouraging children to respond to inferential questions and to rephrase materials that they hear (Zetlin & Gallimore, 1980). Help children set their own purposes for listening by accompanying listening activities with a directed reading–thinking activity, in which children learn to make predictions based on a few cues, either pictorial or textual, then listen to confirm or disprove the prediction (Stauffer, Abrams, & Piluski, 1978). Use materials that are similar to those used for reading comprehension. Develop listening activities for main ideas, details, sequence of events, following directions, making inferences, drawing conclusions, and critical evaluation (Lerner, 2000).
3. Problems in auditory discrimination (Cook, Nolan, & Zanotti, 1980).	Try supplementing instruction with the neurological impress method, in which you and the student read aloud in unison (Cook et al., 1980). Encourage sensitivity to sounds by having the children listen with their eyes closed to environmental sounds, recorded sounds, and other teacher-made sounds. Encourage auditory attending to sounds by having the children listen to or repeat sound patterns. Encourage discrimination of sounds by having the children discriminate loud and soft sounds, high and low sounds, and near and far sounds. Encourage awareness of letter sounds by asking the children to identify words that begin with the same initial consonant or consonant blend, identify words that have the same endings or vowel sounds, and identify words that rhyme (Lerner, 2000).

For Your Development

This chapter discusses a number of methods, suggestions, and illustrative units for teaching attentive listening, listening for a specific purpose, and appreciative listening. Choose one of these topics and develop a lesson for fostering listening. If you are a student teacher or a classroom teacher, use your lesson with children. Allow the children to participate in developing their goals for the lesson and in evaluating their success. Share the activities with your language arts class. If you are not now teaching children, practice your listening lesson with a group of your peers.

Also, develop a learning center to teach some aspects of listening. Form a committee with a group of your classmates to determine objectives for the learning center and design appropriate activities for it. Use the learning center with children in a classroom, or demonstrate the use of the learning center to a group of your peers.

SUMMARY

Listening is an important and complicated skill. It is an active rather than a passive activity, and one in which students participate in their own instructional improvement. They must help set goals for their listening instruction.

The units and lessons in this chapter will help you conceptualize the listening curriculum. Because listening relates to the total language arts program, it cannot be taught in isolation. It must be taught in classroom environments that reflect those outside the classroom. Listening also must be taught continually; it is part of everyone's experience from birth to adulthood.

A complete profile of the listening abilities of children requires understanding of and evaluation of several listening components. For example, tests for auditory acuity may be required because children cannot comprehend oral communication if they cannot hear. Even children who appear to hear well may still have weak auditory perception skills. Diagnosis of these skills may be critical for children who have difficulty recognizing sounds in a reading or spelling approach that relies on phonic analysis. Several methods are available for developing the auditory perception skills necessary to distinguish differences in sounds and words.

There is a positive relationship between attentiveness and listening. Consequently, diagnosis of attentive listening skills may be crucial for a child's future achievement. A profile of listening ability includes how effectively children comprehend what they hear in a wide range of circumstances. You can use both standardized and informal tests for these diagnoses. Some of the informal tests devised by classroom teachers provide the best information for designing effective instructional programs. Develop the attentive listening skills necessary to follow directions and listen for specific purposes, such as identifying main ideas, identifying important details and sequences, and predicting outcomes.

Critical reading and listening demand careful evaluation. In developing critical reading and listening skills in children, you will find that newspapers, television, and radio offer abundant material.

Finally, include listening for appreciation in your instructional planning. Use poetry, music, stories, and plays to develop appreciative listening.

ADDITIONAL LISTENING ACTIVITIES

1. Compile a list of children's books or poems that contain rhyming elements or other interesting sound patterns such as alliteration.
2. Develop an advanced organizer that encourages children to listen for a specific purpose, such as following directions, paraphrasing the main idea of a selection, or identifying the sequential order in a paragraph or longer selection.
3. Create an auditory awareness tape that explores sounds such as nature sounds, animal sounds, street sounds, home sounds, or school sounds. Share the tape with a group of children. Ask them to identify the sounds, classify them according to location, and list other sounds that would fall into the same category.
4. With a group of children, develop a set of guidelines that will help them improve their listening ability. Ask them to identify different listening activities that occur in the day, their purpose for listening, and their requirements for that specific listening activity.

Listening Activity	Purpose	Requirements
Directions for assignments	Accurate, detailed information that I can follow.	Attention to all information
Music	Entertainment and appreciation	Relaxed environment

5. Compile a list of predictable books that rely on repetitive language patterns or repetitive story events. Develop questions that direct children's attention to the repetitive or predictable features of a book. Share the book and questions with children.
6. Select a story or content area materials that provide practice gaining meaning from a listening experience (for example, summarizing, clarifying, predicting, and verifying). Identify appropriate places in the story where children should summarize what they hear, where they might benefit from a clarifying discussion of ideas or content, where they can predict what might happen next, and where they can verify predictions. Share the listening materials with a group of your peers. Evaluate the effectiveness of the listening experience.
7. Compile a card file of poems that allow children to hear the rhythm of language, that have rich metaphors, or that have elements of surprise that delight children.
8. Read a folktale to a group of children. Map or web the characters, settings, and plot.
9. Evaluate a listening learning center. Reinforce listening for the main idea, important details, sequence, and predicting outcomes by using the learning center. The listening center described in this chapter, developed by a group of student teachers, was used in both third and fourth grades. Look carefully at each component. What listening skill is being reinforced by each? How would you introduce the center to children? How would you assist children in using the center? Do you believe the purposes of the center were met? Would you add anything else to the center?

BIBLIOGRAPHY

Ausubel, D. P. "The Use of Advanced Organizers in the Learning and Retention of Meaningful Verbal Material." *Journal of Educational Psychology* 51 (1960): 267–72.

Barrett, Thomas C. "Taxonomy of Reading Comprehension." *Reading 360 Monograph.* Lexington, Mass.: Ginn & Co., 1972.

Barrs, Myra. In "The Reader in the Writer: Reading Hall of Fame." San Francisco: International Reading Association, April 30, 2002.

Barton, James. "Conducting Effective Classroom Discussions." *Journal of Reading* 33 (February 1995): 346–50.

Bryan, Tanis H.; and Bryan, James H. *Understanding Learning Disabilities,* 3rd ed. Mountain View, Calif.: Mayfield Publishing Co., 1986.

Cheyney, Arnold B. *Teaching Reading Skills Through the Newspaper,* 2nd ed. Newark, Del.: International Reading Association, 1984.

Cook, Jimmie E.; Nolan, Gregory A.; and Zanotti, Robert J. "Treating Auditory Perception Problems: The NIM Helps." *Academic Therapy* 15 (March 1980): 473–81.

Cowen, John E. "Conversations with Poet José Garcia Villa on Teaching Poetry to Children." In *Teaching Reading Through the Arts,* edited by John E. Cowen. Newark, Del.: International Reading Association, 1983, pp. 78–87.

Dressel, J. H. "The Effects of Listening to and Discussing Different Qualities of Children's Literature on the Narrative Writing of Fifth Graders." *Research in the Teaching of English* 24 (1990): 397–414.

Durkin, Dolores. *Children Who Read Early.* New York: Teachers College Press, 1966.

Elleman, B.; and LaBarbera, K. *Book Links* 1 (1991): 38–42.

Ferrell, Christopher; and Hipp, Laura. "The TAKS Exam." *Bryan-College Station Eagle* (August 4, 2002): G1, G8.

Funk, Hal; and Funk, Gary. "Guidelines for Developing Listening Skills." *The Reading Teacher* 42 (May 1989): 660–63.

Gearheart, Bill R.; Weishahn, Mel; and Gearheart, Carol J. *The Exceptional Student in the Regular Classroom,* 6th ed. Upper Saddle River, N.J.: Merrill/Prentice Hall, 1995.

GEO News Handbook (November 11–17, 1990): 7.

Hade, D. D. "Children, Stories, and Narrative Transformations." *Research in the Teaching of English* 22 (1988): 310–25.

Hallahan, Daniel P.; and Kauffman, James M. *Exceptional Children: Introduction to Special Education.* Upper Saddle River, N.J.: Prentice Hall, 1986.

Harber, Jean R. "Auditory Perception and Reading: Another Look." *Learning Disability Quarterly* 3 (Summer 1980): 19–29.

———. "Differentiating LD and Normal Children: The Utility of Selected Perceptual and Perceptual-Motor Tests." *Learning Disability Quarterly* 2 (Spring 1979): 70–75.

Harris, Albert J.; and Sipay, Edward R. *How to Increase Reading Ability,* 9th ed. New York: Longman, 1990.

Hart, Verna. *Mainstreaming Children with Special Needs.* New York: Longman, 1981.

Johns, J. *Basic Reading Inventory,* 4th ed. Dubuque, Iowa: Kendall/Hunt, 1997.

Johnson, Doris. "Relationships Between Oral and Written Language." *School Psychology Review* 22 (1993): 595–609.

Lamme, L. "Exploring the World of Music through Picture Books." *The Reading Teacher* 44 (1990): 294–300.

Lerner, Janet W. *Children with Learning Disabilities,* 8th ed. Boston: Houghton Mifflin, 2000.

Leslie, Lauren; and Allen, Linda. "Factors That Predict Success in an Early Literacy Intervention Project." *Reading Research Quarterly* 34 (October–December 1999): 404–24.

Levesque, Jeri. "ELVES: A Read-Aloud Strategy to Develop Listening Comprehension." *The Reading Teacher* 43 (October 1989): 93–94.

Lewis, Rena; and Doorlag, Donald. *Teaching Special Students in the Mainstream,* 5th ed. Upper Saddle River, N.J.: Merrill/Prentice Hall, 1998.

Mandel, M.; O'Connor, E.; and Smith, J. "Effects of a Story Reading Program on the Literacy Development of At-Risk Kindergarten Children." *Journal of Reading Behavior* 22 (1990): 255–75.

O'Connor, Peter D.; Stuck, Gary B.; and Wyne, Marvin D. "Effects of a Short-Term Intervention Resource-Room Program on Task Orientation and Achievement." *The Journal of Special Education* 13 (Winter 1979): 375–85.

Pearson, P. David; and Fielding, Linda. "Research Update: Listening Comprehension." *Language Arts* 59 (September 1982): 617–29.

Pikulski, J. "Informal Reading Inventories." *The Reading Teacher* 43 (1990): 514–16.

Pinnell, Gay Su; and Jaggar, Angela M. "Oral Language: Speaking and Listening in the Classroom." In *Handbook of Research on Teaching the English Language Arts,* 2nd edition, edited by James Flood, Diane Lapp, James R. Squire, and Julie M. Jensen. Mahwah, New Jersey: Lawrence Erlblaum, 2003, 881–931.

Richards, Cathy; Symons, Douglas; Greene, Catherine; and Szuszkiewicz, Tara. "The Bidirectional Relationship Between Achievement and Externalizing Behavior Problems of Students with Learning Disabilities." *Journal of Learning Disabilities* 28 (January 1995): 8–17.

Schmidt, Patricia Ruggiano; Gillen, Susan; Zollo, Teresa Colabufo; and Stone, Rhaenel. "Literacy Learning and Scientific Inquiry: Children Respond." *The Reading Teacher* 55 (March 2002): 534–48.

Silvaroli, N. *Classroom Reading Inventory.* Dubuque, Iowa: William Brown, 1999.

Sipe, Lawrence R. "Talking Back and Taking Over: Using Children's Expressive Engagement During Storybook Read-Alouds." *The Reading Teacher* 55 (February 2002): 476–83.

Spache, George. *Diagnosing and Correcting Reading Disabilities.* Boston: Allyn & Bacon, 1981.

Stauffer, Russel G.; Abrams, Jules C.; and Piluski, John J. *Diagnosis, Correction, and Prevention of Reading Disability.* New York: Harper & Row, 1978.

Stoodt, Barbara D. *Reading Instruction.* Boston: Houghton Mifflin, 1981.

Swanson, H. Lee. "Auditory and Visual Vigilance in Normal and Learning Disabled Readers." *Learning Disability Quarterly* 3 (Spring 1980): 71–78.

Towell, Janet H. "Motivating Students Through Music and Literature." *The Reading Teacher* 53 (December 1999/January 2000): 284–87.

Vosniadou, S.; Pearson, P. D.; and Rogers, T. "What Causes Children's Failures to Detect Inconsistencies in Text? Representation vs. Comparison Difficulties." *Journal of Educational Psychology* 80 (1988): 27–39.

Wallace, Gerald; and Kauffman, James A. *Teaching Students with Learning and Behavior Problems.* Upper Saddle River, N.J.: Merrill/Prentice Hall, 1990.

Wepman, Joseph M. *The Auditory Discrimination Test.* Chicago: Language Research Associates, 1973.

Wepman, Joseph M.; and Morency, Anne. *The Auditory Memory Span Test.* Chicago: Language Research Associates, 1973.

Williams, Joanna P. "Teaching Decoding with an Emphasis on Phoneme Analysis and Phoneme Blending." *Journal of Educational Psychology* 72 (February 1980): 1–15.

Wong, Bernice Y. "Activating the Inactive Learner: Use of Questions/Prompts to Enhance Comprehension and Retention of Implied Information in Learning Disabled Children." *Learning Disability Quarterly* 3 (Winter 1980): 29–37.

———. "Increasing Retention of Main Ideas through Questioning Strategies." *Learning Disability Quarterly* 2 (Spring 1979): 42–47.

Woods, Mary Lynn; and Moe, Alden J. *Analytical Reading Inventory,* 5th ed. Upper Saddle River, N.J.: Merrill/Prentice Hall, 1995.

Ysseldyke, James; and Algozzine, Bob. *Special Education: A Practical Approach for Teachers,* 3rd ed. Boston: Houghton Mifflin, 1995.

Zetlin, Andrea G.; and Gallimore, Ronald. "A Cognitive Skills Training Program for Moderately Retarded Learners." *Education and Training of the Mentally Retarded* 15 (April 1980): 121–31.

CHILDREN'S LITERATURE REFERENCES

Ackerman, Karen. *Song and Dance Man.* Illustrated by Stephen Gammell. New York: Alfred A. Knopf, 1988.

Aragon, Jane Chelsea. *Winter Harvest.* Illustrated by Leslie Baker. Boston: Little, Brown, 1988.

Arnold, Caroline. *Saving the Peregrine Falcon.* Photographs by Richard R. Hewett. Minneapolis: Carolrhoda, 1985.

Beaton, Clare, compiled by. *Mother Goose Remembers.* Cambridge, Mass: Barefoot, 2000.

Bond, Michael. *A Bear Called Paddington.* Illustrated by Peggy Fortnum. Boston: Houghton Mifflin, 1960.

Brandenburg, Jim. *Sand and Fog: Adventures in Southern Africa.* New York: Walker, 1994.

Brighton, Catherine. *Mozart: Scenes from the Childhood of the Great Composer.* New York: Doubleday, 1990.

Brown, Margaret Wise. *Four Fur Feet.* Illustrated by Woodleigh Marx Hubbard. New York: Hyperion, 1994.

Browne, Anthony. *Gorilla.* New York: Watts, 1983.

Burton, Virginia Lee. *The Little House.* Boston: Houghton Mifflin, 1942.

Carroll, Lewis. *Alice's Adventures in Wonderland.* London: Macmillan, 1866, New York: Alfred A. Knopf, 1984.

Christian, Peggy. *If You Find a Rock.* Photographs by Barbara Hirsch Lember. San Diego: Harcourt, 2000.

Clark, Ann Nolan. *Secret of the Andes.* New York: Viking, 1952.

Climo, Shirley. *The Egyptian Cinderella.* Illustrated by Ruth Heller. New York: Thomas Y. Crowell Co., 1989.

Conrad, Pam. *Call Me Ahnighito.* Illustrated by Richard Egielski. New York: HarperCollins, 1995.

Cummings, Pat; and Cummings, Linda. *Talking with Adventurers.* Washington, DC.: National Geographic Society, 1998.

Curlee, Lynn. *Liberty.* New York: Atheneum, 2000.

Day, Alexandra. *Frank and Ernest on the Road.* New York: Scholastic, 1994.

de Paola, Tomie. *Sing, Pierrot, Sing.* San Diego: Harcourt Brace Jovanovich, 1983.

Downing, Julie. *Mozart Tonight.* New York: Bradbury, 1991.

Dunning, Stephen; Lueders, Edward; and Smith, Hugh. *Reflections on a Gift of Watermelon Pickle . . . and Other Modern Verse.* New York: Lothrop, Lee & Shepard, 1967.

Engel, Diana. *Josephina Hates Her Name.* New York: Morrow, 1989.

Facklam, Margery. *And Then There Was One: The Mysteries of Extinction.* Illustrated by Pamela Johnson. Boston: Little, Brown, 1990.

Fleischman, Paul. *Rondo in C.* Illustrated by Janet Wentworth. New York: Harper & Row, 1988.

Floca, Brian. *Dinosaurs at the Ends of the Earth.* New York: Dorling Kindersley, 2000.

Fritz, Jean. *Make Way for Sam Houston.* Illustrated by Elise Primavera. New York: Putnam, 1986.

Galdone, Paul. *The Little Red Hen.* Minneapolis: Seabury, 1973.

Geisert, Arthur. *Pigs from A to Z.* Boston: Houghton Mifflin, 1986.

George, Jean Craighead. *Everglades.* Illustrated by Wendell Minor. New York: HarperCollins, 1995.

Griffith, Helen V. *Grandaddy's Stars.* Illustrated by James Stevenson. New York: Greenwillow, 1995.

Grimm, Brothers. *Rapunzel.* Retold and illustrated by Paul O. Zelinsky. New York: Dutton, 1997.

Harris, Nicholas. *Airplanes: A Fold-Out Book.* Illustrated by Martin Woodward. Chicago: Rand McNally, 1995.

Highwater, Jamake. *Anpao: An American Indian Odyssey.* New York: Lippincott, 1977.

Hoban, Lillian. *Arthur's Great Valentine.* New York: Harper & Row, 1989.

Hoban, Tana. *Shapes, Shapes, Shapes.* New York: Greenwillow, 1986.

Hopkinson, Deborah. *A Band of Angels.* Illustrated by Raul Colon. New York: Atheneum, 1999.

Hutchins, Pat. *Changes, Changes.* New York: Macmillan, 1971.

Johnson, Rebecca L. *Braving the Frozen Frontier: Women Working in Antarctica.* Minneapolis: Lerner, 1997.

Kellogg, Steven. *Tallyho, Pinkerton!* New York: Dial Press, 1982.

Kennedy, X. J.; and Kennedy, Dorothy M. *Knock at a Star: A Child's Introduction to Poetry.* Boston: Little, Brown, 1999.

———, selected by. *Talking Like the Rain: A Read-to-Me Book of Poems.* Illustrated by Jane Dyer. Boston: Little, Brown, 1992.

Koscielniak, Bruce. *The Story of the Incredible Orchestra.* New York: Houghton Mifflin, 2000.

Krementz, Jill. *A Very Young Musician.* New York: Simon & Schuster, 1991.

Lauber, Patricia. *Volcano: The Eruption and Healing of Mount St. Helens.* New York: Bradbury, 1986.

Lear, Edward. *The Complete Nonsense Book.* New York: Dodd, Mead, 1846, 1871, 1946.

———. *The Owl and the Pussycat.* Illustrated by Jan Brett. New York: Putnam, 1991.

Lilligard, Dee. *An Introduction to Musical Instruments: Strings.* Chicago: Children's Press, 1988.

Lindbergh, Reeve. *The Day the Goose Got Loose.* Illustrated by Steven Kellogg. New York: Dial Press, 1990.

Lobel, Arnold. *The Random House Book of Mother Goose.* New York: Random House, 1986.

Marks, Alan, edited by. *Over the Hills and Far Away: A Book of Nursery Rhymes.* New York: North-South, 1994.

McCloskey, Robert. *Time of Wonder.* New York: Viking, 1957.

McCord, David. *Far and Few: Rhymes of the Never Was and Always Is.* Boston: Little, Brown, 1952.

Millard, Anne. *A Street Through Time: A 12,000-Year Walk Through History.* Illustrated by Steve Noon. New York: Dorling Kindersley, 1998.

Miller, Debbie S. *A Wooly Mammoth Journey.* Illustrated by Jon Van Zyle. Boston: Little, Brown, 2001.

Monjo, F. N. *Letters to Horseface: Young Mozart's Travels in Italy.* Illustrated by Don Bolognese and Elaine Raphael. New York: Puffin, 1975.

Mora, Pat. *Tomás and the Library Lady.* Illustrated by Raul Conon. New York: Knopf, 1997.

Pinkney, Andrea Davis. *Duke Ellington.* Illustrated by Brian Pinkney. New York: Hyperion, 1998.

Potter, Beatrix. *The Tale of Peter Rabbit.* New York: Warne, 1902.

Prelutsky, Jack. *A Gopher in the Garden.* New York: Macmillan, 1966.

———, selected by. *The Random House Book of Poetry for Children.* Illustrated by Arnold Lobel. New York: Random House, 1983.

———, selected by. *Read-Aloud Rhymes for the Very Young.* Illustrated by Marc Brown. New York: Alfred A. Knopf, 1986.

Raschka, Chris. *Yo! Yes?* New York: Orchard, 1993.

Raskin, Lawrie; and Pearson, Debora. *My Sahara Adventure: 52 Days by Camel.* Toronto: Annick, 1998.

Sattler, Helen Roney. *Giraffes, the Sentinels of the Savannas.* Illustrated by Christopher Santoro. New York: Lothrop, Lee & Shepard, 1989.

Scieszka, Jon. *The True Story of the 3 Little Pigs.* Illustrated by Lane Smith. New York: Viking, 1989.

Sendak, Maurice. *Where the Wild Things Are.* New York: Harper & Row, 1963.

Seuss, Dr. *The Cat in the Hat.* New York: Random House, 1957.

Silverstein, Shel. *Where the Sidewalk Ends.* New York: Harper & Row, 1974.

Simmons, Jane. *Quack, Daisy, Quack!* Boston: Little, Brown, 2002.

Simon, Seymour. *New Questions and Answers About Dinosaurs.* Illustrated by Jennifer Dewey. New York: Morrow, 1990.

Snyder, Zilpha. *Today Is Saturday.* New York: Atheneum, 1969.

Starbird, Kaye. *The Covered Bridge House and Other Poems.* New York: Four Winds, 1979.

Stevenson, R. L. *A Child's Garden of Verses.* New York: Longman, Green, 1885.

Tames, Richard. *Wolfgang Amadeus Mozart.* New York: Watts, 1991.

Tejima, Keizaburo. *Fox's Dream.* New York: Philomel, 1987.

Thompson, Wendy. *Wolfgang Amadeus Mozart.* New York: Viking, 1991.

Walter, Mildred Pitts. *Brother to the Wind.* Illustrated by Diane and Leo Dillon. New York: Lothrop, Lee & Shepard, 1985.

Weil, Lisl. *Wolferl: The First Six Years in the Life of Wolfgang Amadeus Mozart, 1756–1762.* New York: Holiday, 1991.

Westcott, Nadine. *Peanut Butter and Jelly: A Play Rhyme.* New York: Dutton, 1987.

Whelan, Gloria. *Homeless Bird.* New York: HarperCollins, 2000.

White, E. B. *Charlotte's Web.* Illustrated by Garth Williams. New York: Harper & Row, 1952.

Williams, Margery. *The Velveteen Rabbit.* Illustrated by William Nicholson. New York: Doubleday, 1922, 1958.

Yolen, Jane. *Owl Moon.* Illustrated by John Schoenherr. New York: Philomel, 1987.

———. *The Three Bears Rhyme Book.* Illustrated by Jane Dyer. San Diego: Harcourt Brace Jovanovich, 1987.

Yorinks, Arthur. *Hey, Al.* Illustrated by Richard Egielski. New York: Farrar, Straus & Giroux, 1986.

Zimelman, Nathan. *Treed by a Pride of Irate Lions.* Illustrated by Toni Goffe. Boston: Little, Brown, 1990.

Reading and the Language Arts

After completing this chapter on reading and the language arts, you will be able to:

1. Identify and describe reading approaches that are supported by research.

2. Identify and describe the best practices associated with the teaching of reading.

3. Identify and describe approaches that increase students' phonemic awareness.

4. Describe and develop approaches that increase students' understanding of vocabulary.

5. Describe and develop approaches that increase students' opportunities to use their reading and vocabulary skills when reading real texts.

6. Describe and develop approaches that help students improve their comprehension.

7. Develop a series of lessons that proceed from a vocabulary web, to a literacy web or semantic organizer, to a plot diagram, and finally to a guided discussion.

8. Develop questioning strategies that enhance different types of comprehension and understanding.

9. Describe and develop approaches that encourage students to make predictions about what they read.

10. Develop a unit focusing on reading and literacy.

11. Describe the issues related to the assessment of reading.

12. Evaluating instructional program.

*C*onsiderable confusion and debate currently surrounds ideas about the most effective ways to teach and to assess reading instruction. School districts or even whole states may mandate approaches to reading instruction and to assessment. Reports such as those cited by Duffy and Hoffman (1999) conclude that there is no perfect method for reading instruction. Instead Duffy and Hoffman conclude: "The answer is not in the method; it is in the teacher. It has been repeatedly established that the best instruction results when combinations of methods are orchestrated by a teacher who decides what to do in light of children's needs. Hence, reading instruction effectiveness lies not with a single program or method but, rather, with a teacher who thoughtfully and analytically integrates various programs, materials, and methods as the situation demands" (p. 11). Duffy and Hoffman then describe exemplary teachers who use a combination of approaches including basal readers, authentic literature, and phonemic awareness instruction as needed by the students. As noted in these descriptions, the most effective teachers use a balanced approach to reading instruction. They teach phonemic awareness, but they also provide instruction in which students use their developing phonemic skills to read literature and to write meaningful compositions.

Organizations such as the International Reading Association also emphasize the importance of an excellent classroom teacher who is trained in a variety of reading methodologies. For example, the International Reading Association (2000) describes the qualities of excellent classroom teachers:

1. Teachers understand reading and writing development and believe that all children can learn to read and to write.

2. Teachers continually assess children's individual progress and relate children's reading instruction to children's previous experiences.

3. Teachers know a variety of ways to teach reading, when to use each method, and how to combine the methods into an effective instructional program.
4. Teachers offer a variety of materials and texts for children to read.
5. Teachers use flexible grouping strategies to tailor instruction to individual students.
6. Teachers are good reading coaches who provide help strategically.

Best Practices for Reading Instruction

In this chapter we discuss some of the best practices revealed by reading research. As we proceed through a discussion of and applications for these practices, we will discover that many of these practices have been described in other chapters of this text. There are several sources in which teachers can search for best practices. For example, Zemelman, Daniels, and Hyde (1998) summarize the best practices that relate to reading instruction. They divide these practices by methodologies that should be increased such as reading aloud to students, providing time for independent reading, allowing children to make their own choices for some of their reading materials, exposing children to a wide range of literature, teaching modeling of the reading process, and emphasizing comprehension during instruction.

They emphasize the need to teach reading as a process by using strategies that activate prior knowledge, helping students to make the best predictions, structuring help during reading, providing after-reading applications, grouping by interests or book choices, encouraging silent reading followed by discussion, teaching skills in the context of meaningful literature, writing before and after reading, and measuring success by students' reading habits, attitudes, and comprehension.

One effective teaching practice is exposing children to a wide range of literature.

They also emphasize methodologies that should be decreased such as the exclusive emphasis on whole-class activities, teacher selection of all reading materials, relying only on selections in basal readers, providing primarily instruction on reading subskills such as phonics and word analysis, teaching reading as a one-step act, relying on solitary seatwork, teaching isolated skills through workbooks or drills, providing little or no opportunities for writing, evaluating reading through low-level subskills, and measuring the success of the reading program only on test scores.

In *Classrooms That Work: They Can All Read and Write*, Cunningham and Allington (2003) describe practices that work, including motivating students, building foundations for word attack strategies and vocabulary, developing comprehension, providing guided reading, integrating science and social studies materials into the reading program, choosing effective assessment, and giving extra support for struggling readers.

One of the most quoted sources for best practices is the *Report of the National Reading Panel* (2000). This report concluded the following: Phonemic awareness instruction (phonics) improves students' phonemic awareness, reading, and spelling. Teaching reading fluency through such approaches as guided repeated oral reading and independent silent reading are helpful. Teaching comprehension is critically important to the development of children's reading skills. Both oral and printed vocabulary are essential for the development of reading skills. In the area of comprehension the *Report of the National Reading Panel* reported the following best practices: comprehension monitoring, in which students learn to become aware of their own understanding of the material; cooperative learning, in which students learn reading strategies; use of graphic and semantic organizers to assist comprehension; question answering, in which students answer questions posed by the teacher and receive immediate feedback; question generation, in which students ask themselves questions about aspects of the story; story structure, in which students are taught to use the structure of the story to help them recall the story content and to answer questions; and summarizing, in which students are taught to integrate ideas and to generalize from the text information.

Another source that is useful for assessing best practices is Cole's *Misreading Reading: The Bad Science That Hurts Children* (2000). Cole presents claims made by various studies and then discusses what the research actually shows. For example, one of the claims is that a difficulty in understanding that words are made up of sounds is a primary cause of poor reading. Cole cites research that shows that children trained in phonological awareness make significantly greater gains in phonemic awareness but not in sentence and paragraph comprehension. Again, most of these best practices support the need for a balanced reading program rather than a program that emphasizes only one phase of the complexities required to become a good reader.

The International Reading Association through its newspaper *Reading Today* ("Examining Evidence," 2002) reviewed best practices and developed the following position statement:

1. Teach reading for authentic meaning-making literacy experiences for pleasure, to be informed, and to perform a task.
2. Use high-quality literature.
3. Integrate a comprehensive word study/phonics program into reading/writing instruction.
4. Use multiple texts that link and expand concepts.
5. Balance teacher- and student-led discussions.
6. Build a whole-class community that emphasizes important concepts and builds background knowledge.
7. Work with students in small groups while other students read and write about what they have read.
8. Give students plenty of time to read in class.

9. Give students direct instruction in decoding and comprehension strategies that promote independent reading. Balance direct instruction, guided instruction, and independent learning.
10. Use a variety of assessment techniques to inform instruction. (p. 4)

As you read this position statement, notice that the position toward best practices in the teaching of reading includes the total language arts. There is the use of high-quality literature, the integration of word study into writing instruction, teacher- and student-led discussions, time to read in class, balanced instruction, and a variety of assessment techniques. These best practices are developed throughout this textbook.

For Your Development

Choose one of the sources discussed in this section on best practices. Summarize the findings reported in these sources. With your classmates, develop your own list of best practices that are supported by reading research. Also, develop a list of practices that are not supported by reading research. Consider what practices you would like to use in your own classroom.

Approaches That Increase Phonemic Awareness and Develop Understanding of Phonics

Most early childhood programs include activities that stress the developing understanding of letter–sound relationships. Many of the reading readiness activities found in prekindergarten and kindergarten classes stress reading aloud to children in order to have them develop an ear for language, an increased oral vocabulary, and a respect for the spoken word. This type of instruction is frequently believed to be an introduction to the teaching of phonics as well as a readiness for reading instruction.

According to the *Report of the National Reading Panel,* "Phonics instruction is a way of teaching reading that stresses the acquisition of letter–sound correspondences and their use in reading and spelling. The primary focus of phonics instruction is to help beginning readers understand how letters are linked to sounds (phonemes), to form letter–sound correspondences and spelling patterns and to help them learn how to apply this knowledge in their reading" (2000, p. 8).

Phonics can be taught in any of several ways, including synthetic phonics, which teaches students to convert letters into sounds and then blend the sounds into words; analytic phonics, which teaches students to analyze letter–sound relationships in previously learned words; embedded phonics, which teaches phonics skills through the context of their reading; and analogy phonics, which teaches students unfamiliar words through recognizing the rime segment of a familiar word (*brick* is recognized by the known word *kick*). Phonics is also taught through spelling by teaching students to spell words phonemically.

Disagreements abound about the amount and types of phonics that should be taught. For example, Routman (1996) presents what she calls "commonsense views of phonics" that may be of value to teachers as they approach phonics instruction:

1. Phonics is a tool in the reading process and not an end in itself.
2. Phonics knowledge is necessary to be a competent reader and writer/speller.

3. It is easier to decode a word that you have heard before and know the meaning of.
4. Phonics can be taught and reinforced during shared reading and writing.
5. Phonics can be assessed and taught during writing time.
6. Most of the time set aside for reading in school should be spent reading meaningful texts. (pp. 93–95)

Many of the listening activities discussed in Chapter 4 will be of assistance when developing activities designed to improve phonemic awareness. These activities include auditory perception, auditory awareness, and auditory discrimination. The recommendations and activities included under auditory discrimination of sounds, words, and rhymes and auditory discrimination of beginning, ending, and middle sounds are especially useful for the prekindergarten and kindergarten classrooms.

Young children should have many opportunities to listen to and say rhymes, poetry, and riddles. The following books encourage students to listen for and to use their developing phonemic awareness capabilities:

Jim Aylesworth's *Old Black Fly* (1992)

Byron Barton's *The Wee Little Woman* (1995)

Denise Fleming's *In the Tall, Tall Grass* (1991)

Lloyd Moss's *Zin! Zin! Zin!: A Violin* (1995)

Michael Rosen's *We're Going on a Bear Hunt* (1989)

Walt Whippo's *Little White Duck* (2000)

Jane Yolen's *Off We Go!* (2000)

Jane Yolen's *The Three Bears Rhyme Book* (1987)

Approaches That Increase Understanding of Vocabulary

Studies show that by the time a child with normal language development is four or five years old, he or she has acquired an oral vocabulary of more than 5,000 words (Bear et al., 2000). This child has mastered the word order in English and can recite the days of the week and the months of the year. But, even these children need many opportunities to expand their understandings of the multiple meanings of words and gain an increasing knowledge of new words. Juel (2002) reported that lower ability preschool and kindergarten children are extremely behind in their vocabulary development. They cannot produce such vocabulary-related skills as identifying synonyms and antonyms.

Juel (2002) found that children need a balanced instructional approach for vocabulary to develop. The *Report of the National Reading Panel* (2000) found in their studies of best reading practices that vocabulary should be taught both directly and indirectly. It requires numerous exposures through such practices as exposure to and discussion of words in literature. Studies in reading support both teacher-directed instruction in vocabulary, in which teachers teach words through such activities as associating new words with a variety of concepts, contrasting words to discover relationships, and grouping words into semantic categories. Other studies support the acquisition of vocabulary through incidental reading and that wide reading enhances vocabulary development. Consequently, readers learn many new words by reading them in context. Marzano and Marzano (1988) state their position on the debate between direct and indirect instruction of vocabulary: "A safe middle position appears to be that wide reading should be the primary vehicle for vocabulary learning, yet some selected words can be the focus of direct vocabulary instruction" (p. 11). Many educators believe that the ease of gaining incidental vocabulary knowledge depends on the quality of the writing in the books read by students.

A review of vocabulary research conducted by Carr and Wixon (1986) provides four guidelines for vocabulary instruction and suggests some beneficial strategies. First, they state that instruction should help students relate new vocabulary to their previous experience and background knowledge. (This principle for vocabulary development is similar to schema theory, which is discussed later in this chapter). Activities in which students are asked to think about personal experiences with a word and to respond through written or oral associations are effective. For example, students can make individual vocabulary cards on which they associate words and their definitions with clues from their own experiences.

Second, vocabulary instruction should help students develop word knowledge that extends beyond learning a word in a single context or memorizing a definition. Techniques that allow students to elaborate their word knowledge include examining relationships among new words, introducing words in multiple contexts, introducing new vocabulary and related concepts together, grouping words for semantic categories, developing vocabulary webs, and comparing features of words to decide if the words are mutually exclusive.

Third, instruction should encourage students to become actively involved as they learn the new vocabulary and construct meanings for the new words. Such activities allow students to discuss and explore the meanings of the words rather than merely memorize definitions given to them by the teacher.

Fourth, instruction should develop strategies that students can use to learn the meanings of new words when they are reading independently without adult involvement. Effective strategies teach students a variety of methods for acquiring word meanings, enhance students' abilities to monitor their own understanding of new words, and encourage students to change or modify their strategies for understanding new words when necessary. Carr and Wixon (1986) state that "students become independent learners through instruction that gradually shifts the responsibility for developing new word meanings from the teacher to the student" (p. 592). For example, teachers could instruct students in how to use context cues when the students read independently and then teach them ways to make sure that they actually know what a word means.

Vocabulary Development in the Lower-Elementary Grades

Many concept books also teach vocabulary because the authors of the books rely on well-chosen illustrations to help children grasp both concepts and vocabulary such as *red* and *circle*, and more abstract concepts such as prepositions (*through*, for example) and antonyms (*fast* and *slow*, for example). Concept books come in various degrees of difficulty so teachers should consider a child's level of understanding when selecting, sharing, and discussing the vocabulary in concept books.

Young children can learn the vocabulary and concepts related to colors and shapes through such books as Eric Carle's *My First Book of Colors* (1974), in which children match a block of color with the picture of an object illustrated in that color. In *Of Colors and Things* (1989), Tana Hoban uses both colors and photographs of objects to invite children to search for matching colors. In *Circles, Triangles, and Squares* (1974), Hoban uses large black-and-white photographs to show common shapes in everyday objects. In *Shapes, Shapes, Shapes* (1986), Hoban uses photographs to depict such shapes as circles, rectangles, and ovals. She also uses photographs of familiar objects in *So Many Circles, So Many Squares* (1998). In

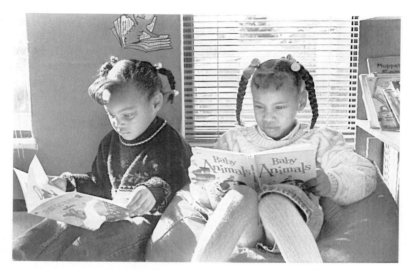

Concept books can increase vocabulary and concept development for young readers.

Over, Under and Through and Other Spatial Concepts (1973) the photographs show children jumping over fire hydrants, walking under outstretched arms, and crawling through large pipes.

Donald Crews familiarizes children with numerous concepts in *Freight Train* (1978). The cars of the train are different colors, and the movement of the train shows concepts such as *across* trestles, *through* cities, and *into* tunnels. The pictures encourage understanding of spatial concepts and of opposites, such as darkness and daylight. Brian Floca uses trucks at an airport in *Five Trucks* (1999) to introduce concepts such as *large* and *heavy*, *small* and *quick*, and *long* and *straight*. The activities of the trucks are shown as airplanes are preparing for takeoff.

Vocabulary and concepts related to seasonal changes are important in children's lives. Anne Rockwell helps children understand seasonal changes and appropriate activities for each season in *First Comes Spring* (1985), while Lisa Westberg Peters in *October Smiled Back* (1996) uses the twelve months of the year to help children understand concepts and vocabulary related to changes in nature. Nancy Tafuri encourages concept and language development with large illustrations of animals in her almost wordless book *Early Morning in the Barn* (1983). These concept books offer pleasure as well as important learning experiences associated with vocabulary development. All of the books should be used to encourage children to talk about the concepts and to identify their own experiences with the concepts.

Individualized dictionaries and vocabulary notebooks can accompany the discussion of concept books. Because students in the lower grades gain considerable vocabulary knowledge from picture books, the students may add their own illustrations to their personalized dictionaries and notebooks. For example, after reading and discussing any of the concept books previously mentioned, they may create their own pictures and text. Pat Hutchins's *What Game Shall We Play?* (1990) encourages many individualized dictionary responses as readers follow the various animals *across* the fields, *among* the grass, *over* the wall, and *into* the hole. Now they can create pages that show themselves using the vocabulary.

Children in the lower-elementary grades benefit from vocabulary activities that encourage their involvement in the vocabulary through activities such as interacting with repetitive language and acting out descriptive words and passages. Barrs (2002) found that reading aloud showed children the language, and that drama increased both their understanding of the text and their imagination. Teachers may use several sources for such an activity. For example, while reading Michael Rosen's *We're Going on a Bear Hunt* (1989) to kindergarten or first-grade students, emphasize the repetitive language and the descriptive words. Show the students that the illustrator, Helen Oxenbury, places the repetitive verses on black-and-white backgrounds and the descriptive action words on colored backgrounds. Ask the students: "Why would an illustrator choose both black-and-white and colored backgrounds in the same book? How should we read this story to show the differences between black-and-white and colored backgrounds?" After orally reading the first series of repetitive text, encourage the students to join in the reading. On the colored action pages ask them to predict the sounds that the family will make as they go through each obstacle. Ask them to notice that each action is repeated three times and that each line increases in size. Ask the students: "Why would an author increase the size of the letters? How could we use our voices and actions to show this increasing size?" Then have the students act out the lines.

Children enjoy joining in the repetitive language and acting out the text using Doreen Cronin's *Click, Clack, Moo: Cows That Type* (2000). Helen Cooper's *Pumpkin Soup* (1999) encourages children to respond to the plight of a cat, a squirrel, and a duck as they try to concoct the best soup that anyone has ever tasted. Barry Moser's retelling of *The Three Little Pigs* (2001) is an ideal tale for children to join in the language through such lines as "No, no, no, not by the hair of my chinny chin chin" and "Then I'll huff and I'll puff and I'll blow your house in!" Children enjoy dramatizing this traditional tale. These techniques are excellent for fostering children's love of literature as well as developing their understanding of vocabulary.

Vocabulary Development in the Middle and Upper-Elementary Grades

Many teachers use journal writing and learning logs to help students use the vocabulary they learn in reading and spelling. Nonfictional sources provide excellent materials for learning logs because students can focus on specific content and vocabulary knowledge gained from informational books, biographies, and autobiographies. Students can write about what they liked best in the book, what information they believe is important, how they will use that information in the future, what new vocabulary words and concepts would be important for them, and what questions still need to be answered or researched. Nonfictional sources frequently include a technical vocabulary that is specific to that subject. For example, after reading Patricia Lauber's *Painters of the Caves* (1998), students may have additional questions that they will want to research and certainly vocabulary words such as *aurochs* (ancestors of today's cattle), *Cro-Magnon* (first modern humans to live in Europe), and *Ice Age*. There are also simpler vocabulary words such as *tundra* and *bison* that may or may not be new to the students.

Teaching students to use context clues is probably one of the most important strategies to increase knowledge of vocabulary and improve comprehension of what is read. Most reading methods books emphasize the development of context clues. The following examples provide some sources that teachers may use to model how to use the various types of context clues:

1. *Definition:* The word is defined within the content of the book. An example of a definition is used by Patricia Lauber in *Painters of the Caves* (1998): "With each change in climate, plant life changed. As the ice advanced, forests gave way to grasslands, then

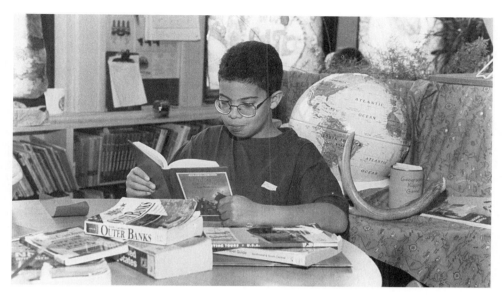

Learning how to use context clues when reading increases student comprehension and vocabulary.

grasslands became *tundra,* frozen land where only sedges, mosses, and lichens grew" (p. 11).

2. *Comparison:* Contrasting words help the reader identify unfamiliar words: "A *fossil* can be many things. The footprints of Stone Age artists who worked in the caves are fossils, as are the footprints of children who played there. But most fossils are skulls, bones, and teeth" (p. 9).

3. *Summary:* The unfamiliar word is a summary of the ideas that precede the word: "Mountain glaciers reach down into valleys. Sheets of ice spread over the land. Once-green lands are swallowed by ice a mile or more thick. Winds blowing over the ice reach far away. Winters are long and cold. Summers are short and cool. These times are known as *ice ages*" (p. 11).

4. *Familiar expression:* Knowledge of a familiar expression helps the reader identify the unknown word: Children who are familiar with space travel will have few difficulties when reading Bryon Barton's *I Want to Be an Astronaut* (1988).

5. *Experience:* The reader's background aids in identifying an unknown word. In *Storms* (1989), Seymour Simon encourages readers to use their knowledge of jet planes and vacuum cleaners to understand a tornado and to clarify the actions of a tornado: "Sometimes a thunderstorm gives birth to a tornado. The wind blows hard and trees bend. Heavy rains or hailstones fall. Lightning and thunder rip the dark sky, and a howling roar like hundreds of jet planes fills the air" (unnumbered).

6. *Synonym:* A known synonym can help the reader identify an unknown word. Authors often repeat a term or idea by referring to a synonym. Sometimes the first word is known and the synonym is unknown, although authors can change this order. In *Dragonflies* (1989) Molly McLaughlin states: "From a special pouch at the front of the male's abdomen, she receives some of his reproductive cells, or sperm" (p. 14); "This larva, or nymph, is quite different from its colorful flying parents" (p. 16); "As the time for the big change, or metamorphosis, comes closer, the nymph's behavior changes too" (p. 22).

After teachers model and discuss these various techniques to help students identify vocabulary in context, they can search for their own examples. They may choose to select one author and search for how the author uses context clues. For example, Seymour Simon, Kathryn Lasky, Patricia Lauber, and Millicent Selsam are all authors who use various context clues to help readers understand more technical content.

Approaches That Develop Comprehension

Most reading authorities agree that comprehension is the ultimate goal of the reading program. All of the strategies that we have previously discussed are quite worthless if students do not gain meaning from what is read. *The Report of the National Reading Panel* (2000) indicates that best practices for increasing comprehension include using graphic and semantic organizers including story maps, in which readers make graphic representations of what they read to assist in their comprehension); questioning and answering, in which teachers pose questions and students receive immediate feedback; questioning, in which readers ask themselves questions; story structures, in which students are taught to use the structure of the story to help them recall the story; and summarization, in which students are taught to integrate ideas and generalize from the text.

Schema Theory

Schema theory has valuable implications for teachers of reading. According to schema theory, the basis for comprehending and remembering ideas in stories and other types of texts is a reader's schema, or organized knowledge. A reader uses prior knowledge of various kinds of texts, knowledge of the world, and the clues supplied by a text to create meaning. According to Anderson (1985), "in schema-theoretic terms, a reader comprehends a message when he is able to bring to mind a schema that gives a good account of the objects and events described in the message" (p. 372).

Prior knowledge and past experiences are extremely important for comprehending and appreciating all types of stories. Afflerbach (1990) found that readers automatically construct main ideas when they have prior knowledge of the content. Likewise, Gauntt (1990) showed that prior knowledge of both text structures and content improves comprehension of expository text. Reading stories to students helps them develop schemas for story structures, vocabulary, language patterns, and other literary elements. These sets of knowledge and expectations are valuable when the students face similar structures, vocabularies, and literary elements in their independent reading. Consequently, teachers and parents should read, tell stories, and talk about a wide variety of literature. To provide the maximum knowledge base, make sure that the literature includes a wide variety of genres and language patterns.

Schema theory emphasizes the importance of activating relevant prior knowledge and helping students fill in gaps in knowledge before they read. Valuable instructional strategies include prereading discussions that review prior knowledge, provide information to help students use their prior knowledge, and identify any gaps in knowledge. If you identify any gaps, or if prerequisite knowledge is lacking, remedy this situation before the students approach the literature. Make use of maps, pictures, films, and historical time lines.

As an example, prior to reading Patricia MacLachlan's *Sarah, Plain and Tall* (1985), focus prereading discussions on prairie life in the 1800s to activate previous knowledge and identify knowledge gaps. You can ask the students to close their eyes and pretend they are living in the 1800s. They are sitting on the front steps of a pioneer house located in one of the prairie states. Ask them to use their imaginations and describe what they see when they look toward the prairie. (They should see prairie grass on gently rolling plains, wheat fields, dirt roads, and expanses of space in which the prairie meets the sky. If there are vehicles on the road, they should be drawn by horses.) Next, ask the students to turn around and describe the house. They can see inside because the door is open. The author of *Sarah, Plain and Tall* frequently contrasts the prairie setting and Sarah's familiar Maine coast. Ask the students to close their eyes and pretend they are on the Maine coast. When they look toward the ocean, what do they see? When they look toward the land, what do they see? Such prereading discussions will help the students understand the settings, conflicts, characters, and comparisons in the story.

Illustrated books are especially good for activating prior knowledge or introducing a time or place. For example, Kathy Jakobsen's paintings of the frontier setting in Reeve Lindbergh's *Johnny Appleseed* (1990) provide details of life in the late 1700s and early 1800s. Wendell Minor's paintings for Diane Siebert's *Heartland* (1989) develop the rural nature of a more contemporary Middle West. Ted Lewin's illustrations for Florence Heide and Judith Gilliland's *The Day of Ahmed's Secret* (1990) provide an excellent introduction to Cairo, Egypt, while Catherine Stock's illustrations in *Armien's Fishing Trip* (1990) introduce students to an African village and the life of people who earn their living from the sea. Alice Provensen's *The Buck Stops Here: The Presidents of the United States* (1990) provides a pictorial representation of the personal and political facts and historical events associated with the presidents of the United States. This book is especially good as an introduction to the time frames of historical fiction selections. Judith St. George's *So You Want to Be President?* (2000) provides a more humorous view of the presidency.

You may also use picture books and easier stories to activate students' prior knowledge or prepare them for the story structures of more difficult texts. For example, use Selina Hastings's *Sir Gawain and the Loathly Lady* (1985) and Margaret Hodges's *Saint George and the Dragon* (1984) to activate prior knowledge or introduce new information about legends, quests, and chivalry before students read longer legends about King Arthur.

Semantic Mapping or Webbing. Many of the approaches for using semantic maps or webs were introduced or will be introduced elsewhere in this text. These approaches are equally beneficial for the reading class. For example, the webbing of literature elements for *Mufaro's Beautiful Daughters* and *Catherine, Called Birdy*, developed in Chapter 6, is an excellent way to improve understanding and stimulate discussion in the reading class. In this section we consider the use of webs for vocabulary development and for creating units around the thematic area of World War II.

WEBBING VOCABULARY.   Webbing the important vocabulary from a book is appropriate at any grade level. The vocabulary and text, however, vary with the grade level. To develop a semantic web around the relevant vocabulary in a piece of literature, place the title of the book in the center of the chalkboard. On arms extending from the center, place the important words from the story. Use a brainstorming session to help the students fill in synonyms and definitions. You may use this activity as a prereading vocabulary introduction. You may also use it to extend understandings. Ask the students to consider exact meanings for the words while reading the story. Have them select terms that seem closest to the meaning developed in the story, add new words or even phrases obtained from the story, and use the words identified in the semantic web for story comprehension.

The following example uses a semantic web with the vocabulary from Tomie de Paola's *The Legend of the Bluebonnet* (1983). Notice the progression from a vocabulary web, to discussion of context clues that relate to the vocabulary words, and finally to a plot diagram that reinforces the vocabulary words and places them in the context of the total book. This lesson was developed and taught with lower achieving fifth- and sixth-grade students (Norton, 1987). However, you can use the procedure for all grades and all ability levels or for other books.

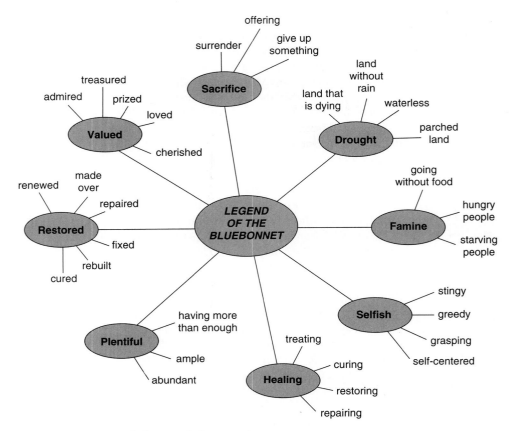

FIGURE 5–1   Vocabulary Web for a Book

Before reading *The Legend of the Bluebonnet*, draw a web on the chalkboard similar to that shown in Figure 5–1. Place the title of the book in the center and extend the vocabulary words *drought, famine, selfish, healing, plentiful, restored, valued,* and *sacrifice.* Before reading, introduce the words and brainstorm with the students to define the words and find synonyms. However, do not complete the extended vocabulary during this first experience. Add meanings after reading and discussing the book. (Note that your final web may be larger. During and following the reading, you may wish to add words. For example, you and the group may consider *Comanche, shaman,* and *miraculous* important for understanding.)

Following the introductory brainstorming, read the story and discuss the vocabulary words within the context of the story. In this story, cause-and-effect relationships as well as opposite meanings are important. For example, write the first paragraph on the chalkboard with the vocabulary word *drought* underlined:

"Great Spirits, the land is dying, your People are dying, too" the line of dancers sang. "Tell us what we have done to anger you. End this <u>drought</u>. Save your people. Tell us what we must do so you will send the rain that will bring back life." (p. 1, unnumbered)

After reading the paragraph, ask the students to identify, circle, and discuss the words that mean *drought:* "land is dying." Next, have them identify, circle, and discuss the words that indicate why the drought must end and show the dangerous consequences of the drought: "Save your people," "bring back life." Now, have them discuss the consequences of drought if something that would save the people and bring back life was requested by the

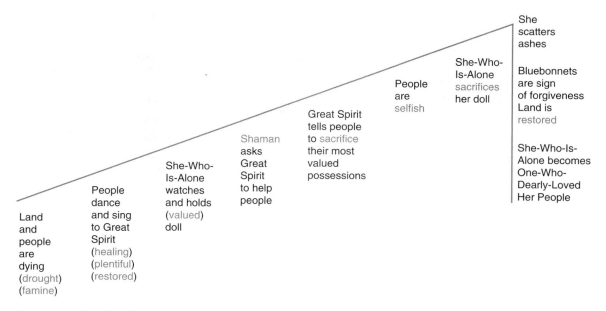

FIGURE 5–2   Plot Development Highlighting Vocabulary

most powerful person in the tribe. Discuss picture clues that show the hot, yellow sun, and the dry, brown earth. As the reading of the story proceeds, extend the meaning of *drought* to include cause-and-effect relationships:

> *drought → famine, starving*
> *rain → grass, plenty*

and opposite meanings:

> *drought → rain; earth will be green and alive*

Continue this procedure until all the vocabulary words are discussed in context. Now view the web again, add terms if necessary, and identify words previously considered for their meanings.

Finally, draw a plot diagram and encourage students to use as many of the vocabulary words as appropriate when they place the important incidents from the story on this structure. Figure 5–2 shows a plot diagram developed with sixth-grade students. The underlined words were identified by the students during this teacher-led activity. The words in parentheses are vocabulary words added by the teacher during the plotting experience. For example, when the group did not identify *drought* in the beginning problem, the teacher said: "What words did you use for the land and the people are dying?"

This approach develops comprehension of vocabulary, emphasizes the importance of context and picture clues in deriving meaning from text, and relates the vocabulary back to the plot of the story. These interrelationships are especially important for poor readers, who may not make the connections.

WEBBING AND THEMATIC UNITS.   Webbing is especially beneficial when developing focus or thematic units that are popular with both literature-based programs and programs that integrate various content areas. Webbing encourages students to identify areas of interest, brainstorm ideas, identify literature selections and other materials that are appropriate for each area, conduct research, authenticate fictional texts through nonfictional sources, work together in groups to report information back to the class, and consider ways in which the thematic unit may integrate the language arts. Because webbing allows students to take part in planning the unit, the technique can motivate interest, reading, and research.

The first steps taken in webbing a unit are to identify topics that the students and teachers would like to investigate, to consider literature that they would like to read under each topic, and to identify ways of sharing their knowledge. For example, the World War II topic identified in Figure 5–3 was chosen by teachers and students in several sixth-grade classrooms as a topic of interest and one that they could use to integrate reading, literature, history, art, and music. Interest was especially high because one of the television stations was highlighting remembrances related to events during World War II. In addition, the subject was of interest because many of the students knew people who were involved in the war.

After identifying the general topic, the students brainstormed various topics that they could study using both historical fiction and nonfiction materials. Their list included the

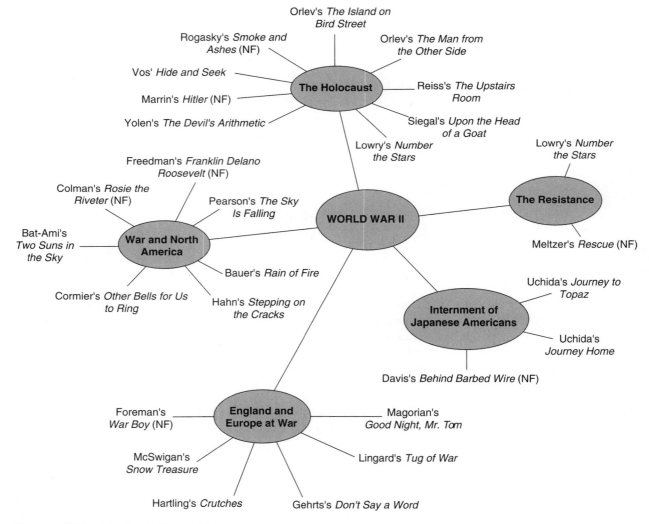

FIGURE 5–3   Unit Web for World War II

Holocaust, the Resistance, the internment of Japanese Americans, England and Europe at war, and living through war in North America. Under each topic, the students listed questions that they would like to have answered about the topic. The students then divided into groups so that each group read about, researched, and reported on their topic. With the help of teachers and librarians, each group investigated sources and chose literature and other materials. When the literature was identified, the groups placed the literature under the appropriate categories on the web as shown in Figure 5–3. Notice that each group identified at least one nonfiction (NF) source for its topic. Additional nonfictional sources included newspapers, magazines, and people who had experienced some phase of the war.

The group members used both the webbing process associated with literary elements (developed in Chapter 6) and the webbing process associated with vocabulary development as they read the books about their topics and developed important concepts related to World War II. These webs were used to assist students as they discussed the books. Figure 5–4 presents

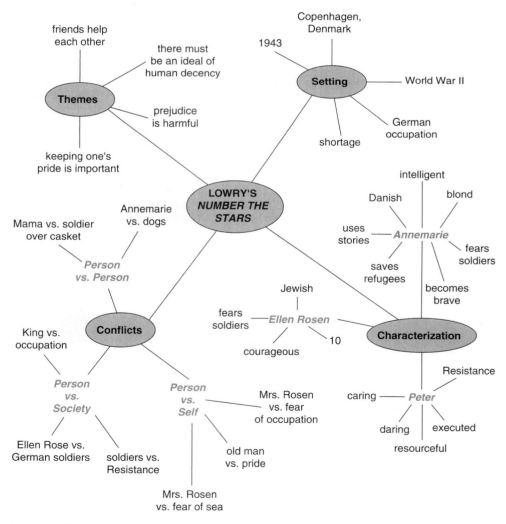

FIGURE 5–4   A Literary Web Using a World War II Book

a literary web using one of the books in the unit, Lois Lowry's 1990 Newbery Medal book, *Number the Stars* (1989). Figure 5–5 presents a vocabulary web using Michael Foreman's *War Boy* (1990).

The groups used various ways to report their findings to the class. For example, they all used nonfictional sources to authenticate settings and conflicts found in the historical fiction. They searched for dates, locations, and historical details that could be verified in nonfictional sources. They also searched for evidence that specific conflicts were common during that time period. Consequently, each group reported on the authenticity and reliability of the books they read. This was an important tie-in with history and showed the students the importance of documenting settings in historical fiction. Each of the groups was able to rate its books according to the authenticity of settings and conflicts developed in the books. Each group used quotes from its books and nonfictional sources to defend its ratings.

Each of the groups also wrote essays on the meaning of courage and bravery. Students debated which characters they thought were the most courageous. This activity proved to be an excellent way to relate literature and writing.

One group chose passages that they thought depicted the prevalent conflicts in the literature. As shown in the literary elements web (Figure 5–4), many were person-versus-society or person-versus-self conflicts. The students accompanied each of the passages with appropriate art and mood music, which was chosen from art and music popular during World War II.

Other groups prepared "You Are There" dramatizations in which they pretended to be reporters describing various scenes from history. Some of these scenes were chosen

FIGURE 5–5   A Vocabulary Web
Using a World War II Book

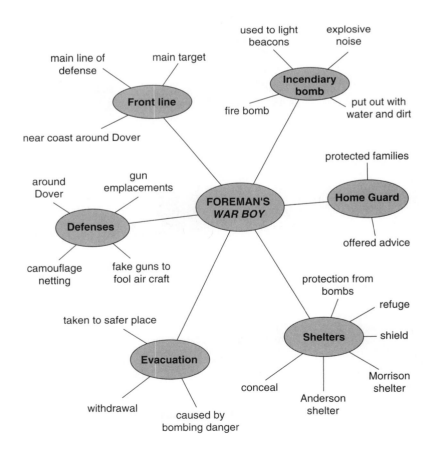

from biographies, with students portraying such characters as Franklin Roosevelt and Hitler.

One group developed a class museum of artifacts that showed items related to war in the United States. Their museum included such memorabilia as posters, stamps for rationed goods, records, tapes of radio shows, and drawings of victory gardens.

Following their presentations, the groups compiled a list of themes that they thought were important in most of the literature selections about World War II. For example, they concluded that most of the books stressed that friends need to help each other, prejudice is a terrible force, freedom is worth fighting for, and moral obligations must be met. They concluded their identification of themes by discussing why they thought each of these themes was important during wartime. They also considered whether these themes are important today.

For Your Development

1. Develop a series of lessons around a literature selection that proceed from a vocabulary web, to a guided discussion of the vocabulary through contextual analysis, and finally to a plot diagram that reinforces the vocabulary.
2. Develop a semantic map or web to lead a literary discussion of the book.
3. Develop a semantic map or web that shows how webbing may be used when developing a thematic unit.

Modeling.   Dole et al. (1991) identify modeling as one of the most effective strategies for developing students' comprehension. Pearson and Camperell (1985) state: "If teachers want students to get the author's message, they are well advised to model for students how to figure out the author's general structure" (p. 338). According to Early and Ericson (1988), research findings indicate that modeling and explaining or describing what students should do during a comprehension lesson is often ignored. They argue that modeling strategies are especially important in teaching students how to draw inferences because failure to make inferences frequently results in poor comprehension.

A modeling approach based on research conducted by Roehler and Duffy (1984) and Gordon (1985) is detailed elsewhere in this text. Chapter 3 presents modeling for inferring characterization using Patricia MacLachlan's *Sarah, Plain and Tall* (1985). Chapter 6 describes a modeling activity designed to develop understanding of similes using Leo Lionni's *Swimmy* (1963). We will now illustrate how you can develop a modeling lesson plan using the 1992 Newbery Medal winner, Phyllis Reynolds Naylor's *Shiloh* (1991).

For Your Plan Book

Lesson Plan

Modeling for Inferring Characterization

Core Book: Shiloh (1991), Phyllis Reynolds Naylor

Objectives

1. To be involved in a modeling activity that shows how to analyze evidence from the text and speculate about characters.

Continued

2. To understand the requirements for effective reasoning.

3. To appreciate and understand how the author implies characterization.

4. To write a response that reflects understanding of the author's implications.

Procedures

1. Identify the requirements for effective reasoning so that the students will understand those requirements. For this lesson, students must be aware that effective inferring of characterization requires them to go beyond the information an author provides in a text. They must use clues from the text to hypothesize about a character's emotions, beliefs, actions, hopes, and fears. Students must also be aware of the techniques that authors use to create well-developed characters.

2. Develop an introduction to the process of inferring characterization. Share with students examples of each type of characterization. You may draw these examples from literature or create your own. Ask the students to show how they can make discoveries about characters through dialogue, narration, a character's thoughts, thoughts of others about the character, and a character's actions.

Explain to students that in this modeling activity they will first listen to you read an excerpt from a book, ask a question, answer the question, provide evidence from the story that supports the answer, and provide the reasoning you used to reach the answer. Tell the students that after they have listened to you proceed through the sequence, they will use the same process to answer questions, identify evidence, and explore their own reasoning. As part of this introduction, discuss the meanings of the terms *evidence* and *reasoning*. Encourage the students to identify evidence about a character in literature and to share how they would use this evidence. They should realize that their own experiences, emotions, and reactions are important aspects of the reasoning process. (This sequence and discussion encourages students to draw on both efferent and aesthetic responses to literature.)

3. Stress the importance of inferring. Ask the students to explain why it is important to be able to make inferences about characters in literature. Encourage them to discuss how understanding characterization makes a story more exciting, enjoyable, and believable. They also should understand that they can infer characterization in their own writing.

4. Provide an introduction to the story. *Shiloh* takes place in the hills of West Virginia and focuses on a boy who tries to save a dog from a cruel owner. The author develops both a strong theme that cruelty to animals is wrong and a personal conflict as the boy tries to save the dog without telling his parents. The boy, Marty, the dog, Shiloh, and Shiloh's owner, Judd, are all well-defined characters.

To introduce the setting, you might use pictures of mountains in the eastern United States. Books such as Cynthia Rylant's *When I Was Young in the Mountains* (1982) allow students to visualize the rural setting. You can ask students how they might respond if they found a dog they believed had been mistreated. How would they try to solve the problem and save the dog? Tell the students they will be reading a book in which a boy tries to save a dog. But, the boy discovers, this is not always easy.

5. Provide the first modeling example. Read from the beginning of the book through this paragraph on page 12:

> I take the .22 rifle Dad had given me in March on my eleventh birthday and set out up the road to see what I can shoot. Like to find me an apple hanging way out on a branch, see if I can bring it down. Line up a few cans on a rail fence and shoot 'em off. Never shoot at anything moving, though. Never had the slightest wish.

Ask: "What do Marty's actions and thoughts reveal about him?" Answer: "I think that Marty likes to practice shooting his gun, but he would never shoot something that is alive. I think Marty cares a great deal for living things and might not like to hunt, hurt, or kill." Provide the evidence from the text: "Marty's actions show that he takes out his gun to practice, but everything that he wants to shoot—the apple and the cans—is not alive. He thinks to himself that he has never shot anything that moves." Provide the reasoning you used to reach your answer: "As I read this story I could see a boy who was comfortable with his rifle. As the author describes Marty's wish to practice his shooting, he refers to harmless actions. I feel that Marty is going out to have a good time with his gun. I also noticed 'never' twice in Marty's thoughts about shooting things that moved. I know from my own experience that when I think 'never,' I really mean what I am thinking. When I read this description, I feel Marty's sadness when he thinks about using the rifle for anything other than hitting cans and apples. I also remember Marty's earlier reactions when he could not eat the rabbit his father had killed with a gun."

6. Provide the second modeling example. At this point, verify that the students understand the procedure. If they do not, model another example completely. When the students understand the process, let them join the discussion by providing answers, evidence, and reasoning. Have the students jot down brief answers to the questions, noting their evidence and reasoning. These notes will improve the quality of the discussion that follows each question.

7. Continue reading the book until you come to the next logical discussion point. Interesting inferences can be drawn from the way in which Marty meets the beagle and responds to the beagle's actions:

> I look, and about fifteen yards off, there's this shorthaired dog—white with brown and black spots— not making any kind of noise, just slinking along with his head down, watching me, tail between his legs like he's hardly got the right to breathe. . . . The dog gets up and backs off. He don't even whimper, like he's lost his bark. Something really hurts inside you when you see a dog cringe like that. You know somebody's been kicking at him. Beating on him, maybe. (p. 14)

Ask: "What do these actions imply about the characters of the dog and Marty? What do we know about each of these main characters in the story?" Ask the students to answer the question. They will probably provide answers similar to this one, although you should encourage a range of speculation and ideas: The dog may be shy around people, or maybe he has been hurt and is afraid of people; the dog does not act like a normal, happy dog; something is wrong; Marty's feelings reveal that he is a very sensitive person and would probably never hurt an animal.

Ask the students to provide evidence for their answers. For example: The author tells us that the dog was slinking and watching the boy, but he did not come to the boy; the dog did not bark—he put his tail between his legs and cringed; Marty's thoughts and feelings show that the cringing dog is very disturbing to him.

Ask the students to provide reasoning. For example: The author gave a very sad description of the dog. I have seen dogs that act like that. I believe that the dog was telling us that he had been hurt by someone and that he was afraid of people; I reacted to the words that the author used; the picture of the dog made me so sad that I thought something was wrong; I know from my own experience what a young dog should look and act like if he is happy— this dog is not happy; I could feel Marty's sadness; I know what it feels like to hurt inside.

8. Continue this process, having the students discuss the many instances of implied characterization in the book. There are numerous examples, such as the following:

> *Text:* After Marty reveals that he would like to become a veterinarian and his father tells him that it would take a lot of money. Marty responds with a simile: "My dream sort of leaks out like water in a paper bag. 'Could be a veterinarian's helper,' I suggest, my second

Continued

choice" (p. 22). *Questions:* "What is the author telling us about Marty's dream and his character? What are his feelings?"

Text: When Marty thinks about why he does not like Shiloh's owner, Judd Travers: "The reason I don't like Judd Travers is a whole lot of reasons, not the least is that I was in the corner store once down in Friendly and saw Judd cheat Mr. Wallace at the cash register. Judd gives the man a ten and gets him to talking, then—when Mr. Wallace gives him change—says he give him a twenty. I blink, like I can't believe Judd done that, and old Mr. Wallace is all confused. So I say, 'No, I think he give you a ten' " (p. 22). *Question:* "What do Judd's actions reveal about his character and what does Marty's response reveal about Marty?"

Text: When Marty's father insists that he must return Shiloh to Judd: "We're in Shiloh now. Dad's crossing the bridge by the old abandoned gristmill, turning at the boarded-up school, and for the first time I can feel Shiloh's body begin to shake. He's trembling all over. I swallow. Try to say something to my dad and have to swallow again" (p. 24). *Questions:* "What do Shiloh's reactions reveal about his feelings? What do Marty's reactions reveal about Marty? At this point, do you believe that Marty is correct about Judd's treatment of the dog? Why or why not?"

Longer stories, such as *Shiloh,* lend themselves to discussions according to chapters. Students can read and discuss several chapters each day. After each session, ask the students to summarize what they know about Marty, Shiloh, and Judd. Ask "What do you want to know about these characters?"

While the students are reading this book, or after they have completed the book, ask them to describe their personal responses to Marty, Shiloh, and Judd in writing.

For Your Development

Develop a modeling lesson and share it with your class. You may complete *Shiloh* or select a new book.

Questioning.   Various types of questioning strategies are appropriate for teaching comprehension. Harniss et al. (1994) state "Effective teachers stop to check for student understanding by asking text-based questions . . . that require the reader to identify critical pieces of information and associations needed to conceptually understand the content area being studied" (p. 244). They state that questions should be designed to focus on critical concepts and principles. They maintain that the asking of questions should be interspersed throughout the reading of the text and should also be used to review important concepts in the text. They also emphasize that these questions should be carefully developed.

Critics of comprehension instruction emphasize, however, that questions too frequently encourage students to respond at the lowest levels of thinking. Ambrulevich (1986) found that questions in literature anthologies focus on the two lowest types of thinking on Bloom's taxonomy. Reading textbooks emphasize the need for developing questioning strategies that require higher level thought processes, and basal readers usually identify the taxonomy level of comprehension questions.

Do not accompany all literature selections with questioning. Nevertheless, develop a framework for designing questions that help students focus on certain aspects of a story and use their higher level thought processes.

You can develop questioning strategies by using Barrett's "Taxonomy of Reading Comprehension" (1972) or another taxonomy of comprehension, or you can focus on developing appreciation of the literary elements of setting, plot, characterization, theme, and style. Both approaches have merit. The following examples are based on Beverly Cleary's 1984 Newbery Medal book, *Dear Mr. Henshaw* (1983). As you read the questions, consider the advantages or disadvantages of each approach. How would the development of both series of questions help students improve their questioning strategies and their ability to focus on important elements in literature?

The first series of questions illustrates how questioning strategies can be developed around Barrett's four levels of reading comprehension: literal recognition or recall, inference, evaluation, and appreciation. The questions listed exemplify each level of the taxonomy. More questions or fewer might be advisable, depending on the book and the instructional purpose.

Literal recognition requires students to identify information provided in the literature. You may require students to recall information after reading or listening to a story, or to locate information while reading. Literal questions often include such words as *who, what, where,* and *when:*

1. *Recall of details*—How old was Leigh Botts when he first wrote to Mr. Henshaw? What is the name of Leigh's dog? What is Leigh's father's occupation? Where does the story *Dear Mr. Henshaw* take place?
2. *Recall of sequence of events*—What sequence of events caused Leigh to place an alarm on his lunch box? What sequence of events caused Leigh to write to Mr. Henshaw and to write in his diary?
3. *Recall of comparisons*—Compare the way that Leigh thought of his mother and the way that he thought of his father.
4. *Recall of character traits*—Describe Leigh's response to Mr. Henshaw when Mr. Henshaw asks Leigh to answer ten questions about himself.

When children infer an answer to a question, they go beyond the information the author provides and hypothesize about such things as details, main ideas, events that might have led to an occurrence, and cause-and-effect relationships. Inference is usually considered a higher level thought process; the answers are not specifically stated within the text. Examples of inferential questions include the following:

1. *Supporting details*—At the end of the book, Leigh says that he "felt sad and a whole lot better at the same time." What do you think he meant by this statement?
2. *Main idea*—What is the theme of the book? What message do you think the author is trying to express?
3. *Comparisons*—Think about the two most important characters in Leigh's life, his mother and his father. How are they alike and how are they different? Compare Leigh at the beginning of the book, when he is writing to Mr. Henshaw, with Leigh at the end of the book, when he is writing in his diary and writing true stories for school.
4. *Cause-and-effect relationships*—If you identify any changes in Leigh, what might have caused those changes?
5. *Character traits*—On page 73, Leigh decides that he cannot hate his father anymore. What does this tell you about Leigh and about his father? Why do you think Leigh's father sent him twenty dollars?
6. *Outcomes*—At one point in the story, Leigh wishes that his mother and father would get back together. What do you think would have happened to the story if that happened? How would Leigh's life have changed? How would his mother's life have

changed? What might have been the outcome of the writing contest at school if Leigh had not had the advantages of his advice from Mr. Henshaw?

Evaluation questions require children to make judgments about the content of the literature by comparing it with external criteria, such as what authorities on a subject say, or internal criteria, such as the reader's own experience or knowledge. Following are examples of evaluative questions:

1. *Adequacy or validity*—Do you agree that an author would take time to write to a child and to take such an interest in him? Why or why not?
2. *Appropriateness*—Do you believe that Leigh's story, "A Day on Dad's Rig," was a good story for the *Young Writers' Yearbook?* Why or why not?
3. *Worth, desirability, or acceptability*—Do you believe that Leigh had the right to feel the way he did toward his father? Why or why not? Do you believe that Leigh was right in his judgment that his father did not spend enough time with him? Why or why not? Was Leigh's mother's judgment right at the end of the book? What would you have done?

Appreciation of literature requires a heightening of sensitivity to the techniques that authors use in order to create an emotional impact. Questions can encourage students to respond emotionally to the plot, identify with the characters, react to an author's use of language, and react to an author's ability to create visual images through words. The following list provides examples of questions that stimulate appreciation:

1. *Emotional response to plot or theme*—How did you respond to the plot of *Dear Mr. Henshaw?* Did the author hold your attention? If so, how? Was the theme of the story worthwhile? Why or why not? Pretend you are either recommending this book for someone else to read or recommending that this book not be read; what would you tell that person?
2. *Identification with characters and incidents*—Have you ever felt like Leigh? Have you ever known anyone who felt like Leigh? What caused you or the person to feel that way? How would you have reacted to the theft of an excellent lunch?
3. *Imagery*—How did the author encourage you to see Leigh's home, neighborhood, and school? Close your eyes and try to describe your neighborhood or town. How would you describe it so that someone else could "see" it?

The preceding examples are not organized according to any sequence for presentation to students, but they do indicate the range of questions to consider when strengthening students' reading comprehension abilities. The next series of questions was written about the same book, *Dear Mr. Henshaw,* but examines specific literary elements within the text.

1. *Setting*—How have Leigh's living conditions changed as a result of his parents' divorce? What are some positive and some negative aspects of where he is now living? What is the importance of having a stable environment in which to live?
2. *Plot*—What problem is causing conflict for Leigh and his family? Why does Leigh write his first letter to Mr. Henshaw? Why does he continue to write letters even after the assigned letter is completed? What does Mr. Henshaw suggest that Leigh do? How do Mr. Henshaw's suggestions help Leigh accept the divorce? What helps Leigh understand his mother's point of view about the divorce? How do we know that he understands his mother's point of view? What happens to help Leigh understand his father's point of view? What does Leigh do to show that he understands his father's point of view? How does Leigh feel about himself and his family at the end of the story?

3. *Characterization*—How does Leigh view himself in comparison to the other children in his school? What three events help improve Leigh's self-image? How does Leigh's self-image change as a result of these events? How does Leigh's real father differ from the father of his dreams? In what ways does Leigh's father disappoint him? How do we know that Leigh's father still cares about Leigh and Leigh's mother? How does the character of Leigh's mother differ from that of his father? What actions show that Leigh's mother wants to care for and to provide for her son?

4. *Theme*—Why did Beverly Cleary write *Dear Mr. Henshaw* in a diary and letter format? Why is this an effective way to present this book? What important messages do the letters and the diary reveal about Leigh and the problems that he faces within himself and his family? At what point do you think Leigh starts to accept his parents' divorce? At what point in the story does Leigh begin to understand that his parents are not going to get back together? Based on the theme, what do you think would be another good title for this book?

5. *Style*—From whose point of view is this story told? How do you know that the story is written from the point of view of a young boy? How does this diary and letter format allow the author to develop the theme, the conflict, and the characters? Does the author's style make you believe that you are reading the writing of a real boy who is facing believable problems? This book deals with some painful and serious emotions. At the same time, the author is able to make readers laugh. How does she accomplish this?

For Your Development

1. Analyze the two series of questions. Are there any overlapping topics? What are the strengths and the weaknesses of each questioning framework? Do you agree that students gain more literary understanding by focusing on the literary elements of setting, plot, characterization, theme, and style? Do you agree that a taxonomy of comprehension helps teachers include all levels of thought processes?

2. Choose a book and develop questioning strategies to accompany that book. Try to include the strengths from a focus on literary elements and the taxonomy of comprehension.

LITERATURE CARD FILES.   Files of questioning strategies, book summaries, difficult words or concepts, and other activities that can accompany a book are beneficial. You will need to know a great deal about specific children's books to use them effectively in recreational reading, individualized instruction, storytelling, or social studies. College students should begin to read a number of children's books from the various categories of literature. It is easier to file pertinent information about a book when you read it than to try to remember it months or even years later. The following format is valuable to many students:

1. Title
2. Author, publisher, date
3. Reading level
4. Interest level
5. Category
6. Difficult words or concepts
7. Short summary

Across Five Aprils   Sixth Grade and Up

Irene Hunt   Historical Fiction: Civil War, Newbery Honor

Summary:

This is the story of the Creighton family and the Civil War as seen through the eyes of Jethro, the youngest member of the family. Jethro never fought in the war, but he saw all his brothers, cousins, and his only surviving sister leave home to fight for either North or South. The book opens in April 1861, and gradually, all of Jethro's brothers go to war. Tom, Eb, and John go to fight for the North, while Bill, Jethro's favorite brother, goes to fight for the South. Jethro is left with his parents to work on the farm. Two families in the community blame the Creightons for Bill's view on the war, and one night their barn is burned and their well filled with kerosene. Jethro's sister leaves to marry her fiance, who was wounded while fighting for the North. Jethro keeps up with the war through newspaper reports provided to him by the newspaper editor, Ross Milton. Jethro becomes lonely for the past and comes to realize how horrible war is. He has to make many decisions and grows up in many ways during the five Aprils in this book.

Factual Questions:

1. In what part of the country does this book take place? (Illinois)
2. Why is the book called *Across Five Aprils*? Is the title appropriate? (The book covers five Aprils of the Civil War.)
3. Why was Jethro the only one who did not go to war? (He was too young.)
4. Why was the Creighton's barn burned and their well contaminated? (One of their sons was fighting for the South.)
5. Why did Jethro want to keep up with his studies? (He idolized Shad, his schoolmaster, and knew study would help him in life.)

Inferential Questions:

1. Why was Ross Milton so special to Jethro? (He was an understanding adult; he understood Jethro's need for education.)
2. If Jethro had spare time, what do you think he would spend it doing? (Educational projects, reading, etc.)
3. How did Jethro feel about the men of the community helping them so much to rebuild their barn? (Very grateful; it felt good to have understanding friends.)

FIGURE 5–6   A Card for a Book Appropriate for Upper-Elementary Grades

8. Questions to ask during a conference. Include factual, inferential, evaluative, and appreciative questions, with possible answers to each question.
9. Several follow-up activities to use with the book
10. Other books on same subject or by same author.

Put the information on a large filing card or a separate page in a loose-leaf notebook, and group the cards or pages by grade level or category. Some students also code their files by color so they can easily choose an appropriate card from a file box. Figure 5–6 is an example of a card developed by a preservice teacher.

You can use literature files with summaries, questions, and activities in numerous ways. The questions provide a framework for discussion for extending understanding of a book, with individual children or during small-group discussions with several children who have

Evaluative Questions:

1. Do you think the author portrays the feelings and problems of the Civil War accurately, even though it is through the eyes of a young boy? Explain.

2. Do you think Jethro should have helped the man who burned down the barn? Why or why not?

3. Do you think Jethro had a right to feel overburdened? Did he?

Appreciative Questions:

1. How did the author present historical facts in an interesting and real way?

2. Did the Civil War seem more interesting to you? In what way?

3. Did you learn more about the Civil War than just the names and dates of the battles? Explain.

Activities:

1. Make a time line of the five years covered by the book. Include on the time line the important things that happened in Jethro's life.

2. Draw a map of the United States and have students code the Union and Confederate states by color.

3. Write a letter that Jethro might have written to Shad in Washington, D.C., after Shad had been injured fighting for the North.

4. Write a letter to a history teacher and recommend the book for teaching about the Civil War. List several reasons why the book would be a good instruction book about the war.

Other Historical Fiction Books or Books About the Civil War:

The Drinking Gourd by F. N. Monjo

Bull Run by Paul Fleischman

The Slave Dancer by Paula Fox

Rifles for Watie by Harold Keith

FIGURE 5–6 Continued

read the same book. You can use the activities for enrichment experiences after a child or a group of children has read the book. At times, you may use the files only to find books to recommend for recreational reading. If you have listed other books, you can recommend additional books to a child who has a specific interest or wants to explore a topic further.

Approaches That Develop Prediction Abilities

Good readers use textual cues and prior knowledge to make predictions. You may stimulate and enhance predictive skills at any level. Books such as John Ivimey's *The Complete Story of Three Blind Mice* (1987) and Scott Cook's *The Gingerbread Boy* (1987) encourage students to join in during repetitive phrases. Predictable story structures such as "The Three Billy Goats Gruff" and "The Three Little Pigs" encourage students to hypothesize about plot developments. Teaching students to identify foreshadowing, a device in which an author suggests plot development before it occurs, is another method for helping students use cues in the text to predict outcomes. A detail in an illustration, the mood of the story, the author's choice of words, a minor episode, or a symbol presented early in the story may foreshadow later action.

Picture storybooks are good introductions to foreshadowing because the illustrations frequently include details that suggest later actions. For example, one of Don Wood's illustrations for Audrey Wood's *Heckedy Peg* (1987) shows the young girl feeding a friendly blackbird through the window; the same blackbird later helps the children by leading their mother to the witch who has transformed them into food. Another illustration shows the boisterous children playing within their cottage, while through the window the witch is approaching. Later, the witch arrives at the door, the children disobey their mother, and the children allow the witch to enter the cottage. Students may try to search for such clues while they read a book, or they may reread a book, searching for clues that foreshadow later developments. You may use many other books in the same way. For example, Richard Egielski's illustrations of a bird with hands in Arthur Yorinks's *Hey, Al* (1986) foreshadow the fate of Al and his dog Eddie.

Illustrations in picture storybooks frequently foreshadow the ending, the type of story, and plot development by creating appropriate moods. For example, Marcia Brown's delicate lines and soft colors suggest a magical setting and foreshadow a fairy-tale ending in Charles Perrault's *Cinderella* (1954). In contrast, Charles Keeping's stark, black lines create ghostly, terrifying subjects and foreshadow the tale's sinister and disastrous consequences in Alfred Noyes's *The Highwayman* (1981). John Schoenherr's illustrations for Jane Yolen's *Owl Moon* (1987) and Marcia Brown's illustrations for Blaise Cendrars's *Shadow* (1982) allow students to look at the illustrations, analyze the mood created by the illustrations, and predict the type of story, type of conflict, and possible ending.

Terms that authors use to describe characters may provide clues to plot changes and even foreshadow themes and endings. For example, students may predict plot development, changing characters, and possible themes as they trace the significance of name changes in Sid Fleischman's historical fiction and 1987 Newbery Medal winner, *The Whipping Boy* (1986). For example, the book uses the following names in reference to the Prince and to his whipping boy, Jemmy. The names in parentheses indicate who is using the specific name:

Prince		*Jemmy*	
p. 1	Prince Brat (King, royalty)	p. 2	Common boy (narrator)
p. 4	Your Royal Awfulness (Jemmy)	p. 6	Jemmy-from-the-Streets (Prince)
p. 5	You fiddle-faddle scholar (tutor)	p. 6	Contrary rascal (Prince)
p. 8	No friends (Jemmy)		
p. 18	Empty-headed prince (Jemmy)	p. 20	My whipping boy (Prince)
p. 21	His Royal Highness (Prince)	p. 21	That ratty street orphan (Prince)

Changing Roles:			
p. 21	Witless servant boy (Jemmy)		
p. 28	Whipping boy (Hold-Your-Nose Billy)		
p. 31	Jemmy-from-the-Streets (Jemmy)		
p. 32	Contrary as a mule (Jemmy)		
p. 33	Prince Blockhead (Jemmy)	p. 33	Imposter (Prince)
		p. 42	Unfaithful servant (Prince)
p. 53	A wounded bird (Jemmy)		
p. 53	Friend (Jemmy)		
p. 61	A brave one (Jemmy)	p. 61	Jemmy (Prince)

p. 61   Friend-O-Jemmy's (Prince)

p. 70   Heir to the throne (Jemmy)   p. 74   My friend (Prince)

p. 88   Friend (Jemmy)

In this example, notice how the changes in names and references to the main characters follow the plot, suggest changes in relationships, and even develop one of the themes of the book. Students and teachers both enjoy this searching for clues provided by the author to help them predict the story line.

Books for older students may use complex symbolism to foreshadow. In such books, students may identify symbols and hypothesize how the symbols foreshadow events. For example, in Cynthia Voigt's 1983 Newbery Honor book, *A Solitary Blue* (1983), students may trace Jeff's changing attitudes toward the heron and predict how these gradual changes in attitude reveal Jeff's growing self-esteem. Likewise, in Voigt's 1983 Newbery Medal book, *Dicey's Song* (1982), students may trace, discuss, and predict the importance of the author's reference to musical selections, a dilapidated boat, and a tree.

For Your Development

1. Select a grade level and develop a list of books to encourage students to make predictions.
2. Develop a lesson in which you lead students in a search for clues that will help them predict plot development, character development, theme, or story ending.

For Your Plan Book

Lesson Plan

A Literary Approach to the Study of Biography

This unit includes activities to enhance students' appreciation of biography, to encourage students to read carefully, and to help students evaluate critically what they read. The unit objectives come from all of the language arts, including reading, speaking, listening, and writing. The bibliography includes books for a range of ability levels—from picture biographies to biographies appropriate for upper-elementary and middle-school students. The literary approach to biography emphasizes an understanding of and appreciation for the techniques that authors use to tell about real people. The approach is concerned primarily with character development, but it also involves plot, setting, theme, and style.

Choose the literature and activities that are appropriate for your specific grade level. Use teacher-directed activities with the class and a specific book, and use other activities with individual students to encourage them to read widely and independently. Also include content and concepts from the social studies, history, and geography. Fleming and McGinnis's *Portraits: Biography and Autobiography in the Secondary School* (1985) contains additional ideas. Although the activities are designed for secondary students, you may adapt many of the excellent ideas for younger children.

Objectives

1. To develop an appreciation for biography.
2. To analyze and critically evaluate plot in biography.

Continued

3. To analyze and critically evaluate characterization in biography.
4. To analyze and critically evaluate setting in biography.
5. To analyze and critically evaluate theme in biography.
6. To analyze and critically evaluate style in biography.
7. To integrate the language arts and English skills of reading, speaking, listening, and writing within a literature focus.

Biographies Discussed in This Approach

Adler, David. *Martin Luther King, Jr.: Free at Last* (1987)

Brooks, Polly. *Queen Eleanor: Independent Spirit of the Medieval World* (1983)

Coerr, Eleanor. *Sadako and the Thousand Paper Cranes* (1977)

Dalgliesh, Alice. *The Columbus Story* (1955)

D'Aulaire, Ingri, and D'Aulaire, Edgar. *Columbus* (1955)

Freedman, Russell. *Eleanor Roosevelt: A Life of Discovery* (1994 Newbery Honor, 1993)

Freedman, Russell. *Lincoln: A Photobiography* (1988 Newbery Medal, 1987)

Fritz, Jean. *Where Do You Think You're Going, Christopher Columbus?* (1980)

Goodnough, David. *Christopher Columbus* (1979)

Levinson, Nancy Smiler, *Christopher Columbus: Voyager to the Unknown* (1990)

Roosevelt, Elliot. *Eleanor Roosevelt, with Love* (1984)

Sis, Peter. *Follow the Dream: The Story of Christopher Columbus* (1991)

Ventura, Piero. *Christopher Columbus* (1978)

Cover photograph of Russell Freedman's book Lincoln: A Photobiography.

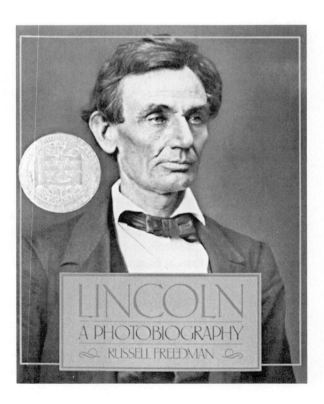

West, Delno, and West, Jean. *Christopher Columbus: The Great Adventure* (1991)

Whitney, Sharon. *Eleanor Roosevelt* (1982)

Yates, Elizabeth. *Amos Fortune, Free Man* (1951 Newbery, 1950)

Yates, Elizabeth. *My Diary, My World* (1981)

Yates, Elizabeth. *My Widening World* (1983)

Procedures

Read, analyze, and discuss a biography according to the following literary elements:

I. Plot Development
  A. What is the order for the plot development? Does author use chronological order?
     Flashbacks? How does the author present important information from the past that
     influences the biographical character?
  B. What time frame does the author emphasize? Why do you believe the author chose
     that time period in the character's life?
  C. What types of conflict does the biographer develop? Find examples of these conflict
     types. Why do you believe the biographer chose to emphasize these types of conflict?
     1. Person versus self
     2. Person versus person
     3. Person versus society
     4. Person versus nature
  D. What pattern of action does the author develop?
     1. Rising action with identifiable climax and end of conflict.
     2. Action moves from one incident to another incident. (There is a final climax but
        author leaves reader with a sense of uncertainty.)
     3. Action moves with a tension that does not develop a climax. There is minimal
        suspense.
     4. Action moves in a line that does not have one dramatic climax but may have sev-
        eral dramatic episodes.
  E. How does the author develop readers' interest in the plot?
     1. Find examples of interest-creating introductions. For example, how does Brooks
        attract your attention in this introductory paragraph to *Queen Eleanor: Indepen-
        dent Spirit of the Medieval World:* "The French King, Louis the Fat, lay dying in his
        hunting lodge where he had been taken to escape the summer heat, the flies, the
        stench of Paris. His hands shook with palsy, and his bleary eyes could hardly see.
        Recently he had grown so fat that he could no longer mount a horse or bend
        over to tie his shoes" (p. 7).
     2. Find examples of direct quotes from the biographical character or photographs
        that the author uses to stimulate interest. For example, how does Freedman at-
        tract attention in the introduction to Chapter 1 in *Lincoln: A Photobiography:* "If
        any personal description of me is thought desirable, it may be said, I am, in height,
        six feet, four inches, nearly; lean in flesh, weighing, on average, one hundred and
        eighty pounds; dark complexion, with coarse black hair and grey eyes—no other
        marks or brands recollected" (p. 1).
     3. Find examples of any other techniques, such as foreshadowing of events to come.
  F. Additional activities can help students analyze plot development in biography:
     1. Draw and label the lifeline of a character such as Yates's *Amos Fortune, Free Man.*
        Draw and label the pattern of action developed by the author. Compare the two

Continued

drawings. How are they alike, and how are they different? Try to account for any differences.

2. Compare the pattern of action for two biographies written about the same person but written by two different authors. For example, choose two of the biographies listed about Christopher Columbus or about Eleanor Roosevelt. Try to account for any differences.

3. Compare introductory paragraphs in several biographies. Choose the example that you think is the most effective. Prepare the paragraph as an oral reading, share it with your class, and tell why you believe the introduction is effective.

4. Develop a class chart of types of conflict found in biographies. Categorize the biographies according to their predominant conflict. Are there any similarities among biographies in a specific category? For example, are person-versus-society conflicts found more often in biographies about civil rights leaders?

II. Characterization

   A. How does the author reveal the character of the biographical person? Find and discuss examples of any of the following ways in which authors reveal character:

      1. Actions of the character.

      2. Dialogue that reveals the speech of the character.

      3. Thoughts of the character.

      4. Thoughts of others toward the character.

      5. Narrative comments about the character made by the author.

   B. Using each of the aforementioned examples, what did you learn about the character? Was each technique appropriate for the biography? Could the author substantiate that each way of revealing character was authentic? (Look for references in the biography and for sources used by the author.)

   C. How did the person change over the course of the biography? What caused any changes? How did the author show the changes?

   D. Who influenced the biographical subject? How did the author develop these supporting characters?

   E. Who is telling the biographical story? What is the relationship of the author to the biographical subject? How does this relationship influence the tone of the biography and the attitude toward the biographical subject? For example, answer these questions for Elliot Roosevelt's *Eleanor Roosevelt, with Love.*

   F. Additional activities can help students analyze characterization in biography:

      1. Identify scenes in the biography that include dialogue between characters. Dramatize the scenes using the dialogue presented in the literature. Discuss the impact of the dialogue with the class.

      2. Compare the characterizations developed in two biographies written about the same person but by different authors.

      3. Rewrite a scene from a biography but choose to write the scene from a different point of view. Discuss how this different point of view changes the presentation of the character. How do the tone and the attitude change?

III. Setting

   A. How important is the setting in biography? Why is the setting important or not important?

B. What role does the setting have in biography? Locate examples, if used, and discuss the importance of each of these purposes for a biography:
  1. Providing historical background.
  2. Setting the mood.
  3. Providing an antagonist.
  4. Providing symbolic meanings.
  5. Providing illumination for character and clarifying conflict.
C. What are the various settings developed in a biography? How much detail is included?
D. Is the setting in the past or present? How does the author inform readers of the time period?
E. How much influence does the setting have on character?
F. Additional activities that help students understand and evaluate setting in biography:
  1. Find the specific locations mentioned in a biography on a map. Locate descriptions of these places in geography texts or other nonfictional sources. How do the descriptions compare with the settings in the biography?
  2. Locate the specific dates and historical happenings identified in a biography. Check the accuracy of these dates and happenings in other nonfictional sources.
  3. Choose a specific setting described in a biography. Draw the setting as if it were a backdrop for a stage production. Is there enough detail to complete the drawing? If not, what information would improve your drawing?

IV. Theme
A. There may be one primary theme in a biography and several secondary themes. Search for and identify any primary and secondary themes in a biography. How are these themes integrated into the biography? Does the title of the biography reflect the theme? For example, what could Adler's title *Martin Luther King, Jr.: Free at Last* imply?
B. An author may literally state a theme or merely imply it. Search for evidence of each method. Why do you believe the author used each approach? What was the impact?
C. Themes in biographies frequently depict the biographical person's ability to triumph over obstacles or to struggle for identity. Search for evidence of either of these themes.
D. Additional activities can help students analyze theme in biography:
  1. The themes in biographies frequently include didacticism, or instruction. The lives of great people often provide models for readers and suggest proper values, attitudes, and actions. Analyze several biographies to identify any instructional purposes. Why do you believe the author chose that specific person's life to teach a lesson?
  2. Compare biographies written for younger children with biographies written for young adults. Analyze any differences in themes. Are any themes more consistently developed at either level?
  3. Identify and compare the themes developed in several biographies written about the same person. If the themes are not the same, how do you account for the differences? Could the differences relate to the author's purpose for writing the biography or the age level of the readers?

V. Author's Style
A. Author's style refers to how an author says something rather than what the author says. Authors may vary sentence length, repeat words, or choose descriptive words to suggest mood and create interest. For example, in her biography *The Columbus Story*, written for younger readers, Alice Dalgliesh repeats words to create interest

Continued

and excitement. The waves beckon Columbus, "Come, Come, Come!" White sails chant, "Adventure, adventure, adventure!" "day after day after day." Excitement is enhanced by "Land! Land! Land" and "Climbing, climbing, -higher-higher-higher." By repeated words, such as "Nothing but sea—and—sea—and sea," Dalgliesh lengthens the days and creates an image of vast open sea. Identify examples in which an author's choice of words enhances the mood of a biography.

B. Symbolism is a complex literary technique. It allows authors to suggest deeper meanings. For example, a dove may symbolize peace and a flag may symbolize patriotism. Authors of biographies, especially those for older readers, may choose symbols that relate to the people, conflict, and theme. For example, Eleanor Coerr uses considerable symbolism in her biography, *Sadako and the Thousand Paper Cranes*. The cranes are an ancient Japanese symbol for honor, humility, respect, hope, and protection. An ancient Japanese myth reveals that the gods will grant a long and happy life to a sick person who can make one thousand paper cranes. Coerr uses both the symbolic meaning for crane and belief in the myth to develop Sadako's character and the plot, as Sadako tries to overcome the personal ravages caused by the atomic bomb. The symbolism of the crane also suggests and reinforces themes. Search for examples of symbolism in a biography. How does the symbolism relate to the people, plot development, and theme? Do you believe the symbolism is appropriate? Why or why not?

C. Authors may use figurative language, such as similes and metaphors, to clarify and enhance descriptions of settings and people. For example, in *Sadako and the Thousand Paper Cranes,* Coerr uses a simile when she states, "There was a flash of a million suns. Then the heat pricked my eyes like needles" (p. 18). She uses a metaphor to imply a comparison between the atomic bomb and a thunderbolt. In *The Columbus Story,* Dalgliesh uses numerous similes to describe the setting in which the sea is smooth and "quiet as a river," the colors are as beautiful "as feathers of birds," and the trees are "as green and beautiful as the trees of Spain in the month of May." Search for examples of similes and metaphors. How do the comparisons relate to the setting or the people? Are they appropriate? Why or why not?

D. Additional activities can help students understand style in biography:

1. Authors of biographies are frequently prolific writers. Identify a biographer who has written numerous books, including, if possible, nonfictional materials that reveal information about the author. Analyze the works according to any similarities in style, themes, and characterizations. Elizabeth Yates is an excellent example. Her 1950 biography *Amos Fortune, Free Man* won the Newbery award for literature; her autobiographies *My Diary, My World* and *My Widening World* received critical acclaim. Her many other books are available in libraries, and her biographical profile and acceptance speech for the Newbery award are available in *Horn Book* magazine.

2. Reviews of biographies usually emphasize the author's literary style and ability to develop accurate characters. Search in sources such as *Horn Book, Booklist, School Library Journal,* and *The New York Times Book Review* to find reviews of biographies that you have read. What do the critics who wrote the reviews emphasize? Do you agree or disagree with the book critic? Why or why not?

3. Attitudes toward some biographers and biographies differ. Attitudes toward a biography and the author's writing style may also change over time. Yates's *Amos Fortune, Free Man,* which won the Newbery award for excellence in literature, illustrates such diversity and changing attitudes. The book is still highly acclaimed by numerous critics. For example, Zena Sutherland (1986) describes the book as "written with warmth and compassion.... The details are grim, but Amos Fortune

carried suffering lightly because his eyes were on the freedom of the future. It is this characteristic of Fortune's, so clearly depicted by Yates, that causes some modern critics to disparage the book. They disapprove of the quiet way Amos Fortune bore his enslavement with courage and dignity, forgetting the circumstances under which he achieved his own personal integrity and offered the chance to live free to other blacks" (p. 459). In contrast, Donnarae MacCann (1985) states that the book is written with a "white supremacist attitude" (p. 169) and that "the author's descriptions are condescending, but beyond that they make the African appear almost subhuman" (p. 170). Read a book such as *Amos Fortune, Free Man* and decide for yourself which viewpoint you endorse. Defend your reasons for this viewpoint.

Learning to Read by Reading

Students who demonstrate mastery of higher level reading skills do considerable reading; choose books from a variety of genres, including both fiction and nonfiction; and select books beyond required reading. Reading widely and frequently allows students to develop knowledge about the world and literature that helps them comprehend new experiences. Students who read widely and frequently also develop appreciation for literature and increase the likelihood that they will become lifelong readers. This section considers three approaches to reading: recreational reading groups, computer-assisted reading programs, and focus units. Many of these approaches provide several of the best practices identified by Zemelan et al. (1998) including time for independent reading, children's choices in reading matters, use of collaborative activities with discussion and interaction, and grouping by interests or book choices. They also encourage a decrease in only using basal readers and teaching subskills.

Recreational Reading Groups

Recreational reading groups encourage students to self-select literature around a specific theme or topic, and include opportunities for the students and teachers to respond verbally to their reading experiences. Students may select books from a wide range of literature or focus on a narrower range of topics, genres, or characteristics.

In a survey of teachers and recreational reading, Block and Mangieri (2002) found that teachers who incorporated recreational reading groups into their literacy curriculum had a high knowledge of children's books, were lifelong readers, and provided students with a rich array of pleasurable experiences with books. "These teachers routinely (a) offer numerous opportunities for children to read books of choice silently, (b) provide incentives to read at home, and (c) ask for pupils' responses to books read during recreational reading activities in class. They reported that they did so in spite of the pressures to prepare for state-mandated literacy assessments" (p. 577).

If topics are the focus, form groupings according to interests rather than achievement levels, and include a range of literature to meet the reading levels of all of the students in the group. If the materials are totally self-selected, divide the class into about three groups. Designate a leader for each group. Have the students bring their books to one of these three reading circles and read for about thirty minutes. (Vary the time according to attention spans and reading interests.) Then, have the students relate something interesting about the books they have been reading.

When you first form recreational reading groups, make one large group with you as leader. Model independent reading behavior for the total group and begin the discussion by relating something interesting about the book you are reading. After students understand the procedures, more interaction develops in smaller groups. Place competent readers next to less efficient readers to help with unknown words. Groups may stay together until their books are finished, or the groups may change from one session to the next.

Recreational reading groups structured around specific topics encourage reading of a wider variety of materials and genres than students might otherwise select. They also encourage literary appreciation, as students and teachers consider why they enjoy or dislike the selected literature. For example, the topic humor appeals to students. As they read humorous books, they learn to appreciate the various ways in which authors develop humor. Have the students begin by selecting, reading, and sharing humorous incidents in picture books. These books are excellent choices for stimulating aesthetic responses. Have the students share their enjoyment of the humor developed by both author and illustrator. For example, the various books by Theodore Geisel (Dr. Seuss) develop humor through nonsensical characters and word play. Surprising and unexpected situations provide the humor in Doreen Cronin's *Click, Clack, Moo: Cows that Type* (2000), Reeve Lindbergh's *The Day the Goose Got Loose* (1990), Audrey Wood's *King Bidgood's in the Bathtub* (1985), and Eric A. Kimmel's *The Chanukkah Guest* (1990). Exaggeration provides the humor in Patricia Polacco's *Meteor!* (1987) and in Anne Isaacs's *Swamp Angel* (1994). Caricature and ridiculous situations provide the humor in James Marshall's illustrations for Grimm's *Red Riding Hood* (1987) and in Florence Parry Heide's *The Bigness Contest* (1994). The language and situations provide the humor in Mem Fox's *Hattie and the Fox* (1987). Language, situations, and illustrations all provide humor in Jon Scieszka's *The Stinky Cheese Man and Other Fairly Stupid Tales* (1992).

Recreational reading groups may explore preposterous characters and situations in such modern fantasy selections as Carl Sandburg's *Rootabaga Stories* (1922), Astrid Lindgren's *Pippi Longstocking* (1950), and Richard and Florence Atwater's *Mr. Popper's Penguins* (1938). Other groups may experience and explore humor in contemporary realistic fiction; for example, in the humorous person-versus-person conflict in Beverly Cleary's *Ramona and Her Father* (1977), in the exaggerations in Helen Cresswell's various "Bagthorpe Saga" books, and in the role reversals in Lois Lowry's *Anastasia on Her Own* (1985). After reading and responding to numerous humorous books in the recreational reading groups, students can read or listen to stories selected by Pamela Pollack in *The Random House Book of Humor for Children* (1988). Now, they can decide why these books might have been chosen to exemplify humor. The students may also choose to develop their own book of humor.

Authors who interest students may also be the focus of recreational reading groups. Maurice Sendak, Beverly Cleary, Virginia Hamilton, Lloyd Alexander, and Tomie de Paola are authors who have numerous books in print. Likewise, poets such as Myra Cohn Livingston, Byrd Baylor, Edward Lear, and Jack Prelutsky have sufficient poetry collections in print to serve as choices for recreational reading groups. A search through the index of a children's literature text will help you identify numerous authors and their books (for example, Norton, 2003).

Computer-Assisted Instruction in Reading

The *Report of the National Reading Panel* (2000) found too few studies related to computers and reading to make recommendations about best practices. The panel concluded: "In sum, the Panel is encouraged by the reported successes in the use of computer technology for reading instruction, but relatively few specific instructional applications can be gleaned from the research. Many questions still need to be addressed" (p. 18). The report cited several trends that show promise such as the use of highlighted text that links definitions and supporting text and the use of computers as word processors because reading instruction is most effective when combined with writing instruction. The panel found no research that incorporated Internet applications with reading instruction.

Chapter 13, "Library and Reference Skills," provides suggestions for using technology in the language arts. The section includes activities that may be used by the reading teacher such as introducing technology through literature, writing and publishing book reviews on the web, bringing specialists into the classroom through the Internet, and issues connected with using and teaching through websites.

Focus, or Thematic, Units

Focus units help teachers and students focus on specific reading skills and literary attributes. Units also improve achievement levels when compared with students who learn from text-books (Jones & Coombs, 1994–95). Units encourage considerable individual reading, as students choose literature for either unit-related projects or enjoyment. If one of the objectives of a unit is to provide opportunities for students to expand their reading, then include independent reading activities and expanded reading lists. Norton's (1996) publication, *The Impact of Literature-Based Reading*, develops units on topics entitled "Comparing Different Versions of the Same Folktale," "Developing Understanding and Appreciation for the Native American Culture," "Developing Understanding and Appreciation of the Black Culture," "Responding to Contemporary Issues Through Science Fiction," "Friendship Themes in Literature," "Survival Themes in Literature," and "Overcoming Obstacles and Hardships." In this chapter, there is a unit for teaching reading skills and literary appreciation associated with biography.

You may develop focus topics or themes that include one genre of literature or several genres. You may also combine knowledge from various content areas within your unit. For example, Norton and Kracht (1991) developed a unit combining literature and the following themes from geography: (1) location: position on the earth's surface; (2) place: landscape and people; (3) relationships within places: cultural and physical relationships and how relationships develop; (4) movement: movement of people, materials, and ideas; and (5) regions: how they form and change. Books were identified that exemplified the themes, and a series of activities was developed in which students used their knowledge of geography to locate and analyze each of the themes in literature. The literature included a wide range of genres, including folklore, contemporary realistic fiction, biography, and informational literature.

A fifth-grade teacher developed a "Pioneer Spirit" unit to help students consider the personal, psychological, physical, spiritual, and social qualities that fostered early exploration. The literature included historical fiction, biographies, autobiographies, informational materials, and poetry. Teacher-directed lessons helped students read the literature, gain insights, and draw possible conclusions from the past and present. Smaller group activities encouraged students to consider the kind of pioneer spirit that would be required to explore universes of the future or to restructure environments on planet Earth. Other activities required independent reading and considerable research. The teacher, librarian, and students identified literature from as many genres as possible related to the topic.

Assessment and the Reading Program

Two types of tests are usually considered when evaluating a student's reading abilities: informal and standardized tests. The informal test, such as an Informal Reading Inventory, is a test given to an individual student in which the child reads graded passages and answers questions related to the passages. This test may have both oral and silent sections. The test may also measure areas like phonics abilities. These inventories provide extensive information about each student's level of reading and suggest appropriate levels for texts for reading instruction. The results of this test may identify an independent reading level that is appropriate for self-selected and recreational reading, an instructional level that indicates the level for formal reading instruction in groups or individually, and a frustration level that shows the level at which reading may be too difficult for the student. Reading clinics often use a series of such tests to measure various levels of reading difficulty and to develop a plan of action for instruction or remediation.

Portfolios are another type of informal assessment used by many teachers and school districts. Allington and Cunningham (2002) describe a portfolio process that they believe is effective for assessing each child's literacy development. Each portfolio includes the following:

1. Self-portraits that each child creates at the beginning and ending of the year
2. Interviews conducted each September that include questions on personal interests such as favorite pastimes, reading at home, and responses to school
3. A parents questionnaire in which parents provide information on their child
4. Concepts About Print developed by Marie Clay in which students are assessed about their understandings of print and books
5. A word awareness writing activity given at the close of kindergarten and in first grade
6. Unedited writing samples
7. Running records of three reading samples collected at the beginning, middle, and end of the year
8. Three records of each child retelling a story

For portfolios to work, children need time to conference with the teacher. Consequently, the development of portfolios should be integrated into the classroom schedule. Allington and Cunningham stress that involving parents in the portfolio process is important. The contents of a portfolio is a discussion starter with parents and can be the basis for a parent–teacher conference.

The second type of testing, the schoolwide and often state-mandated achievement tests, are receiving considerable attention in professional journals and in newspapers. Articles in professional journals such as "High-Stakes Testing in Reading: Today in Texas, Tomorrow?" (Hoffman, Assaf, & Paris, 2001) discuss the implications of and the often detrimental consequences associated with statewide testing.

Articles in local newspapers frequently list the achievement test scores of schools within the district and label them according to their achievement levels. These articles may report comparisons between achievement levels from one year to the next. Other articles such as "The Elderly Man and the Sea? Test Sanitizes Literary Texts" (N. R. Kleinfield, 2002) question the content of tests in which the test developers may be altering the content of passages written by well-known authors.

Questions associated with high-stakes testing include these:

1. What are the best ways to make schools and teachers accountable for higher levels of achievement for all children?
2. Do the tests reflect the educational goals of the school curriculum?
3. What are the consequences of teaching to the test? Is time lost from actual instruction or from content that is not being tested?
4. Do test items match what is known about the reading process?
5. Are test results helpful in designing a reading program that meets the needs of all children?

6. What controls the curriculum—the contents of the test or the goals and objectives of a sound educational plan?
7. Do test scores reflect the actual achievement levels of students at each grade level?
8. Are the results of the test overemphasized by the administration?
9. What are the consequences for students who do poorly on the tests? Promotion or retention?
10. What are the consequences for teachers whose students do poorly on the tests?
11. Do the test results help teachers improve instruction?

For Your Development

In class conduct a debate on the pros and cons of high-stakes testing:

1. Place slips of paper in a container. On the slips identify the roles of various participants: "Teacher—for high-stakes testing," "Parent—for high-stakes testing," "Administration—for high-stakes testing," "School board member—for high-stakes testing," "Teacher—against high-stakes testing," "Parent—against high-stakes testing," "Administration—against high-stakes testing," "School board member—against high-stakes testing." Let the participants each choose one slip.
2. Research the role that is on the paper. Find support for your position and be ready to debate your point.
3. Prior to the debate, each side should meet to discuss their strategies.
4. Set up the rules for the debate such as five minutes for pro teacher, five minutes for against teacher, and two minutes for rebuttal on each side. Continue until everyone has presented and had an opportunity for a rebuttal. Conclude the debate with each side summarizing their strongest points.
5. This activity generates considerable discussion about testing. Summarize your own conclusions and beliefs about high-stakes testing.

Evaluating Instructional Programs in the Reading Program

We have identified best practices for teaching reading that have been supported by research studies. There is one more area of reading that may or may not be backed by research studies. These are schoolwide approaches such as "Accelerated Schools" and "High Schools That Work" that the developers promise will improve student learning. Some of these programs cost school districts very little money; yet while others cost thousands of dollars.

One source that schools may use to evaluate some of these programs is *An Educators' Guide to Schoolwide Reform* (American Institutes for Research [AIR], 1999). This source, published by the Educational Research Service, evaluates the claims of twenty-four schoolwide reform approaches. This evaluation includes evidence of positive effects on student achievement, year introduced in schools, numbers of schools in which the program is used, support the developer provides to the schools, first-year costs, and first-year costs with current staff reassigned. This text includes descriptions of each program, identification of sources that evaluated the program, the measurement instruments that were used in the evaluation, the dimension of education that was measured, and the effect of the research results. Even a brief glance at the statistics related to each program shows that many programs do not live up to their claims. Teachers need to be interactive in the decision making about approaches that are being considered that could influence their teaching for many years to come.

You may also search the journals to find evaluations of various programs. For example, Chenoweth (2001) asks the question "Do Accelerated Reader and Reading Counts Work?" The author of the article states, "Increasingly popular 'reading management programs' give kids points for every book they read. But do they turn kids into readers?" (p. 48).

For Your Development

Search the journals and sources such as *An Educators' Guide to Schoolwide Reform* (AIR, 1999). What are the claims of various schoolwide programs or basal reading programs such as "Open Court"?

1. What proof can you find that the programs are as effective as the publishers claim them to be?
2. What are the characteristics of programs that are effective?
3. How do you know that they will be effective with the students you teach or plan to teach?
4. Pretend that you are presenting one of these programs to a group of teachers. Develop your argument for or against the program.

Mainstreaming

Reading is one of the most important subjects for students with learning disabilities. Lerner (1989) states that approximately 80 percent of students with learning disabilities experience reading problems. Authorities on learning disabilities also stress the importance of providing structure to help students comprehend literature through such techniques as modeling, organizing, questioning, and background knowledge. Table 5–1 provides specific characteristics of students with learning disabilities that may influence reading achievement and some of the techniques that have proven to be successful.

Table 5–1   Mainstreaming and reading for children with learning disabilities

Characteristics of Children with Learning Disabilities	Teaching Techniques for Language Arts Instruction
1. Some students may have weak decoding abilities but good comprehension (Jordan, 1994).	1. Provide many opportunities to apply word attack skills in a variety of contexts such as sentences, poems, and short stories; teach them to use multiple strategies for reading such as words as whole units, phonics, and context clues (Jordan, 1994). Add clues to help students decode troublesome words—mark long vowels, cross out silent letters, and divide words into syllables (Lewis & Doorlag, 1998).

Characteristics of Children with Learning Disabilities	Teaching Techniques for Language Arts Instruction
2. Some students have difficulty with automatic word recognition and reading fluency (Jordan, 1994).	2. To gain fluency and speed, encourage reading aloud from a variety of familiar materials, stress reading comprehension in the content areas, and give shorter reading assignments or increase the time limits. Use oral vocabulary activities to improve general knowledge (Jordan, 1994). Use assisted reading and modeling (Stahl & Kuhn, 2002). Strong focus on student learning outcomes (Adler & Fisher, 2001). Use computer software in which multimedia programs "talk," allowing students to develop sight vocabularies as they read and listen to stories and poems (Lewis & Doorlag, 1998).
3. Many students lack the basic skills needed to read textbooks independently in content areas (Gleason, 1995; Harniss et al., 1994).	3. To improve students' understanding of expository text use an explicit problem–solution–effect text structure for history; use concept maps and graphic organizers; use text-based interspersed questions and cues to focus attention on critical concepts and principles (Harniss et al., 1994). Provide explicit instruction in note taking, underlining, and skimming; relate instruction directly to content-area subjects (Jordan, 1994). Use thematic units to encourage integration of reading with other areas.
4. Many students have less background knowledge than their normal peers (Harniss et al., 1994).	4. Use content enhancements such as elaborate maps (Brigham, Scruggs, & Mastropieri, 1995). Provide sufficient background knowledge to help students comprehend materials (Harniss et al., 1994). Activate prior knowledge, use predicting and organizing ideas (Englert, Rozendal, & Mariage, 1994).
5. Many students have problems comprehending narrative themes (Williams et al., 1994) and understanding figurative language in literature (Johnson, 1993).	5. Activate prior knowledge, use questioning, predicting, and modeling (Simmons et al., 1995; Williams et al., 1994). Integrate systematic direct instruction into literature lessons (Mandlebaum, Lightbourne, & VandenBroek, 1994). Use inquiry learning to assist in developing literacy (Schmidt et al., 2002).

SUMMARY

This chapter reviews the best practices for reading instruction as found in studies that evaluate effective approaches for teaching reading. The chapter focuses on approaches that increase phonemic awareness and develop understanding of phonics, approaches that increase understanding of vocabulary, and approaches that develop comprehension. Approaches that develop vocabulary are divided according to vocabulary development in the lower-elementary grades and vocabulary development in the middle and upper-elementary grades.

The presentation of approaches that develop comprehension begins with a discussion about the importance of schema in using prior knowledge and past experiences to increase comprehension. The comprehension approaches include semantic mapping or webbing, modeling inferencing of characterization, questioning strategies, prediction approaches, and theme development. Approaches that increase students' independent reading include recreational reading groups, computer-assisted instruction, and focus units.

The chapter includes a section on assessment in the reading program that focuses on informal and formal methods of assessment. The informal assessment includes portfolios. The chapter discusses questions and issues related to high-stakes testing. The assessment section concludes with a discussion on evaluating instruction programs.

ADDITIONAL READING AND LANGUAGE ARTS ACTIVITIES

1. Read an article in a current journal such as *The Reading Teacher, The Journal of Reading,* or *Language Arts* that describes a reading program. Report your findings to the class.
2. Develop an introduction to a book that helps students activate prior knowledge or provides important background information before the students read the book.
3. Analyze how you use prior knowledge of texts, knowledge of the world, and clues supplied by text to create meaning (schema theory). Read several pieces of unfamiliar literature chosen from different genres, such as traditional literature, poetry, modern fantasy, and nonfictional information. Keep a journal account of how you created meaning during your reading.
4. Conduct a recreational reading group with a group of students or a group of your peers.
5. Develop a lesson plan in which students must use the text to find and support a theme or trace the developing conflict in the story.
6. Develop a file of semantic webs or questioning to accompany specific books. Emphasize the development of higher comprehension skills.
7. Develop a file of books and accompanying activities to encourage students to make predictions.
8. Develop a thematic unit.

BIBLIOGRAPHY

Adler, Martha A.; and Fisher, Charles W. "Early Reading Programs in High-Poverty School: A Case Study of Beating the Odds." *The Reading Teacher* 54 (March 2001): 616–19.

Afflerbach, P. P. "The Influence of Prior Knowledge on Expert Readers' Main Idea Construction Strategies." *Reading Research Quarterly* 25 (1990): 31–46.

Allington; Richard; and Cunningham, Patricia M. *Schools That Work: Where All Children Read and Write,* 2nd ed. Boston: Allyn & Bacon, 2002.

Ambrulevich, A. K. "An Analysis of the Levels of Thinking Required by Questions in Selected Literature Anthologies for Grades Eight, Nine, and Ten." Doctoral Dissertation, University of Bridgeport; 1986. *Dissertation Abstracts International* 47: 03A. (University Microfilms No. 86-13,043).

American Institutes for Research. *An Educators' Guide to School Reform.* Arlington, Va.: Educational Research Service, 1999.

Anderson, Richard C. "Role of the Reader's Schema in Comprehension, Learning, and Memory." In *Theoretical Models and Processes of Reading,* 3rd ed., edited by Harry Singer and Robert Ruddell. Newark, Del.: International Reading Association, 1985.

Barrett, Thomas. "Taxonomy of Reading Comprehension." In *Reading 360 Monograph.* Lexington, Mass.: Ginn, 1972.

Barrs, Mayra. "The Reader in the Writer." San Francisco: International Reading Association, 2002.

Bear, Donald R; Invernizzi, Marcia; Templeton, Shane; and Johnston, Francine. *Words Their Way,* 2nd ed. Upper Saddle River, N.J.: Merrill, 2000.

Block, Cathy Collins; and Mangieri, John M. "Recreational Reading: 20 Years Later." *The Reading Teacher* 55 (March 2002): 572–80.

Brigham, Frederick; Scruggs, Thomas; and Mastropieri, Margo. "Elaborative Maps for Enhanced Learning of Historical Information: Uniting Spatial, Verbal, and Imaginal Information." *The Journal of Special Education* 28 (1995): 440–60.

Carr, E; and Wixon, K. "Guidelines for Evaluating Vocabulary Instruction." *Journal of Reading* 29 (1986): 588–95.

Chenoweth, Karin. "Keeping Score." *School Library Journal* 47 (September 2001): 48–51.

Clay, Marie. *Observation Survey of Early Literacy Achievement.* Portsmouth, N.H.: Heinemann, 1993.

Cole, Gerald. *Misreading Reading: The Bad Science That Hurts Children.* Portsmouth, N.H.: Heinemann, 2000.

Cunningham, Patricia M; and Allington, Richard L. *Classrooms That Work: They Can All Read and Write,* 3rd ed. Boston: Allyn & Bacon, 2003.

Dole, J.; Duffy, G.; Roehler, L.; and Pearson, P. D. "Moving from the Old to the New: Research on Reading Comprehension Instruction." *Review of Educational Research* 61 (1991): 239–64.

Duffy, Gerald; and Hoffman, James V. "In Pursuit of an Illusion: The Flawed Search for a Perfect Method." *The Reading Teacher* 53 (September 1999): 10–16.

Early, Margaret; and Ericson, Bonnie O. "The Act of Reading." In *Literature in the Classroom: Readers, Texts, and Contexts,* edited by Ben F. Nelms. Urbana, Ill.: National Council of Teachers of English, 1988, pp. 31–44.

Englert, Carol Sue; Rozendal, Mary; and Mariage, Mary. "Fostering the Search for Understanding: A Teacher's Strategies for Leading Cognitive Development in 'Zones of Proximal Development.'" *Learning Disability Quarterly* 17 (Summer 1994): 187–204.

"Examining Evidence: New IRA Position Statement on Evidence-Based Reading Instruction." *Reading Today* 20 (August/September 2002): 1, 4.

Fleming, Margaret; and McGinnis, Jo, eds. *Portraits: Biography and Autobiography in the Secondary School.* Urbana, Ill.: National Council of Teachers of English, 1985.

Gauntt, H. L. "The Process of Prior Knowledge of Text Structure and Prior Knowledge of Content in the Comprehension and Recall of Expository Text." 1990. *Dissertation Abstracts International* 50: 11A (University Microfilms No. 90–10,405).

Gleason, Mary. "Using Direct Instruction to Integrate Reading and Writing for Students with Learning Disabilities." *Reading & Writing Quarterly: Overcoming Learning Difficulties* 11 (1995): 91–108.

Gordon, Christine J. "Modeling Inference Awareness Across the Curriculum." *Journal of Reading* 28 (February 1985): 444–47.

Harniss, Mark; Hollenbeck, Keith; Crawford, Donald; and Carnine, Douglas. "Content Organization and Instructional Design Issues in the Development of History Texts." *Learning Disability Quarterly* 17 (Summer 1994): 235–48.

Hoffman, James V.; Assaf, Lori Czop; and Paris, Scott G. "High-Stakes Testing in Reading: Today in Texas, Tomorrow?" *The Reading Teacher* 54 (February 2001): 482–92.

International Reading Association. "Research-Based Description of the Distinguishing Qualities of Excellent Classroom Teachers." *Reading Today* 19 (April/May 2000).

Johnson, Doris. "Relationships Between Oral and Written Language." *School Psychology Review* 22 (1993): 595–609.

Jones, H. Jon; and Coombs, William T. "A Themed Literature Unit versus a Textbook: A Comparison of the Effects on Content Acquisition and Attitudes in Elementary Social Studies." *Reading Research and Instruction* 34 (Winter 1994–95): 85–96.

Jordan, Nancy C. "Developing Perspectives on Reading Disabilities." *Reading and Writing Quarterly: Overcoming Learning Difficulties* 10 (1994): 297–311.

Juel, Connie. "The Importance of Preschool and Kindergarten Language Development in Reading Acquisition." San Francisco: International Reading Association, 2002.

Kleinfield, N. R. "The Elderly Man and the Sea? Test Sanitizes Literary Texts." *The New York Times* (June 2, 2002): 1, 30.

Lerner, Janet W. "Educational Intervention in Learning Disabilities." *Journal of the American Academy of Child and Adolescent Psychiatry* 28 (1989): 326–31.

Lewis, Rena; and Doorlag, Donald. *Teaching Special Students in the Mainstream,* 5th ed. Upper Saddle River, N.J.: Merrill/Prentice Hall, 1998.

MacCann, Donnarae. "Racism in Prize-Winning Biographical Works." In *The Black American in Books for Children: Readings in Racism,* edited by Donnarae MacCann and Gloria Woodard. Metuchen, N.J.: Scarecrow Press, 1985, pp. 169–79.

Mandlebaum, Linda Higbee; Lightbourne, Leslie; and VandenBroek, Judy. "Teaching with Literature." *Intervention in School and Clinic* 29 (January 1994): 134–50.

Marzano, R.; and Marzano, J. *A Cluster Approach to Elementary Vocabulary Instruction.* Newark, Del.: International Reading Association, 1988.

National Reading Panel. *Report of the National Reading Panel.* Washington, D.C: U.S. Department of Health and Human Services, 2000.

Norton, Donna E. "An Evaluation of the BISD/ TAMU Multiethnic Reading Program." Research Report, College Station: Texas A&M University, 1987.

———. *The Impact of Literature-Based Instruction.* Upper Saddle River, N.J.: Merrill/Prentice Hall, 1996.

———. *Through the Eyes of a Child: An Introduction to Children's Literature,* 6th ed. Upper Saddle River, N.J.: Merrill/Prentice Hall, 2003.

————; and Kracht, J. "Developing Understanding of Geography Themes through Literature." Washington, D.C.: National Conference for Social Studies, 1991.

Pearson, P. David; and Camperell, Kay. "Comprehension of Text Structures." In *Theoretical Models and Processes of Reading,* edited by Harry Singer and Robert Ruddell. Newark, Del.: International Reading Association, 1985, pp. 323–42.

Pollak, Judy. "A Workshop Approach to Reading and Writing: Why Does It Work for Middle Level Learners?" *Reading Improvement* 31 (Fall 1994): 145–48.

Roehler, Laura; and Duffy, Gerald G. "Direct Explanation of Comprehension Processes." In *Comprehension Instruction,* edited by Gerald G. Duffy, Laura R. Roehler, and Jana Mason. New York: Longman, 1984, pp. 265–80.

Routman, Regie. *Literacy at the Crossroads.* Portsmouth, N.H.: Heinemann, 1996.

Schmidt, Patricia Ruggiano; Gillen, Susan; Zollo, Teresa, Colabufo; and Stone, Rhaenel. "Literacy Learning and Scientific Inquiry: Children Respond." *The Reading Teacher* 55 (March 2002): 534–48.

Simmons, Deborah; Baker, Janice; Fuchs, Lynn; Fuchs, Doug; and Zigmond, Naomi. "Teacher-Directed Reading Instruction in the Mainstream: A Call for Instructional Reform." *Reading & Writing Quarterly: Overcoming Learning Difficulties* 11 (1995): 19–36.

Stahl, Steven A.; and Kuhn, Melanie R. "Making It Sound Like Language: Developing Fluency." *The Reading Teacher* 55 (March 2002): 582–84.

Sutherland, Zena; and Arbuthnot, May Hill. *Children and Books.* Glenview, Ill.: Scott, Foresman & Co., 1986.

Williams, Joanna; Brown, Laura; Silverstein, Ada; and deCani, John. "An Instructional Program in Comprehension of Narrative Themes for Adolescents with Learning Disabilities." *Learning Disability Quarterly* 17 (Summer 1994): 205–21.

Zarrillo, J. "Teachers' Interpretations of Literature-Based Reading." *The Reading Teacher* 43 (1989): 22–28.

Zemelman, Steven; Daniels, Harvey; and Hyde, S. *Best Practice: New Standards for Teaching and Learning in America's Schools,* 2nd ed. Portsmouth, N.H.: Heinemann, 1998.

CHILDREN'S LITERATURE REFERENCES

Adler, David. *Martin Luther King, Jr.: Free at Last.* Illustrated by Robert Casilla, New York: Holiday, 1987.

Atwater, Richard; and Atwater, Florence. *Mr. Popper's Penguins.* Boston: Little, Brown, 1938.

Aylesworth, Jim. *Old Black Fly.* Illustrated by Stephen Gammel. New York: Holt, 1992.

Barton, Byron. *The Wee Little Woman.* New York: HarperCollins, 1995.

————. *I Want to Be an Astronaut.* New York: Crowell, 1988.

Bat-Ami, Miriam. *Two Suns in the Sky.* Chicago: Front Street, 1999.

Bauer, Marian. *Rain of Fire.* New York: Clarion, 1983.

Brooks, Polly. *Queen Eleanor: Independent Spirit of the Medieval World.* Philadelphia: J. B. Lippincott Co., 1983.

Carle, Eric. *My First Book of Colors.* New York: Crowell, 1974.

Cendrars, Blaise. *Shadow.* Illustrated by Marcia Brown. New York: Charles Scribner's Sons, 1982.

Cleary, Beverly. *Dear Mr. Henshaw.* Illustrated by Paul O. Zelinsky. New York: William Morrow & Co., 1983.

———. *Ramona and Her Father.* New York: William Morrow & Co., 1977.

Coerr, Eleanor. *Sadako and the Thousand Paper Cranes.* New York: Putnam, 1977.

Colman, Penny. *Rosie the Riveter: Women Working on the Home Front in World War II.* New York: Crown, 1995.

Cook, Scott. *The Gingerbread Boy.* New York: Alfred A. Knopf, 1987.

Cooper, Helen. *Pumpkin Soup.* New York: Farrar, Straus & Giroux, 1999.

Cormier, Robert. *Other Bells for Us to Ring.* New York: Delacorte, 1990.

Cresswell, Helen. "The Bagthorpe Saga," *Ordinary Jack* (1977), *Absolute Zero* (1978), *Bagthorpes Unlimited* (1978), and *Bagthorpes Abroad* (1984). New York: Macmillan.

Crews, Donald. *Freight Train.* New York: Greenwillow, 1978.

Cronin, Doreen. *Click, Clack, Moo: Cows That Type.* Illustrated by Betsy Lewin. New York: Simon & Schuster, 2000.

Dalgliesh, Alice. *The Columbus Story.* New York: Charles Scribner's Sons, 1955.

D'Aulaire, Ingri; and D'Aulaire, Edgar. *Columbus.* New York: Doubleday, 1955.

Davis, Daniel. *Behind Barbed Wire.* New York: Dutton, 1982.

de Paola, Tomie. *The Legend of the Bluebonnet.* New York: Putnam, 1983.

Fleischman, Paul. *Bull Run.* Illustrated by David Frampton. New York: HarperCollins, 1993.

Fleischman, Sid. *The Whipping Boy.* New York: Greenwillow, 1986.

Fleming, Denise. *In the Tall, Tall Grass.* New York: Holt, 1991.

Floca, Brian. *Five Trucks.* New York: Dorlong Kindersley, 1999.

Foreman, Michael. *War Boy.* Boston: Little, Brown, 1990.

Fox, Mem. *Hattie and the Fox.* New York: Bradbury, 1987.

Fox, Paula. *The Slave Dancer.* Illustrated by Eros Keith. New York: Bradbury, 1973.

Freedman, Russell. *Eleanor Roosevelt: A Life of Discovery.* New York: Clarion, 1993.

———. *Franklin Delano Roosevelt.* New York: Clarion, 1990.

———. *Lincoln: A Photobiography.* New York: Clarion, 1987.

Fritz, Jean. *Where Do You Think You're Going, Christopher Columbus?* Illustrated by Margot Tomes. New York: Putnam, 1980.

Gehrts, Barbara. *Don't Say a Word.* New York: Macmillan, 1987.

Goodnough, David. *Christopher Columbus.* Mahwah, N.J.: Troll, 1979.

Grimm, Brothers. *Red Riding Hood.* Retold and illustrated by James Marshall. New York: Dial Press, 1987.

Hahn, Mary Downing. *Stepping on the Cracks.* New York: Clarion, 1991.

Hartling, Peter. *Crutches.* New York: Lothrop, Lee & Shepard, 1988.

Hastings, Selina. *Sir Gawain and the Loathly Lady.* New York: Lothrop, Lee & Shepard, 1985.

Heide, Florence Parry. *The Bigness Contest.* Illustrated by Victoria Chess. Boston: Little, Brown, 1994.

————; and Gilliland, Judith. *The Day of Ahmed's Secret.* Illustrated by Ted Lewin. New York: Lothrop, Lee & Shepard, 1990.

Hoban, Tana. *Circles, Triangles, and Squares.* New York: Macmillan, 1974.

————. *Of Colors and Things.* New York: Greenwillow, 1989.

————. *Over, Under and Through and Other Spatial Concepts.* New York: Macmillan, 1973.

————. *Shapes, Shapes, Shapes.* New York: Greenwillow, 1986.

————. *So Many Circles, So Many Squares.* New York: Greenwillow, 1998.

Hodges, Margaret. *Saint George and the Dragon.* Boston: Little, Brown, 1984.

Hunt, Irene. *Across Five Aprils.* Chicago: Follett, 1964.

Hutchins, Pat. *What Game Shall We Play?* New York: Greenwillow, 1990.

Isaacs, Anne. *Swamp Angel.* Illustrated by Paul O. Zelinsky. New York: Dutton, 1994.

Ivimey, John. *The Complete Story of the Three Blind Mice.* Illustrated by Paul Galdone. New York: Clarion, 1987.

Keith, Harold. *Rifles for Watie.* New York: Thomas Y. Crowell Co., 1957.

Kimmel, Eric A. *The Chanukkah Guest.* Illustrated by Giora Carmi. New York: Holiday, 1990.

Lauber, Patricia. *Painters of the Caves.* Washington, D.C.: National Geographic, 1998.

Levinson, Nancy Smiler. *Christopher Columbus: Voyager to the Unknown.* New York: Dutton, 1990.

Lindbergh, Reeve. *The Day the Goose Got Loose.* Illustrated by Steven Kellogg. New York: Dial, 1990.

————. *Johnny Appleseed.* Illustrated by Kathy Jakobsen. Boston: Little, Brown, 1990.

Lingard, Joan. *Tug of War.* New York: Lodestar, 1989.

Lindgren, Astrid. *Pippi Longstocking.* New York: Viking Press, 1950.

Lionni, Leo. *Swimmy.* New York: Pantheon, 1963.

Lowry, Lois. *Anastasia on Her Own.* Boston: Houghton Mifflin, 1985.

————. *Number the Stars.* Boston: Houghton Mifflin, 1989.

MacLachlan, Patricia. *Sarah, Plain and Tall.* New York: Harper & Row, 1985.

Magorian, M. *Good Night, Mr. Tom.* New York: Harper & Row, 1981.

Marrin, Albert. *Hitler.* New York: Viking, 1987.

McLaughlin, Molly. *Dragonflies.* New York: Walker, 1989.

McSwigan, Marie. *Snow Treasure.* New York: Dutton, 1942.

Meltzer, Milton. *Rescue: The Story of How Gentiles Saved the Jews in the Holocaust.* New York: Harper & Row, 1988.

Monjo, F. N. *The Drinking Gourd.* Illustrated by Fred Brenner. New York: Harper & Row, 1970.

Moser, Barry. *The Three Little Pigs.* Boston: Little, Brown, 2001.

Moss, Lloyd. *Zin! Zin! Zin!: A Violin.* Illustrated by Marjorie Priceman. New York: Simon & Schuster, 1995.

Naylor, Phyllis Reynolds. *Shiloh.* New York: Atheneum, 1991.

Noyes, Alfred. *The Highwayman.* Illustrated by Charles Keeping. New York: Oxford, 1981.

Orlev, Ur. *The Island on Bird Street.* Boston: Houghton Mifflin, 1984.

————. *The Man from the Other Side.* Boston: Houghton Mifflin, 1991.

Pearson, Kit. *The Sky Is Falling.* New York: Viking, 1989.

Perrault, Charles. *Cinderella.* Illustrated by Marcia Brown. New York: Charles Scribner's Sons, 1954.

Peters, Lisa Westberg. *October Smiled Back.* Illustrated by Ed Young. New York: Holt, 1996.

Polacco, Patricia. *Meteor!* New York: Dodd, Mead & Co., 1987.

Pollack, Pamela, selected by. *The Random House Book of Humor for Children.* Illustrated by Paul O. Zelinsky. New York: Random House, 1988.

Provensen, Alice. *The Buck Stops Here: The Presidents of the United States.* New York: Harper & Row, 1990.

Reiss, Johanna. *The Upstairs Room.* New York: Thomas Y. Crowell Co., 1972.

Rockwell, Anne. *First Comes Spring.* New York: Crowell, 1985.

Rogasky, Barbara. *Smoke and Ashes.* New York: Holiday, 1988.

Roosevelt, Elliot. *Eleanor Roosevelt, with Love.* New York: Dutton, 1984.

Rosen, Michael, edited by. *We're Going on a Bear Hunt.* Illustrated by Helen Oxenbury. New York: Macmillan, 1989.

Rylant, Cynthia. *When I Was Young in the Mountains.* New York: Dutton, 1982.

St. George, Judith. *So You Want to Be President?* Illustrated by David Small. New York: Philomel, 2000.

Sandburg, Carl. *Rootabaga Stories.* San Diego: Harcourt Brace Jovanovich, 1922.

Scieszka, Jon. *The Stinky Cheese Man and Other Fairly Stupid Tales.* Illustrated by Lane Smith. New York: Viking, 1992.

Seuss, Dr. *Horton Hears a Who.* New York: Random House, 1954.

Siebert, Diane. *Heartland.* Illustrated by Wendell Minor. New York: Thomas Y. Crowell Co., 1989.

Siegal, Aranka. *Upon the Head of a Goat.* New York: Farrar, Straus & Giroux, 1981.

Simon, Seymour. *Storms.* New York: Morrow, 1989.

Sis, Peter. *Follow the Dream: The Story of Christopher Columbus.* New York: Alfred A. Knopf, 1991.

Stock, Catherine. *Armien's Fishing Trip.* New York: William Morrow & Co., 1990.

Tafuri, Nancy. *Early Morning in the Barn.* New York: Greenwillow, 1983.

Uchida, Yoshiko. *Journey Home.* New York: Atheneum, 1978.

———. *Journey to Topaz.* New York: Charles Scribner's Sons, 1971.

Ventura, Piero. *Christopher Columbus.* New York: Random House, 1978.

Voigt, Cynthia. *Dicey's Song.* New York: Atheneum, 1982.

———. *A Solitary Blue.* New York: Atheneum, 1983.

Vos, Ida. *Hide and Seek.* Boston: Houghton Mifflin, 1991.

West, Delno C.; and West, Jean M. *Christopher Columbus: The Great Adventure.* New York: Atheneum, 1991.

Whippo, Walt. *Little White Duck.* Music by Bernard Zaritzky. Illustrated by Joan Paley. Boston: Little, Brown, 2000.

Whitney, Sharon. *Eleanor Roosevelt.* New York: Watts, 1982.

Wood, Audrey. *Heckedy Peg.* Illustrated by Don Wood. San Diego: Harcourt Brace Jovanovich, 1987.

————. *King Bidgood's in the Bathtub.* Illustrated by Don Wood. San Diego: Harcourt Brace Jovanovich, 1985.

Yates, Elizabeth. *Amos Fortune, Free Man.* New York: Dutton, 1950.

————. *My Diary, My World.* Philadelphia: Westminster, 1981.

————. *My Widening World.* Philadelphia: Westminster, 1983.

Yolen, Jane. *The Devil's Arithmetic.* New York: Viking, 1988.

————. *Off We Go!* Illustrated by Laurel Molk. Boston: Little, Brown, 2000.

————. *Owl Moon.* Illustrated by John Schoenherr. New York: Philomel, 1987.

————. *The Three Bears Rhyme Book.* Illustrated by Jane Dyer. San Diego: Harcourt Brace Jovanovich, 1987.

Yorinks, Arthur. *Hey, Al.* Illustrated by Richard Egielski. New York: Farrar, Straus & Giroux, 1986.

Literature and the Language Arts

After completing this chapter on literature, you will be able to:

1. Describe an environment that stimulates interest in literature.
2. Select literature that considers appropriateness, balance, and children's interests.
3. Prepare and tell an appropriate story.
4. List benefits of reading aloud to children, discuss selection of books for reading aloud, and read a selection aloud to children.
5. Describe how art adds to appreciation of literature.
6. Describe methods and develop lessons that increase students' understanding of literary elements through webbing, modeling, and plot diagramming.
7. List the instructional possibilities for a children's book.
8. Describe ways for developing students' understanding of and appreciation for literary genres.
9. Understand that literature provides a means of integrating the language arts and may be used with all areas of the language arts.
10. Describe how to increase world understanding through folktales.
11. Develop a unit around literature.

*T*he many books written especially for children open up new and wonderful worlds. Through books, children experience the enchantment of Cinderella, the adventure of Huckleberry Finn, and the loneliness and challenge of living on the Island of the Blue Dolphins. Most adults have favorite books from childhood that remain vivid in their memories. Mary Poppins, Pooh Bear, or Caddie Woodlawn may seem like personal friends. Not all children, however, regard literature as a source of pleasure and as a way of meeting new friends. The goal of this chapter is to show you how to help children develop a love of reading and an appreciation for a variety of literary genres. In addition, the chapter stresses using literature in the language arts curriculum and suggests ways to integrate literature and language arts objectives into other subject areas. Chapter 5 emphasized approaches that bring literature into the reading curriculum. These two chapters are placed early in the text so that you will be able to select literature and literature-related activities in all of the language communication areas included in speaking, writing, listening, and reading.

Using literature in the curriculum and teaching about literature in the classroom are two exciting yet complex areas. Choosing literature that motivates students to read requires knowledge about literature, awareness of the interests of students, and knowledge about instructional approaches that motivate and stimulate interest. Likewise, teaching about literature requires knowledge about literature and instructional approaches that encourage understanding of various genres, story structures, and such literary elements as style, characterization, and theme.

As you approach literature and methodologies related to literature keep in mind the following five objectives for the literature program identified by Norton (2003). The literature program should:

1. Help students realize that literature is for entertainment and can be enjoyed throughout their lives.

2. Acquaint students with their own literary heritage as well as the heritage of other students and foster the value of preservation of knowledge.
3. Help students understand the formal elements of literature, lead them to prefer the best that our literature has to offer, and encourage them to appreciate authors who not only have something to say but say it extremely well.
4. Help students understand themselves and the rest of humanity and to identify with literary characters who are confronting and overcoming problems like their own. Hopefully, they will see both themselves and their world in a new perspective.
5. Help students evaluate what they read as educators help them compare, question, and evaluate the books that they read.

If students are to gain these values associated with enjoyment, knowledge of their heritage, recognition and appreciation of good literature, and understanding of themselves and others, they must explore balanced selections of literature. Consequently, the literature program should include classics and contemporary stories, fantasy as well as realistic stories, prose as well as poetry, biographies, and books containing factual information.

Curriculum documents from various school districts frequently develop this multifaceted nature of literature. For example, a kindergarten through sixth-grade literature curriculum may have the following goals: (1) to introduce children to their literary heritage; (2) to encourage children to read for pleasure and knowledge; (3) to provide children with knowledge about literary elements and structure; (4) to allow children to give creative responses to literature; (5) to develop children's ability to evaluate literature; and (6) to develop independent readers and learners.

Literature programs have broad educational and personal goals. Folklore from around the world, the writings of Mark Twain and Robert Louis Stevenson, and the poetry of Langston Hughes and Edward Lear, for example, help children understand and value cultural and literary heritage. Historical fiction and nonfiction chronicling early explorations and frontier expansion allow children to live vicariously through history. Books on outer space and scientific breakthroughs open doors to new knowledge and expand interests. Fantasy and science fiction nurture and expand imaginations and allow children to visualize worlds that have not yet materialized. Biography and autobiography allow children to explore human possibilities while promoting their personal and social development. Interactions with many types of literature allow children to expand their language and to develop their cognitive skills. The time spent with literature is among the most rewarding. Smith (1991) argues that a variety of genres are necessary to promote emotional growth as the children learn to appreciate literature and identify with fictional characters. In addition, the analysis of different literary genres promotes cognitive development as children identify themes discussed in one genre and find similar themes in other genres.

The Environment

A strong literature program includes an environment in which children can easily locate and read books. In a study of children's access to print, Neuman and Celano (2001) focused on the settings in which literacy begins for young children. They challenged the assumption that "books and other literacy-related resources are easily and equally accessible to all children and their families" (p. 11). They argue that the access or lack of access to literacy materials influences the ultimate achievement for young children and that differences in access could influence the degree of children's familiarity with book language and cognitive behaviors associated with reading. Studies such as this one as well as reports by Galda and Beach (2001) highlight the importance of a rich literature environment if students are to gain understanding of such literature-associated abilities as predicting story outcomes and understanding story structures and themes.

Now let us consider what a literacy-rich environment should look like. In *Classrooms That Work*, Cunningham and Allington (2003) describe a classroom in which all of the children are destined to succeed in learning to read and to write. They describe a room filled with books and other reading materials such as newspapers and a teacher who reads or refers to books or parts of books throughout the day. Weather poems may be a springboard into a science unit. Art books may be used to begin an art lesson. Books about a specific historical era may be part of the social studies lesson. Children share the books they are currently reading and provide responses to the books.

Cunningham and Allington (2003) conclude: "Children who are successful at becoming literate view reading and writing as authentic activities from which they get information and pleasure, and by which they communicate with others. They know what reading and writing are really for and they want to be successful at it. The literacy-rich classroom communicates the importance of real reading and writing activities and not relegating reading and writing to a brief period" (p. 21).

Teachers should provide time for children to listen to, read, and discuss books. Tell them about the authors and summarize plots, characters, and settings. Provide opportunities for children to select books themselves. Children throughout the elementary grades enjoy having books read to them, so read to children frequently. Also, provide opportunities for them to read to other children. Encouraging children to read outside of school is also very important. Anderson, Wilson, and Fielding (1988) found that reading books outside of school was the best predictor of students' future reading achievement.

Educators who use or recommend literature-based programs emphasize a dynamic environment. Taxel (1988) describes a literature-based classroom as "fluid and dynamic, . . . a place where educators see literature as central to the curriculum, not as an occasional bit of enrichment undertaken when the 'real' work is completed" (p. 74).

An environment where students have ready access to books encourages interaction in a strong literature program.

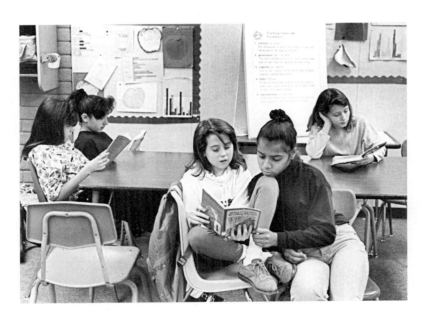

Understanding and enjoying literature are the major goals in a first- through sixth-grade program that May (1987) describes. May's program for exploring different literature genres begins in kindergarten, where students and teachers explore books containing personification and compare these books to other fantasy stories and folktales. At this level, students consider how the characters and their actions seem real. First graders explore literary patterns within folktales, look at variances among folktales found in different cultures, and examine different versions of the same folktale. They also explore realistic fiction and relate the literature to a unit on the family. Second graders discuss repeated patterns, magical numbers, and settings in folktales. They compare additional versions of folktales and explore folktale adaptations. Third graders read E. B. White's *Charlotte's Web* (1952) and discuss animal characters, personification, fantasy, and point of view. They compare fantasy and realistic stories about animals. Fourth graders explore literature around a social studies unit on India. Fifth graders explore literature as part of a social studies unit on medieval Europe and discuss historical fiction as literature and interpretation of history. They also consider the importance of setting, symbolism, and stereotypical characters in legends and work with myths and fables. Sixth graders explore differences between autobiography and biography, conduct oral interviews, write short biographies, and share them with the class.

May (1987) is enthusiastic about this literature program and shares the following response from a teacher: "By the end of the first year the children were reading more library books than before. They were also talking about literature and were 'borrowing' an author's style or symbolism when they admired it. They were more appreciative of an author's writing style. All of the students, even the slow learners, were writing and reading for enjoyment" (p. 136).

The teacher of a fifth-grade literature program shows equal enthusiasm. Five (1988) describes a literature-based program in which she begins each session with a mini-lesson on an element of fiction: "Often I use the books that I read aloud to them each day as the basis for my mini-lessons, allowing time for discussions, for making predictions, and interpretations, and for discovering characteristics of a particular author's style that students may wish to apply to their own writing. Different genres are also introduced during these lessons" (p. 105). The mini-lessons involve discussion, direct teaching, and sharing of specific activities. Mini-lessons focus on such topics as book selection, copyrights, plot structures, and time lines of characters. After the mini-lessons, students read related books of their own choosing, discuss the books, and write about their choices. Five enthusiastically evaluates her program: "Today my reading program is dramatically different and so are the results. Today my students read between 25 and 144 books a year. Children listen to each other and seek recommendations for their next book selections. They wonder about authors and look for feelings, for believable characters, for interesting words, and they are delighted with effective dialogue. And my students and I always talk books before school, during school, at lunch and after school, something we never did in my 'workbook' days" (p. 104).

Both programs emphasize an environment that is rich with literature, encourages children to explore various literary devices in a number of ways, and includes both teacher- and student-directed activities with literature. The programs also show that teachers may use literature to combine reading, writing, and other content areas.

Literature in the Curriculum

The previously described language arts programs illustrate the importance of including a variety of genres of literature in the curriculum. Smith (1991) identifies a conceptual shift in education that requires the use of numerous books and develops an environment in which students pursue topics of personal interest.

Literature selections must include books that can be read to and by children and books that meet the goals for developing literary appreciation and understanding. A language arts curriculum should include picture books, folklore, modern fantasy, poetry, contemporary realistic fiction, historical fiction, biography, autobiography, and informational literature selected to help students develop an understanding of and an appreciation for specific genres. The literature within these genres should reflect varied cultural and literary heritage, and should provide insights into personal and social development. Knowledge about appropriateness, balance, resources to help teachers choose literature, and children's interests are basic to achieving these objectives.

What Is Appropriate?

Much concern surrounds contemporary realistic fiction. During times of changing values, such concern is not surprising. Current controversy regarding realistic fiction centers around issues related to literary merit and appropriate content. The heroes and heroines in today's realistic fiction face problems related to sexism, racism, violence, drugs, sexual activities, and such family disturbances as separation, divorce, and abuse. Quan's analysis (1990) of social values in adolescent literature published between 1940 and 1980 indicates a shift from social conservatism to a more liberal interpretation of traditional values. Such shifts cause some groups to question the appropriateness of the literature read in schools.

Shifts in contemporary realistic fiction in which the characters and the conflicts more closely mirror the people and the problems in society also cause concerns related to censorship. Certain groups believe in censoring books or authors they suspect are capable of subverting children's religious, social, or political beliefs. According to a survey by People for the American Way, censorship attempts "increased by 20 percent during the 1986–87 school year and by 168 percent in the last five years" (Wiessler, 1987, sec. 1, 1). A report by Dronka (1987) indicates that organized groups are increasingly advocating censorship. As more publishers develop literature-based textbooks, they too face the challenges of censorship. For example, Meade (1990) quotes advocates who view a literature-based series as "a blend of sophistication and wholesomeness" and opponents who detect "a not-so-subtle emphasis on violence, death, and the occult" (p. 38). In an article in *Education Week*, Rothman (1990) states that "school districts can protect their literature curriculum by having in place procedures that ensure that the materials selected are educationally sound" (p. 5). (For guidelines for evaluating literature and meeting problems related to censorship such as those related to sexism, sexuality, and violence, see Norton, 2003.)

Sexism in children's literature is frequently denounced by critics. Frasher (1982) found that literature published after 1970 reflects a heightened sensitivity toward women. Literature published prior to 1970 not only includes more male main characters, but also more negative comments about females than the more recent literature. Anita P. Davis and Thomas R. McDaniel (1999) analyzed the percentages of male and female characters in more recent Caldecott Medal winners. They found that 39 percent of the characters in books published in the 1990s were female. School libraries should certainly offer books that portray women and girls in nonstereotyped roles. They should offer biographies of famous women to provide models for girls, just as they offer biographies of well-known men. Libraries should also offer stories about girls who are active and inventive and who do not always follow the initiative of boys.

As mentioned previously, many contemporary books deal with real problems many children face, such as divorce, death, special needs, and various difficulties associated with growing up. Polese (1994) is so emphatic about using books to help children survive difficulties that she maintains, "books can help youngsters survive and even thrive through extremely difficult childhoods" (p. 156). Books based on specific problems include the following:

- *Divorce:* Beverly Cleary's *Dear Mr. Henshaw* (1983): Corresponding with his favorite author helps a sixth-grade boy overcome problems associated with his parents' divorce. Gary Paulsen's *Hatchet* (1987): Surviving in the Canadian wilderness helps a boy face problems associated with his parents' divorce.
- *Death:* Eleanor Cameron's *That Julia Redfern* (1982): A girl develops a close relationship with her father and then accepts his death. Marion Dane Bauer's *On My Honor* (1986): A boy faces both his own disobedience and the death of his best friend. Audrey Couloumbis's *Getting Near to Baby* (1999). A family faces the death of their family's baby. Norma Fox Mazer's *After the Rain* (1987): A girl develops a close relationship with her grandfather and then mourns his death.
- *Special needs:* Ellen Howard's *Edith Herself* (1987): A girl faces and solves her problems associated with epilepsy in a story set in the 1890s. Jeanne Lee's *Silent Lotus* (1991): A young mute girl learns to perform the story dances of Cambodia.
- *Growing up:* Karen Cushman's *Catherine, Called Birdy* (1994): A girl in medieval England fights the role placed on females in her society as does the heroine in *Matilda Bone* (2000), also set in medieval times. Jean Little's *Different Dragons* (1986): A boy and a girl discover that they both have fears that they must overcome.

Literature selections should take into account the needs of children of different ages and abilities. Although many books are geared to the varied interests of children with average or above-average reading ability, there are not as many designed for children with beginning skills or children whose reading ability is several years below grade level. The interests of students who are below grade level are similar to those of children who read at grade level, but teachers must select easier-to-read books for the slower children.

Criteria for the evaluation of children's books that are appropriate for adults who experience reading problems (Thistlethwaite, 1994) is also helpful when selecting easier books that are acceptable for older readers. For example, the theme should be relevant to the age of the readers and allow readers to relate to the theme. The depth of experience should allow readers to explore experiences related to different races, ethnic groups, and social classes. The artwork should be appealing to older readers. Finally, the ages of some of the characters in the book should be closer to the ages of the readers.

Literature collections should include books on science, art, social studies, and music topics. Margery Facklam's *Spiders and Their Web Sites* (2001) and Susan E. Goodman's *Stones, Bones, and Petroglyphs* (1998) enrich the science curriculum. Jan Greenberg and Sandra Jordan's *The Painter's Eye: Learning to Look at Contemporary Art* (1991), Nancy Willard's *Pish, Posh, Said Hieronymus Bosch* (1991), and Zheng Zhensun and Alice Low's *A Young Painter: The Life and Paintings of Wang Yani—China's Extraordinary Young Artist* (1991) are excellent for increasing appreciation for art. The social studies curriculum is enriched by such books as Russell Freedman's *Eleanor Roosevelt: A Life of Discovery* (1993) and Laurence Yep's *Dragon's Gate* (1993). Books such as Violette Verdy's *Of Swans, Sugarplums, and Satin Slippers: Ballet Stories for Children* (1991) add interest to the study of music.

Materials on specific topics should be available at a wide range of reading levels, even when they are studied at only one grade level. The reason for this is obvious from the test results of several sixth-grade classes. Reading levels in six classrooms ranged from second through twelfth grade. In addition, because specific musical selections can enhance the study of a period of history, and because filmstrips or sets of pictures can promote understanding of written content in the subject areas, library materials should reflect the needs of the overall curriculum.

A Comprehensive Collection

Literature selections for libraries, as well as for individual children, should include picture books, traditional literature, modern fantasy, poetry, contemporary realistic fiction, historical fiction, biography, and nonfiction. Picture books, alphabet books, and storybooks that develop plot and characters afford children their earliest encounters with literature. Teachers and parents usually read these books to younger children because picture storybook reading levels are usually at least for third grade. Excellent alphabet books include Betsy Bowen's *Antler, Bear, Canoe: A Northwoods Alphabet Year* (1991), Chris Van Allsburg's *The Z Was Zapped* (1987), Suse MacDonald's *Alphabatics* (1986), and Peter Dodson's *An Alphabet of Dinosaurs* (1995). These books expand language and encourage interaction with the text. Picture storybooks should include old favorites, such as Dr. Seuss's *The 500 Hats of Bartholomew Cubbins* (1938), Robert McCloskey's *Make Way for Ducklings* (1941), and Maurice Sendak's *Where the Wild Things Are* (1963). As new books are published, you can select titles to add to the collection. Faith Ringgold's *Tar Beach* (1991), Anne Isaacs's *Swamp Angel* (1994), and Barbara Kerley's *The Dinosaurs of Waterhouse Hawkins* (2001) encourage children to interact with both the illustrations and the text. Picture storybooks, such as Denys Cazet's *A Fish in His Pocket* (1987), show children that even young characters can solve problems in satisfying and creative ways.

A well-balanced collection includes picture storybooks illustrated in a variety of ways. The collection should include photographs, woodcuts, collages, painted pictures, ink drawings, and crayon illustrations. Children frequently enjoy creating their own collages as well as viewing those of professional artists. The following books are illustrated through collage: Simms Taback's *Joseph Had a Little Overcoat* (1999), Judith Heide Gilliland's *Steamboat! The Story of Captain Blanche Leathers* (2000), and Steve Jenkins's *The Top of the World: Climbing Mount Everest* (1999).

A collection should also include well-loved traditional literature—folktales handed down from earlier generations, such as "Little Red Riding Hood," "The Three Billy Goats Gruff," and "Cinderella," along with mythology and stories of epic heroes, such as King Arthur and Robin Hood. Traditional literature should include folklore from numerous cultures. Olaf Baker's *Where the Buffaloes Begin* (1981), Van Dyke Parks's adaptation of Joel Chandler Harris's *Jump Again! More Adventures of Brer Rabbit* (1987), and Demi's *The Stonecutter* (1995) are excellent selections.

Children should be introduced to classics in modern fantasy, such as E. B. White's *Charlotte's Web* (1952), C. S. Lewis's *The Lion, the Witch and the Wardrobe* (1950), A. A. Milne's *Winnie-the-Pooh* (1926), and Beatrix Potter's *The Tale of Peter Rabbit* (1902). Authors such as Lloyd Alexander, Hans Christian Andersen, Michael Bond, Lucy Boston, Lewis Carroll, Susan Cooper, Kenneth Grahame, Rudyard Kipling, Ursula LeGuin, Madeleine L'Engle, and Margery Williams bring excitement to this genre of literature. In addition to these, collections should include newer fantasies, such as J. K. Rowling's *Harry Potter and the Sorcerer's Stone* (1997), Robin McKinley's *The Hero and the Crown* (1984), and Brian Jacques's *Redwall* (1986).

Study of the past might be very dull without historical fiction. Such stories allow children to live vicariously in the past and to understand important themes and values. Children can learn about the Revolutionary War by reading Esther Forbes's *Johnny Tremain* (1943), visit the Pilgrims by reading Patricia Clapp's *Constance: A Story of Early Plymouth* (1968), be persecuted as a witch in Elizabeth Speare's *The Witch of Blackbird Pond* (1958), live in the pioneer wilderness in Laura Ingalls Wilder's *Little House in the Big Woods* (1932), discover Victorian London in Philip Pullman's *The Ruby in the Smoke* (1987) and Leon Garfield's *The December Rose* (1986), or feel what it might be like to be a slave in Belinda Hurmence's *A*

Girl Called Boy (1982). They may visit the ancient Korean culture by reading Linda Sue Park's *A Single Shard* (2001) to discover how a boy makes his dreams come true.

Biographies add another dimension to literature programs by allowing children to learn more about past and present heroes and heroines. You can introduce children to biographies in the early grades with picture storybook biographies, such as David Adler's *Martin Luther King, Jr.: Free at Last* (1986). Middle-elementary students can read autobiographies such as Lillian Gish's *An Actor's Life for Me!* (1987) and biographies such as Jean Fritz's *Make Way for Sam Houston* (1986). Encourage older children to read biographies such as Russell Freedman's *Lincoln: A Photobiography* (1987), Polly Brooks's *Queen Eleanor: Independent Spirit of the Medieval World* (1983), and Catherine Reef's *Walt Whitman* (1995).

Informational books are available in all areas of knowledge. There are books about the history and culture of the ancient and modern worlds. Books about the laws of nature encourage children to learn about their own bodies, observe nature, explore the life cycles of animals, consider the impact of endangered species, experiment with plants, and explore the geology of the earth. Informational books answer children's questions about discoveries of the past and present or explain how many kinds of machines work. Informational books also allow children to learn more about their hobbies and interests. Such books often include directions, provide guidelines for choosing equipment or other materials, and give interesting background information.

Sources of Information

Many resources are available to help teachers select literature. Children's literature textbooks are the best source of information for genre-specific literature. *Through the Eyes of a Child: An Introduction to Children's Literature* (Norton, 2003), *The Impact of Literature-Based Reading* (Norton, 1992), *Children and Books* (Sutherland & Arbuthnot, 1997), and *Children's Literature* (Huck, Hepler, & Hickman, 1997) discuss literature according to genre and recommend hundreds of titles useful for literature programs. These texts list Caldecott and Newbery award-winning books. Specialized books, such as Cianciolo's *Picture Books for Children* (1990), present criteria for evaluation and recommend specific books. For example, Cianciolo recommends books that are categorized according to the themes of "Me and My Family," "Other People," "The World I Live In," and "The Imaginative World."

Literature journals are excellent resources for new books and for specialized collections and topics. For example, the *School Library Journal, Booklist,* and *Hornbook* contain book reviews and starred reviews for excellent books. *Booklist* publishes yearly lists of "Notable Children's Books" and "Children's Editors' Choice." In addition, *Booklist* publishes specialty lists, such as "Popular Reading—Chapter Books" (Bennett, 1987); "Popular Reading—After Henry Huggins" (Cooper, 1986); "Storytelling Sources" (Corcoran, 1986); "Picture Books for Older Children" (Kiefer, 1986); "Poetry for Young Children" (Phelan, 1988); and "Contemporary Issues—Intergenerational Relationships" (Wilms, 1986). The *School Library Journal* publishes a "Best Books" list each year and specific recommendations for literature and media, such as "Modern Classics" (Breckenridge, 1988), "Cultural Diverse Videos: African-Americans" (Mandell, 1992), and "Letters, Numbers, Shapes, & Colors" (Carlson, 1995).

Social Education provides a yearly source of "Notable Children's Trade Books in the Field of Social Studies." For example, the 1994 notable book list includes an annotated list of biography, contemporary issues, folklore, geography, social interactions, U.S. history and culture, world history and culture, reference works, and story and poetry collections.

Book Links also publishes lists of recommended books, such as "Book Links Salutes 'A Few Good Books' of 1991" (Elleman, 1992), as well as lists that relate to specific themes, such as "Our Emerging Nation—The Late 1800s" (Chatton, 1992). The *Children's Litera-*

ture Association Quarterly publishes articles on specific genres of literature, authors, literary criticism, and issues. It also lists "Touchstone" books—books the editors consider so good that they provide the criteria by which all other books are evaluated. *Language Arts, The Reading Teacher,* and *The New Advocate* also review children's literature. Each October, *The Reading Teacher* publishes a list of books that children from across the United States select as their favorites for the year.

For Your Development

1. Visit an elementary classroom in which literature is an important part of the curriculum. Describe the environment, the teacher's attitude toward literature, and the interactions of the children with books.
2. Choose a resource for selecting literature. Review the information about books that you gain from the resource.

Children's Interests

Understanding why and what children read is necessary to help them select books that stimulate interests and provide enjoyment. You can learn about children's interests by reviewing studies of children's interests and preferences and by talking to children and evaluating their responses on interest inventories.

Each year, a joint project of the International Reading Association and the Children's Book Council allows approximately 10,000 children from around the United States to evaluate children's books published during a given year. Each year, the council records the reactions and a research team uses this information to compile a list of "Children's Choices." These lists of children's favorites give teachers a better understanding of the characteristics of books that appeal to children.

The various lists of children's choices suggest particular types of stories that appeal to young readers. For example, in a recent list, the "beginning independent reading" category contains comical stories about more or less realistic family situations, humorous animal stories, stories that develop emotional experiences, action-filled fantasies, traditional stories, counting books, rhymes, and riddles. The "younger reader" category includes realistic stories about families, friends, school, and personal problems; animal stories; fantasies; fast-paced adventures; folktales; and humorous stories. Stories that children chose in the middle grades include realistic stories about sibling rivalry, peer acceptance, fears, and lack of conformity to stereotypes; fantasies; suspense stories; and humorous stories. Popular information books include factual and nonsensical advice about human health, factual information about animals, and biographical information about sports stars. Popular poetry includes collections by Judith Viorst, Shel Silverstein, and William Cole. The choices include books from a wide variety of genres.

Research also indicates that reading ability influences the reading interests of children. Swanton's (1984) survey comparing gifted students with students of average ability reports that gifted children prefer mysteries (43 percent), fiction (41 percent), science fiction (29 percent), and fantasy (18 percent). In contrast, the top four choices for students of average ability are mysteries (47 percent), comedy/humor (27 percent), realistic fiction (23 percent), and adventure (18 percent). Gifted students indicated that they like science fiction and fantasy "because of the challenge . . . [and] its relationship to Dungeons and Dragons" (p. 100).

1. What do you like to do when you get home from school?
   _____

2. What do you like to do on Saturday?
   _____

3. Do you like to watch television? _____ If you do, what are the names of your favorite programs?
   _____

4. Do you have a hobby? _____ If you do, what is your hobby?
   _____

5. Do you like to make or collect things? _____ If you do, what have you made or collected?
   _____

6. What is your favorite sport? _____
7. What games do you like best? _____
8. Do you like to go to the movies? _____ If you do, what is your favorite movie?
   _____

9. Do you have a pet? _____ If you do, what is your pet? _____
10. Where have you spent your summer vacations? _____
    _____

11. Have you ever made a special study of rocks? _____ space? _____ plants? _____
    animals? _____ travel? _____ dinosaurs? _____ other? _____
12. What are your favorite subjects in school?
    art? _____ handwriting? _____ social studies? _____ English? _____
    physical education? _____ science? _____ music? _____ creative writing? _____
    spelling? _____ arithmetic? _____ other? _____

FIGURE 6–1   An Informal Interest Inventory

Gifted students listed Judy Blume, Lloyd Alexander, J. R. R. Tolkien, and C. S. Lewis as favorite authors. Average students listed Judy Blume, Beverly Cleary, and Jack London. As you can see, there are similarities and differences within these favorites. Many additional types of literature may become favorites if understanding and knowledgeable teachers provide opportunities for students to listen to, read, and discuss literature.

Although information from research and children's choices provides general ideas about what subjects and authors are preferred by children of certain ages and reading abilities, we must not develop stereotyped views about children's preferences. Without asking questions about interests, there is no way to know about children's specific and unusual interests. Informal conversation is one of the simplest ways to uncover children's interests—ask a child to describe what he or she likes to do and read about. You will need some way of recording the information when you work with a number of children. Develop interest inventories in which students answer questions about their favorite hobbies, books, sports, television shows, and other interests. Write down young children's answers. Older children can read the questionnaire themselves and write their own responses. Such an inventory might include some of the questions asked in Figure 6–1. (Make changes according to age levels, and add information if children tell why they like certain books.) After the interest inventory is complete, use the findings as the basis for helping children select books and extend their enjoyment of literature.

13. What subject is the hardest for you? _____
14. What kinds of books do you like to have someone read to you?
    animal stories? _____ fairy tales? _____ true stories? _____ science fiction? _____
    adventure? _____ mystery stories? _____ sports stories? _____ poems? _____
    humorous stories? _____ other kinds of stories? _____
15. What is your favorite book that someone read to you? _____
16. What kinds of books do you like to read by yourself?
    animal stories? _____ picture books? _____ fairy tales? _____ true stories? _____
    science fiction? _____ adventures? _____ mystery stories? _____ sports stories? _____
    poems? _____ funny stories? _____ other kinds of stories? _____
17. What is your favorite book that you read by yourself? _____
    _____
18. Would you rather read a book by yourself or have someone read to you?
    _____
19. Write the title of a book that you read this week.
    _____
20. What books or magazines do you have at home? _____
    _____
    _____
21. Do you ever go to the library? _____
    How often do you go to the library? _____
    Do you have a library card? _____

FIGURE 6–1   Continued

For Your Development

Administer an interest inventory to several elementary children. Tabulate their interests and select several books that you feel match their interests.

Storytelling

Have you ever sat around a campfire and listened to a storyteller take you to all kinds of magical places? Have you watched as children become entranced listening to a story? What makes storytelling more effective than merely reading the story aloud? A great deal of magic results from the amount of preparation that goes into the activity. Storytelling encourages children to understand the oral tradition in literature. Through storytelling children can become actively involved in the story experience. When adults tell stories, they also motivate children to tell their own stories.

This last point was made clear to one of my college classes when we invited a group of kindergarten and first-grade children to our class to take part in a story time. One child was particularly delighted with the stories, but was apparently too shy to become involved in any activity or discussion. Her mother informed us a few days later that the child was so stimulated by the experience that when she went home, she told her family all the stories she had heard. She also made flannel-board and puppet figures to accompany some of the stories. Then, she started to practice new stories, and wanted to tell them to anyone who would take a few minutes to listen. Any activity with the power to motivate a child in this way is certainly worth the effort.

Selection

When you select a story for telling, choose one that is appropriate for the age of the audience and the time allotted. Choose a story that has a strong beginning, to capture your listeners' attention quickly. Also, choose something suspenseful. Your story should have a lot of action; children enjoy an active plot. Usually three or four characters are enough because both you and the children may have difficulty keeping track of a greater number. Rapunzel, for example, has a wicked witch, a beautiful maiden, and a rescuing prince. In addition, be sure that the dialogue in the story appears natural. As with all stories for young children, choose a story with a climax that both you and the children can recognize. Finally, choose a story with a satisfactory conclusion.

Consider both the age and experience of the children. For example, preschool- through kindergarten-age children need stories that are short and to the point. The stories should include familiar things—animals, children, homes, machines, and people. Humorous and nonsense stories and cumulative tales are good choices, including "The Three Little Pigs," "The Three Billy Goats Gruff," and "Henny Penny." Ancient and modern fairy tales usu-

Sometimes teachers will involve children in storytelling.

ally appeal to children ages six through ten; therefore, consider "The Elves and the Shoe-maker," "Rumpelstiltskin," and "The Bremen Town Musicians." Animal tales and stories of children from other lands are also appropriate. Older-elementary-age children usually like true stories, hero tales, and stories that teach something about personal ideals. Such children also enjoy adventure, so myths, legends, and epics are popular. Consider, for example, "Aladdin," "How Thor Found His Hammer," "Robin Hood," "Pecos Bill," and "Paul Bunyan."

Some storytellers enjoy telling several stories around a specific theme. For example, a Hans Christian Andersen storytelling festival could include "The Steadfast Tin Soldier," "The Nightingale," "The Tinderbox," and "The Swineherd." The theme of forgetfulness could include "Soap, Soap, Soap" in Richard Chase's *Grandfather Tales* (1948), the story of a boy who can't remember what he is shopping for, and "Icarus and Daedalus," a Greek legend, in which Icarus forgets that his wings are attached with wax. If you are interested in choosing several stories about a certain subject, Anne Pellowski's *Hidden Stories in Plants* (1990) and *The Family Story-Telling Handbook* (1987) include recommended stories and suggestions for how to use them. Carolyn N. Cullum's *The Storytime Sourcebook* (1999) divides stories around specific subjects. Rex M. Ellis's *Beneath the Blazing Sun* (1997) presents both African-American stories and introductory material for the folklore.

Preparation

An experienced storyteller, Patti Hubert, recommends the following sequence, which has proven successful for her:

1. Read the story completely through about three times.
2. List mentally the sequence of events. You are giving yourself a mental outline of the important happenings.
3. Reread the story, noting the events you didn't remember.
4. Go over the main events again and add the details you remember. Think about the meaning of the events and ways to express that meaning, rather than memorize the words in the story.
5. When you feel you know the story, tell the story to a mirror. (You will be surprised at how horrible the story sounds the first time.)
6. After you have practiced two or three more times, the wording will improve, and you can change vocal pitch to differentiate characters.
7. Change your posture or hand gestures to represent different characters.
8. Don't be afraid to use pauses to separate scenes.[1]

Introduction

Many storytellers set the mood for story time with a symbol. One librarian uses a small lamp. When the lamp is lit, it is also time to listen. If you have a certain place in your classroom for storytelling, movement to that corner may prepare the children and set the mood. Your storytelling corner might include an easel on which to place a drawing from the story or a motivating question written on cardboard. Some storytellers create a mood with a record or a piano. One student teacher successfully used a guitar for this purpose. As soon as he went

---

[1] This sequence is used with permission of Patti Hubert, drama teacher, San Antonio.

into the storytelling corner and played a specific song on the guitar, the students came over, anticipating an enjoyable activity.

There are numerous ways to introduce your story. Ask a question, or tell the students why you enjoy a particular story. Offer something interesting about the author. Give background information about a country or a period of history to add interest to a folktale. Display prominently the book from which your story is taken, along with other stories by the same author and other stories on the same subject. One of the reasons for storytelling is to motivate children to tell stories themselves, so a display adds visual interest.

Many student teachers effectively introduce a story with objects. One student used a stuffed toy rabbit to introduce *The Velveteen Rabbit* by Margery Williams (1922). You could use a toy or figure of a cat with *Puss in Boots* by Charles Perrault (1952). Use a lariat to introduce a tall tale about Pecos Bill. Use artifacts from a country to introduce folktales. One of my favorite objects is a small, painted jewelry case from Japan. I often bring out the case when I am telling stories to young children, and we talk about the magic of stories that is contained in the case because it has been to so many story hours. Then, I open the box slowly while the children catch the magic in their hands. This magic is wonderful, so they hold it carefully while they listen to the story. When the story ends, each child carefully returns the magic to the box until it is time to use it for another story.

Actual Telling

Once you have prepared your story and developed ways to introduce it or to set a mood, you are ready to face your expectant students. Patti Hubert offers the following suggestions for telling your story:

1. Find a place in the room where all the children can see and hear you.
2. Either stand in front of the children or sit with them.
3. Select an appropriate introduction. Use a prop, tell something about the author, discuss a related event, or ask a question.
4. Maintain eye contact with the children. This engages them more fully in the story.
5. Use your voice rate and volume for effect.
6. Take a short step or shift your weight to indicate a change in scene or character or to heighten the suspense. If you are sitting, lean toward or away from the children.
7. After telling your story, pause to give the audience a chance to soak in everything you have said.

Pictures and Objects

Effective storytelling does not require props, but you may want to add variety with felt boards, flip charts, roll stories, objects, or chalk talks.

Felt Boards.   For visual interest, cut out representations of the main characters from felt, flannel, or pellon, and put them on a board covered with felt or flannel. Figures provide cues to the story and give beginning storytellers added security. It is better to tell a felt-board story rather than read it because manipulating both figures and a book at the same time is awkward.

It is easy to make a flannel or felt board. Cover an artist's cardboard portfolio with felt or flannel. Make a firmer felt board by covering a rectangle of lightweight wood, such as fiberboard or plywood, with a large piece of felt or flannel. Hinge two smaller squares of board together if you will need to transport the board. You can make backdrops for different scenes and locations by chalking in scenery on a loose piece of flannel large enough to cover the board. These scenic flannel pieces are easy to store, and they add interest without cluttering the appearance of a felt story.

Certain types of stories are more suitable for felt boards than others. Stories with a great deal of physical action or detailed settings are inappropriate. Simple stories with only a few major figures and definite scenes are easy to handle. Cumulative tales, which add elements throughout the story, are extremely good. Some stories that meet these requirements are "Goldilocks and the Three Bears," "The Three Little Pigs," "The Three Billy Goats Gruff," "Jack and the Beanstalk," and "The Emperor's New Clothes." You can show these traditional favorites with a few simple characters.

When you tell a story, place the board so the whole group can see it. An easel is a good place to position the board for a large group. Place the figures in proper order before you begin the story, and keep the figures out of the children's sight until you place them on the board. You will need to practice several times so you will be talking to the children, not to the board.

Felt stories allow the students to become involved. Children can retell the felt stories, reinforcing oral language and comprehension skills. After they have seen one or two such stories, many children want to make their own. These stories are excellent means of giving oral book reports or illustrating creative writing stories. If you leave the felt board in a room so the children have easy access to it, you will find they use it frequently. (A felt board is also an excellent visual aid for developing concepts in math and science.)

Flip Charts.   Another technique that adds visual interest to storytelling is illustrating a story on several large sheets of poster board (see Figure 6–2). As with felt boards, use flip charts with stories in which you can develop the main ideas with a series of pictures. Draw the charts by hand or with the aid of an opaque projector. The most successful flip charts use three-dimensional materials. Yarn, fabric, sandpaper, small stones, bark, and straws add tactile dimensions to flip charts, and invite children to touch the pictures.

One student teacher drew a flip-chart story entitled "Freddie's Private Cloud." She used rice for shingles on a house, cloth for clothing, real feathers on birds, nylon net for clouds, sandpaper for a lawn-mower engine, spaghetti for a ladder, bark for tree trunks, rolls of real paper for newspaper, beans for stones, sponge for waves, and felt for animals.

FIGURE 6–2   A Flip-Chart Picture

FIGURE 6–3   A Picture for a
Roll Story

Roll Stories.   Roll stories are also sequentially illustrated. Draw the pictures on a large roll of paper, then unroll them as you tell the story. Place the completed roll story inside a box with an opening cut out like a television screen. The roll should have dowels at either end so that it is easy to roll and unroll (see Figure 6–3).

Roll stories are excellent culmination activities after you have read or told a story. Children can form groups to draw pictures and retell a story with their own pictures. Roll stories reinforce reading skills as well as storytelling skills. For example, after one first-grade teacher told "Peter and the Wolf" to her students, the students listed the scenes from the story, and each of them chose two sequential scenes to illustrate. The teacher cut a long roll of paper into sections that fit the length of the work tables in the classroom, and the children, with the teacher's assistance, measured the distance needed for each picture. Then, the children drew their illustrations, in correct sequence, onto the roll. When each child had completed his or her illustrations, the child dictated to the teacher the part of the story that corresponded to the illustrations. Then, the teacher used these individually dictated stories for reading instruction. The children practiced reading their own contributions so they could present a "movie" of "Peter and the Wolf." Next, the class taped together the table-length rolls and attached dowels to each end. They placed the long roll inside a box with a rectangular viewing area, and the children practiced reading their parts as they unrolled the story. They added background music from "Peter and the Wolf," and invited another grade to come in and view their presentation. This is an excellent motivating activity for remedial reading instruction.

Object Stories.   Certain stories lend themselves to showing objects from the story. For example, while telling Marcia Brown's *Stone Soup* (1947), a teacher or students can place the ingredients in a soup kettle.

Chalk Talks.   It is fascinating to watch someone illustrate a story while telling it. One student teacher invited a cartoonist to visit her fourth-grade class. The cartoonist quickly

FIGURE 6–4   Chalk Figure

Peter, Peter, pumpkin eater
Had a wife and couldn't keep her
He put her in a pumpkin shell
And there he kept her very well.

Humpty Dumpty sat on a wall
Humpty Dumpty had a great fall
All the king's horses
And all the king's men
Couldn't put Humpty Dumpty
together again.

sketched cartoon figures while telling a corresponding story. This highly motivating activity led many students to try the technique with simple figures. Although you may not have a cartoonist's rapid drawing ability, you might enjoy trying the activity with stick-figure characters or simple shapes. Figure 6–4 shows simple sketches to accompany familiar nursery rhymes. One teacher made up a story about the adventures of an Easter egg, with simple shapes that could be sketched quickly on the chalkboard.

For Your Development

Choose a story to prepare for storytelling according to the suggestions in this section of the chapter. Use pictures or objects if you wish. Tell your story to a group of children or a group of your peers. You may find additional suggestions in Ramon Royal Ross's *Storyteller* (1996) and in David Holt and Bill Mooney's *Ready-to-Tell Tales* (1994).

Reading Aloud

Reading aloud to children is one of the most beneficial activities that adults do with children. Allison and Watson (1994) found in a study of emergent literacy among young children: "The earlier a parent began reading to their child, the higher the child's emergent reading level was at the end of kindergarten" (p. 68). Reading aloud is so important that Allison and Watson recommend that early childhood educators encourage all parents to read to their children.

Reading aloud is also one of the most beneficial activities that adults do with school-age children. Brown (1999) emphasizes that because younger children's listening level is greater than their reading level, reading aloud builds background knowledge, teaches new words, and provides a positive role model. Dowhower (1994) summarizes research indicating that adult interaction in the form of questioning and scaffolding during reading a story aloud is important for recall, comprehension, and vocabulary development. Fortunately, Walmsley

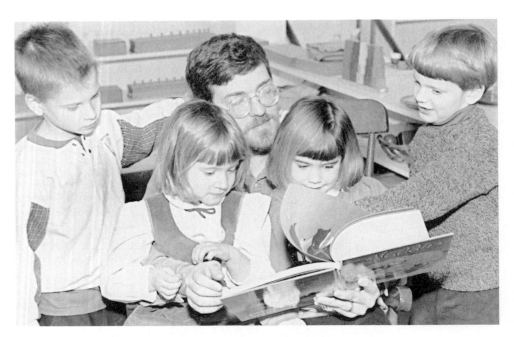

Reading aloud is not only pleasurable but teaches children about story structure.

and Walp (1989) found that reading aloud to students is the activity teachers use the most to involve students in literature. There is probably no better way to interest children in the world of books than to read to them. This is one way for children to learn that literature is a source of pleasure. For children who are just struggling to learn to read, a book may not yet be a source of happiness. In fact, the sight of books may actually arouse negative feelings in some children. Thus, instructional techniques that improve attitudes are highly desirable. Is there a better way for children to see the pleasure they can derive from books than by sharing books in a relaxed environment with a teacher who obviously enjoys good literature? Nilsen and Donelson (2001) make a strong case for reading aloud to older students in order to present the students with materials "that just might interest, intrigue, amuse, or excite them, material that might make young people aware of new or old books or writers or techniques or ideas. . . . Poetry must be read aloud. So must drama. Reading fiction aloud is half the fun of teaching short stories" (p. 358).

In addition to deriving pleasure, students learn about story structures from the books they hear. They hear language patterns and words that may be unfamiliar to them. These listening experiences increase appreciation for and understanding of different story and sentence structures and prepare children when they encounter them in their own reading. Herrell (1990) found that interactive reading aloud to kindergarten children had positive effects on the children's reading. In *Becoming a Nation of Readers: The Report of the Commission on Reading,* Anderson et al. (1985) state: "The single most important activity for building the knowledge required for eventual success in reading is reading aloud to children" (p. 23).

Another important benefit of reading aloud is that it motivates children to do their own reading. After children are excited by hearing a selection, they usually want to read it to themselves; thus, interaction between an enthusiastic teacher and interested peers is especially important.

Style and illustrations are both considerations when choosing books to read aloud. The language in Michael Rosen's *We're Going on a Bear Hunt* (1989) stimulates interaction between the reader and the listeners. Other good choices for young listeners include A. A. Milne's *Winnie-the-Pooh* (1926) and Dr. Seuss's *The 500 Hats of Bartholomew Cubbins* (1938). Young children also enjoy the illustrations in a story, such as those in Maurice Sendak's *Where the Wild Things Are* (1963) and those in Arthur Yorinks's *Hey, Al* (1986).

Age, attention span, and level of reading ability are important considerations when selecting stories to read aloud. The books should challenge children to improve their reading skills as well as increase their appreciation of literature. Leave the numerous easy-to-read books for children to read independently. Younger children respond to short stories that you can finish in one reading. Books such as Faith Ringgold's *Tar Beach* (1991), Kevin Henkes's *Chrysanthemum* (1991), Amy Schwartz's *Oma and Bobo* (1987), and Ann Grifalconi's *Darkness and the Butterfly* (1987) are favorites with children in first and second grade. Katherine Paterson's *The Tale of the Mandarin Ducks* (1990) and Jane Yolen's *The Girl in the Golden Bower* (1994) have sufficiently developed plot to appeal to second graders. By the time children reach third grade, you can read continued stories, although you should complete a chapter during each story time rather than leave a segment unfinished. Third graders usually enjoy E. B. White's *Charlotte's Web* (1952) and Laura Ingalls Wilder's "Little House" series. Fourth and fifth graders often respond to Madeleine L'Engle's *A Wrinkle in Time* (1962) and C. S. Lewis's *The Lion, the Witch and the Wardrobe* (1950). Armstrong Sperry's *Call It Courage* (1940) and Esther Forbes's *Johnny Tremain* (1943) often appeal to sixth and seventh graders.

Enthusiasm is a vital ingredient during story time. If you are uninterested and unprepared, you will spoil the story time for the children. Preparation requires reading the story silently so that you understand the sequence of events, the mood, the subject, the vocabulary, and other concepts. Next, read the story aloud to practice pronunciation, pacing, voice characterizations, and so forth. Beginning oral readers should listen to themselves on a tape recorder before they read to an audience. Enunciation, pacing, and volume are especially important for young children's understanding. Finally, consider how to introduce the story using such techniques as those mentioned previously under storytelling.

An appropriate environment for story time is also essential. Children in the early elementary grades need to sit close to you, especially if the story is a picture book that you will show as you read. Also, prepare the children for the listening experience by getting their attention and providing appropriate goals for the experience. If necessary, clarify a concept or a vocabulary word to help the children understand the story. Introduce the story with a question, a discussion about the title, a prediction about the story, or background information about the author. As you read the story aloud, encourage the students to interact with the story.

Just as you should draw on various categories of literature, you should also use various methods for sharing stories with groups—recordings; films; storytelling; and visual techniques, such as puppets, felt boards, and chalk talks. Keep records of the stories you share with the children and note their reactions. These records will help you balance the types of books you select and understand the interests of the children.

For Your Development

Choose a book and prepare it for reading aloud. Read the book to a group of children or a group of your peers.

Art

Strange and curious worlds, imaginary kingdoms, animal fantasies, space explorations, and historical settings lend themselves to artistic interpretations. Illustrated books using various artistic media and containing descriptive passages stimulate artistic expression, encourage enjoyment of literature, enhance aesthetic development, and stimulate understanding of various literary elements, such as setting and plot. (A word of caution: Art should allow children to expand their enjoyment of a story through self-expression. Do not force an art activity with every story.)

Use illustrated books to show children that artists see their subjects in different ways and use different media to interpret mood and setting. Help children discover that artistic interpretations are individual qualities. For example, you could read and discuss Molly Bang's illustrations showing the impact of form, line, and color in *Picture This: Perception & Composition* (1991). Because Bang uses various forms and colors to develop an illustrated version of "Little Red Riding Hood" and discusses the impact of any changes she makes in the illustrations, you may share, compare, and discuss additional illustrated versions of "Little Red Riding Hood." Excellent examples for this activity include Trina Schart Hyman's illustrations for Grimms' *Little Red Riding Hood* (1983), James Marshall's illustrations for *Red Riding Hood* (1987), Sarah Moon's photographs for Perrault's *Little Red Riding Hood* (1983), William Wegman's photographs of dogs for *Little Red Riding Hood* (1993), and Ed Young's illustrations for *Lon Po Po: A Red-Riding Hood Story from China* (1989). In these examples, illustrations reinforce a "once upon a time" traditional setting, develop a humorous mood, and create a stark, terrifying mood. Children can experiment with form, line, color, and artistic medium to create their own moods.

Use books illustrated with a particular artistic medium to stimulate students to try that medium in their own illustrations. For example, in collage, any object or substance that can be attached to a surface can be used to develop a design. Artists and student artists may use paper, cloth, cardboard, leather, wood, leaves, flowers, or even butterflies. They may cut up and arrange their own paintings or use paint and other media to add background. When photographically produced in a book, collages still communicate texture. Children's literature selections that show children how adult authors use collage include Jeannie Baker's *Where the Forest Meets the Sea* (1988) and *Window* (1991); Molly Bang's illustrations for Sylvia Cassedy and Kunihiro Suetake's *Red Dragon on My Shoulder* (1992); Ezra Jack Keats's *Peter's Chair* (1967), *The Snowy Day* (1962), and *The Trip* (1978); Eric Carle's *The Very Hungry Caterpillar* (1971); Marcia Brown's illustrations for Blaise Cendrars's *Shadow* (1982); and Lois Ehlert's *Red Leaf, Yellow Leaf* (1991).

Books that are filled with descriptive passages and vivid characters entice children to try their own artistic explorations and interpretations. For example, vivid settings from Beatrix Potter's *The Tale of Squirrel Nutkin* (1903), Kenneth Grahame's *The Wind in the Willows* (1908), and E. B. White's *Charlotte's Web* (1952) encourage individual drawings or group-developed murals. Nancy Farmer's *The Ear, the Eye and the Arm* (1994) can motivate depiction of a science fiction setting in a world yet to materialize. Likewise, Janet Lunn's *Shadow in Hawthorn Bay* (1986) can motivate pictorial comparisons between the hills of Scotland around Loch Ness and Hawthorn Bay, Ontario, in the early 1800s.

Many stories encourage students to hypothesize about what could happen next and to create visual interpretations. Let younger students expand on one of the nursery rhymes in Tomie de Paola's *Mother Goose* (1985). For example, how do Peter, Peter, Pumpkin Eater and his wife live in the pumpkin shell? Students can extend Keizaburo Tejima's *Fox's Dream* (1987) by illustrating the same forest in the spring rather than winter. Older students can extend Robert O'Brien's *Mrs. Frisby and the Rats of NIMH* (1971) by drawing Thorn Valley, the colony that the intelligent rats want to develop. Then, they can compare their drawings with the written descriptions in Jane Leslie Conly's sequel, *Rasco and the Rats of NIMH* (1986). Mythology can inspire students, like illustrators of picture books, to depict the settings for mythological places, such as the sacred lake where a Native American boy waits for the buffalo to appear (Olaf Baker's *Where the Buffaloes Begin,* 1981) or the foaming sea that produces the goddess Aphrodite (Doris Gates's *Two Queens of Heaven: Aphrodite and Demeter,* 1974).

Reading stories aloud, storytelling, and artistic interpretations of literature are stimulating ways to develop appreciation for and understanding of literature. These activities also motivate students to read literature and even write and illustrate their own books.

Literary Criticism

At one time in the history of education, choosing selections from a wealth of children's literature was not a problem. Rather the problem was finding anything at all for children. In 1800, only 270 books were published for the juvenile market. Fortunately, this situation has changed dramatically. Currently, more than 3,000 books for children are published annually. This increase in quantity, however, has led to concern for the quality of literature that students read. Quality is important for several reasons that relate to the language arts. For example, Dressel (1990) found that children who read and discuss higher quality literature produce higher quality written stories. Likewise, Lehr (1988) reported that children's ability to identify themes correlates with their exposure to quality literature.

This section discusses ways to help students become critical of the books they read. To reinforce the exposure to quality literature, the examples of literature used in this section and the subsequent sections in this chapter are selected from three sources that reflect standards for quality: Newbery Medal and Honor Awards selected yearly by the American Library Association for the most distinguished contributions to children's literature published in the United States, the Caldecott Medal and Honor Awards selected annually by the American

Of more than 3,000 books published for children each year, how will you help children select books to read?

Library Association for the illustrators of the most distinguished picture books published in the United States, and the Touchstones in Children's Literature selected by the Children's Literature Association. These Touchstones include many classics in children's literature that were selected because they reflect the quality by which all other literature should be evaluated. In addition to being examples of quality literature, these books are almost always available because they do not go out of print. In addition, most libraries order the Newbery and Caldecott books for each year. (When referring to the books in these next sections the abbreviations NM will mean Newbery Medal, NH will mean Newbery Honor, CM will mean Caldecott Medal, CH will mean Caldecott Honor, and T will mean a Touchstone book. The dates for the Newbery and Caldecott Awards are also one year beyond their publication dates. The awards are given for outstanding literature published the previous year.)

Literary Elements

Literature is usually evaluated in terms of plot, conflict, characterization, setting, theme, and style. Consequently, you need to recognize these literary elements in the books you share with students. We will review them quickly here because they are usually covered in detail in children's literature courses. The quotes and examples used to illustrate each of the literary elements are from recent Caldecott Medal and Honor Books and the Newbery Medal and Honor Books.

Plot.   The plot of a story develops the action. Plots should provide excitement, suspense, and conflict. The development of events usually follows a chronological order, although flashbacks may answer questions about a character's background or reveal information about the past. The plots of most children's stories follow a structure in which characters and problems are introduced at the beginning of the story, conflict builds until a climax is reached, a turning point occurs, and then the conflict is resolved.

This type of plot development is found in Julius Lester's *John Henry* (CH 1995, 1994). The story is introduced through John Henry's exceptional birth when the animals come from the woods to glimpse the new baby. The events follow a chronological order in which John Henry rapidly grows to maturity as shown when the baby jumps out of his mama's arms and starts growing. The next day he is strong enough to rebuild the house and chop down an acre of trees. The plot advances rapidly as John Henry races the meanest man in the state and wins even though the man is on his horse and John Henry is on foot. John Henry's might with a hammer is shown to be superior to dynamite in moving a boulder and he challenges a steam drill on the Chesapeake and Ohio Railroad in West Virginia. The climax is reached when John Henry wins the race. The turning point is reached as John Henry's heart bursts from exhaustion. The conflict is resolved, however, when people discover that dying is not important, it is how well you live that counts. The story concludes with the belief that John Henry's spirit still sings.

Longer books frequently follow the same type of plot development, although there is considerably more detail developed around problems, building of conflict, climax, turning point, and resolution. Notice in the following example from Nancy Farmer's *The Ear, the Eye and the Arm* (NH 1995, 1994) how the author reviews the major incidents in the plot that take the reader almost to the climax and resolution:

> The children have proven strong beyond our wildest expectations. They escaped from Dead Man's Vlei. They got in and out of Resthaven. They eluded the Masks in the subway. According to Mrs. Horsepool-Worthingham, after they recovered from the chicken pox, they practically ran her house. (p. 252)

Conflict.   Excitement in a story occurs when the main character experiences a struggle or overcomes conflict. Conflict is the usual source of plots in literature. Children's literature includes four kinds of conflict: (1) person versus person, (2) person versus society, (3) person versus nature, and (4) person versus self. Authors must describe and develop conflicts so as to make them believable. A good plot lets children share the action, feel the conflict, recognize the climax, and respond to a satisfactory ending.

In picture storybooks the conflict is usually developed through both the illustrations and the text. For example, in Eve Bunting's *Smoky Night* (CM 1995, 1994), the text and illustrations develop a person-versus-society conflict as a mother and her son experience the Los Angeles riots that break out in the streets of their neighborhood. The illustrations reinforce the increasing conflict through a combination of paintings and collage that show shattered windows, stolen appliances and other goods, and smoke and flames that finally cause the family to flee from their apartment to a shelter. The author's use of a neighbor's and the boy's lost cats, which are finally found by a firefighter, shows both the personal tragedies that may result from conflicts with society and the power of such conflicts to bring people together in times of mutual need.

The longer Newbery Awards frequently develop several types of conflicts. The conflicts developed in Karen Cushman's *Catherine, Called Birdy* (NH 1995, 1994) result because the main character rebels against the female role demanded by society in medieval England. Notice in the following example how the author suggests person-versus-society, person-versus-person, and even person-versus-self conflict:

> The stars and my family align to make my life black and miserable. My mother seeks to make me a fine lady—dumb, docile, and accomplished—so I must take lady-lessons and keep my mouth closed. My brother Edward thinks even girls should not be ignorant, so he taught me to read holy books and to write, even though I would rather sit in an apple tree and wonder. Now my father, the toad, conspires to sell me like a cheese to some lack-wit seeking a wife. (p. 5)

Characterization.   Characters should seem believable and should develop throughout the course of a story. The credibility of characters depends on the author's ability to reveal their natures, including both strengths and weaknesses. Characters are developed through descriptions of their thoughts and actions and records of their conversations. The most memorable characters usually have several sides—like real people, they are not all good or all bad. Characters who are developed well, so that readers understand their many sides, are called "round." Characters that remain unchanged in a story are called "flat" or "static."

Picture storybooks for younger children frequently focus on characteristics of characters that make them very similar to their readers, consequently young readers relate to both their needs and the characters. In Kevin Henkes's *Owen* (CH 1994, 1993), the author develops a mouse child who acts very much like a normal child: He loves a favorite blanket and refuses to give up this security even though his parents try numerous schemes to make him give up the blanket before he starts school. The author develops a believable character who has real needs that are understandable. In a happy conclusion, the parents and Owen resolve the conflict in a way that is satisfactory to all. In this text, both the illustrations and the text develop the many sides of the mouse child.

One of the characteristics of most of the Newbery books is the development of well-rounded characters who change in the course of the story. In the following example from Cynthia Rylant's *Missing May* (NM 1993, 1992), notice how the author develops characterization by describing how Summer feels about herself in the beginning of the book:

> Back in Ohio, where I'd been treated like a homework assignment somebody was always having to do, eating was never a joy of any kind. Every house I had ever lived in

was so particular about its food, and especially when the food involved me. There's no good way to explain this. But I felt like one of those little mice who has to figure out the right button to push before its food will drop down into the cup. Caged and begging. That's how I felt sometimes. (p. 7)

Setting.   Setting refers to the geographic location of the story and the time—past, present, or future—in which the events take place. If a location is identifiable as a real place, the author should present it accurately. Authors of historical fiction, for example, must make the backgrounds for their stories as authentic as possible. In addition to a complete historical background, settings may provide instantly recognizable backgrounds, such as "a certain kingdom" or "deep in the forest." Settings can create a mood, develop conflict, or provide symbolic meaning.

Both the illustrations and the text in picture storybooks must reflect the purpose of the setting developed in the story. For example, the illustrations in Elisa Bartone's *Peppe, the Lamplighter* (CH 1994, 1993) reflect an earlier time in history when lamplighters were required to light gas lights on the streets. These illustrations reflect an historical time period and suggest the environment more effectively than words.

In the longer Newbery books, the text, and not illustrations, presents the mood and the time period. Notice in the following example from Lois Lowry's *The Giver* (NM 1994, 1993) how the author introduces you to the time, but also to a setting that creates conflict and emotions that may be associated with terror:

> It was almost December, and Jonas was beginning to be frightened. No. Wrong word, Jonas thought. Frightened meant that deep, sickening feeling of something terrible about to happen. Frightened was the way he had felt a year ago when an unidentified aircraft had overflown the community twice. He had seen it both times. Squinting toward the sky, he had seen the sleek jet, almost a blur at its high speed, go past, and a second later heard the blast of sound that followed. Then one more time, a moment later, from the opposite direction, the same plane. (p. 1)

Theme.   The theme of a story is the underlying idea that ties the plot, characters, and setting together into a meaningful whole. Themes are frequently implied rather than directly stated. They are revealed by studying the actions of the characters, analyzing the central conflict, and considering the outcome of a story. When looking for theme, it is important to consider how the main character changes in the story, what types of conflict exist, what actions are rewarded or punished, and what the main character learns as a result of the conflict. Even the title may provide clues to the theme.

The themes in picture storybooks are not as complex as in longer novels. In addition, there are usually one or two themes that are carefully developed. For example, in Eve Bunting's *Smoky Night* (CM 1995, 1994) a happy resolution occurs when two neighbors who had not previously been friends decide to meet in the future. This resolution is enhanced as their two cats, who had previously fought also, become friends. Through the content of the story, the characters' actions, and the story's resolution, the author develops the theme that difficult times bring people together.

The longer Newbery books frequently have multiple themes that are layered throughout the books. Notice in the following example from Laurence Yep's *Dragon's Gate* (NH 1994, 1993) how the characters' actions and dialogue develop the theme that cooperation is important. In fact cooperation may save your life:

> "There isn't one of us who hasn't wanted to run away," he explained. "It could have been any of us. And it could have been any of us who were blinded. All we have is one another. We have to cooperate if we're going to get off this mountain alive."

It was true that the crew worked even more smoothly and efficiently than before. My punishment and Father's blinding had shown them that they would have to depend on one another. (p. 184)

Style.   Style refers to the way in which an author uses language to develop a story that allows readers to hear, see, and feel the setting, conflict, and characters. The author Paula Fox (1995) makes a strong statement about the power of language in literature: "Great stories give us metaphors that flash upon the mind the way lightning flashes upon the earth, illuminating for an instant an entire landscape that had been hidden in the dark" (p. 122). Style, of course, should also be appropriate for the characters, setting, and plot. Does the language seem in keeping with what the characters would really say? If there is figurative language, will the children be able to grasp the meaning? Reading aloud is a good way to see if the author has a pleasing and appropriate style.

The language style in picture storybooks written for younger children frequently enhances children's language development and interest in such language style as repetitive language and rhyming words. Denise Fleming's *In the Small, Small Pond* (CH 1994, 1993) uses repetitive language as the author repeats the title of the book and also uses words that are appealing to young children. Read the following quote aloud and feel the appeal of the language:

In the small, small pond . . .
wiggle, jiggle, tadpoles wriggle. (unnumbered)

The style in the longer Newbery books is frequently much more complex as authors create settings, moods, and characterizations through their style. In the following quote from Karen Cushman's *Catherine, Called Birdy* (NH 1995, 1994), notice how the author uses language to create both visual and sound pictures of a medieval English manor:

Now that I am about to leave, I feel how dear this place is to me. I sat in the field next to the village this morning, trying to memorize the sounds—the squeal of cart wheels and the bawling of babies, the shouts of children and peddlers and cross old women, the hissing of the geese and the roosters' crow. The dogs were barking, the water wheel splashed, and the smith's hammer rang like a church bell. I took it all into my heart so I can play it like music whenever I need to. (p. 156)

Format.   Format refers to the physical aspects of the book—cover, printing and binding, illustrations, and size. Illustrations should help the story come alive. The printing should be clear and easy to read. Some bindings are more appropriate for school libraries than others. Although paperbacks are more readily affordable, hardcover editions last longer and usually appear in permanent collections.

For Your Development

Read the Caldecott and Newbery books discussed in the previous section on literary elements. Locate additional examples of the literary elements and discuss them with your language arts class. Or share the books with children of the appropriate age and record their reactions to the books. Read additional examples such as the following: Search for examples of plot and conflict in Christopher Paul Curtis's *The Watsons Go to Birmingham—1963* (NH 1996, 1995), examples of characterization in Carol Fenner's *Yolonda's Genius* (NH 1996, 1995), and examples of setting in Linda Sue Park's *A Single Shard* (NM 2002, 2001).

Lesson Plan

For Your Plan Book

An Evaluation-of-Literature Unit

Sixth-Grade Level

A sixth-grade teacher introduced her students to this unit by having the children interview their parents and other adults to find out what favorite books the adults remembered reading when they were in elementary school. On a large chart, the children listed the books and the adults who chose them. Then, the students checked book awards, such as the Newbery and Caldecott, to see how many of the books appeared on these lists. Next, each student read a book his or her parents had mentioned and discussed the book with the parents in terms of what made it special. The teacher introduced the concepts of plot, characterization, setting, theme, and style, and the students examined the books they had read for examples of each of these elements. Finally, the sixth graders listed questions to ask in evaluating a book:

1. Is this a good story?
2. Is the story about something I think could really happen?
3. Did the main character overcome the problem, but not too easily?
4. Did the climax seem natural?
5. Did the characters seem real?
6. Did the characters grow in the story?
7. Did I find out about more than one side of the characters?
8. Did the setting present what is actually known about that time or place?
9. Did the characters fit into the setting?
10. Did I feel that I was really in that time or place?
11. What did the author want to tell me in the story?
12. Was the theme worthwhile?
13. When I read the book aloud, did the people sound like real people actually talking?
14. Did the rest of the language sound natural?

As a follow-up activity, the students wrote stories and asked these questions about their own writing. Use this type of activity to introduce a more extensive study of literature.

Instruction

Developing understanding of literary elements is both a challenge to the teacher and an exciting approach to literature. Several strategies may be used to help students appreciate the importance of literary elements in the stories they encounter. Activities such as webbing, modeling, and drawing plot structures are especially effective. These approaches also integrate the language arts through oral language, listening, writing, and reading.

Webbing.   When you use webbing during guided book discussions, not only do you help students understand important characteristics of the story, you also help them appreciate literature and improve their reading and writing competencies. Prior to the webbing experience, introduce the literary elements. Then, draw simple webs that include each of these components while leading discussions that help the students identify the important ideas associated with the components. For example, place "The Three Billy Goats Gruff" in the center of a web and then draw each of the literary elements from the center. As you read

Webbing of a concept during a guided book discussion improves children's reading and writing competence.

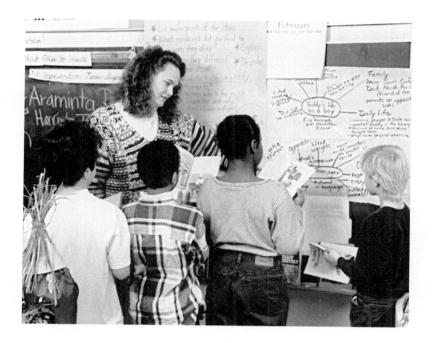

the story, ask the students to listen for the components. After completing the story, lead a discussion in which the students fill in the main ideas on the web. If necessary, reread sections to help the students identify specific elements. You may also ask students to focus on one element. This technique is effective when you first introduce literary elements and webbing. A short story may need to be reread several times to complete all of the literary elements.

Another approach is to ask groups of students to be responsible for specific elements on a web. Each group then listens for specific information and webs a specific element before oral discussion takes place. This approach frequently leads to in-depth analysis as students listen attentively for their own areas of concern.

After completing this activity with several simple books and webs, you and the students may progress to webbing of more complex books. John Steptoe's *Mufaro's Beautiful Daughters: An African Tale* (CH 1988, 1987) is a logical next choice. The story is short enough to read several times within one class session and the basic literary elements are easy to identify. First, introduce the story. Next, draw a web on the board with *Mufaro's Beautiful Daughters* in the center. Extend the terms *setting, characters, conflict, plot,* and *theme,* as shown in Figure 6–5. Now, read the story to the students and have them listen for information to place on the web. Following this reading, either reread the story, stopping at appropriate places to consider information that should go on the web, or lead a discussion in which the students fill in the web. If you do not reread the total book before filling in the web, you may need to reread parts of the story to help students decide what should be placed on the web. The choice of approach will depend on the students' listening capabilities and experiences with literary elements. Whichever approach you use, have the students develop a web on their own papers as you complete the web on the board using the information they supply. Some webs become quite large and may cover several chalkboards. In another class period following the development of the web, ask the students to write their own stories about the book using information on the web to help them construct the stories.

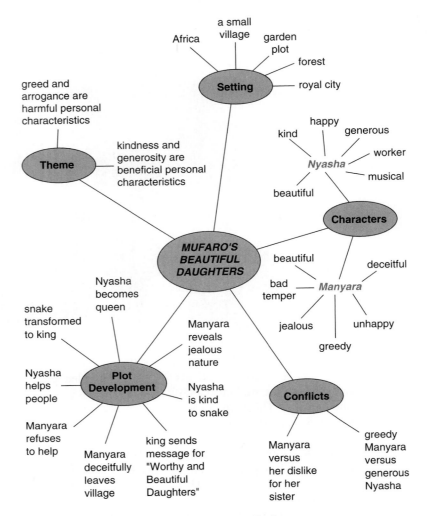

FIGURE 6–5   A Literary-Discussion Web for a Folktale

They may experiment with changing certain literary elements and writing the story to match those changes.

Figure 6–5 shows only the first level of information. When this web was completed with third- and fourth-grade students it extended to several chalkboards. Students supplied additional information for each of the settings. The webbing activity stimulates considerable discussion about literary elements when students must support their ideas with evidence from the text, discuss relationships between the identified elements, and discuss their reasons for certain inferences. For example, the author does not directly state the themes shown on the web in Figure 6–5. The text, however, provides clues to these themes by describing characteristics of people who are rewarded and people who are punished. Also, some of the terms describing the characters are words that the students derived from descriptions of the characters' actions.

Webbing may also be used with longer books. A more complex web can be developed for Karen Cushman's *Catherine, Called Birdy* (NH 1995, 1994). Figure 6–6 develops a web summarizing the literary qualities of this historical fiction novel.

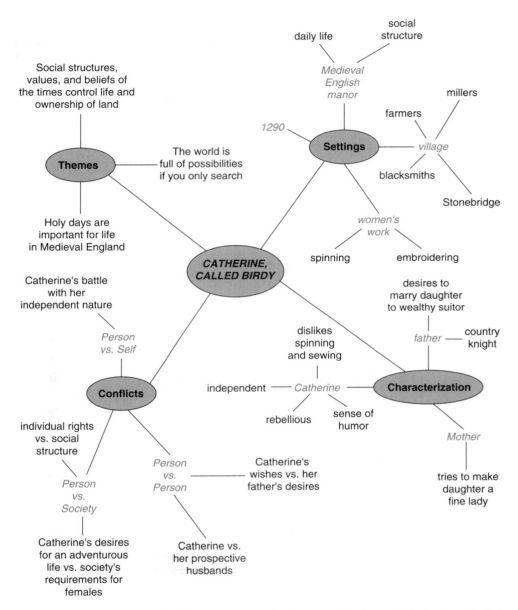

FIGURE 6–6 A Semantic Web Summarizing the Literary Qualities of *Catherine, Called Birdy*

For Your Development

Choose a book that would be good for a literary discussion. Make a web according to the literary elements found in the book.

Modeling.   Modeling is a technique that allows teachers to interact actively with students and show them how to approach thought processes. Modeling also integrates the language arts as students use oral language in their discussions, analyze evidence found in literature, and write responses. Modeling is developed in several chapters in this text. For example, an in-depth look at modeling was developed in Chapter 3 as a way of teaching students how to become actively involved in and aware of their thought processing. The example used there describes the steps in modeling inferencing of characterization using Patricia MacLachlan's *Sarah, Plain and Tall* (NM 1986, 1985). Look at the in-depth lesson plan described for that book in Chapter 3. Notice how the teacher in that example guides the students through an understanding of characterization. The same approach may be used to model the understanding of any of the literary elements. This chapter considers how to use modeling to help students understand the author's style. A lesson plan format similar to that developed in Chapter 3 is used in the following example.

For Your Plan Book

Lesson Plan

Modeling for the Understanding of Similes Using the 1964 Caldecott Honor Book

Grade Level: Lower Elementary   *Book: Leo Lionni's* Swimmy *(CH 1965, 1963)*

Requirements for Effective Reasoning

1. Going beyond the information the author provides in the text.
2. Knowing that similes are comparisons that authors make between something in the text and something that is not in the text.
3. Knowing that similes are introduced with the clue words *like* and *as*.
4. Knowing that authors use similes to develop vivid descriptions and characterizations.
5. Thinking about how one object is like another object.

Introduction

1. *Introduce similes through a dialogue like this:* "Sometimes when authors write, they use a special kind of writing called figurative language. This kind of language is a way for authors to use fewer words but to write more vividly. Similes are a form of figurative language. In similes, authors compare one thing with another thing. Today, we will listen for ways that authors use similes to encourage us to see pictures in our minds."

2. *Provide examples and nonexamples of similes:* "Similes are stated comparisons in which an author tells us how two things are alike. We say a simile is a stated comparison because the author uses the clue words *like* or *as* to signal the comparison. Many times, an author will compare one object you know and one object that you do not know. For example, in 'Sandy is as quiet as a mouse,' the author is using *as* to clue the comparison. A mouse is shy around people, so I can visualize that Sandy is a very shy person. She does not talk very much. In another example, 'Giraffes have ears like giant leaves,' the author is using *like* to clue the comparison. Even without seeing a giraffe, I know that the ears are shaped like big leaves. I can almost 'see' the giraffe with big, pointed, leaf-shaped ears that stick up above its head. We must listen carefully, however, because *as* or *like* in a sentence does not always signal a comparison. For example, in 'We will watch as the moon rises' are there any comparisons? Likewise, in 'I like hamburgers' is there a comparison?"

3. *Tell students why similes are important:* "We need to know about similes and what they can tell us as we read or listen to stories so that we can understand what we read. Similes help us appreciate the story. Authors use similes to paint vivid pictures with words just as artists paint vivid pictures with paints. We can use similes to make our own writing more vivid and more meaningful. Today, I am going to read a story about a fish. Listen for the similes, tell what you think the comparison means, and explain how you reached the answer. Listen carefully as I do the first one for you. By listening to how I thought through the meaning of the simile, you will know what I expect of you when it is your turn."

Example One

Read page 1 but do not show the illustration. Ask the question: "What does Swimmy look like?" Answer the question: "Swimmy is shiny and deep black." Provide the evidence: "The author uses the simile clue *as*. The author compares one of the fish to the black of a mussel shell." State the reasoning that you used to reach the answer: "The author is telling me to think about more information. The comparison is between Swimmy's color and the black of a mussel shell. There are many shades of black. I also know from seeing mussel shells at the beach that a mussel shell is dark black and shiny. If I close my eyes, I can see a small, black, shiny fish swimming among many other fish who are not black." (After modeling the simile, ask the students to listen to the page again with their eyes closed. Can they see Swimmy's color? Then share the illustration and compare their visualized pictures with that in the illustration.)

Example Two

Read pages 4 through 10, stopping with the sentence, "One day . . . a lobster, who walked like a water-moving machine." (Show the illustrations after modeling, or the students will use the illustrations to gain visual images rather than the words and their imaginations.) Ask the question: "How does a lobster move?" Answer the question: "A lobster walks mechanically through the water, pushing the water ahead of it." Provide evidence: "The author uses the simile clue *like*. The author compares the lobster and a water-moving machine." Provide the reasoning for reaching the answer: "The machine that I see in my mind would move mechanically through the water rather than darting and gliding like a fish. This machine would have to push forward against the water. I imagine it moving like a robot, with its claws moving the water and its feet plodding along. I am also impressed with how many words the author saved and how vivid a picture he depicted by using just the right comparison."

At this point, make sure that all of the students understand the process involved in answering questions, giving evidence, and providing reasoning used to reach the answer. Follow the same procedures, but change the involvement as you ask the questions but the students enter into the discussion with answers, evidence, and reasoning.

Example Three

Read pages 11 through 17, stopping with "sea anemones . . . pink palm trees swaying in the wind." Ask the question: "What do the sea anemones look like?" Ask the students to answer the question: "The sea anemones are pink and have thin bodies (trunks). The top of an anemone has thin stringy arms that wave in the water." Continue the discussion, letting the students provide the evidence for the answer and discuss the reasoning that they used to reach the answer. Continue this procedure, reading and stopping at page 18 after the simile comparing the new school of fish to Swimmy's school. Read to the end of the text, where the comparison is with the biggest fish in the sea. Encourage looking for evidence and using the reasoning process. Students' visualizations of the similes may be different from the artist's illustrations, so let the students draw their own interpretations. They frequently decide that their own interpretations are more exciting than are the artist's.

Modeling may be used to improve the understanding of any of the literary elements. Modeling is effective at any grade level because of the wide selection of books available. Modeling is also another opportunity to introduce students to Newbery and Caldecott Medal and Honor books. The following award-winning books and literary elements suggest some of the modeling activities that you may develop:

- *Setting:* Karen Hesse's *Out of the Dust* (NM 1998, 1997), setting as antagonist; Armstrong Sperry's *Call It Courage* (NM 1941, 1940), setting as antagonist; Jean Craighead George's *Julie of the Wolves* (NM 1973, 1972), setting as antagonist; Karen Cushman's *Catherine, Called Birdy* (NH 1995, 1994) and *The Midwife's Apprentice* (NM 1996, 1995), setting as historical background; Christopher Paul Curtis's *Bud, Not Buddy* (NM 2000, 1999); Laurence Yep's *Dragon's Gate* (NH 1994, 1993), setting as historical, cultural, and geographical background; Kate Seredy's *The White Stag* (NM 1938, 1937), setting as mood; Marcia Brown's illustrations and Blaise Cendrars's poetry in *Shadow* (CM 1983, 1982), setting as mood.
- *Conflict:* Byrd Baylor's *Hawk, I'm Your Brother* (CH 1977, 1976), person-versus-person and person-versus-nature conflicts; Lois Lowry's *The Giver* (NM 1994, 1993) and *Number the Stars* (NM 1990, 1989), person-versus-society conflict; Katherine Paterson's *Bridge to Terabithia* (NM 1978, 1977), person-versus-society and person-versus-self conflicts.
- *Style:* Virginia Lee Burton's *The Little House* (CM 1943, 1942), personification of objects; Sharon Bell Mathis's *The Hundred Penny Box* (NH 1976, 1975), symbolism through music and pennies; Cynthia Voigt's *Dicey's Song* (NM 1983, 1982), symbolism through music and boat; Jane Yolen's *Owl Moon* (CM 1988, 1987), similes; Anne Isaacs's *Swamp Angel* (CH 1995, 1994), exaggeration.
- *Theme:* Chris Van Allsburg's *The Polar Express* (CM 1986, 1985), importance of keeping our beliefs in miracles; Byrd Baylor's *Hawk, I'm Your Brother* (CH 1977, 1976), importance of having a dream and freedom; Cynthia Rylant's *The Relatives Came* (CH 1986, 1985), sharing of happy memories while establishing bonds across the generations; Sharon Creech's *Walk Two Moons* (NM 1995, 1994), importance of not judging others; Barbara Kerley's *The Dinosaurs of Waterhouse Hawkins* (CH 2002, 2001), the importance of working for a dream; Emily Arnold McCully's *Mirette on the High Wire* (CM 1993, 1992), overcoming fear and personal problems.

Plot Diagramming.   As we have mentioned, in most stories for younger readers the characters and problems are introduced at the beginning, the conflict builds until a climax is reached, a turning point occurs, and then the conflict ends. This type of structure is usual in stories in which the main character faces problems caused by external forces. Help students understand this plot development by having them place key incidents from a story on a plot diagram such as that shown in Figure 6–7. Stories ranging from "The Three Billy Goats Gruff" to the high fantasy of Lloyd Alexander follow this type of structure.

To develop an activity around plot diagramming using John Steptoe's *Mufaro's Beautiful Daughters: An African Tale,* draw the plot diagram shown in Figure 6–7 on the board. Introduce the book and ask students to listen for the conflict and the characters in the story. Encourage them to discuss their reactions to the conflict and the characters. Next, have the students diagram the story according to the plot diagram. Ask, "Did each of the characters respond in the same way to the major incidents in the story?" "Why do you believe the greedy, selfish sister and the generous, kind sister reacted differently?" "What do we call this type of conflict in literature?" Be sure that they understand that this is a person-versus-person conflict because the two main characters have different motives and desires that are in conflict.

FIGURE 6–7   A Plot Diagram

FIGURE 6–8   Plot Diagram for *Mufaro's Beautiful Daughters: An African Tale*

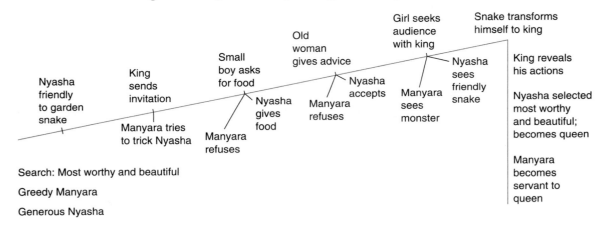

Ask the students to not only plot the major incidents in the story, but also to identify how each of the two characters responded to the incidents. This activity will allow the students to better understand the motivation of the characters and how the characters' motives relate to the conflict. You can reread the story to the children or allow them to reread it themselves. The diagram in Figure 6–8 (Norton, 1992) was completed with middle-elementary students. Notice how the students identified both the common plot structures and the different character responses to each incident.

Additional books that are excellent for this type of plot diagram include Ed Young's *Lon Po Po: A Red-Riding Hood Story from China* (CM 1990, 1989); Julius Lester's *John Henry* (CH 1995, 1994); and Arthur Ransome's *The Fool of the World and the Flying Ship* (CM 1969, 1968).

When characters try to overcome problems caused by inner conflicts, use the same type of diagram but change the terminology. Cohen (1985) identifies four major components in the development of person-versus-self conflicts: (1) problem, (2) struggle, (3) realization, and (4) achievement of peace or truth: "The point at which the struggle wanes and the inner strength emerges seems to be the point of self-realization. The point leads immediately to the final sense of peace or truth that is the resolution of the quest. The best books are those which move readers and cause them to identify with the character's struggle" (p. 28). Place Cohen's components on a plot diagram, such as that in Figure 6–9, and let the students record major incidents on the diagram. Books such as Paula Fox's *One-Eyed Cat* (NH 1985, 1984) and Marion Dane Bauer's *On My Honor* (NH 1987, 1986) are examples of person-versus-self struggle.

FIGURE 6–9   A Person-Versus-
Self Plot Diagram

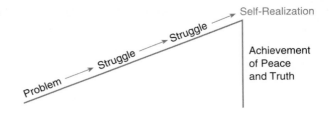

Listing Possibilities.   Explore various ways to use a book for instructional purposes. Categories include art interpretation, drama, clarification of values, personal response, characterization, plot development, symbolism, and related literature. A group of college students used this technique to identify the instructional potential of several children's books. The following example illustrates the many activities that arise from Scott O'Dell's 1961 Newbery Medal winner, *Island of the Blue Dolphins:*

Art Interpretation

a. Make a model of Karana's weapons.
b. Make a shadowbox of Karana's home on the island.
c. Make a model of the Aleuts' ship.
d. Make a salt map of the Island of the Blue Dolphins and mark the places Karana went.

Drama

a. Make masks and dramatize the opening scene between Karana's father and the Aleuts.
b. Pantomime Karana's attempts to make weapons.
c. Pantomime the meeting between Karana and Tutok.

Clarification of Values

a. What took more courage for Karana—to stay on the boat, or to jump off the boat and stay with her brother?
b. Should Karana have broken the tribal taboos about weapons?
c. Was Karana's judgment about the Aleutian otter killing a fair one?

Personal Response

a. Have you ever felt as alone as Karana did? Explain.
b. How did Karana respond after her brother died and after Rontu died? Compare her responses in terms of the loneliness she felt.
c. What factors would have persuaded you to go or to stay on the island?

Characterization

a. How did Tutok see Karana?
b. How did the missionaries see Karana?
c. How did Rontu see Karana?
d. How do you see Karana?

Plot Development

a. What are the major incidents or decisions that influence the plot development?
b. How do each of these decisions influence the story?

  to leave or to stay at the beginning of the story.
  to make weapons.
  to trap Rontu.

to talk to Tutok.
to leave or to stay at the end of the story.

Symbolism

  a. To reveal a secret name causes it to lose its magic.
  b. The island is the shape of a dolphin.
  c. Blue clay is symbolic of eligibility for marriage.
  d. Dolphins are protectors.

Related Literature

  a. Tests of courage today:

> *Eleanor Roosevelt: A Life of Discovery* (Freedman)
> *Number the Stars* (Lowry)
> *Shabanu: Daughter of the Wind* (Staples)
> *My Side of the Mountain* (George)
> *Hatchet* (Paulsen)

  b. Kinds of courage:

> *Lincoln: A Photobiography* (Freedman)
> *Sounder* (Armstrong)
> *Old Yeller* (Gipson)
> *The True Confessions of Charlotte Doyle* (Avi)

  c. Incredible journeys:

> *Commodore Perry in the Land of the Shogun* (Blumberg)
> *A Wrinkle in Time* (L'Engle)
> *The Wright Brothers: How They Invented the Airplane* (Freedman)

For Your Development

  1. Develop a modeling activity in which you identify a literary element and provide instruction in the understanding of that literary element.
  2. With a group of your peers, select a book appropriate for children and identify its possibilities for instructional activities. Share your suggestions with the entire class.

Developing an Understanding of Picture Books

Picture books are excellent choices for initial analysis of literature. According to Lacy (1986), they may be used to stimulate visual exploration, interpretation, and reflection. Although most children's books are illustrated, not all illustrated books are classified as picture books. Activities such as looking at illustrations, discussing the importance of text and illustrations within a book, comparing picture books and illustrated books, and classifying books as either picture books or illustrated books foster an appreciation of picture books. These activities also stimulate cognitive development.

Picture Books versus Illustrated Books

In their discussion of picture books, Schwarcz and Schwarcz (1991) state: "One must take a close look in order to discover what can be found in, and culled from a picture book.

Further, the careful scrutiny of one particular book will aid in the analysis of others" (p. 14). A logical progression for this activity begins by defining picture books, continues by analyzing examples and examining criteria, and finishes by comparing picture books and illustrated books and justifying why particular books are placed within either category. This progression emphasizes discussion, analysis, and support for various decisions. It also shows students that there are no right or wrong answers. Some books lend themselves to lively discussions because students may justifiably classify them in more than one way.

Introduce picture books by asking students to define a picture book. Next, share several definitions developed by either children's literature authorities or illustrators/authors of picture books and discuss the implications of those definitions. For example, Sutherland and Hearne (1984) define a picture book as one in which the illustrations are either as important as the text or more important than the text. Illustrator Uri Shulevitz (1985) states that picture books are closely related to theater and film because picture books are dramatic experiences that include "actors" and "stages." In picture books, the characters, settings, and actions are shown through the pictures. Lukens (1999) emphasizes that "Because illustration has the characteristics of an art form, however, it should be regarded as art. Illustrators use the techniques of representation, expressionism, impressionism, and surrealism, of cubism and pointillism, of naive, folk, and collage styles as well as photography. Like other art forms, illustration uses symbolic language for communication. It has both meaning and content created from visual and usually verbal symbols as well" (p. 41).

Next, share and discuss examples of picture books. Begin your discussion with wordless books such as Eric Rohmann's *Time Flies* (CH 1995, 1994) and David Wiesner's *Free Fall* (CH 1989, 1988). Ask the students to tell you the story from the illustrations and to describe the setting, characters, and conflict (if any) that they find in the stories. They should conclude that all of these elements are revealed through the illustrations. Consequently, these books meet the previously stated definitions for picture books.

Proceed from wordless books to books that have minimal texts, such as Maurice Sendak's *Where the Wild Things Are* (CM 1964, 1963), David Wiesner's *Tuesday* (CM 1992, 1991), and Audrey Wood's *King Bidgood's in the Bathtub* (CH 1986, 1985). Ask the students to note that the illustrations present information that the written text does not. For example, the illustrations in Sendak's book portray the magnitude and type of mischief of the wild things, as well as their appearance. In addition, the illustrations provide drama as they increase in size until finally the land of the wild things appear in double-page spreads, without text. This book clearly matches Shulevitz's definition for a picture book, which includes both actors and stages. Likewise, the illustrations in Wood's book provide maximum detail for minimal text. For example, the text states, "Today we lunch in the tub!" (p. 11, unnumbered). The double-page illustrations show an elegant luncheon with a cake centerpiece that is a model of the king's castle. Ask the students to describe the illustrations, either orally or in writing. They will discover that without the illustrations, pages of descriptive material would be required. Furthermore, the author would have to create a humorous and exaggerated mood through words alone. Students should conclude from this discussion that picture books with minimal text contain numerous details in the illustrations that are essential to the meaning of the story.

Next, proceed to picture books in which the illustrations and the text play equal roles, such as Wanda Gág's *Millions of Cats* (T 1928) and Arthur Yorinks's *Hey, Al* (CM 1987, 1986). Gág's book is an excellent choice because the written text complements the illustrations and repetitive style by creating a feeling of movement. Even though there is more written text in *Hey, Al* than in *Where the Wild Things Are,* the illustrator of *Hey, Al,* Richard Egielski, uses some of the same techniques as Sendak. The illustrations become larger as the conflict develops, cover a double-page spread at the height of the interest, and include considerable information about setting and characters. After reading the texts and looking at the illustrations, students should discover that the illustrations and the written text are equally important.

Next, proceed to highly illustrated books that are not classified as picture books. For example, Russell Freedman's *Lincoln: A Photobiography* (NM 1988, 1987) contains a photograph or other type of illustration on about every second page. After the students listen to or read the text and analyze the illustrations in relation to the text, they should discover that although the illustrations add both information and interest, they cannot stand alone or are not as important as the written text.

Finally, ask the students to develop a list of activities and questions to help them decide if a book is a picture book or an illustrated book. For example:

1. Try to retell the story without looking at the words. Does the sequence of illustrations allow me to understand the story? (picture book)
2. Read the text. Is the story self-sufficient without the illustrations? (illustrated book)
3. Compare the illustrations and the text. Are the illustrations so important that they provide information about the setting, actions, and characters that the written text does not provide? (picture book)

Additional examples that you may use for this final comparison include the following picture books: Uri Shulevitz's *Snow* (CH 1999, 1998), Denise Fleming's *In the Small, Small Pond* (CH 1994, 1993), David Macaulay's *Black and White* (CM 1991, 1990), Nancy Tafuri's *Have You Seen My Duckling?* (CH 1985, 1984), and Allen Say's *Grandfather's Journey* (CM 1994, 1993). These may be compared with the following illustrated books: Patricia McKissack's *The Dark-Thirty: Southern Tales of the Supernatural* (NH 1993, 1992) and William Steig's *Abel's Island* (NH 1977, 1976).

Books such as Bill Peet's *Bill Peet: An Autobiography* (CH 1990, 1989) show how important it is to emphasize support for categories rather than right and wrong answers. Lively discussions accompany this book because students can support it as either picture book or illustrated text.

A study of picture books may also add an evaluation of historical settings in both the illustrations and the text. Harms and Lettow (1994) develop criteria for evaluating picture books with historical settings and provide a list of recommended books. Their criteria include authenticity of both text and illustrations, illustrations that complement and clarify the meaning of the text, and three-dimensional characters who help children identify with the conflicts of the time period.

Picture story books that might be used for such an activity include Elisa Bartone's *Peppe, the Lamplighter* (CH 1994, 1993), Allen Say's *Grandfather's Journey* (CM 1994, 1993), Alice and Martin Provensen's *The Glorious Flight: Across the Channel with Louis Bleriot* (CM 1984, 1983), and Sherely Anne Williams's *Working Cotton* (CH 1993, 1992).

For Your Development

1. Develop a lesson plan in which you teach students to differentiate between picture books and illustrated books.
2. Read Bruce McMillan's article "Photographer or Photo-Illustrator: What's the Difference?" (1991). Select books that you would classify under each category. Develop a lesson in which you help students compare and contrast the categories.

Table 6–1   Characteristics of literary genres

	Modern Fantasy or Science Fiction: *The Giver*	Contemporary Realistic Fiction: *Walk Two Moons*	Historical Fiction: *Catherine, Called Birdy*	Biography: *Eleanor Roosevelt*
Characters:	Personified toys Little people Supernatural beings People who have imaginary experiences Animals who behave like people People who live in worlds controlled by technology	Fictional human characters who behave like real people Fictional animal characters who behave like real animals	Fictional humans who behave like real people and express understanding of historical period	Real people
Literary evidence:	People have eliminated conflict, poverty, inequality	Sal behaves like a real teenager with all the problems and conflicts	Strong heroine who expresses her attitudes about female expectations in medieval England	Draws on memoirs of her life and includes incidents that really happened
Setting:	Past, present, or future Imaginary world created by the author May travel through time and space	Contemporary world as we know it May have fictional location but must be possible in contemporary world	Authentic for historic time period Supported by facts	True for time the person actually lived Supported by facts
Literary evidence:	Future society devoid of conscience, emotion, and color	Locations in Ohio: describes travel in real places from Ohio to Idaho	Details associated with daily life on an English manor, 1290	True settings that follow her life, 1884–1962

Literary Genres

Children's literature is often categorized as traditional literature, modern fantasy, poetry, contemporary realistic fiction, historical fiction, biography and autobiography, and informational books. Each of these genres has special characteristics related to characters, settings, plots, and techniques the authors use to create believable stories. Discussing and comparing various genres help students appreciate an author's ability to write within a genre and enhance their understanding of the nature of that genre. Table 6–1 compares several genres with respect to characters, setting, plot development, and believability.

To develop an understanding of and appreciation for differences and similarities, introduce one genre and help students identify its characteristics. After thoroughly investigating this genre by having the students listen to and read literary examples and identify and discuss

	Modern Fantasy or Science Fiction: *The Giver*	Contemporary Realistic Fiction: *Walk Two Moons*	Historical Fiction: *Catherine, Called Birdy*	Biography: *Eleanor Roosevelt*
Plot development:	Conflict may be against supernatural powers or technology Problems may be solved through magical powers or scientific advancement	Author creates plot as fictional characters face contemporary situations, such as growing up, survival, family problems	Author creates plot as fictional characters cope with problems that are authentic for the historical time	Plot follows life of a real person Conflict follows real problems and dates
Literary evidence:	Jonas's conflicts result as he ponders the consequences of the society's actions and reexamines his beliefs	Sal faces her mother's leaving her father and herself and tries to make discoveries about her mother	The plot focuses on personal conflicts caused by society's demands on a young girl	The plot follows the chronological order of her life
Creating believable stories:	Authors encourage readers to suspend disbelief	Author relies on relevant subjects, everyday occurrences, or realism	Authors use research to create historically authentic settings and problems	Authors use research and documentation and objectivity
Literary evidence:	Detailed descriptions of futuristic setting and the history of society as Jonas experiences visions from the past	Author relies on problems facing Sal as she tries to understand her mother	Author's text and notes emphasize characteristics of medieval England, the social structure, and importance of the church	Photographs and documentation add to authenticity of the book

the characteristics of the genre, continue the same type of listening, reading, and discussing activities with the next genre. Then, ask the students to compare and contrast the genres.

There are numerous, clearly defined differences between modern fantasy and contemporary realistic fiction; this is a logical place to begin the study of literary genres. First, share and discuss several modern fantasy selections and encourage students to identify characteristics of modern fantasy that are similar to those listed in Table 6–1. Within any genre, read texts or portions of texts to students and then identify and discuss various characteristics and examples of those characteristics from the literature. After this initial activity, either you or the students may read additional books from the genre and add them to the charts.

Modern Fantasy

Modern fantasy is fiction in which the author transports readers into a time period and setting where the impossible becomes convincingly possible. Authors of modern fantasy create their settings by altering one or more of the literary elements that would be expected in the real world. Authors of modern fantasy frequently choose to have their characters depart from known possibilities. The characters themselves may be contrary to reality or may experience preposterous situations (Norton, 2003).

Modern fantasy selections should include stories that reflect the various types of characters in the modern fantasy genre, such as personified toys (A. A. Milne's *Winnie-the-Pooh,* T 1926, 1954); little people (Mary Norton's *The Borrowers,* T 1952); people who have imaginary experiences (C. S. Lewis's *The Lion, the Witch and the Wardrobe,* T 1950; Lewis Carroll's *Alice's Adventures in Wonderland,* T 1866, 1984; and Madeleine L'Engle's *A Wrinkle in Time,* T, NM 1963, 1962); and animals who behave like people (Beatrix Potter's *The Tale of Peter Rabbit,* T 1902; Robert Lawson's *Rabbit Hill,* NM 1944; and E. B. White's *Charlotte's Web,* T, NH 1953, 1952). (Notice how many of these recommendations are considered classics in children's literature.)

Modern fantasy selections should show students that settings may be in the past, present, or future. Settings may also be in worlds that are totally created by the author, such as Narnia in *The Lion, the Witch and the Wardrobe,* Prydain in Lloyd Alexander's *The Book of Three* (T 1964), and Demar in Robin McKinley's *The Hero and the Crown* (NM 1984). Characters may also go through time warps such as those found in Philippa Pearce's *Tom's Midnight Garden* (T 1958) in which the settings shift from present to past.

Likewise, conflict may be against supernatural powers, as in *The Lion, the Witch and the Wardrobe* or *The Hero and the Crown.* In modern fantasies, the problems are solved through magical or supernatural powers.

Science fiction is also an important part of modern fantasy. Authors of science fiction rely on hypothesized scientific advancements and imagined technology to create their plots. To achieve credibility, they provide detailed descriptions of this technology, portray characters who believe in the technology or the results of the technology, and create a world where science interacts with every area of society. Such a world of the future is depicted in Lois Lowry's *The Giver* (NM 1994, 1993). Technology has eliminated poverty, inequality, and unemployment, but the society is devoid of conscience, emotion, and even color. Accompanying twelve-year-old Jonas as he discovers the truth about his society, readers must ponder and reexamine many of their own beliefs.

The books should help students understand and appreciate that authors of modern fantasy must make readers believe in worlds, characters, and actions that are not possible in the world as they know it. In literary terms, an author must encourage readers to suspend disbelief. These key questions must be considered by the student: Did the author make me believe that the characters, settings, and conflicts were possible? How did the author create the world, the people, and the conflict so that I believed they were possible?

Contemporary Realistic Fiction

After students develop a clear understanding of modern fantasy, extend the study of genres into contemporary realistic fiction. In contemporary realistic fiction, everything in the story, including characters, setting, and plot, could happen to real people or animals living in the contemporary world. Contemporary realistic fiction does not mean that the story is true; it means only that it could have happened (Norton, 2003).

Use an instructional approach for the study of contemporary realistic fiction similar to that for modern fantasy. Select books such as the following to help students identify and develop characteristics of contemporary realistic fiction: Beverly Cleary's *Dear Mr. Henshaw* (NM 1984, 1983) and *Ramona Quimby, Age 8* (NH 1982, 1981); Jane Leslie Conly's *Crazy Lady!* (NH 1994, 1993); Sharon Creech's *Walk Two Moons* (NM 1995, 1994); Katherine Paterson's *Bridge to Terabithia* (NM 1978, 1977); Kate DiCamillo's *Because of Winn-Dixie* (NH 2001, 2000); Louis Sachar's *Holes* (NM 1999, 1998); and Gary Paulsen's *Hatchet* (NH 1988, 1987).

After identifying and developing the characteristics of contemporary realistic fiction, encourage students to compare modern fantasy and contemporary realistic fiction.

Historical Fiction

Continue with an analysis of historical fiction. Historical fiction is fiction written about an earlier time, in which the setting is authentic in every respect; the actions, beliefs, and values of the characters are realistic for the time period; and the conflicts reflect the historical time period. Although the characters did not actually live, they could have lived during that time period (Norton, 2003).

Follow the sequence of events described under modern fantasy. Select books to help students develop an appreciation for and understanding of the characteristics shown in Table 6–1: Linda Sue Park's *A Single Shard* (NM 2002, 2001); Karen Cushman's *Catherine, Called Birdy* (NH 1995, 1994) and *The Midwife's Apprentice* (NM 1996, 1995); Patricia MacLachlan's *Sarah, Plain and Tall* (NM 1986, 1985); Scott O'Dell's *Sing Down the Moon* (NH 1971, 1970); Elizabeth George Speare's *The Sign of the Beaver* (NH 1984, 1983); Mildred Taylor's *Roll of Thunder, Hear My Cry* (NM 1977, 1976); Christopher Paul Curtis's *The Watsons Go to Birmingham—1963* (NH 1996, 1995); and Laura Ingalls Wilder's *Little House in the Big Woods* (T 1932).

After analyzing the literature and identifying and discussing characteristics, compare similarities and differences between historical fiction, contemporary realistic fiction, and modern fantasy.

Biography

Finally, extend the study of genre into biography. A biography is a book written about a real person, living or dead. A biography must be a true story about the person and the other people and the incidents that influenced that person's life. The characters, their actions, and the settings reflect what actually happened and not what could have happened. Biographies that could be used to help students identify and develop characteristics of the genre include Russell Freedman's *Lincoln: A Photobiography* (NM 1988, 1987) and *Eleanor Roosevelt: A Life of Discovery* (NH 1994, 1993) and Elizabeth Yates's *Amos Fortune, Free Man* (NM 1995, 1950).

After you and the students find examples from biographies to support the characteristics and you conclude discussions of them, compare characteristics of biography as a genre with the characteristics of other genres.

For Your Development

Choose another genre of children's literature, such as poetry, traditional literature, or informational literature, and develop an activity that encourages students to develop appreciation and understanding of the characteristics of that genre.

Poetry

Poetry is not easily defined because there is no single accepted definition of poetry. Some definitions specify the characteristics of poetry, including the poetic elements and the functions of words, while other definitions emphasize the emotional impact of poetry. Ask your students to develop their own definition of poetry as they read and respond to various examples of poetry. One of my own favorite quotes about the importance of poetry is stated by John Adams in his biography: "You will never be alone with a poem in your pocket" (Mc-Cullough, 2001, p. 19).

In addition to developing their own definitions of poetry, they may search for and share orally the various elements of poetry including rhythm, rhyme and other sound patterns, repetition, imagery, and shape. Some excellent examples of poetry that may be used for this activity include *Reflections on a Gift of Watermelon Pickle . . . and Other Modern Verse*, compiled by Stephen Dunning, Edward Lueders, and Hugh Smith (T 1967); *Joyful Noise: Poems for Two Voices* by Paul Fleischman (NM 1989, 1988); *One at a Time: Collected Poems for the Young* by David McCord (T 1977); and *A Visit to William Blake's Inn: Poems for Innocent and Experienced Travelers* by Nancy Willard (NM 1982, 1981).

Traditional Literature

Folklore is that wonderful part of literature handed down by the storytellers of many cultures. In contrast to a modern story, a traditional tale has no identifiable author. Instead, storytellers tell what they have received from previous tellers of tales. Folklore includes folktales, myths, and legends. Folktales are probably the most common type of folklore shared with younger children. Folktales are regarded as fiction by the original tellers of the tales. The stories are set in any time or place. Settings such as "Once upon a time" in a great forest make the stories timeless and placeless. Folktales usually tell the adventures of animal or human characters. They contain common motifs such as supernatural adversaries, supernatural helpers, magic, and marvels. Many of the award-winning picture storybooks are folktales. For example, students may discover the characteristics of folktales by reading and discussing stories such as Grimm's *Little Red Riding Hood* retold by Trina Schart Hyman (CH 1984, 1983); Charles Perrault's *Puss in Boots* illustrated by Fred Marcellino (CH 1991, 1990); John Steptoe's *Mufaro's Beautiful Daughters: An African Tale* (CH 1988, 1987); Paul O. Zelinsky's *Rapunzel* (CM 1998, 1997); and Ed Young's *Lon Po Po: A Red-Riding Hood Story from China* (CM 1990, 1989).

Myths are stories that, in the society in which they are told, are considered to be truthful accounts of what happened in the remote past. Myths are important in every culture because they account for the origins of the world and humans, for everyday natural phenomena, and for human emotions and experiences. The main characters in myths are usually deities. The actions take place in an earlier world or another world, such as the underworld or the sky. Many ancient Greek myths, for example, explain the creation of the world, the creation of the gods and goddesses who ruled from Mount Olympus, and the reasons for natural phenomena. Examples of myths that may be used to help students understand the characteristics of myths include Padraic Colum's *The Golden Fleece* (T 1921, NH 1922); Ingri and Edgar D'Aulaire's *Norse Gods and Giants* (T 1967); and Virginia Hamilton's *In the Beginning: Creation Stories from Around the World* (NH 1989, 1988).

Legends, like myths, were regarded as true by the original storyteller and the audience. Legends are set in a period that is less remote, when the world was much as it is

Folklore contributes to a child's understanding of cultural traditions.

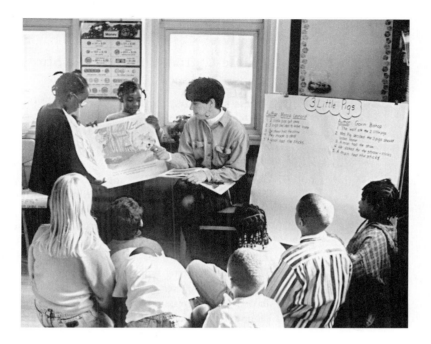

today. The main characters in legends are human. Many legends embroider the historical facts of human wars and migrations, brave deeds, and royalty. Legends are important because they present characteristics of heroes that are important to the culture. Examples of legends that may be used to help students understand their characteristics include Margaret Hodges's *Saint George and the Dragon* (CM 1985, 1984); Julius Lester's *John Henry* (CH 1995, 1994); and Howard Pyle's *The Story of King Arthur and His Knights* (T 1903).

Folklore enables teachers to instill an understanding of other cultures and an appreciation for cultures that differ. Folklore is the mirror of a culture and looks at that culture from the inside instead of the outside.

See Norton's *Through the Eyes of a Child: An Introduction to Children's Literature* (2003) for additional ways to involve children in traditional literature. The text includes ways to compare different versions of a folktale and how to investigate folktales from a single country.

For Your Development

1. Select a group of folktales from a particular country. Read the folktales and note the information you find about values, beliefs, occupations, transportation, animals, and agriculture.

2. Select a story type or motif from folktales, such as the various "Little Red Riding Hood" stories. Find as many folktales as you can from different cultures that tell basically the same story. Compare the different versions. How are they alike? How are they different? How do you account for the similarities?

For Your Plan Book

A Folktale Unit: A Comparative Study of "Cinderella" Stories from Different Cultures

(Due to the specialized nature of these stories, the stories are not all award-winning books.) (Norton, 1992)

General Objectives

1. To encourage children to appreciate a literary form, the folktale, and to realize that they share common interests, attitudes, and values with their counterparts in other lands.
2. To have children verbalize generalizations—such as the strongly contrasted values of good and evil—regarding the nature of folktales.
3. To share enthusiasm for folktales by reading certain selections aloud.
4. To develop listening skills by asking children to listen for specifics in each story.
5. To motivate children to search for more folktales to read and enjoy.
6. To provide opportunity for children to enjoy silent reading of the folktales of their choice.
7. To encourage children, once they are acquainted with the "Cinderella" type of folktale to generalize about commonalities across "Cinderella" stories from different cultures and to identify differences among the "Cinderella" stories that may relate to the specific culture.
8. To encourage children to share what they learn with one another.
9. To have children, individually and as a group, demonstrate their knowledge of and appreciation for folktales to their classmates by creating a bulletin board display and presenting a puppet play, a reader's theater, or other type of drama, thereby inviting others to read and share in the enjoyment of such stories.

Examples of "Cinderella" Versions That May Be Used with This Unit:

Shirley Climo's *The Egyptian Cinderella* (1989)

Brothers Grimm's German "Cinderella" found in *Household Tales* (T 1979)

William Hooks's eastern North Carolina version, *Moss Gown* (1987)

Charlotte Huck's English version, *Princess Furball* (1989)

Joseph Jacob's English "Tattercoats" found in Sutherland and Livingston's *The Scott, Foresman Anthology of Children's Literature* (1984)

Rafe Martin's Native American version, *Rough-Faced Girl* (1992)

Ai-Ling Louie's *Yeh-Shen: A Cinderella Story from China* (1982)

Charles Perrault's French version, *Cinderella* (CM 1955, 1954)

Procedures

To begin this unit tell the students that some folktales have common story types found in cultures throughout the world. These folktales are called variants because they have basic elements in common, but frequently differ in such areas as settings, names of characters, magical objects, tasks to be completed, and obstacles to be overcome.

After students have read or listened to several "Cinderella" stories, ask them to identify the common elements in the different versions, such as those retold by Grimm and Perrault. Remind the students that common elements should be general such as "The heroine has a lowly position in the family." After students have identified several common elements, begin the study of variants by reading or rereading the Brothers Grimm and French versions of "Cinderella" during the same class period. Ask the students to notice the common important elements in these tales and add them to the list they compiled earlier. Such a list might include the following:

1. The heroine has a lowly position in the family.
2. The heroine is persecuted by stepsisters or other members of the household.
3. The heroine accomplishes difficult tasks.
4. The heroine has an opportunity to meet a person who has great worth within the culture.
5. The heroine is kept from meeting the person of great worth because she lacks clothing to attend a function.
6. The heroine is helped by a supernatural being.
7. The heroine is warned to return by a certain time.
8. The person of great worth is attracted to the heroine.
9. There is a test for the rightful heroine.
10. The heroine passes the test and marries the person of great worth.

Next, ask the students to identify how each of these common elements is developed in the German and French tales. For example, in both tales the girl's lowly position is caused by the mother's death and the father's remarriage. There are some specific differences, however. For example, the girl in the German version receives her wishes from a bird on the tree on her mother's grave and the girl in the French version receives wishes from a fairy godmother. The endings are also different: The German version ends unhappily for the stepmother and stepsisters while the French version ends in forgiveness of the stepsisters and their marriage to noblemen.

After the students have identified common elements and specific examples across the German and French "Cinderella" tales, ask them to read or listen to variants from other cultures. During this activity they should identify the elements that are similar and those that are different. Why do the elements in the stories change? How are these changes related to the cultures in which the tales were told? They should also analyze any illustrations for cultural information. For example, both the Native American and the Chinese "Cinderella" tales develop considerable cultural background through the illustrations. When reading these stories, the students should identify the elements in the story that are common to the previously listed elements. Then ask them to identify the elements that reflect the other cultures. They will discover, for example, that the Native American story has many of the "Cinderella" elements but it is also set firmly in the culture of the Woodlands Indians. As do many Native American tales, the story has a close relationship with nature.

After reading and discussing numerous variants from various cultures, ask older students what they think would happen if the people who told the stories and listened to the stories moved to a new land. Ask, "Would they take their oral stories with them? How do you think the stories might change over the years to reflect different settings or cultures?" Encourage the students to speculate about such areas as differences in settings, occupations, foods, and activities. Tell the students that as they listen to or read *Moss Gown,* another variant of the "Cinderella" story, they should search for (1) Cinderella elements, (2) references to time and place, and (3) evidence of the European country from which the early storytellers came. (If desired, students also can search for King Lear elements in this tale.)

Continued

Students should discover the following Cinderella elements:

1. The heroine, a generous young girl, has two greedy older sisters.
2. The heroine has a helper with supernatural powers.
3. The heroine has a gown that changes to rags at a specified time.
4. The heroine is given the hardest kitchen work.
5. An important person holds a dance.
6. The heroine cannot attend the dance because she lacks a dress.
7. A supernatural being casts a spell and provides a dress.
8. An order is given about the dress.
9. The important person dances only with the heroine.
10. The important person and the heroine are married.

The references to time and place include the following:

1. A great plantation
2. A house with eight marble columns
3. Fine fields
4. Riding and hunting in the mysterious swamp
5. Black-green cypress treetops
6. Gray Spanish moss
7. The word used to cast a spell is a French word used in the Carolinas
8. Important person holds a frolic

The students should discuss how these references to time and place reflect the new environment of the original storytellers. They should also identify where they think the story takes place. Students might identify the following evidence to show that the original storytellers had English backgrounds: (1) Similarities to British "Tattercoats" include servants who mistreat the girl and a man of wealthy position who loves her even though she is dressed in rags, (2) activities such as riding and hunting are commonly found in England, and (3) King Lear elements reflect knowledge of English Shakespeare.

Additional Activities That Integrate the Unit throughout the Curriculum:

1. *Creative writing:* Ask the students to pretend they are storytellers who are telling a variant of Cinderella that reflects their own culture, their school, or even their family. They should use the common Cinderella elements, but make the audience understand and picture the new culture.
2. *Written personal response:* Ask the students to choose a Cinderella variant and explain why they like or dislike the plot and the characters.
3. *Artistic response:* Ask the students to choose a folktale variant that is not highly illustrated. Through their own illustrations, they should show the setting and other cultural references. Encourage them to research the area and the culture so they will be as accurate as possible. Students could create a bulletin board display to show the settings and other cultural references.
4. *Geography insights:* Ask the students to point out on a map of the world the locations of the various Cinderella variants. Ask, "What does the map reveal about the importance of the Cinderella story?"
5. *Creative drama:* As a group project, ask the students to select several Cinderella characters from different cultures. Pretend that the characters are having a conversation. What information would the characters exchange? What questions would they ask each other?

What advice would they give? Or pretend that the more cruel members of the story or the supernatural beings could exchange ideas. What advice would they give? Another enjoyable drama project is the preparation and presenting of one of the variants through reader's theater.

6. *Puppetry project:* As a group project, ask the students to select one of the variants and prepare it for a presentation for the other members of the class.

7. *Oral interviewing and collecting of tales:* Ask the students to interview people in their community, and ask them which Cinderella tale or tales they remember. Summarize the information to discover which Cinderella variant is the most popular in the community.

For Your Plan Book

Lesson Plan

A Newbery Award Unit That Relates Literature, Art, Music, and Other Historical Occurrences

General Objectives

1. To encourage students to appreciate a time period developed by an author.
2. To develop an understanding of a time period by considering art, music, and historical occurrences that would have influenced the time period.
3. To integrate the curriculum across literature, art, music, and social studies.
4. To develop an appreciation for well-written literature and for the research skills required by an author.
5. To develop the ability to conduct research related to a time period in history as identified through specific Newbery Award books.
6. To develop a culminating activity that allows students to share their findings with an audience.

Examples of Newbery Literature to Be Used with This Unit:

Karen Cushman's *Catherine, Called Birdy* (NH 1995, 1994)

Esther Forbes's *Johnny Tremain* (NM 1944, 1943)

Procedures

Explain to the students that historical authenticity is considered one of the most important criteria when evaluating books set in time periods that are different from our own. To make you believe that the story and the characters could have really existed, the author must use accurate language, depict the details of everyday life, and be faithful to the historical record of what really happened. Some authors write about their own experiences or the experiences of relatives. Other authors write about time periods that are far removed from their own experiences. To write this kind of book, authors must conduct extensive research so that readers can vicariously see, hear, smell, and feel the environment.

Explain to the students that they will be reading several award-winning books that are set in time periods different from their own. To increase their understanding of a time period, they will be doing some of the research activities required of the authors. For example, they may be expanding their understanding of a time period by discovering additional information about the time period such as the music, art, and literature that would have been heard and

Continued

seen during the time period. They will also search for any additional information about the social structures of the times and the education that they would have experienced if they had lived during the time period. (This unit is divided according to the books to be shared. The class may focus on only one of the books or may continue with activities around each of the books. The books and activities are described in chronological order according to time periods. This should give students a better understanding of changes in history and the requirements of authors who write novels set in different time periods.)

Catherine, Called Birdy

For the first experience, explain to the students that they will be reading a book set in medieval England. After they have read and discussed the book they will be using the time frame to learn more about the history, the literature, the art, the music, the education, and the social structure of that time period. After they read the book they will divide into interest groups and each group will conduct research on one of the areas. Discuss with the students that each group will have an opportunity to share their findings with the class. These findings might be in the form of activities such as a skit, a reading, a puppet play, a re-creation of a market day or a fair, or artwork.

Background Information to Share with Students

The setting for *Catherine, Called Birdy* is 1290 in medieval England. The setting takes place in an English manor and within a knight's family. Part of the conflict results because of Catherine's desire for independence and an adventurous life versus society's requirements for females and her father's desire to marry his daughter to a wealthy suitor. The heroine discovers, through her own actions, that the world is full of possibilities, but in order to realize these possibilities she must continue trying. To provide additional background information read the Author's Note on pages 165–168. Have the students read and discuss the book. They may choose to develop their own areas of additional inquiry after reading the book and analyzing the author's note.

The Following Areas Suggest Possibilities for Group Inquiry

Literature that would have been read or told during the times: "King Arthur Legends" or tales of the Knights of the Round Table and other examples of folklore (*Sources:* Margaret Hodges's *Saint George and the Dragon,* CM 1985, 1984; Howard Pyle's *The Story of King Arthur and His Knights,* T 1903; Joseph Jacobs's *English Fairy Tales,* T 1942)

Music/entertainment of the times: dancing around the maypole, market days and fairs, chess, choral chapels with Gregorian chants being sung, madrigals accompanied by harps, folksongs

Art/architecture: Major themes were related to Christianity and the praise of God; Gothic architecture in cathedrals; (*Source:* David Macaulay's *Cathedral: The Story of Its Construction,* CH 1974, 1973); royalty lived in castles (*Source:* David Macaulay's *Castle,* CH 1978, 1977); tapestries included medieval allegory; illuminated manuscripts (*Source:* Johnathan Hunt's *Illumination,* 1989); sculpture, stained glass, and embroidery

Education: monastery schools for students going into a monastic order; cathedral schools taught wealthy laymen a curriculum including grammar, logic, rhetoric, arithmetic, music, geometry, and astronomy

Social structures: craft guilds, voluntary protective associations; everyone lived in a tight social structure, girls and women were controlled by their fathers or their husbands; knighthood: At seven a knight's son was sent to a castle to serve as a page. He received lessons in riding and swordsmanship. At fourteen he became a squire to an individual knight. At twenty-one he was named a knight.

Culminating Activity

Students may choose from many exciting activities to help them visualize the time period. Reenactment of a possible day in a cathedral school or the re-creation of a market day or a fair allow numerous possibilities. A storytelling festival could allow many students to prepare one of the tales for an appreciative audience. Ask the students to summarize what they have learned about medieval England and to evaluate the ability of Karen Cushman to re-create a setting, characters, and plot that they believe could be true. Ask them to consider their own research into the time period as they make this judgment.

Johnny Tremain

Background Information to Share with Students

Explain to the students that they will be reading a book set in the time period of the Revolutionary War. The story begins in Boston in 1773. Forbes makes her leading character a fictional silversmith, while real characters such as Paul Revere and Samuel Adams are background characters. To create a believable story Forbes must integrate the details of colonial life into the setting. The sights, sounds, and smells of revolutionary Boston must be woven into the characters' daily routines. Through these details readers know that Johnny sleeps in a loft, wears leather breeches and a coarse shirt, likes the bustling wharf, and is proud of his work in the silversmith shop. Through Johnny's observations, actions, and thoughts, Forbes emphasizes the issues of the times, the values of the people, and the feelings about freedom. Johnny discovers the political thinking of the time when he hears a minister preach sermons filled with anger against taxation without representation, delivers messages for the secret anti-British Boston Observers, and rides for the Boston Committee of Correspondence. Johnny is one of the "Indians" who throw tea into Boston Harbor. He experiences the anger and resulting unity when British troops close the harbor. He is there when British troops and colonial rebels clash at Concord. He discovers that a sixteen-year-old is considered a boy in times of peace and a man in times of war.

For additional background information you may read the biographical note about Esther Forbes in Miller and Field's *Newbery Medal Books, 1922–1955* (1955). This text also includes Forbes's acceptance speech when she won the Newbery Medal for *Johnny Tremain*. Of particular interest is the information that Forbes won the Pulitzer Prize for her adult biography, *Paul Revere and the World He Lived In,* and the fact that when she was conducting her research for the adult biography she became interested in the life of the apprentices. Consequently, after finishing her biography she wrote a fictional account of one of the apprentices. Students should realize that she used her considerable previous research to create a believable historical fiction story. In addition, "*Johnny Tremain* may well be counted the first classic story of Boston for young people. This is not alone because of the accurate picture of the pre-Revolutionary town, with its wandering streets and busy wharves, its crafts and trades, markets and merchants, not because of the rich abundance of details about the manners of the period, its ways of living and customs of trade, nor even because it is an arresting portrayal of the stubborn resistance of the Patriots and townspeople against arbitrary acts of the British Parliament. It is a distinguished book, primarily, because the people in it are vigorously endowed with the human quality which binds one generation to another" (p. 247).

As with *Catherine, Called Birdy,* after students have read and discussed *Johnny Tremain* they may make their own list of possibilities for group inquiry. Because this time period is often referred to as "The Age of Enlightenment" that led into the "Age of Political Revolution" there are many areas for investigation.

Continued

The Following Areas Suggest Possibilities for Group Inquiry

Literature that would have been written, read, or told during the times: 1719: Daniel Defoe's *Robinson Crusoe;* 1726: Jonathan Swift's *Gulliver's Travels;* 1755: Samuel Johnson published his *English Dictionary;* 1762: Jean Jacques Rousseau's *Emile* [*Sources:* There are editions of *Robinson Crusoe* and *Gulliver's Travels* that can be shared with students. An excellent source for numerous books is *Fifteen Centuries of Children's Literature* (Bingham & Scholt, 1980). The section "Restoration to American Independence (1660–1799)" provides historical background for both Britain and America as well as an annotated chronology of books.]

Music/entertainment of the times: Many of the great names in classical music began their careers during this time period. Wolfgang Amadeus Mozart (1756–1791) wrote numerous selections. In 1762 he wrote the "Minuet in G" when he was only six years old. This was the beginning of a huge classical music career as he completed compositions such as *The Magic Flute* and *The Marriage of Figaro.* Music of Bach and Haydn was popular. The dance called the minuet would have been performed by elegant ladies and gentlemen. In England in 1728 a satirical opera, *The Beggars Opera,* entertained audiences with a combination of English and Scottish folk tunes. In 1750 the harpsichord was challenged by the piano as the most popular instrument. In 1771 Thomas Jefferson was given one of the first pianos to be imported to America. (*Sources:* The music of these composers is readily available.)

Art/architecture: Students may study both art in children's books published during this time and artists whose works are now found in museums. Woodcuts were used in the early books illustrated for children and may be found in reproductions of books such as Thomas Bewick's illustrations in *The New Lottery Book of Birds and Beasts,* published in 1771, and *A Pretty Book of Pictures for Little Masters and Misses: or Tommy Trip's History of Beasts and Birds,* published in 1779. [*Sources:* Examples of these illustrations are found in Chapter 2, "The History of Children's Literature" in Norton's *Through the Eyes of a Child: An Introduction to Children's Literature* (2003). Books on art history include colored reproductions and discussions of art. For example, the chapter "Neoclassicism and Romanticism in Europe and the United States" in Stokstad's *Art History, Volume Two* (1995) includes numerous paintings from this period.]

Education: The Puritans had considerable influence on education in America. By the 1640s, Massachusetts law required heads of families to teach their children and apprentices to read. *Pilgrim's Progress* was required reading for colonial children in North America. Another important book would have been *The New England Primer,* a combination alphabet and catechism designed to teach Puritan ideals. The primer was written in such a way that spiritual instruction was the main theme. The primer appeared around 1690 and was printed in hundreds of editions until 1830. John Newbery's books for children began appearing in the 1740s.

Politics of the time period: An age of exploration was taking place in 1768–1779 as Captain James Cook explores the islands of the Pacific. (*Source:* Rhoda Blumberg's *The Remarkable Voyages of Captain Cook,* 1991)

1762–1796: Catherine the Great increases the power, territory, and influence of Russia.
1775: Battles of Lexington and Concord begin the American Revolution.
1775–1783: The American Revolution occurs.
1776: Declaration of Independence is written.
1787–1788: United States Constitution is ratified.

(*Sources:* Numerous nonfictional information books and biographies have been written about this time period including Milton Meltzer's *The American Revolutionaries: A History in Their Own Words, 1750–1800,* 1987; *George Washington and the Birth of Our Nation,* 1986; *Thomas Jefferson: The Revolutionary Aristocrat,* 1991; and Jean Fritz's *Traitor: The Case of Benedict Arnold,* 1981.)

Culminating Activity

As with the previous book, many exciting activities can be used to culminate this portion of the unit. One of the most interesting activities was conducted by one of my students as a conclusion to a study of the Revolutionary period. Her students developed a "Living Biography" to show what they had learned about the time period. Each of the students chose a Revolutionary War character, prepared words that he or she might have said, and presented those words as part of a presentation in a school gymnasium. The audience went from subject to subject and chose the ones that they wanted to hear. In addition, the classes presented demonstrations of poetry, literature, art, and music to identify the time period.

This type of activity may be developed with literature from any time period. There are numerous award-winning books about other time periods such as "The Salem Witch-Hunts," "Pioneer America," "The Civil War," and "World War II."

SUMMARY

Teach students that they can read literature for both pleasure and understanding. The foundations for a good literature program include an environment in which books are easy to locate and read. Teachers should love books, share them daily with students, and encourage interaction with a variety of books. This chapter includes suggestions for judging appropriateness of books, balancing literature selections, using various sources to find out about books, and identifying the interests of students.

To develop enjoyment of literature through storytelling, consider story selection, preparation, introduction, and the actual telling. Also consider using pictures and objects along with your storytelling. When reading aloud to children, consider their interests, ages, and experiences with literature. Pick books of high quality that are worthy of the time spent both by reader and listeners.

This chapter includes techniques to increase understanding of literature: webbing, modeling, and plot diagramming. List various instructional possibilities for the books you consider using. Also, explore the various literary genres. These include modern fantasy, contemporary realistic fiction, historical fiction, biography, poetry, and traditional literature. In an effort to assist students in the appreciation of books that are considered of high quality, the sections on literary elements and literary genres focused on books that have won Caldecott, Newbery, or Touchstone awards.

ADDITIONAL LITERATURE AND THE LANGUAGE ARTS ACTIVITIES

1. Ask a librarian about the literature children enjoy during story time and the literature they check out of the library. Are there any differences or similarities between these two groups? Speculate about reasons for either differences or similarities.
2. If possible, visit a library or classroom during story time. Note any effective techniques the storyteller uses to obtain students' interest, introduce the story, and interact with listeners during the story presentation.
3. Read a journal article about the use of literature in the classroom or in the library, such as those found in *The New Advocate, Children's Literature in Education,* and the *School Library Journal.* What is the main emphasis of the article? Share the article and your review of the article with your class.

4. Referring to the journals listed in activity 3, review the articles published during one year. What are the major topics covered during that time period? Are there any recurring issues or themes? What are the recommendations for using literature in the curriculum?

5. Choose a grade level. Develop a list of books that you believe to be appropriate for that grade level. Be sure to balance the selections to include the major genres of literature.

6. Refer to a journal, such as *Booklist, Hornbook,* or *School Library Journal,* that includes critical reviews of literature and recommends children's books. Locate three books that received starred reviews within the journal. Read the books and consider why the journal board of reviewers recommended the books. Do you agree with the reviews? Share the books, your reviews, and the journal reviews with your language arts class.

7. Interview a student about his or her interests. Then develop a list of books that you would recommend to that student.

8. Patricia Wilson (1985) studied the preferences of fifth- and sixth-grade students for literature that is both highly recommended and considered classic in children's literature. She found that the students' favorites included *Charlotte's Web, Little House in the Big Woods, The Hobbit, The Secret Garden, The Lion, the Witch and the Wardrobe, Heidi,* and *The Borrowers.* Either lead a discussion with a student about one of these books or read one of the books to a group of students. What is the reaction of the students to the book? Why do you believe Wilson's subjects chose these books as favorites? If one of these books is also your favorite children's book, why is it your favorite book?

9. Develop a file of books appropriate for stimulating students' enjoyment through art. Include ways to use the books to stimulate enjoyment.

10. Using Table 6–1, identify books for each genre of literature and identify the literary evidence that places the books within that genre. (Choose books that are not discussed in this chapter.)

11. Develop a modeling lesson to help students understand and appreciate one of the literary elements.

12. Using either of the plot diagrams in Figures 6–7 and 6–9, choose a book and place the key events from the book on the diagram.

BIBLIOGRAPHY

Allison, Dorothy; and Watson, J. Allen. "The Significance of Adult Storybook Reading Styles on the Development of Young Children's Emergent Reading." *Reading Research and Instruction* 34 (1994): 57–72.

Anderson, R. C.; Hiebert, E. H.; Scott, J. A.; and Wilkinson, I. A. *Becoming a Nation of Readers: The Report of the Commission on Reading.* Champaign, Ill.: Center for the Study of Reading, 1985.

Anderson, R. C.; Wilson, P. T.; and Fielding, C. G. "Growth in Reading and How Children Spend Their Time Outside of School." *Reading Research Quarterly* 23 (1988): 285–303.

Bennett, Kathleen. "Popular Reading—Chapter Books." *Booklist* (November 1, 1987): 488–90.

Bingham, Jane; and Scholt, Grayce. *Fifteen Centuries of Children's Literature.* Westport, Conn.: Greenwood, 1980.

Breckenridge, Kit. "Modern Classics." *School Library Journal* 34 (April 1988): 42–43.

Brown, June. "Critical Questions." *The Reading Teacher* 52 (February 1999): 520–21.

Carlson, Ann D. "Letters, Numbers, Shapes, & Colors." *School Library Journal* 41 (May 1995): 30–33.

Chatton, B. "Our Emerging Nation—The Late 1800s." *Book Links* 1 (1992): 48–53.

Children's Literature Association. *Touchstones: A List of Distinguished Children's Books.* Lafayette, Ind.: Purdue University, Children's Literature Association, 1985.

Cianciolo, P. J. *Picture Books for Children,* 3rd ed. Chicago: American Library Association, 1990.

Cohen, Caron Lee. "The Quest in Children's Literature." *School Library Journal* 31 (August 1985): 28–29.

Cooper, Ilene. "Popular Reading—After Henry Huggins." *Booklist* (November 1, 1986): 415–16.

Corcoran, Frances. "Storytelling Sources." *Booklist* (April 15, 1986): 1234–35.

Cullum, Carolyn N. *The Storytime Sourcebook.* New York: Neal-Schumanz, 1999.

Cunningham, Patricia M.; and Allington, Richard L. *Classrooms That Work: They Can All Read and Write,* 3rd ed. Boston: Allyn & Bacon, 2003.

Davis, Anita P.; and McDaniel, Thomas R. "You've Come a Long Way, Baby—Or Have You: Research Evaluating Gender Portrayal in Recent Caldecott-Winning Books." *The Reading Teacher* 52 (February 1999): 532–36.

Dowhower, Sarah. "Repeated Reading Revisited: Research into Practice." *Reading & Writing Quarterly: Overcoming Learning Difficulties* 10 (1994): 343–58.

Dressel, J. H. "The Effects of Listening to and Discussing Different Qualities of Children's Literature on the Narrative Writing of Fifth Graders." *Research in the Teaching of English* 24 (1990): 397–414.

Dronka, P. "Forums for Curriculum Critics Settle Some Disputes: Clash Persists on Students' Thinking about Controversy." *Update* (March 1987): 1, 6, 7.

Elleman, B. "Book Links Salutes 'A Few Good Books' of 1991." *Book Links* 1 (1992): 4–8.

Ellis, Rex M. *Beneath the Blazing Sun.* Little Rock: August House, 1997.

Five, Cora Lee; "From Workbook to Workshop: Increasing Children's Involvement in the Reading Process." *The New Advocate* 1 (Spring 1988): 103–13.

Fox, Paula. "On Language." *School Library Journal* 41 (March 1995): 122–26.

Frasher, Ramona. "A Feminist Look at Literature for Children: Ten Years Later." In *Sex Stereotypes and Reading: Research and Strategies,* edited by E. Marcia Sheridan. Newark, Del.: International Reading Association, 1982.

Galda, Lee; and Beach, Richard. "Response to Literature as a Cultural Activity." *Reading Research Quarterly* 36 (January–March 2001): 64–73.

Harms, Jeanne McLain; and Lettow, Lucille J. "Criteria for Selecting Picture Books with Historical Settings." *Social Education* 58 (March 1994): 152–54.

Herrell, A. L. "A Child and an Adult Interact with a Book: The Effects on Language and Literacy in Kindergarten." 1990. *Dissertation Abstracts International* 50: 10A (University Microfilms No. 90-04,995).

Holt, David; and Mooney, Bill, edited by. *Ready-to-Tell Tales.* Little Rock: August House, 1994.

Huck, Charlotte; Hepler, Susan; and Hickman, Janet. *Children's Literature.* New York: Holt, Rinehart & Winston, 1993.

Kiefer, Barbara. "Picture Books for Older Children." *Booklist* (September 15, 1986): 138–39.

Lacy, Lyn. *Art and Design in Children's Picture Books.* Chicago: American Library Association, 1986.

Lehr, S. "The Child's Developing Sense of Theme as a Response to Literature." *Reading Research Quarterly* 23 (1988): 337–57.

Lukens, Rebecca J. *A Critical Handbook of Children's Literature,* 6th ed. New York: Longman, 1999.

Mandell, P. L. "Cultural Diverse Videos—African-Americans." *School Library Journal* 38 (1992): 49–51, 54–56.

May, Jill P. "Creating a School Wide Literature Program: A Case Study." *Children's Literature Association Quarterly* 12 (Fall 1987): 135–37.

McCullough, David. *John Adams.* New York: Simon & Schuster, 2001.

McMillan, B. "Photographer or Photo-Illustrator: What's the Difference?" *School Library Journal* 37 (1991): 38–39.

Meade, J. "A War of Words." *Teacher* (November/December 1990): 37–45.

Miller, Bertha Mahony; and Field, Elinor Whitney, edited by. *Newbery Medal Books, 1922–1955.* Boston: The Horn Book, 1955.

National Council of Teachers of English. "Forum: Essentials of English." *Language Arts* 60 (February 1983): 244–48.

Neuman, Susan B.; and Celano, Donna. "Access to Print in Low-Income and Middle-Income Communities: An Ecological Study of Four Neighborhoods." *Reading Research Quarterly* 36 (January–March 2001): 8–26.

Nilsen, Alleen Pace; and Donelson, Kenneth L. *Literature for Today's Young Adults,* 6th ed. New York: Longman, 2001.

Norton, D. E. *The Impact of Literature-Based Reading.* Upper Saddle River, N.J.: Merrill/Prentice Hall, 1992.

———. *Through the Eyes of a Child: An Introduction to Children's Literature,* 6th ed. Upper Saddle River, N.J.: Merrill/Prentice Hall, 2003.

"Notable Children's Trade Books in the Field of Social Studies: 1994." *Social Education* 58 (April/May 1994): 241–54.

Pellowski, Anne. *The Family Story-Telling Handbook.* New York: Macmillan, 1987.

———. *Hidden Stories in Plants.* New York: Macmillan, 1990.

Phelan, Carolyn. "Poetry for Young Children." *Booklist* (January 1, 1988): 790–92.

Polese, Carolyn. "Resilient Readers: Children's Literature in the Lives of Abuse Survivors." *School Library Journal* 40 (March 1994): 156–57.

Quan, N. A. "Social Values in Popular Adolescent Literature, 1940–1980." 1990. *Dissertation Abstracts International* 50: 10A (University Microfilms No. 90-06,480).

Ross, Ramon Royal. *Storyteller,* 3rd ed. Little Rock: August House, 1996.

Rothman, R. "Experts Warn of Attempts to Censor Classic Texts." *Education Week* (February 1990): 5.

Schwarcz, J.; and Schwarcz, C. *The Picture Book Comes of Age.* Chicago: American Library Association, 1991.

Shulevitz, Uri. *Writing with Pictures: How to Write and Illustrate Children's Books.* New York: Watson-Guptill, 1985.

Smith, C. "The Role of Different Literary Genres." *The Reading Teacher* 44 (1991): 440–41.

Stokstad, Marilyn. *Art History* (Vol. 2). New York: Abrams, 1995.

Sutherland, Zena; and Arbuthnot, May Hill. *Children and Books.* New York: Longman, 1997.

———; and Hearne, Betsy. "In Search of the Perfect Picture Book Definition." In *Jump Over the Moon,* edited by Pamela Barron and Jennifer Burley. New York: Holt, Rinehart & Winston, 1984.

Swanton, Susan. "Minds Alive: What and Why Gifted Students Read for Pleasure." *School Library Journal* 30 (March 1984): 99–102.

Taxel, Joel. "Notes from the Editor." *The New Advocate* 1 (Spring 1988): 73–74.

Thistlethwaite, Linda. "Literature for All Ages in the Adult Education Program." *Reading Research and Instruction* 34 (1994): 136–48.

Walmsley, S. A.; and Walp, T. P. *Teaching Literature in Elementary School: A Report on the Elementary School Antecedents of Secondary School Literature Instruction.* Report Series 1.3. Albany, N.Y.: Center for the Teaching and Learning of Literature. University at Albany, State University of New York, 1989 (ERIC No. ED 315 754).

Wiessler, J. "Book Censorship Attempts Are Soaring, Group's Survey Says." *Houston Chronicle* (August 28, 1987): Sec. 1, p. 8.

Wilms, Denise. "Contemporary Issues—Intergenerational Relationships." *Booklist* (May 1, 1986): 1318–20.

Wilson, Patricia Jane. "Children's Classics: A Reading Preference Study of Fifth and Sixth Graders." Doctoral Dissertation, University of Houston, 1985. *Dissertation Abstracts International* 47: 454A.

CHILDREN'S LITERATURE REFERENCES

Adler, David. *Martin Luther King, Jr.: Free at Last.* Illustrated by Robert Casilla. New York: Holiday, 1986.

Alexander, Lloyd. *The Book of Three.* New York: Holt, Rinehart & Winston, 1964.

Armstrong, William H. *Sounder.* New York: Harper & Row, 1969.

Avi. *The True Confessions of Charlotte Doyle.* New York: Orchard, 1990.

Baker, Jeannie. *Where the Forest Meets the Sea.* New York: Greenwillow, 1988.

———. *Window.* New York: Greenwillow, 1991.

Baker, Olaf. *Where the Buffaloes Begin.* Illustrated by Stephen Gammell. New York: Warne, 1981.

Bang, Molly. *Picture This: Perception & Composition.* Boston: Little, Brown, 1991.

Bartone, Elisa. *Peppe, the Lamplighter.* New York: Lothrop, Lee & Shepard, 1993.

Bauer, Marion Dane. *On My Honor.* New York: Clarion, 1986.

Baylor, Byrd. *Hawk, I'm Your Brother.* Illustrated by Peter Parnall. New York: Charles Scribner's Sons, 1976.

Blumberg, Rhoda. *Commodore Perry in the Land of the Shogun.* New York: Lothrop, Lee & Shepard, 1985.

———. *The Remarkable Voyages of Captain Cook.* New York: Bradbury, 1991.

Bowen, Betsy. *Antler, Bear, Canoe: A Northwoods Alphabet Year.* Boston: Little, Brown, 1991.

Brooks, Polly. *Queen Eleanor: Independent Spirit of the Medieval World.* Philadelphia: J. B. Lippincott Co., 1983.

Brown, Marcia. *Stone Soup.* New York: Charles Scribner's Sons, 1947.

Bunting, Eve. *Smoky Night.* Illustrated by David Diaz. San Diego: Harcourt Brace Jovanovich, 1994.

Burton, Virginia Lee. *The Little House.* Boston: Houghton Mifflin, 1942.

Cameron, Eleanor. *That Julia Redfern.* Illustrated by Gail Owens. New York: E. P. Dutton, 1982.

Carle, Eric. *The Very Hungry Caterpillar.* New York: Thomas Y. Crowell Co., 1971.

Carroll, Lewis. *Alice's Adventures in Wonderland.* Illustrated by John Tenniel. Macmillan, 1866, New York: Alfred A. Knopf, 1984.

Cassedy, Sylvia; and Suetake, Kunihiro, translated by. *Red Dragon on My Shoulder.* Illustrated by Molly Bang. New York: HarperCollins, 1992.

Cazet, Denys. *A Fish in His Pocket.* New York: Watts, 1987.

Cendrars, Blaise. *Shadow.* Illustrated by Marcia Brown. New York: Charles Scribner's Sons, 1982.

Chase, Richard. *Grandfather Tales.* Boston: Houghton Mifflin, 1948.

Clapp, Patricia. *Constance: A Story of Early Plymouth.* New York: Lothrop, Lee & Shepard, 1968.

Cleary, Beverly. *Dear Mr. Henshaw.* Illustrated by Paul O. Zelinsky. New York: William Morrow & Co., 1983.

———. *Ramona Quimby, Age 8.* New York: William Morrow, 1981.

Climo, Shirley. *The Egyptian Cinderella.* Illustrated by Ruth Heller. New York: Thomas Y. Crowell Co., 1989.

Colum, Padraic. *The Golden Fleece.* New York: Macmillan, 1921, 1962.

Conly, Jane Leslie. *Crazy Lady!* New York: HarperCollins, 1993.

———. *Rasco and the Rats of NIMH.* New York: Harper & Row, 1986.

Couloumbis, Audrey. *Getting Near to Baby.* New York: Putnam's, 1999.

Creech, Sharon. *Walk Two Moons.* New York: HarperCollins, 1994.

Curtis, Christopher Paul. *Bud, Not Buddy.* New York: Delacorte, 1995.

———. *The Watsons Go to Birmingham—1963.* New York: Delacorte, 1995.

Cushman, Karen. *Catherine, Called Birdy.* New York: Clarion, 1994.

———. *Matilda Bone.* New York: Random House, 2000.

———. *The Midwife's Apprentice.* New York: Houghton Mifflin, 1995.

D'Aulaire, Ingri; and D'Aulaire, Edgar Parin. *Norse Gods and Giants.* New York: Doubleday, 1967.

Demi. *The Stonecutter.* New York: Crown, 1995.

de Paola, Tomie. *Mother Goose.* New York: Putnam, 1985.

DiCamillo, Kate. *Because of Winn-Dixie.* Cambridge: Candlewick, 2000.

Dodson, Peter. *An Alphabet of Dinosaurs.* Illustrated by Wayne D. Barlowe. New York: Scholastic, 1995.

Dunning, Stephen; Lueders, Edward; and Smith, Hugh, edited by. *Reflections on a Gift of Watermelon Pickle . . . and Other Modern Verse.* New York: Lothrop, Lee & Shepard, 1967.

Ehlert, Lois. *Red Leaf, Yellow Leaf.* San Diego: Harcourt Brace Jovanovich, 1991.

Facklam, Margery. *Spiders and Their Web Sites.* Illustrated by Alan Male. Boston: Little, Brown, 2001.

Farmer, Nancy. *The Ear, the Eye and the Arm.* New York: Orchard, 1994.

Fenner, Carol. *Yolonda's Genius.* New York: Simon & Schuster, 1995.

Fleischman, Paul. *Joyful Noise: Poems for Two Voices.* New York: Harper & Row, 1988.

Fleming, Denise. *In the Small, Small Pond.* New York: Henry Holt, 1993.

Forbes, Esther. *Johnny Tremain.* Illustrated by Lynd Ward. Boston: Houghton Mifflin Co., 1943.

Fox, Paula. *One-Eyed Cat.* New York: Bradbury, 1984.

Freedman, Russell. *Eleanor Roosevelt: A Life of Discovery.* New York: Clarion, 1993.

———. *Lincoln: A Photobiography.* New York: Clarion, 1987.

———. *The Wright Brothers: How They Invented the Airplane.* New York: Holiday, 1991.

Fritz, Jean. *Bully for You Teddy Roosevelt.* Illustrated by Mike Wimmer. New York: Putnam, 1991.

———. *Make Way for Sam Houston.* New York: Putnam, 1986.

———. *Traitor: The Case of Benedict Arnold.* New York: Putnam, 1981.

———. *Where Do You Think You're Going, Christopher Columbus?* Illustrated by Margot Tomes. New York: Putnam, 1980.

Gág, Wanda. *Millions of Cats.* New York: Coward-McCann, 1928.

Garfield, Leon. *The December Rose.* New York: Viking Press, 1986.

Gates, Doris. *Two Queens of Heaven: Aphrodite and Demeter.* Illustrated by Trina Schart Hyman. New York: Viking Press, 1974.

George, Jean Craighead. *Julie of the Wolves.* New York: Harper & Row, 1972.

———. *My Side of the Mountain.* New York: Dutton, 1959.

Gilliland, Judith Heide. *Steamboat! The Story of Captain Blanche Leathers.* Illustrated by Holly Meade. New York: Dorling Kindersley, 2000.

Gipson, Fred. *Old Yeller.* New York: Harper & Row, 1956.

Gish, Lillian. Told to Selma Lanes. *An Actor's Life for Me!* New York: Viking Press, 1987.

Goodman, Susan E. *Stones, Bones, and Petroglyphs: Digging into Southwest Archaeology.* Photographs by Michael J. Doolittle. New York: Simon & Schuster, 1998.

Grahame, Kenneth. *The Wind in the Willows.* Illustrated by E. H. Shepard. New York: Charles Scribner's Sons, 1908, 1940.

Greenberg, Jan; and Jordan, Sandra. *The Painter's Eye: Learning to Look at Contemporary Art.* New York: Delacorte, 1991.

Grifalconi, Ann. *Darkness and the Butterfly.* Boston: Little, Brown, 1987.

Grimm, Brothers. *Household Tales.* Illustrated by Mervyn Peake. New York: Schocken, 1979.

———. *Little Red Riding Hood.* Retold and Illustrated by Trina Schart Hyman. New York: Holiday, 1983.

———. *Red Riding Hood.* Retold and illustrated by James Marshall. New York: Dial Press, 1987.

Hamilton, Virginia. *In the Beginning: Creation Stories from Around the World.* San Diego: Harcourt Brace Jovanovich, 1988.

Harris, Joel Chandler. *Jump Again! More Adventures of Brer Rabbit.* Adapted by Van Dyke Parks. Illustrated by Barry Moser. San Diego: Harcourt Brace Jovanovich, 1987.

Henkes, Kevin. *Chrysanthemum.* New York: Greenwillow, 1991.

———. *Owen.* New York: Greenwillow, 1993.

Hesse, Karen. *Out of the Dust.* New York: Scholastic, 1997.

Hodges, Margaret. *Saint George and the Dragon.* Illustrated by Trina Schart Hyman. Boston: Little, Brown, 1984.

Hooks, William. *Moss Gown.* Illustrated by Donald Carrick. New York: Clarion, 1987.

Howard, Ellen. *Edith Herself.* New York: Atheneum, 1987.

Huck, Charlotte. *Princess Furball.* Illustrated by Anita Lobel. New York: Greenwillow, 1989.

Hunt, Jonathan. *Illuminations.* New York: Bradbury, 1989.

Hurmence, Belinda. *A Girl Called Boy.* Boston: Houghton Mifflin Co., 1982.

Isaacs, Anne. *Swamp Angel.* Illustrated by Paul O. Zelinsky. New York: Dutton, 1994.

Jacob, Joseph. *English Fairy Tales.* London: Fredrick Muller, T 1942.

Jacques, Brian. *Redwall.* New York: Philomel, 1986.

———. *The Top of the World: Climbing Mount Everest.* Boston: Houghton Mifflin, 1999.

Jenkins, Steve. *The Top of the World: Climbing Mount Everest.* Boston: Houghton Mifflin, 1999.

Keats, Ezra Jack. *Peter's Chair.* New York: Harper & Row, 1967.

———. *The Snowy Day.* New York: Viking Press, 1962.

———. *The Trip.* New York: Greenwillow, 1978.

Kerley, Barbara. *The Dinosaurs of Waterhouse Hawkins.* Illustrated by Brian Selznick. New York: Scholastic, 2001.

Lawson, Robert. *Rabbit Hill.* New York: Viking Press, 1944.

Lee, Jeanne. *Silent Lotus.* New York: Farrar, Straus & Giroux, 1991.

L'Engle, Madeleine. *A Wrinkle in Time.* New York: Farrar, Straus & Giroux, 1962.

Lester, Julius. *John Henry.* Illustrated by Jerry Pinkeny. New York: Dial, 1994.

Lewis, C. S. *The Lion, the Witch and the Wardrobe.* New York: Macmillan, 1950.

Lionni, Leo. *Swimmy.* New York: Pantheon, 1963.

Little, Jean. *Different Dragons.* New York: Viking Press, 1986.

Louie, Ai-Ling, retold by. *Yeh-Shen: A Cinderella Story from China.* Illustrated by Ed Young. New York: Philomel, 1982.

Lowry, Lois. *The Giver.* Boston: Houghton Mifflin Co., 1993.

———. *Number the Stars.* Boston: Houghton Mifflin, 1989.

———. *Shadow in Hawthorn Bay.* New York: Charles Scribner's Sons, 1986.

Lunn, Janet. *Shadow in Hawthorn Bay.* New York: Scrobner, 1986.

Macaulay, David. *Black and White.* Boston: Houghton Mifflin, 1990.

———. *Castle.* Boston: Houghton Mifflin, 1977.

———. *Cathedral: The Story of Its Construction.* Boston: Houghton Mifflin, 1973.

MacDonald, Suse. *Alphabatics.* New York: Bradbury, 1986.

MacLachlan, Patricia. *Sarah, Plain and Tall.* New York: Harper & Row, 1985.

Martin, Rafe. *Rough-Faced Girl.* Illustrated by David Shannon. New York: Putnam, 1992.

Mathis, Sharon Bell. *The Hundred Penny Box.* Illustrated by Leo and Diane Dillon. New York: Viking Press, 1975.

Mazer, Norma Fox. *After the Rain.* New York: William Morrow, 1987.

McCloskey, Robert. *Make Way for Ducklings.* New York: Viking Press, 1941.

McCord, David. *One at a Time: Collected Poems for the Young.* Boston: Little, Brown, 1977.

McCully, Emily Arnold. *Mirette on the High Wire.* New York: Putnam, 1992.

McKinley, Robin. *The Hero and the Crown.* New York: Greenwillow, 1984.

McKissack, Patricia. *The Dark-Thirty: Southern Tales of the Supernatural.* Illustrated by Brian Pinkney. New York: Alfred A. Knopf, 1992.

Meltzer, Milton. *The American Revolutionaries: A History in Their Own Words, 1750–1800.* New York: Thomas Y. Crowell Co., 1987.

———. *George Washington and the Birth of Our Nation.* New York: Watts, 1986.

———. *Thomas Jefferson: The Revolutionary Aristocrat.* New York: Watts, 1991.

Milne, A. A. *Winnie-the-Pooh.* Illustrated by Ernest Shepard. New York: E. P. Dutton, 1926, 1954.

Norton, Mary. *The Borrowers.* San Diego: Harcourt Brace Jovanovich, 1952.

O'Brien, Robert. *Mrs. Frisby and the Rats of NIMH.* New York: Atheneum, 1971.

O'Dell, Scott. *Island of the Blue Dolphins.* Boston: Houghton Mifflin Co., 1960.

———. *Sing Down the Moon.* Boston: Houghton Mifflin Co., 1970.

Park, Linda Sue. *A Single Shard.* New York: Clarion, 2001.

Paterson, Katherine. *Bridge to Terabithia.* New York: Thomas Y. Crowell Co., 1977.

———. *The Tale of the Mandarin Ducks.* Illustrated by Leo and Diane Dillon. New York: Dutton, 1990.

Paulsen, Gary. *Hatchet.* New York: Bradbury, 1987.

Pearce, Philippa. *Tom's Midnight Garden.* New York: J. B. Lippincott Co., 1958.

Peet, Bill. *Bill Peet: An Autobiography.* Boston: Houghton Mifflin, 1989.

Perrault, Charles. *Cinderella.* Illustrated by Marcia Brown. New York: Charles Scribner's Sons, 1954.

———. *Little Red Riding Hood.* Illustrated by Sarah Moon. Mankato, Minn.: Creative Education, 1983.

———. *Puss in Boots.* Illustrated by Marcia Brown. Charles Scribner's Sons, 1952.

———. *Puss in Boots.* Illustrated by Fred Marcellino. New York: Farrar, Straus & Giroux, 1990.

Potter, Beatrix. *The Tale of Peter Rabbit.* New York: Warne, 1902.

———. *The Tale of Squirrel Nutkin.* New York: Warne, 1903, 1986.

Provensen, Alice; and Provensen, Martin. *The Glorious Flight: Across the Channel With Louis Bleriot.* New York: Viking, 1983.

Pullman, Philip. *The Ruby in the Smoke.* New York: Alfred A. Knopf, 1987.

Pyle, Howard. *The Story of King Arthur and His Knights.* New York: Charles Scribner's Sons, 1903, 1978.

Ransome, Arthur. *The Fool of the World and the Flying Ship.* New York: Farrar, Straus & Giroux, 1968.

Reef, Catherine. *Walt Whitman.* New York: Clarion, 1995.

Ringgold, Faith. *Tar Beach.* New York: Crown, 1991.

Rohmann, Eric. *Time Flies.* New York: Crown, 1994.

Rosen, Michael, retold by. *We're Going on a Bear Hunt.* Illustrated by Helen Oxenbury. New York: Macmillan, 1989.

Rowling, J. K. *Harry Potter and the Sorcerer's Stone.* Illustrated by Mary Grandpre. New York: Scholastic, 1997.

Rylant, Cynthia. *Missing May.* New York: Orchard, 1992.

———. *The Relatives Came.* Illustrated by Stephen Gammell. New York: Bradbury, 1985.

Sachar, Louis. *Holes.* New York: Farrar, Straus & Giroux, 1998.

Say, Allen. *Grandfather's Journey.* Boston: Houghton Mifflin, 1993.

Schwartz, Amy. *Oma and Bobo.* New York: Bradbury, 1987.

Sendak, Maurice. *Where the Wild Things Are.* New York: Harper & Row, 1963.

Seredy, Kate. *The White Stag.* New York: Viking Press, 1937, Puffin, 1979.

Seuss, Dr. *The 500 Hats of Bartholomew Cubbins.* New York: Vanguard, 1938.

Shulevitz, Uri. *Snow.* New York: Farrar, Straus & Giroux, 1998.

Speare, Elizabeth George. *The Sign of the Beaver.* Boston: Houghton Mifflin, 1983.

———. *The Witch of BlackBird Pond.* Boston: Houghton Mifflin, 1958.

Sperry, Armstrong. *Call It Courage.* New York: Macmillan, 1940.

Staples, Susan Fisher. *Shabanu: Daughter of the Wind.* New York: Alfred A. Knopf, 1989.

Steig, William. *Abel's Island.* New York: Farrar, Straus & Giroux, 1976.

Steptoe, John. *Mufaro's Beautiful Daughters: An African Tale.* New York: Lothrop, Lee & Shepard, 1987.

Sutherland, Zena; and Livingston, Myra. *The Scott Foresman Anthology of Children's Literature.* Glenview, Ill.: Scott Foresman & Co., 1984.

Taback, Simms. *Joseph Had a Little Overcoat.* New York: Viking, 1999.

Tafuri, Nancy. *Have You Seen My Duckling?* New York: Greenwillow, 1984.

Taylor, Mildred. *Roll of Thunder, Hear My Cry.* New York: Dial Press, 1976.

Tejima, Keizaburo. *Fox's Dream.* New York: Philomel, 1987.

Van Allsburg, Chris. *The Polar Express.* Boston: Houghton Mifflin Co., 1985.

———. *The Z Was Zapped.* Boston: Houghton Mifflin, 1987.

Verdy, Violette. *Of Swans, Sugarplums, and Satin Slippers: Ballet Stories for Children.* Illustrated by Marcia Brown. New York: Scholastic, 1991.

Voigt, Cynthia. *Dicey's Song.* New York: Atheneum, 1982.

Wegman, William. *Little Red Riding Hood.* New York: Hyperion, 1993.

White, E. B. *Charlotte's Web.* Illustrated by Garth Williams. New York: Harper & Row, 1952.

Wiesner, David. *Free Fall.* New York: Lothrop, Lee & Shepard, 1988.

———. *Tuesday.* Boston: Clarion, 1991.

Wilder, Laura Ingalls. *Little House in the Big Woods.* Illustrated by Garth Williams. New York: Harper & Row, 1932, 1953.

Willard, Nancy. *Pish, Posh, Said Hieronymus Bosch.* Illustrated by Leo and Diane Dillon. Orlando: Harcourt Brace Jovanovich, 1991.

———. *A Visit to William Blake's Inn: Poems for Innocent and Experienced Travelers.* Illustrated by Alice and Martin Provensen. San Diego: Harcourt Brace Jovanovich, 1981.

Williams, Margery. *The Velveteen Rabbit: Or How Toys Become Real.* New York: Doubleday, 1922, 1958.

Williams, Sherely Anne. *Working Cotton.* Illustrated by Carole Byard. San Diego: Harcourt Brace Jovanovich, 1992.

Wood, Audrey. *King Bidgood's in the Bathtub.* Illustrated by Don Wood. San Diego: Harcourt Brace Jovanovich, 1985.

Yates, Elizabeth. *Amos Fortune, Free Man.* New York: Dutton, 1950.

Yep, Laurence. *Dragon's Gate.* New York: HarperCollins, 1993.

Yolen, Jane. *The Girl in the Golden Bower.* Illustrated by Jane Dyer. Boston: Little, Brown, 1994.

————. *Owl Moon.* Illustrated by John Schoenherr. New York: Philomel, 1987.

Yorinks, Arthur. *Hey, Al.* Illustrated by Richard Egielski. New York: Farrar, Straus & Giroux, 1986.

Young, Ed. *Lon Po Po: A Red-Riding Hood Story from China.* New York: Philomel, 1989.

Zelinsky, Paul O. *Rapunzel.* New York: Dutton, 1997.

Zhensun, Zheng; and Low, Alice. *A Young Painter: The Life and Paintings of Wang Yani—China's Extraordinary Young Artist.* Photographs by Zheng Zhensun. New York: Scholastic, 1991.

Composition:
The Writing Process

After completing this chapter on composition, you will be able to:

1. Discuss several viewpoints on the teaching of writing.
2. Describe the theoretical bases for the writing process.
3. Identify classroom procedures related to the processing approach to writing.
4. Describe and develop prewriting activities.
5. Describe and develop activities that focus on writing the first draft.
6. Describe and develop activities that focus on revision.
7. Describe and develop methods for evaluating writing.

*W*ritten composition is receiving increasing attention in research studies and in non-technical publications as well. For example, Hillocks's (1986) text *Research on Written Composition: New Directions for Teaching* reviews research studies, selects the most effective approaches to teaching writing, and adds strategies for teaching within the writing process. Professional organizations such as the National Council of Teachers of English are publishing texts that examine the role of teachers in the writing process, the various stages in the process, and activities to help improve writing.

This chapter and Chapter 8 explore the writing process and develop activities that enhance the writing of children. These two chapters consider the development of narrative, expository, descriptive, and persuasive writing. Chapter 7 focuses on the writing process and outlines each of the steps in detail. In addition, it discusses assessment of composition, research on effective modes of instruction, teacher–pupil and peer-editing-group conferencing, and sharing of students' work. Chapter 8 deals with specific strategies that are useful for children in the upper grades. Expressive, imaginative, and expository writing are featured.

According to Dyson and Freedman (2003), writing is a complex process, one involving the orchestration of many kinds of skills. "For example, when writing an essay in school, the writer must solve the subproblems of how to form letters, how to punctuate and spell, how to construct felicitous written sentences, how to get ideas, how to order those ideas, and so on. Some of these processes become quite automatic and unconscious as the writer matures, while others take time, attention, and skill, even for experienced adults" (p. 975). To develop as writers, students need to discover that writing is a way to communicate with others, to adapt their writing to various audiences, to master techniques to make their writing appealing and persuasive, to develop their talents for creative and imaginative expression, and to recognize that the various mechanics of writing are part of the goal of becoming effective writers.

Viewpoints

There is no one favored approach to teaching writing. Some educators recommend approaches that emphasize the process of writing, whereas others recommend those that emphasize the goals of writing. Cunningham and Allington (1999) contrast various types of instruction when they state, "Unfortunately, writing instruction in schools often has focused primarily on the editing skills of penmanship, spelling, mechanics, and grammar. Schools used language books, handwriting books, and spelling books as the base for the writing curriculum. In these schools, children rarely had the opportunity to think, compose, or write. Instead, they spent most of their time concentrating on the skills. Recently, many schools have moved away from commercial programs and have set out to create their own writing curriculum in which the emphasis is on writing. . . . In most schools, children write more now than they did a few years ago, but there are still concerns about whether writing is actually being taught—especially thoughtful writing" (p. 86). These authors ask: Are children being taught the wide range of writing that is necessary in and out of school? Are children being taught to search out, gather, and organize information? Are they being taught to revise? Are they also learning how to spell?

Kulberg (1993) emphasizes that there is a trend from descriptive, product-oriented writing to an explanatory, process-oriented approach. Applebee (1984) argues for an approach that considers both the process and the resulting products of writing: "We must develop models of writing that more explicitly take account of topic knowledge and of interaction between the writing process and the goals of the writing event. The separation of process and product, though perhaps a needed step in the development of our research, seems now to be a major stumbling block to future progress" (p. 591).

Following a review of the findings gained from the National Writing Project, Myers and Gray (1983) state that teachers use writing activities that include processing (problem-solving that includes specific stages, such as prewriting, writing, and postwriting), modeling (imitating written samples), and distancing (focusing on the relationships between writer and subject and between writer and audience). Effective writing practices frequently include elements from processing, modeling, and distancing. According to Myers and Gray,

> . . . writing to an audience has both a processing function (the words often flow more easily in social interaction) and a distancing function. Imitation of texts has a modeling function (the student is modeling the pattern in the text) and a distancing function (the student is adopting a particular point of view). The best classroom techniques probably include all three approaches. Writing groups and a classroom publication program are two ways to combine approaches. Both techniques encourage discussion of the ideas (processing), provide an actual audience that one can study (distancing), and generate a variety of student models that other students can imitate (modeling). (p. 43)

It is interesting to note that the most effective mode of instruction identified by Hillocks (1986) accounts for topic knowledge and interaction between the writing process and the goals of the writing event. This effective mode may also include components from processing, modeling, and distancing.

Hillocks's comprehensive review (1986) of research on composition is one of the most frequently cited studies related to effective approaches and implications for the types of activities that should be included in the writing process. A brief review of Hillocks's findings illustrates the importance of many of the activities and principles discussed in this chapter. First, Hillocks found that the least effective mode of instruction was characterized by teacher lectures and teacher-dominated discussions. The next most effective mode was characterized by considerable free writing about personal interests, by writing for audiences of peers, and by teachers' responses to whatever students write. The most effective mode was characterized by instruction emphasizing (a) processes such as prewriting, composing, and revising; (b) prewriting activities that help develop the skills to be applied during the ensuing writing; (c) specific objectives for learning; (d) activities that help students learn the procedures for using those forms during the writing process; and (e) interaction with peers and feedback during the total writing process rather than primarily at the end of a composing activity.

In summary, according to Hillocks (1986), the most effective instruction is characterized by specific objectives (for example, to increase the use of figurative language in writing), materials and problems selected to engage the students in the processes important for that specified aspect of writing, and activities such as small-group problem-centered discussions. In effective instruction, teachers frequently give brief introductory lessons about the principles to be studied and applied during small-group activities and then during independent work. It is worthwhile to note Hillocks's assumptions about the most effective composition approaches:

1. Teachers should actively seek to develop identifiable writing skills in students.
2. Students develop skills by using them orally before using them in writing.
3. One major function of prewriting activities is to develop writing skills.
4. The use of skills such as generating criteria to define a concept are complex, and therefore may require collaboration with and feedback from others.

Many of Hillocks's findings were also found to be the most effective writing strategies in research conducted by Sadoski, Wilson, and Norton (1997). These strategies are included in both Chapters 7 and 8. In addition, Norton and Sadoski (1992–1996) have conducted writing institutes for five years. The most effective strategies from these writing institutes are also emphasized in these writing chapters.

Teachers as Writers

Scholars whose work emphasizes the writing process frequently discuss the importance of developing teachers as writers. For example, Atwell (1991) believes that teachers need to write so that they understand how and why students write and can create conditions in which students become successful writers. It is believed that teachers who are excited and positive about their own writing model that excitement for their students. This positive modeling is as important as demonstrating techniques for good writing. Such enthusiasm models the teacher's own beliefs and inspires and guides students to consider writing vital in their lives. In contrast, teachers who are fearful and reluctant writers may model aversion and apprehension about writing.

Through a workshop approach with teachers, Frager (1994) provides valuable information about both the types of writers that teachers perceive themselves to be and the experiences that seem to be instrumental in formulating identities as writers. By analyzing responses of teachers, Frager characterized the teacher writers as mainly reluctant writers, practical writers, or integral writers. Reluctant writers expressed distaste for writing by describing writing as painful and not pleasurable. This group identified several reasons for negative feelings about writing such as parents' misinterpretation of messages, memories of hurtful criticism, and lack of experience in selecting their own topics or ways of writing. Practical writers characterized themselves as writers by reason of necessity such as writing to fulfill personal, professional, social, and family obligations. The third group, the integral writers, identified writing as vital to their identities and lives. The writing experiences of the integral writers were both more varied and more positive than the experiences of the previous two groups. They identified various compositions such as diaries, essays, letters, and notebooks as adding to their own learning process. Writing also provided this group of teachers with a sense of pleasure or wonder.

Frager (1994) found the following four types of prior experiences influence teachers' positive or negative identities as writers: (1) criticism teachers receive about their writing; (2) opportunities or lack thereof to make choices about their writing; (3) types of writing done in response to the workplace; and (4) writing completed for a public audience including grant writing, publishing an article, or writing a newspaper editorial.

Frager (1994) recommends that teacher-education programs provide instruction in the various types of writing that teachers will need to perform. In addition, he believes that they need writing workshop experiences that allow them to write on topics of their choice, write for public audiences, and receive positive feedback about their writing. Frager concludes: "Ultimately, improvements in the writing curriculum may not only rest on teachers' conceptions about writing but also on teachers' ability to demonstrate those conceptions, a function of their identities as writers" (p. 278). Developing the teacher as writer is also a major aspect of our summer writing institute (Norton and Sadoski, 1992–1996). Hopefully, the suggestions developed in these two writing chapters will also be used by teachers to increase their own experiences as teachers and writers.

Theories

Current practice in written composition is shifting away from total emphasis on the products of writing to concern for the processes of writers during the act of writing. The information-processing model for written composition is based on the work of cognitive psychologists such as Bruner (1956), Gagné (1970), and Ammon (1977). Researchers in this area ask what the act of writing involves, how skilled and unskilled writers approach the different tasks faced in a writing project, and how educators can assist writers as they perform various writing tasks.

Cognitive psychologists view the brain as a system for processing and storing information that is very much like a computer. In this view, a computer program is a map or an internal hierarchy (Simon, 1981). Cognitive research focuses on the writer's mind, and researchers identify, analyze, and describe steps that writers go through during various phases of the writing process. Researchers also try to identify and describe the qualities of mental maps that writers use to organize information into meaningful units. Lapp and Flood (1993) describe writing as a "cognitively demanding, complex, multifaceted task. Writers must deal with issues such as assessing topical knowledge, organizing that knowledge, taking audience and purpose into account along with associated rhetorical requirements, paying attention to linguistic features of written text, and managing the motor skills required to put words on paper" (p. 254).

Researchers have identified and analyzed the processes involved in writing by observing writers and asking them to think aloud as they approach various writing tasks. The writing process model defined by Flower and Hayes is one of the most frequently cited. Flower and Hayes (1978) define writing as a problem-solving cognitive process that includes making plans, operating, searching memory, using procedures that get things done, and testing or evaluating the results of the plans and operations. Figure 7–1 shows the structure of the Hayes and Flower (1980) model. Notice the interactions of the processes as writers approach the problem and then engage in planning that emphasizes generating ideas, organizing, and setting goals. At the same time, writers draw from their memories to obtain knowledge of the topic, audience, and writing plans. As the process continues, writers compose or translate with interactions still taking place. Finally, they review, evaluate, and revise their writing. Again interactions take place because the reviewing stage requires information considered during other stages in the writing process.

Many researchers who observe the writing process have developed definitions and models that differ only slightly from the one envisioned by Hayes and Flower. For example, following the observation of primary-age students, Graves (1981) defined the writing process as "a series of operations leading to the solution of a problem. The process begins when the writer consciously or unconsciously starts a topic and is finished when the written piece is published" (p. 4).

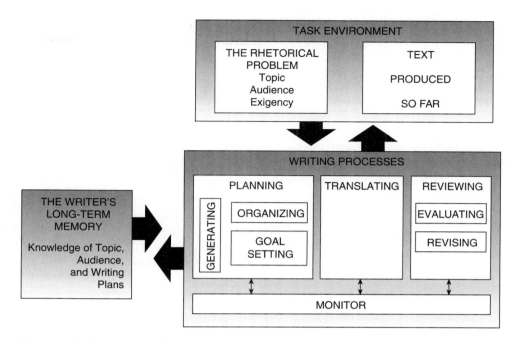

FIGURE 7–1   Stages in the Writing Process

Source: From "Writing and Problem Solving" by J. Hayes and L. Flower, 1980, *Visible Language*, 14, pp. 388–390. Reprinted by permission.

Britton et al. (1979) identify the stages in the writing process as (1) conception, which is a long or a brief time during which a specific incident provokes the decision to write; (2) incubation, which is the preparatory period; and (3) production, which includes the actual writing. In addition, they identify memory, influences of written and printed sources, and revision as other important aspects of the writing process.

Lapp and Flood (1993), in a review of the writing process, emphasize that the stages of writing are not neat sequences of events because writers may be in more than one stage at a time. In addition, the starting and ending points of writing are not fixed. Lapp and Flood caution, "Writers who are engaged in writing will determine their own paths and eventually will develop an approach to writing that is uniquely their own" (p. 255).

Considerable advances in understanding of writing have occurred in the past thirty years. In an effort to identify conclusions reached from research, Jensen (1993) summarized questionnaire responses of sixteen educators who conduct research in writing. According to these experts, we now know that "(1) writing during the early years is a natural 'gateway to literacy'; (2) all children can be writers; (3) understanding writing and writers means understanding complex and interrelated influences—cognitive, social, cultural, psychological, linguistic, and technological; and (4) we write so that both we and others can know what we think, who we are" (p. 291).

Recent research into children's writing is beginning to consider children's perceptions and attitudes about writing. In a study in Great Britain, Wray (1993) considered developmental changes in children's perceptions and attitudes about writing in a sample of 475 children ranging in age from seven to eleven. Wray found that children's perceptions about writing change with age and literacy abilities. For example, young children mention aspects of writing related to the mechanics of spelling, neatness, and punctuation. Older students, however, began to focus on ideas and other areas related to composition such as structure, characters, and style. Wray believes that these changes highlight a possible developmental trend in children's views about writing. In addition, children may focus on aspects of writing that at the time seem difficult to them. Consequently, children who are having difficulty with the technical aspects of writing focus their attention on those aspects. Later, when the technical aspects are mastered and less of a problem, they focus on the composition aspects of writing.

Instruction

Instruction for processing emphasizes the steps in the writing process. Many of the effective procedures used during this sequence of events were developed as a result of large writing projects, such as the Bay Area Writing Project and the National Writing Project. For example, Proett and Gill's (1986) sequence of events and recommended activities resulted from information compiled during the Bay Area Writing Project and the University of California Project.

Proett and Gill (1986) sequence the steps in the writing process according to activities that teachers and students should do before students write, while students write, and after students write. The before-writing activities encourage students to discover and explore, choose a focus for writing, gather and record ideas, classify information, structure information, and apply general truths to specific cases. The during-writing activities encourage students to record ideas into a tentative, first-draft shape; make choices depending on the audience, purpose, and desired form of writing; and consider such concerns as choice of words and sentence structure. The after-writing activities encourage students to scrutinize their first drafts, get peer responses from editing groups, rethink, revise, polish, and proofread. Finally, students share their writings through various activities. Figure 7–2 shows this process as envisioned by Proett and Gill and presents activities appropriate for each phase.

In addition to the steps in the writing process, Proett and Gill (1986) identify the following principles to guide the selection of activities under the process approach:

1. Neither guided composition on an occasional basis nor frequent unguided writing produces marked growth in writing skill. Experience strongly argues for frequent, clearly purposeful, guided writing experiences.
2. Students need to produce more writing than a teacher of classes of twenty-five to thirty can possibly evaluate carefully. Some compromise with the practice of thoroughly marking every paper as necessary.
3. Students can profitably practice the steps in the writing process (brainstorming, focused timed writing, sentence combining, small-group editing, and so forth) one at a time, but they also need to experience the entire process on a single writing project in order to develop a sense of working from start to finish on a paper on their own. When the steps in the process are undertaken separately, you must connect them to an understanding of the whole process so that students can see how each step is independent but also integral in the production of a final written piece.
4. Although writing is a legitimate homework activity, all elements of the writing process should be undertaken at some time during class so that teachers can coach and monitor progress. Real teaching must continue after the assignment is given, through all stages of the process.
5. Writing is a tremendously complex activity. It involves the simultaneous application of a series of intellectual and physical activities. In the classroom, teachers must break these activities into manageable segments to give learners a chance to handle them successfully in some consecutive fashion (for example, clustering of ideas, then

	Content and Idea Building		
BEFORE STUDENTS WRITE	Observing	Brainstorming	Dramatizing
	Remembering	Clustering	Reading
	Researching	Listing	Mapping
	Imagining	Detailing	Outlining
	Experiencing	Logging	Watching films and other media

Content and Idea Building

BEFORE STUDENTS WRITE

Observing	Brainstorming	Dramatizing
Remembering	Clustering	Reading
Researching	Listing	Mapping
Imagining	Detailing	Outlining
Experiencing	Logging	Watching films and other media

Development and Ordering

Developing details, reasons, examples, or incidents

Ordering by chronology, space, importance, logic

Classifying

Applying a general truth to a specific case (deductive)

Generalizing from supporting details (inductive)

Structuring by cause and effect

WHILE STUDENTS WRITE

Rhetorical Stance

Voice:	Who am I? How do I feel? What do I know? How sure am I?
Audience:	Who's listening? What are they ready for? What help do they need? How are they feeling?
Purpose:	What do I want to happen? What is likely to result? What effect do I seek? What am I willing to accept?
Form:	What form fits this message?

Linguistic Choices

Specific, concrete word choice

Figurative language

Sentence structure: length, opener, verb structure

Sentence type: simple, expanded, complex, compound, cumulative

Syntax: phrase and clause structures, word order; connections and transitions; modification and subordination

AFTER STUDENTS WRITE

Revision

Getting responses: editing groups, read-arounds

Raising questions, expanding, clarifying

Testing against criteria; using a rubric

Proofreading and polishing

Highlighting

Sharing	Posting	Mailing
Publishing	Filing	Reading

FIGURE 7–2   The Writing Process

Source: From Jackie Proett and Kent Gill, *The Writing Process in Action: A Handbook for Teachers.* Copyright © 1986 by the National Council of Teachers of English. Reprinted with permission.

seeking coherence through some logic of organization, then identifying controlling elements of stance, then drafting paragraphs for peer review, and finally revising in light of valid criticism).

6. Teachers and curriculum experts have long sought the ideal linear sequence for the writing program, asking what logically must precede what in a course or a series of grade levels. However, there has been no clearly accepted linear sequence for writing-skill development, either in textbooks or in curriculum guides. Because writing is a holistic act, requiring application of the whole range of skills to every writing project, a recursive model seems more appropriate. It gives students experience with most of what a writer does early on, but then circles back periodically to give maturing learners another, perhaps more sophisticated, experience with the skill employed earlier.

Activities

In this section we consider some of the activities that take place during the writing process (presented in outline form in Figure 7–2) and try to develop an understanding of the writing process. We include both unstructured and structured activities as students and teachers progress through the stages of prewriting, composing, and postcomposing. Before we begin developing specific aspects of the writing process for instruction, we should consider Suhor's (1984) warning: "The sequence in the Writing Process Model, as flexible as it is, cannot be followed slavishly. The sequence is not a stairway progression. . . . It should be thought of as 'looped,' not tightly linear, since certain aspects—discussion, conferencing, note-taking, revising, proofreading—may take place at several points, not just in the slots assigned on the visual model" (p. 101). In addition, many of the following sections include advice from professional writers. For instance, insights into their own writing processes are provided by authors of children's books.

Before you try to teach writing to students, develop your own understanding of the writing process. Hayes and Flower's model in Figure 7–1 developed by asking experienced writers to describe what they did as they approached and completed a writing task. Proett and Gill developed their model (Figure 7–2) through various writing workshops and research with students. Daniels and Zemelman (1985), who developed workshops for training teachers in the writing process, state that asking adults to create their own models of the writing process is "one of the main mechanisms by which participants formalize the discoveries they have made from their own writing experiences" (p. 78).

For Your Development

Before you proceed with this chapter, try one or two approaches for developing your own model of the writing process. Remember that your model does not need to be identical to one presented in this text. Your model may vary somewhat, depending on your purpose for writing, your topic, your background knowledge, and your audience.

1. Assuming you have a writing assignment in one of your classes, keep a log describing your activities and actions as you approach the writing assignment, write various drafts, and finish the paper in the form to be handed in to the professor.

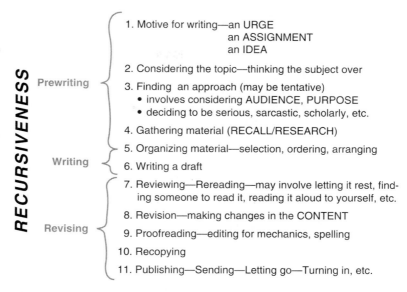

1. Motive for writing—an URGE
   an ASSIGNMENT
   an IDEA

2. Considering the topic—thinking the subject over

3. Finding an approach (may be tentative)
   • involves considering AUDIENCE, PURPOSE
   • deciding to be serious, sarcastic, scholarly, etc.

4. Gathering material (RECALL/RESEARCH)

5. Organizing material—selection, ordering, arranging

6. Writing a draft

7. Reviewing—Rereading—may involve letting it rest, finding someone to read it, reading it aloud to yourself, etc.

8. Revision—making changes in the CONTENT

9. Proofreading—editing for mechanics, spelling

10. Recopying

11. Publishing—Sending—Letting go—Turning in, etc.

Prewriting

Writing

Revising

RECURSIVENESS

FIGURE 7–3   Writing Process Model
Source: From Harvey Daniels and Steven Zemelman, *A Writing Project: Training Teachers of Composition from Kindergarten to College.* Copyright © 1985 by Heinemann Educational Books. Reprinted with permission.

2. Within your language arts class, complete a writing task that is to be eventually shared with a group of your peers through your college or university newspaper. Choose an issue of concern on your campus. You may share your writing with your language arts class to gain recommendations before you submit your article to the newspaper.

3. After you have completed either one of the preceding tasks, form groups within your language arts class. List the steps you went through as you approached and completed your writing task. You may find it helpful to first list all of your actions, then categorize them into types of activities, and finally put them into a chronological order. Like Hayes and Flower, you may find that you performed various interactions and repetitive actions during different stages in your writing process.

4. Share and discuss your model of the writing process in your language arts class. Are there any commonalities among the models? Look especially at what you did before writing, while writing the first draft, and while revising and reviewing before you were satisfied with your paper.

5. Finally, compare your model of the writing process with the one developed by a group of teachers during Daniels and Zemelman's (1985) writing workshop (see Figure 7–3). What are the similarities and differences?

6. After you have compared your model with the one by Daniels and Zemelman, compare the Hayes and Flower (1980) model and the Proett and Gill model (1986). What are the commonalities across models? Why do you believe there are such similarities? Do all of the models have categories that take into account prewriting, writing, and postwriting activities? Are these stages important when you teach writing composition to a group of students? Why are they important? How could this knowledge influence your teaching?

Before Writing

This first stage in the writing process includes activities that motivate students to write, generate ideas for writing, and focus the attention of students on the subject or objective of the writing. This phase allows students to become engrossed in a topic, extend their knowledge, heighten their awareness, and develop appropriate thinking skills. Proett and Gill (1986) include in this prewriting phase activities such as semantic mapping and webbing, brainstorming, dramatizing, experiencing, observing, reading, and watching films. These activities help students build ideas and create content. They frequently stimulate students to pull knowledge from long-term memory and apply it to the writing experience. They include developing details and reasons, ordering by chronology or space, classifying, applying, generalizing, and structuring cause–effect relationships.

Prewriting activities vary according to the age of the students and the objectives for the writing. Activities may include going on a class excursion and then talking about the experience, planning and then drawing a picture, or reading and then discussing a model story or poem written around a specific structure that students identify, try to duplicate, and evaluate in their own writing. Prewriting activities also may be extensions of ongoing school work, such as a science or social studies unit. They may result from common experiences, such as birthdays or family vacations. They may be new experiences created by the teacher. It is at this point in the writing process that you should question and interview students to clarify their ideas, assist them in thinking about procedures for gathering information, and help them make plans for future writing. Whatever activities you include, planning is extremely important. Carey (1989) found a positive relationship between the amount of initial planning and the quality of the finished writing. Blohm and Benton (1991) showed that generating questions prior to writing enhances the quality of informative writing. Haas (1990) found that note taking and predraft planning are critical when writing technical reports. Extensive oral exchanges of ideas during such activities as brainstorming and semantic mapping help students clarify and extend their ideas.

Interesting guidelines to help writers during their prewriting stage may also be gained from authors of children's literature as they describe their own writing processes. For example, James Cross Giblin (1990), an author of nonfiction books, emphasizes the importance of getting ideas for writing. He maintains that authors should search for ideas within their own interests, enthusiasms, knowledge, and personal experiences. Patricia Beatty (1990), an author of historical fiction, gets ideas from numerous sources such as magazine articles, figures in biographies, and the history of a locale that interests her.

Both Giblin and Beatty emphasize the importance of gathering information and conducting research prior to writing. Giblin (1990) uses 4- × 6-inch cards on which he places important research information and the source of the information. Giblin maintains that checking the accuracy of facts is so important that each fact is checked against at least two other sources before he includes it in a nonfictional book. Beatty (1990) is extremely fascinated by research in libraries and actual locations for her books. She states, "It's the minutiae of the period that chiefly bring the past alive in historical fiction. I find the little things I research matter most of all; in fact, the research I do often gives me more pleasure than the actual process of writing" (p. 408).

Jean E. Karl (1994), both an editor and author of children's books, provides guidelines for authors of nonfiction literature that can also be shared with school-age children. Karl presents steps in the writing process that begin with choosing a subject. The potential author makes a list of topics that he or she would like to write about (these topics may include ones that the writer knows a great deal about or ones that the writer would like to research and write about) and then narrows the topic to a subject that can be covered. The author then checks the library to discover what else has been written on the topic and decides if he or she cares enough about the topic to conduct further research. Karl stresses that prior to writing an author needs to "Read as much as you can, talk with experts if you can, absorb as much information as is possible. Make notes to yourself so you will not forget salient points—either on cards that may be filed by topic or in a notebook. Jot down names of especially helpful books so that you can come back to them as needed. Keep track of where you found pictures and charts that might be of help to an illustrator" (p. 80).

Drawing.   Artwork created by students is one of the earliest motivators used to stimulate writing and to help young students plan written compositions. Prewriting activities include planning the artwork, creating it, and talking about it. As students draw something that interests them, they have opportunities to think about the details in the picture, the person or the object in the picture, and the things they want to disclose. Stories develop naturally from such experiences. In addition, students enjoy sharing both their artwork and their dictated or individually written stories.

Connecting art and writing seems to be a natural way to increase children's self expressions. Ernst (1994) describes an artists' workshop approach with elementary children in which she combines art and writing because both are ways of thinking, knowing, and making meaning. She maintains that writing helps students express their thinking about art, evaluate and revise their work, describe their process, and reflect on their learning and thinking.

Ernst (1994) describes parallel activities that are similar to those found in a writers' workshop. For example, as a preart and prewriting activity, she begins an art lesson in which students and teachers look at the work of artists to understand what artists do, read a picture book to understand how words and pictures work together and to inspire and encourage imagination, and discuss students' art. Ernst states that literature is especially important in this art and writing workshop approach because literature gives students ideas for pictures and projects and helps them choose topics. Next, she provides a mini-lesson on techniques of painting or pasting, drawing, or writing. During this time students identify the media they will use or the topic for their pictures. Writing is added to the artists' workshop as students record their thinking about their art in their artists' notebooks. Early writing may answer questions such as "What did you discover?" or "What is your picture about?" Later writing includes longer responses to their art as they express their feelings and reflect on their art. These writings may take many forms including poetry.

Literature is an important element in this artists' and writers' workshop approach. Illustrations in books may help children identify types of art media and techniques that may be especially rewarding for them. For example, if the mini-lesson presents the development of collage, the teacher might share and discuss books illustrated with collage such as Holly Meade's Collages for Judith Heide Gilliland's *Steamboat! The Story of Captain Blanche Leathers* (2000) and Eric Carle's *The Very Clumsy Click Beetle* (1999). Children may create their own collage illustrations to illustrate a story or a poem. They may also write about their feelings and responses as they work with collage.

Children's author Eve Bunting (1990) provides an important relationship between text and illustrations that can be shared with children. She states that when writing a picture storybook, authors should "think pictures. Perceive your story as a moving slide show, vivid, arresting, and dramatic" (p. 441). Children might consider such relationships between text and illustrations in Bunting's *Smoky Night* (1994), *Ghost's Hour, Spook's Hour* (1987), and *I Am the Mummy Heb-Nefert* (1997).

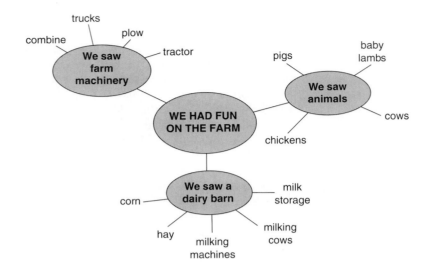

Figure 7–4 A Semantic Map about a Farm Trip

Semantic Mapping.   Semantic maps are good for idea building and organizing ideas during the prewriting phase of composition. Semantic mapping helps students identify main ideas and supporting details of a topic of interest, organize prior knowledge, and write paragraphs.

You may use semantic mapping or webbing prior to writing as a total-class, small-group, or individual activity. For a total-class or small-group activity, write the desired topic in the center of the chalkboard or large sheet of paper. Next, lead a discussion in which you elicit main ideas or categories from the students and draw in circles that extend from the center. Add supporting ideas and details as the discussion continues. Then, let the students review the information and write or dictate their stories.

The first processing experience with mapping and writing is usually a group activity. Demonstrate how easily ideas developed during the brainstorming may be charted and expanded, and how easily writing may be organized. For example, a writing activity for first and second graders was generated from a group trip to a farm. The teacher asked for a logical title, such as "We Had Fun on the Farm," and then began the map. She asked questions to help students remember important events during the visit: "What machinery did we see?" Figure 7–4 illustrates this semantic map.

After developing the map, the class wrote a group story following the organization presented on the chalkboard. Through this procedure, the mapping and the group-written story acted as models for future group and individual activities. The students learned a great deal about organization, grouping ideas into paragraphs, and supporting main ideas with important details. The teacher extended individual writing, asking students to write descriptive accounts of each of the main ideas. Students could choose to write about the animals, the buildings, or the machinery. Each of these areas can be further extended using a mapping and discussing process.

The semantic mapping technique is equally helpful before an individual writing activity. Figure 7–5 was generated by an older student whose assignment was to write a humorous story about her summer vacation. Notice that this type of activity encourages students to self-select their own topics and to write about something of special interest to them.

FIGURE 7–5 A Semantic Map that Helped an Older Student Develop Her Story

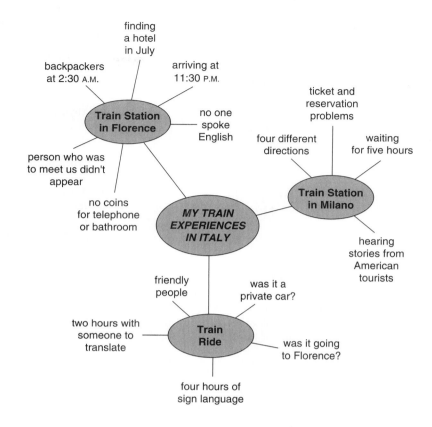

Modeling.   Many of the activities listed under Proett and Gill's development and ordering phase of prewriting (1986) (see Figure 7–2) lend themselves to brief instruction in which a teacher models certain kinds of paragraph development, plot structure, or figurative language. The students then apply what they have learned as they go through the writing phase and use it to provide criteria during the revision process as they share their writing with peer groups, editing groups, and teachers, and then revise their first drafts.

The structure of a limerick or diamante illustrates the need for models during some prewriting activities. To understand this requirement, stop and write a limerick or a diamante. Can you do it without referring to either a model or a specific definition for each type of poetry form? Unless you have been studying and writing these forms of poetry recently, you probably cannot accomplish the task. This is equally true for elementary students.

Use the following models for limericks, cinquains, and diamantes with elementary students. First, read numerous examples of limericks to students. Edward Lear's *Nonsense Omnibus* (1943, 1846), David McCord's *One at a Time: Collected Poems for the Young* (1977), and N. M. Bodecker's *A Person from Britain Whose Head Was the Shape of a Mitten and Other Limericks* (1980) provide excellent examples for this activity. Next, discuss the form of the limerick as shown below. Then, lead a brainstorming activity, during which the students list words that rhyme with several possible key words to use in their own writing. Have the students write their own limericks, share them with the class, and make any revisions after this initial exchange. Then have the students place their limericks into their own class book of limericks.

Limericks are short, funny, five-line poems in which the first, second, and last lines rhyme with each other. The third and fourth lines are shorter and rhyme only with each other. This form results in a poem that looks approximately like this:

Line 1. _____ *a*   *a* lines rhyme
Line 2. _____ *a*
Line 3. _____ *b*   *b* lines rhyme
Line 4. _____ *b*
Line 5. _____ *a*

The following limerick was written by a fifth-grade student:

> There once was a computer named Zeke
> Who turned out to be quite a freak.
> When you told him to add,
> He would call for his Dad
> So his outlook in life was quite bleak.

During other class periods, follow the same reading, modeling, brainstorming, writing, and sharing formats with the cinquain and diamante formats for poetry. In the cinquain, the lines are not difficult to write, and they stress certain types of vocabulary. Unlike the limerick, the cinquain does not use rhyming words. The cinquain is composed of five lines that meet the following requirements:

1. A word for a title
2. Two words to describe the title
3. Three words to express action
4. Four words to express feeling
5. The title again, or a word like it.

A diagram of the cinquain looks like this:

title

describe   title

action   action   action

feeling   about   the   title

title

The cinquain offers a chance for inductive teaching of such language concepts as descriptive words and action words. Students can improve their cinquains if they talk about the kinds of words that make up each line and brainstorm examples. The following cinquains were written by fourth-grade students:

Clouds   Scrubbrush
Fluffy, white   Low, brown
Floating, moving, falling   Tumbling, scratching, dying
Clouds are pillowy soft   Scrubbrush is painfully ugly
Clouds   Scrubbrush

The diamante is another form of poetry that has certain requirements for each line that result in a diamond-shaped poem:

line 1: noun

line 2: two adjectives

line 3: three participles

line 4: four nouns or a phrase

line 5: three participles indicating change

line 6: two adjectives

line 7: contrasting noun (p. 222)

It is helpful if teachers draw a sample and illustrate the types of words used, rather than merely using the terminology of the parts of speech. Thus, in line one, you will have to present examples of a noun; in line two, examples of adjectives related to the first-line noun; in line three, of participles, as verb forms ending in *-ing, -ed, -en*. The nouns or phrase in the fourth line provide a transition from the subject of the first noun to the subject of the contrasting noun on line seven. The fifth line contains three participles that correspond with the seventh-line noun and indicate change from the first noun. The sixth line contains two adjectives that correspond with the final noun and, thus, contrast with line two. The final noun contrasts with line one. A diagram of the diamante looks like this:

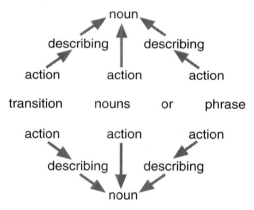

Besides illustrating the parts of speech used in the diamante, you must make clear the concept of contrasts. Contrasting nouns are necessary, in addition to contrasting adjectives and contrasting verb forms that correspond with the appropriate nouns. An instructional activity leading up to this form of poetry begins with identifying the form and suggesting contrasting nouns, such as *war–peace, freedom–slavery,* and *giant–dwarf.* The class should also discuss contrasting descriptive words and contrasting action words. The students will find a thesaurus helpful when working with this form of poetry.

The following diamante was written by a fifth-grade student:

fantasy

magical,   mysterious

dreaming,   fooling,   inventing

An   Unidentified   Flying   Object

proving,   trying,   testing

genuine,   true

reality

As you can see, *fantasy* and *reality* are opposites. *Magical* and *mysterious* describe *fantasy*, and contrast with *genuine* and *true*. The participles *dreaming, fooling,* and *inventing* show action related to fantasy, and contrast with *proving, trying,* and *testing*. This student chose for the middle line the phrase "An Unidentified Flying Object," which might be either fantasy or reality and thus provides transition between the two words.

Literature selections also provide excellent subjects for writing limericks, cinquains, and diamantes. Students may choose a character, a setting, a conflict, or a theme in literature and write poetry that develops these literary elements. For example, a cinquain format might be used to describe the various settings found in Karen Cushman's *Catherine, Called Birdy* (1994). The poetry might portray what it was like living in a medieval English manor in 1290, the village associated with the manor, or the various activities that are considered women's work. The more complex nature of the diamante as it depicts opposites might be an excellent format to depict various Shakespearian characters, conflicts, and themes. Retellings of Shakespeare's stories written for younger audiences include *William Shakespeare's The Tempest* retold by Bruce Coville (1994), Geraldine McCaughrean's *Stories from Shakespeare* (1995), and Leon Garfield's *Shakespeare Stories II* (1995). The illustrations in these three versions may also be used to add feeling to the poetry. Julius Lester's retelling of *Othello* (1995) is a good source for older students.

Listing and Categorizing.   Activities that encourage students to list and categorize, classify, or order information provide opportunities for content building and idea building. For example, a third-grade teacher used this strategy to help students identify and categorize the incidents that occurred before, during, and after a field trip. The class decided that division by time would be most appropriate. It developed the following three categories of events:

1. Things we did to get ready for our train ride.
2. Things we did on the day of our train ride.
3. Things we did for several days after the train ride.

Next, the class changed these categories into questions, and wrote each question on a separate section of the chalkboard:

1. What did we do to get ready for our train ride?
2. What did we do on the day of our train ride?
3. What did we do for several days after the train ride?

In the next step, the children answered the three questions by listing information under the appropriate question. They developed the following sentence outline:

A Ride on the Train

  I. What did we do to get ready for our train ride?
   A. We studied about railroads.
   B. We called the railroad depot to get train times and ticket cost.
   C. We wrote a note to our parents asking permission to go on the train ride.
   D. We called the school bus company to get a bus to pick us up at school, take us to the depot, and pick us up at the next train depot.
 II. What did we do on the day of our train ride?
   A. We rode on the bus to the train depot.
   B. We bought our train tickets.
   C. We each got a seat on the train.
   D. The conductor took our tickets.

Listing and categorizing are excellent prewriting activities because they stimulate ideas.

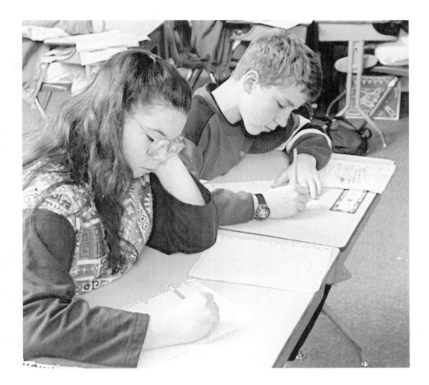

    E. The conductor told us about the train.
    F. We saw the dining car, the observation car, and the Pullman cars.
    G. When we got off the train we looked at the engine.
    H. We rode the bus back to school.
III. What did we do for several days after the train ride?
    A. We drew pictures of the train and the depot for a bulletin board.
    B. We wrote thank-you notes to the train conductor.
    C. We wrote a story so we could remember the train ride.
    D. We read more books about trains.
    E. We learned some songs about trains.

After developing this outline, the students wrote individual stories about their trip. The children used the outline, but added their own details to make the story personal. As you can see, this activity also became an introduction to outlining and writing a longer factual report.

Another way to motivate interest and help students categorize ideas, know what references they need from library sources, and organize materials is to list some questions that the children want answered about a general topic. One graduate student, who also teaches fourth grade, used this approach before her students wrote reports about Native Americans. The students first listed a number of questions they wanted answered. Then, they grouped the questions into categories. Part of the list appears in Figure 7–6 (the full list contained more than 100 questions). When the students selected a category they wished to investigate, the questions on the list provided both a starting point for the information search and a topic for writing.

Native Americans

1. Clothing
   a. What did Native Americans wear?
   b. How did they get their materials?
   c. How did they sew?
   d. Did all Native Americans dress alike?
2. Education
   a. Did Native Americans have to go to school?
   b. What did they need to learn?
   c. Who taught the Native American children?
   d. What did they write on?
3. Houses
   a. What were tepees made from?
   b. How did they cook and wash?
   c. Did all Native Americans live in the same kinds of houses?
4. Medicine
   a. Did Native Americans get sick?
   b. Why did the medicine men dance?
   c. Did Native Americans take medicine?

5. Food
   a. What did the Native Americans eat?
   b. Where did they get their food?
   c. Was their food tasty?
   d. How did they store their food?
   e. What else did they use for hunting besides bows and arrows?

6. Tribes
   a. How did you get to be a chief?
   b. Where did the different Native American Tribes live?
   c. How were they alike or different?

7. War and Peace
   a. Why did the Native Americans fight the settlers?
   b. Were any Native Americans friendly with the settlers?
   c. How did the settlers treat the Native Americans?
   d. What would happen if you went on a reservation today?

FIGURE 7–6   Outline of Questions Asked by Fourth-Grade Students about Native Americans

Writing

Prewriting experiences allow students to explore, imagine, consider initial structure, and think about details to go into their writing. Writing, however, demands some additional considerations. Proett and Gill (1986) state:

> The writing stage needs to be viewed in two very different ways. Seen in one way, it is the flowing of words onto the page, easily, naturally, rapidly. But it is also a time of making decisions, of choosing what to tell and what to leave out, or thinking about who is speaking and who is listening, of determining what order, what structure, what word works best. In some ways these functions even seem contradictory; the first needs to be fluid and fast while the other calls for deliberation and reason. The teaching task is to help the writer coordinate these two functions. (p. 11)

As we did with prewriting, let us consider the advice of the professional editor and author Jean E. Karl (1994) as we approach the writing stage. Karl states that after completing your research you must decide what will go into the text. You must ask yourself "What is the most important point that you want to make?" Then ask yourself "What information do I need to include that will help the audience understand my subject?" To help an author focus the writing Karl recommends that an author should "Build a pyramid of information, each new idea building on what went before, until you reach the top, the understanding you wanted to convey. It should set a pattern and follow it. It should begin at what you have decided is the beginning—at the easiest information to understand—and move slowly into the more difficult material. It should make each new step of knowledge interesting as well as understandable. The ongoing progress from one idea to the next should always be sharp and evident" (pp. 81–82).

Karl (1994) recommends that authors make a final outline in which they review all they have done and consider again the pattern that the writing should take. Now they are ready to write a first draft in which they consider the requirements of the audience and the overall tone of the work. During this first draft, the author should try to make every word and every sentence count and build on the work that came before. As we discuss the various activities recommended for the writing stage, notice how many of these activities correspond with Karl's recommendations.

Author Ayn Rand (2001) also emphasizes the need to develop an outline. Rand states, "No beginner should write without an outline. If I could enforce this as an absolute, I would. Most writing problems—the psychological barriers, setbacks, discouragements—come from the absence of a proper outline. One reason for the dreadful articles in our media is that they are written without outlines, and thus fall apart structurally" (p. 41). As you read the outline of questions in Figure 7–6, consider how these questions could be used to create an outline.

This section begins with a discussion of ways to help students create an outline by making decisions about audience, purpose, form, organizational pattern, and linguistic style. Next, we consider ways to help students write a first draft rapidly.

Audience and Purpose.   To entertain an audience or to inform the audience about a new scientific development, would you write a composition in the same way? Should you write a composition for a second-grade audience using the same words you would use for an adult audience? The answer to both of these questions is an obvious no. To help students realize the importance of audience and purpose, you must provide them with many opportunities to write for different types of real audiences, ranging from themselves, to their peers, to you, to other known audiences, to unknown audiences. (This concern is important in both processing and distancing approaches to writing.)

Unfortunately, many studies indicate that students have few audiences except the teacher. About one-third of papers result in some type of teacher–learner dialogue. The rest are addressed to the teacher as an examiner. Only 10 percent of writing is read regularly by other students, but students should be given many opportunities to write for varied real audiences, for purposes other than to be examined on their knowledge, and for audiences that respond to the writing in ways that go beyond the examination.

There are many opportunities in school to encourage students to write for real audiences and for different purposes. For example, students can write letters or stories to and for their families. They can have pen pals in other classrooms and even other school districts. They can write stories and other types of articles to be displayed in the library, on bulletin boards, and in a school or classroom newspaper. They can write diaries and autobiographies for their own pleasure. They can send reports to and correspond with local historical societies, newspapers, television stations, government officials, and businesses. They can develop their own books, literary magazines, comic books, newspapers, and other types of journals. They can share these products with larger audiences. Students themselves will think of many additional ways to create real audiences for their writing.

Table 7–1 Writing activity, purpose, requirements, and audience

Writing	Purpose	Requirements	Audience
1. Weather and temperature charts	Compare conditions over a nine-month period.	Thermometer to take temperature. Observe clouds at same time of day. Accuracy.	Science class.
2. Personal letters	Exchange accounts of experiences with friend.	Interesting personal information. Informal writing level.	A friend who knows me.
3. Invitations	Inform and invite audience to a program, party, etc.	What, who, why, when, where. (Proofreading is important.)	Parents, neighbors, friends.
4. Puppet plays	Entertain.	Original story that entertains. Puppets.	Class, parents, other invited guests.
5. Diaries	Record daily experiences and feelings.	Short notes on things important to me.	Me.
6. News stories	Inform about news, events, sports, etc.	Accuracy—who, what, when, where. Clear, brief reporting. (Editing and proofreading are important.)	Whole school. If city paper, large unknown audience that wants information.
7. Forms	Obtain social security card, driver's license. Send for information.	Accurate information, clear handwriting. (Proofreading is important.)	People who don't know me. Government.
8. Imaginative	Entertain, enjoy.	Fresh ideas, imagination, feelings.	Class. If published, a large, unknown audience.

Students need to realize the importance of audience characteristics and purposes when they are making decisions about writing. To help them realize the importance of audience and purpose, encourage students to list questions they need to answer about the characteristics of the audience and the purpose of the composition. A group of fifth graders developed the following list:

1. How old is my audience?
2. How much knowledge of the subject does my audience have?
3. Is the subject going to be interesting to my audience?
4. Would the subject add new knowledge to my audience?
5. Does the audience want to be informed or entertained?
6. How do I want the audience to react? Do I want them to be persuaded to my viewpoint? Do I want them to laugh? Do I want them to follow directions? Do I want them to have new ideas? Do I want them to have new information? Do I want them to be sad?

After they developed the questions, they discussed why and how the answers to the questions would influence their writing.

Writing	Purpose	Requirements	Audience
9. Autobiographies	Tell others about myself. Compile class book.	Facts about myself, feelings, wishes. (Proofreading is Important.)	Class and parents. If published, a large, unknown audience.
10. Book reports	Report author, title information, summary, and personal reactions.	Careful reading and writing for summary. (Proofreading is important.)	Class. If book review in a paper, people who might want to read the book.
11. Reports and projects in social studies, science, etc.	Share new facts and information.	Research from several sources, data, main ideas, and details. Accuracy of facts, best order for ideas. (Proofreading is important.)	Class. If journal or magazine article, people wanting that information.
12. Biographies	Report knowledge about well-known person.	Research from several sources. Comparisons of information. Accuracy. (Proofreading is important.)	Class. If published, a large, unknown audience.
13. Editorials	Persuade someone to my viewpoint.	Knowledge of ways to persuade and use facts. Rewriting to clearly persuade.	People who read the newspaper. Some will agree with the writer, some will disagree.
14. Minutes for meetings	Keep a record of what happened.	Accurate listening and reading.	Class, group, or organization.

Another processing and distancing activity that helps students understand requirements for audience and purpose is having the students list several different types of writing and then discuss the purpose of that type of writing, the requirements for it, and the intended audience. One group of fourth-grade students put this information into table form (Table 7–1).

Form. After discussing information similar to that shown in Table 7–1, students have clearer ideas about possible content for each type of writing, as well as about purpose and audience. They also understand that writing can take on numerous forms. You can expand this list to include other forms of writing, such as poetry, cartoons, picture storybooks, nonfictional textbooks, essays, interviews, reviews, songs, and sketches. Next, bring to class examples of these various forms for writing. Share the forms with students as they consider the differences and why certain forms may be more appropriate for specific purposes and audiences.

It is also interesting to try to change forms and then compare the content and impact on the audience. For example, after reading historical fiction about early British heroes, some college students wrote book reports in the form of ballads and then asked fifth- and sixth-grade students to complete a similar task. The students learned that ballads were appropriate for sharing heroic character information during the colonial time period, discovered information about the ballad as a form of writing, determined that content might be similar or different depending on the form, and recognized that the influence on an audience may depend on the form chosen to deliver the message.

Other interesting activities with form include writing telegrams from news articles, science fiction from scientific factual information, diary entries from novels, letters from biographies, and cartoons from any type of literature. Whatever the motivation, students conclude the activity by comparing information, characteristics of form, and appropriateness of different forms for different purposes and audiences.

Organizational Pattern.   Students frequently pay little attention to the organizational patterns used in their own writing or the writing of others. The organizational patterns in limericks, cinquains, and diamantes are obvious and must be followed for authenticity. However, there are other, less obvious and less structured organizational patterns that provide logical order. Writers frequently use several of these patterns within the same paper or book. As shown by the titles, these major organizational patterns lend themselves to writing in many of the content areas. You may introduce these forms through activities in which you model the identification of various organizational approaches, diagram paragraphs according to the organizational pattern, and lead discussions in which students identify and describe the organizational pattern. Then, the students should write compositions using organizational patterns that they believe are appropriate. Our example of the train ride used a chronological order of events. Compositions such as those reporting historical events or autobiographies lend themselves to ordering in which the earliest events are reported first.

A second method of organization is through spatial concepts. The order might proceed from inside to outside, from right to left, or from bottom to top. Such a pattern might look like this:

Bottom	The Old Man in the Park
↓	↓ New and shiny black shoes
Top	↓ Bare white ankles
	↓ Cuffed, baggy, and torn pants
	↓ Faded flannel shirt
	↓ Expression of contentment and satisfaction

Or this:

Inside	Water distribution
↓	↓ On the inside of the earth.
Outside	↓ On the earth's surface.
	↓ In the atmosphere.

A third method starts with the simplest or most familiar ideas and progresses to the most complex or unfamiliar ideas. A writer may begin by reviewing information or concepts the audience already knows and then progress to new information that is harder to understand without background information. Following is a diagram of this order:

Familiar	Wind energy
↓	↓ Trees swaying
Unfamiliar	↓ Kites flying
	↓ Windmill pumping water
	↓ Wind turbine connected to a generator

Social studies and science writers often use two other patterns of organization to develop main ideas and supporting details. A report might first identify a problem, continue by suggesting causes for the problem, and conclude with possible solutions. A diagram would look like this:

Problem	Air pollution
↓ Cause of problem	↓ Automobiles—industrial waste
↓ Possible solutions of the problem	↓ Catalytic converters—filtering smoke in factories

After identifying a problem, a report might discuss its effects rather than its causes. This report form also concludes with possible solutions to the problems, for example:

Problem	Air pollution
↓ Effect of problem	↓ Lung diseases—plant diseases
↓ Possible solutions to the problem	↓ Catalytic converters on cars—filtering smoke in factories

A final useful arrangement is question and answer. In this pattern, a writer asks a question and answers it, asks another question and answers it, and so forth; for example:

Question ↓	What clothes should you take to keep dry when camping?
Answer	Discuss characteristics of a good raincoat or poncho

Most professional authors use a combination of several organizational patterns. The patterns help authors develop their ideas and readers follow the ideas. Understanding the advantage of various organizational patterns helps students write their own compositions. You can provide many opportunities for students to identify organizational patterns used by authors and analyze the effectiveness of the patterns for the particular content. For example, ask students to search for and identify examples of chronological order in Russell Freedman's *Franklin Delano Roosevelt* (1990) as the author describes the life of the former president from boyhood through his experiences as commander in chief. In Katherine Leiner's *First Children Growing Up in the White House* (1996), the author uses chronological order to trace the history of the White House. The chronological order in Rhoda Blumberg's *The Incredible Journey of Lewis and Clark* (1987) is reinforced with maps that trace the journey from east to west and then from west to east.

An organizational pattern based on a spatial concept is evident in the following example from James Cross Giblin's *The Riddle of the Rosetta Stone: Key to Ancient Egypt* (1990):

> What makes this stone so special? Step closer, and you'll see. Spotlights pick out markings carved into the surface of the stone, and close up you can tell that these markings are writing. At the top are fourteen lines of hieroglyphs—pictures of animals, birds, and geometric shapes. Below them you can make out thirty-two lines written in an unfamiliar script. And below that, at the bottom of the slab, are fifty-four more lines written in the letters of the Greek alphabet. (p. 7)

Also notice how Stewart Ross uses spatial concepts associated with directions in his description of 1605 London in his *Shakespeare and Macbeth: The Story Behind the Play* (1994):

> Church spires and the stone buildings of the mighty overlook wooden houses set in a maze of winding streets. To the west lie the great cathedral and the palace of Westminster; to the east the massive bulk of the Tower of London stands sentinel beside crowded wharves and jetties. And in the heart of the ancient city, St. Paul's rises like a great rock amid a sea of tiled and thatched roofs. (p. 7)

In Patricia Lauber's *The News About Dinosaurs* (1988), the author presents familiar information about dinosaurs and follows with new and unfamiliar information. Various patterns that begin with problems and include solutions are evident in Laurence Pringle's *Global Warming: Assessing the Greenhouse Threat* (1990), Charlotte Wilcox's *Trash!* (1988), and Carole Vogel and Kathryn Goldner's *The Great Yellowstone Fire* (1990). A question-and-answer organizational pattern is used by Seymour Simon in *New Questions and Answers About Dinosaurs* (1990). Sometimes the title of the book provides the question while the text answers the question. This format is found in Robert Snedden's *What Is a Reptile?* (1994) and in Celia Godkin's *What About Ladybugs?* (1995).

Because authors use many different organizational patterns within the same book, students can analyze the effectiveness of each pattern. After students have identified and analyzed the effectiveness of the various organizational patterns, have them write their own stories and reports based on one or more of these patterns.

Linguistic Style.   The sentence-combining and modeling activities developed in Chapter 10 help students explore various linguistic styles, develop fluency in writing, and develop a variety of appropriate solutions to linguistic choices. You may use these approaches during group lessons, introductory activities, or individual conferences when students need help making linguistic decisions. Teachers frequently use examples from students' writing to show how sentence combining, other transformations, and word choices can improve fluency and clarity. You may write your own compositions to reflect any student problems, place the compositions on transparencies or handouts, and lead discussions during which students identify and use various sentence-combining strategies to improve their writing.

Literature provides good sources for observation and discussion. Through models, students can discover various techniques used by authors to create interest and achieve fluency and clarity. For example, have the students observe how Armstrong Sperry develops vivid descriptions of setting and conflict in *Call It Courage* (1940). In the following passage, Sperry decreases the length of his sentences as the tension rises and the conflict increases. This changing of sentence length not only stresses developing tension, it also reflects the rhythm of the angry ocean:

> There was a wave lifting before the canoe. Many the boy had seen, but this was a giant—a monster livid and hungry. Higher, higher it rose, until it seemed that it must scrape at the low-hanging clouds. Its crest heaved over with a vast sigh. The boy saw it coming. He tried to cry out. No sound issued from his throat. Suddenly the wave was upon him. Down it crashed. Chaos! Mafatu felt the paddle torn from his hands. Thunder in his ears. Water strangling him. Terror in his soul. The canoe slewed round into the trough. The boy flung himself forward, wound his arms around the midthwart. It was the end of a world. (p. 24)

Literary models are especially important for demonstrating the importance of carefully chosen words. Authors Paula Fox and Jan Hudson, for example, develop strong characterizations through the use of similes, metaphors, and other types of figurative language. In *One-Eyed Cat* (1984), notice how Fox uses a simile to describe the main character's guilt: "When there was a splinter in his foot, it was all he could think about; he would forget that every part of his body except where the splinter was felt fine. That's the way it was now with the attic. The gun was like a splinter in his mind" (p. 90). Later, Fox compares Ned's secret to a mountain of snow: "All the lies he had told, the subterfuge, were piled up over the gun like a mountain of hard-packed snow. He felt his secret had frozen around him. He didn't know how to melt it" (p. 162).

The author's choice of language in Hudson's *Sweetgrass* (1989) is especially appropriate for a story about a Blackfoot Indian girl who lived on the northern prairies in the 1800s. Students can discuss the carefully chosen words for this character's thoughts: "When thinking about her life, Sweetgrass thinks: 'All things moved as they should. Our lives seemed fixed as in a beaded design or the roundness of an old tale told on winter nights'" (p. 10).

Author Eve Bunting (1990) emphasizes the importance of using poetic, descriptive language, especially in shorter picture storybooks. Bunting asks, "Isn't it more breathtaking to read, 'The air hissed to the beat of the wings' (*The Man Who Could Call Down Owls*) than, 'There was the sound of wings in the air'? Try to use the actual 'sound' word. The air hissed; the bus wheezed; the leaves flurried in the wind" (p. 413).

First Draft.   The objective of this phase of the writing process is the fairly rapid writing of ideas generated, developed, and refined during the prewriting phase. The objective is not to produce finished compositions; that objective takes place in the postwriting, or revision, phase. (All writing, however, does not need to lead to a finished composition.)

Your students may find it helpful if you show them how you write your own first drafts. For example, my own first drafts are written with pencil on legal-size pads. I leave enough space between lines to make changes in word choices or to rewrite sentences. I draw arrows if I change my mind about the ordering of sentences in paragraphs or the ordering of paragraphs. I frequently insert ideas between sentences, on the next page, or even on the back of the page. Again, arrows show me where to locate and place this material. I erase and cross out words, sentences, and even paragraphs. If I cannot think of a specific word or need to add a specific reference, I draw a line. The word will come later; the reference must be found and added. I draw lines if I need to check spelling or a convention in punctuation or grammar. In this case, I draw a line under the questionable word or punctuation, place an abbreviation (*sp., gr.,* or *pn.*) above the line, and continue with my flow of ideas. The lines and abbreviations are cues for areas to check during revision. From an example such as this, students should see that first drafts are frequently tentative and messy. They require editing and revisions. Students should also understand some of the techniques they may use in developing their first, or rough, drafts.

I use semantic mapping to develop my ideas and organize my writing, so I frequently go back and forth between the map and the first draft. As I write, I ask myself questions such as these: Did I include those ideas and develop those points? What should come next in the development of the writing? Do I have more information on my map than I can develop thoroughly in a paper? Would it be better if I omitted this portion? If I omit this portion, do I need to change my introduction or my conclusions? A semantic map helps jog memory, improves organization, and provides key evaluators for the revision process. Working with the map and the written composition in this way may also suggest that the original ideas are not working, that major modifications are necessary, and that it is necessary to start over. As we all know, writing is not easy.

Using Computers.   Computer-assisted programs may help students organize their ideas before writing, compose their stories, and revise and edit their selections. Computers with various software programs for writing and word processing motivate writing because the children can focus on content rather than penmanship, easily edit their ideas, interact with peers, see what the finished product looks like before it is printed, and produce attractive final drafts. At the prewriting stage, Gomez (1987) recommends three prewriting modules published by Milliken. These modules allow students to brainstorm and organize their ideas on disks, print the results, and either write with pen and paper or merge ideas with their files on word processors. Other programs that have prewriting capabilities include *The Writers Helper* published by Conduit, *Bank Street Writer Activity Files* published by Scholastic, and *Quill* published by D. C. Heath.

At the composing level, various word processor programs encourage students to compose first drafts and then revise without recopying. Some programs have unique motivating capabilities: *That's My Story,* published by Learning Well, includes story starters;

Using computers promotes longer compositions and motivates children to do careful editing.

Kidwriter, published by Spinnaker, includes pictures that children may choose to write about; and *Super Story Tree,* published by Scholastic, has a choose-your-own adventure format.

Several studies emphasize the advantages of student interaction during the composing process. For example, Dickinson (1986) used computer teams and encouraged children to talk with each other about their writing plans, discuss their actual writing, and consider their teammates' reactions and feedback when they made their revisions. The capabilities of the *Quill* program extend to the composing level. Describing students' interactions while using this program, Bruce, Michaels, and Watson-Gegeo (1985) state: "Students' writing is public and available to be read as it is entered into the computer (looking over the writer's shoulder as it appears on the screen). Later, using an information storage and retrieval system, students can retrieve their own or someone else's writing stored in the computer. Writing comes off the printer typed and formatted like published print (newspapers, magazine ads). It can then be seen on the wall (where its neatly typed format makes it easier to read and hence more accessible to classmates and outside visitors)" (p. 148). Interactions during this observation occurred as students wrote on the computer, read and discussed other students' writing and revisions, and used the computers to send messages to each other.

At the revising and editing levels, word processing programs allow students to respond to the text of others, encourage spelling checks, and make it easier for students to revise and edit their own writing. Texts by Selfe (1986) and Wresch (1984) provide detailed directions for using computers in all stages of the writing process.

Educators also emphasize computer applications to teach sentence combining and to increase and improve the writing skills of children with special needs. Bradley (1982) helped students improve their sentence structures by teaching them sentence combining through a computer program. Rubenstein and Rollins (1978) developed a letter-writing project with deaf children. Over a year's time, forty previously reluctant writers used computers to generate more than 1,500 letters to each other. The authors concluded that electronic mail is a powerful motivator for children's writing. Likewise, Kleiman and Humphrey (1982) found that children with learning disabilities, ranging in age from seven to sixteen, enthusiastically increased their writing when encouraged to use word processors.

Although many educators are enthusiastic about using computer programs for writing, several potential problems warrant consideration. If children are to make full use of the capabilities of computers during the writing process, they must have numerous opportunities to use the computers. This means they must have frequent access to computers. In addition, they must learn how to type on a computer keyboard, use a word processor, use various software packages, and use a printer. The greatest need may be for students and teachers to understand that word processing programs will not magically solve writing problems and provide instruction in all phases of writing. In a study of the quality and writing capabilities of seventh- through ninth-grade students, Dauite (1986) emphasizes this point: "This study suggests that word processing features for revising are most useful for writing development when combined closely with cognitive and instructional aids that draw students into reading their texts and developing revising strategies such as self-questioning. Experienced writers who have benefited from the basic processing features already know what good writing looks like and how to evaluate their texts critically. If our students are to benefit from automatic recopying and reformatting, we have to continue to help them learn what good writing is and how to improve their own draft texts" (p. 158).

After Writing

After the writing phase, major portions of the writing process still remain. During the final phase, help students develop self-evaluative skills as they reread, review, and revise their compositions. Provide opportunities to share the writings with peer editing groups and with you during teacher conferences. Encourage the students to proofread their writings and share their finished examples orally or through various publishing and presentation techniques.

Revising. Under the revising portion of the writing process, Karl (1994) recommends that an author evaluate the writing by looking at it as a whole and asking herself or himself the following questions: "Does the beginning set the tone, and does that tone follow through? Do ideas follow each other in a logical progression? Can you now see that segments of your text do not belong there and should be cut out? In some places do you need to say a bit more to make yourself understood? Are your transitions from one idea to the next true bridges from one passage to another, carrying the reader from one idea to the next? Does your summary at the end convey the essence of the whole and the thought that for those really interested there is more to be learned?" (p. 93).

Karl (1994) recommends that during this phase the writing should be evaluated carefully. This is also the time to let others read the writing and let them point to places that do not convey the meaning that you hoped to convey. She maintains that this is also the time to read the material aloud to yourself as well as to others. Now there may be a need to revise again in order to smooth the writing, to alter the patterns of paragraphs, to clarify the meaning of the sentences, or to respond to concerns of the listening and reading audience. Professional author Rand (2001) also emphasizes the importance of applying grammatical rules to clarify meaning. She states: "The ability to think precisely and thus to write precisely cannot be achieved without observing grammatical rules . . . the whole secret of grammar is clarity" (p. 99).

Working with older writers, Wallace and Hayes (1991) found that students who are given instruction in revision produce superior compositions when compared to students who are simply asked to make the text better. Experienced writers use several revision techniques that are equally effective with less experienced student writers. For example, author Donald Murray (1990) believes that it is possible to break down the revision process as writers study their own works. Murray maintains that in his early revisions he reads to locate the effectiveness of seven elements: subject, audience, form, structure, development, dimension, and tone. Under subject, he asks questions such as "Do I have anything to say? Did I say it clearly?" In the area of audience he asks, "Is there an audience for what I have written? Will anyone need or enjoy what I have to say?" Under form, he considers whether the form of the paper or book is the most appropriate for the writing. "Is the form—short story, biography, essay, and so forth—suitable for the work?" In the area of structure, he considers the order for what is written. "Is the structure built on a solid framework of logic, argument, narrative, or motivation?" Under development, Murray analyzes whether each part builds in a way that prepares the reader for the next part. Under dimensions, he considers if there is a pleasing proportion among all of the parts. The final element is tone, in which he listens for voice and the development of his own style. "Is there a coherent tone holding the whole writing together?"

After he has made sure that his draft has these seven elements, Murray (1990) is now ready for the careful process of line-by-line editing in which he reads the work aloud and considers the appropriateness of words, sentences, and paragraphs. He reads his sentences for variety and balance. He plays with figurative language and other language structures "until he achieves a manuscript which appears effortless to the reader" (p. 27).

Although Murray is a professional writer, many of his suggestions are equally valid for student writers. You can duplicate the areas of the revision process in the classroom. Sharing your own writing experiences with students places you in the role of a model. Demonstrate to the students how you changed a written project because you read it aloud to yourself and then shared it with another individual or group. This activity helps students understand the importance of the revision phase of writing.

Teacher–Student Conferencing.   Conferencing with peers and teachers is important during the revision process. Tompkins and Hoskisson (1991) identified and briefly described various types of conferences used during this stage, as illustrated in Figure 7–7.

Research indicates that conferences and editing groups are beneficial at all grade levels. In an investigation of the revision process of first-grade students, Fitzgerald and Stamm (1990) found group conferences to be most helpful for those students who had the least knowledge about revision and who needed the most assistance in their writing. Nelson (1990) found that peer response between drafts produces better quality final drafts.

Three types of teacher–student conferences are frequently mentioned in the literature: (1) informal conferences, in which teachers provide immediate help for students who require assistance; (2) regularly scheduled conferences for individual students; and (3) scheduled conferences, in which groups of students are given lessons on writing conventions. Graves (1983) recommends both informal conferencing (teachers moving around the room, stopping at individual desks) and regularly scheduled conferencing (individual students coming to teachers prepared to discuss their work, ask and answer questions, and receive motivation and guidance). Graves believes that teachers should have regularly scheduled conferences with students at least once a week.

You may structure conferences on general, open-ended questions or on questions dealing with specific details, paragraph organization, and purpose for the writing. General, open-ended questions include the following: What do you like best about this piece of writing? What questions would you like to ask me? What surprised you as you were writing this draft? Are you having any problems? Which part is giving you problems? In a conference dealing with more specific elements, you might say, "I like the way you described the dog in your story. I could really see and hear him. I knew he was unhappy because he was lost. How do you think you could make your readers know more about his master, Davey? How do you think you could make your readers understand how Davey is feeling because his dog is lost?" Similar comments and questions may lead to discussions on ways to work with setting and plot.

Other possible topics for discussion are paragraph development, vocabulary choices, transitional phrases or sentences, story conclusions, and literary form. You could focus on the objectives of the lesson and refer to specific lessons taught as part of the prewriting phase, such as lessons on organizational patterns.

1. On-the-Spot Conferences

   The teacher visits briefly with a student at his or her desk to monitor some aspect of the writing assignment or to see how the student is progressing. The teacher begins by asking the student to read what he or she has written and then asks a question or two about the writing. Usually the teacher has several questions in mind before having the conference with the student. These conferences are brief; the teacher spends less than a minute at a student's desk before moving away.

2. Drafting Conferences

   Students bring their rough drafts and meet with the teacher at a table set up in the classroom specifically for that purpose. Students bring to the conference examples of specific writing problems that they would like to talk to the teacher about. These short, individual conferences often last less than 5 minutes so it is possible for a teacher to meet with 8 to 10 students in 30 minutes. Often students sign up for these conferences in advance.

3. Revising Conferences

   A small group of students and the teacher meet in writing group conferences. Students read what they have written and ask for specific suggestions from classmates and the teacher about how to revise their compositions. These conferences offer student writers an audience to provide feedback on how well they have communicated. These small-group conferences last approximately 30 minutes or as long as necessary for each student to share his or her writing. Many elementary teachers schedule these conferences periodically in place of reading groups. After all, the purpose of reading and writing groups is virtually the same: to read and react to a piece of writing.

4. Editing Conferences

   Students meet with the teacher for an editing conference. In these individual or small-group conferences, the teacher reviews students' proofread compositions and helps them to correct spelling, punctuation, capitalization, and other mechanical errors. The teacher takes notes during these conferences about the problems students are having with mechanical skills in order to plan individual, special instruction conferences.

5. Instructional Conferences

   Ten- to fifteen-minute conferences are scheduled with individual students to provide special instruction. Teachers prepare for these conferences by reviewing students' writing folders and by planning instruction on one or two skills (e.g., capitalizing proper nouns, using commas in a series) that are particularly troublesome for individual students.

6. Conferences with Classmates

   Students meet with one or two classmates to ask for advice, to share a piece of writing, or to proofread a composition in much the same way that they hold a conference with the teacher. In these student conferences, students are expected to maintain a helpful and supportive relationship with their classmates.

7. Class Conferences

   Conferences with the entire class are held periodically to write and revise class collaboration compositions, to practice new conferencing strategies, and to discuss concerns relating to all students. Sometimes, these conferences are planned, and at other times they occur spontaneously as the need arises.

FIGURE 7–7   Types of Writing Conferences

Source: From Gail E. Tompkins and Kenneth Hoskisson, *Language Arts: Content and Teaching Strategies,* 2nd ed. (Upper Saddle River, N.J.: Merrill/Prentice Hall, 1991).

During these conferences, you should keep in mind that teachers who are supportive are likely to be the most effective. An experiment by Spaulding (1989) underscores the importance of teacher interaction during the writing process. One group of students was given a writing assignment without having had any class lessons on the assigned topic. Another group was first provided a lecture on the topic and then assigned a writing task in which the students used their notes to write about the topic. Spaulding's findings showed that those students who were given the lecture first were more engaged with their writing tasks than the students who had not been provided with instruction. She concluded: "The students generally manifested greater persistence, more reflective behaviors, and less self-doubt in the lecture condition than they did in the no instruction conditions. . . . The importance of instructional support, both content-related and procedural, in explaining the students' task-related engagement is evident throughout this study" (p. 157).

As suggested by the variety of questions and discussion topics, teachers play a variety of roles during writing conferences. According to Harris (1986), teachers encourage student writers by playing the role of coach, commentator, counselor, listener, and diagnostician. As coach, a teacher uses such comments as "You've done a good job describing the boy in the picture. Can you do the same thing when you describe the girl?" The coach, Harris states, "uses comments to help writers identify what they have to watch out for, what they have to work harder on, what has been working well for them, and what to build on" (p. 35).

In the commentator role, a teacher helps students see where they are in the writing process and where they need to move in the next draft. Comments may include statements such as "Good. The first draft helped you focus your subject on _____. You are now ready to try your idea to add more detail about _____." In the counselor role, a teacher considers the whole person, including previous experience, motivation, prior learning, attitudes, and interests. This role is especially important when a teacher is trying to help students counteract writing blocks or other problems that are interfering with writing.

As a listener, a teacher plays several changing roles (Murray, 1979). At prewriting conferences, the teacher is a friendly listener who is interested in each student as an individual with ideas to express. As students develop drafts, the teacher becomes a fellow writer who tries to focus, shape, and form the written composition. As the writing progresses, the teacher listens closely to the language of the paper. Throughout this sequence, the teacher listens carefully to discover what the student needs to know.

As diagnostician, a teacher probes, asks questions, engages in exploratory conversations, and encourages students to make final decisions about their writing. Harris (1986) warns, however, that in this role, a teacher should not "unwittingly assume total control, wresting from the student all responsibility for what happens and closing off all avenues for student participation. When this happens, chances for students to improve their writing decrease dramatically" (p. 40). This final role may be the most difficult. Students may expect teachers to provide the major input. The purpose of a teacher–student conference is to encourage writers to participate in the discussion and develop independent writing skills. This role is not met when students respond passively to teacher comments without becoming involved in the process.

Eve Bunting (1990), an author of picture storybooks, provides guidelines for adult authors that are also beneficial for student authors who are writing and revising picture books. These guidelines may be shared with students during teacher–student conferences. She states:

> When you've finished your manuscript divide it by drawing lines across the text to mark what you see as the natural ending of a page. Or set up a dummy by taking eight sheets of blank paper and folding them horizontally to make a 32-page book (32 pages is the usual picture book length, less three or four for front matter: title page, copyright, and

A group of peers can help a young author revise her writing by asking clarifying questions.

dedication). Write your text on each dummy page. Do you have enough pictures? Do you have too many words? Work for balance. Visualize your little reader, or listener, impatient to get on with it, to turn the page to find out what happens next. (p. 412)

When revising the text, Bunting also states that the picture book is usually 1,000 words or less, so the writing needs to be concise but also it needs to sound poetic.

Peer Editing.   Peer editing groups are effective in the revision process because groups of three to five students provide a known audience for student writers. They encourage writers to sense the impact of their work, answer questions about their writing, clarify points, and revise writing to meet the needs of real audiences. Moreover, they allow student editors to hone their own editing and revising techniques, ask clarifying questions about content, and apply their new skills to their own writing.

Before peer editing groups can function, students need to develop trust. They must be willing to share their work with others and provide critical dialogue when it is their turn to respond to writing. The teacher should model the first editing group as a participant to help the students understand that the role of the editing group is to respond to specific things that they like about the paper, to ask questions about parts that are unclear, and to consider what could be added or changed to clarify or increase enjoyment and understanding. You may use sample papers to encourage this interaction and show students how to respond effectively as both presenter and editor. The complexity of the tasks expected of the peer editing groups and even the length of such activities depends on the ages, writing capabilities, and understandings of the students. Younger elementary students may focus on what they like about a paper, ask questions to clarify details in the paper, and respond to the effectiveness of revisions. Older students may become much more involved in the connections between the objectives of the lesson, form of the writing, and evaluation of the drafts during stages in the revision process.

From their work with older students during the National Writing Project, Daniels and Zemelman (1985) generated many useful suggestions for peer editing groups. They recommend that you form peer editing groups by tentatively ranking students from 1 (best prepared for writing) to 25 or whatever number is in the total class (least prepared for writing). Then, list students numerically in three columns. Form groups by selecting students across columns. In this way, each group includes above-average, average, and poor writers. You may alter these groups to balance students according to sex or to make changes because of inability to work together. You may keep the groups intact for long periods or re-form them monthly.

Several guidelines improve the function of these groups. First, peer editing groups are most effective when writers read their papers aloud so that both the writers and listeners hear the effect of the language. In addition, group members as well as writers should sign the drafts presented and discussed in the peer editing groups. These signatures show that both the author and the group members share responsibility for the writing. Furthermore, peer editing groups may benefit from checklists of criteria or forms that relate to the specific writing assignment being revised. Forms may be as simple as spaces to show examples of what the editing group liked about the writing and where clarification could take place to improve the writing, or they may consider such elements in a writing project as characterization, plot development, settings, or cause–effect relationships. The Holistic Scoring Scale (Table 7–2) and other such scales may help editing groups focus on important aspects of the writing task.

Daniels and Zemelman (1985) suggest that editing groups should meet for three different purposes. First, they should meet to discuss the assignment. Second, they should meet to edit each other's rough drafts. Finally, they should meet to proofread the final drafts. Daniels and Zemelman propose the weekly schedule shown in Figure 7–8. It incorporates the three functions of the peer editing groups and includes focus lessons on particular elements in writing.

For Your Development

Read the following editing checklist and note the dates (Cunningham and Allington, 1999):

1. Name and date (9/3)
2. Title in center (9/7)
3. Sentences make sense (9/24)
4. Possible misspelled words (10/17)
5. Ending Punctuation . ? ! (11/25)
6. Capitals in right places (1/14)
7. Stays on topic (2/14) (p. 92)

The dates reflect what was being emphasized in mini-lessons taught during a writer's workshop. Also notice that the editing checklist builds on prior knowledge until the children have a good grasp of a skill before a new one is added.

Sharing.   Students should share their writing with a genuine audience. For example, they should mail letters to the appropriate person. They should read poetry and short stories to peers. They should place stories in the library or post them on the bulletin board. They should publish class newspapers and magazines. Although it is not necessary to extend writing to any other activity, students often enjoy using their own writing for choral-reading and reader's theater arrangements, art interpretations, or dramatizations.

Table 7–2   Holistic scoring scale for writing

Point Score	Characteristics
6	Has a thesis
	Concrete details used effectively
	Fluent in words and ideas
	Varied sentence structure
	Satisfactory closing statement
	Generally clear mechanics
5	Has a central idea
	Specific facts, details, or reasons
	Consistent development
	Less insightful, imaginative, concrete, or developed than a 6
	Generally clear mechanics, errors do not interfere with overall effectiveness
4	Has several clear ideas
	Relevant and specific details
	Evidence of fluency, but not of unified development
	May be overly general or trite
	May have simple sentence structure or vocabulary
	Mechanical errors do not affect readability
3	Has at least one idea; few, if any, supporting details
	Less fluent, developed, or detailed than a 4
	Sentences, vocabulary, and thought may be simplistic
	Mechanical errors do not affect readability
2	No thesis
	Has a sense of order, but order may be only that of plot summary
	Fluency and thought are minimal
	Has at least one relevant idea
	May have many mechanical errors but paper is readable
1	No thesis and, of course, no support for thesis
	No sense of organization
	Simplistic or vague language
	May be unreadable due to spelling, handwriting, or other mechanical problems

Source: "Effects on Student Writing of Teacher Training in the National Writing Project Model" by R. J. Pritchard, 1987, *Written Communication,* 4, p. 58. Reprinted with permission.

Students enjoy making permanent collections of their poems and stories. One teacher had each child develop an accordion-pleated poem book. To construct the books, the students folded large sheets of heavy drawing paper in half, connected several sheets with tape, and printed their poems and an accompanying illustration on each page. Other classes made their own books by constructing covers in various appropriate shapes, cutting paper to

Mondays

1. Rough drafts are due for assignment given the previous Friday.

2. Groups meet immediately and begin work. Each paper is read aloud by its author. The other group members ask questions about the content of the paper, which the author records on his rough draft, without actually answering any of them at this time. Both positive comments and constructive suggestions are expected at this time. Students have the entire period for this purpose and are instructed to think over the questions that were asked and make any changes that seem appropriate before coming to class on Tuesday.

Tuesdays

1. "Final" drafts are due.

2. Ten-minute free writing.

3. Groups meet again, this time actually exchanging papers and looking over them silently. Their focus today is on content and grammar/mechanics. No marks are made on another person's paper; instead, group members are to point the problems out and allow the author to decide what he/she wants to do about them.

4. Papers are turned in, signed by the author, and cosigned by the readers. Those who wish to do further rewriting simply sign a list on the teacher's desk and are automatically granted an extension.

Wednesdays

1. Ten-minute free writing.

2. People who have done further rewriting may have their group members go over their new "final" drafts instead of doing the ten-minute free writing on this day.

3. Focus lesson on subject matter, writing process, or grammar item.

Thursdays

1. Ten-minute free writing.

2. Complete the focus lesson.

Fridays

1. Student evaluation (alternating between self-evaluation and group evaluation).

2. Vocabulary due.

3. Students are allowed to work independently, reading their novels, working on the next paragraph, or revising papers. Individual conferences are held at this time. (pp. 167–68)

FIGURE 7–8   Weekly Schedule for Writing Activities

Source: From Harvey Daniels and Steven Zemelman, *A Writing Project: Training Teachers of Composition from Kindergarten to College.* Copyright © 1985 by Heinemann Educational Books. Reprinted with permission.

match the shapes, and binding the cover and pages together. A group of second graders placed Halloween stories inside a jack-o-lantern book, fourth graders wrote city poems and stories inside a book resembling a skyscraper, and third graders placed humorous mythical animal stories and poems inside a book resembling a Dr. Seuss beast.

Many teachers use a study of newspapers as an introduction to creating a class-written newspaper or to introduce editing and proofreading of a child's own writing. Newspapers can motivate almost limitless writing activities and are also useful for developing learning centers.

Collaborative Writing.   Collaborative writing projects frequently include all of the areas of the writing process. These projects may pair older students with younger students or divide same-age students into small groups of about three students each in which the members coauthor a piece of writing. Teachers and researchers who work with collaborative writing groups recommend them as means for increasing positive attitudes toward writing. As you read the following descriptions of two examples of collaborative writing, notice how the writing activities emphasize various phases of the writing process.

In a cross-age collaboration between sixth-grade students and kindergarten students, Leland and Fitzpatrick (1994) taught sixth graders to read effectively to younger students and to encourage their kindergarten partners to talk about the stories and to write their own stories. Meeting for forty-five minutes once a week, the older students read to and discussed the stories with their younger partners. Prior to the reading, the sixth-grade teacher modeled expressive reading and other means of discussing books such as using story mapping with words and pictures. Following several months of activities with literature, the sixth-grade students used story mapping and discussions to help their kindergarten partners plan and write their own stories. Leland and Fitzpatrick state that after the basic story was mapped, the partners drafted their stories. The kindergarten children dictated to the older students who served as recorders, facilitators, and audience. The sixth graders typed the drafts on computers and worked with their partners on revision and editing.

Leland and Fitzpatrick (1994) describe these collaborative sessions: "Each time they met with their kindergarten partners, the sixth graders first read and discussed a library book which they had prepared ahead of time, then reread their coauthored drafts and worked on the revision process together. Teachers conferred with the various teams and encouraged children to ask questions about the sense of the stories they were writing. Editing was primarily the responsibility of the sixth graders, who were assisted during their regular language arts instruction" (p. 298).

Dale (1994) describes an effective collaborative writing activity in which ninth-grade students formed groups of three in order to write essays that supported a specific stand. Prior to this assignment, Dale spent several class periods introducing collaboration by discussing the rationale for coauthoring, modeling collaborative writing with another teacher, and discussing argumentative writing. Dale concludes: "The most effective collaborative writing discourse occurred among students writing in a positive social environment who were engaged with each other, the writing process, and the topic. Coauthors worked with others productively and prompted each other to generate ideas, plan effectively, engage in discussion of ideas, and evaluate their choices at the word, structure, and idea levels" (p. 342).

For Your Plan Book

Lesson Plan

Learning Center Activities Based on Newspapers

Meet the Press

Purpose: To increase reading and writing ability through the use of newspapers.

Grade level: Intermediate upper elementary. Appropriate for individual, small-group, and large-group activity. Suggested limit: 30

General materials: Newspapers, paper, pencil, manila folders, computer or typewriter (optional), picture file. More specific materials are listed for each activity.

Continued

Plan to progress: Give the students a photocopied handout with their assignments, determining level placement (for example, Reporter One). Allot space for "Extra, Extra" activities to meet individual needs. The handout should indicate the activities that the students will complete as they progress through the learning center. Post these general instructions and explain them orally to the students:

Dear Reporter,

I have given you some assignments for our next newspaper. You may do the assignments in any order you wish. When you complete each assignment, check your answers. Then place your finished work in the "Ready for Print" box. When all of the assignments are completed, sign up for an activity in the school newspaper. (The following categories are suggested: Lifestyle, Dennis the Menace, Editorials, Sports, News, Dear Abby, and Wedding.) In order to write your activity, interview a person in your field of interest. Place the article in the "Ready for Print" box. When all of your work is completed, you may begin work on the "Extra, Extra" box.

Good Luck,
The Editor

Instructions: Besides the general instructions, write specific instructions for each activity on its manila envelope.

Evaluation: Provide an answer box or envelope so the students can easily locate the answer keys they need. Keep the students' work in a class file. Have the students indicate by a check mark the activities they have completed. Observe the students' work and initial each student's handout upon approval.

Activities:

Reporter One (low-level)

Dear Abby

Objective: To match the advice column with the correct solution.

Materials: Glue "Dear Abby" advice columns to a manila envelope with the problems separated from the solutions. Number the problems and letter the solutions.

Activity: Have the students match the correct solution with the problem by writing their answers on a sheet of paper.

Evaluation: Answer key.

Capture the Caption

Objective: To match pictures with the correct captions.

Materials: Manila folders, each containing several pictures and captions. Number the pictures and letter the captions.

Activity: Have the students choose one of the manila folders. Have them match pictures with the captions and write their answers on paper.

Evaluation: Answer key.

Headline Scramble

Objective: To match each article with the correct headline and picture.

Materials: Manila folders, each containing several articles with matching headlines and pictures if possible. Place the articles separately from the headlines in the manila folders. Number the articles and letter the captions.

Activity: Have each student choose one of the folders, place the words in a line, and then classify each picture under the appropriate word.

Evaluation: Student self-check.

Feeling, Feelings

Objective: In one word, to describe how each person feels.

Materials: A manila folder with several pieces of construction paper. Each piece of construction paper has a picture of a person glued to it. Number each picture.

Activity: Have each student choose three of the sheets of construction paper with the pictures. In one word, each student must describe how each person feels. The students must use a different word for each person.

Evaluation: Pupil self-check.

Getting the Meaning

Objective: To match the article with the main idea.

Materials: A manila folder with numerous low-level, high-interest articles. Each article should contain strips of paper with three possible main ideas.

Activity: Have the students choose four articles from the manila folder. Have them match the strip of paper that contains the main idea with the appropriate article.

Evaluation: Answer key.

Sequencing Cartoons

Objective: To sequence cartoon frames.

Materials: Five multiframed cartoons, each backed with different-colored construction paper. Cut these into separate frames, and number them in the correct order on the back.

Activity: Have the students group the cartoon frames according to color and then sequence them.

Evaluation: The students will check their answers by turning them over. The correct order is indicated by the numbers on the back.

Reporter Two

Headlines

Objective: To write an article to go with a specific headline.

Materials: Headlines placed in a manila folder.

Activity: Have each student choose one headline from the manila folder and then write an article in journalistic form.

Evaluation: Rating scale (see Figure 7–A).

Continued

Rating Scale

Student's name: _____

	Low				High	
1. Originality	1	2	3	4	5	NA*
2. Creativity	1	2	3	4	5	NA
3. Expressive	1	2	3	4	5	NA
4. Form or Style (Newspaper)	1	2	3	4	5	NA

    a. Who _____
    b. What _____
    c. When _____
    d. Where _____
    e. Why _____

5. Sentence structure	1	2	3	4	5	NA
6. Paragraph structure	1	2	3	4	5	NA
7. Consistency in theme	1	2	3	4	5	NA
8. Grammatical structure	1	2	3	4	5	NA

    a. Spelling
    b. Punctuation
    c. Capitalization

Notes

_____

_____

NA means nonapplicable for this assignment.

FIGURE 7–A Rating Scale

Main Ideas

Objective: To write out the main idea of an article students have read.

Materials: Articles without the headlines. Manila folders.

Activity: Have the students read the articles and write out the main idea of each.

Evaluation: Rating scale.

Article Artistry

Objective: To write an article and a caption for a photograph.

Materials: A picture file.

Activity: Have the students choose a picture from the picture file and then write an article for the picture and a caption for the article.

Evaluation: Rating scale.

Catchy Cartoons

Objective: To write a caption for each of several pictures.

Materials: A picture file.

Activity: Have the students choose several pictures from the picture file and then write one caption for each of the pictures.

Evaluation: Rating scale.

Don't Be Conned

Objective: To identify propaganda techniques contained in advertisements.

Materials: Several advertisements illustrating propaganda techniques.

Activity: Have the students read the advertisements and identify in writing the propaganda techniques used.

Evaluation: Answer key.

Cartoon Talk

Objective: To fill in cartoon balloons with appropriate words.

Materials: Several cartoons, each mounted on construction paper with their ballooned message opaqued out.

Activity: Have the students fill in the cartoon balloons with appropriate dialogue.

Evaluation: Rating scale.

Article Sequencing

Objective: To sequence an article.

Materials: Several articles cut into sections, each mounted on different-colored construction paper. Cut these into separate pieces, and number them in the correct order on the back.

Activity: Have the students group article pieces according to color and then sequence them.

Evaluation: Self-checked; answers on the back.

Advice Editor

Objective: To write advice to a given problem.

Materials: A variety of advice columns mounted on tagboard.

Activity: Have each student choose one problem and write an original solution.

Evaluation: Rating scale.

Extra, Extra

Writing Cartoons

Objective: After drawing a cartoon, to write a script to accompany it.

Materials: Blank cartoon frames, colored pencils.

Activity: Have each student create a cartoon sequence using his or her favorite cartoon character. The students should write scripts to go along with their drawings.

Evaluation: Rating scale.

Continued

Junior Jumble

Objective: To unscramble words.

Materials: Several junior jumbles mounted on poster board.

Activity: Have the students choose three junior jumbles, unscramble the words, and solve the puzzle.

Evaluation: Answer key.

TV Quiz

Objective: Using the TV listings, to answer several questions.

Materials: TV listings, typed questions mounted on tagboard.

Activity: Have the students read the questions on the tagboard and skim the magazine to answer them.

Evaluation: Answer key.

Brain Twisters

Objective: To solve the problem in the brain twister.

Materials: Several brain twisters mounted on construction paper.

Activity: Have the students read the brain twisters and then solve each problem.

Evaluation: Self-checked; answers on the back.

Advertising

Objective: To write an original advertisement using some propaganda technique.

Materials: Various pictures of products mounted on tagboard.

Activity: Have the students choose at least one of the pictures and write an advertisement for it using one of the propaganda techniques.

Evaluation: Rating scale.

Fact or Opinion Game

Objective: To classify headlines into fact or opinion.

Materials: Game board made from construction paper. On it, a definition of fact and a definition of opinion. Under each definition, staple a pocket to the construction paper. Provide twenty headlines, some of which are facts, the remainder of which are opinions.

Activity: Have each student choose a headline and read it. Then have the student decide whether it is a fact or an opinion and place the headline into the correct pocket on the game board.

Evaluation: Self-checked; answers on the back.

Fun Facts for Browsing

Objective: To read fun facts for enjoyment.

Materials: An envelope that contains fun facts items, such as facts from Ripley's *Believe It or Not,* Wrigley's "Fun Fact," and *Guinness Book of World Records* excerpts.

Activity: This activity is merely for the enjoyment of reading. Let the students read these materials during free time.

Evaluation: None

Used with permission of Nancy Mangano, Debra Penkert, and Jacqueline Thurston, graduate students at Texas A&M University.

Assessment

Studies that analyze the composing process of skilled and unskilled writers provide important insights for language arts teachers. In addition, the studies identify characteristics of writers who might benefit from activities stressing the writing process.

Glatthorn (1982) synthesized the results from several studies and reached several conclusions about the writing processes of skilled and unskilled writers. The following observable characteristics describe the actions of skilled and unskilled writers during each of Glatthorn's four stages of the writing process:

1. *Exploring*—the beginning stage, in which writers think about a topic, discover what they know, collect information, consider audience, and reflect about approaches.

   Skilled Writers: Take time to explore the topic and use many strategies.
   Unskilled Writers: Do little exploring and do not consider it important or useful.

2. *Planning*—the stage in which writers make preliminary choices about content, organization, and proportion.

   Skilled Writers: Take time to plan and use a variety of techniques, such as listing, sketching, and diagramming.
   Unskilled Writers: Do little planning either before writing or while writing.

3. *Drafting*—the psychomotor process by which writers choose the words and craft the sentences.

   Skilled Writers: Write in ways that are less like speech and show sensitivity to the reader. Usually, they spend more time drafting than do unskilled writers.
   Unskilled Writers: Write in ways that imitate speech, show little concern for readers, and seem preoccupied with spelling and punctuation.

4. *Revising*—the stage in which writers evaluate what they wrote and make changes in the form and content.

   Skilled Writers: Either revise very little or revise extensively. When they make extensive revisions, they examine larger issues, such as content and reader appeal.
   Unskilled Writers: Either revise very little or revise only at the word level. They see revising as error hunting and copying over in ink.

Students who exhibit the characteristics of unskilled writers might benefit from a processing approach to composition. In addition, Myers and Gray (1983) state that writers who lack fluency and have difficulty generating or expanding ideas should engage in processing activities. One of the most effective ways to assess growth is accumulation of writing samples. You may keep each child's examples in a folder, compiled over long periods of time, so that both you and the child can look at and evaluate changes in the writing. If changes are not occurring, you should suspect that the instruction is probably not appropriate for that particular child. Phelps (Gleason and Mano, 1986), an advocate of teaching the writing process, emphasizes that writing instructors should analyze drafts in terms of potential for writing development, not in terms of errors. Such an analysis looks for clues to changes going on within the writing and considers ways to help students proceed toward the next step in writing development.

Effective teachers analyze writing in terms of its strengths and weaknesses rather than merely circle errors.

Effective evaluation considers the purpose for each writing activity. For example, if the objective of a poetry-writing lesson is for children to become aware of their uniqueness through self-expression, the instruction is effective to the degree that children write their own thoughts and emotions in poetic form. You should evaluate poetic originality by comparing a child's poetry with the previous poetry for that child, not some standard for all children.

To analyze the influence of both audience and purpose, Goodman (1985) recommends that teachers keep copies of children's letters written to different audiences for different purposes. You should analyze the letters according to the following considerations: the appropriateness of the language for the specific purpose, the degree to which children change their language and style to meet the needs of the specific audience, the increase in conventional spellings, the changes in grammatical complexity of the sentences, and the concern for legibility.

In an evaluation of teaching composition in open classes in England, Williams (1978) concluded that merely dating the children's materials allows them to see their own improvement over a period of time. As she put it, "the teacher could not have developed a more motivating feedback system than this chronological record of the student's composition efforts. Handwriting and quantity and quality of work had all improved noticeably" (p. 3). A writing folder should include samples of many types of writing. You may compile a checklist of some of the areas to observe for written composition. Such a checklist would look something like Figure 7–9.

For Your Development

Collect several written compositions from the same child and evaluate the writing using the Holistic Scoring Scale (Table 7–2) and the checklist for informal evaluation of writing (Figure 7–9). Tabulate your findings.

Ideas:	Yes	Sometimes	No
1. Sentences express his or her ideas.	_____	_____	_____
2. Ideas flow from one sentence to another.	_____	_____	_____
Purpose and Audience:			
3. Understands the purpose for an audience when writing.	_____	_____	_____
4. Age, knowledge, and interest of audience influence the composition.	_____	_____	_____
5. Purpose of the composition influences the writing.	_____	_____	_____
Organizing Ideas—Paragraphs:			
6. Groups and classifies related ideas.	_____	_____	_____
7. Understands need for and chooses main idea that unifies a paragraph.	_____	_____	_____
8. Supports main ideas with necessary facts and details.	_____	_____	_____
9. Puts main idea and supporting details into logical order.	_____	_____	_____
Organizing Ideas—Longer Compositions:			
10. Narrows subject to one that can be realistically covered.	_____	_____	_____
11. Gathers ideas and information before trying to write composition.	_____	_____	_____
12. Understands and develops important questions on the topic.	_____	_____	_____
13. Organizes important questions and supporting data into logical sequence.	_____	_____	_____
14. Demonstrates progress in ability to write composition with interesting introduction, main ideas, supporting details, and logical conclusion.	_____	_____	_____
Rewriting:			
15. Reads orally while developing composition and makes changes to improve clarity of writing.	_____	_____	_____
16. Responds to teacher questions and makes appropriate writing changes.	_____	_____	_____
17. Reads composition silently while developing it and makes changes.	_____	_____	_____
Vocabulary:			
18. Has extensive writing vocabulary.	_____	_____	_____
19. Uses context clues to develop new vocabulary understanding.	_____	_____	_____
20. Uses precise vocabulary in factual writing.	_____	_____	_____
21. Uses few slang expressions in factual writing.	_____	_____	_____
22. Does not rely on trite expressions.	_____	_____	_____

FIGURE 7–9 Checklist for Informal Evaluation of Writing

Table 7–3   Mainstreaming and writing for children with learning disabilities

Characteristics of Children with Learning Disabilities	Teaching Techniques for Language Arts Instruction
1. Students tend to be passive learners and avoid participation for fear of failure (Wong, 1994). There may be motivational problems caused by repeated failure (MacArthur et al., 1993). They may be inattentive and easily distracted (Harris, Graham, Reid, McElroy, & Hamby, 1994).	1. Involve students in active learning by modeling for them how to think systematically during strategy learning (Wong, 1994). Encourage students to self-monitor their performance (Harris et al., 1994). Use checklists to guide students (Ysseldyke & Algozzine, 1995). Teach narrative writing and emphasize ideas that show students that writing can be enjoyable (Rueda, 1990). Use visual imagery (Polloway & Patton, 1997).
2. Students may have difficulty transferring strategies to new situations (Wong, 1994).	2. Encourage them to think about how they could use the strategy in new situations such as other content areas (Wong, 1994). Show how graphic organizers can be used in various content areas (Ellis, 1994).
3. May have difficulty with higher level cognitive processes such as setting goals, generating appropriate content, organizing their writing, and evaluating and revising their text (MacArthur et al., 1993).	3. Use mnemonic aids such as C = SPACE: C = characters, S = setting, P = problem or purpose, A = action, C = conclusion, and E = emotion to help them generate content, make notes, and focus on details (MacArthur et al., 1993). Use story maps to plan elements of their stories; provide guided practice until students are proficient in using the maps (Gleason, 1995; Harniss, Hollenbeck, Crawford, & Carnine, 1994; Lewis & Doorlag, 1995 Marchisan & Alber, 2001). Provide story prompts and story grammar cueing systems (Graves, Montague, & Wong, 1990).
4. Students may have difficulty with the mechanics of writing (Graves, Semmel, & Gerber, 1994). They may work slowly and have difficulty composing on paper (Lewis & Doorlag, 1995).	4. Use computers and word processing tools (Ysseldyke & Algozzine, 1995). Have students compose on a tape recorder and then transcribe what they have dictated (Lewis & Doorlag, 1995). For students who work slowly, reduce the length of the written task or extend the time limits (Lewis & Doorlag, 1995).

Mainstreaming

Studies of children with learning disabilities frequently show that these students may have difficulty with the physical demands and conventions of writing; the fluent production of sentences; and the higher level cognitive processes of setting goals, generating appropriate content, organizing writing, and evaluating and revising text. MacArthur, Graham, and Schwartz (1993) found that an approach to writing in which students work at meaningful tasks, receive responses to their writing from peers and teacher, and publish their work for real audiences is effective. In addition, the classroom structure needs to support extended cycles of planning, drafting, and revision. Within this cycle teachers support the development of writing strategies through conferencing and explicit instruction in strategies for planning and revising. They emphasize that writing instruction needs to follow the same general format including asking individual students about their plans for writing, mini-lessons, writing time, and group sharing.

Marchisan and Alber (2001) explore strategies that may be used to help students with writing difficulties. They conclude: "Resistant writers can be taught to write using the writing process approach paired with the tools of technology, direct instruction, and a committed, well-trained teacher" (p. 161). Some of the strategies they find helpful include the following suggestions for each part of the writing process:

- *Prewriting stage:* Motivate students to think about topics that are of special interest to them; use visual imagery to help them visualize the details associated with a place or an experience; model prewriting procedures such as story webs and self-questioning strategies.
- *Writing stage:* Provide word banks to help with vocabulary; cowrite a story with them; help them use word processing programs to write; gradually reduce assistance.
- *Revision stage:* Provide direct instruction for writing errors through mini-lessons; provide a self-evaluation checklist; use conferencing; provide guidance for revising a draft; teach students to use the computer for editing; keep writing portfolios.
- *Publishing and sharing stage:* Display compositions in the room or in hallways, have an author's chair in which students can read their works; create class newsletters or newspapers.

Table 7–3 presents the characteristics of and effective techniques for developing writing with students who have learning disabilities.

SUMMARY

Current research in written composition analyzes approaches to teaching written composition. Studies of the writing process and corresponding models examine the tasks of writers as they identify the topic for a writing project, generate ideas, plan and organize their writing, write rough drafts, review and evaluate their writing, and revise their writing.

You can develop composition skills through the writing process by emphasizing activities that help students during each phase. During the prewriting phase, activities can motivate students to write, generate ideas, and focus their attention on desired subjects or objectives. Prewriting activities include drawing, semantic mapping, outlining and listing and categorizing.

Activities designed to improve progress during the writing phase include deciding on audience and purpose, deciding about form, deciding about organizational pattern, deciding about linguistic style, and writing the first draft. After-writing activities include revising, teacher–student conferencing, peer editing, and sharing writing with an audience.

ADDITIONAL WRITING PROCESS ACTIVITIES

1. Observe an elementary student. Identify the activities of the student in approaching and completing a writing task.

2. Interview an elementary, a middle-school, and a high-school language arts or English teacher. Ask how often the students should write, the purpose for writing, and the appropriate audience for writing. Share your findings in your language arts class. How do these results compare with both the American and the British studies discussed in this chapter?

3. Develop a file of ideas and resources to use during the prewriting stage of the writing process.

4. Develop a modeling activity appropriate for the prewriting or writing stage. Share your activity with your language arts class.

5. Lead a prewriting activity in which you help a group of children or an individual child develop a semantic map or web for a writing assignment.

6. Collect examples of various forms of writing, such as diaries, editorials, and short stories, that are appropriate for writing projects. List the characteristics of each form and identify writing assignments in which the forms would be appropriate.

7. If possible, visit a classroom during a teacher–student conference or during peer editing groups. What is the focus of the activity? How do teachers or peers respond to papers? How do students respond when they present or discuss their writings? What questions do they ask? Can you identify where the students are in the writing process? What are the major writing problems experienced by the students? How are the students receiving help with those writing problems?

8. Develop a file of different ideas for sharing writing with an audience. Your file might include directions for making books, developing writing bulletin boards, and making oral presentations that emphasize original work.

9. Develop a collection of articles written by professional authors. What recommendations do they make that could help student or teacher authors?

BIBLIOGRAPHY

Ammon, Paul. "Cognitive Development and Early Childhood Education: Piagetian and Neo-Piagetian Theories." In *Psychological Processes in Early Education,* edited by H. L. Hom and P. A. Robinson. New York: Academic Press, 1977.

Applebee, Arthur N. "Writing and Reasoning." *Review of Educational Research* 54 (Winter 1984): 577–96.

Atwell, Nancy. "Writing and Reading from the Inside Out." In *Literacy in Process: The Heinemann Reader,* edited by B. Power and R. Hubbard. Portsmouth, N.H.: Heinemann, 1991, pp. 227–43.

Beatty, Patricia. "Writing the Historical Novel for Young Readers." In *The Writer's Handbook,* edited by Sylvia K. Burack. Boston: The Writer, Inc., 1990, pp. 406–10.

Blohm, P. J.; and Benton, S. C. "Effect of Prewriting Interventions on Production of Elaboration in Informative Writing." *Journal of Research and Development in Education* 24 (1991): 28–32.

Bradley, Virginia N. "Improving Students' Writing with Microcomputers." *Language Arts* 59 (October 1982): 732–43.

Britton, James; Burgess, Tony; Martin, Nancy; McLeod, Alex; and Rosen, Harold. *The Development of Writing Abilities (11–18).* Schools Council Research Studies. London: Macmillan, 1979.

Bruce, Bertram; Michaels, Sarah; and Watson-Gegeo, Karen. "How Computers Can Change the Writing Process." *Language Arts* 62 (February 1985): 143–49.

Bruner, Jerome; Goodnow, Jacqueline; and Austin, G. A. *A Study of Thinking.* New York: John Wiley & Sons, 1956.

Bunting, Eve. "Think Picture Book." In *The Writer's Handbook,* edited by Sylvia K. Burack. Boston: The Writer, Inc., 1990, pp. 411–15.

Carey, L. *Differences in Writers' Initial Task Representation.* 1989. Technical Report No. 35. Center for the Study of Writing. ERIC Document Reproduction Service No. ED 310 403.

Cunningham, Patricia M.; and Allington, Richard L. *Classrooms That Work: They Can All Read and Write,* 2nd ed. New York: Longman, 1999.

Dale, Helen. "Collaborative Writing Interactions in One Ninth-Grade Classroom." *Journal of Educational Research* 87 (July/August 1994): 334–44.

Daniels, Harvey; and Zemelman, Steven. *A Writing Project: Training Teachers of Composition from Kindergarten to College.* Portsmouth, N.H.: Heinemann, 1985.

Dauite, Colette. "Physical and Cognitive Factors in Revising: Insights from Studies with Computers." *Research in the Teaching of English* 20 (May 1986): 141–59.

Dickinson, David K. "Cooperation, Collaboration, and a Computer: Integrating a Computer into a First-Second Grade Writing Program." *Research in the Teaching of English* 20 (December 1986): 357–78.

Dyson, Anne Haas; and Freedman, Sarah Warshauer. "Writing." In *Handbook of Research on Teaching the English Language Arts,* edited by James Flood, Diane Lapp James R. Squire, and Julie M. Jensen. New York: Macmillan, 2003.

Ellis, Edwin. "Integrating Writing Strategy Instruction with Content-Area Instruction: Part 1—Orienting Students to Organizational Devices." *Intervention in School and Clinic* 29 (January 1994): 169–79.

Ernst, Karen. "Writing Pictures, Painting Words: Writing in an Artists' Workshop." *Language Arts* 71 (January 1994): 44–52.

Fitzgerald, J.; and Stamm, C. "Effects of Group Conferences on First Graders' Revision in Writing." *Written Communication* 7 (1990): 96–135.

Flower, Linda; and Hayes, John. "The Dynamics of Composing: Making Plans and Juggling Constraints." In *Cognitive Processes in Writing,* edited by Lee W. Gregg and Erwin R. Steinberg. Hillsdale, N.J.: Lawrence Erlbaum Associates, 1978.

Frager, Alan M. "Teaching, Writing, and Identity." *Language Arts* 71 (April 1994): 274–78.

Gagné, Robert. *The Conditions of Learning,* 2nd ed. New York: Holt, Rinehart & Winston, 1970.

Gibbs, E. B. "Peer Response Groups: Implications for Writing Development in a Fifth-Grade Classroom." 1990. *Dissertation Abstracts International* 51: 05A. (University Microfilms No. 90-11, 331)

Giblin, James Cross. "Writing Nonfiction Books for Young Readers." In *The Writer's Handbook,* edited by Sylvia K. Burack. Boston: The Writer, Inc., 1990, pp. 395–400.

Glatthorn, Allan A. "Demystifying the Teaching of Writing." *Language Arts* 59 (October 1982): 722–25.

Gleason, Barbara; and Mano, Sandra. "Issues in Development: An Interview with Wetherbee Phelps." *The Writing Instructor* 5 (Winter 1986): 45–50.

Gleason, Mary. "Using Direct Instruction to Integrate Reading and Writing for Students with Learning Disabilities." *Reading & Writing Quarterly: Overcoming Learning Difficulties* 11 (1995): 91–108.

Gomez, Mary Louise. "Using Microcomputers in the Language Arts." In *Language Arts Instruction and the Beginning Teacher*, edited by Carl Personke and Dale Johnson. Upper Saddle River, N.J.: Prentice Hall, 1987.

Goodman, Yetta. "Kidwatching: Observing Children in the Classroom." In *Observing the Language Learner*, edited by Angela Jaggar and M. Trika Smith-Burke. Urbana, Ill.: National Council of Teachers of English, 1985, pp. 9–18.

Graves, Anne; Montague, M.; and Wong, Y. "The Effects of Procedural Facilitation on Story Composition of Learning Disabled Students." *Learning Disabilities Research* 5 (1990): 88–93.

———; Semmel, Melvyn; and Gerber, Michael. "The Effects of Story Prompts on the Narrative Production of Students with and without Learning Disabilities." *Learning Disability Quarterly* 17 (Spring 1994): 154–64.

Graves, Donald. *A Case Study Observing the Development of Primary Children's Composing, Spelling, and Motor Behaviors during the Writing Process*. Final Report, NIE Grant No. G-78-0174. Durham, N.H.: University of New Hampshire, 1981. ED 218 653.

———. *Writing: Teachers and Children at Work*. Exeter, N.H.: Heinemann, 1983.

Haas, C. "Composing in Technological Contexts: A Study of Note-Making." *Written Communication* 7 (1990): 512–47.

Harniss, Mark; Hollenbeck, Keith; Crawford, Donald; and Carnine, Douglas. "Content Organization and Instructional Design Issues in the Development of History Texts." *Learning Disability Quarterly* 17 (Summer 1994): 235–48.

Harris, Karen; Graham, Steve; Reid, Robert; McElroy, Karen; and Hamby, Robin Stern. "Self-Monitoring of Performance: Replication and Cross-Task Comparison Studies." *Learning Disability Quarterly* 17 (Spring 1994): 121–39.

Harris, Muriel. *Teaching One-to-One: The Writing Conference*. Urbana, Ill.: National Council of Teachers of English, 1986.

Hayes, John; and Flower, Linda. "Writing and Problem Solving." *Visible Language* 14 (1980): 388–90.

Hill, Julianne. "Walter Cronkite." *Writer's Digest* 81 (September 2001): 42–43.

Hillocks, George. *Research on Written Composition: New Directions for Teaching*. Urbana, Ill.: National Conference on Research in English, 1986.

Jensen, Julia M. "What Do We Know About the Writing of Elementary School Children?" *Language Arts* 70 (April 1993): 290–94.

Karl, Jean E. *How to Write and Sell Children's Picture Books*. Cincinnati: Writer's Digest, 1994.

Kleiman, Glenn; and Humphrey, Mary. "Word Processing in the Classroom." *Compute* 22 (March 1982): 96–99.

Kulberg, Janet. "What School Psychologists Need to Know About Writing Disabilities." *School Psychology Review* 22 (1993): 682–84.

Lapp, Diane; and Flood, James. "Are There 'Real' Writers Living in Your Classroom? Implementing a Writer-Centered Classroom." *The Reading Teacher* 48 (November 1993): 254–58.

Leland, Christine; and Fitzpatrick, Ruth. "Cross-Age Interaction Builds Enthusiasm for Reading and Writing." *The Reading Teacher* 47 (January 1994): 292–301.

Lewis, Rena; and Doorlag, Donald. *Teaching Special Students in the Mainstream*, 4th ed. Upper Saddle River, N.J.: Merrill/Prentice Hall, 1995.

MacArthur, Charles; Graham, Steve; and Schwartz, Shirley. "Integrating Strategy Instruction and Word Processing into a Process Approach to Writing Instruction." *School Psychology Review* 22 (1993): 671–81.

Marchisan, M.; and Alber, S. R. "The Write Way: Tips for Teaching the Writing Process to Resistant Writers." *Intervention in School and Clinic* 36.3 (2001): 154–162.

Murray, Donald. "The Listening Eye: Reflections on the Writing Conference." *College English* 41 (1979).

———. "The Maker's Eye: Revising Your Own Manuscripts." In *The Writer's Handbook,* edited by Sylvia K. Burack. Boston: The Writer, Inc., 1990, pp. 24–28.

Myers, Miles; and Gray, James. *Theory and Practice in the Teaching of Composition: Processing, Distancing, and Modeling.* Urbana, Ill.: National Council of Teachers of English, 1983.

Nelson, R. R. "The Revision Processes of Male Tenth Graders: Qualitative Differences in Revision Activities in Expository Modes." 1990. *Dissertation Abstracts International* 51, 90–08, 005.

Norton, Donna E.; and Sadoski, Mark. "Summer Writing Institute." Texas A&M University, 1992–1996.

Polloway, E. A.; and Patton, J. R. *Strategies for Teaching Learners with Special Needs,* 6th ed. Upper Saddle River, N.J.: Merrill/Prentice Hall, 1997.

Pritchard, Ruie Jane. "Effects on Student Writing of Teacher Training in the National Writing Project Model." *Written Communication* 4 (January 1987): 51–67.

Proett, Jackie; and Gill, Kent. *The Writing Process in Action: A Handbook for Teachers.* Urbana, Ill.: National Council of Teachers of English, 1986.

Rand, Ayn. *The Art of Nonfiction: A Guide for Writers and Readers,* edited by Robert Mayhew. New York: Putnam, 2001.

Rubenstein, R.; and Rollins, A. *Demonstration of the Use of Computer Assisted Instruction with Handicapped Children: Final Report.* Cambridge, Mass.: Bolt Beranek & Newman, 1978.

Rueda, R. "Assisted Performance in Writing Instruction with Learning Disabled Students." In *Vygotsky and Education: Instructional Implications and Applications of Sociohistorical Psychology,* edited by L. Moll. Cambridge, Mass.: Cambridge University Press, 1990, pp. 403–26.

Sadoski, Mark; Wilson, Victor; and Norton, Donna. "Effective Approaches in Written Composition." Paper presented at the National Reading Conference, San Diego, December 1994.

Sadoski, Mark; Wilson, Victor L.; and Norton, Donna E. "The Relative Contributions of Research-Based Composition Activities to Writing Improvement in Lower and Middle Grades." *Research in the Teaching of English* 31 (February 1997): 120–50.

Selfe, Cynthia. *Computer-Assisted Instruction in Composition: Create Your Own.* Urbana, Ill.: National Council of Teachers of English, 1986.

Simon, Herbert A. *The Sciences of the Artificial,* 2nd ed. Cambridge, Mass.: The MIT Press, 1981.

Smoot, W. Scott. "An Experiment in Teaching Grammar in Context." *Voices from the Middle* 8 (March 2001): 34–42.

Spaulding, C. "The Effects of Ownership Opportunities and Instructional Support on High School Students' Writing Task Engagement." *Research in the Teaching of English* 23 (1989): 139–62.

Suhor, Charles. "Thinking Visually about Writing: Three Models for Teaching Composition, K–12," in *Speaking and Writing, K–12*, edited by Christopher Thaiss and Charles Suhor. Urbana, Ill.: National Council of Teachers of English, 1984, pp. 74–103.

Tompkins, Gail; and Hoskisson, Kenneth. *Language Arts: Content and Teaching Strategies*, 2nd ed. Upper Saddle River, N.J.: Merrill/Prentice Hall, 1991.

Wallace, D.; and Hayes, J. R. "Redefining Revision for Freshmen." *Research in the Teaching of English* 25 (1991): 54–66.

Weaver, Constance. *Teaching Grammar in Context*. Portsmouth, N.H.: Boynton/Cook, 1996.

Weaver, Constance; McNally, Carol; and Moerman, Sharon. "To Grammar or Not to Grammar: That Is Not the Question!" *Voices from the Middle* 8 (March 2001): 17–33.

Williams, Laura E. "Methods of Teaching Composition in Open Classes—England, Canada, and the United States." *Innovator* 9 (January 1978): 1–3.

Wong, Bernice. "Instructional Parameters Promoting Transfer of Learning Strategies in Students with Learning Disabilities." *Learning Disability Quarterly* 17 (Spring 1994): 110–20.

Wray, David. "What Do Children Think About Writing?" *Educational Review* 45 (February 1993): 67–77.

Wresch, William, ed. *The Computer in Composition Instruction: A Writer's Tool*. Urbana, Ill.: National Council of Teachers of English, 1984.

Ysseldyke, James; and Algozzine, Bob. *Special Education: A Practical Approach for Teachers*, 3rd ed. Boston: Houghton Mifflin, 1995.

CHILDREN'S LITERATURE REFERENCES

Blumberg, Rhoda. *The Incredible Journey of Lewis and Clark*. New York: Lothrop, Lee & Shepard, 1987.

Bodecker, N. M. *A Person from Britain Whose Head Was the Shape of a Mitten and Other Limericks*. London: Dent, 1980.

Bunting, Eve. *Ghost's Hour, Spook's Hour*. Illustrated by Donald Carrick. New York: Clarion, 1987.

Bunting, Eve. *I Am the Mummy Heb-Nefert*. Illustrated by David Christiana. San Diego: Harcourt, 1997.

———. *Smoky Night*. Illustrated by David Diaz. San Diego: Harcourt Brace Jovanovich, 1994.

Carle, Eric. *The Very Clumsy Click Beetle*. New York: Philomel, 1999.

Cushman, Karen. *Catherine, Called Birdy*. New York: Clarion, 1994.

Fox, Paula. *One-Eyed Cat*. New York: Bradbury, 1984.

Freedman, Russell. *Franklin Delano Roosevelt*. New York: Clarion, 1990.

Garfield, Leon, retold by. *Shakespeare Stories II*. Illustrated by Michael Foreman. Boston: Houghton Mifflin, 1995.

Giblin, James Cross. *The Riddle of the Rosetta Stone: Key to Ancient Egypt*. New York: HarperCollins, 1990.

Gilliland, Judith Heide. *Steamboat! The Story of Captain Blanche Leathers.* Illustrated by Holly Meade. New York: Dorling Kindersley, 2000.

Godkin, Celia. *What About Ladybugs?* San Francisco: Sierra Club, 1995.

Hudson, Jan. *Sweetgrass.* New York: Philomel, 1989.

Lauber, Patricia. *The News about Dinosaurs.* New York: Bradbury, 1988.

Lear, Edward. *Nonsense Omnibus.* New York: Warne, 1943 (from earlier editions dating from 1846).

Leiner, Katherine. *First Children: Growing Up in the White House.* Illustrated by Katie Keller. New York: Tambourine, 1996.

Lester, Julius. *Othello.* New York: Scholastic, 1995.

McCaughrean, Geraldine, retold by. *Stories from Shakespeare.* Illustrated by Anthony Maitland. New York: McElderry, 1995.

McCord, David. *One at a Time: Collected Poems for the Young.* Boston: Little, Brown, 1977.

Pringle, Laurence. *Global Warming: Assessing the Greenhouse Threat.* New York: Little, Brown, 1990.

Ross, Stewart. *Shakespeare and Macbeth: The Story Behind the Play.* Illustrated by Tony Karpinski. New York: Viking, 1994.

Shakespeare, William. *The Tempest.* Retold by Bruce Coville. Illustrated by Ruth Sanderson. New York: Doubleday, 1994.

Simon, Seymour. *New Questions and Answers about Dinosaurs.* Illustrated by Jennifer Dewey. New York: Morrow, 1990.

Snedden, Robert. *What Is a Reptile?* Photographs by Oxford Scientific Films. San Francisco: Sierra Club, 1994.

Sperry, Armstrong. *Call It Courage.* New York: Macmillan, 1940.

Vogel, Carole G.; and Goldner, Kathryn A. *The Great Yellowstone Fire.* Boston: Sierra Club and Little, Brown, 1990.

Wilcox, Charlotte. *Trash!* Photographs by Jerry Bushey. Minneapolis: Carolrhoda, 1988.

Composition: Expressive, Imaginative, and Expository Writing

After completing this chapter on expressive, imaginative, and expository writing, you will be able to:

1. Define terms related to expressive, imaginative, and expository writing.
2. Identify and develop writing approaches that encourage expressive writing.
3. Identify and develop writing approaches that encourage imaginative writing.
4. Describe the importance of the environment for developing creative writers.
5. Describe and develop writing approaches that improve ability to create plots, settings, and characters.
6. Describe how creative writing is enhanced through an understanding of symbolism.
7. Identify writing approaches to encourage poetic expression.
8. Describe writing approaches that develop and improve expository writing.
9. Develop an authentication project.

*T*his chapter emphasizes expressive, imaginative, and expository writing. In the expressive function, writers, especially young children, write in the same way they speak. In the imaginative function, writers use language as an art medium to simultaneously inform and entertain. In the expository function, writers inform, record, report, and explain. Yet, there are no absolute divisions between expressive, imaginative, and expository writing. As you approach this chapter, remember that the ideas for stimulating writing are more important than the divisions.

Expressive Writing

Expressive writing is very close to speech and, consequently, very close to the writer. It is relaxed and intimate. It reveals the writer and verbalizes his or her consciousness. It is also the mode in which, generally speaking, we frame the tentative first drafts of new ideas.

Expressive writing, with its close relationship to speech, is the most accessible form of writing for young children. Children come to school with knowledge of speech and are used to speaking to known audiences on intimate terms. In the early stages, writing should be in the form of expressive speech. From this starting point, children can proceed into the imaginative and expository forms.

Expressive writing is frequently characterized as thinking aloud on paper. Expressive writing activities encourage writers to explore their reactions and to express their moods, feelings, and opinions. The form for this personal expression may be a diary, journal, or letter written to a friend. Expressive writing frequently encourages children to write personal narratives about their own lives. Shared beyond oneself, the writing is addressed to a known audience, or at least to an audience that shares the values, opinions, and interests of the writer. On the adult level, such writing may take the form of gossip columns or special-interest articles.

Journals and Diaries

Journal writing is recommended at all levels of education. Even adult writers keep journals in which they write or draw. When Maurice Sendak was a boy, he drew pictures of other students playing. Later, he used these pictures to get ideas for his books.

Watson (1987) describes a kindergarten journal activity in which teachers first prepare journals for each student by folding eight sheets of 12- by 18-inch paper in half, adding a cover of heavier paper, and stapling the pages so that they lie flat when the journal is opened. You may introduce the journal to students by explaining to them that they will be keeping a journal in which they will write stories, personal anecdotes, or summaries of and reactions to various school activities. They will be using inventive spellings or dictating the entries to you or an aide. Volunteers will "publish" their entries by reading them aloud to the class. The students will be writing in a different journal during each month of the year. These journals will remain in school until the end of the year, at which time the students may take them home. However, the journals will be available to the students and may be used for parent–teacher conferences. You may also use them to extend the writing process by asking students to select short entries to expand and refine. Kept on a monthly basis, the journals provide a means of assessing individual growth.

Teachers use journal writing to encourage students to express ideas and to react in personal ways. For example, Armstrong (1990) found that journals show how students think about literature and composition. Some teachers have students write about topics of their choosing during short daily writing periods. For example, Bromley (1985) describes a technique called sustained spontaneous writing (SSW), in which students write for five to fifteen minutes on subjects of their choice. This writing, in the form of a personal journal or diary, is dated, but it is not shared with anyone unless the student volunteers to share it. Bromley recommends dating so that students can review their entries from different time periods.

Journal writing may be more structured and encourages students to think about what they already know or feel about a subject. Ideas for journal writing may include listing pleasant smells or sights, describing wishes, identifying favorite colors or music and explaining

Journals can be used to begin and extend the writing process.

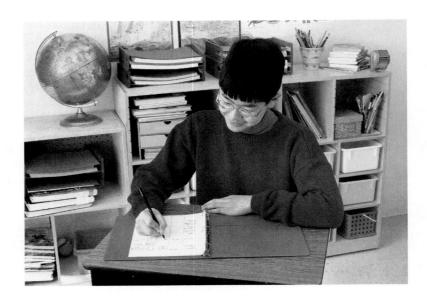

why they are favorites, listing memorable characters from books and explaining why they are memorable, and recording impressions following a walk.

Dialogue journals (Gambrell, 1985) are specifically designed to increase the interaction between students and teachers. As the name implies, students write questions and comments about something happening in their personal lives or in school with the knowledge that the teacher will read their entries. The teacher then writes brief responses directly in the journal. Rasinski (1994–95) describes an experience in which student teachers interact with students through dialogue journals. He concludes that the dialogue journals are especially positive because the "personalness and permanence of the dialogue journal communications provide an ideal opportunity to promote literacy learning and develop the in-depth relationship and sense of trust and caring that are essential for fully effective teaching" (p. 60). Due to time constraints, teachers frequently read and respond to journals on a rotating basis.

Learning Logs

Learning logs focus on specific content. Students respond to and reflect on what they learned in a lesson, project, or unit of study. They make their entries at the end of the class, although perhaps not every day. In many ways, learning logs form bridges between expressive writing and expository writing. From the expressive viewpoint, students can respond to what they liked best about a lesson or how the lesson could be improved. They can explain why they think the lesson is important, how they will use it in the future, and what they would like to know more about. From the expository viewpoint, students can respond to the main points of the lesson, state what they learned during the lesson, and list questions about content that they would like answered.

You may use learning logs or writer's logs to help students reflect on what they have learned from their writing and about how their writing is progressing. Swartzendruber-Putnam (2000) defines writer's logs as a way to focus on one week of writing. She states "The section of their notebook labeled 'Writer's Log' is a weekly opportunity for students to step back, think, and write a paragraph about how their writing is progressing and what they are learning" (p. 89). She prepares students to write in their writer's logs by explaining to them that it is an opportunity for them to think about what they have written during the week. She encourages students to focus on one aspect of their writing such as a mini-lesson topic that they have found to be useful in their own writing. These logs may also be used to help the teacher monitor students' progress and to meet their individual needs as writers.

You may also use learning logs to help students retain material and develop understanding. MacVaugh (1990) found that journal writing facilitates learning in the content areas. The logs may also generate ideas for writing projects and help students realize that their viewpoints and responses are worthwhile. This format, as discussed later, is especially appropriate for responding to literature.

Writer's Journals

A writer's journal forms a natural bridge between expressive and imaginative writing. The information in a writer's journal provides a source for story ideas, characterizations, language choices, and sensory experiences. Although a few students may create writer's journals on their own, most need to be encouraged to do so.

In *The Young Writer's Handbook: A Practical Guide for the Beginner Who Is Serious About Writing* (1984), Susan and Stephen Tchudi provide ideas for students and teachers who are developing writers' journals. The Tchudis recommend that writers of all ages use journals to explore their experiences, their world, and their language. The descriptions and reactions frequently become bases for fictional stories, poetry, and other forms of writing. Writers should probe their memories, record early experiences, and think about how those experiences shaped their lives. They should record their dreams, daydreams, and nightmares, and their opinions about various topics. Finally, they should sit in various places and record everything around them. They should describe in detail what they see, hear, smell, feel, and taste. They should also compare things in their environment; these comparisons may later be used as similes and metaphors in their writings.

In exploring their world, writers should move beyond their own experiences and day-to-day events and seek new ideas and new ways of looking at things. They should describe impressions of new experiences and analyze broad concepts, such as fear and friendship. They should extend their experiences through newspapers and write their reactions to news stories, editorials, features, and sports articles.

To explore language, writers should listen for and record unusual or interesting expressions. They can write down dialects and word choices to later add authenticity to characterizations in their writings. They can collect interesting expressions and quotes to add vitality to stories.

The Tchudis recommend that writers set aside a few pages of their journals to list areas of special interest (hobbies, reading interests, locations); landmarks in their lives (first day of school, trip to a dentist, ride on an airplane); people who are important in their lives and imaginary characters of interest; places that are real or imaginary; memories of pleasant and unpleasant experiences; things they would like to change; and questions that fascinate them.

Letters

Writing letters to friends, relatives, teachers, authors, or even imaginary people is an excellent way to encourage expressive writing in children. Numerous experiences motivate such writing. For example, stories that include situations in which characters write letters can be used to motivate children to write letters of their own. Younger students could be introduced to letters through Janet and Allan Ahlberg's *The Jolly Postman* (1986). In this book, the postman delivers letters to fairy-tale characters, such as Cinderella and The Three Bears. Several books use trips or moving as reasons for letter writing. For example, in *Your Best Friend, Kate* (1989), Pat Brisson develops a story in which Kate writes letters to her best friend describing her experiences during a car trip with her family. In *Stringbean's Trip to the Shining Sea* (1988), Vera Williams bases her story on a series of postcards written during a camping trip across the western United States. In *Jenny's Journey* (1991), Sheila Sampton's character writes a letter to a friend and fantasizes about sailing to the friend's new island home. In *Little Dog Lost* (1991), Inga Moore develops a character who discovers that letter writing helps when she moves away from her friends.

There are many excellent stories in which characters write to relatives. For example, in Marc Brown's *Arthur Goes to Camp* (1982), Arthur tells of his adventures in letters to his mother and father. In Judith Caseley's *Dear Annie* (1991), the author uses letters to develop the relationship between Annie and her grandfather. In Philippe Dupasquier's *Dear Daddy* (1985), a girl writes to her father who is away at sea. Patricia MacLachlan's *Sarah, Plain and Tall* (1985) begins with a series of letters written to children by a woman who later becomes their mother.

Some books that include letters are based on comical or exaggerated situations. These books may motivate humorous letters. For example, Simon James's *Dear Mr. Blueberry*

(1991) involves a series of letters that explores the improbable situation of finding a whale in a backyard pond. In Nathan Zimelman's *Please Excuse Jasper* (1987), a series of letters explains the fantastic events that prevent Jasper from attending school.

There are also many stories in which characters write letters based on historical events. Leong Va's *A Letter to the King* (1991) is set in ancient China and revolves around a letter that a girl delivers to persuade the king to release her father. Patricia Reilly Giff's *The War Began at Supper: Letters to Miss Loria* (1991) includes letters written about the Persian Gulf war to a former student teacher. Yoshiko Uchida's "Letter from a Concentration Camp" in *The Big Book for Peace* (Durrell & Sachs, 1990) is a fictional letter written by a Japanese American boy from an American internment camp during World War II.

Students frequently enjoy writing letters to their favorite authors. Such books as Beverly Cleary's *Dear Mr. Henshaw* (1983) may be used to interest students in writing to authors.

A draft letter is a longer piece of writing that focuses on a single piece of work. Swartzendruber-Putnam (2000) asks her students to write a draft letter at the end of each unit in which students turn in a draft of their best writing for the teacher's feedback. She states, "Before I will accept this draft, it must be accompanied by a reflective letter. The letter should reflect on several aspects of the student's writing. The students may write about favorite parts of the piece, any weaknesses they see in this particular piece, what new techniques they tried that differed from their regular process, or any number of other aspects that we brainstorm together. The letters are to be more polished and thoughtful than the logs" (p. 90). Swartzendruber-Putnam concludes: "Both writers logs and draft letters offer students an opportunity to practice writing techniques, as well as an opportunity to practice reflection" (p. 92). She also asks students to write portfolio letters in which they analyze a series of writing assignments that are included in writing portfolios. She concludes "My students may groan when I mention the word reflection. They know as well as I that it takes a great deal of brain power, but as with anything that takes effort, the rewards are great" (p. 93).

Personal Narratives

Writing personal narratives is a frequent activity found in elementary classrooms. In this type of activity, children write stories from their own personal experiences. These stories may be in the form of autobiographical experiences or stories about people who are very close to the child. In a case study of a fifth/sixth-grade classroom that emphasizes the writing process and the writing of personal narratives, McCarthey (1994) found both opportunities and risks when writing focuses on personal narratives. The case studies detailed by McCarthey illustrate both positive and negative aspects of personal or autobiographical writing. Both the positive and negative aspects should be understood by teachers. On the positive side, McCarthey includes the opportunities for authenticity when writing from personal experience, the experience of finding one's own voice, and the therapeutic value of writing about something or someone close to oneself. McCarthey also warns of potential risks related to writing from personal experience. For example, McCarthey found five potential risks that should be understood by teachers: (1) focusing on deeply personal responses may create unintentional emotional consequences in the classroom; (2) writing mostly from personal experience may limit some students' voices; (3) writing personal experiences may cause conflicts between teachers and values of students from other cultures; (4) because of differences in background knowledge and experience, some students may not be ready to write their personal experiences for a larger audience; and (5) emphasizing autobiographical and personal writing to the exclusion of other forms of writing may cause students to conclude that all writing is autobiographical in nature.

1. Choose an area in which learning logs are appropriate. What questions would you use to heighten expressive writing? Try keeping a learning log for one week in one of your college classes. Include both expressive and expository reactions. Try writing reflective letters that focus on your own writing.

2. Reread the description of a writer's journal. How would you modify the journal for younger elementary students? What would you emphasize in upper elementary and middle school? Begin a writing journal of your own observations. Include entries that encourage you to explore your experiences, world, and language. What topics could stimulate you to write a paper using details and information from your journal?

Imaginative Writing

Terms such as *poetic writing, creative writing,* and *imaginative writing* describe fictional prose, poetry, or drama. In Horace's terms, the purpose for such writing is "to inform and delight." The creative process involves awareness of all aspects of life, as well as discovery of meaning in life. Good writers use these perceptions to create meaning through words and to communicate both their feelings and information.

Poetic and imaginative writing, then, includes original writing that uses both imaginative and experimental thinking. The child who writes an original poem, a fairy tale, a puppetry script, or develops a personal experience is engaging in this creativity. Unfortunately, creativity does not develop without a great deal of nurturing. Through experiences that lead to creative writing, a child's creative expression can be stimulated. Vocabularies can be enriched when children describe experiences related to sight, touch, smell, hearing, and taste. Vocabularies can be refined when they search for and discover the most appropriate word to express an idea. Writing poetry and original drama allows experimentation with the sounds and impact of well-chosen words. Writing an original story helps students understand the development of plot and characterization. As we will see in this chapter, writing can be improved by teaching students to respond to story structure and to elaborate on descriptive details. Finally, writing improvement can be taught in the context where it actually belongs—in the process of meaningful writing.

Developing the Creative Writer

In this section we present some of the factors that encourage creative writing development. We discuss the environment; useful types of stimulation; an example of a creative writing activity, including a motivational period, discussion time, a writing period, and a sharing experience; and the development of the creative poetry writer. You will see that the previously discussed stages related to the writing process apply in the development of the poetic imaginative writer. The prewriting phases may include stimulation of creative processes, models for literary forms, and lessons designed to teach various conventions that may be applied and evaluated during writing and revision (Hillocks, 1986).

Many of the activities recommended in this chapter and in the previous chapter are also based on the findings of research conducted by Sadoski, Willson, and Norton (1994). This research showed that teachers can produce dramatic gains in writing quality and quantity with their students. Particularly effective is a combination of instructional practices including inquiry activities, prewriting activities, critically analyzing or responding to literature, and the use of scales or similar types of criteria.

The Environment.   Just as a rich environment is necessary for the development of oral language skills, so, too, does the development of creative writing depend on such an environment. Oral expression flourishes in an atmosphere that allows many opportunities for purposeful communication; this is true as well with creative writing. The environment should offer opportunities to write for many different purposes and many different audiences. You would not, for example, write in the same way when composing an informal note as you would when writing an original story for publication. Thus, development of an audience sense, or distancing, is clearly important for skillful writing.

An educational environment that fosters creativity allows children to progress through seven stages of development at their own pace. First, children need to develop an awareness of life. This means developing sensitivity through activities in which they experience visual stimulation, sounds, smells, tastes, movements, and feelings. Take the children outside to experience a tree or a busy city street. Have them look, listen, feel, and then share descriptive language about their sensations. Developing descriptive vocabularies requires this type of activity. Fine literature, poetry, and music also expand sensitivity. Art and building materials also allow children to manipulate and feel before they discuss and write.

Second, the environment should encourage children to care about others. Many awareness experiences help children develop empathy for the feelings and experiences of others. Role-playing activities allow children to experience what it would be like to be in another's position and can often lead to exciting creative writing.

Third, the environment should allow time for children to consider new awareness. This may be thought of as an "incubation period." It allows the mind to think both consciously and unconsciously. Many of you have had the experience of thinking about an almost impossible task, until all of a sudden, the solution seemed very clear. This is applicable to writing. It often requires longer than half an hour for a child to create a product that he or she feels is satisfactory. Some children may need much longer awareness periods than others. Some children need many awareness and oral language experiences before they tentatively dictate or write a piece that demonstrates feeling and originality. Graves (2002) emphasizes the need to provide many and longer opportunities for children to develop writing that is meaningful to them.

Fourth, the environment should allow children to make their own discoveries. Children need opportunities to ask questions and find answers. Children need opportunities to be involved in discussions in which there is not one correct answer but from which many questions arise and many answers appear.

Fifth, the environment should stimulate writers to create meaning with words. You must provide many opportunities to try various types of writing in all content areas. You must be involved in the students' writing during writing conferences and other phases of composing. When necessary, provide guidelines for writing that children can apply during writing and revision. This is especially important when introducing certain types of poetry writing and literary elements.

Sixth, after children have created meaning by writing, the environment should allow for the development of detachment, so the authors can involve themselves in the evaluation process through reexamination and rewriting until their writing most effectively portrays the feelings and meanings.

Finally, the environment should allow writers opportunities to test the effectiveness of their communication. Do the compositions convey both the intended information and the feelings when they are presented to an audience? Children need many opportunities to write and evaluate their work with specific audiences in mind and to present their writings to these audiences. Something wonderful happens when a child's finished product expresses the child's feelings effectively and meets with awe and pleasure from an audience.

Topics.   Many topics provide motivation for writing. If students are already involved in a unit or study of a topic, they have in-depth experience and information on which to base their writings. Kindergarten and first-grade students write both longer and higher quality compositions if their writing originates from firsthand experiences rather than textbook assignments. Science, social studies, and literature units are excellent sources for stimulation. If students are already reading, talking about, and listening to the topic, it is logical to have them write about it as well.

For example, one of my second-grade student teachers developed a unit on the post office and mail service. As the unit progressed, students constructed a classroom mailbox, learned about zip codes, went to a post office, and investigated mail transportation from the pony express days to the present. This unit stimulated a great deal of writing. The children wrote and mailed letters in the real and classroom post offices, wrote creative stories about what happened to letters when Mr. Zip was ignored, wrote diaries from the viewpoint of a pony express rider crossing dangerous mountains and traversing Indian territory, and wrote stories depicting the journey of a letter down the Mississippi on a riverboat. Some children wrote about the adventures of pilots in the early airmail service, and other students looked into the future to write fanciful versions of mail service in the year 3000. Instead of conducting a unit that was dull and ordinary, this teacher provided many opportunities for creative writing and stimulated further study and investigation. In turn, that study motivated still more writing. The children wrote from a background rich in knowledge, and the classroom activities provided enough diversity that all of the students were motivated by at least a portion of the topic. (Early planes, the pony express, and futuristic travel especially appealed to the boys.)

Everyday Experiences.   Stimulation can come from everyday experiences, from the common things that children know best: their neighborhood, their street, shopping, their family, their hopes and fears, and their likes and dislikes. For example, some fanciful stories came out of a reading of Dr. Seuss's *And to Think That I Saw It on Mulberry Street.* After hearing the story, the children discussed their own streets. They talked about what they saw every day and how the street and the things on it might appear to a person with a vivid imagination. Finally, they wrote stories from this new perspective.

Personal feelings also stimulate creative writing. A third grader lets you know very clearly what he considers trouble (the spelling is as in the original):

Trouble Is

Trouble is runing in the hall becase the principal will cach you.
Trouble is I can't wright a poem becase its hard.
Trouble is getting a tooth pulled becase it hurts.
Trouble is when someone yells at you becase you get punished.
Trouble is ending a poem becase its hard.

Happiness is another emotion close to children. The following dictated poem was created by a group of five first-grade students:

Happiness Is

Happiness is having pets.
Happiness is having a cat.
Happiness is going skiing.
Happiness is riding a horse.
Happiness is loving a snake.
Happiness is having food to eat.
Happiness is going ice skating.
Happiness is having your own bike.
Happiness is having your own puppy.
Happiness is having your own bedroom.
Happiness is learning how to ride a bike.
Happiness is jumping in a pile of leaves.
Happiness is getting your allowance every week.
Happiness is catching a frog in a swimming pool.
Happiness is being nice to your brother and sister.
Happiness is sharing your jelly beans with no fighting.
Happiness is going snake hunting and finding big snakes.
Happiness is having your own swimming pool in your backyard.
And best of all, happiness is being alive.

Another topic close to the everyday experience of children is recess. The following imaginative writing resulted when a third-grade teacher asked each child to imagine that he or she was a ball and to write a story from the ball's point of view:

The Life of a Ball

Hi, I am a ball. And you know what balls are used for, bouncing. Well, I'm not. I just sit in the closet all day long.

Hey, here comes somebody and they're taking me outside. Ouch! You kicked me. I'm not going to make a basket for you. Oh no, they're going inside and that was the last recess. Now they're getting on the bus and going home.

Burrr. It's starting to snow. Ouch! A big hunk of ice hit me. I wish I had a set of ball muffs and a jacket. It's starting to rain and I wish I had some galoshes and a raincoat. Oh. Here comes some wind and I'm blowing under the car. Ouch! I hit the tire. I'm going to try to get into the school.

At last I got inside with my friends the football, and the baseball and my mom the basketball. It was so warm that I went to sleep.

Something just woke me up. Oh no, it's those kids again. I'm being taken outside, but last night was so hard on me that I'm flat and I won't bounce. They say I'm dead and they are putting me back in the closet. I guess I'll just have to stay here until someone blows me up again. But there are worse places than this closet.

New Experiences.   Another stimulation is new experiences. These experiences may be in the form of short lessons such as those described in Hillocks's environmental mode (1986) for teaching composition. They may include models of writing and literature to be applied during writing experiences. Many sense awareness activities fall into this category: going for a walk; listening to, smelling, and touching the environment; discussing sensations and writing descriptive phrases; and, finally, composing stories or poems about the experience. You may also bring in unique objects, or use music, literature, or pictures and photographs for stimulation.

Many of the research studies that Hillocks (1986) identifies as the most effective approaches for teaching writing fall under teacher-introduced approaches: The teacher first introduces a concept in a short structured lesson and then the students apply that concept during the writing and revision stages of the writing process. Hillocks refers to Sager's study. In this study, Sager increased the abilities of sixth-grade students to elaborate details. For example, Sager (1973) asked students working in small groups to read the following story:

The Green Martian Monster
The Green Martian monster descended on the USA. He didn't have a mouth. "Who goes?" they said. There was no answer. So they shot him and he died.

After reading the story, which the students had been told scored 0 on elaboration, Sager asked the students to do the following:

1. Quickly list all the reasons why a mouthless green Martian monster might land in the USA.
2. List all the places the Martian could have landed.
3. Who could "they" have been? List all possibilities.
4. List all the thoughts "they" could have been thinking when they saw the Martian.
5. What could have happened between the time the Martian was shot and the time he died? List all possibilities.
6. Look at your lists. To be interesting and easy to understand, a story needs details such as you have written. Add some of these details to the story and take turns reading the story the way you would have written it. (p. 95)

Hillocks (1986) emphasizes the importance of this example because students did far more than rate a composition. He says: "They found problems with the writing, generated ideas which would help to correct those problems, and synthesized those problems with the existing frame. Finally, they considered the principles underlying what they had done. Using such materials as the above composition, the experimental groups in the study worked with scales dealing with vocabulary, elaboration, organization, and structure" (p. 123). These same techniques were found to be especially beneficial in the research conducted by Sadoski et al. (1994).

As a result of her research, Sager (1977) identifies the following four factors that contribute to effective writing in the upper elementary grades:

1. A rich and varied vocabulary that allows a writer to hold the reader's interest. A rich vocabulary uses exact words, synonyms, words that appeal to the senses, descriptive words and expressions, and word combinations and comparisons.
2. An organizational ability that presents ideas in a logical arrangement, stays with the subject, and follows an effective sequence.
3. The ability to elaborate and fully develop ideas so that they flow smoothly from one to the next. The ability to elaborate reveals itself in an abundance of related ideas and vivid details.
4. The ability to use a variety of sentences and thus state ideas both accurately and fluently.

Cartoons are especially reliable for developing narrative writing with young children. Cartoons featuring Charlie Brown and Snoopy are excellent. Charlie Brown coloring books are also highly motivating, especially for reluctant readers. Photographs are also effective for stimulating writing if children can identify with them.

Another stimulus is music. A few bars are often enough to stimulate creative response, although the whole selection may be required with narrative records such as *Peter and the Wolf*. One university student used "Night on Bald Mountain," by Mussorgsky, which stimulated an imaginative sixth grader to write the following description:

Night on Bald Mountain

It is midnight, everyone is asleep, except, bald mountain! As the church bell strikes, the devil of mountaintops opens his wings and smiles evilly onto the small graveyards, the evil gleaming of his eyes seems to say, "Thou shalt come out of hiding and appraise the devil of bald mountain!" As if in answer, ghostly shadows and skeletons begin to float up. When seeing this he cackles in delight, and suddenly thrusts his fingers at a huge boulder, and where the boulder had been, there was a fiery pit of flame.

Still another stimulus involves objects that provoke discussion and speculation. Children need opportunities to think about what an object is, who made it, how and why it was used, who owned it, and so forth. As an example, for a class studying frontier America, you might bring in a collection of dolls and other toys characteristic of the period. Some might be handmade, such as a cornhusk doll, whereas others might be replicas of period toys. The children would have background and knowledge of the period. They could look at the toys and describe them and discuss the adventures the toys might have shared with their owners and the feelings the owners might have had about their toys. They could talk about which toy they would choose if they could take only one on a covered-wagon journey. After discussion, they could write their stories—from the viewpoint of either the toy or the child.

Literature is not only an excellent stimulus for creative writing but also a model for writing improvement. One fourth-grade teacher used a study of fables to stimulate creative writing. Because a child cannot write a fable without understanding what it is, the teacher first did a modeling activity in which she read a number of Aesop's fables to the class. Good adaptations of Aesop's works for elementary students include *The Aesop for Children* (1919, 1947), Heidi Holder's *Aesop's Fables* (1981), Tom Paxton's *Aesop's Fables Retold in Verse* (1988), Michael Hague's *Aesop's Fables* (1985), and Mitsumasa Anno's *Anno's Aesop* (1989). John Bierhorst's *Doctor Coyote: A Native American Aesop's Fables* (1987) shows students how fables can be adapted to a different culture and environment. Several picture storybook versions of fables, such as Lorinda Bryan Cauley's *The Town Mouse and the Country Mouse* (1984) and Janet Stevens's *The Tortoise and the Hare* (1984), illustrate how authors use the fable idea to develop longer stories by expanding the original fables.

The students learned that fables have the following characteristics: (1) they are fictional, (2) they are meant to entertain, (3) they are poetic, (4) they have a double or an allegorical meaning, and (5) they are moral tales, usually about animal characters who behave and act like human characters (Norton, 2003).

The class developed their own criteria for fables: They are short tales in which animals talk as humans; the animals represent human nature (for example, a fox is sly and cunning); and fables have a moral. These criteria also became a scale for evaluating their own writing. The class read and discussed many fables. Finally, the teacher had the children write their own fables. The teacher typed and reproduced the finished fables in a booklet so that each student had the accumulated class collection. The following example is from this fourth-grade collection.

> The Cat and the Birds
> Once there was a cat that picked on all the birds in his neighborhood because they were smaller than he was. One afternoon the cat was chasing a bird when suddenly he felt a striking pain in his back. He turned around and saw a little sparrow on his back. From that day on he never judged anyone by his size.

For creative writing, the instructional sequence is as important as the type of stimulation. Therefore, you must place stimulation activities within the framework of the writing process discussed in Chapter 7.

Vocabulary Development.   Choice of words is extremely important in creative writing. Mason, Herman, and Au (1991) state that students who have extensive vocabularies have a vast array of concepts about meaning-related connections among words. These students use vocabulary skills appropriately in numerous situations as they write, listen, speak, and read. As mentioned previously, creative writing is often termed visual writing. Consequently, students must make readers visualize a character, scene, or incident without using trite expressions. Vocabulary is the key, and students need practice in describing objects, scenes, and people. To develop descriptive vocabulary, have children reach into a bag containing a ball, a penny, a pencil, a rubber band, sandpaper, and a glass. Each child describes an item without looking at it. The description may include the texture, size, shape, and firmness of the item. The rest of the group then guesses what the item is.

One class listed a number of phrases that they thought were too vague. These included "a beautiful scene," "a handsome man," "a big dog," "a lovely girl," and "an exciting moment." "A beautiful scene" conjured up as many different images as students in the group. The activity showed a need for precision if readers are to perceive the visual images that writers intend. Strunk and White (1979), in their popular *The Elements of Style,* state that one of the elementary principles of composition is to use definite, specific, and concrete language: "If those who have studied the art of writing are in accord on any one point, it is on this: the surest way to arouse and hold the attention of the reader is by being specific, definite, and concrete. The greatest writers . . . are effective largely because they deal in particulars and report the details that matter. Their words call up pictures" (p. 21).

Overuse of adjectives and adverbs is a common problem in writing. For example, "The great green expanse of meadow was filled with stately, brown, soft-eyed deer eating their sweet-smelling breakfast" is a description so overdone that it is ineffective. To avoid this pitfall, children need a variety of descriptive techniques. An important technique is use of vivid action words, in both story writing and poetry. Strunk and White (1979) state that writers should write with nouns and verbs rather than with adjectives and adverbs.

How can you help children learn to choose more descriptive verbs? If you look at children's writing, especially in the early elementary grades, you will find certain words used over and over. One such word is *said.* You see "Mother said," "Father said," and so forth repeatedly. But does *said* describe how a person is saying anything? One class compiled a list of over 100 words to use in place of *said.* They decided that *argued, yelled, growled, whined, declared,* and so forth were much more descriptive of how a person talked and felt than the overused *said.* The children became aware of visual verbs, looked for them in their reading, and used them in their writing.

The children talked about other verbs that do not communicate as well as they should. They read sentences, such as "The boy walked down the street," and they discussed why and

Children can expand their vocabularies by producing word "banks" on charts.

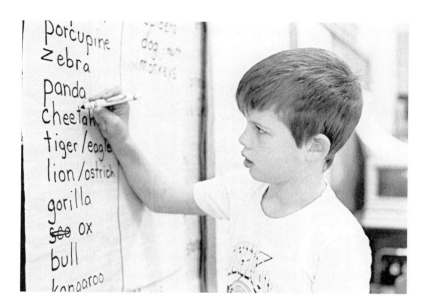

where he might be walking. Then, they substituted other, more visual verbs. For example, consider these substitutions:

The boy *strolled* down the street.   (He was not in a hurry and just wanted to go for a walk.)

The boy *strutted* down the street.   (He had just won a baseball game and was very proud.)

The boy *tramped* down the street.   (He was angry because his father told him he couldn't go to a movie.)

The children worked with other verbs, such as these:

The girl *drank* a large glass of lemonade.
The girl *sipped* a large glass of lemonade.   (She was at a party and wanted to be polite.)

The girl *gulped* a large glass of lemonade.   (She had been running and was very hot and thirsty.)

Jim *sat* in the large chair.
Jim *sprawled* in the large chair.   (He was tired and by himself and he wanted to relax.)

Jim *crouched* in the large chair.   (Jim was ready to leave the chair in a hurry.)

This kind of exercise helps students use visual verbs and makes them more observant when they read literature.

For Your Development

Design a series of activities to help children develop more descriptive vocabularies. Present the activities to a group of children or share them with a group of your peers.

Story Writing

There is a strong connection between reading and listening to literature and writing stories. Schema theory supports reading and telling stories to children and helping children understand such literary elements as plot, setting, and characterization. To apply schema implications to creative writing, read literature to children. Literature provides models for the literary elements and helps children increase their understanding and appreciation of them.

In addition to all of the excellent examples of children's literature, there is a fairly new phenomenon in book publishing that may be used to motivate children's writing. In a *Publishers Weekly* article, Bailey (1993) discusses the growing number of published books written by children. One of these books, Nila K. Leigh's *Learning to Swim in Swaziland: A Child's-Eye View of a Southern African Country* (1993), was written and illustrated by a fourth-grade girl. According to the introduction to the book, it is based on a series of letters that the author wrote to her former classmates in New York City while she lived in Swaziland. Children may read and discuss this book and consider how they might write and illustrate a book, at least for a classroom audience.

Plot.   Use very simple stories to introduce the concept of plot. Teachers at a writing institute identified this type of prewriting activity as one of the most beneficial for improving students' writing (Sadoski et al., 1994). Stories that have a strong, logical sequence are good for this beginning activity. For example, one teacher used the following sequence of instruction with a fifth-grade class. First, the teacher read a simple story, "The Three Billy Goats Gruff." He asked the children to listen carefully so they could identify the characters and incidents in the story. After listening to the story, the children identified its four characters: (1) the littlest billy goat, (2) the middle-sized billy goat, (3) the great big billy goat, and (4) the troll. Next, the class listed the incidents that occur in the story:

1. The goats want to eat the grass on the other side of the bridge, but there is a terrible troll under the bridge.
2. After being threatened by the troll, the littlest goat crosses successfully.
3. The middle goat crosses successfully, also after being threatened by the troll.
4. The largest billy goat is confronted by the troll and knocks the troll off the bridge.
5. The three goats eat grass on the other side of the bridge.

The teacher had the class investigate the order of the five incidents by acting them out. Then, he asked whether the action had to be in that specific order. The students rearranged the order in several ways and tried to act out each new order. The five incidents were written on strips of cardboard and arranged in the order being demonstrated. The students concluded that if the story is to retain logical development, the incidents cannot be presented in a different order. Some of their reasons follow: (1) the beginning must start with the goats on one side of the bridge and a need to cross the bridge; (2) the littlest goat must cross the bridge first, so that he can tell the troll to wait for his middle-sized brother, who is fatter and will taste better; (3) the middle-sized goat must come next, so that a larger goat will remain; (4) the biggest goat must cross in order to eliminate the troll; and (5) the goats must eliminate the troll in order to eat happily on the other side. The group also concluded that if the biggest goat eliminates the troll in the beginning, the story is not interesting, because there is too little conflict.

Through this activity, the students realized that plot connects actions in a logical sequence. The students listened to other short stories and identified the sequence of events, from which they began to realize that many stories develop their plots through conflict.

In the next activity, the class looked again at "The Three Billy Goats Gruff." They identified which characters were in conflict: the three goats against the ugly old troll. They identified the reason for the conflict: the goats wanted grass on the other side of the bridge, but the troll lived under the bridge and wanted to eat the goats. They identified the series of conflicts: first, the little goat against the troll; next, the middle-sized goat against the troll; and finally, the biggest goat against the troll.

The teacher then read Alexander Nikolayevich Afanasyev's folktale, *The Fool and the Fish* (1990). The students listened for the major characters: a lazy man named Ivan, an enchanted fish, a tsar, and a princess. They listened for the source of conflict: the furious tsar tries to eliminate Ivan and the princess. They identified the series of incidents that develop the plot:

1. Ivan draws an enchanted fish out of the stream.
2. The fish offers Ivan unlimited wishes in return for freedom.
3. Ivan asks the fish for help carrying water, fetching wood, and beating off angry villagers.
4. Ivan is transported to the tsar's palace.
5. The angry tsar orders Ivan and the princess placed in a barrel and thrown into the sea.
6. The fish saves Ivan and the princess and grants Ivan a fine palace.
7. The tsar accepts Ivan as his son-in-law and they all live in peace.

The teacher introduced the concept that a plot has beginning incidents, middle incidents, and ending incidents. With the teacher's assistance, the class drew a diagram to show the progress of a plot (Figure 8–1). After they drew the diagram and discussed plot development, they placed the incidents from *The Fool and the Fish* on the diagram (Figure 8–2).

Finally, students wrote their own stories, using beginning, middle, and ending incidents. The teacher interacted with each student during the composing phases, and the children shared their finished products. The class used the plot-development model during different phases of the writing process. During prewriting, students listened to stories, developed a model, and applied the model to other stories. During the writing phase, the students referred to the model to develop stories with beginning, middle, and ending incidents and to include rising action. After writing their first drafts, the students referred to the model during teacher conferences and peer editing groups. The model helped the students determine areas that were well developed as well as those that needed to be revised for clarity. The model encouraged self-evaluation because the students were able to refer to specific components and analyze whether their writings included those components.

Additional plot structures that are useful in writing are illustrated in Chapters 5 and 6. The plot structure in person-versus-self conflicts (problem → struggle → struggle → self-realization → achievement of peace and truth) is diagrammed in Figure 6–9. Three other patterns of action are used in plot structures: (1) the action moves from one incident to another incident (final climax leaves the reader with a sense of uncertainty); (2) the action

FIGURE 8–1   The Diagram of a Plot

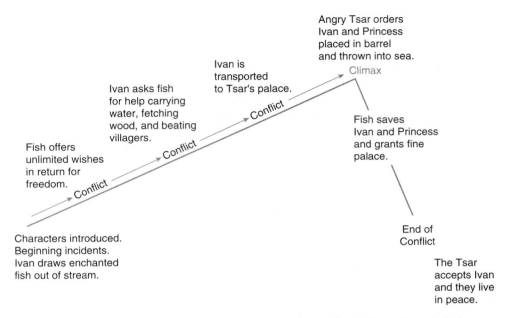

FIGURE 8–2   Plot Diagram with Incidents from *The Fool and the Fish* Included

moves with a tension that does not develop a climax (minimal suspense); and (3) the action moves in a lifeline that does not have one dramatic climax, but may have several dramatic episodes. These additional plot structures are especially interesting when working with older students. Literature written for younger students usually follows the plot structure shown in Figures 8–1 and 8–2.

Using Teacher Think-Aloud Techniques to Help Students Write Plot Structures and Conflicts.   Authors such as Cunningham and Allington (2003) maintain that to have effective writing instruction in a classroom, children must watch and listen to teachers think aloud about the various topics of which they are asking children to write. This may be especially important as students advance in the grades and are expected to write imaginative pieces that include believable plots and conflicts.

The following excerpts show how several student teachers in my classes prepared think-alouds to accompany the writings of award-winning authors. Notice in these examples how they are focusing on the different types of conflict and how the authors develop these conflicts in books for upper-elementary classes. The students are also showing how the authors relate the conflicts to important themes in their writing. The first example was prepared by Ashley Aldridge (2002) to accompany Gary Paulsen's *Woodsong* (1990):

> This book is exciting because it is an account of the author's real life story and his experiences with nature. Paulsen takes readers through his encounters with nature and shares his own personal opinions of the outdoors and exactly how readers should respect them. However, halfway through the story there is a major turning point that is absolutely crucial because at this point Paulsen enters the race for his life. He has traveled to Alaska and entered the Iditarod.

> Although the book begins with Paulsen's obvious internal battle with himself, it quickly begins to involve person against nature. This turning point is quite ironic because his battle of person against nature also begins to involve his inner struggle about how he views nature. He is out on an average morning with his dog team and witnesses a deer being attacked by a group of seven wolves. He watches the entire attack and begins to actually feel the deer's sense of fear and death. For the first time he thinks about what it might be like to be in the helpless animal's position, or even perhaps that of the hungry wolves. He witnesses nature in all of its glory, although it's quite a horrific scene. After this experience Paulsen describes the wondrous dance of nature. He speaks of the dance many times and each time he speaks in such a way that he is continuing his internal battle within himself and also that of his battle with nature. Paulsen had forced himself to see only the beauty and peacefulness of nature, and now for the first time he sees nature in all its cruelty.
>
> The theme of this book remains connected throughout its entirety. There are parallels that show us the connection between the inner self and nature. The major turning point in this book occurs when Paulsen enters the Iditarod in Alaska. This is truly where the entire theme comes together by showing this constant correlation between self and nature. It is filled with his descriptions of the bitter cold and nights with no sleep. He describes the scene in Alaska as complete madness and chaos. We learn his true feelings as he describes nature and experiences during his journey in such graphic detail, so that we begin to realize the connections he is making. Once again it is the correlation between man and nature that Paulsen wants his readers to understand.
>
> As I read this book I thought about how Paulsen's adventure made me feel. I also thought about how my feelings about nature and life in the woods have changed. I also thought about the types of animals that I might encounter if I visited Alaska. Paulsen's text provides a greater understanding of nature and also the relationship between person against self and person against nature. Many connections and parallels can be taken from this text, along with many different interpretations of Paulsen's inner view of his life in the woods. For me, the book opens an entire realm of ideas and possible writing topics.

In addition, Aldridge includes in her think-aloud quotes from the book that develop both Paulsen's inner conflicts and his person-against-nature conflicts. She talks about how the book made her feel. She also stresses how Paulsen's use of language encourages her to visualize and feel the plot and conflicts in the story. Following this experience, she used the book to motivate both herself and her students to write about personal experiences that stressed a conflict with nature. The students discussed what they learned from Paulsen's writing and how they could use these discoveries in their own writings.

The second example is a portion of Celeste McPhee's (2002) think-aloud for Elizabeth Coatsworth's *The Cat Who Went to Heaven* (1930), a book for slightly younger readers. Notice in her think-aloud that she begins with a background of the Japanese setting and the Buddhist culture:

> The Cat Who Went to Heaven is a book that changes mood toward the end of the story. At the beginning of the book, the author develops a setting in Japan in which a starving artist and his housekeeper live in a little house. It is important to know that in the Buddhist culture cats are considered evil, and the first conflict, person versus society, emerges when the housekeeper goes to the market for food and buys a pet cat instead of food. The artist is angry with the housekeeper, but he soon sees the kind nature of the cat and names her Good Fortune thinking she is unlike any other cat and may bring luck.

Soon after Good Fortune joins the household, the artist is blessed with tremendous good luck. The Priest in their town needs an artist to paint a picture of the Death of Buddha to hang in the temple. The Priest decides it is the will of Buddha that the starving artist will be chosen to paint the picture. As the artist paints the Buddha with his blessed animals, the author creates a strong person-versus-self conflict. He must paint the tiger, which is wicked in nature yet blessed by Buddha, but he cannot put a cat like Good Fortune in the painting because cats are considered evil. The artist loves his cat deeply, and this troubles him because he "knew that the tiger, too, had come to bid farewell to Buddha, and he too had received the master's blessing. How could that be? The fierceness and cruelty of tigers. . . the killers among the reeds" (p. 45).

The society in which he lives believes that the cat does not belong in the painting because "all people know that cats, though lovely, are usually proud and self satisfied" (p. 47). The climax of the person-versus-self and person-versus-society conflict results when the artist goes against society and his need to please the priest, and paints the cat into Buddha's painting in spite of the consequences of possible rejection and starvation. Soon the priest comes for the painting and shows his rejection saying, "I will take your painting tomorrow and officially burn it. Some other artist's picture must hang in our temple" (p. 51). The artist was depressed after putting so much effort into the painting, although he did not regret painting his cat into the picture.

The turning point occurs when the artist finds out that the painting was not burned, but it amazingly hung in the temple, "with incense and candles. . . for where the last animal had stood, now was only white silk that seemed never to have felt the touch of ink, and the great Buddha, the one whom he painted with hands folded upon his breast, had stretched out an arm in blessing, and under the holy hand knelt the figure of a tiny cat, with pretty white head bowed in happy adoration" (p. 53). The artist is now filled with gratitude for the Lord Buddha. He became a respected artist and Buddha had given his little cat, ironically named Good Fortune, recognition.

I especially like this book because the theme relates to the person-against-society and person-against-self conflicts. Through the actions of the artist we learn that being true to a friend, the cat, and standing up for what we believe is not always an easy thing to do, yet sometimes the reward is greater than can be foreseen. The author develops the artist's guilt about not painting his cat into the picture so well through repeated spells of anxiety. The housekeeper is used as a mirror to show us the artist's state of mind. For example, when he is frustrated she talks to the reader by saying, "My master will weary himself into a fever" (p. 32). He uses her songs to give us a taste of the mood for every chapter. At the beginning of every chapter is a "Song of the Housekeeper" written as rhyming poetry. In the beginning of the book she sings, ". . . the fat god of luck never enters our door. . . " and at the ending chapter she sings, ". . . the mercy of Buddha has no end; this is too beautiful a thing to understand. . . " (p. 54). The author brilliantly uses the small songs as points on a time line of the artist's life; the little songs follow the format of a plot diagram, building on one another until a climax, turning point, and resolution are reached. We can compare each Song of the Housekeeper, and use the songs to understand the development of plot and conflict. I believe that Elizabeth Coatsworth's book reveals an engaging story displaying the union of conflict and theme through the author's creative style.

If using this book with a more mature audience, the teacher could ask the students to conduct cultural studies to authenticate the Buddhist faith. They can learn about art in Japan at this time in history and compare the art to the paintings created in the book. They can also search for examples of Japanese folklore that develop the importance of the various animals depicted in the story.

For Your Development

1. Develop a writing lesson that follows the plot development shown in Figures 8–1 and 8–2. Develop a model using examples other than the two presented in this chapter. Develop a list of children's literature selections that follow that specific plot development. What types of children's books develop this plot structure?
2. Choose another plot structure. Identify several literature selections that follow that specific plot structure and place the incidents from the story on the plot structure. Develop a writing lesson that helps students understand and apply the plot structure.
3. Choose a book and create a think-aloud activity in which you identify how the author develops plot and conflict. Stress how the various techniques used by the author may also be used in the imaginative writing of students.

Setting.   Several of the ideas for entries in a writer's journal emphasize describing a specific location or new experience by writing vivid details related to sight, sound, smell, and touch. Similar activities provide valuable prewriting experiences before students write settings for stories. For example, ask students to jot down details as they are walking through a park, looking at a busy city street, or looking at the sky during different weather conditions.

The RADAR approach to writing (Davis, 1988) uses a structured approach to help students describe both settings and characters. In this approach, students look at a picture, divide the picture into three parts, and then circle each part. For example, if the picture includes a dog chasing a cat into the woods, the students circle the dog, the cat, and the woods. Next, the students number each part and describe it in detail. They start with the first part and write their descriptions moving from top to bottom. The students also use terms to indicate location, such as *beside, over,* and *under,* in writing their descriptions.

Picture storybooks are among the best classroom sources for developing observational and writing skills related to setting. Introduce the books, read the stories while encouraging the students to look carefully at the settings, and then ask the students to describe the settings in detail. Emphasize the students' words and phrases that they believe describe the settings. Encourage them to make comparisons through simile and metaphor. Finally, ask them to write their own descriptions, incorporating what they learned during the discussion. It is advisable to develop the first setting description as a group activity in which you use descriptive words and phrases and highlight various things the students should look for.

Books that have familiar settings are excellent for younger students. If the settings are within their experiential backgrounds, the students may even compare the settings in the illustrations with similar settings in their own environments. At least some of the following settings should be familiar to many children: Bruce McMillan's *One Sun: A Book of Terse Verse* (1990)—a beach in summer; Jane Yolen's *Owl Moon* (1987)—rural woods in winter; Dayal Khalsa's *I Want a Dog* (1987)—city neighborhood and home; Lois Lenski's *Sing a Song of People* (1987)—city environment; Merle Peek's *The Balancing Act: A Counting Song* (1987)—an amusement park; Marc Brown's *Arthur's Baby* (1987)—family home, preparing for a baby; and Valerie Flournoy's *The Patchwork Quilt* (1985)—a close, three-generation African-American family.

After students master writing simple descriptive settings, let them describe and write settings that have specific purposes. For example, many settings create the mood of a story. Students may try to match the feeling of a setting through their choice of words. Marcia Brown's illustrations for Cendrar's *Shadow* (1982) are excellent for exploring how setting can create a frightening, spooky mood. The illustrations in sharp collage seem to reach out menacingly.

After students try to describe the settings in their own words, have them analyze how the author creates the mood as the shadow staggers, grabs, and teems like snakes and worms. Cynthia Rylant's *When I Was Young in the Mountains* (1982) creates a warm, gentle, nostalgic mood. Descriptions of Grandfather's kiss on a front porch and of Grandmother holding a child's hand in the dark enhance the mood. Pictures of country kitchens, country stores, and swimming holes suggest a leisurely, secure, and happy way of life for children. In Catharine O'Neill's *Mrs. Dunphy's Dog* (1987), the illustrations that show lampposts and fenceposts at angles, animals in caricature, and literal interpretations of the news create a humorous mood.

Students can explore how both illustrations and text create moods. They can brainstorm lists of words and phrases that suggest different moods and try to match the mood of the illustrations in their own writings. You may share only the illustrations in books and ask students to describe the mood they think the illustrations suggest, write descriptions reflecting this mood, and then compare their descriptions with those developed by the author. After completing several writing activities of this sort, a fifth-grade class listed and categorized words that reflected specific moods in books and in their own writings that accompanied the illustrations. The students included words that depicted mood in both setting and characterizations. Table 8–1 illustrates part of this activity.

Books with illustrations that show setting as the antagonist include the previously mentioned *Shadow*. In Margaret Hodges's *The Wave* (1964), Blair Lent creates a large, dark swirl of a tidal wave. Robert McCloskey's *Time of Wonder* (1957) shows the destructive force of a hurricane as it bends the lines of the trees. Students can use these illustrations to write settings that reflect danger.

Picture books that you may use to stimulate historical setting include Donald Hall's *Ox-Cart Man* (1979)—early nineteenth-century New England; John Goodall's *The Story of a Main Street* (1987)—England from the medieval period through contemporary time; Tomie de Paola's *An Early American Christmas* (1987)—New Hampshire, early 1800s; Byrd Baylor's *The Best Town in the World* (1983)—nineteenth-century rural Texas; Reeve Lindbergh's *Johnny Appleseed* (1990)—frontier America from Massachusetts to Indiana; and Diane Stanley's *Peter the Great* (1986)—Russia, late 1600s through early 1700s. These books provide excellent sources because students can see how an illustrator provides authenticity through illustrations. Then, students can try to make readers see the same historical settings through words.

Table 8–1   Words that suggest moods for settings

Frightening Mood	Warm, Happy Mood	Funny Mood
Cendrar's *Shadow:*	McPhail's *The Dream Child:*	Small's *Imogene's Antlers:*
prowler, stolen like a thief, body dragging, teeming like snakes	moon like warm breath, Tame Bear, Dream Child, drift, sleepy, hugs, licks	Imogene had grown antlers, antlers decked with doughnuts, antlers drying towels
Our Words:	Our Words:	Our Words:
squirming black fingers, clawing branches, ghostly white silent shapes	cuddly little bear, secure in mother's lap, cradling boat, drifting in sky	silly, preposterous, unbelievable, stupefied, speechless

Using Teacher Think-Aloud Techniques to Help Students Write About Settings.
This excerpt from an example developed by Jennifer Fall (2002) shows a think-aloud using
settings in Dorothy Rhoads's *The Corn Grows Ripe* (1956):

> In the beginning of the book the author uses setting as historical background to show the
> lifestyle of the Maya Indians who lived in the Yucatan, which is part of modern day Mexico.
> The houses of the Maya are described as having one room: "The sides were made of young
> trees cut from the bush, placed upright and fastened with vines. The floor was earth. The
> roof was thatched leaves of guano palm. The furniture too . . . was made from trees cut
> from the bush. Everything Dionisio's family used and needed came from the forest that
> closed in around the small village and closed out the outside world" (p. 16). This shows the
> importance that the setting of the forest has for these people because all of the things they
> depend on for survival come from the forest.
>
> Throughout the book, Rhoads uses descriptions of setting to demonstrate the mood of
> the story. "The Corn Grows Ripe" relies on descriptions of the seasons of the year to further
> illustrate the events of the plot. For this reason, much of the setting describes the changing
> of the various seasons as they relate to the process of planting, growing, and harvesting
> corn. In the beginning of the book, the start of the spring season is described: ". . . trees
> around them, birds sang full throated and hopped along branches. Green vines and thin
> green tree snakes hung from the trees. New leaves from the recent rains crowded bushes.
> Bright-colored flowers as gay as the tissue-paper decorations in the churches were caught
> among the green. . . . Everything was beginning" (p. 22). This scenery is full of words such
> as "green" and "bright-colored," which bring to mind happy and lively thoughts of
> springtime. The author proceeds to describe other seasons of the year such as when
> drought is in the land and the people and the land are thirsty. During the drought the
> author describes the setting in this way: "Every day was hotter than the day before. Gray
> dust settled on the houses and in the streets and clung to the shriveled leaves like swarms
> of tiny insects. The trees of the bush were only skeleton trees, gray bony trunks and limbs.
> Everything gasped for water" (p. 58). This is a very vivid description of the setting that
> helps the reader visualize the degree of thirst and the desperate need for water. By these
> descriptions of setting, the reader realizes the importance of the water for the corn.
>
> Rhoads concludes her book in a way that brings the seasons back to the beginning of
> the cycle. The rains eventually come and it is now late September, time to harvest the corn.
> The new description of the setting tells how the ". . . air was cool and fresh after the recent
> rains. The trees were crowded with new leaves. Flowers were everywhere—morning glories
> in rainbow colors, yellow orchids caught in the tops of trees. Birds, bright-colored as
> flowers, sang gaily and flashed in and out among the green leaves" (p. 82). This picture
> helps portray the mood of renewal and revival in nature. It also creates a positive, happy
> mood that is very appropriate because Tigre and his father are going to harvest their corn
> and other vegetables. This is definitely a happy time for the family, and the beautiful
> springtime setting helps reinforce their feelings of happiness. Now the cycle of planting,
> growing, and harvesting corn has been completed. The book ends with the news of the
> wonderful harvest that the family will have.

Fall highlighted the importance of painting a word picture when developing an effective setting. She also emphasized how the author had used personification to make the setting come
to life. She stressed the importance of the contrasting settings in order to develop the conflicts associated with living so closely to the cycles of nature. After reading and discussing
such vivid passages related to setting, it is a logical next step to have students develop their
own descriptions of setting within their imaginative writings.

The Author Tells About the Character

Look for:
1. The author tells you what he thinks about the character.
2. The author describes what the character looks like.
3. The author describes the setting to let you know more about the character.

Example: Little Town on the Prairie (Laura Ingalls Wilder)
   A description of Mary, after she becomes blind— "Even in the days before scarlet fever had taken the sight from her clear blue eyes, she had never liked to work outdoors in the sun and wind. Now she was happy to be useful indoors." (p. 8)

**The Author Records Conversations
with Other Characters (Dialogue)**

Look for:
1. Speech lets you know about attitudes, dialect (where the character lives), education, mood, wisdom, and so forth.
2. What does the character actually say?
3. How does the character say it?

Example: Little Town on the Prairie
   Ma's attitude toward drinking— " 'It's a pity more men don't say the same,' said Ma. 'I begin to believe that if there isn't a stop put to the liquor traffic, women must bestir themselves and have something to say about it.'
   Pa twinkled at her. 'Seems to me you have plenty to say, Caroline. Ma never left me in doubt as to the evil of drink, nor you either.' " (p. 55)

The Author Describes the Person's Thoughts

Look for:
1. The thoughts describe the person's inner feelings.
2. Do they agree with the dialogue, or does the character have a hidden side?

FIGURE 8–3   Methods of Developing Characters

Excerpts from *Little Town on the Prairie* by Laura Ingalls Wilder. Copyright, 1941, as to text, by Laura Ingalls Wilder. Renewed 1969 by Roger L. MacBride. By permission of Harper & Row, Publishers, Inc.

Characterization.   Another problem emerges for young authors when they try to write stories by weaving incidents together to form a plot. The characters in a story are intrinsic to the incidents that occur. The characters may be people or animals, but young authors often have problems developing their characters so they seem real. Again, you may use literature to help students. How do authors of some of the children's favorite books make the characters seem so real? Most authors use the following methods to develop characters:

1. Tell about the person through narration.
2. Record the character's conversation with others in the story (dialogue).
3. Describe the person's thoughts.
4. Show others' thoughts about the character.
5. Show the character in action.

You can use these five methods to explore characterization and add new dimensions to students' writing. In preparation, have the students read books about memorable characters

Example: Little Town on the Prairie

Laura is not sure that there is always something to be thankful for—"Laura thought, 'Ma is right, there is always something to be thankful for.' Still, her heart was heavy. The oats and the corn crop were gone. She did not know how Mary could go to college now. The beautiful new dress, the two other new dresses, and the pretty underwear, must be laid away until next year. It was a cruel disappointment to Mary." (p. 106)

The Author Shows Others' Thoughts About the Character

Look for:

1. How do other people react to the character? Do they like him or her? Do they trust him or her? Do all people react the same way?

2. How does your reaction change after you read another's reaction?

Example: Little Town on the Prairie

Laura's various reactions to her sister Mary—"Mary had always been good. Sometimes she had been so good that Laura could hardly bear it." (p. 11)

" 'Oh, Mary,' Laura said. 'You look exactly as if you'd stepped out of a fashion plate. There won't be, there just can't be, one single girl in college who can hold a candle to you.' " (p. 96)

The Author Shows the Character in Action

Look for:

1. Actions suggest what the character is really like, what he or she is doing, and what he or she is planning.

2. Do the actions agree with the dialogue?

Example: Little Town on the Prairie

Laura is very conscientious and trustworthy—"Laura stopped, aghast. Suddenly she had realized what she was doing. Ma must have hidden this book, Laura had no right to read it. Quickly she shut her eyes, and then she shut the book. It was almost more than she could do, not to read just one word more, just to the end of that one line. But she knew that she must not yield one tiny bit to temptation." (p. 141)

FIGURE 8–3   Continued

with whom they are familiar and notice how the authors develop the characters. They will undoubtedly discover basically the same techniques listed previously.

One class, for example, developed large charts, each of which depicted one of the methods of characterization. On the charts, the class described each method in greater detail and recorded examples from various pieces of literature. Finally, the students experimented with that type of character writing. Figure 8–3 gives examples of this activity as it was conducted with a fifth-grade group of accelerated students. The charts and examples provided references throughout the writing process, as the students wrote character sketches using the various techniques. Students can choose undeveloped characters from literature, such as Snow White or Cinderella. It is interesting to take an in-depth look at Cinderella through her thoughts and the thoughts of her stepsisters, her stepmother, and the prince. Older students can read Robin McKinley's *Beauty* (1978) to discover how an author developed a full-length novel from the characters and plot of a folktale. Character sketches may also come from people students know or people they learn about from newspapers or television. It is interesting to speculate about what two sports stars are thinking as they shake hands or what two world leaders are like.

Children with learning disabilities may require considerable help in planning their stories and verifying that they have included each of the story elements. Martin and Manno (1995) describe a successful technique that they use with students who have learning disabilities: They teach the students to use a story planner form to plan their stories and to monitor their writing. The planner includes three columns. The first column lists six essential story elements including main character, other characters, setting, problem, plan (action), and ending. The second column provides space for the students to write brief notes while planning their stories. The third column provides a space for students to check off the elements when they are included in the story.

For Your Development

Select plot, setting, or characterization. Develop a series of lessons to improve understanding of the components of plot, the purposes for setting, or the methods authors use to show character. Use your lessons with children, and share the results with your language arts class, or present your lessons to a small group of your peers.

Symbolism and Allusion

Both creative writing and literature appreciation profit from an understanding of symbolism and allusion. Greek and Roman mythology presents heroes and gods as symbols for certain human characteristics. Jane Yolen (1977) believes that the study of mythology is important for building an understanding of ancient cultures and for acquiring the background necessary to understand many of the allusions in writing. For example, a child cannot fully understand why some mountains are called volcanoes, or what "as strong as Atlas" or "as swift as Mercury" means if he or she has no experience with mythology.

For Your Plan Book

Lesson Plan

A Mythology Unit to Develop Symbolic Writing

The following series of lessons allows children to study mythology, understand the symbolism in mythology, relate the mythological characters to well-known present-day or historical people, and relate the characteristics portrayed by the mythological characters to their self-images. The activities were developed with sixth-grade students who had been studying Greek and Roman mythology in reading/language arts; thus, the lessons were a natural outgrowth of a classroom activity. First, the students reviewed characters from Greek mythology, discussed the characteristics, and looked at what they symbolized:

Poseidon   God of the sea; Greeks prayed to him to protect them when they took a sea voyage.

Ares   God of war, symbolized by the vulture; Hades liked him because he increased the underworld population.

Heracles   Extremely strong Greek hero; accomplished such tasks as killing the nine-headed Hydra.

Zeus	Ruler of Mount Olympus, supreme ruler, god of the wealthy.
Apollo	God of the sun, truth, music, medicine, and prophecy.
Aphrodite	Goddess of love and beauty; presided over girlish babble and tricks.
Hermes	Swift messenger of the gods; god of commerce, orators, and writers.
Demeter	Goddess of crops.
Artemis	Goddess of the moon; guardian of cities, young animals, and women.
Athena	Goddess of wisdom.
Dionysus	God of wine, symbol of revelry; he gave Greece the gift of wine; driven mad by Hera.
Hephaestus	God of fire and artisans; an inventor.

The students then searched for advertisements that used mythological characters and discussed why they were good symbols. For example: Why is Mercury a good symbol for a car? Why is Atlas used as a symbol for a tire company? Why has a camera company chosen the name Argus? (Argus was a giant with a hundred eyes.) They then described what products might use names such as Heracles, Hermes, Apollo, and Poseidon as advertising symbols, and wrote advertisements for their created products.

In the next part of the sequence, the students discussed well-known personalities from the present and past. Each chose a personality and listed the characteristics that they felt described the person. As a final activity in that session, they wrote short descriptions of a person in terms of Greek heroes. One of the students wrote the following symbolic description of Hitler:

Characteristics of Hitler: Paranoid, insane, greedy, hated the Jewish people, powerful speaker, influential, a killer, an egotist, thought his was the master race.

Hitler and Mythology

Since Hitler was a madman who envisioned conquering the world, I would say that Ares and Dionysus would describe Hitler well. Ares was the god of war; since Hitler started World War II, Ares would be a good mythical symbol. I believe that Hades would have also liked Hitler because the war would have sent so many new people to the underworld. Dionysus also is an excellent symbol for Hitler because Dionysus caused a great deal of revelry with his gift of wine but he later went insane. Hitler also caused revelry when he first influenced the German people, but he went insane and his actions caused a great deal of misery.

Finally, the students thought about themselves and identified characteristics that might be used to describe them. They wrote short symbolic descriptions of themselves in terms of mythology. One boy wrote:

The Way I See Myself and Mythology

I personally think that the Greek gods who closely resemble my beliefs are Apollo, Athena, and Hephaestus. Apollo was the god of music and medicine. I hopefully will become a doctor and an accomplished musician. Apollo was also the patron of truth, which is essential for friends to have between one another. Athena was the goddess of wisdom. I always want to know more about everything. Hephaestus was the god of fire and the artisans. He was a great engineer. Hopefully I'll be able to invent patentable items.

For Your Development

1. Read several selections from mythology. (Do not use Greek mythology.) Make a chart showing the characteristics of the heroes and what they might symbolize. Describe yourself in terms of these characteristics.
2. Make a collection of current advertisements that use symbols from mythology. Are they appropriate? Why or why not?

Poetic Writing

Why do some children produce quality poetry, while others do not? The answer probably lies primarily with a teacher's dedication to the development of poetic self-expression. Just as in presenting other forms of creative writing, teachers must structure the environment so that children are not punished for novel and creative thinking. The school experience is often criticized because many children apparently learn to conform and, thus, they learn at an early age not to express themselves.

What are some instructional approaches that you can use to develop creative poetry writers? First, stimulate an interest in and a love for poetry. Nobody can write poetry without first developing a feel for it. Consequently, read good poetry to children. Teachers should begin by reading humorous poems, which establish a positive image, and simple free-verse poems, which serve as models for beginning writing. Popular humorous poets include Jack Prelutsky, Shel Silverstein, William Jay Smith, John Ciardi, and Laura Richards. Sources for poetry selections include textbooks by Huck, Hepler, and Hickman (1997), Norton (2003), and Sutherland (1996).

Awareness and Observation.   In addition to reading poetry to children, teachers must structure activities that nurture both awareness and powers of observation in children. For example, one third-grade student teacher planned a lesson around an orange. He began by asking the children where oranges came from, what oranges are used for, and whether they liked oranges. Then, he gave an orange to each child and explained that the children were to take their time discovering all they could about an orange through touch, taste, sight, and smell. He told them: "Discover all you can about the outside of your orange by looking at it; look at the pores, the color, the shape, the scars, and the soft spots. Now feel it. Roll it in your hands and on the table, squeeze it, rub your fingers over the pores, close your eyes and feel it. Smell it. Slowly begin to peel it; how does it smell? Contrast the feel and sight of the outside of the skin to the inside; taste the inside of the skin. Now look at the inside of the orange. What shape is it? What color is it? Feel the inside, gently squeeze it, taste the inside of the orange. What is inside some of the sections? Put one in your hand. What color is it? What shape is it? Is it hard or soft?"

After the students talked about all the things they had discovered about an orange, the teacher asked them to write a poem, beginning each line with "An orange." Some observations that resulted from this activity follow:

An Orange

An orange is round like a ball
An orange is the color of the sun
An orange is bumpy on the outside
An orange is squeezy and yummy

An orange rind is bitter as a lemon
An orange has squishy pulp
An orange has tough, slippery seeds

This type of observation and poetry development was influenced by Kenneth Koch's (1971) *Wishes, Lies, and Dreams,* in which he describes his experiences teaching poetry to children in New York City. The book describes such techniques as developing wish poems, noise poems, and color poems, and it includes examples of poetry written on these themes by first- through sixth-grade children. Listening to poetry written by other children stimulates enthusiasm in elementary students. Koch found that the theme of wishes is one that all children are able to relate to. The same format used in "An Orange" can help children develop their wishes into poems. The following poem developed after a teacher read a number of "Wish" poems from Koch's book. After hearing the poems, the students talked about various wishes of their own, then wrote their own wish poems.

I Wish . . .

I wish I was a towering giraffe
So I could see everything
I wish I was a swift cheetah
So I could run like the wind
I wish I was a majestic tree
So all the birds could rest on me
—A fourth-grade wish

Effective teachers provide an environment that encourages creative writing time.

In another type of observation lesson, the students were to write a visually descriptive piece about a fall afternoon. But the teacher did not just tell them to take out paper and pencil and write a page about a fall day; instead, she began in a field. The students made lists of sight, sound, and smell words and word clusters (distinguishing between insect, plant, and mechanical life). They listed the images that they saw in the clouds. They investigated their surroundings—finding, catching, and describing daddy longlegs, crickets, and katydids. This activity resulted in observations that later took a poetic form. After observing a cricket, one student wrote the following poem:

Cricket
creeping, putting
one leg first,
then another,
and another,
till all six
have moved
and he starts
again.
ing, le
p   a
m   p
u   i
j   n
g

flying through
the air
and then
Bump
he lands
and
jumps
again.

Notice how this sixth-grade student has captured the essence of the cricket. Another student used her powers of observation to watch an eagle in the sky. She jotted down her feelings as she watched and later put her observations and feelings into this poetic form:

Eagle

I like to watch an eagle soar,
How he just glides alone,
I wonder what it's like,
gliding freely through the air,
his wings spread widely,
and, he looks so nice and proud
but, pretty soon he'll be extinct,
and he'll glide and soar no more.

Imagery.   Much of poetry revolves around imagery. Poets often create word pictures by comparing their thoughts to experiences and likenesses and differences in life. The following third-grade author uses various comparisons to describe a giggle:

Giggles

Giggles are good-tasting fellows
They smell like brownies
Just coming out of the oven
They feel like a new Bugs Bunny doll
Giggles look like a red clown at the circus
Giggles are shaped like bubbles.

Another child developed the image of a gulp:

Gulps

A gulp is very heavy,
    especially on rainy days.
A gulp tastes like chocolate,
    smells like coffee,
    and feels like a magnet.

To develop imagery, children must practice describing objects in terms of other objects. One teacher introduced color description through a brainstorming activity in which the class rapidly provided associations with a color. For example:

It is as red as . . .   a stop sign, blood, a valentine, danger, a lobster, a sunset, an apple, a strawberry

Similarly, with another concept:

As quick as . . .   drinking a glass of lemonade on a hot day, a shooting star, a mongoose

Children can also make comparisons with the following expressions: as tired as, as hungry as, as thin as, as quiet as, as silly as, as sneaky as, as soft as. After this kind of practice, one student described a house as "so empty, you could hear the spiders spin webs."

The experiences of these classes demonstrate the interaction of a stimulation activity and the brainstorming of ideas and concepts prior to writing. Stimulation and discussion activities not only develop creative awareness but also the descriptive vocabularies necessary for creative writing. Student teachers as well as classroom teachers report that their creative writing activities are not very successful when they ignore the oral exchange of ideas.

Poetry Forms.   Several of the student poems presented in this chapter use a basic form, such as starting each line with "Happiness is" or ending each line with a rhyming word. Children enjoy several other forms of poetry and find them not too difficult to write. Such forms may also provide some children with a little more guidance and structure. Chapter 7 presents forms for limericks, cinquains, and diamantes as examples of poetry forms that you could use as models during the writing process.

Using Poetry to Answer the Question "Does Poetry Reveal the Life of the Poet?"   Is it possible to analyze poetry to discover autobiographical information about the poet? Can the life of the poet be authenticated through the poetry written or selected by the poet? Norton and Norton (2002) analyzed the poetry of Jack Prelutsky, Emily Dickinson, Walt Whitman, and Jacqueline Kennedy Onassis to try and answer this question. They then compared their conclusions drawn from the poetry with biographical and autobiographical information about the poets.

You may also use the poetry of various children's poets to try to reveal the life of the poet. For this activity we will consider the poetry of Jack Prelutsky, who is very popular with children and has published over fourteen volumes of his own poetry and three anthologies of selected poetry.

To begin this project, explain to the students that they will use examples from poetry to exemplify autobiographical information. First, discuss with students that Jack Prelutsky has published numerous volumes of poetry for younger readers. These volumes are frequently on best-seller lists and have been identified as among the 100 most influential publications for juvenile audiences. To allow students to have a better understanding of Jack Prelutsky you might read "Through the Eyes of a Poet" featured in *Through the Eyes of a Child: An Introduction to Children's Literature* (Norton, 2003). After listening to this interview, children will discover that Prelutsky writes mostly humorous poems and many of them deal with humorous, not frightening, monsters.

Share with students additional biographical information such as that found in Sharron L. McElmeel's *100 Most Popular Children's Authors* (1999) and *The Poet Tree* (1993) and Allen Raymond's "Jack Prelutsky . . . Man of Many Talents" (1986). By reading these sources we discover considerable information that is verified through his poetry. For example, biographers reveal that Prelutsky lived with his family on the top floor of an apartment in Brooklyn and he was known as an absent-minded, strange-looking, clumsy kid. Poems in *The New Kid on the Block* and *Something Big Has Been Here* reflect many of these experiences. He loved everything about dinosaurs and he enjoyed reading about animals. His poems about dinosaurs and other monsters such as *The Dragons Are Singing Tonight* (1993), *The Gargoyle on the Roof* (1999), and *Tyrannosaurus Was a Beast* (1988), however, reflect his humor and his enjoyment of language. Biographers also reveal that Prelutsky frequently writes about the exploits of his childhood friends. We discover that his four best friends were Harvey, Lucky, Tony, and Willie. These experiences motivated the poetry in *Rolling Harvey Down the Hill*. Provide students with a collection of Prelutsky's poetry and ask them to search for poems that support this information.

In addition to using Prelutsky's poetry to try to identify various characteristics of his personality, you may ask students to use Prelutsky's poetry to write their own biographies of Prelutsky. For this activity, they should use lines from his poetry to support their beliefs about the poet. I have used this activity with all ages of students. University students also enjoy writing the biography and then comparing their conclusions with information in more factual biographical writings.

Older students may use the poetry published in *The Best-Loved Poems of Jacqueline Kennedy Onassis* (2001), edited by her daughter, Caroline Kennedy, to search for biographical data. This collection includes poems that she loved as well as several of her own poems. Students can learn a great deal about the woman who was the First Lady and one of the most influential advocates of the arts. Caroline Kennedy's comments in the introduction to the book reveal Mrs. Kennedy's love of poetry: "One of the greatest gifts my brother and I received from my mother was her love of literature and language. In this anthology, I have tried to include poems that reflect things that were important to her—a spirit of adventure, the worlds of imagination and nature, and the strength of love and family. . . . My mother was lucky to have a grandfather who loved poetry. When she was a little girl, she would visit him every Wednesday evening after dancing class, and they would memorize poems together. I feel fortunate that she passed this gift along to John and me, teaching us poems she loved as well as encouraging us to discover poems on our own" (pp. xi–xiii).

Expository Writing

Expository writing is probably the most common writing used in classrooms. According to Frye, Baker, and Perkins (1985), expository writing is "explanatory writing, the presentation of facts, ideas, or opinions, as in short forms like the article or essay, or in longer nonfictional forms like the history, scientific treatise, travel book, biography, or autobiography. Expository writing is often treated as a larger category including exposition as a major element, but making use also of argument, description, and narration. It is contrasted with imaginative writing or creative writing" (p. 184).

Cognitive abilities are frequently discussed in relation to writing. For example, a study conducted by Webster and Ammon (1994) found that certain types of cognitive development may be more crucial for writing that requires comparisons. They discovered that students' ability to classify is especially relevant to the organization of attributes in children's reading and writing of comparisons. Making comparisons are very important in many areas of the curriculum.

Some activities use content-area sources to improve understanding of writing and the writing process, whereas other activities emphasize the writing process as a way to learn in the content areas. Many writing activities reflect both goals, although one or the other may be more important for a specific teacher and a specific content area. Writing-to-learn strategies should develop writing fluency, foster abstract thinking, and guide students in their quest for knowledge. There are numerous ways in which you can accomplish learning through writing.

Research Reports

The third-grade students who wrote an outline of their class trip, using questions and answers, were actually developing a report (see Chapter 7). The structure of the report included a central theme: the train ride. Each paragraph had a main idea relating to the central theme. The answers to the main-idea questions provided supporting ideas, which developed the three main ideas under the central theme. This exercise was an excellent readiness activity for the time when the students would have to produce individual, well-planned reports or other expository compositions. As elementary students progress into longer expository writing, they must decide on the audience and purpose for the writing. Once they have chosen their subject, they must narrow it to one they can cover realistically in a short composition, gather ideas and information, organize the ideas and information, write the report, and revise it.

Audience and Purpose.   Activities that focus on expository writing requirements include charting weather and temperature; filling out forms; and writing news stories, autobiographies and biographies, book reports, editorials, class minutes, and reports for projects in science and social studies classes. Audiences range from known class members, teachers, parents, and friends to wider, unknown audiences. The purposes for most of these projects are to inform, compare, compile, convince, and report.

Subject.   Conducting research and writing about subjects of considerable interest to each student may be extremely motivating. Researching and writing family history make interesting topics. Books such as Daisy Corning Stone Spedden's *Polar the Titanic Bear* (1994) provide an exciting motivator for this type of writing. Spedden tells the history of the family through the viewpoint of a toy bear. In this way, the bear reveals the various experiences as he accompanies the family in their travels and describes their adventures. The text presents

The writing process will help young writers focus on audience and purpose.

an historical depiction of the family by including items such as photographs, postcards, and tickets along with the family history.

Students must be able to uncover information about the subjects for their research. They should look for information in textbooks, journals, magazines, encyclopedias, newspapers, and so forth. Students should look through class, school, and public libraries to see how much information is available to them on various subjects.

Many subjects are just too broad for elementary students. For example, energy, transportation, air travel, and the Revolutionary War are obviously too broad to approach in a short composition. Students should narrow the scope of these subjects. There are several ways to help students narrow a subject. Brainstorming helped a group of fifth graders look at the general subject of water and find specific topics and main ideas to develop in short compositions. The fifth graders developed a web of interest, narrowing the broad subject of water to four topics: (1) sports, (2) energy, (3) sea life, and (4) weather. Each specific topic had several main ideas that students could use in organizing a composition. This technique is successful with elementary students, but you can use it with various grade levels by changing the subject matter.

Students can also narrow topics by studying the tables of contents in several books on a general subject. For example, the subject of camping is interesting to many elementary children because they often go camping with their families or scout troops. After looking through books on camping, a fourth-grade class developed the list in Figure 8–4. This search yielded many specific, interesting topics that the students could turn into meaningful compositions. The approach also teaches students how to use tables of contents for locating information. Many students need such practice in reference skills.

Another way to narrow a subject is to have children list some questions they want answered about a general topic. For example, a group of fourth graders became concerned because a stream near their homes was cluttered with bottles, cans, and other offensive garbage. They investigated the dangers of this kind of pollution and what other communities had done in similar circumstances. Then, they recommended ways to improve their stream. They developed good reports from their study, and they even wrote some letters to the editor of the local newspaper and to community groups to generate community interest.

Camping

1. Camp cooking
   a. campfires
   b. camping stoves
   c. cooking utensils
   d. food
   e. recipes
2. Equipment for sleeping
   a. tents
   b. sleeping bags
   c. cots and air mattresses
   d. pickup campers
   e. trailers
   f. motor homes
3. Special clothes
   a. hiking shoes and clothing
   b. raincoats or ponchos
   c. cold-weather wear
   d. clothing for horseback riding
4. Skills
   a. using an ax
   b. using knives
   c. using a rope—knots, hitches, splices
   d. reading a map and compass
   e. building a fire
   f. packing a backpack
   g. setting up and taking down camp

5. Safety in camp
   a. first aid
   b. pure water
   c. water safety
   d. insects
   e. snakes
   f. wild animals
6. Survival
   a. navigation
   b. getting help
   c. emergency food
   d. emergency shelter
   e. water
7. Transportation
   a. backpacking
   b. canoes
   c. bicycles
   d. horses
   e. boats
   f. trailers
8. Where to camp
   a. national parks
   b. state parks
   c. wilderness areas
   d. private campgrounds

FIGURE 8–4   A List of Camping Topics

Ideas and Information.   The methods for narrowing a topic proceed naturally into the next step: searching for ideas and information to include in the composition. For example, after students who were studying Native Americans changed or added questions to the categories they had chosen, the teacher explored the library with them. They looked through card files, tables of contents, indexes, websites, and so forth to discover sources of information. From these resources, the students compiled information to answer each of their questions.

After narrowing the subject and developing important questions, students should write each of their questions on a separate index card or sheet of paper. Then, when they find information that pertains to the question, they should write it, in their own words, on the appropriate card or paper. Placing the items on separate cards helps students rearrange their questions and information into the most logical order. They find it easier to deal with one main idea at a time rather than a disorganized pile of information. For example, a card asking a main-idea question about camping might look like Figure 8–5.

Organization.   After students finish gathering information and ideas on cards, they are ready to start analyzing, selecting, and ordering their information. Webbing, discussed previously, is a good way to accomplish this task. Students may find they have too little or too

---

How can you make an emergency shelter if you are lost?

Start looking for your shelter in the day.

Shelter should protect from cold, wind, and rain.

Build a lean-to from about 1-inch-thick poles tied together with vines or fishline.

- Draw a picture to show this in my report.

Put evergreens or leaf branches on poles to protect yourself from rain.

- Draw a picture to show this in my report.

Make the lean-to very steep.

A cave or overhanging rock makes a shelter.

Build a fire in front of the shelter.

A fire will make you warm and be a signal.

If you are in snow, dig a cave in the side of a drift.

Put pine boughs on the floor of the snow cave.

A snow cave is a good insulator.

Leave air holes in the cave.

Mark the outside of the cave so searchers will know you're there.

- Draw a picture to show this in my report.

FIGURE 8–5   A Card Asking a Main-Idea Question about Camping

much information about one main idea. Some information may be important, some may be trivial. Some information may require verification from sources other than those they have already used. As students arrange and rearrange their information cards, they frequently discover the best organizational patterns to use. The various organizational patterns include chronological; spatial; familiar to unfamiliar; problem, to cause of problem, to possible solutions; problem, to effect of problem, to possible solutions; and question to answer. These formats provide logical organizations for reports in many content areas.

Writing.   Now, the students must develop the main ideas and important details into a closely related unit. In literature, the plot has a beginning, a middle, and an end. The same progression appears in factual writing, but it does not build the action to a climax. Instead, the beginning introduces readers to what the writing will be about and catches attention, the middle develops the main ideas and supporting information, and a summary or concluding paragraph pulls together the ideas in the composition and gives readers the feeling that the composition is finished.

The introductory paragraph is important. When you pick up a magazine, how do you choose the articles that you read? The author may ask a question that arouses your interest, make a startling statement, or present an interesting, little known fact. The author may show how important something is to you personally. Questions such as "Would you like to save $100 a month on your grocery bill?" or "Do you know that the new cars are considered unsafe and are being recalled?" usually attract attention because the subject matter of the article affects you in a highly personal way. You would expect the introductory paragraph of the first example to introduce a piece about various ways to save money in the grocery store, and that of the second article to introduce a critical report on the dangers of a specific new car. The writer has pre-

FIGURE 8–6   A Diagram Identifying the Major Parts of a Composition

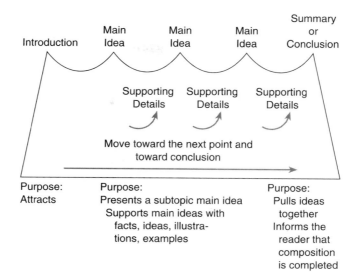

sented the issue, and you expect the remainder of the article to develop facts and information that will help solve the problem. No matter how attention-getting the opener is, it is a poor introduction if it raises false expectations about the content of the composition that follows.

The body of a work develops the main ideas related to the introductory paragraph. If students grasp the concept of a paragraph, writing the body is not too difficult. If students understand the need for rational sequencing of ideas, they can move logically from one point to the next. Some vocabulary terms help writing move from one idea to another. If students are writing in chronological order, for example, they may use such words as *first, second, third, before, during, after, yesterday, today, tomorrow, next,* and *last.* Or they may use dates, such as "in 1990," "in 1993," and "in 2003." These words signal the developing order of ideas. If students organize their thoughts according to problem, causes, effects, and solutions, they can show relationships between ideas. Words such as *because, therefore, since, too,* and *when* signal relationships in this kind of organization.

Certain phrases signal that a composition is drawing to a close. Phrases such as "in conclusion" and "to summarize" indicate that the writer is going to end a report.

To review the three parts of the composition, look at them in diagram form in Figure 8–6. This diagram is quite different from the diagram for a story. A written report presents an introduction that quickly interests readers and develops ideas that move toward a conclusion or summary.

Revision.   In teaching composition skills, you should help students develop clear ideas, organize them, and elaborate on them. Consequently, teacher feedback, student evaluation of writing, and any rewriting should emphasize these aspects.

Interact with students during the entire writing process. Provide both positive feedback and an opportunity to make improvements during each step of the process. Do not wait for the finished product. Writing conferences can provide opportunities to interact with students when they select a topic, narrow the topic, gather information, organize information, develop an outline, and write the final composition. React as students discuss and write during each part of the process.

MacArthur, Graham, and Schwartz (1993) teach a revising strategy to students with special needs that specifies the roles of author and editor and provides specific evaluation criteria and revising strategies. During this strategy, students meet in pairs to discuss each others' papers. The revising strategy includes the following steps:

1. LISTEN and read along as the author reads.
2. TELL what it was about and what you liked best. (After the second step, the two students change roles and the second student reads his or her paper.)
3. READ and make NOTES about the work.
   CLEAR? Is there anything that is hard to understand?
   DETAILS? Where could more information be added? (Students separately reread each others' papers and note questions and suggestions on the paper.)
4. DISCUSS your suggestions with the author and try to develop solutions.
5. The author makes revisions on the computer.

Writing and the Content Areas

As we have already stated, some activities use content-area sources to improve understanding of writing and the writing process; other activities emphasize using writing to learn in the content areas. O'Day (1994) emphasizes the use of writing in social studies to encourage thinking and independent learning in middle-school children. For example, O'Day recommends that teachers provide a few minutes for students to gather their ideas in notebooks before a discussion in order to increase both the level of discussions and the number of participants. In this example, prewriting functions as prethinking. O'Day states: "In my classes, more passive students who rarely entered discussions in the past usually now, through a prewrite, have the time and ability to carefully think out a concept or question" (p. 39). Other writing activities that improve understanding in social studies include finding evidence of author bias and then using these notes to create their own slanted language to present a point of view that is opposite to the author.

Informational Text (Nonfiction).   Hairston (1986) uses simulation activities with older students to place them in the role of a specific professional writer and to have them consider how that author may have responded during the writing process. For example, Hairston selects a good example of nonfictional literature and then helps students construct scenarios in which they try to reconstruct the writer's actions, both mental and physical, from the time of the initial idea to the time of the completed product. Within these scenarios, the students consider what motivated the author to write the text; how and why the author chose a certain approach to attract attention and gain sympathy or understanding; what techniques the author used to substantiate the specific point of view, including examples, experiences, comparisons, details, and images; why the author chose those techniques; and how the author shaped the text to develop that specific point of view.

During this analysis and simulation, students should discover that good professional authors of nonfiction support their writing with facts and specific details rather than with generalizations and unsupported opinions. In addition, students should discover how professional authors deal with some of the same problems that cause them difficulty. To extend understanding of specific writing techniques used by authors, develop files of examples that illustrate solutions to various writing problems, such as gaining attention, developing support for positions, shaping articles to develop positions, using figurative language and images to persuade, and developing conclusions. Then, ask the students to apply these techniques in their own writing.

The following books are useful in helping students discover how authors use various organizational patterns to shape their ideas and improve their writing (Norton, 1992): Seymour Simon's *New Questions and Answers About Dinosaurs* (1990)—question and answer; Laurence Pringle's *Global Warming: Assessing the Greenhouse Threat* (1990)—problem–effect—cause–solution; Peter and Connie Roop's *Seasons of the Cranes* (1989)—chronological order; and Helen Roney Sattler's *Giraffes, the Sentinels of the Savannas* (1990)—main idea to supporting details.

Additional authors of nonfictional information literature that may be used for extending understanding of specific writing techniques include Franklyn Branley, Joanna Cole, Patricia Lauber, Hershell and Joan Nixon, Dorothy Patent, Jack Denton Scott, Millicent Selsam, and Jerome Wexler.

Children with learning disabilities may require additional structured strategies to help them write informational material. MacArthur et al. (1993) recommend a mnemonic strategy for helping these students develop various types of writing. For example, when writing a simple opinion essay, they may use the mnemonic TREE (Topic or what you believe, Reasons, Examples, Ending).

For Your Plan Book

Lesson Plan

Authentication of Literature and Expository Writing

Two types of authentication projects lend themselves to expository writing and are excellent ways to help students discover the importance of and even the fun associated with searching for clues related to the authenticity of a text. The first type of project focuses on document authentication of folklore (Norton, 1998), and the second type of project relates to the authentication of historical fiction, biography, autobiography, and informational books. The second type of writing project may be closely related to content-area subjects.

Document Authenticity of Folklore

My students and I have used this strategy with students as young as second grade and as old as those at university levels. The first step of this approach is to evaluate the quality of source notes that are found in folktales, myths, or legends. To make this evaluation, teachers may use suggestions developed by Hearne (1993a, 1993b). Hearne proposes the evaluation of source notes by categorizing them into five-point evaluation source notes that proceed from the worst examples to the best examples.

In the first article, Hearne (1993a) asks "How do you tell if a folktale in picture-book format is authentic or true to its cultural background?" (p. 22). Hearne then explores the necessity for authors and publishers to provide source notes so that reviewers and readers may judge the authenticity of the folktale. She categorizes the author's provision of source notes into five levels based on certain criteria. At the lowest, or fifth level, are nonexistent source notes. At this level the subtitle may identify the book as a folktale from a specific culture, but no additional information is given. A text such as Ed Young's *Lon Po Po: A Red Riding Hood Tale from China* (1989) includes only subtitle information.

The fourth level provides a background-as-source-note in which the author provides some background information such as the history of the tale or the location of the story without providing sources that identify the book or books from which the tale was adapted. For example, the only information provided in Alexander Nikolayevich Afanasyev's *The Fool and the Fish: A Tale*

Continued

from Russia (1990) mentions a brief history of Afanasyev, who lived from 1826 to 1871. Although the information provided is interesting, it is not sufficient to evaluate the authenticity of the tale.

The third level is the fine-print source note that appears in such tiny print that the reader considers it irrelevant to the text. An example of this type of source note is found in Ruth Sanderson's retelling of *The Twelve Dancing Princesses* (1990). The source note states: "The text for *The Twelve Dancing Princesses* was retold from the Brothers Grimm." This information at least provides a starting point for comparative research, but, unfortunately, the fine print causes many readers to ignore it.

The highest two levels of source notes provide information that readers may use to begin their own authentication research. For example, well-made source notes that cite specific sources in highly visible print that is also integrated into the book's design fall into the second level. This source note may include descriptions of how the story fits into a culture. The first level of source note is a model source note that cites specific sources, describes the cultural context, and elaborates on how the adapter or reteller may have changed the tale, with explanations about why these changes were made. This final type of source note provides readers with information related to authenticity and allows students to verify the tale's accuracy or make a study of the adaptations.

For example, the author's note in Aaron Shepard's *Master Man* (2001) states: "'Master Man' is a tale of the Hausa, the largest ethnic group of northern Nigeria. The Hausa live mainly on the Savannah (grassland with scattered trees). Though most Hausa live in rural villages—as portrayed in this story—the larger Hausa towns have possessed a sophisticated urban culture since long before European colonization. . . . The main source for my retelling is number 12, 'A story about a giant, and the cause of thunder,' in *Hausa Folk-Lore, Customs, Proverbs, Etc.,* by R. Sutherland Rattray (Oxford: Clarendon Press, 1913, volume 1). I also drew on several other Hausa variants of the tales, collectively titled 'The Story of Manly-Man' and translated by Neil Skinner (Madison: University of Wisconsin Press, 1977)" (Author's Note).

Using these criteria for source notes, students can review the source notes in folklore found in the school or public library, collect examples of each level of source note, and draw conclusions that support the importance of high-quality source notes when judging the authenticity of published folklore in single volumes or in collections. Students can use these judgments to respond to the importance of source notes in order to answer Hearne's question: "How do you tell if a folktale in picture-book format is authentic, or true to its cultural background?" If desired, students can locate the original sources for the tales and compare them with the new adaptations.

Hearne's second article (1993b) focuses on the authenticity of illustrations in the folklore. Now Hearne asks: "How do contemporary adaptation and art reflect a folktale's culture of origin?" (p. 33). Hearne maintains that the art or design should be authentic for the culture. This means that illustrators should not use motifs misappropriated from a culture or misapplied from one culture to another. Stott (1990) also emphasizes the need for illustrations that reflect both the culture and the geographical location.

Again, the source notes in some of the illustrated folktales provide enough information to begin a search and to evaluate the authenticity of the illustrations. For example, John Steptoe identifies the original source, the culture, and the geographical location for *Mufaro's Beautiful Daughters: An African Tale* (1987) as "The tale was collected from people living near the Zimbabwe ruins, a site that archaeologists now consider to have been a magnificent trade city built and occupied by indigenous Africans. Details in the illustrations for *Mufaro's Beautiful Daughters* are based on the architecture of the ruins and on the flora and fauna of the Zimbabwe region" (unnumbered back cover).

Students can use this information to begin their research of nonfiction articles and books. For example, they could study the reality of the city. Great Zimbabwe is found in ruins as documented and photographed in a *National Geographic* article, "Rhodesia: A House Divided," by

Allan C. Fisher (1975). The huts illustrated by Steptoe are similar to those shown in Barnes-Svarney's *Places and Peoples of the World: Zimbabwe* (1989). The soapstone birds illustrated by Steptoe are found in Patricia Cheney's photographs in *The Land and People of Zimbabwe* (1990). Many additional examples showing the authenticity of the illustrations are available.

Teachers may ask students to choose illustrated books, search for informational sources that suggest that the illustrations are either authentic or nonauthentic, and write a response to Hearne's (1993b) question: "How do contemporary adaptation and art reflect a folktale's culture of origin? And, what are the implications when these origins are—and are not—reflected accurately?" (p. 33).

This type of authentication project may be completed as a group activity in which the illustrations in a book are divided among members of the group. Now each group is responsible for searching for and reporting on the authenticity of the illustrations. Students frequently enjoy locating errors in illustrations as much as they do substantiating authentic sources. This type of activity is also excellent for helping students learn about various cultures or expanding their knowledge about geography and time periods.

Authentication of Historical Fiction, Biography, and Informational Books

This type of authentication and writing is excellent for slightly older students depending on the availability and reading level of the materials. This authentication activity may also use websites as part of the evaluation process.

This activity is based on categories modified from Altick and Fenstermaker's *The Art of Literary Research* (1993). The categories are placed in question format to help the students. The example we will use to authenticate is the 1999 National Book Award winner, Louise Erdrich's *The Birchbark House,* an historical fiction novel about a young Ojibwa girl living on an island in Lake Superior in 1847. Let us start this activity by evaluating the author's source notes and deciding if there is information in these notes that will help during the authentication. For example, the author creates credibility for the story by identifying herself as a member of the Turtle Mountain Band of Ojibwa and stating that she became interested in writing the book while researching her own family history. In her acknowledgments Erdrich states: "My mother, Rita Erdrich, and my sister Lise Erdrich, researched our family life and found ancestors on both sides who lived on Madeline Island during the time in which this book is set. One of them was Gatay Manomin, or Old Wild Rice. I'd like to thank him and his descendants, my extended family.... This book and those that will follow are an attempt to retrace my own family's history" (unpaged acknowledgments). Ask the students to respond to the level of information discovered in this note. How could it help them begin their research?

Now introduce each of the questions. Following each question is a summary of the type of information that students may find to authenticate the book:

1. *What are the geographical and social settings for the book and are they authentic?* Students should use nonfictional sources to evaluate this area. According to the book the story is set on an island in Lake Superior near the village of La Pointe. The author includes a map of Lake Superior that includes an island and La Pointe. Informational books such as Tanner's *The Ojibwa* (1992) confirm that the Ojibwa lived in this area. Maps show an island called Madeline Island and a major mission called La Pointe. Warren's *History of the Ojibwa People* (1984) includes a chapter on the town of La Pointe and describes the interactions of the people. Using such sources, students may analyze the lifestyles of the people, their living conditions including types of homes in summer and in winter, and the descriptions of the geographical locations and compare these with descriptions found in *The Birchbark House.* Erdrich's drawings include

Continued

illustrations of peeling the birchbark, a birchbark house, a winter cabin, and maps that may be used for comparisons and authentication.

2. *What are the values and beliefs of the people in the book and are they authentic?* Two of the evaluative criteria for Native American literature are that the Native American characters belong to a specific identified tribe and are not grouped together under one category referred to as "Indian" and that customs, values, and beliefs for the specific tribe are authentic and respected (Norton, 2003).

In this book the Ojibwa tribe is identified and Ojibwa values are especially meaningful. The author reinforces Ojibwa values and beliefs through traditional stories told by the girl's father and grandmother. One of the stories told by the grandmother is "Nanabozho and Muskrat Make an Earth." The text develops the importance of using oral stories to pass on various beliefs and to educate the members of the tribe. In addition, the "Earth Diver" story as told by grandmother is one of the oldest and most common creation stories told among North American tribes living around the Great Lakes.

Teachers may ask students to authenticate this part of the story by searching for an example of an "Earth Diver" type of story such as "The Earth on Turtle's Back" found in Michael J. Caduto and Joseph Bruchac's *Keepers of the Earth* (1989).

3. *What are the major events that make up the plot of the story?* Many of the major events that can easily be authenticated follow the seasons and the associated tasks performed by the Ojibwa people, for example, building the birchbark house to live in during the warmer seasons during which time the people peel the birchbark from the trees, create a frame from wood saplings, and cover the frame with sheets of birchbark. This process can be authenticated by reading Lucas's *The Ojibwas: People of the Northern Forests* (1994) and Tanner's *The Ojibwa* (1992).

Another major event includes collecting the sap from maple sugar groves and boiling the sap into maple sugar. *The Ojibwa* describes this process. The collection of wild rice is also described in *The Birchbark House*.

The interactions with the fur traders and missionary schools are important events as is overcoming the smallpox epidemic. These events are also easily authenticated.

4. *What are the major conflicts in the book and are they authentic for the time period?* The major conflict that the village must overcome is the smallpox epidemic of 1847 during which time eighteen Ojibwa died from the disease. This overcoming of a smallpox epidemic is also a major conflict in Jan Hudson's *Sweetgrass* (1989).

Another major conflict results because of the European intrusion through trading posts and mission schools. Sources such as *The Ojibwas: People of the Northern Forests* and *History of the Ojibwa People* describe the impact of the British and French fur traders.

5. *What are the major themes and are they found in other literature written about the time period or the people?* Several themes are developed in *The Birchbark House* that are also developed in other Native American literature. For example, important messages are revealed in dreams and voices heard in nature. This ability is revealed as "Nokomis understood the meaning of what had happened, understood why the voices had spoken, understood what it meant for Omakaya's future and was proud and glad to have a granddaughter chosen to be a healer" (p. 209). Many autobiographies and biographies of early Native American leaders such as *Black Elk Speaks: Being the Life Story of a Holy Man of the Ogala Sioux* (1979) show respect for messages revealed in dreams and the hearing of voices found in nature. Consequently, this ability reinforces the information that only people of great stature within a tribe are given this special ability. This ability also suggests that the grandmother is correct when she is proud of her granddaughter's future.

Another theme shows that being responsible for one's family is important. Students may conduct an interesting comparison of this theme found in *The Birchbark House* and in Jan Hudson's *Sweetgrass* (1989), a story about a young Blackfoot girl who grows up during the winter of a smallpox epidemic in 1837. (For references to Native American literature see Chapter 3, "Native American Literature," in Norton's *Multicultural Children's Literature,* 2001, pp. 68–131.)

For a group activity in authentication and expository writing, students may divide into five groups and each group conduct research into one of the questions. They should search for support for the topics and compare the information found in the text with other nonfictional sources. The search for folklore that supports the values is especially enjoyable as students combine an oral activity with a writing activity.

A University Student's Response to Her Authentication Project

Carolyn Graham (2002) wrote the following evaluation after completing an authentication project:

> I learned so much from authenticating Sabin's book, *Amelia Earhart: Adventure in the Sky.* Sabin's inaccuracies seemed to be minor and of little consequence. However, when I started adding up all the minor errors it irritated me. I was surprised at how many little errors could be in a book. Before I have always believed the facts in a book were all true. I know enough to take an author's opinion in stride, but I expect an author to accurately present facts. . . . It caused me to see the huge amount of research that must go into biographies and other books with nonfictional material.
>
> I also like this project because it taught me how to use books and fun materials to teach children. As we learned in class, you do not always have to use textbooks, which often bore children. I feel like I know a lot about Amelia Earhart now and I have not read a single textbook. I found it easier to remember the information while reading all of the biographies about Amelia Earhart. I am also quite sure that I have learned a lot more about her than I ever would have from an account in a textbook. I do not think that I have ever seen more than a paragraph or two in any of my textbooks about her.
>
> I think that this would be a great book to use in the classroom. I think that children could benefit from authenticating this book because there are some inaccuracies in the book and it would teach them not to take what is given to them for granted without checking it out themselves. I also personally like the book because it tells kids that no matter the boundaries set by society, anyone who sets their mind to it can achieve their dreams. (p. 27)

Summaries.   Identifying a main idea in a book is often difficult for elementary students. Taylor (1986) found that fourth- and fifth-grade students had difficulty finding and expressing main ideas when they were asked to write summaries. Teaching children to write summaries integrates reading, writing, listening, and speaking with the various content areas. Hidi and Anderson (1986) found that effective summary writing teaches students how to discover information important to the author and how to analyze and paraphrase this information. Key elements in this approach require identification of topic sentences, main ideas, and important details; identification of key phrases, such as "in summary"; identification of text clues, such as underlining, italics, and boldface print; and ability to supply synonyms and paraphrase text.

Hidi and Anderson (1986) recommend that teachers begin with short passages and gradually increase passage length as students improve their summarizing skills. In addition, early experiences should use simple narratives and texts that are well organized so that important text elements are obvious to students.

Coffman (1994) studied sixth-grade students' ability to write summaries and techniques that improve their summary writing. He found that children experience few difficulties when summarizing short stories. However, they have greater difficulty creating summaries of longer stories that contain more content and require making important judgments. Coffman found that summary writing could be improved if teachers ask questions that focus on major goals, attempts, and outcomes in each episode of complex stories because these story-focused questions guide the students in making text-connected inferences from the beginning to the end of the story.

Teaching summary writing is enhanced by modeling and by approaches that proceed from introduction of the skill, to direct instruction by the teacher, to teacher-guided application, and finally to independent practice. Notice how this sequence is incorporated into the following effective strategies identified by Bromley and McKeveny (1986) for teaching summary writing: (1) Establish purposes and provide rationales for using summary writing; (2) use demonstrations and simulations to develop understandings and to provide opportunities to study such topics as paragraph organization and location of main ideas; (3) use verbal practice to help students to identify key words, supply synonyms, and paraphrase text; (4) try group composition of summaries before expecting students to write individual summaries; (5) use models of acceptable summaries to help students compare, evaluate, and revise their own summaries; (6) use folders in which students keep their summaries for review and study; and (7) provide study time during which students can use their summaries to review important information from various content areas. Bromley and McKeveny emphasize the importance of long-term instruction in summary writing. Their research showed that "using precise writing twice weekly over an entire semester was more effective than daily 45-minute lessons for three or four weeks" (p. 393).

Writing that requires paraphrasing and summarizing may take place within any content area and may emphasize various types of activities. Shugarman and Hurst (1986) provide the following additional suggestions for paraphrasing and summarizing:

1. Have students elaborate on paraphrasing and summarizing by creating captioned cartoons, graphs, or maps that reflect the information in the text.
2. Ask students to paraphrase and summarize compositions written by other students. Then, have them share and discuss their summaries with the original authors.
3. Divide the class into teams and choose a panel of experts. Assign text passages to be read and paraphrased by each team. Have the panel select the best paraphrased text.
4. Have students bring in relevant text from library materials, newspapers, and magazines. Ask them to write summaries of the materials and to compare and discuss the various solutions.

Book Reports

Almost every elementary teacher uses book reports, whether oral or written. Through the creative use of book reporting, you can provide opportunities for many types of writing as well as strengthen the connections between writing, reading, and literature. Literature includes books from all content areas; thus, book reporting also heightens learning in the content areas.

For expressive book reports, instruct students to do the following:

1. Write a personal response to a book in your journal. Include in your reaction to the book what you liked or did not like about a character, the plot of the story, or the language. How would you change any of these elements if you could rewrite the book?
2. Choose one of the characters in the book and keep a dialogue journal with that character. Write questions you would like to ask that character about feelings, reactions,

beliefs, motives, or actions. Exchange your dialogue journal with someone else in the class who has read the same book. Ask the other person to write the answers to your questions as if he or she were that person.

3. Keep a learning log about a piece of nonfictional literature. Write reactions to the author's ability to interest you in the subject and to present information so that you believed it was true. What points was the author trying to make? Did he or she accomplish this task?

4. Keep a diary as if you were one of the characters in a book. Include personal reactions to things that happened to you in the story.

5. Pretend that you are the author of the book you just finished and that you were motivated to write the book because of entries in your writer's journal. Write entries that might have motivated you to develop the setting, characters, plot, or theme of the book.

6. Pretend that you are the author of a book you have read. Write an inventory of experiences from your writer's journal that you would need before you wrote the book.

For imaginative and poetic writing, instruct students to:

1. Write sequels to books you have read or tell stories of your own about characters in books. Choose a book that could have a next installment. Choose one of the characters from the book and tell what happens after the first story ends.

2. Choose a character from your book. Write a letter that character might write to another character in the story. Be sure that you write the letter from the viewpoint of that character. You might choose a problem that your character must solve and have the character write to a friend or relative in the book asking for advice or explaining why your character responded in a certain way.

3. Write a limerick about one of the characters in your book. (This activity should follow writing limericks in class.)

4. Identify the main theme in your book. Write a cinquain about that theme. For the title, select one word that expresses that theme. On the next line, write two words that describe the theme. On the third line, write three action words that express the theme. On the fourth line, write four words that express your feelings about the theme. Complete your cinquain with the title or a word that has the same meaning as the title. (This activity should follow writing cinquains in class.)

5. Identify the major conflicting forces in your book (for example, good versus evil). Write a poem in the diamante format that expresses the conflict in your book. Line 1 should be one of the conflicting forces. Line 2 should have two words that describe the force. Line 3 should have three action words related to the force. Line 4 should have four transitional nouns or a phrase about the conflict. Line 5 should have three action words related to the opposite force. Line 6 should have two words that describe the opposite force. Line 7 should be the opposite force. (This activity should follow the writing of diamante formats in class.)

6. Draw and label the plot development in your book.

7. Pretend that you are the set designer who will construct the set when your book becomes a stage play. Divide the book into three acts. Write detailed descriptions of the settings for each of the acts. Make your readers "see" the stage settings.

8. Choose a picture book and describe the setting as if you could not use illustrations in the book. Make your readers "see" and "feel" the settings through your choice of words.

9. Create a dictionary of words and phrases that suggest the mood of the story. Add words and phrases that you believe would be appropriate in addition to those chosen by the author.

10. Choose a character from your book and write a character sketch showing how the author feels about the character, how the character feels about him- or herself, and how other characters feel about that character.

11. Choose an incident in the book in which you would like to interact with the character. Pretend that you are one of the new characters introduced in the story. Write the incident in which you interact with the character. You may use your incident to clarify information or to try to persuade the character to do something. You may not, however, change the character from the characterization developed by the author.

12. Create a postcard that one of the characters might have sent in the story. Select one of the scenes from the book to draw on the front. Write the postcard as if you are that character.

For expository writing, instruct students to:

1. Write an appropriate weather report for several scenes in the book or for each chapter in the book.

2. Pretend you are the author of an informational book or a biography you have just read. Write a paragraph describing the audience for your book. How old is your audience? How much information on your subject does your audience have? How did you obtain information about your audience? How did this information influence the way you wrote your book?

3. Pretend you are the author of an informational book or a biography you have just read. Write a paragraph about your purpose for writing the book. What decisions did you have to make in order to write for that purpose? After you read your completed book, did you still think you were successful in presenting your purpose? How would you know if you were successful?

4. Pretend that you are the author of an informational book or a biography. Write three paragraphs about your book: (a) a paragraph describing how you decided on your subject, (b) a paragraph describing how you narrowed your subject to one that could be covered in your book, and (c) a paragraph describing how you conducted research on your book.

5. Pretend you are the author of an informational book. Draw a web of interest that you might have developed to help you organize the book.

6. Choose an exciting incident in the story. Write the incident as a news article. Include accurate information on who, what, when, where, and why.

7. Choose an incident in the book that could be controversial. Pretend you are one of the characters in the book and write a letter to the newspaper editor to persuade readers that your point of view is correct.

8. Write a summary of your book in the form of a cartoon, graph, or map. Write a caption explaining your content.

9. Diagram your book according to the major organizational patterns that the author used. The organizational patterns include chronological; spatial; familiar to unfamiliar; problem, to cause of problem, to possible solutions for the problem; problem, to effect of problem, to possible solutions for the problem; and question/answer.

For Your Development

1. Select a content area and develop a lesson plan for teaching beginning summarizing skills within that content area. Include in your lesson a rationale for teaching summarizing, a modeling in which you write a summary, a guided application, and an independent prac-

tice that encourages students to apply the summary skills within the content area. (*Note:* This lesson may require several days to complete.)

2. Develop a file of examples of expository writing to share with students who are having difficulty writing introductions, substantiating facts, organizing information, presenting arguments, or drawing conclusions.

SUMMARY

This chapter looks at three specific types of writing: (1) expressive writing; (2) imaginative writing, including stories and poetry; and (3) expository writing. Expressive writing is very close to speech. It is relaxed and intimate. It is personally relevant to the writer and reveals the writer's feelings. Expressive writing encourages personal responses and emotional reactions. Such writing includes journals and diaries, learning logs, writer's journals, and letters.

Imaginative writing includes fictional prose and poetry. You can develop creative writers by stimulating fictional story writing. Develop students' vocabularies by studing plots, settings, and characterizations. Also explore symbolism and allusions to mythology. For poetic writing, encourage students to observe and to study imagery and poetic forms.

Expository writing presents facts, ideas, or opinions. Researchers show that expository writing is dominant in the schools. For research reports, students should consider their audience and purpose for writing. They should determine their topic, making sure that it is narrow enough to be appropriate for the length of the report. In addition, they should gather and organize their ideas and information. Think-alouds and authentication projects provide excellent means for teaching students research skills. After writing their reports, students should revise. In the content areas, specific activities can help students understand the process of writing and learn the subject matter. Within expository writing, summary writing is an important skill.

Book reporting can take on an expressive, a poetic, or an expository function. A biography unit that integrates the language arts through reading, literature, writing, and oral language concludes the chapter.

ADDITIONAL ACTIVITIES TO ENHANCE UNDERSTANDING OF EXPRESSIVE, IMAGINATIVE, AND EXPOSITORY WRITING

1. Develop a lesson in which you introduce journal writing, learning logs, or writer's journals to students. Explain why these writing sources are important and how students might be able to use them to expand and enhance other types of writing.
2. Interview a student about imaginative writing. What subjects does the student like to write about? How does the student approach a creative writing task? Ask to see examples of writing that the student would like to share with you.
3. Diagram several books according to plot development.
4. Develop a characterization reference file in which you include examples of how authors tell about a character through narration, record the dialogue of a character, describe the thoughts of a character, show the thoughts of others about a character, and show a character in action. Choose references to model characterization with students in the grade levels in which you teach or would like to teach.

5. Write a lesson plan for story or poetry writing. Account for the various stages in the writing process.
6. Interview a teacher about how he or she teaches poetry writing. How often does the teacher ask students to write poetry? How does the teacher stimulate students' interests? What instructional techniques does the teacher consider effective? How does the teacher encourage students to share poetry?
7. Develop a file of poetry sources that you could use to stimulate poetry writing.
8. Develop a file of ideas that encourage expressive, poetic, and expository book reports.

BIBLIOGRAPHY

Aldridge, Ashley. "Think Aloud to Accompany Woodsong." Paper presented at Texas A&M University, 2002.

Altick, Richard; and Fenstermaker, John. *The Art of Literary Research.* New York: Norton, 1993.

Armstrong, D. B. "A Teacher Reflects on a High School English Class: The Dialogue Journal's Contributions to Learning and to Interpersonal Relations." 1990, *Dissertation Abstracts International* 51: 02A. (University Microfilms No. 90-04,261.)

Bailey, Diane. "From the Pens of Babes. . . ." *Publishers Weekly* (March 15, 1993): 25–26.

Barnes-Svarney, Patricia. *Places and Peoples of the World: Zimbabwe.* New York: Chelsea House, 1989.

Black Elk. *Black Elk Speaks: Being the Life Story of a Holy Man of the Ogala Sioux.* Lincoln: Univ. of Nebraska Press, 1979.

Brand, A. G.; and Chibnall, J. "The Emotions of Apprentice Poets." *Empirical Studies of Arts* 7 (1989): 45–49.

Bromley, Karen. "SSW: Sustained Spontaneous Writing." *Childhood Education* 62 (1985): 23–29.

———; and McKeveny, Laurie. "Precise Writing: Suggestions for Instruction in Summarizing." *Journal of Reading* 29 (February 1986): 392–95.

Cheney, Patricia. *The Land and People of Zimbabwe.* New York: Lippincott, 1990.

Cunningham, Patricia M.; and Allington, Richard L. *Classrooms that Work: They Can All Read and Write,* 3rd. ed. Boston: Allyn & Bacon, 2003.

Coffman, Gerry. "The Influence of Question and Story Variations on Sixth Graders' Summarization Behaviors." *Reading Research and Instruction* 34 (1994): 19–38.

Davis, Stephanie. "How Radar Writing Works." *Dallas Morning News* (May 22, 1988): 8F.

Fall, Jennifer. "Think-Aloud for Writing About Settings in *The Corn Grows Ripe.*" Paper presented at Texas A&M University, 2001.

Fisher, Allan C. "Rhodesia: A House Divided." *National Geographic* (May 1975).

Frye, Northrop; Baker, Sheridan; and Perkins, George. *The Harper Handbook to Literature.* New York: Harper & Row, 1985.

Gambrell, L. B. "Dialogue Journals: Reading–Writing Interaction." *The Reading Teacher* 38 (1985): 512–15.

Graham, Carolyn. "Authentication of *Amelia Earhart.*" Paper presented at Texas A&M University, 2002.

Graves, Donald. "Featured Panel—Writing." Paper presented at the International Reading Association Conference, San Francisco, April 29, 2002.

Hairston, Maxine. "Using Nonfiction Literature in the Composition Classroom." In *Convergencies: Transactions in Reading and Writing,* edited by Bruce T. Petersen. Urbana, Ill.: National Council of Teachers of English, 1986, pp. 179–88.

Hearne, Betsy. "Cite the Source: Reducing Cultural Chaos in Picture Books, Part One." *School Library Journal* 39 (July 1993a): 22–27.

Hearne, Betsy. "Respect the Source: Reducing Cultural Chaos in Picture Books, Part Two." *School Library Journal* 39 (August 1993b): 33–37.

Hidi, Suzanne; and Anderson, Valerie. "Producing Written Summaries: Task Demands, Cognitive Operations, and Implications for Instruction." *Review of Educational Research* 56 (Winter 1986): 473–93.

Hillocks, George. *Research on Written Composition: New Directions for Teaching.* Urbana, Ill.: National Conference on Research in English, 1986.

Huck, Charlotte; Hepler, Susan; and Hickman, Janet. *Children's Literature.* Brown & Benchmark, 1997.

Koch, Kenneth. *Wishes, Lies, and Dreams.* New York: Vintage Book/Chelsea House Publishers, 1971.

Lucas, Eileen. *The Ojibwas: People of the Northern Forests.* Brookfield, Conn.: Millbrook, 1994.

MacArthur, Charles; Graham, Steve; and Schwartz, Shirley. "Integrating Strategy Instruction and Word Processing into a Process Approach to Writing Instruction." *School Psychology Review* 22 (1993): 671–81.

MacVaugh, P. Q. "Writing to Learn: A Phenomenological Study of the Use of Journals to Facilitate Learning in the Content Areas." 1990. *Dissertation Abstracts International* 51: 04A. (University Microfilms No. 90–24, 465).

Martin, Kerri F.; and Manno, Carla. "Use of a Check-Off System to Improve Middle School Students' Story Compositions." *Journal of Learning Disabilities* 28 (March 1995): 139–49.

Mason, J.; Herman, P.; and Au, K. "Children's Developing Knowledge of Words." In *Handbook of Research on Teaching the English Language Arts,* edited by J. Flood, J. Jensen, D. Lapp, and J. Squire. New York: Macmillan, 1991, pp. 721–31.

McCarthey, Sarah J. "Opportunities and Risks of Writing from Personal Experience." *Language Arts* 71 (March 1994): 182–90.

McPhee, Celestine. "Think-Aloud for *The Cat Who Went to Heaven.* Paper presented at Texas A&M University, 2002.

Norton, Donna E. *The Impact of Literature-Based Reading.* Upper Saddle River, N.J.: Merrill/Prentice Hall, 1992.

———. "Document Authentication of Folklore." *Encyclopedia of Library and Information Science* 61 (1998): 109–121.

———. *Through the Eyes of a Child: An Introduction to Children's Literature,* 6th ed. Upper Saddle River, N.J.: Merrill/Prentice Hall, 2003.

———. *Multicultural Children's Literature Through the Eyes of Many Children.* Upper Saddle River, N.J.: Merrill/Prentice Hall, 2001.

———; and Norton, Saundra E. "Does Poetry Reveal the Life of the Poet?: Analyzing Poetry in Search of Autobiographical Data." Paper presented at International Society for Educational Biography Conference, San Antonio, Texas, April 18–20, 2002.

O'Day, Kim. "Using Formal and Informal Writing in Middle School Social Studies." *Social Education* 58 (January 1994): 39–40.

Rasinski, Timothy V. "Literacy and Relationship Building Through Dialogue Journals." *Journal of Reading Education* 20 (Winter 1994-95): 53–60.

Sadoski, Mark; Willson, Victor; and Norton, Donna. "Effective Strategies for Written Composition." Paper presented at the National Reading Conference, San Diego, December 1994.

Sager, Carol. "Improving the Quality of Written Composition in the Middle Grades." *Language Arts* 54 (October 1977): 760–62.

———. "Improving the Quality of Written Composition through Pupil Use of Rating Scale." Doctoral Dissertation, Boston University, 1973. *Dissertation Abstracts International* 34: 04A.

Shugarman, Sherrie L.; and Hurst, Joe B. "Purposeful Paraphrasing: Promoting a Nontrivial Pursuit for Meaning." *Journal of Reading* 29 (February 1986): 396–99.

Stott, Jon C. "In Search of Sedna: Children's Versions of a Major Inuit Myth." *Children's Literature Quarterly* 15 (Winter 1990): 199–201.

Strunk, William, Jr.; and White, E. B. *The Elements of Style,* 3rd ed. New York: Macmillan, 1979.

Swartzendruber-Putnam, Dawn. "Written Reflections: Creating Better Thinkers, Better Writers." *English Journal* 90 (September 2000): 88–93.

Sutherland, Zena. New York: Longman 1996.

Tanner, Helen Hornbeck. *The Ojibwa.* New York: Chelsea House, 1992.

Taylor, K. K. "Summary Writing for Young Children." *Reading Research Quarterly* 21 (1986): 193–208.

Tchudi, Susan; and Tchudi, Stephen. *The Young Writer's Handbook: A Practical Guide for the Beginner Who Is Serious About Writing.* New York: Charles Scribner's Sons, 1984.

Warren, William W. *History of the Ojibwa People.* St. Paul, Minn.: Minnesota Historical Society, 1984.

Watson, Dorothy, ed. *Ideas and Insights: Language Arts in the Elementary School.* Urbana, Ill.: National Council of Teachers of English, 1987.

Webster, Linda; and Ammon, Paul. "Linking Written Language to Cognitive Development: Reading, Writing, and Concrete Operations." *Research in the Teaching of English* 28 (February 1994): 89–109.

Yolen, Jane. "How Basic Is Shazam?" *Language Arts* 54 (September 1977): 645–51.

CHILDREN'S LITERATURE REFERENCES

Aesop. *Aesop's Fables.* Illustrated by Heidi Holder. New York: Viking, 1981.

———. *Aesop's Fables.* Selected and illustrated by Michael Hague. New York: Holt, Rinehart & Winston, 1985.

———. *Aesop's Fables Retold in Verse.* Retold by Tom Paxton. Illustrated by Robert Rayevsky. New York: Morrow, 1988.

———. *The Aesop for Children.* Illustrated by Milo Winter. Chicago: Rand McNally, 1919, 1947.

Afanasyev, Alexander Nikolayevich. *The Fool and the Fish.* Retold by Lenny Holt. Illustrated by Gennady Spirin. New York: Dial Press, 1990.

Ahlberg, Janet; and Ahlberg, Allan. *The Jolly Postman.* Boston: Little, Brown, 1986.

Anno, Mitsumasa. *Anno's Aesop.* New York: Orchard, 1989.

Baylor, Byrd. *The Best Town in the World.* Illustrated by Ronald Himler. New York: Charles Scribner's Sons, 1983.

Bierhorst, John. *Doctor Coyote: A Native American Aesop's Fables.* Illustrated by Wendy Watson. New York: Macmillan, 1987.

Brisson, Pat. *Your Best Friend, Kate.* Illustrated by Rick Brown. New York: Bradbury, 1989.

Brown, Marc. *Arthur's Baby.* Boston: Little, Brown, 1987.

———. *Arthur Goes to Camp.* Boston: Little Brown, 1982.

Caduto, Michael J.; and Bruchac, Joseph. *Keepers of the Earth.* Golden, CO: Fulcrum, 1989.

Caseley, Judith. *Dear Annie.* New York: Greenwillow, 1991.

Cauley, Lorinda Bryan, retold by. *The Town Mouse and the Country Mouse.* New York: Putnam, 1984.

Cendrars, Blaise. *Shadow.* Illustrated by Marcia Brown. New York: Charles Scribner's Sons, 1982.

Cleary, Beverly. *Dear Mr. Henshaw.* Illustrated by Paul Zelinsky. New York: Morrow, 1983.

Coatsworth, Elizabeth. *The Cat Who Went to Heaven.* Illustrated by Lynd Ward. New York: Simon & Schuster, 1930, 1958.

de Paola, Tomie. *An Early American Christmas.* New York: Holiday House, 1987.

Dupasquier, Philippe. *Dear Daddy.* New York: Bradbury, 1985.

Durrell, Ann; and Sachs, Marilyn, eds. *The Big Book for Peace.* New York: Dutton, 1990.

Erdrich, Louise. *The Birchbark House.* New York: Hyperion, 1999.

Flournoy, Valerie. *The Patchwork Quilt.* Illustrated by Jerry Pinkney. New York: Dial Press, 1985.

Freedman, Russell. *Lincoln: A Photobiography.* New York: Clarion, 1987.

Giff, Patricia Reilly. *The War Began at Supper: Letters to Miss Loria.* Illustrated by Betsy Lewin. New York: Delacorte, 1991.

Goodall, John. *The Story of a Main Street.* New York: Macmillan, 1987.

Hall, Donald. *Ox-Cart Man.* Illustrated by Barbara Cooney. New York: Viking Press, 1979.

Hodges, Margaret. *The Wave.* Illustrated by Blair Lent. Boston: Houghton Mifflin, 1964.

Hudson, Jan. *Sweetgrass.* New York: Philomel, 1989.

James, Simon. *Dear Mr. Blueberry.* New York: Macmillan, 1991.

Kennedy, Caroline, edited by. *The Best Loved Poems of Jacqueline Kennedy Onassis.* New York: Hyperion, 2001.

Khalsa, Dayal. *I Want a Dog.* New York: Potter, 1987.

Leigh, Nila K. *Learning to Swim in Swaziland: A Child's-Eye View of a Southern African Country.* New York: Scholastic, 1993.

Lenski, Lois. *Sing a Song of People.* Illustrated by Giles Laroche. Boston: Little, Brown, 1987.

Lindbergh, Reeve. *Johnny Appleseed.* Boston: Little, Brown, 1990.

MacLachlan, Patricia. *Sarah, Plain and Tall.* New York: HarperCollins, 1985.

McCloskey, Robert. *Time of Wonder.* New York: Viking Press, 1957.

McElmeel, Sharron L. *100 Most Popular Children's Authors.* Englewood, Col: Libraries Unlimited, 1999.

McElmeel, Sharon L. *The Poet Tree.* Englewood, CO: Teacher Ideas Press, 1993.

McKinley, Robin. *Beauty.* New York: Simon & Schuster, 1978.

McMillan, Bruce. *One Sun: A Book of Terse Verse.* New York: Holiday House, 1990.

McPhail, David. *The Dream Child.* New York: Dutton, 1985.

Moore, Inga. *Little Dog Lost.* New York: Macmillan, 1991.

O'Neill, Catharine. *Mrs. Dunphy's Dog.* New York: Viking Press, 1987.

Paulsen, Gary. *Woodsong.* New York: Bradbury, 1990.

Peek, Merle. *The Balancing Act: A Counting Song.* New York: Clarion, 1987.

Prelutsky, Jack. *The Dragons Are Singing Tonight.* Illustrated by Peter Sis. New York: Greenwillow, 1993.

———. *Something Big Has Been Here.* Illustrated by James Stevenson. New York: Greenwillow, 1990.

———. *The Gargoyle on the Roof.* Illustrated by Peter Sis. New York: Greenwillow, 1999.

———. *The New Kid on the Block.* Illustrated by James Stevenson. New York: Greenwillow, 1984.

———. *Tyrannosaurus Was a Beast.* Illustrated by Arnold Lobel. New York: Greenwillow, 1988.

Pringle, Laurence. *Global Warming: Assessing the Greenhouse Threat.* New York: Arcade, 1990.

Rattray, R. Sutherland. *Hausa Fold-Lore, Customs, Proverbs, Etc. Volume 1.* Oxford: Clarendon Press, 1913.

Raymond, Allen. "Jack Prelutsky . . . Man of Many Talents." *Early Years.* (Nov/Dec. 1986): 38–42.

Rhoads, Dorothy. *The Corn Grows Ripe.* Illustrated by Jean Charlot. New York: Viking, 1956.

Roop, Peter; and Roop, Connie. *Seasons of the Cranes.* New York: Walker, 1989.

———. *Rolling Harvey Down the Hill.* Illustrated by Victoria Chess. New York: Greenwillow, 1980.

Rylant, Cynthia. *When I Was Young in the Mountains.* Illustrated by Diane Goode. New York: Dutton, 1982.

Sabin, *Amelia Earhart: Adventure in the Sky.* Additional Children's.

Sampton, Sheila. *Jenny's Journey.* New York: Viking Press, 1991.

Sanderson, Ruth. *The Twelve Dancing Princesses.* Boston: Little, Brown, 1990.

Sattler, Helen Roney. *Giraffes, the Sentinels of the Savannas.* New York: Lothrop, Lee & Shepard, 1990.

Seuss, Dr. *And to Think That I Saw It on Mulberry Street.* New York: Vanguard, 1937.

Shepard, Aaron. *Master Man.* Illustrated by David Wisniewski. New York: HarperCollins, 2001.

Simon, Seymour. *New Questions and Answers About Dinosaurs.* Illustrated by Jennifer Dewey. New York: Morrow, 1990.

Skinner, Neil, translated by *The Story of Manly-Man.* Madison, WI: University of Wisconsin Press, 1977.

Small, David. *Imogene's Antlers.* New York: Crown, 1985.

Spedden, Daisy Corning Stone. *Polar the Titanic Bear.* Boston: Little, Brown, 1994.

Stanley, Diane. *Peter the Great.* New York: Four Winds, 1986.

Steptoe, John. *Mufaro's Beautiful Daughters: An African Tale.* New York: Lothrop, Lee & Shepard, 1987.

Stevens, Janet, retold by. *The Tortoise and the Hare.* New York: Holiday House, 1984.

————, retold by. *The Town Mouse and the Country Mouse.* New York: Holiday House, 1987.

Stewart, Sarah. *The Gardener.* Illustrated by David Small. New York: Farrar, Straus Giroux, 1997.

Sutherland, R. Rattray. *Hausa Folk-Lore, Customs, Proverbs, Etc.,* Vol 1 Oxford, Clavendon Press, 1913.

Va, Leong. *A Letter to the King.* New York: HarperCollins, 1991.

Wilder, Laura Ingalls. *Little Town on the Prairie.* New York: Harper & Row, 1941.

Williams, Vera B. *Stringbean's Trip to the Shining Sea.* Illustrated by Vera B. Williams and Jennifer Williams. New York: Greenwillow, 1988.

Yolen, Jane. *Owl Moon.* Illustrated by John Schoenherr. New York: Philomel, 1987.

Young, Ed. *Lon Po Po: A Red Riding Hood Tale from China.* New York: Philomel, 1989.

Zimelman, Nathan. *Please Excuse Jasper.* Illustrated by Ray Cruz. Nashville: Abingdon, 1987.

After completing this chapter on spelling, you will be able to:

1. Define the objectives of elementary spelling programs.
2. Understand the importance of developmental stages that influence spelling.
3. Understand the relationship between spelling and writing.
4. Place students on their proper instructional spelling levels.
5. Analyze how standardized spelling tests can help you evaluate a student's spelling.
6. Use informal spelling inventories to evaluate a student's spelling strengths and weaknesses.
7. Evaluate a student's application of spelling generalizations.
8. Understand the two most commonly used criteria for selecting spelling words.
9. Use the best developmental approach for spelling instruction, including the corrected-test method and the most efficient self-study method.
10. Design a weekly spelling program.
11. Understand the importance of proofreading to the spelling activity.
12. Develop accelerated spelling activities for gifted students.
13. Understand the step-by-step procedures needed to instruct students who require an effective remedial approach.

*L*ike handwriting, spelling is a tool to improve written communication and reading ability. There is an obvious connection between spelling and writing. For example, students frequently begin writing with invented spellings and then progress to more accurate spellings. Young students who are encouraged to use invented spellings in their early writing produce longer or better first drafts. This approach allows them to experiment with words, to explore their thoughts, and to become aware of patterns within words. It is hoped that these experiences will prepare them for conventional spelling instruction.

There is an obvious connection between spelling and reading and spelling and writing. When reporting results of their long-range survey of spelling, Hughes and Searle (2000) state, "Through frequent reading of varied texts, a reader is exposed to an extensive vocabulary, to how sound is represented in print, to the orthographic patterns of language, to the 'look' of correctly spelled words, and to the ways that meaning influences English spelling" (p. 203). They make the spelling and writing connection when they conclude, "It became evident that our best spellers were not only excellent, avid readers, but were also committed writers at home as well as at school. It was their approaches toward their writing, including their behaviors and attitudes toward their spelling, that distinguished these good spellers from children who . . . had stalled in their spelling development" (p. 204). They found that writing creates a purpose for learning to spell correctly and that early writing provides opportunities to explore understandings of print including the relationships among sounds and letters when making spelling decisions.

Hughes and Searle (2000) identified several characteristics of children who become good spellers by the end of the sixth grade. These characteristics include showing an interest in the meanings and spellings of words encountered in their environment, understanding that spelling is important because it allows readers to understand their writing, and developing self-reliance in monitoring and correcting their own spellings.

How spelling is taught and evaluated in schools depends on how spelling is viewed by educators. In a review of various spelling approaches, Weiner (1994) identifies four views of spelling that influence how spelling is taught and evaluated. The first view of spelling is that spelling accuracy can be achieved through mastery of a sequence of skills. Students are given grade-level word lists and engage in a variety of study activities related to the words. Achievement of spelling is measured through formal assessment. A second, related view is that spelling instruction can be individualized by giving students placement tests before being assigned sequenced word lists on an individualized basis. Students then proceed at their own rate and spelling is measured by formal assessment. Within both of these views, teachers may encourage students to transfer their spelling achievement by being involved in daily reading and writing activities.

A third view is that spelling instruction cannot be separated from language instruction. Consequently, spelling instruction focuses children's attention on words in context. Evaluation takes place during individual conferences in which students are directed to the appropriate strategy for spelling the word.

A fourth view, which may or may not underlie the first three views, focuses on a developmental function of language that shows predictable stages of spelling acquisition. In this view, spelling instruction occurs after students have had numerous experiences with reading, writing, and spelling. Instruction reflects and builds on these developmental stages. Consequently, evaluation of spelling includes evaluation of where children are within these developmental stages.

As you approach this chapter on spelling instruction, you will discover that effective spelling instruction may use components of several of these views toward spelling, including attitudes, skills, abilities, and habits:

Attitudes
Each child should:
1. Recognize the necessity and responsibility for correct spelling in effective communication.
2. Show a desire to spell words correctly.
3. Believe that spelling correctly is something he or she can accomplish.

Skills and Abilities
Each child should be able to:
1. Recognize all the letters of the alphabet in capital and lowercase forms in both printed and handwritten materials.
2. Write all the letters of the alphabet in a legible manner in both capital and lowercase forms.
3. Alphabetize words.
4. Hear words accurately as they are spoken.
5. Pronounce words clearly and accurately.
6. See printed words accurately.
7. Group and connect the letters of a word properly.
8. Use punctuation elements that are necessary for spelling.
9. Use a dictionary, including diacritical markings and guide words.
10. Pronounce unfamiliar words properly.
11. Use knowledge of sound and symbol relationships.
12. Use knowledge of orthographic patterns that recur in language.
13. Use the most effective spelling rules (generalizations).
14. Use personally effective procedures in learning to spell new words.

Habits

Each child should habitually:
1. Proofread all writing carefully.
2. Use reliable sources to find the spellings of unknown words.
3. Follow a specific study procedure in learning to spell new words.

The major objective of spelling is effective written communication. Mature spellers can correctly write a great number of words without conscious effort. Consequently, to develop effective spellers, a spelling program must enhance the independent spelling skills of students. In addition, the spelling program must include many opportunities to write for an audience. Bear and Templeton (1998) conclude: "Spelling is much more than a courtesy to one's reader; understanding how words are spelled is a means to more efficient and proficient writing and reading. To read and write words appropriately and fluently and to appreciate fully how words work in context, instruction must balance authentic reading and writing with purposeful word study. Word study instruction integrates spelling, phonics, and vocabulary instruction" (p. 223).

Developmental Stages

In a review of research pertaining to developmental patterns in spelling, Adams (1990) states: "Over time, children's writing gradually but clearly reflects increasing knowledge of the spelling of particular words and of general orthographic conventions. In addition, it reflects increasing sensitivity to the phonemic structures of words. Of particular interest, young writers have special difficulty in hearing the separate phonemes of consonant clusters, suggesting that the spellings of consonant blends warrant explicit instruction attention" (p. 96).

Researchers in the 1970s and 1980s, such as Read (1971), Henderson and Beers (1980), Gentry (1982), Henderson (1985), and Henderson and Templeton (1986), investigated developmental stages through which children proceed as they acquire spelling ability. Henderson and Templeton (1986) concluded that "developmental theory validates the skills we should teach and provides a rationale for the pacing and maintenance of instruction in a more detailed and clearly stated manner than has been possible before" (p. 314). These researchers used children's inventive spellings to identify the following five stages in developing spelling competence:

1. *Stage I*—Preliterate stage, in which young children spontaneously use symbols to represent words; there is, however, no knowledge of letter–sound correspondence.
2. *Stage II*—In approximately first grade, children begin to spell alphabetically, matching sounds and letters systematically. Their spellings reflect errors such as MAK = make.
3. *Stage III*—In approximately third and fourth grades, children begin to assimilate word knowledge and conventional alternatives for representing sounds, include vowels in every syllable, use familiar spelling patterns, and intersperse standard spelling with phonetic spelling. Their spellings reflect errors such as CREME = cream.
4. *Stage IV*—In approximately fourth through sixth grades, children increase their understanding of word patterns. Their spellings reflect errors such as INOCENT = innocent.
5. *Stage V*—Children understand that words related in meaning are often spelled similarly; children's knowledge of the English orthographic system and the accompanying rules is established; children's knowledge of base and root words is extensively developed.

Henderson and Templeton (1986) provide suggestions for instruction that apply at each of these stages. For example, at stage II, children should begin to examine systematically groups of words that are organized around common features such as short-vowel phonograms, beginning consonant digraphs, and common long-vowel patterns. Use short lists of words that are chosen from reading vocabularies for examination and memorization. At the same time, instruct children in letter formation and provide them with many opportunities for creative and purposeful writing.

At stage III, Henderson and Templeton (1986) maintain that spelling instruction should emphasize basic pattern features of words, including review of the long-vowel patterns taught in stage II (for example, /a/:bait), introduction of common digraphs (for example, *ow, oi*), study of *r*- and *l*-influenced vowel patterns (for example, *card, fall*), study of relationships between words in compounds, learning of functions of homophones in spelling, examination of common inflections and their joining to base words (for example, *ed, ing, ly*), presentation of base words that can stand alone after prefixes and suffixes are removed, and study of the sounds and meanings of common prefixes and suffixes.

At stage IV, Henderson and Templeton (1986) emphasize continued study of common and uncommon vowel patterns, scanning of words syllable by syllable, examination of prefixes and suffixes for meaning rather than sound (for example, when to use *able* or *ible, ant* or *ance, ent* or *ence*), exploration of homophones, and study of consonant doubling as it applies to a broader range of vocabulary.

At stage V, Henderson and Templeton (1986) emphasize study of silent and sounded consonant patterns (for example, *resign, resignation*); study of different vowel-alternation patterns sequenced from long to short (for example, *sane–sanity*), long to schwa (for example, *inflame–inflammation*), short to schwa (for example, *explain–explanation*), and examination of contributions of Greek and Latin forms to the spelling and meaning connection in English.

According to Bear and Templeton (1998), students' development in spelling reflects a growth in knowledge about letters and sounds, letter and syllable patterns, and how meaning is represented through spelling. This knowledge, consequently, reflects three layers of information about spelling: alphabetic, pattern, and meaning. The alphabetic layer matches letters and sounds. The pattern layer provides information about groupings of letters such as the vowel–consonant–silent *e* pattern. The meaning layer reflects the spelling of meaning elements despite sound change such as define/definition.

Bear and Templeton (1998) provide the following implications for using the developmental model for spelling instruction and word study:

1. Students should be grouped for spelling and word study. Most classrooms require three or four spelling groups. An instructional spelling level is one in which the student spells between 40 and 90 percent of the words correctly.
2. Students should examine known words that represent developmentally appropriate patterns.
3. During the examination of words, students should be guided toward the discovery of patterns and generalizations. Activities such as word sorts, word hunts, word study notebooks, and word games are recommended during guided examination.

School Spelling Programs

In this section we consider recommendations for encouraging invented spellings in your writers and instructional approaches that lead to phonological awareness and finally to spelling mastery.

Encouraging Invented Spellings in Young Writers

Research indicates that young children who are encouraged to write words so that they can read them, or to use their own invented spellings, will write longer stories than those children who are encouraged to use only correct spellings. Adams (1990) concludes: "In overview, classroom encouragement of invented spellings and independent writing from the start seems a very promising approach toward the development of phonemic awareness and orthographic skills. Beyond this, early writing seems an incomparable means of developing children's abilities to reflect on their own thoughts, to elaborate and organize their ideas, and to express themselves in print. Moreover, such challenges require children to think actively about print" (p. 99). Richard Gentry (2000) argues that a knowledge of stages of invented spelling leads to better assessment of children and to more informed literacy instruction.

Invented spelling is especially important in process writing. According to Cunningham (1991), "children who are allowed and encouraged to 'spell it so you can read it,' write longer and better first drafts than children who only write words they know how to spell" (p. 91). Cunningham maintains that when writing a first draft students should be encouraged to say the words and write down the letters they hear. Many teachers encourage invented spellings during first drafts and then help students spell the words correctly for their final writing. Bob Yukster (personal communication, October 1991), a trainer in the Reading Recovery program, sometimes encourages students to use invented spellings; at other times, he tells them that invented spellings are not acceptable. For example, during early drafts of creative writing, students are encouraged to use their own invented spellings. However, when the students are using their writings to learn to read, correct spellings are used. Likewise, teachers at a 1991 writing and literature workshop indicated that they allow invented spellings for first drafts, but then encourage the development of correct spellings during the editing process.

You can help young children understand the usefulness of invented spellings by modeling the process for them. Hansen (1985) describes how she introduces invented spelling to kindergarten children. She begins by using an overhead projector and drawing a picture on a transparency. After drawing the picture, she writes a sentence across the top by sounding out the words and writing the letters for the most prominent sounds. She explains that she is writing the way most children write when they begin. Then she writes the same sentence in conventional spelling along the bottom of the page. She explains that this is the kind of

Invented spelling is encouraged in free writing activities, but when writing is "published," attention to correct spelling becomes important to clear communication.

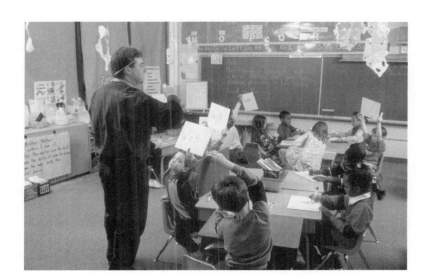

writing that adults do, and that is found in books. Next, the children draw a picture and write a story using their own invented spellings. She then talks to each child about his or her story and writes a sentence or two in conventional spelling at the bottom of each page.

Cunningham (1991) describes another strategy to help children experiment with invented spellings. The teacher asks students to suggest words they might use to write a paper on a specific topic. When a student suggests a word, everyone says the word slowly and writes a possible spelling. When the task is completed, the teacher calls on students to tell how they might spell the word. After writing several possibilities on the board, the teacher points out to the students that these are words they could read, which is their goal when writing a first draft; however, if they are writing a finished paper, they would need to edit and correct their spellings. The teacher ends the lesson by writing the conventional spelling above each column and talking about which spellings were closest to the conventional spelling.

Cunningham and Cunningham (1992) also recommend an approach that enhances invented spelling by using a strategy called "Making Words" in which students are given specific letters and asked to make two-letter words and to continue with three-, four-, and five-letter words until the final word is made. Such a strategy might begin by asking the children to select the consonant letters *d, p, r,* and *s* (written in black print with lowercase on one side and capital letters on the other side) and the vowels *i* and *e* (written in red print with lowercase on one side and capital letters on the other side) from individual cards. At the same time, the teacher places identical letters in a pocket chart at the front of the room. The children proceed through a sequence of activities in which they use the letters to develop words that use an increasing number of the letters. For example, Cunningham and Cunningham recommend that this activity might proceed from the initial word *Ed* to the final word *spider.* To accomplish this sequence, the teacher could use the following progression: *Ed, red, rid, sip, pie, pies, dies, side, ride, ripe, rise, pride, drips,* and *spider.* After children create each word, they also show it on the teacher's pocket chart and discuss the creation of the word.

Developing Phonological Awareness

Researchers who investigate characteristics of good spellers report the importance of developing students' awareness of words because good spellers seem to depend on sensitivity to patterns of letters within words and seem more sensitive to whether a spelling looks correct. Adams (1990) concludes that difficulty with either phonemic analysis or knowledge of spelling patterns interferes with good spelling.

Several studies conducted in Europe indicate the benefits of programs that encourage phonological awareness in students. For example, Lundberg, Frost, and Petersen (1988) developed such a program for Danish preschool children. The children in this program were superior in spelling at the end of both first and second grades. The instruction includes daily sessions in which children take part in listening games that emphasize nonverbal and verbal sounds and in rhyming games that focus on nursery rhymes, rhymed stories, and games for rhyme production. Following the introduction of these games, children respond to syllables in their own names and in other known multisyllabic words by clapping their hands and by dancing, marching, and walking in pace with the various patterns.

A Norwegian study suggests that lower ability students may gain the most from phonological training. Lie (1991) found that spelling achievement of first-grade students was superior when they were involved in a program that encouraged phonemic awareness of the initial, final, and medial sounds in spoken words. As part of this awareness training, teachers and students discuss the meaning of language and the fact that words can be divided into sounds that can be heard when the words are pronounced. Students then identify initial phonemes in words. Lie concludes: "The evidence . . . suggests that a systematic training program for stimulating skills in word analysis in first-grade children facilitates both reading and spelling acquisition" (p. 247).

Adams (1990) reinforces the importance of helping students look for and listen for patterns in words. After reviewing the research in spelling, she concludes:

> Successful spelling improvement depends on getting children to attend to unfamiliar patterns. . . . Research indicates that the experience of seeing a word in print is not only superior to hearing it spelled but, further, is an extremely powerful and effective means of acquiring its spelling. In addition, the experience of seeing or imagining a word's spelling, as contrasted with repeatedly hearing the word or even rehearsing it aloud, has been shown to be a superior means toward remembering its pronunciation, even among first graders. One obvious instructional implication of this evidence is that teachers should habitually encourage students to look at the spellings of words. Teachers should write the words of interest on the board or point to them on the page. Merely spelling words aloud, relatively speaking, is a waste of time. . . . Research demonstrates that the process of copying new words strengthens students' memory for those words. . . . Perhaps this should not be surprising—the writing of a word forces attention to its full sequences of letters. For students, the thought that somebody else might evaluate their products may encourage such attention even more. (p. 102)

Francine R. Johnston (1999) highly recommends the study of word families in order to develop phonological awareness. Her guidelines for the study of word families follow a developmental approach in which she teaches one word family at a time such as the *at* family or the *an* family. Then she compares word families containing different short vowels such as those found in *cat, but,* and *sit.* This study continues with a study of common or familiar words that include blends and digraphs. Blends and digraphs may be added to the one-family words as students go from *pack, rack,* and *sack* to *black, track,* and *snack.*

Johnston (1999) recommends that when silent vowels begin to appear in children's invented spellings, the children are ready to study the patterns that spell the other vowel sounds of English such as those found in *bail, jail,* and *mail.* Johnston concludes, "There is no hard and fast sequence to this instruction. Teachers should use children's invented spellings to determine what they know and what they are ready to learn" (p. 74).

Patricia Cunningham (1998) presents a program for increasing students' ability to build meaning, spell, and read multisyllable words. Her recommendations include first helping students become word detectives as they search for the meaning, spelling, and decoding relationships shared by words. She states, "There are two questions I would like to put into the mouths of every teacher of children from third grade through high school. These two questions are: 'Do I know any other words that look and sound like this word?' and 'Are any of these look-alike/sound-alike words related to each other?' The answer to the first question should help students with pronouncing and spelling the word. The answer to the second question should help students discover what, if any, meaning relationships exist between this new word and others in their meaning vocabulary stores" (p. 204).

Her second recommendation is to teach the prefixes that are most useful from a meaning standpoint such as *re* in *rebound, return,* and *replace.* Teachers would help students categorize words that have similar meanings according to their prefixes. The third recommendation is to teach the suffixes that are the most useful because suffixes are predictable indicators of pronunciation and sometimes signal a meaning relationship. Fourth, she would teach a few useful root words such as *play, work, agree,* and *create.* Students would suggest words that contain each of these root words and discuss how the meaning of the word changes when found in, for example, *workable, homework, network,* and *rework.* Finally, Cunningham (1998) recommends that teachers teach students to spell a set of big words that have high utility for meaning, spelling, and decoding. She includes a list of fifty words that contain the most useful prefixes, suffixes, and spelling changes. You may find it useful to study the sample lessons that Cunningham includes for each of her recommendations.

Guidelines for Spelling Instruction

In addition to studies conducted by Henderson and Templeton (1986), considerable research in spelling diagnosis, instructional programs, and teaching techniques provides clear guidelines for spelling instruction. Following a review of research spanning more than fifty years, Hillerich (1982) identified the following effective procedures and instructional approaches:

1. Determine the appropriate instructional spelling level for each student.
2. Teach the list of high-frequency words using a research-based approach.
3. Teach generalizations about apostrophes and word endings.
4. Provide experiences with homophones.
5. Teach dictionary skills along with ways of spelling various sounds.
6. Develop a desire to spell correctly when writing for an audience other than an informal group.
7. Encourage considerable writing to help children develop an understanding that writing is the only reason for learning to spell.
8. Provide children with many meaningful writing experiences that reinforce the automatic spelling of their security lists.

These recommendations will be apparent throughout the forthcoming discussions on assessment and instruction.

Using Computers

Computer programs may be especially useful for helping children improve their spelling accuracy and increase their knowledge of spelling patterns. Gustafson (1982) compared the spelling achievement scores and spelling retention ability of students who learned to spell with a computer spelling program with children who learned to spell with a teacher-directed approach. Both achievement and retention were higher in the computer-based group.

Mason (1983) maintains that computer programs are excellent accuracy trainers. When students type in words incorrectly, they must find their errors before continuing. He states: "Teachers using this approach report dramatic improvement in spelling in addition to greater accuracy in reading words. They also report incidents of student jubilation when pesky bugs are found and corrected and programs finally run as they should. This joy in accomplishment is so profound that it often shocks teachers who had thought nothing in school could excite these children" (p. 506).

The ease of changing words in a word processor prior to printing can motivate proofreading for spelling and mechanical errors as well as improvement of other aspects of composition. This potential is not yet reached. Becker, director of the Johns Hopkins classroom-technology study, states that one of the best uses for computers with older children is the teaching of writing (McGrath, 1983). He estimates, however, that less than 7 percent of computer time in high-school programs involves word processing activities.

Balajthy (1986) provides the following guidelines to use when selecting spelling software: It should allow teachers to add new words, contain colorful and interesting programs, use voice synthesis to present words, provide feedback, review misspelled words, and assist with recordkeeping.

Assessment

Spelling offers an excellent opportunity for diagnostic teaching. Assessment is necessary to discover at what grade level to begin spelling instruction and to evaluate each student's specific spelling strengths and weaknesses.

Formal Assessment

Because there is no economy in teaching words children can already spell correctly, it is important to determine each child's appropriate spelling level. It is equally important to diagnose the level of students who are having spelling problems. Students will not make adequate gains if they are expected to spell words of an unrealistically high level of difficulty. For example, children should receive instruction in a word list for which they can spell approximately 75 percent of the words; children who are not able to correctly spell 50 percent of a graded word list have not mastered the prerequisite spellings taught at lower grade levels.

It is not difficult to place elementary students on appropriate spelling levels. First, select approximately twenty-five words from each graded spelling list. Do not choose only the most difficult or the easiest words from that level. Many teachers find the best procedure is to choose every tenth word from a list of spelling words for each grade. Table 9–1 illustrates the result of this procedure, using a graded word list from the *Skills in Spelling* series published by the American Book Company.

After compiling the lists, administer the tests to the class to determine spelling levels. Administer the first-grade list to all students. Do not administer a further test to children who spell fewer than 75 percent correctly; you will have discovered their level of spelling ability. Use first-grade instruction for these children.

Test students who have mastered the first-grade list with the second-grade list. If the students have not mastered this list, provide them with second-grade instruction. Then, test students who demonstrate mastery of the second-grade list with the third-grade list. Test the children on consecutive days until you have placed all of them in their most efficient instructional level. This diagnostic procedure is not overly time consuming, and it ensures that each child will receive instruction at the correct spelling level.

For Your Development

Compile a spelling test list, using the graded lists from one of the spelling series. Administer the list to a group of children and estimate the spelling instructional level for each member of the group.

Table 9–1   Word list from the *Skills in Spelling* series

Grade 1	Grade 2	Grade 3	Grade 4
pig	after	Monday	act
pretty	wet	fed	dream
send	win	trip	drove
she	block	week	eight
five	top	name	tip
purple	game	Friday	base
can	five	these	penny
like	boat	sent	cook
there	stay	cent	paid
come	nest	full	all right
not	friend	keep	everywhere
	fall	then	careful
	band	add	everybody
	dinner	bread	country
	girls	where	church
	dress	fight	comb
	there	asked	coal
	when	things	bow
	thanks	tall	busy
	open	use	ocean
	call	with	circus
	our	stopped	hurry
	at	nuts	master
	calling	snowball	lucky
	something	throw	popcorn

Source: From Bremer, Bishop, and Stone, *Skills in Spelling* (Dallas: American Book Co., 1976). Reprinted by permission of American Book Co.

Informal Assessment

Informal spelling assessment, including teacher-made tests and observations, will give you the most useful information for designing a spelling program. Informal evaluation techniques are vital when you require specific information about a child's spelling. Moreover, informal diagnosis is essential for designing a program to remediate spelling difficulties. Questions you might consider during informal observation include the following: Does the child accurately produce letter and sound symbols when writing? Can the child blend sounds to make words? Does the child reverse letters? Can the child remember words written on the board? Can the child hear minimal differences in words such as *pin* and *pen?*

Maximize informal spelling assessment by systematic study of a child's spelling errors. If a child follows a pattern in misspelling certain words, expect that child to make the same type of error when spelling similar words. Spache's Spelling Errors Test provides a list of types of errors often reflected in children's spelling:

1. A silent letter is omitted: *take–tak.*
2. A sounded letter is omitted: *stand–stan.*
3. A double letter is omitted: *letter–leter.*
4. A single letter is added: *park–parck.*
5. Letters are transposed or reversed: *angel–angle.*
6. There is a phonetic substitution for the vowel: *green–grean.*
7. There is a phonetic substitution for the consonant: *bush–buch.*
8. There is a phonetic substitution for the syllable: *flies–flys.*
9. There is a phonetic substitution for the word: *hare–hear.*
10. There is a nonphonetic substitution for the vowel: *bats–bots.*
11. There is a nonphonetic substitution for a consonant: *camper–canper.*

Use this list to analyze test papers and other written work. Various creative writing and written assignments in content areas provide sources for informal spelling assessment.

Besides observing written work, also analyze a child's oral spelling and speech performance. How does the child approach oral spelling? Does the child sound words out one letter at a time, by syllables, or as whole-word units? Are the child's oral errors similar to his or her written errors? Does the child enunciate words carefully? How does the child pronounce the words he or she spells incorrectly? Does the speech of the child reflect a dialect? Does the dialect interfere with spelling patterns? Is the child able to blend sounds orally into a whole word?

You can compile other useful information by observing study skills with regard to spelling. Does the child apply an effective method of study to spelling-word lists? A positive attitude toward spelling is essential. Does the child feel that spelling is important? Does the child carefully proofread his or her papers for spelling errors? Does the child use a dictionary to verify spelling questions? Does the child use new spelling words in other daily assignments?

You can also obtain valuable diagnostic information by questioning children. Ask children to tell you how they spell an unknown word. Question them about their best method for remembering a spelling word. Many children say they must carefully write a word several times before they are able to remember it. One child with a learning disability indicated that he traced words with his hands when his teacher asked him to spell orally. Other children say they benefit from spelling words aloud while writing. One fourth-grade girl explained her method for overcoming a dialect difference between herself and her teacher. She solved her difficulty by whispering each word before writing a dictated word. Children can frequently describe their greatest spelling problems, so make this information a vital part of your informal spelling assessment.

Another useful informal assessment diagnoses a child's ability to apply spelling generalizations. Horn (1963) recommends teaching rules that apply to a large number of words and have few exceptions. Administer a cloze test to assess a child's knowledge of the more reliable generalizations. A cloze test for specific spelling generalizations might include the following examples:

1. *Generalization:* Words that end with a silent *e* usually drop the *e* before adding a suffix beginning with a vowel.

   Cloze: Jim was rak_____ the leaves. (ing)

2. *Generalization:* Words ending in silent *e* retain their *e* when adding a suffix beginning with a consonant.

   Cloze: The president lives in a stat_____ mansion. (ely)

3. *Generalization:* If a word ends with a consonant plus *y,* change the *y* to *i* before adding suffixes except those beginning with *i.* Do not change the *y* to *i* when adding suffixes to words ending in a vowel plus *y.*

   Cloze: The bab_____ were all crying at once. (ies)
   Cloze: The horse was carr_____ a heavy load. (ying)
   Cloze: The boy scouts were enjo_____ the football game. (ying)

4. *Generalization:* Double the final consonant in one-syllable words or words accented on the last syllable, ending in a single consonant preceded by a single vowel before adding a suffix beginning with a vowel.

   Cloze: The horse was run_____ a very fast race. (ning)
   Cloze: Sunday is the begin_____ of the week. (ning)

5. *Generalization:* The letter *q* is always followed by the letter *u* in the English language.

   Cloze: At night it is q_____iet in the house. (u)

6. *Generalization:* Proper nouns should begin with capital letters.

   Cloze: The dog's name is _____over. (R)

For Your Development

1. The following examples are excerpts from a third-grade student's daily written work. The first selection is an outlining activity following a reading lesson. The second example is from a social studies assignment. Study the child's papers and find the spelling errors. Classify the errors according to the Spache spelling error categories and then according to Henderson and Templeton's stages (1986) in developmental spelling. How do the errors compare with Henderson and Templeton's stages? At what stage or stages is this student? What proof do you have for your answer? Do you see any consistent errors? Discuss the implications of these errors for remedial instruction.

I. Daytime
   A. a sailor showd Mark around
   B. there was a spider
   C. Mark went to play with his frends
   D. the boys climed around
   E. the sailer toke the spider to a sientest
II. Nighttime
   A. the tarantual was luse
   B. Marks Mother was wered
   C. he wated until 9 o'clock with the spider
   D. Tim quickly looked at the spider
   E. Tin cauld another polece

Fur Seals

Seals are excellent swimers and they spend lots of time in the water. They have fur all over them.

The mail seals are cauld bulls and femail seals are cauld cows. They have there pups on land and they usually have one pup but sometimes two.

Seals spend much of there time on land or on floating chunks of ice.

Fur seals stay at sea for 6 to 8 months.

They are found along the costes of continents in most parts of the world.

A few kinds live in fresh water lakes and cloes to inland seas.

2. Mary Jo Fresch (2001) uses examples of journal entries written by one child in kindergarten through fourth grade to show the child's changing developmental level in spelling. Access Fresch's article and compare her findings over the years. If possible, try to collect and categorize your own examples of developmental levels in spelling.

Word Selection

An examination of the word lists in major spelling books illustrates two different viewpoints on the selection of spelling words. According to some experts, the English language system is irregular; consequently, spelling instruction should emphasize gradual accumulation of the most useful words. In contrast, others believe that the English language is remarkably regular, and that efficient spelling programs should have greater phonetic emphasis.

A Frequency-of-Use Approach

Many spelling programs concur with the philosophy that the English language system is irregular and that instruction should be based on the words most frequently used. Ernest Horn, whose writings and research span the past fifty years in education, is the most influential proponent of this view. As early as 1919, Horn stated: "One must show that a rule can be easily taught, that it can be remembered, and that it will function in the stress of actual spelling. Evidence seems to cast a doubt on all three of these assumptions." In 1954, he said, "The limited success in attempts to teach pupils to learn and apply even a few spelling rules suggests that we should not be too optimistic about the practicality of teaching the more numerous and complicated rules or principles in phonetics," and in 1957, "There seems no escape from the direct teaching of the large number of common words which do not conform in their spelling to any phonetic or orthographic rule." By 1963, Horn believed that some emphasis on phonics should be included in the spelling program. He cautioned, however, that "instruction in phonics should be regarded . . . as an aid to spelling rather than a substitute for the systematic study of words in the spelling list."

The words Horn believed should compose the spelling list are those most frequently used by children and adults. In selecting these high-frequency words, Horn (1963) recommended the following:

1. The easiest words should be taught in the beginning grades and the most difficult words in the advanced grades.
2. Words most frequently used in writing should be taught first.

High-frequency words are often emphasized in the spelling program.

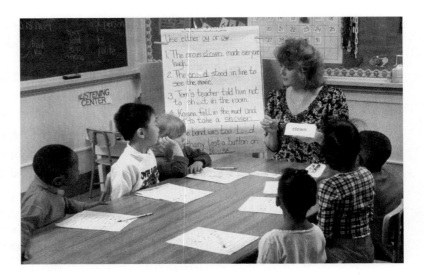

3. Words commonly used by children in a specific grade should be taught in that grade.
4. Words needed in other content subjects should be taught in the appropriate grades.

Researchers have compiled several spelling lists that can be useful for evaluating and selecting high-frequency spelling words. The first 10 words on Horn's list (*I, the, and, to, a, you, of, in, we, for*) constitute 25 percent of the words used in various kinds of writing. The first 100 words in the list account for 65 percent of the words written by children and adults. Encouraging mastery of meaningful lists is appropriate because spelling efficiency increases when children are taught the words they need to spell most frequently.

A Phonetic Emphasis

Some linguists disagree with Horn's opinion that the English language system is irregular; they maintain that there is a high degree of regularity between the graphemic presentation of a written word and its corresponding sounds. In 1965, Hodges and Rudorf investigated the relationship between phonemes (sounds) and graphemes (printed letters) in more than 17,000 words; they found a high degree of regularity between the sounds and the written letters.

Hanna and Hanna (1965) recommend that a spelling program reflect the finding of the Hodges and Rudorf investigation; they believe that children should learn to spell words using a phonic approach. In an earlier article, Hanna and Moore (1953) recommended putting aside some time for a concentrated attack on translating sounds into written symbols, during which a child would learn phonic patterns inductively. The simple patterns, such as the consonant–vowel–consonant in *cat*, would be learned first, and the complex phonic patterns later. Hanna and Moore argue that the English words that follow a rarely occurring phonic pattern should be memorized.

An Emphasis on Meaning

Chomsky (1970) suggests that words that mean the same tend to look the same, even though they may have different pronunciations. Thus, the words *nation* and *national* have similar spellings, and the meanings are consistent even though the phonetic pronunciations are different. Likewise, certain spelling patterns are considered consistent because they indicate a specific part of speech. From this perspective, the writing system seems both sensible and systematic.

Zutell (1978) suggests that teachers apply linguistic and psycholinguistic findings by helping children develop their understanding of the writing system. To do so, "teachers must consciously construct environments in which children have the opportunity to systematically examine words and to freely generate, test, and evaluate their own spelling strategies" (p. 847). Such a spelling program allows children to examine their own writing; provides experiences for reading and vocabulary development; and provides activities that allow children to compare, contrast, and categorize words according to root words, word origins, and similarities in structural patterns.

Instruction

In a developmental spelling program, teachers must consider such questions as the following: How many words should be taught? How many minutes a day should be spent on spelling instruction? What words should be studied? What is the most efficient individual study method? How often should review be included? How should students receive instruction in spelling generalizations?

Several factors contribute to a decision about how many words to teach during spelling lessons. You must consider the number of words that students can learn efficiently in a specific grade as well as how much emphasis is placed on spelling in other content areas. Most spelling series contain fewer than 4,000 words. One spelling authority describes this accumulation of words in terms of daily tasks. If 2 new words a day are presented in second and third grades, 3 new words a day in fourth and fifth grades, and 4 new words a day in sixth, seventh, and eighth grades, students can master the spelling of 4,180 words. If the words are chosen according to high frequency, this accumulation accounts for 98 percent of the words written by children and adults. It does not seem an impossible task for most students to master the essential spelling lists if spelling is systematically taught. Most authorities believe that students can learn these spelling words during concentrated daily spelling instruction periods of approximately fifteen minutes.

Your problem now is deciding what words each student should master. It would be inefficient to have students work on words that are either too easy or too difficult, so begin the program with assessment procedures to ascertain each student's individual spelling instructional level. After assessment, divide the class into appropriate groupings. The average elementary class will have, perhaps, four spelling groups. Initiate spelling instruction with the corrected-test method.

The Corrected-Test Method

Horn (1963) indicates that the single best method for learning to spell is the corrected-test method. Personke (1987) states that the approach "has been reexamined many times and remains the single best method for learning to spell words. The reason for its success is simple: it provides immediate, positive feedback" (p. 79). Following research on self-corrected spelling test methods, Harward, Allred, and Sudweeks (1994) conclude that "The results reaffirm research findings that document self-corrections as an effective technique for increasing students' spelling proficiency (p. 263).

In an earlier study, Hillerich (1977) indicates that the use of a pretest, with immediate correction by the child, accounts for about 95 percent of all learning that takes place in spelling. In the corrected-test method, the teacher administers a spelling test before the students study the words. This procedure liberates students from systematic study of words they already know. Immediately after the test, have the pupils self-correct their tests; they may self-correct from their own spelling lists, from typed lists that you provide, or by listening to you slowly read the correct test. Have the pupils immediately write the correct spelling of any words they have missed. This method gives students essential positive feedback. If you collect the tests, correct them, then return them to the children, they may retain the misspellings rather than the correct spellings. Monitor the corrected-test procedure carefully to ensure that the students are checking their work accurately and correcting their misspelled words.

Classroom teachers have found two successful techniques for administering more than one spelling list to a class. Some teachers test the various ability groupings simultaneously. These teachers read, in turn, one word from each spelling list. For example, the teacher dictates the first-grade word *pretty* to one group, the second-grade word *block* to the next group, the third-grade word *Friday* to the third group, and the fourth-grade word *everywhere* to the last group. After each group receives a word, the teacher returns to the initial group's next word and follows the same sequence until all students have been tested on their lists. Other teachers prefer to test one group at a time, which takes longer but gives a smaller group to monitor. Self-correction and immediate writing of misspelled words follow both methods of administration. Each child's misspelled words form the list of words that the child systematically studies for that week.

The Self-Study Method

The self-corrected test procedure gives students an individualized list of words to master. Now, each student must learn these misspelled words efficiently. Teachers know that students do not automatically use the most effective study methods. In fact, proper study methods should be reviewed at the beginning of each grade.

Horn (1963) recommends teaching the following self-study procedure:

1. Pronounce the word correctly. Correct pronunciation is important in learning to spell. Enunciate each syllable distinctly while looking closely at the word.
2. Close your eyes and try to recall how the word looks, syllable by syllable. Pronounce the word in a whisper while you try to visualize the word.
3. Open your eyes and make sure you have recalled the word correctly. Repeat these steps two or three times.
4. When you feel that you have learned the word, cover it and write it without looking. Check your written word with the correct, covered word.
5. Repeat this writing procedure until you have correctly spelled the word three times. Check the correct spelling after each writing.

Students who have a lot of trouble with spelling need to overlearn their spelling words—they may need more than three correct repetitions of each spelling word, and some of these students may benefit from a more rigorous remedial technique.

The Weekly Spelling Plan

A study plan might result in a Monday through Friday arrangement similar to the following:

1. On Monday, give a pretest to each spelling group. The pretest should consist of all the words that the group is expected to master during the week. Have the children

check their own words, using the corrected-test approach. Have them study each misspelled word immediately. Templeton and Morris (1999) find that the Monday pretest is the most important measure because the pretest tells the teacher how much prior knowledge individual students bring to the task of learning a list of fifteen to twenty words. They again stress that this pretest should test words in which the students can already spell approximately 50 percent of the words.

2. On Tuesday, have the children continue to study misspelled words. Also, have them work on exercises to expand the meaning of the spelling words. Such exercises might consist of writing phrases with each word or adding affixes to the words. For example, affixes to the word *decide* produce *decided, deciding,* and *undecided.*

3. On Wednesday, give a midweek test of all the words given on Monday to each spelling group. If children spell the list correctly on Wednesday, do not require them to take an additional test. If children miss words, have them immediately use the self-study method again with their words.

4. For Thursday's spelling lesson, include enrichment activities that use the words in various situations. Unless children use the spelling words they learn, they quickly forget them. Some students will need self-study time before the Friday test.

5. On Friday, have students who missed spelling words on both Monday and Wednesday take a final test. Add words they miss on Friday to the students' spelling lists for periodic review.

Have students keep charts to help them visualize their individual growth in spelling. They should chart their spelling scores from the Wednesday or Friday tests with charts resembling that of Figure 9–1.

Horn (1963) emphasizes periodic review as an essential aspect of an efficient spelling program. The first review should occur within a day or two after the words are taught; the Wednesday test provides this review. The second review should take place during the following month. Place missed words on a special list and review them regularly. Finally,

FIGURE 9–1 Individual Pupil Spelling Progress Chart

include words the children find especially difficult during the year on the instructional list for the following grade.

In a developmental spelling program, remember six important factors when planning the spelling curriculum. The initial step is diagnostic testing to find the most efficient spelling level for each student. Second, the weekly program begins with a pretest, followed immediately by the corrected-test procedure. Third, each child should work only on the words that are difficult for him or her, and you should show the child a definite method for learning these words. Fourth, rigorous reviews will emphasize the more difficult words. Fifth, the pupil should chart his or her daily, weekly, monthly, and yearly progress. Finally, students need to apply their spelling words in various contexts.

The Inductive Method

Most spelling authorities believe that the instructional program should include some spelling generalizations. Disagreement over the teaching of spelling generalizations pertains to the number of generalizations considered reliable; you should definitely include the more reliable generalizations in a developmental spelling program. Students will be better able to apply these generalizations if they learn them inductively.

Using an inductive method, initiate the learning experience by writing on the board several words that demonstrate the particular generalization. Then, ask the children to supply more words like those listed, and add them to the list. Write any exceptions to the rule on a separate list. Then, guide the class to look carefully at the words to discover the generalization involved. After they discover the generalization, the children should turn to their spelling books or lists to verify their discovery. Inductive teaching tends to be active; consequently, it both motivates and provides positive reinforcement.

For Your Plan Book

Lesson Plan

A Spelling-Generalization Lesson Using an Inductive Approach

An excellent third-grade teacher developed this lesson plan. Begin by placing the following words on the board in two columns. Put singular forms in the left-hand column, plural forms in the right-hand column:

key	keys
day	days
monkey	monkeys
boy	boys
donkey	donkeys
baby	babies
cherry	cherries
lady	ladies
berry	berries
daisy	daisies

Pronounce all the words with the children. Have individual children say sentences aloud, using the listed words, and then ask the children to add similar words to the list. Put the children's words on the board next to the appropriate row.

Have the class examine the left-hand column and decide on a common element for all the words (all words end with *y*). Next, have the class look at the right-hand column and determine how the first five words were made plural (*s* was added to each word). Ask how the second five words were made plural (*es* was added and the *y* was changed to *i*). Also, ask why the *y* was changed in some words but not in others. The question should lead the children to formulate a generalization similar to the following:

Generalization: If a word ends in *y*, add *s* to make the plural if a vowel is before the *y*. If a consonant is before the *y*, change the *y* to *i* and add *es* to form the plural.

Then, have the students test their generalization on new words. The following words conform to the above generalizations:

sky	lorry	ferry	penny	play	tray
bay	trolley	body	country	toy	

Finally, ask the class to open their spelling, reading, and literature books to find additional words that fit the *y* generalization.

For Your Development

1. Administer a list of appropriate spelling words to an elementary class. Following the corrected-test activity, instruct the class in the most efficient method for self-study. Develop a chart with student assistance to remind the students how to use the study procedures.
2. Develop a lesson plan that teaches a spelling generalization step by step. If you are a preservice teacher, demonstrate your activity to a group of peers in your college class. If you are an in-service teacher, instruct a group of children with your lesson plan.
3. Read an article about spelling instruction such as "Adapting the Spelling Basal for Spelling Workshop" (Opitz and Cooper, 1993). Write a response to the article or share a summary of the article with your language arts class.
4. Read an article on the categories of spelling instruction such as "Three Paradigms of Spelling Instruction in Grades 3 to 6" (Heald-Taylor, 1998). Which of these types of spelling instruction do you observe in classrooms? What types of instructional strategies accompany each approach?

Spelling and Proofreading

Jan Turbill (2000) uses results from a series of case studies to emphasize the importance of developing a spelling conscience through teaching proofreading. She concludes that proofreading should be an integral part of learning to read, write, and spell. She maintains that instruction in proofreading requires a classroom culture that emphasizes the social purposes for standard spelling, a teacher who helps students understand the decisions made during the proofreading process, a teacher who provides explicit instruction during writing conferences and spelling activities, and teacher expectations that students will spell words correctly. Turbill concludes that to be effective spellers students need to develop a spelling conscience that includes their development as effective proofreaders. She states, "Proofreading should be seen, therefore, not simply as a set of procedural skills, but rather as an integral part of the literacy curriculum from the time children begin to learn to read and write" (p. 216).

Virginia Smith, a fourth-grade teacher, developed the following unit to teach the proofreading skills associated with spelling improvement. She taught the unit to her class. This unit is based on research by Personke and Yee (1971). They conclude that students must attain an attitude toward spelling that they label "spelling conscience" and must be instructed in the techniques necessary for proofreading their own compositions efficiently. The dictionary is the primary reference tool for such proofreading. Smith's unit begins with an informal diagnostic test, followed by proofreading activities that stress dictionary skills, proofreading spelling lists, proofreading a story, and writing a paragraph from dictation.

For Your Plan Book

Lesson Plan

Proofreading Unit for Grade 4

I. Informal Diagnostic Test
   A. Objectives:
      1. To introduce the importance of proofreading for increasing spelling accuracy in compositions.
      2. To discover a student's proofreading skills.
   B. Procedures: Give each child a copy of the following letter. Explain that there are spelling errors in the letter, and you want the children to look carefully at the words and draw a line under each incorrect spelling. Explain that the procedure of reading written material and correcting spelling is called *proofreading*. After children underline the words, have them write the correct spelling above each word, if they know it. Ask the children to write "proofread for spelling" at the end of the letter.

Deer Tom,	1
Have you playd much basbal	2
lately? I am Know on the Red	1
Arows teem. My bruther is two.	4
We both bated Fryday nite. I	3
gut a hit but he diddn't.	2
We are coming to yur town	1
next week to viset. I hope we	1
cen play basbal together then.	2
Yur frend,	2
Tony	
	19 errors

   C. Materials:
   D. Evaluation: Make a proofreading folder for each child. Check each child's proofreading accuracy, noting which errors the child does and does not detect. Return the papers to the class and discuss the need for proofreading skills.

II. Dictionary Skills—Arranging Words in Alphabetical Order
   A. Objective: To review the use of a dictionary in order to improve proofreading skills.
   B. Procedures: Explain to the children that the dictionary is used to check all guesses they make in spelling. Review the procedures for arranging words in alphabetical order. First, alphabetize words according to the first letter of the word: *cattle, bottle, safety, another, timber, doctor, meat, laughter*. Next, alphabetize words according to the second letter of the word: *builder, better, brake, battle, blimp, box, bicycle*. Finally, review the practice that if two words begin with the same letters, you alphabetize according to the first letter that is different. Example: *clever, clatter, clergy, climate, cloudy, cloak, clothes, clump, club, claw, click*.
   C. Materials: Divide the class into teams. Give each team a set of words written on cards to put into alphabetical order. The first team to put their words into correct order scores a point. Players may move about with the cards, or they can place cards on the chalk tray. The cards should progress from easier to more complicated alphabetizing tasks. Eventually, have the children put lists of words such as these into alphabetical order: *interesting, interested, interests*.

III. Dictionary Skills—Using Guide Words
   A. Objective: To learn that speed of dictionary use can be improved through the use of guide words.
   B. Procedures: Have the students open their dictionaries to a specific page. Discuss the two words at the top of the page. Example: On page 955 are the words *rally* and *rang*. Have the students look at the page and decide the purpose of the two words. Help them understand that *rally* is the first word on the page and *rang* is the last word. Discuss the benefits of using guide words.
   C. Materials: Each team or individual student needs a copy of the same dictionary. Ask the students how rapidly they can find the guide words on the page where the word *horse* is found. Continue that procedure with various words. For another activity with individual dictionaries, provide the guide words for a page and ask the students if certain words would be found on that page. Example: Is the word *know* on the same page with the guide words *knight* and *knotting*? Have the students look the words up in the dictionary to verify their answers.
   D. Evaluation: Evaluate each student's ability to use guide words accurately. Provide a worksheet on which students must find the pages where specific guide words appear. Informally test the students' ability to find specific words rapidly.

IV. Proofreading Spelling Lists
   A. Objective: To learn to apply proofreading skills to a list of spelling words.
   B. Procedures: Have the students write down a list of words that you read to them slowly. Ask the students to pronounce the words carefully to themselves before they write the words. Tell them to underline the words they don't know how to spell. After dictating the list, allow the students about fifteen minutes to check the spellings in their dictionaries. Have them write the correct spellings above misspelled words. When they have made their corrections, have them write "proofread for spelling" on their papers.
   C. Materials: Use the following words for dictation. (The words were taken from a fourth-grade text.)

read	glow	alone	nice
case	twice	fool	hour
afraid	noisy	chair	fear
eager	worst	pearl	harbor
seed	collar	thread	cover

Continued

D. Evaluation: How well did the students check their guesses? Were they able to distinguish between words that they knew were correctly spelled and those that were not?

V. Proofreading a Story
A. Objective: To improve the students' ability to apply proofreading skills to a written composition.
B. Procedures: Give each child a copy of a poorly written story. Have the children read through the story, then proofread for spelling errors, underlining each incorrect spelling once and writing the corrected word above. Have the children use the dictionary to verify any guesses and ask them to write "proofread for spelling" when they are finished.
C. Materials:

The fat cat ran swiftly across	1
the gras. He was chaseing a mous.	3
Wood he cetch it? The mouse ran bak	3
and fourth by the flower bed.	1
Suddenly the cat jumbd. The mous	2
dashd behind the roze bush, then	2
dizappeared from site. He wuz safe	3
frum the fat cat.	1

16 errors

D. Evaluation: Observe how well students are able to find errors and to use their dictionaries to find correct spellings. Go over the corrections in class so the students can see how they have done.

VI. Writing a Paragraph from Dictation and Proofreading It
A. Objective: To practice proofreading skills following a dictated paragraph.
B. Procedures: Dictate a short paragraph to the class. Tell the students to underline any unknown spellings as they write the paragraph. After the dictation, allow time for the class to check their guessed spellings in the dictionary. Have them write the correct spellings above the word. Have them write "proofread for spelling" on the paper when they are finished.
C. Materials:

Mary and her brother Tom went to the beach last Thursday. The sun was hot, the sea was cold and the sand was clean. Mary and Tom had fun swimming and playing. When they came home they were both very tired and very happy.

D. Evaluation: Observe how well the students check their guesses using the dictionary. Have the students state the steps that they should follow when proofreading a story or a list of spelling words. They should practice these steps in every subject area.

Used with permission of Virginia Smith, teacher at St. Michael's Academy, Bryan, Texas.

Gifted Spellers

When you use a diagnostic and pretest approach, accelerated students will not waste class periods on words they can already spell. Gifted spellers can thus take part in a spelling period without excessive boredom. Because accelerated students may learn their words very rapidly, they will have time during the spelling period to increase their vocabularies and work on word lists that suit their particular interests. As an example, one gifted third-grade student was especially interested in astronomy and another in dinosaurs. The children learned to spell subject-related words that allowed them to write about their favorite topics. The words are not normally taught in the third-grade spelling curriculum, but these students used them frequently.

Successful spelling programs for gifted spellers are usually individualized. Gifted students should not be punished by having to master a second list of words after they have learned one list. One student who described her spelling experience indicated that her spelling teacher always gave her an additional twenty-five spelling words if she spelled the first twenty-five correctly. The second list proved to be punishment for this girl, rather than an award for accurate spelling. The girl solved her problem by intentionally missing words on the first list so she would not have to write an additional list of words. Obviously, the teacher had not placed this child on the correct spelling level and had not used a pretest to determine the words she did not need to study.

You can enrich the spelling curriculum with vocabulary-building activities. Help students find synonyms for overworked words and discover when the meaning of a sentence would be improved by the use of a more exact word. For example, the word *small* has several different meanings. Students who are investigating synonyms would find three categories of words relating to *small:*

Little	*Minor*	*Small-minded*
diminutive	unimportant	ignoble
wee	trivial	narrow
miniature	insignificant	bigoted
dwarfish	modest	petty
Lilliputian	inconsiderable	stingy
minute	secondary	limited
tiny	inconsequential	provincial
	trifling	intolerant

Have the students categorize the various synonyms according to their proper meanings and discuss the context for using each of them. Among other words with multiple meanings and numerous synonyms are *strong, big, rub, rude, nice, real, look, safe,* and *fair.*

Spelling and Literature

All types of literature may be used to select spelling words or to reinforce students' understandings of spelling words. Teachers who are using literature-based approaches to reading often relate the vocabulary words in the literature and the spelling words that the children are studying. Teachers in the content areas frequently choose spelling words taken from the literature of that content. For example, the lower grade spelling lists are also found in the vocabularies of easy-to-read books such as Cynthia Rylant's *Henry and Mudge and the Bedtime Thumps* (1991), *Henry and Mudge and the Happy Cat* (1990), and *Henry and Mudge and the Long Weekend* (1992); Jean Van Leeuwen's *Oliver, Amanda, and Grandmother Pig* (1987) and *Oliver Pig at School* (1990); Katherine Paterson's *The Smallest Cow in the World* (1991); Nancy Smiler Levinson's *Snowshoe Thompson* (1992); Mary Ann Hoberman's *You Read to Me, I'll Read to You* (2001); and Joanna Cole and Stephanie Calmenson's *Ready . . . Set . . . Read!: The Beginning Reader's Treasury* (1990). Children can search for their spelling words and also select additional words that they would like to learn to spell.

Nonfictional information books provide numerous sources for content-area spelling words associated with literature. For example, spelling related to shapes may be reinforced through Ed Emberley's *The Wing on a Flea: A Book About Shapes* (2001). Older students might select spelling words related to science, geography, and mathematics from Kathryn Lasky's *The Librarian Who Measured the Earth* (1994). In this story set in ancient Greece they will make discoveries about Eratosthenes, the first man to measure the circumference of the earth. A spelling list might include the following words: *accurate, angle, calculate, chronology, circumference, constellations, dictionaries, encyclopedias, geography, laboratories, libraries, mathematics, measuring, museum, philosophy, science, scrolls, sections, sphere,* and *surveyors.* Now students would not only study the words, they would also identify meanings and relate the terms to a content area. During a study of the Mayan culture, spelling words might be selected from Laurie Coulter's *Secrets in Stone: All About Maya Hieroglyphs* (2001). A glossary provides sources for words.

For Your Development

Search through either easy-to-read books or books that are appropriate for a specific content area. Develop a lesson in which you help students identify spelling words that are appropriate for either type of book. Encourage students to use the spelling words in their own writing.

Approaches for Slow Spellers

Slower spellers in a class may need special consideration. Accurate diagnosis of spelling ability levels and specific strengths and weaknesses is especially important for effective remedial instruction. You may need to reduce by half the list of words that you expect remedial spellers to master because a more detailed study method may be necessary. Templeton and Morris (1999) state that students who experience difficulty with spelling may need to be provided spelling instruction at a slower pace that is geared to the appropriate development level regardless of the student's grade or age. This instruction frequently requires focusing on fewer words at a time, teaching spelling patterns in an explicit manner, and providing large amounts of practice and review.

The Fernald Approach

Fernald's multisensory approach has been successful with many less able spellers (Campbell, 1976). Begin by writing a word on a card in large letters. (Use cursive writing for older children and manuscript for younger students.)

Next, show this card to the child and name the word. Ask the child to look carefully at the word and say it with you. Trace the word with two fingers while the child repeats the word. Next, have the child trace the word with two fingers while he or she pronounces each syllable; the child does not spell the word. Have the child repeat this tracing and verbalizing until he or she feels ready to write the word without copying it.

When the child is ready, have the child turn the card face down and write the word without looking at it. After writing the word, have the child turn the card over to verify the spelling. If the child spells the word correctly, have the child go through the writing and verification procedures three more times without copying either the card or the previously written words. If unsuccessful, have the child trace and verbalize again. Do not permit the child to erase part of the word; the child must rewrite the whole word if he or she makes an error. The following day, retest words learned in this manner.

You can use the Fernald approach individually or with small groups. One teacher who used this approach with severely remedial spellers reported that her pupils increased mastery of their spelling words by 80 percent. They learned fewer words, but used the words they learned in daily work and remembered them.

Reinforcement Games

Less able spellers need reinforcement activities. Games offer diversion from the more drill-centered remedial approaches. The tic-tac-toe and the sports and spelling games enrich and motivate remedial instruction.

Tic-Tac-Toe. In the tic-tac-toe game, print the week's spelling words on one side of tagboard cards. One player shuffles the cards while the second player draws a tic-tac-toe grid. The players decide who is to be X and who is to be O. Player X draws the first card, and asks player O to spell the word on the card. If player O spells the word correctly, he or she places an O on the grid and draws a card for player X to spell. When a player is unable to spell a word, he or she places the card on the bottom of the card pile and is not allowed to place a marker on the grid. The winner is the player who places three of his or her markers in a row.

Sports and Spelling. For the sports and spelling game, have the students divide into pairs. Give each pair the sports section from the daily newspaper. The children must find as many words from their spelling list as possible. The winners are the team or teams who find the most words.

For Your Development

Develop a spelling game for reinforcing a weekly spelling list. Play the game with children of the appropriate age. *Caution:* When you use games to reinforce learning, be sure to supervise the play. Children may circumvent the rules of the game and make up their own. When this happens, the objective for the game is not realized.

Mainstreaming

With its demands for visual and auditory perception, short- and long-term memory, attention to details, and fine-motor capabilities, spelling instruction causes considerable problems for children with learning and mental disabilities. Fulk and Stormont-Spurgin (1995) identify the following possible reasons for the persistence of severe spelling deficits for students with learning disabilities: "First, teacher preparation for spelling instruction may be overlooked, due to an overriding emphasis on the instruction of reading and mathematics. Second, minimal instructional time may be allocated to spelling due to beliefs that spelling is of secondary importance in today's extensive curriculum. Third, believing that students acquired these techniques in the primary grades, teachers may neglect instruction in effective spelling strategies" (p. 488).

Table 9–2   Mainstreaming and spelling for children with learning disabilities

Characteristics of Children with Learning Disabilities	Teaching Techniques for Language Arts Instruction
1. Lower scores than those for normal children on spelling both predictable and unpredictable words (Fulk & Stormont-Spurgin, 1995).	1. Limit the number of new words introduced each day. Teach effective study strategies such as the test–study–test method (Fulk & Stormont-Spurgin, 1995; Lewis & Doorlag, 1995; McNaughton, Hughes, & Clark, 1991; Templeton & Morris, 1999).
2. Poor visual short-term memory and problems with auditory and/or visual memory (Fulk & Stormont-Spurgin, 1995; Wallace & McLoughlin, 1988).	2. Try the VAKT approach, which emphasizes seeing, saying, hearing, and feeling in order to learn spelling words (Gearheart, Weishahn, & Gearheart, 1992). Try "Spelling Cheerleading" (Rogers, 1999).
3. Phonemic discrimination problems may be reflected in spelling difficulties because children have difficulty hearing fine differences of sounds within words (Johnson, 1993).	3. Avoid phonics approaches and try a linguistic spelling or whole-word system. Provide auditory discrimination training. Use rhyming words (Johnson, 1993; Otto & Smith, 1980; Ysseldyke & Algozzine, 1995). Try the auditory discrimination suggestions for listening development for children with learning disabilities. Use word boxes to help children match sounds to print (Joseph, 1999). Use word sorting techniques (Zutell, 1998).
4. May be inattentive, easily distracted, and off-task during academic activities (Harris, Graham, Reid, McElroy, & Hamby, 1994).	4. Encourage students to self-monitor their performance on graphs and so forth (Fulk & Stormont-Spurgin, 1995; Harris et al., 1994). Combine Add-A-Word spelling procedure with a public posting of successful student performance (Struthers, Bartlamay, Bell, & McLaughlin, 1994).

Table 9–3   Mainstreaming and spelling for children with mental disabilities

Characteristics of Children with Mental Disabilities	Teaching Techniques for Language Arts Instruction
1. Below-average ability in spelling as well as other academic areas; spelling ability may be even lower than reading ability (Otto & Smith, 1980).	1. Test the student's reading vocabulary with the Dolch Basic Word List or the Johnson Word List. Then test the student's spelling ability on the same list. The initial target words for spelling growth are the words a student can read but cannot spell (Otto & Smith, 1980).
2. Lack of phonic-analysis ability.	2. Try a multisensory approach for spelling instruction. Try an approach emphasizing spelling patterns or word families with high utility value (Otto & Smith, 1980). Use informal and formal tests and trial teaching to determine the best method for spelling instruction (Harris & Sipay, 1985). Try color cues (Frostig, 1984).

Many teachers provide special instruction in spelling and provide many opportunities for children to dictate their stories to scribes. Table 9–2 presents characteristics of children with learning disabilities that might interfere with spelling, and corresponding teaching techniques for language arts instruction. Table 9–3 presents the same information for children with mental disabilities. The characteristics and techniques for language arts instruction result from a search of the research literature and recommendations of authorities who work with mainstreamed children.

SUMMARY

In the many articles dealing with the writing crisis in American schools, poor spelling is often cited as a major problem. School programs must proceed from sound diagnosis; help students learn to spell the words they need to know; provide instruction in reliable spelling generalizations; develop an understanding of word meanings; equip spellers with more than one strategy; incorporate spelling into all areas of the curriculum; and provide for motivation, positive attitudes, and sound habits.

Use diagnostic approaches to place students on appropriate instructional levels. Analyze the types of errors each child makes in writing and use this information to individualize your spelling program. You should test to place students at appropriate levels and determine an understanding of spelling generalizations. In addition, you should analyze errors.

You may select spelling words according to several different criteria. The frequency-of-use approach bases spelling instruction on the words used most frequently. Consequently, with this approach, you would teach first the words most frequently used in writing. In a specific grade, you should also teach words commonly used by children in that grade, including words from the content areas.

A quite different criterion emphasizes the phonic regularity of words. Words in this approach follow consistent spelling patterns. Some linguists and psycholinguists stress consistency of spelling patterns in words of similar meaning. Thus, spelling instruction should allow students to compare, contrast, and categorize words according to root words, word origins, and similarities in structural patterns.

Several techniques are valuable in spelling instruction. The corrected-test method provides immediate feedback and liberates students from systematic study of words already mastered. The self-study method allows students to master their individualized spelling words. The inductive method allows students to discover and use the reliable spelling generalizations.

Use special spelling approaches for less able spellers. The Fernald approach is useful for children with learning disabilities. In this multisensory method, children look at the word, say the word, trace the word, then write the word without looking at it. Spelling games are useful for reinforcing and motivating remedial spelling students. However, do not teach spelling as an isolated subject. Students, whether regular, gifted, or remedial, require many opportunities to use spelling in meaningful situations.

ADDITIONAL SPELLING ACTIVITIES

1. Collect writing samples of three- to ten-year-olds. Identify the stages in spelling development according to Henderson and Templeton's (1986) five stages.
2. Compare an informal spelling-level test that you compile from one specific spelling program with one from a second spelling program. Evaluate the similarities and the

differences between the two tests. What information does each test provide? Is there a difference in word difficulty or word selection?

3. Develop a spelling lesson designed to teach an apostrophe generalization.
4. Interview several good, average, and poor spellers. Determine their perceptions about their spelling ability, their attitudes toward spelling, their study approaches, and their techniques for spelling an unknown word.
5. Develop a spelling unit designed to improve proofreading abilities.
6. Develop a series of spelling lessons that would accompany a literature-based approach to reading.

BIBLIOGRAPHY

Adams, M. J. *Beginning to Read: Thinking and Learning About Print.* Urbana–Champaign, Ill.: University of Illinois, Center for the Study of Reading, 1990.

Balajthy, E. "Using Microcomputers to Teach Spelling." *The Reading Teacher* 39 (1986): 438–43.

Bear, Donald; and Templeton, Shane. "Explorations in Developmental Spelling: Foundations for Learning and Teaching Phonics, Spelling, and Vocabulary." *The Reading Teacher* 52 (November 1998): 222–42.

Bremer, Neville; Bishop, Katherine; and Stone, Lucile. *Skills in Spelling.* Dallas: American Book Co., 1976.

Campbell, Dorothy. "Mode of Response to Tactual Stimuli and Learning Disabled and Normal Pupils Learning New Words with Phoneme–Grapheme Equivalence." *Journal of Research and Development in Education* 9 (Winter 1976): 29.

Chomsky, Carol. "Reading, Writing, and Phonology." *Harvard Educational Review* 40 (1970): 287–309.

Cunningham, Patricia M. "The Multisyllabic Word Dilemma: Helping Students Build Meaning, Spell, and Read 'Big' Words." *Reading & Writing Quarterly: Overcoming Learning Difficulties* 14 (April–June 1998): 189–218.

————. *Phonics They Use: Words for Reading and Writing.* New York: HarperCollins, 1991.

————; and Cunningham, James W. "Making Words: Enhancing the Invented Spelling–Decoding Connection." *The Reading Teacher* 46 (October 1992): 106–15.

Fresch, Mary Jo. "Journal Entries as a Window on Spelling Knowledge." *The Reading Teacher* 54 (February 2001): 500–13.

Frostig, Marianne. "Corrective Reading in the Classroom." In *Readings on Reading Instruction,* 3rd ed., edited by Albert J. Harris and Edward R. Sipay. New York: Longman, 1984.

Fulk, Barbara; and Stormont-Spurgin, Melissa. "Spelling Interventions for Students with Disabilities: A Review." *The Journal of Special Education* 28 (1995): 488–513.

Gearheart, Bill R.; Weishahn, Mel W.; and Gearheart, Carol J. *The Exceptional Student in the Regular Classroom,* 5th ed. Upper Saddle River, N.J.: Merrill/Prentice Hall, 1992.

Gentry, J. Richard. "An Analysis of Developmental Spelling in GNYS AT WRK." *The Reading Teacher* 36 (November 1982): 192–200.

————. "A Retrospective on Invented Spelling and a Look Forward." *The Reading Teacher* 54 (November 2000): 318–32.

Gustafson, B. "An Individualized Teacher-Directed Spelling Program Compared with a Computer-Based Spelling Program." Doctoral Dissertation, Iowa State University, 1982. *Dissertation Abstracts International* 991A–992A. (University Microfilms No. DA 8221191.)

Hanna, Paul R.; and Hanna, Jean S. "Applications of Linguistics and Psychological Cues to the Spelling Course of Study." *Elementary English* 42 (November 1965): 753–59.

———; and Moore, James. "Spelling—From Spoken Word to Written Symbol." *Elementary School Journal* 53 (February 1953): 329–37.

Hansen, J. *Breaking Ground.* Portsmouth, N.H.: Heinemann, 1985.

Harris, Albert J.; and Sipay, Edward R. *How to Increase Reading Ability*, 8th ed. New York: Longman, 1985.

Harris, Karen; Graham, Steve; Reid, Robert; McElroy, Karen; and Hamby, Robin Stern. "Self-Monitoring of Performance: Replication and Cross-Task Comparison Studies." *Learning Disability Quarterly* 17 (Spring 1994): 121–39.

Harward, Stan V.; Allred, Ruel A.; and Sudweeks, Richard R. "The Effectiveness of Four Self-Corrected Spelling Test Methods." *Reading Psychology* 15 (October–December 1994): 245–71.

Heald-Taylor, B. Gail. "Three Paradigms of Spelling Instruction in Grades 3 to 6." *The Reading Teacher* 51 (February 1998): 404–13.

Henderson, Edmund. *Teaching Spelling.* New York: Houghton Mifflin, 1985.

———; and Beers, James W., eds. *Developmental and Cognitive Aspects of Learning to Spell: A Reflection of Word Knowledge.* Newark, Del.: International Reading Association, 1980.

———; and Templeton, Shane. "A Developmental Perspective of Formal Spelling Through Alphabet, Pattern, and Meaning." *The Elementary School Journal* 86 (January 1986): 305–16.

Hillerich, Robert L. "Let's Teach Spelling—Not Phonetic Misspelling." *Language Arts* 54 (March 1977): 301–07.

———. "Spelling: What Can Be Diagnosed?" *Elementary School Journal* 83 (1982): 138–47.

Hodges, R. E.; and Rudorf, E. H. "Searching Linguistics for Cues for the Teaching of Spelling." *Elementary English* 42 (May 1965): 527–33.

Horn, Ernest. "Phonetics and Spelling." *Elementary School Journal* 57 (May 1957): 424–32.

———. "Phonics and Spelling." *Journal of Education* 136 (May 1954): 233–35.

———. "Principles of Methods in Teaching Spelling as Derived from Scientific Investigation." In *18th Yearbook of the National Society for the Study of Education, Part II.* Bloomington, Ill.: Public School Publishing Co., 1919, pp. 52–77.

———. *Teaching Spelling.* American Educational Research Association, Department of Classroom Teachers Research Pamphlet. Washington, D.C.: National Education Association, 1963.

Hughes, Margaret; and Searle, Dennis. "Spelling and the Second 'R'." *Language Arts* 77 (January 2000): 203–08.

Johnson, Doris. "Relationships Between Oral and Written Language." *School Psychology Review* 22 (1993): 595–609.

Johnston, Francine R. "The Timing and Teaching of Word Families." *The Reading Teacher* 53 (September 1999): 64–75.

Joseph, Laurice M. "Word Boxes Help Children with Learning Disabilities Identify and Spell Words." *The Reading Teacher* 52 (January 1999): 348–56.

Lewis, Rena; and Doorlag, Donald. *Teaching Special Students in the Mainstream,* 4th ed. Upper Saddle River, N.J.: Merrill/Prentice Hall, 1995.

Lie, A. "Effects of a Training Program for Stimulating Skills in Word Analysis in First-Grade Children." *Reading Research Quarterly* 26 (1991): 234–50.

Lundberg, I.; Frost, J.; and Petersen, O. "Effects of an Extensive Program for Stimulating Phonological Awareness in Preschool Children." *Reading Research Quarterly* 23 (1988): 263–84.

Mason, George E. "The Computer in the Reading Clinic." *The Reading Teacher* 36 (February 1983): 504–07.

McGrath, Ellie. "Education: The Bold Quest for Quality." *Time* (October 10, 1983): 58–66.

McNaughton, David; Hughes, Charles; and Clark, Karen. "Spelling Instruction for Students with Learning Disabilities: Implications for Research and Practice." *Learning Disability Quarterly* 17 (Summer 1991): 169–85.

Opitz, Michael F.; and Cooper, Donna. "Adapting the Spelling Basal for Spelling Workshop." *The Reading Teacher* 47 (October 1993): 106–13.

Otto, Wayne; and Smith, Richard. *Corrective and Remedial Teaching.* Boston: Houghton Mifflin, 1980.

Personke, Carl. "Spelling as a Language Art." In *Language Arts Instruction and the Beginning Teacher,* edited by Carl Personke and Dale Johnson. Upper Saddle River, N.J.: Prentice Hall, 1987.

————; and Yee, Albert. *Comprehensive Spelling Instruction.* Scranton, Pa.: Indext Educational Publishers, 1971.

Read, Charles. "Pre-School Children's Knowledge of English Phonology." *Harvard Educational Review* 41 (February 1971): 1–34.

Rogers, Linda K. "Spelling Cheerleading." *The Reading Teacher* 53 (October 1999): 110–12.

Struthers, J. P.; Bartlamay, Helen; Bell, S.; and McLaughlin, T. F. "An Analysis of the Add-A-Word Spelling Program and Public Posting Across Three Categories of Children with Special Needs." *Reading Improvement* 31 (Spring 1994): 28–36.

Templeton, Shane; and Morris, Darrell. "Questions Teachers Ask About Spelling." *Reading Research Quarterly* 34 (January/February/March 1999): 102–12.

Turbill, Jan. "Developing a Spelling Conscience." *Language Arts* 77 (January 2000): 209–17.

Wallace, Gerald; and McLoughlin, James A. *Learning Disabilities: Concepts and Characteristics,* 3rd ed. Upper Saddle River, N.J.: Merrill/Prentice Hall, 1988.

Weiner, Sue. "Four First Graders' Descriptions of How They Spell." *The Elementary School Journal* 94 (January 1994): 315–30.

Ysseldyke, James; and Algozzine, Bob. *Special Education: A Practical Approach for Teachers*, 3rd ed. Boston: Houghton Mifflin, 1995.

Zutell, Jerry. "Some Psycholinguistic Perspectives on Children's Spelling." *Language Arts* 55 (October 1978): 844–50.

————. "Word Sorting: A Developmental Spelling Approach to Word Study for Delayed Readers." *Reading & Writing Quarterly: Overcoming Learning Difficulties* 14 (April–June 1998): 219–38.

CHILDREN'S LITERATURE REFERENCES

Cole, Joanna, and Calmenson, Stephanie, compiled by. *Ready . . . Set . . . Read!: The Beginning Reader's Treasury.* New York: Doubleday, 1990.

Coulter, Laurie. *Secrets in Stone: All About Maya Hieroglyphs.* Illustrated by Sarah Jane English. Toronto, Ontario: Madison Press, 2001.

Emberley, Ed. *The Wing on a Flea: A Book About Shapes.* Boston: Little, Brown, 2001.

Hoberman, Mary Ann. *You Read to Me, I'll Read to You.* Illustrated by Michael Emberley. Boston: Little, Brown, 2001.

Lasky, Kathryn. *The Librarian Who Measured the Earth.* Illustrated by Kevin Hawkes. New York: Little, Brown, 1994.

Levinson, Nancy Smiler. *Snowshoe Thompson.* Illustrated by Joan Sandin. New York: HarperCollins, 1992.

Paterson, Katherine. *The Smallest Cow in the World.* Illustrated by Jane Clark Brown. New York: HarperCollins, 1991.

Rylant, Cynthia. *Henry and Mudge and the Bedtime Thumps.* Illustrated by Sucie Stevenson. New York: Bradbury, 1991.

———. *Henry and Mudge and the Happy Cat.* Illustrated by Sucie Stevenson. New York: Bradbury, 1990.

———. *Henry and Mudge and the Long Weekend.* Illustrated by Sucie Stevenson. New York: Bradbury, 1992.

Van Leeuwen, Jean. *Oliver, Amanda, and Grandmother Pig.* Illustrated by Ann Schweninger. New York: Dial, 1987.

———. *Oliver Pig At School.* Illustrated by Ann Schweninger. New York: Dial Press, 1990.

Grammar, Usage, and the Mechanics of Language

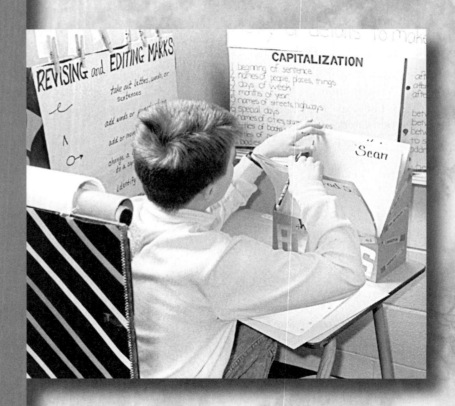

After completing this chapter on grammar, usage, and mechanics, you will be able to:

1. Develop a definition of grammar that includes the three parts of grammar.
2. Describe several characteristics of traditional grammar and list several instructional activities included in a study of traditional grammar.
3. Describe several characteristics of structural grammar and list several instructional activities included in a study of structural grammar.
4. Describe several characteristics of transformational grammar and list several instructional activities included in a study of transformational grammar.
5. Define the levels of usage and list the goals for a level of usage appropriate for classrooms.
6. Develop an inductive lesson for helping children understand a usage concept.
7. List the punctuation skills usually taught in the elementary grades.
8. List the capitalization skills usually taught in the elementary grades.

*L*ike handwriting and spelling, grammar is not an end in itself. Rather, it should be viewed as a means to achieve clarity in both oral and written language. In an interview with news correspondent Walter Cronkite, Hill (2001) reports on changes that he has observed in writing and reporting styles. Hill concludes: "What he finds truly appalling is grammar. Cronkite states: 'The problem is that even newspapers are not edited as well as they should be'" (p. 43). Grammar has been an important part of the language arts curriculum for many years, although the emphasis it receives varies from time to time. There have been revolutionary changes in the approaches of educators to grammar and grammar instruction. These innovations, however, have not gone unchallenged. Grammar is frequently mentioned in the back-to-basics movement, and some critics of American education feel that instruction would profit from a return to a more traditional approach to grammar. To be prepared to answer the critics and to provide better instruction, teachers need to understand the different aspects of grammar and appropriate methods for improving students' grasp and application of grammar and usage.

Many college students admit, rather sheepishly, that they have forgotten a great deal about grammar, so this chapter starts with a definition. Francis (1964) provides a useful, three-part definition of grammar:

> *Grammar 1:* The first thing we mean by grammar is the set of formal patterns in which the words of a language are arranged in order to convey larger meanings. It is not necessary that we be able to discuss these patterns consciously in order to be able to use them. In fact, all speakers of any language above the age of five or six know how to use its complex forms of organization with considerable skill. In this sense of the word they are thoroughly familiar with its grammar.
>
> *Grammar 2:* The second meaning of grammar is that branch of linguistic science which is concerned with the description, analysis, and formalization of language patterns.
>
> *Grammar 3:* The third sense in which people use the word grammar is that of linguistic etiquette. The word in this sense is often coupled with a derogatory adjective; the expression "He ain't there" is "bad grammar." What we mean is that such an expression is bad linguistic manners in certain circles. (pp. 69–70)

413

Grammar 1

The first part of this definition includes the intuitive knowledge of sentence structure that most children demonstrate by the time they enter school. This is the major subject of Chapter 2, "Language and Cognitive Development." Hartwell (1985) builds on Francis's definition when he identifies this first part of grammar as a set of formal patterns that speakers of a language use automatically to construct meaning. Hillocks and Smith (1991) define knowledge of grammar as "the ability to produce and understand a wide range of grammatical structures" (p. 595). Consequently, students have a substantial knowledge of grammar before they receive any formal instruction. Hillocks and Smith add, however, "the fact that students enter school with this knowledge already in place does not imply that they do not develop during their years of formal schooling" (p. 595). This intuitive knowledge is the basis for further grammar instruction in school. Many state guidelines, such as the *English Language Art and Reading Standards* from Texas, emphasize both the need for developing oral language fluency and the more formal instruction that helps children use writing conventions. You can emphasize grammar 1 by providing many opportunities for children to explore their language through oral language activities. These activities help children discover the flexibility of language and its uses for communication.

Grammar 2

Grammar 2, the linguistic branch of grammar, is concerned with the description, analysis, and formalization of language patterns. Traditional grammar, structural grammar, and transformational grammar are various approaches within this branch. The National Council of Teachers of English (1996) standards for language arts include this about grammar 2: "Students apply Knowledge of language Structure, language conventions (e.g., spelling and punctuation), media techniques, figurative language, and genre to create, critique, and discuss print and nonprint texts" (p. 36).

Traditional Grammar

Traditional grammar has its roots in the eighteenth-century works of Joseph Priestly, Robert Lowth, George Campbell, and Lindley Murray. These writers were prescriptive. They based their rules on Latin, which they saw as a perfect language. Baker (1989) states: "These rules owe their place in school grammars to a project that began in the English Renaissance. At that time, it was felt that the best of all possible languages would be one in which the grammatical rules of the language could be identified with the rules of reasoning that humans everywhere use. Classical Greek and Latin appeared to Renaissance thinkers to be the languages that most clearly embodied this idea" (p. 24).

Traditional grammar is called *prescriptive* because it attempts to tell people how to speak or write. Traditional grammar classifies words as verbs, adjectives, nouns, adverbs, pronouns, prepositions, conjunctions, or interjections. Instructional activities in traditional grammar might require children to underline all the nouns in a sentence, draw an arrow between a pronoun and its antecedent, mark the verb in a sentence, define the classification of the verb, change the verb to passive or active voice, conjugate verbs, identify adverbs in a sentence, indicate the words that adverbs modify, find the prepositions in a sentence, or identify the conjunctions in a sentence.

Structural Grammar

Structural grammar began with the work of Leonard Bloomfield. It was further developed by linguists such as Charles Fries and James Sledd. The structuralists suggested a new way to classify language. Consequently, structural grammar is not prescriptive, as is traditional grammar; instead, it is descriptive.

With the development of structural grammar, structural linguists began to study the structure of individual languages. According to Baker (1989), structural linguistics provided two basic truths that are extremely important: First, contrary to what was believed at the time, there are no "primitive" languages. Instead, oral languages are "governed by coherent systems of rules in exactly the same way that the better known written languages were" (p. 13). Second, there is a much wider diversity among different languages than had been suspected. Consequently, "language scholars abandoned the practice of trying to fit the description of every newly encountered language into the mold provided by the rule systems of Latin and Greek. Instead, they increasingly adopted the view that each language deserved to be described in its own terms" (p. 13).

Form Classes.   Structuralists divide words into groups according to the ways in which the words change form, the positions of the words in a sentence, and the structure of the words preceding them. Structuralists identify four form classes, resembling nouns, verbs, adjectives, and adverbs. Consider nouns, for example, for how they might be described in structural grammar:

1. Nouns change form by adding *s* or *es* to show plural and *s* or an apostrophe (') to show possession. For example:

   father—fathers (plural)—father's (possessive)

   Other groups of words, such as verbs, adjectives, and adverbs, cannot be made either plural or possessive.

Children need to recognize that each occasion, audience, and purpose requires different language standards or usage.

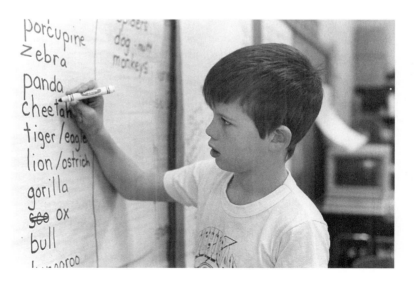

2. Nouns also occur in certain positions in sentences. For example, in the sentence "This (determiner) boy (noun) ran (verb) away (adverb)," the noun falls after the determiner and before the verb. Any word placed in this specific position is a noun:

This _____ ran away.

Nouns also occur after verbs as objects (as in "Jerry mailed *letters*" and after prepositions as objects (as in "We are at *home*").

3. Nouns often appear with structure words called determiners. These determiners frequently precede nouns. For example:

articles:	*an* airplane
	a story
	the city
possessives:	*my* sister
	your brother
	their wagon
demonstratives:	*this* house
	that tree
	these balls

Verbs may also be described in terms of changes in form, positions in sentences, and relationships to certain structure words. For example:

1. Simple verbs may change form by adding *s* for present tense (she walk*s*) and *ed* for past tense (she walk*ed*). However, there are many irregular verbs, which are changed to past tense without adding *ed*, as in *ring, rang,* and *rung.*
2. Verbs usually are located after the subject of a sentence (a noun). In the sentence "Jimmy ran to school," only verbs fit into this position:

Jimmy _____ to school.

3. The structure words that come before verbs are auxiliaries, such as *can, would, were,* and *has been,* as in the sentence "Mother *has been* painting all morning."

Structuralists describe adjectives in the following ways:

1. Adjectives containing one or two syllables usually change form to show comparison by adding *er* and *est.* For example:

small, smaller, smallest

Adjectives containing more than two syllables usually change form by adding the structure words *more* and *most.* For example:

appealing, more appealing, most appealing

2. Adjectives often occur before the nouns they modify, as in "Let's climb the big*gest* tree." Only adjectives may be placed in this position:

Let's climb the _____ tree.

Adjectives may also appear after linking verbs, as in the sentence "The sky is *cloudy.*" (Note that nouns, too, may come after linking verbs.)

3. Intensifiers, such as *very* and *quite,* frequently come before adjectives. (In addition, adverbs may come before adjectives.)

The final form class is adverbs.

1. Adverbs, like adjectives, may change form by adding *er* and *est.*
2. Adverbs are often found at the end of a sentence, as in "Call your mother *immediately!*"
3. Adverbs, like adjectives, may also be marked by intensifiers.

Instructional activities in a structural grammar text might require the students to change the forms of verbs by adding *s, ed,* or *ing.* (These may be taught inductively.)

Sentence Patterns.   Structural grammar also describes grammar according to sentence patterns. Roberts (1962) developed a sequence of ten patterns to describe existing sentences. These sentence patterns are frequently used in textbooks that use a structural grammar approach. Pattern 1, for example, follows:

Determiner	*Noun*	*Verb (Intransitive)*	*Adverb*
The	woman	walks	rapidly

Students might identify existing sentences as to their appropriate sentence pattern. Teachers might place on the board a sentence such as "The tree was tall and _____" and let the children discuss the characteristics of words that fit the empty position and provide examples of appropriate words. Classes might develop similar sentences with empty positions for each of the patterns in the grammar. According to Goodman (1965), patterns are frequently provided as models for the analysis of existing sentences.

Transformational Grammar

Transformational grammar is based on the work of Noam Chomsky (1957). It builds on the work of the structuralists but extends structural grammar into the meaning of language. Whereas structural grammar is concerned primarily with syntax, transformational grammar is concerned primarily with semantics and the generation of sentences. According to Lamb (1977), "transformational grammar purports to provide rules for producing new sentences as well as patterns for the analysis of existing sentences. Although sentence patterns are suggested in transformational grammars, these serve a different function than they do in structural grammars" (p. 100).

Menyuk (1991) discusses the importance of transformational grammar when she states that one of the most dramatic changes in the understanding of language occurred some thirty years ago: "This was the advent of transformational, or more accurately, generative grammar. Previously language theories were influenced by behaviorists' theories of learning. Language was described as a set of learned habits. . . . Generative theories hold that language knowledge is represented in the mind as a system of rules, and that language is acquired by an active learner" (p. 24). She maintains that these are now the aspects of current linguistic theory that are the most germane to the teaching of the language arts.

The term *transformational* refers to basic sentences and the transforms, or variations, that can be developed from these basic sentences. The basic sentences, or kernel sentences, have several definite characteristics. They are formed by placing words together in certain patterns. The second part of transformational grammar consists of directions or rules for rearranging or combining the kernel sentences into new, more complicated structures.

Kernel Sentences.   The formula for a kernel sentence is:

Sentence = noun phrase + verb phrase

Diagram this sentence formula as follows:

Noun Phrase	Verb Phrase
The car	is red

Kernel sentences have several definite characteristics:

1. In a kernel sentence, the subject is followed by the predicate.

   Subject (The car) Predicate (is red)

2. A kernel sentence is a statement, not a question. (All questions are transforms.)
3. A kernel sentence is affirmative. (All negative sentences are transforms.)
4. A kernel sentence is in the active voice. (All passive-voice sentences are transforms.)
5. A kernel sentence contains a single predicate.

Sentence Patterns.   Transformationalists also suggest patterns, or basic-sentence types. Mellon (1964) named five basic-sentence patterns, whereas Kean and Personke (1976) identified four types of sentences, according to the positions or slots that words may fill. Any sentence that does not follow one of the four patterns is considered a transformation:

1. The *be* sentence:

Noun Phrase	Verb (Be class)	Noun Phrase, Adjective, or Prepositional Phrase	Optional Adverb
The squirrel	is	a rodent	
The squirrel	is	lively	today
The squirrel	is	in the tree	

2. The intransitive verb sentence:

Noun Phrase	Verb (Intransitive)	Open Adverb or Prepositional Phrase	Optional Adverb
Jerry	ran		rapidly
Jerry	ran	outside	quickly
Jerry	ran	into the field	

3. The transitive verb sentence:

Noun Phrase	Verb (Transitive)	Noun Phrase (Direct Object)	Optional Adverb
The girls	mailed	the package	yesterday

4. The linking verb sentence:

Phrase	Verb (Linking)	Noun Phrase or Adjective	Optional Adverb
Judy	became	the president	
Judy	became	frightened	today

Basic-Sentence Transformations.   Both single-base transformations, which act on one kernel sentence, and double-base transformations, which combine two kernel sentences, are possible with the rules of transformational grammar (Kean & Personke, 1976). The following single-base transformations are possible:

1. *Question transformation*—The kernel sentence "The car is red" may be easily transformed into a question by rearranging the words into "Is the car red?" The sentence also becomes a question by changing the intonation to "The car is red?" The words *do, does,* or *did* may transform the kernel into a question; for example, "Did Judy become the president?" Question transforms may begin with *who, what, when, where,* and *why.* Thus, the kernel "Jerry ran into the field" could become "Why did Jerry run into the field?" or "When did Jerry run into the field?"

2. *Passive transformation*—The kernel sentence must be in the active voice, so this change affects sentences that contain transitive verbs. The sentence must be transformed so that the subject receives, rather than performs, the action expressed in the verb. The kernel sentence "The teacher read the book" would become the transformation "The book was read by the teacher." As you can see, the direct object of the original kernel sentence is now the subject of the transformation.

3. *Negative transformation*—The original kernel sentence, "The car is red," becomes a transformation merely by inserting *not* or *n't* after the verb. This transformation results in the sentence "The car is not red." *Do, does,* or *did* may be used along with the *not* to transform the sentence "Jerry ran outside quickly" to the negative transform "Jerry did not run outside quickly."

Sentences may also be transformed through double-base transformations, in which the transformations result from combining two kernel sentences into one transformation. More complex sentences result from this transformation. The following double-base transformations are possibilities:

1. *Coordinating transformation*—Coordinating transformations often use coordinating conjunctions, such as *and, but, or,* or sentence connectors, such as *however, therefore, moreover,* to combine kernel sentences in equal or coordinating positions. For example, the two kernel sentences "Jerry has a bicycle" and "Jerry has a kite" combine in the transform to become "Jerry has a bicycle and a kite."

2. *Adjective insert*—Two kernel sentences may also be joined to form a more interesting and complex transform by combining a kernel sentence containing an adjective with a kernel sentence containing a noun phrase. For example, the two kernel sentences "The squirrel is a rodent" and "The squirrel is lively today" may be transformed into "The squirrel is a lively rodent today."

3. *Subordinating transformation*—This transformation is more complex than the coordinating transformation. Subordinating connectors, such as *although, whenever, until,* or *because,* are used to connect the two kernel sentences. For example, the two kernel sentences "The boy was quiet" and "He was happy" might combine in the transform "The boy was quiet, although he was happy," or "Although he was happy, the boy was quiet."

4. *Relative clause transformation*—A relative clause begins with a relative adverb or relative pronoun and is inserted in or at the end of the sentence. For example, the kernel sentences "The car is red" and "I have a car" may combine to form the transform "I have a car that is red." Similarly the two kernels "The man is old" and "The man lives on our street" may combine to form the transform "The man who lives on our street is old."

Instructional activities in a transformational grammar should relate closely to the descriptive elements of the grammar. Because the basic sentence is *noun phrase plus verb phrase,* instructional activities should help children develop an understanding of noun and verb phrases. The major emphasis of instruction should be to guide children in experiencing and working with grammar by helping them examine their own sentences, as well as those written by others. Children should learn how sentences are formed, changed, combined, and improved.

‿For Your Development

1. With a group of your peers, select several language arts textbooks designed for elementary and middle-school children. Analyze the texts to see whether they are based on a traditional, structural, or transformational grammar philosophy. Find examples of learning activities that represent a particular viewpoint. Compare their similarities and differences. Which do you feel is most teachable? Which do you feel would result in the best understanding of language? Share your findings with the rest of your language arts class and be prepared to support your conclusions about the grammar with which you would feel most comfortable in the classroom.

2. Seventh and eighth-grade teacher Joan Berger (2001) provides her schedule for grammar instruction. Compare her schedule given here for seventh graders with the information you found in language arts books:

September	Compound sentences
October	Compound sentences, adverb clauses
November	Adverb clauses
December	Appositives and adjective clauses
January/February	Review words or phrases inserted into a sentence
March	Parenthetical, series, dates, and addresses
April/May	Review all material

Assessment

In the chapters on language and cognitive development and oral language development in this text we discuss informal methods for evaluating oral language that encourage the gathering of oral language samples and that provide sources for the analysis of how children use word patterns and how they convey meaning with those patterns.

You may analyze children's knowledge of and application of grammar through informal approaches. Many of the activities suggested later in this chapter may provide source material for this analysis. Test applications only by analyzing actual speech or written samples produced by the individual child. According to Savage (1977):

> Evaluation of grammatical application centers on the sentences that the children themselves produce: whether they can produce individual sentences based on models, the sentence types and sentence variety that are evident in their written work, how ideas are combined into sentences and how sentences are grouped into paragraphs, and how effective the writing is through the use of grammatical constructions. (p. 380)

Topic variance, however, may influence the quality of written samples. Hirsch (1982) maintains that sentences are more varied and coherent, spelling and punctuation are better, and syntax is improved if the topic is easy rather than difficult or unfamiliar. Consequently, he believes that students may need to write on as many as five different topics before one can make valid judgments.

Assessment procedures vary according to state and local requirements. Many local school districts are developing methods of assessment, such as informal assessments of students' writings. Other schools rely on state-developed and mandated tests. In any case, proceed with caution to ensure that whatever type of assessment you use matches the goals for instruction and assesses the application of grammar during realistic writing situations. As Lamb (1977) notes, "those responsible for selecting tests should recognize the possible discrepancy between what is taught and what is tested" (p. 114).

One test for evaluating a child's ability to combine sentences is the Syntactic Maturity Test, by Roy O'Donnell and Kellogg Hunt (*Measures for Research and Evaluation in the English Language Arts,* Urbana, Ill.: National Council of Teachers of English, 1975). This test relates to transformational grammar. You may use it before teaching sentence combining, or afterward, to evaluate instructional effectiveness. You can administer the Syntactic Maturity Test to students from beginning fourth graders to adults. It contains a paragraph of thirty-two very short, three- to five-word sentences (for example, "Aluminum is a metal. It is abundant."). Students are asked to rewrite the paragraph by combining the sentences without omitting any information. The new paragraph is then analyzed for mean T-unit length (independent clauses and their modifiers).

Instruction

Research does not show that teaching formal rules of grammar improves either speaking or writing (Hillocks & Smith, 1991). Kylene Beers (2001) concludes: "Repeated research studies have confirmed what teachers saw in their classrooms: isolated grammar instruction did not improve students' written or oral English. . . . In this issue we take the stance that grammar and usage instruction do belong in the middle school. The question isn't 'Do we teach grammar,' but instead 'How do we teach grammar in context?' " (p. 4).

Educators emphasize the knowledge that children gain from reading literature and from writing because there is a strong correlation between reading and writing. Researchers such

Children need many opportunities for meaningful writing.

as Krashen (1984) and Stotsky (1983), who investigated writing competence, emphasize that reading ability and experience consistently correlate with writing skill and that the abstract knowledge that proficient writers have about text comes "from large amounts of self-motivated reading for interest and/or pleasure" (Krashen, 1984, p. 20).

In fact, there is a great deal of argument over the value of teaching grammar and which grammar, if any, to teach. Research reveals no advantage in teaching traditional grammar, but there has been some indication that instruction in sentence combining yields positive results in writing. Mellon (1969) found that a technique using transformational sentence combining and grammar produced beneficial results. O'Hare (1973) also used a sentence-combining approach to improve the quality of students' writing. In a review of research, Hillocks and Smith (1991) conclude that the overwhelming majority of sentence-combining studies have been positive and that sentence-combining activities improve writing quality.

The National Council of Teachers of English (1983) believes that grammar should be taught not only to improve writing but also to increase understanding of the language. According to Kean and Personke (1976), "the only justifiable reason for teaching grammar is to lead children to want to explore their language and discover how it works" (p. 313). They explain that the process of communication is the objective of all language study, and that "grammar can play a significant role in such a program if children are guided to experience and work with grammar directly rather than studying it as a complex system that must be memorized" (p. 313). Krashen (1984) maintains that "conscious knowledge of rules of grammar and usage helps only at the editing stage and is limited to straightforward, learnable aspects of grammar" (p. 27). Christenbury (1996) presents several agreed-on opinions including that grammar "cannot be taught effectively in discrete, unconnected units; cannot be taught effectively in massive doses; cannot be taught divorced from student writing; cannot be taught effectively if students see no real need for it and if teachers cannot persuade them to see a need" (p. 12). Lamb (1977) recommends that teachers compare the various grammars, note their similarities and differences, and judge for themselves which is most teachable and will result in better understanding and appreciation of language. She feels each of the newer grammars has merit.

Several authors recommend choosing the best aspects of several grammars. Savage (1977), for example, recommends an eclectic grammar:

> In grammar, eclecticism involves drawing on some of the content and techniques that characterize new grammar in helping children master the grammar they are expected to learn as part of the language arts. It involves, for example, using the signals employed by the structural grammarian as an aid in helping children identify parts of speech, or engaging in some of the sentence-combining activities used by the transformational grammar in helping children generate sentences. It attempts to "plug up" some of the leaks in traditional grammar. (p. 338)

The instructional activities we describe next use an eclectic approach for helping students understand and use their language. Sentence-combining activities are emphasized.

Activities for Early Elementary Grades

In the early elementary grades, use linguistic blocks, cloze sentences, and scrambled sentences to build understanding of sentence patterns. Also, have students change order but retain meaning and have them expand sentences.

Linguistic Blocks.   Use linguistic blocks to help develop and reinforce the basic sentence patterns in English, and help children understand the movable and immovable parts of language. A linguistic block has a different word printed on each of its sides; all of the words on the block belong to the same form class. You can make these blocks out of wooden blocks or even milk cartons. Use words the children have learned in reading or language experience activities. Coding the blocks by color will help children see relationships and patterns within a sentence. For example, you might use blue for nouns, red for verbs, green for adjectives, white for noun determiners, yellow for conjunctions, orange for adverbs, gray for prepositions, purple for pronouns, and brown for punctuation.

You can use linguistic blocks for a great many experiments with sentence construction and meaning. For example, beginning with the simplest noun–verb pattern of a kernel sentence, have students create sentences, such as "Jerry swam." By changing the noun block, students will discover that all the names on the noun blocks fit that same position; for example, "Jane swam," "Tag swam," and "Bill swam." They will also discover they cannot reverse the words in this sentence and still make sense (swam Jerry). Next, have the children try other words in the second position and talk about the words that fit that position; for example, "Jerry sang," "Jerry called," and "Jerry moved." Allow the students to suggest other simple combinations.

Next, have the students try noun blocks that are not people's or pets' names. They can substitute a noun block with the words *dog, cat, man,* and *girl* for the proper-noun block. Look at the resulting sentence: "dog swam." Decide whether it sounds appropriate. By trying each of the common-noun blocks, students will discover that they must add something to make a complete sentence. They usually provide examples such as "My dog swam," "This dog swam," and "The dog swam." Then, introduce another block marked with determiners, such as *the, my, this, your,* and *these,* and lead the students, inductively, to the realization that certain types of words are used before nouns that are not names.

Allow the children to experiment with other sentence patterns. Can they add more to the simple noun, verb, and noun-determiner blocks? (It is not necessary to use these terms with children.) Encourage the children to expand orally by telling *how* someone ran, swam, sang, moved, and so forth. Having thus introduced the adverb, discuss what this kind of word does and how it adds information to the kernel sentence. The children will develop sentences such as "Jerry swam quickly" and "Jane moved quietly."

To help children understand the changes in meaning that result when some sentence sequences are reversed, introduce, with the linguistic blocks, the transitive-verb sentence. Remember that all the verbs on a given block must belong to the same verb class. Sentences such as "The girls mailed the letter" can be formed with transitive-verb blocks. Then, ask the children to experiment by exchanging the noun blocks, "girls" and "letter," so that the sentence reads "The letter mailed the girls." Finally, discuss how the meaning changed when the two words were exchanged. This activity demonstrates how closely meaning is related to a specific sequence of words.

You also can use linguistic blocks to transform kernel sentences into questions, negatives, and so forth. Linguistic blocks allow students to experiment with expanding sentences and to visualize how expansion changes meaning. Data show that such manipulation activities tend to improve written sentence structures for even young students. In an unpublished doctoral dissertation evaluating children's writing achievement after a special language program using linguistic blocks in first, second, and third grades, Baele (1968) found that children in a reading program that included the language supplement showed a significant increase in language quality in sentence structures compared to students who did not use the supplementary program.

Cloze Sentences.   You may use a cloze technique for building an understanding of sentence patterns. In this approach, write a model sentence, omitting a specific type of word, and ask the students to suggest words that fill the position. Such an approach inductively builds knowledge of form classes. For example, a second-grade teacher used the following examples to introduce the noun class:

The _____ was in the zoo.

The teacher asked the children to think of words that would fit in the blank. They provided *zebra, monkey, lion,* and so forth. The class read the sentences and discussed the types of words that fit into the blank. You can also introduce another pattern for nouns, in which the noun is the object, as in the following:

I could see the _____.

Ask the children to offer and discuss words such as *car, train, house,* and *clouds.* Also, have them work with the pattern in which the noun is the object of a preposition:

The man was in the _____.

You can use the cloze technique for other class forms; for example:

Verbs:	Susan _____ (*ran, walked, limped, hopped*) home.
Adjectives:	The _____ (*big, small, blue*) car was on the street.
	The food tasted _____ (*good, hot, spicy, delicious*).
Adverbs:	The cat ran _____ (*quickly, rapidly, quietly*) after the bird.

Use the various patterns of form class to devise similar exercises.

Sentence Transformations.   Students in lower elementary grades can do simple transformations as oral activities and, later, use the same principles in written activities. The sentence transformations described with transformational grammar provide the information for this activity. For example, you might present the coordinating transformation by showing and discussing the following kernel sentences:

Susan has a ball.
Susan has a bat.

Next, lead a discussion of how the two sentences could be combined into one better sentence; for example, "Susan has a ball and bat." You and the students may suggest numerous combinations.

Sentence Scrambling.   Sentences may be scrambled, then rearranged to make sense. This activity is much like a game, because the scrambled sentences can be quite humorous; in fact, you may present it as a game. For example:

walked the slowly turtle (The turtle walked slowly.)
hopped rabbit the (The rabbit hopped.)
her lost Amy game (Amy lost her game.)

Let children scramble their own sentences for another student to unscramble. Their sentences may become quite complex as they progress in ability and grade levels.

Changing Word Order.   Ask students to practice rearranging word order in a sentence without changing the original meaning:

I ate my breakfast this morning. = This morning I ate my breakfast.
The third-grade girls won the race yesterday. = Yesterday the third-grade girls won the race.

Sentence Expansion. Start with a simple sentence and expand it to supply more information. Pantomime and pictures are good introductions to this activity. For example, one second-grade teacher wrote "Mrs. Brown" on the chalkboard, and asked the children to watch her to see if they could fill in the blank. First, she walked to the door. The sentence now became "Mrs. Brown walked." Then, "Mrs. Brown walked to the door." Next, she asked the children, "How did Mrs. Brown walk?" The children watched a second time, and responded, "Mrs. Brown walked slowly to the door." Then, she asked, "When did Mrs. Brown walk slowly to the door?" The class now responded with "Mrs. Brown walked slowly to the door this morning" and "This morning Mrs. Brown walked slowly to the door." The teacher continued the activity by having some of the children pantomime. They expanded each sentence to include not only who, but also what, where, when, how, and why.

Another time, the group looked at large pictures and expanded simple sentences that introduced a subject without telling anything about the subject, such as "Snoopy slept," "The bear ran," and "Mother cooked." The children also drew their own pictures and expanded sentences to describe them.

Activities for Middle-Elementary and Upper-Elementary Grades

Many of the preceding activities are useful, also, in the middle- and upper-elementary grades. The normal rate of syntactic development can be hastened with sentence-combining activities such as those developed for fourth graders by Hunt and O'Donnell (1970). Stoddard (1982) found that sentence-combining activities developed for fifth- and sixth-grade students improved both the overall quality of writing and syntactic maturity. Research by O'Hare (1973) showed that seventh-grade children improved their writing when sentence combining appeared in the curriculum. Weaver (1996) found that sentence combining helps students write more syntactically sophisticated and effective sentences.

In addition to improving the quality of written composition, Mackie (1982) improved the reading comprehension of fourth-grade students who used a sentence-combining approach. In a review of sentence-combining research, Hillocks (1986) reported that the majority of studies indicate that sentence combining promotes syntactic fluency. Remember, however, that the goals of sentence combining are (1) to improve syntactic control and (2) to make sentence construction more automatic. Both goals allow students to focus on writing content rather than the mechanics of sentence construction. Hillocks and Smith (1991) conclude that sentence combining is effective for all types of students—from remedial students to those who are above average.

For Your Plan Book

Lesson Plan

Improving the Writing of Fourth Graders Using a Sentence-Combining Approach

The series of lessons that Kellogg Hunt and Roy O'Donnell (1970) presented to fourth graders required about fifteen minutes per day, about three times a week, over the school year. Hunt and O'Donnell did not use grammatical terms during the classroom activities.

Continued

They described the instruction only as combining two or more sentences into one. The first lesson required them to show the following two sentences on the chalkboard or a transparency:

> I rode in a boat.
> The boat leaked a little.

They read the two sentences as they presented them, and presented a third sentence that combined the first two:

> I rode in a boat that leaked a little.

Next, they read aloud a similar pair of sentences and called on the children to combine the second pair as demonstrated by the model. They covered twelve such combinations in the first lesson.

The transformation lessons progressed in the following sequence:

1. Relative clause modifying object:

> Judy lost a book.
> The book was red.
>> Judy lost a book that was red.
>> Judy lost a red book.

2. Relative clause modifying subject:

> The girl is selling cookies.
> The girl is tall.
>> The girl who is tall is selling cookies.
>> The tall girl is selling cookies.

3. Relative clause reduced to adverb of place:

> The monkey eats bananas.
> The monkey is in the tree.
>> The monkey that is in the tree eats bananas.
>> The monkey in the tree eats bananas.

4. Relative clause reduced to past participle:

> The boy won the race.
> The boy is named Joe.
>> The boy who is named Joe won the race.
>> The boy named Joe won the race.

5. Relative clause reduced to present participle:

> The lion is scary.
> The lion is sitting on the log.
>> The lion that is sitting on the log is scary.
>> The lion sitting on the log is scary.

6. Relative clause reduced to nonrestrictive appositive:

> Mr. Jones directs traffic.
> Mr. Jones is a policeman.
>> Mr. Jones, who is a policeman, directs traffic.
>> Mr. Jones, a policeman, directs traffic.

7. Relative clause with nonsubject relativized:

   The sunset was beautiful.
   We saw the sunset.
   >The sunset that we saw was beautiful.
   >The sunset we saw was beautiful.

8. Free combining of sentences (children may combine them however they wish):

   Children have Christmas stockings.
   The stockings are red.
   The stockings hang by the fireplace.
   Santa fills the stockings.
   Nuts and candy are in the stockings.

   (This activity covered several lessons.)

9. Coordination of noun phrase, verb phrase:

   Mortimer plays football.
   Henry plays football.
   >Mortimer and Henry play football.

10. Review of coordination and modifiers of nouns.
11. Free writing, combining three sentences.
12. *That* plus subject as object:

    He said something.
    His name is John.
    >He said that his name is John.
    >He said his name is John.

13. Extraposition with *it:*

    We lost.
    This disappointed me.
    >It disappointed me that we lost.

14. Free writing, combining four sentences.
15. Nonembedded yes–no questions:

    The cat will play the flute.
    >"Will the cat play the flute?"
    Embedded in direct quotation:
    >He asked, "Will the cat play the flute?"
    Embedded as indirect question:
    >He asked (if, whether) the cat would play the flute.

16. Changing statements to questions by replacing some with a word such as *who, what, which, where, when:*

    Someone will eat the trainer.
    >Who will eat the trainer?

17. Adverb clauses: *as, before, after, until, if, unless, because:*

    The game started.
    My friend came in.

Continued

> As the game started my friend came in.
> Before the game started my friend came in.
> After the game started my friend came in.

18. A story of twenty-six short sentences. The students combined the sentences in free writing.

The complete series of lessons is presented in Hunt and O'Donnell's *An Elementary School Curriculum to Develop Better Writing Skills* (1970). A sentence-combining program for seventh graders, which includes examples of sentences for each lesson, can be found in O'Hare's *Sentence Combining: Improving Student Writing Without Formal Grammar Instruction* (1973).

Sentence Combining.   Sentence-combining activities are found in numerous textbooks designed for use in elementary through college courses. William Strong (1986) provides guidelines and examples that use sentence-combining approaches to teach twenty different types of activities. Some of these activities are similar to the structured sentences developed by Hunt and O'Donnell (1970). In other activities, students generate a range of responses. These activities help students explore, discuss, and evaluate various stylistic options. Strong recommends the following guidelines for developing sentence-combining activities:

1. Discuss purposes for sentence combining. Include creating good sentences, becoming flexible in writing, and exploring ways to transform sentences.
2. Encourage students to try new patterns and to take risks with solutions to sentence-combining problems.
3. Provide a positive environment for risk taking by accepting various solutions. When students offer marginal solutions, refer the solutions to the class for judgment.
4. Use signal exercises, context clues, and oral prompts to help students understand the functions of sentence combining.
5. After modeling sentence-combining exercises, place students in pairs to work through exercises orally.
6. When students are working in pairs, have one student act as scribe for the other; then reverse roles. Have the students discuss problems and work out solutions.
7. Have pairs of students develop options for a sentence-combining activity and then agree on the best solution. Ask the students to explain why they prefer particular sentences.
8. In round-robin combining, encourage students to listen closely and then give as many solutions to a sentence-combining cluster as they can. Ask the students to vote on the solutions and discuss reasons for their choices.
9. Be specific in your praise of good sentences. Tell the students what you like about these sentences.
10. Welcome mistakes as opportunities for group problem solving and use mistakes as bases for skill development in editing workshops.
11. Use transformations handed in by students for in-class workshops.
12. Assign an exercise for homework and then ask several students to put their work on transparency film. Compare their versions in class.
13. Brainstorm with the class to make an exercise more specific and detailed by adding information. Put these details between exercise sentences or elaborate sentence-combining clusters and then compare results.
14. Have students write out solutions to various sentence-combining clusters on note cards. Shuffle the cards and ask the students to rearrange them into a clear, coherent paragraph.

15. Use sentence combining as a springboard for journal writing. Have the students do an exercise each day and then extend that exercise with sentences of their own.

16. Have students combine sentences in a lean, direct style. Contrast the effects of active and passive voice.

17. Ask students to compare their style with that of professional writers. Rewrite a passage into kernel sentences and ask the students to recombine the kernel sentences and then compare their versions with the original.

18. Analyze a sentence-combining exercise for tone, cohesion, method of development, and logical patterns.

19. Create original sentence-combining exercises for specific transformations, course content, or discourse patterns.

20. Emphasize transfer learning by drawing sentence-combining activities from student texts and literature. Have the students revise their writing with particular sentence-combining techniques. Follow sentence-combining lessons with parallel writing tasks for application.

Using Literature for Models of Effective Sentences and Paragraphs. Weaver, McNally, and Moerman (2001) conclude that teaching grammar in isolation is not a practical act; instead, they propose: "What we have found practical, though, is drawing upon literature for models of effective sentences and paragraphs, while incorporating only the most useful grammatical concepts (and even less terminology) into our teaching of writing. This enables us to help students improve sentences as they learn to recognize skilled use of detail, style, voice, and, of course, the conventions of edited American English" (p. 18).

The idea of using literature as models for effective sentences and paragraphs is further reinforced by Noden (2001) who compares the writing of amateur and professional writers: "Readers want a picture—something to see, not just a paragraph to read. A picture made out of words. That's what makes a pro out of an amateur. An amateur writer tells a story. A pro shows the story, creates a picture to look at instead of just words to read. A good author writes with a camera, not with a pen" (p. 10). For example, Noden describes how he uses images of form in which he encourages students to feel grammatical rhythms by imitating the grammatical patterns in well-constructed paragraphs. Noden concludes, "Images act as a doorway into the writer's art and have the power to enchant students like a pied piper into the imaginative world of grammar" (p. 16).

McNally (Weaver et al., 2001) describes how she takes well-written paragraphs from award-winning books and rewrites them in a way that might be in papers written by her students. She then has her students discuss the rewritten materials, rewrite the altered passage into what they believe would appear in the author's passage, and finally share and discuss the author's actual writing. McNally uses Lois Lowry's *The Giver* (1993) as her example, but you can try this activity with any well-written text. For example, you might rewrite the first paragraph in Philip Pullman's *The Golden Compass* (Carnegie Medal, 1995):

> *Lyra and her daemon walked through the hall.*
> *They stayed out of sight of the kitchen.*
> *Three tables were laid in the hall.*
> *Silver and glass were on the tables.*
> *Portraits hung on the walls.*
> *The high table had gold.*
> *The seats were mahogany.*

Ask students to discuss these sentences and to write a paragraph that they think might be in Pullman's text. After discussion and rewriting, share the following first paragraph from Pullman's text with the students:

> Lyra and her daemon moved through the darkening hall, taking care to keep to one side, out of sight of the kitchen. The three great tables that ran the length of the hall were laid already, the silver and the glass catching what little light there was, and the long benches were pulled out ready for the guests. Portraits of former Masters hung high up in the gloom along the walls. Lyra reached the dais and looked back at the open kitchen door, and seeing no one, stepped up beside the high table. The places here were laid with gold, not silver, and the fourteen seats were not oak benches but mahogany chairs with velvet cushions. (p. 3)

Ask students to compare the short choppy sentences that had little description with the painting of the scene created by Pullman.

Using examples of award-winning literature, ask students to find and share well-written paragraphs in books. Ask them to consider what makes these writings excellent. In addition to books that are chosen for various literary awards such as the Newbery, the Carnegies, and the Hans Christian Andersen Award, you can ask your students to consider the merits of books identified by Breen et al. (2000) on their list of the most significant books for children and young adults in terms of shaping the twentieth century. When citing their criteria for these books, they state: "We decided that our list should include books with literary and artistic merit, as well as books that are perennially popular with young readers, books that have blazed new trails, and books that have exerted a lasting influence on the world of children's book publishing" (p. 50).

Of the 100 books on the list, 23 were selected unanimously by all four of the experts on the first round of balloting: Natalie Babbitt's *Tuck Everlasting* (1975), Ludwig Bemelmans's *Madeline* (1939), Judy Blume's *Are You There, God? It's Me, Margaret* (1970), Margaret Wise Brown's *Goodnight Moon* (1947), Robert Cormier's *The Chocolate War* (1999), Louise Fitzhugh's *Harriet the Spy* (1964), Anne Frank's *Anne Frank: The Diary of a Young Girl* (1995), Russell Freedman's *Lincoln: A Photobiography* (1987), Jean Craighead George's *Julie of the Wolves* (1972), Ezra Jack Keats's *The Snowy Day* (1962), E. L. Konigsburg's *From the Mixed-Up Files of Mrs. Basil E. Frankweiler* (1967), Madeleine L'Engle's *A Wrinkle in Time* (1962), C. S. Lewis's *The Lion, the Witch, and the Wardrobe* (1950), Arnold Lobel's *Frog and Toad Are Friends* (1970), Patricia MacLachlan's *Sarah, Plain and Tall* (1985), A. A. Milne's *Winnie-the-Pooh* (1926/1954), Scott O'Dell's *Island of the Blue Dolphins* (1960), Katherine Paterson's *Bridge to Terabithia* (1977), Beatrix Potter's *The Tale of Peter Rabbit* (1902), Maurice Sendak's *Where the Wild Things Are* (1963), Dr. Seuss's *The Cat in the Hat* (1954), E. B. White's *Charlotte's Web* (1952), and Laura Ingalls Wilder's *Little House in the Big Woods* (1932).

Collect as many of these books as possible and ask students to evaluate the books according to style and grammar. Why do they think these books were chosen for their excellence? The students may want to select their own books that they think should be on such a list.

Open-Response Exercises.   You can structure sentence-combining activities with definite correct responses or with open responses in which students generate a range of acceptable responses. Open responses help students explore, discuss, and evaluate various stylistic options. During sentence-combining exercises, you can challenge writing teams by giving oral prompts. For example, give prompts such as begin with "carefully," begin with "not wanting to," begin with "the paper," begin with "to keep," use *because* as a connector, use a semicolon and *therefore,* use "so that" as a connector, and use "in order to" as a connector.

Use prompts to help teach sentence variety. In addition, help students realize that some sentences sound better than others, and that judgments about quality frequently depend on the surrounding sentences. Have students hand in sentence-combining activities for credit; share them in small groups for proofreading, judging, or comparing; enrich them with details generated during prewriting activities; or use them as springboards for in-class follow-up assignments.

You may choose sentence-combining activities from content areas and literature. For example, sentences to combine might include information from social studies or science, recommendations from writing style books, and kernel sentences rewritten from literature paragraphs. You can cluster kernel sentences into groups, or you can list them without clustering. Clustering provides more structure for young students and students who may require extra guidance. When you use kernel sentences from literary sources, let the students compare their solutions with the source material and discover the impact of various literary techniques.

When introducing open-response exercises, Strong (1986) first explains to students that there are many right answers when combining sentences and that making mistakes is expected because people learn from their errors. Next, he asks students to think of different ways to combine two sentences, such as "Carol was working hard on her test. Sue slipped her a note." Before they do this task, he tells the students that they can (1) add connecting words, (2) take out unnecessary words, (3) move words around, and (4) change word endings. Then, he shows students how to combine sentences by modeling various transformations, such as "Carol was working hard on her test, and Sue slipped her a note," "As Carol worked hard on her test, Sue slipped her a note," and "Carol was working hard on her test when Sue slipped her a note." During this modeling, he presents and discusses several awkward or confusing transformations, such as "Working hard on her test, Carol was slipped a note by Sue," "It was Carol, hard at work on her test, who was slipped a note by Sue," and "A note was slipped from Sue to Carol, who was working hard on her test." Finally, he models and discusses unacceptable sentence transformations, such as "Carol working hard on her test, Sue slip her a note," "On her test Carol was hardly working, and a note Sue slipped to her," and "Slipping a note to Carol was Sue, who was working hard on her test" (p. 26).

Next, Strong (1986) leads an oral discussion during which the students try sentence combining with several other examples, such as those found in Figure 10–1. Strong then pairs students as they search for various sentence-combining solutions to additional short sentences from Figure 10–1. After five minutes, the students transcribe two or three transformations on the board. Strong expands this activity by having students combine the sentence transformations into extended text, such as "Carol was hard at work on her test when Sue slipped a note to her. Not wanting her teacher to see, she unfolded it carefully" or "Carol was working hard on her test when Sue slipped her a note, which she carefully unfolded because she didn't want her teacher to see" (p. 27).

For Your Development

1. Develop a series of kernel sentences from the following paragraph selected from Molly Cone's science information text *Come Back, Salmon* (1992):

   When the obstacle is a dam, a salmon can often jump from one pool to another up a series of "steps," called a "fish ladder," built at the side of the dam. To get over a waterfall,

Continued

salmon have been known to leap as high as eleven feet. If the first leap fails, the homebound salmon will try again. And again. And again. Some salmon lose their lives trying. (p. 34)

2. Model the introduction to a sentence-combining activity for your class.
3. Identify materials from literature and social studies. What would you emphasize with each sentence-combining activity? Develop kernel sentences to accompany the materials. Share your activity with a group.

Lexical Access.   Lexical access refers to the process of getting information about a word, such as its meaning and its pronunciation, from one's mental dictionary. According to Samuels and Naslund (1994), lexical access refers to three kinds of processes associated with accessing information:

1. The meaning of a word in the dictionary sense.
2. Categorical concepts, such as lexical category (Is this an English word or a pseudo-word?), semantic category (Is this word an example of an animal, vegetable, or mineral?), and grammatical category (Is this word a direct or indirect object?).
3. Phonemic and morphemic representation (pronunciation of the word on the basis of its printed form).

Value Judgment

1.1 Carol was working hard on her test.

1.2 Sue slipped her a note.

2.1 Carol unfolded the paper carefully.

2.2 She didn't want her teacher to see.

3.1 The note asked for help on a question.

3.2 The question was important.

4.1 Carol looked down at her paper.

4.2 She thought about the class's honor system.

5.1 Everyone had made a pledge.

5.2 The pledge was not to cheat.

6.1 Carol didn't want to go back on her word.

6.2 Sue was her best friend.

7.1 Time was running out.

7.2 She had to make up her mind.

8.1 Her mouth felt dry.

8.2 Her mouth felt tight.

Assignment. Finish the story. Explain the reasons behind Carol's judgment.

FIGURE 10–1   Sentence-Combining Exercises

Source: From William Strong, *Creative Approaches to Sentence Combining.* Urbana, Ill.: National Council of Teachers of English, 1986. Reprinted by permission.

Slow access to such word meanings and usages leads to problems in comprehension. Consequently, students need both accuracy in the lexical access of word meanings and fast and easy access to their mental dictionaries. It appears that both cognitive development and experience influence the efficiency with which children access and recode information. After reviewing research on lexical access, Samuels and Naslund (1994) conclude:

> There are two avenues individuals can take to access information rapidly and with little attention and effort. Some children have a general ability to access information in their mental dictionary with speed and accuracy, and they have arrived at this position because they have read more than other children. Another group of children have domain-specific knowledge, and this gives them the ability to access lexical information rapidly in the specific area in which they are knowledgeable; however, they do not have the ability to access lexical information rapidly across the board, as those with general rapid access do. (p. 294)

In their instructional implications for improving lexical access, Samuels and Naslund recommend that students increase their speed and automaticity by increasing the amount of time spent reading for general knowledge and for the specialized expertise that some students acquire through reading. Consequently, the educational environment should encourage them to gain a wealth of knowledge through books. Language arts teachers may increase this general knowledge as they read to children, encourage children to increase their breadth of reading, and interact with children in ways that help them understand what they read.

Cohesive Devices.   Words such as *he, she, it, we* (personal pronouns); *this, these, those* (demonstrative pronouns); *who, whom, whose* (relative pronouns); *here, there* (location noun substitutions); and *now, then, former,* and *later* (temporal noun substitutions) are used frequently in writing. Such terms reduce redundancy, clarify relationships, and link ideas within the text. These cohesive devices tie together information within sentences, paragraphs, and longer passages. When authors provide clear, logical cohesive devices (for example, referents such as pronouns, conjunctions that link two ideas, substitutions that replace one word with another word to add to the meaning of the first word, and repetitions that restate information), comprehension of a text increases. In contrast, when the connectors are vague or inferred, comprehension decreases for many students. Cox, Shanahan, and Sulzby (1990) found that cohesive harmony characterizes well-written and coherent text. Moe and Irwin (1986) state that teachers must not only be aware of these cohesive devices within texts, but also help students understand and use cohesive devices.

Baumann and Stevenson (1986) recommend the following four-step procedure for teaching cohesive devices. The approach moves from full teacher responsibility to shared student/teacher responsibility to full student responsibility.

1. Introduce the lesson by telling the students what skill related to cohesive devices you will teach, by providing an example of the cohesive device, and by explaining why the acquisition of that skill is important.
2. Provide direct instruction, in which you model, show, demonstrate, and lead the instruction in the skill.
3. Provide students with guided application of the skill, but use materials not used during previous instruction.
4. Provide independent practice, in which the students apply the skill in their comprehension of text. Trade books and other primary sources as well as content-area texts are effective materials for this activity and increase the transfer of the skill to additional contexts. Trade books also allow students to practice their skills within passage-length texts rather than isolated sentences that do not consider prior information.

Lesson Plan

For Your Plan Book

A Lesson Plan on Cohesive Devices

Objectives

To teach students to comprehend personal pronouns and to apply this knowledge when reading or listening to picture storybooks.

Introduction

Teacher:　When people write they often use words that stand for other words. These words allow writers to repeat an idea without repeating the same words. Look at the following sentences written on the board and read the sentences with me:

Barbara likes to write stories. She writes funny stories about animals.

In the first sentence, find the word *Barbara.* In the second sentence, find the word *she.* This is an example of a sentence in which one word replaces another word. *She* means the same thing as *Barbara.* Words like *she* are called pronouns. Check to see if we are right in our identification of the meaning of the word by reading both sentences, but replacing *she* with *Barbara* in the second sentence. Now read these sentences with me:

Barbara likes to write stories. Barbara writes funny stories about animals.

Notice that the two sentences still mean the same thing. If we replace *she* with another girl's name, the second sentence has a different meaning. These sentences are examples of what we will learn about today. We will learn that words such as *she, he, we, her, you, they, their,* and *it* stand for other words. This is important because it helps you understand what writers are trying to tell you. It is also important because you can use this skill in your own writing.

Teacher-Directed Instruction

(Write sentences on the board that include the pronouns to be emphasized. Choose the sentences according to the reading and interest levels of your students.)

Teacher:　Look at the sentences written on the board:

1. Cinderella lived with *her* stepmother and *her* stepsisters. *She* sat in the ashes in the kitchen, and that is how *she* got *her* name.
2. The prince wanted to marry one of the girls in the kingdom. *He* gave a ball to meet the girls.
3. The stepsisters and the stepmother dressed in *their* best clothes. *They* went to the ball.
4. Cinderella was unhappy because *she* wanted to go to the ball. *She* was granted a wish by *her* fairy godmother.
5. A magical carriage took *her* to the ball. *It* turned back into a pumpkin at midnight.

Read the sentences in number 1 with me. Look for the words used in place of Cinderella. Notice that the words are in italics. Now, listen as I tell you how I figured out the meanings of the words. First, I noticed that *her* was used twice in the first sentence. I thought about whose stepmother and whose stepsisters the sentence meant. I replaced both of the *hers* with *Cinderella* and the sentence made sense. Then I noticed that *she* was used twice in the next sentence. I thought about the first sentence and I asked myself if *she* and *her* meant Cinderella, the stepmother, or the stepsisters. I knew that *she* could not mean the stepsisters because the word would have to be *they.* I used the meaning of the first sentence to help me identify that *she* meant Cinderella. I knew from the story about Cinderella that Cinderella was given her name because she sat in the cinders and ashes in the kitchen fireplace. Now, let's read the two sentences together and replace *she* and *her* with *Cinderella*. Do the sentences have the correct meaning? Also, notice how much better the sentences sound when *she* and *her* replace *Cinderella*. These sentences also show that we often need to read the sentences before or after a pronoun to understand what the author means.

Now look at the sentences in number 2. Read the sentences with me. I want you to think through the meaning of the sentences. What word is substituted? (He) Good. Who gave the ball? (The prince) Good. How do you know that *he* refers to the prince? (Students provide evidence and reasoning.)

(Continue with a teacher-led discussion for the sentences in numbers 3 through 5. Add additional sentences if the students do not master this portion of the lesson.)

Teacher: We are now going to read some examples of these pronouns used by authors of the books in our school library. I have written several paragraphs on transparencies. Look at these paragraphs from *Millions of Cats* (Gág, 1928, 1956):

> "But *we* can never feed them all," said the very old woman, "*They* will eat us out of house and home."
>
> "I never thought of that," said the very old man, "What shall *we* do?"
>
> The very old woman thought for a while and then *she* said, "I know! *We* will let the cats decide which one *we* shall keep."
>
> "Oh yes," said the very old man, and *he* called to the cats, "Which one of *you* is the prettiest?"
>
> "*I* am!"
>
> "No, *I* am!" (p. 20, unnumbered)

In the Cinderella example, we discovered that we sometimes have to read sentences before a pronoun or sentences after a pronoun to know what the pronoun means. In this example from *Millions of Cats* we will need to read into the paragraph before we know what the first pronoun means. Read the first sentence with me. What is the first word that is in italics? (We) Good. Can anyone tell me what *we* refers to? In this example, we need to read beyond the word. Now, let's read the whole selection together. Then, we'll go back and try to identify what each underlined word means. Who can tell me what *we* means and how you know what *we* means? (Student response and reasoning.) Now who can write the words that mean *we* on the right place on the transparency? (Student writes *woman* and *man* above *we* on the transparency or on the board if board work is preferred to a transparency.) Good. Now who can read the sentence by replacing *we* with the words that mean the same as we? (Student response.) Good.

(Continue with the remainder of the story, stopping at each underlined word to discuss the meaning and to write the word above the pronoun. Reread the total selection to verify the meaning of the underlined words. Discuss how the use of pronouns improves the beauty of the text.)

Teacher-Guided Application

Teacher: We are going to look at different paragraphs taken from library books. The words that you need to identify are in italics. I want you to read the paragraphs, think about the meanings for the pronouns, and write the correct meaning over each underlined word.

Continued

We'll do the first one together to make sure that we all understand what to do. Then, I want you to do the rest of the sentences by yourself. Be sure to read the whole selection to make sure that your choice makes sense and is accurate. When you are finished, we'll read the paragraphs together and discuss your answers.

The Mother's Day Mice (Eve Bunting, 1986)

Biggest Little Mouse wakened first. It was early in the morning and still almost dark. *He* tugged gently on the whiskers of Middle Mouse, who slept next to *him*. "It's Mother's Day," *he* whispered. "Time to get up and go for our presents."

Middle Mouse tugged gently on the whiskers of Little Mouse, who slept between *him* and the wall. "Mother's Day," *he* whispered.

They crept out of bed and tiptoed past Mother's room. (p. 1)

The Man Who Could Call Down Owls (Eve Bunting, 1984)

By day the man worked in *his* owl barn. There were wings to be mended and legs to be splinted.

"How do *you* find the owls that need your help?" the boy asked.

The man smiled. "*They* find me." *He* held a screech owl. "When an owl is sick and frightened *you* must hold *it* firmly. Then *it* can't hurt *itself* or *you*. Always remember that." (p. 7)

(After the students complete this activity independently, conduct a guided discussion of this phase of the lesson. Encourage discussion that looks at the reasons for the replacements as well as at the correct answers.)

Independent Practice

Teacher: We have completed several paragraphs in which authors use pronouns to replace other words in the stories. I have a selection of books in which I want you to find examples of pronouns. When you find an example of a pronoun, write the sentence on your paper. Leave space to write the meaning of the word above the pronoun. We'll share these examples in class tomorrow. Be ready to read your selection to the class and to tell the class what each pronoun means.

You may use the following books for this activity:

Eve Bunting's *I am the Mummy Heb-Nefert* (1997)

Lois Ehlert's *Moon Rope: A Peruvian Folktale* (1992)

Florence Parry Heide and Judith Heide Gilliland's *The Day of Ahmed's Secret* (1990)

Barbara Kerley's *The Dinosaurs of Waterhouse Hawkins* (2001)

Julius Lester's *John Henry* (1994)

Michael Morpurgo's *Wombat Goes Walkabout* (2000)

Cynthia Rylant's *Henry and Mudge and the Happy Cat* (1990)

Allen Say's *Grandfather's Journey* (1993)

Sarah Stewart's *The Gardener* (1996)

Rosemary Wells's *Yoko* (1998)

Andrea Zimmerman and David Clemesha's *My Dog Toby* (2000)

For Your Development

Develop a cohesive comprehension lesson plan appropriate for older students. To identify an area for instruction, analyze several books written for middle- and upper-elementary students. What cohesive devices do the authors use? For example, Patricia Lauber's 1987 Newbery Honor book *Volcano: The Eruption and Healing of Mount St. Helens* uses the referent "it" nine times in the first two paragraphs. "It," however, may refer to volcano, Mount St. Helens, earthquake, rock, molten rock, or magma. The meanings of the referents are clear as long as you read the text carefully.

Include in your lesson plan the following four titles: introduction, direct instruction, teacher-guided application, and independent practice. Whenever appropriate, include modeling in the lesson plan.

Grammar 3 (Usage)

Language usage concerns the various language standards considered appropriate for different occasions, audiences, and purposes. Usage instruction should help children make proper decisions both in speaking and in writing.

Discussions related to usage generate considerable controversy. According to De-Haven (1983), "the controversy stems from a lack of agreement in (1) defining an acceptable level of usage and (2) setting instructional goals" (p. 69). People make usage choices in response to forces external to the language. Everyone's language varies, depending on the formality of the occasion. For example, you would use words differently when conversing casually or when writing to a friend than you would when presenting a formal speech or when writing a letter of inquiry to a prospective employer. Stewig and Nordberg (1995) maintain that "The dilemma faced by the elementary teacher is how to balance the need for students to be able to express their ideas freely and vigorously with the need to learn standard English usage. This question has been hotly debated, and its resolution is not easy" (p. 464).

The number of usage levels differs according to which grammarian is speaking. Lodge and Trett (1968) postulate three levels of usage: (1) nonstandard English, (2) general English, and (3) formal English. Language standards change from one group to another and with time. What was considered almost illiterate a number of years ago may be virtually ignored today; for example, when to use *may* and *can,* or *shall* and *will.* According to Savage (1977), "In the final analysis, the 'correctness' or appropriateness of usage must be judged in the social context in which the language is used" (p. 369). Elementary schools usually design usage instruction to help children move from one usage situation to another because different levels are appropriate for different audiences and purposes. Instead of teaching that some form is incorrect, modern usage instruction stresses appropriateness for certain purposes and audiences. Modern usage instruction, then, is flexible, and tries to increase the range of levels of usage available to children.

Tiedt and Tiedt (1975) recommend that "we teach educated forms of standard English without undue stress on picayune points that really achieve little" (p. 30). What are these educated forms of English? According to Kean and Personke (1976), "among the many attempts to sort out the more important usage 'violations' for teachers who guide children's language development, perhaps the most noteworthy to date is a list of twenty-five goals for elementary language instruction prepared by English educator Robert Pooley" (p. 290). Pooley compiled his list in 1960 and warned at the time that some of the goals would eventually require modification. Read and decide which are still valuable for classroom usage:

1. The elimination of all baby talk and "cute" expressions.
2. The correct uses in speech and writing of *I, me, he, him, she, her, they, them.* (Exception: It's me.)
3. The correct uses of *is, are, was, were,* with respect to number and tense.
4. Correct past tense of common irregular verbs such as *saw, took, brought, bought, stuck.*
5. Correct use of past participles of the same verbs and similar verbs after auxiliaries.
6. Elimination of the double negative: "We don't have no apples," etc.
7. Elimination of analogical forms: *ain't, hisn, hern, ourn, theirselves,* etc.
8. Correct use of possessive pronouns: *my, mine, his, hers, theirs, ours.*
9. Mastery of the distinction between *its,* possessive pronoun, and *it's, it is.*
10. Placement of *have* or its phonetic reduction to *ve* between *I* and a past participle.
11. Elimination of *them* as a demonstrative pronoun.
12. Elimination of *this here* and *that there.*
13. Mastery of use of *a* and *an* as articles.
14. Correct use of personal pronouns in compound constructions: as subject (*Mark and I*), as object (*Mary and me*), and as object of preposition (*to Mary and me*).
15. The use of *we* before an appositional noun when subject; *us* when object.
16. Correct number agreement with the phrases *there is, there are, there was, there were.*
17. Elimination of *he don't, she don't, it don't.*
18. Elimination of *learn* for *teach, leave* for *let.*
19. Elimination of pleonastic (redundant) subjects: *my brother he, my mother she, that fellow he.*
20. Proper agreement in number with antecedent pronouns *one, anyone, everyone, each, no one.* With *everybody* and *none* some tolerance of number seems acceptable now.
21. The use of *who* and *whom* as references to persons. (But note, "Who did he give it to?" is tolerated in all but very formal situations. In the latter, "To whom did he give it?" is preferable.
22. Accurate use of *said* in reporting the words of a speaker in the past.
23. Correction of *lay down* to *lie down.*
24. The distinction between *good* as an adjective and *well* as an adverb: "He spoke well."
25. Elimination of *can't hardly, all the farther* (for "as far as"), and *Where is he (she, it) at?*"[1]

In addition, Pooley listed eight items that are no longer considered "incorrect," and that may even be in quite general use:

1. Any distinction between *shall* and *will.*
2. Any reference to the split infinitive.
3. Elimination of *like* as a conjunction.
4. Objection to the phrase "different than."
5. Objection to "He is one of those boys who is. . . ."
6. Objection to "the reason . . . is because. . . ."

---

[1]From Robert Pooley, "Dare Schools Set a Standard in English Usage?" *English Journal* 49 (March 1960): 176. Copyright © 1960 by the National Council of Teachers of English. Reprinted by permission of the publisher.

7. Objection to *myself* as a polite substitute for *me,* as in "I understand you will meet Mrs. Jones and myself at the station."
8. Insistence upon the possessive case standing before a gerund.[2]

Assessment

To evaluate usage, look at a child's ability to use appropriate forms of grammar according to occasion, audience, and purpose. Listen to the child's speech in several different situations and analyze the writing that the child produces for various purposes. An informal checklist (see, for example, Figure 10–2) may be the most valuable evaluation guide. Base your checklist on the understanding and demonstrated use of several levels of usage and on Pooley's (1960) list of appropriate usage for classrooms.

Instruction

Instruction in usage usually emphasizes that there are several appropriate levels of usage for oral or written communications depending on the purposes and the audiences. For example, what is appropriate on the playground may not be appropriate when addressing the principal or mayor, or when writing a formal letter requesting a job interview. Activities such as role-playing, inductive teaching of usage, and analyzing levels of usage exemplified by characters in books or on television help students improve their understanding of usage.

Role-Playing.   Role-playing activities can help children improve their understanding of various levels of usage. Role-playing also allows children opportunities to think about and discuss the roles of speaker or writer, audience, and subject matter in regard to appropriate levels of usage. You and the students can suggest a number of situations requiring different levels of usage. A middle- or upper-elementary class might try the following roles:

1. Jerry's friend Jimmy has joined a neighborhood softball team. Jimmy has invited Jerry to go with him to meet the team, because the team needs a pitcher. Jerry wants them to accept him as the newest member of the team. Pretend Jerry and Jimmy are talking on their way to a vacant lot or park. Make up the conversation that might occur between Jimmy, Jerry, and the rest of the team.
2. You have just found out that your school will have a science fair. The winner of the science fair will receive a microscope that you have wanted for a long time. In addition, the winner will represent the school in the regional science fair. You have an idea for a project and want to talk about it with the science teacher. You want to convince him that you have thought about your ideas, and you want him to give you some additional out-of-school help.

After role-playing, have the students discuss the appropriateness of the communication according to subject matter and audience. What are the consequences of an inappropriate level of usage?

---

[2]Ibid., p. 176.

	Name _____			
	Grade _____			
		Yes	Sometimes	No
1.	Understands that there is more than one level of appropriate usage	_____	_____	_____
2.	Is able to change level of spoken usage according to occasion, audience, and purpose	_____	_____	_____
3.	Is able to change level of written usage according to occasion, audience, and purpose	_____	_____	_____
4.	Has eliminated baby talk	_____	_____	_____
5.	Uses correct form of *I, me, he, him, she, they, them*	_____	_____	_____
6.	Uses correct form of *is, are, was, were*	_____	_____	_____
7.	Uses correct past tense of irregular verbs	_____	_____	_____
8.	Uses correct past participle	_____	_____	_____
9.	Does not use double negative	_____	_____	_____
10.	Does not use *ain't, hisn, hern,* etc.	_____	_____	_____
11.	Uses correct possessive pronouns	_____	_____	_____
12.	Uses *it's* and *its* correctly	_____	_____	_____
13.	Does not use *them* as a demonstrative pronoun	_____	_____	_____
14.	Does not use *this here* and *that there*	_____	_____	_____
15.	Uses *a* and *an* correctly	_____	_____	_____
16.	Uses correct personal pronouns in compound constructions	_____	_____	_____
17.	Uses *we* (subject) and *us* (object) correctly	_____	_____	_____
18.	Does not use *he don't, she don't, it don't*	_____	_____	_____
19.	Uses correct number agreement in *there is, there are, there was, there were*	_____	_____	_____
20.	Uses *learn* and *teach* and *leave* and *let* correctly	_____	_____	_____
21.	Does not use *my brother he,* etc.	_____	_____	_____
22.	Uses proper agreement with antecedent pronouns	_____	_____	_____
23.	Uses *said* in past tense	_____	_____	_____
24.	Uses *good* as adjective and *well* as adverb	_____	_____	_____
25.	Most critical usage problems are:			

_____

_____

_____

FIGURE 10–2   Informal Checklist for Usage

Inductive Teaching.   Inductive approaches that help children analyze their problems are more helpful than isolated drills, in which the children merely underline choices on a worksheet. As an example, look at a lesson built around one of the appropriate usages recommended by Pooley (1960)—the correct use of *is, are, was,* and *were* in number agreement (singular and plural) and tense (present tense, past tense).

For Your Plan Book

Lesson Plan

An Inductive Approach to *Was* and *Were*—Singular and Plural Forms in Past Tense

First, write the following sentences on the chalkboard:

1. Carol *was* at the movie last night.
2. Jane and Julie *were* also at the movie last night.
3. They *were* at the movie together.
4. Jim *was* at home last night.
5. I *was* also at home.
6. We *were* at home together.
7. You *were* at the park.

Next, read the sentences (use numbers 1–6 first) to the students, asking them to listen carefully. Then ask the students to read the sentences to you. Now, tell the students to look carefully at the italic words in sentences 1–6. Then ask, "When did the activity in each sentence take place?" The students should conclude that it was last night, which is in the past, and not something that is happening right now, in the present. Next ask "How many people were in each of the sentences?" The students should conclude that sentences 1, 4, and 5 concern one person, and that sentences 2, 3, and 6 concern more than one person. Write just this portion of each sentence on the board, in two columns:

One Person	**More Than One Person**
Carol *was*	Jane and Julie *were*
Jim *was*	They *were*
I *was*	We *were*

Now, ask the students if they can think of a guiding suggestion to help them remember when to use *was* and when to use *were*. They will usually produce a generalization like this:

> When we are talking about something that happened in the past, we use *was* if we are talking about one person and we use *were* if we are talking about more than one person.

Now, ask the students to look at sentence 7. "Does this sentence follow our guide? What is wrong?" The students should conclude that the word *you* refers to only one person, but uses *were* in the past tense as if the word *you* referred to more than one person. Ask the students where to place the sentence on the list. They will usually suggest that, because it is an exception, placing it in a third column will help them remember. Now, ask if there is anything the students need to add to their guiding rule. The fact that *were* follows the word *you* can be added as an exception. Finally, ask the students to create additional sentences that conform to the same patterns. Remember that they will need frequent opportunities to practice with oral and written activities rather than with worksheet drills.

Continued

Analyzing Usage in Literature.   What levels of usage are exemplified by characters in literature or on television? Are the levels formal or informal? Do characters change their level of usage depending on their purposes and audiences? Use tape-recorded examples from television to show various levels of usage. Older students may make discoveries about changing levels of usage by comparing books written during different time periods. For example, students might compare the language usage in the contemporary writings of such authors as Betsy Byars, Barbara Corcoran, and Walter Dean Myers with language usage in the classic writings of Frances Hodgson Burnett, Kenneth Grahame, and Lucy M. Montgomery.

For Your Development

Select one of Pooley's (1960) recommendations for classroom usage. Develop an inductive lesson (on something other than *was* and *were*) that will help children understand the usage level. Also, provide suggestions for ways of reinforcing the lesson.

The Mechanics of Writing

The mechanics of writing includes punctuation and capitalization. Remember, as with other aspects of composition, children learn punctuation and capitalization most effectively in conjunction with meaningful writing activities.

Hodges (1991) emphasizes the need for writers to be familiar with graphic features, such as punctuation, segmentation, and capitalization: "Punctuation sets apart syntactic units, and provides intonational cues and semantic information. Segmentation (the spaces between words in print) identifies word boundaries. In conjunction with periods, capital letters have both semantic and syntactic uses in indicating proper names and sentence boundaries" (p. 779).

Punctuation

Punctuation is important because it clarifies meaning. During oral interchanges, listeners hear signals—pauses, speech stops, rising and falling voice tones—that help them comprehend meaning. Writers replace these vocal signals with punctuation. The early activities in which children dictate short stories or sentences to place under pictures provide readiness for and instruction in punctuation.

Studies show that punctuation—particularly with commas and periods—is frequently a problem for elementary-age children (Hazlett, 1972; Porter, 1974). The punctuation usually taught in the elementary grades is listed in Table 10–1.

For Your Development

Look at a scope-and-sequence chart in a language arts textbook. Make a punctuation chart to use with a specific elementary-school level. Design your chart to show the signal given by the punctuation mark and its placement. For example, you might finish the following chart:

Name	Example	Signal	Where Used
Period		Come to a full stop	At the end of a sentence that tells something

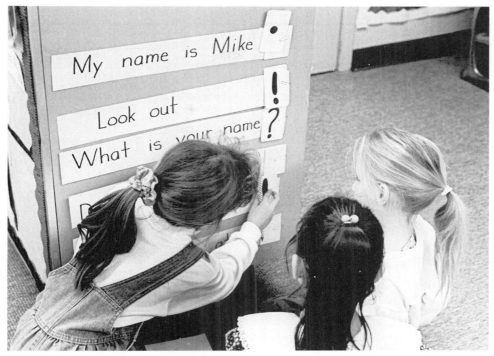

Learning about punctuation can be fun.

Capitalization

Capitalization is another signal that clarifies meaning. Writers signal the beginning of a sentence with a capital letter and the end of a sentence with a period, question mark, or exclamation mark. Writers also signal important titles and names by capitalization. If a writer capitalizes Northeast, he or she is referring to a specific section of the country; if the writer does not capitalize northeast, the reference is to a direction.

Most children seem to have fewer problems applying capitalization rules than applying punctuation rules. The National Assessment of Educational Progress concluded: "Capitalization errors tended to appear less frequently in the 9-year-old papers than most of the other kinds of errors" (Hazlett, 1972, p. 12). The National Assessment found that most high-quality papers were free of capitalization errors; this was also true of middle-quality papers. The low-quality papers were, however, inconsistent; the first word in a sentence was often left uncapitalized, and many common nouns, such as *deer* and *tree,* were capitalized. The judges concluded that children who wrote the low-quality papers had some idea of when to use capitals and when not to, but their ideas were incomplete. It thus appears that most children learn about and apply appropriate capitalization in their writing, while a few will require more concentrated assistance.

Introduce children to capitalization in their early, dictated stories. A teacher who writes a sentence on the board or chart can point out the capital letter at the beginning of each sentence. When writing names of people, cities, states, or holidays, teachers can again indicate the importance of the capital letter. Capitalization rules usually taught in the elementary grades are listed in Table 10–2.

Table 10–1   Punctuation taught in elementary grades

Punctuation Rule	Example
1. A period is used at the end of a sentence.	1. We went to the zoo.
2. A period is used after numbers on a list.	2. 1. Show and Tell 2. Reading
3. A period is used after abbreviations.	3. Sun. Mon. Tues. Mr. Mrs.
4. A question mark is used after a sentence that asks a question.	4. What was the name of Billy's dog?
5. A comma is placed between the day of the month and the year.	5. Today is October 1, 2003.
6. A comma is used between the names of a city and a state.	6. We live in Ithaca, New York.
7. A comma is used after the salutation in a letter.	7. Dear Sandy,
8. A comma is used after the closing of a letter.	8. Your friend, Jimmy
9. Commas divide items in a list.	9. Susan brought an acorn, a colored maple leaf, and an ear of Indian corn.
10. A comma is used before a coordinating conjunction (upper elementary).	10. He wanted to eat the whole pie, but he knew he would be sick.
11. A comma is used to signal the subject of the sentence (upper elementary).	11. Even though the day was hot, we all decided to go on a picnic.
12. A comma is used when a slight interruption offers additional information (upper elementary).	12. Jim Black, our basketball coach, is a very nice man.
13. A comma is used between two equal adjectives that modify the noun (upper elementary).	13. That swimmer is a strong, healthy athlete.
14. An exclamation mark follows a statement of excitement.	14. Help! Help! Jimmy is chasing me with a snake!
15. An apostrophe shows that letters have been omitted in a contraction.	15. I will = I'll
16. An apostrophe is used to show possession.	16. This is Judy's basketball.

Instruction

Both punctuation and capitalization clarify written communication. Children need to understand why mechanical skills are necessary, but they must also be aware that writing is primarily concerned with the development of content and ideas. In this context, punctuation and capitalization are very important during the editing process.

How can you maintain balance without overemphasizing one aspect of writing to the detriment of the other? Kean and Personke (1976) offer three general guidelines for instruction in mechanics:

Table 10–2   Capitalization taught in elementary grades

Capitalization Rule	Example
1. Capitalize the first word in a sentence.	1. The first grade is planning a puppet show.
2. Capitalize the first and last names of people.	2. Sandy Smith
3. Capitalize the pronoun *I*.	3. I do not think I will go.
4. Capitalize the name of a street.	4. Our school is on Southwest Parkway.
5. Capitalize the name of the city and state.	5. We live in San Francisco, California.
6. Capitalize the names of months, days, holidays.	6. Today is Monday, June 1. Christmas Hanukkah
7. Capitalize the first word and other important words in titles.	7. We are reading A Snowy Day.
8. Capitalize a title such as Mr., Mrs., Miss, or Ms.	8. Our teacher is Mrs. Chandler.
9. Capitalize the greeting in a letter.	9. Dear Martin,
10. Capitalize the first word in the closing of a letter.	10. Your friend,
11. Capitalize the titles of persons (upper elementary).	11. Doctor Erickson General Washington
12. Capitalize all cities, states, countries, continents, and oceans (upper elementary).	12. United States North America Pacific Ocean
13. Capitalize proper adjectives (upper elementary).	13. French
14. Capitalize the names of organizations (upper elementary).	14. Girl Scouts, Boy Scouts
15. Capitalize the names of sections of the country but not directions (upper elementary).	15. The Northeast has many large cities. Lake Superior is northeast of Minneapolis.
16. Capitalize words referring to the Bible and the Deity (upper elementary).	16. The Bible God

1. Several of the mechanics of written language are learned as children write, read, and observe, making formal classroom presentations unnecessary in many cases. Students who did not naturally learn them may require individual help.
2. Individual variation in readiness makes it likely that learning will be most efficient when instruction is conducted among small groups of children who are at similar stages of readiness. (This means small-group instruction of children who demonstrate similar needs, rather than whole-class instruction.)
3. Instruction in mechanics needs to begin and culminate in a real writing situation; if isolated practice is necessary, it should be in the intermediate learning stage.[3]

[3]From John M. Kean and Carl Personke, *The Language Arts: Teaching and Learning in the Elementary School* (New York: St. Martin's Press, 1976). Reprinted by permission.

Table 10–3   Steps in instruction for "a comma separates words in series"

Guideline	Example
1. Call attention to the rule in reading or dictated stories.	1. Find sentences that contain words in series in reading. Point them out in language experience. Example: Oranges, grapefruit, and lemons grow in Florida.
2. Observe a mechanical need in an actual writing situation.	2. Students are writing series of words without using the appropriate punctuation.
3. Develop individual or small-group instruction designed to eliminate the problem.	3. Have the students read four or five sentences with words in series. Ask the students to inductively state the rule. Write new sentences on the chalkboard without commas. Have the students put in the commas, using colored chalk. Reinforce the principle with games.
4. Assign a real writing task that requires application of the skill.	4. "Write a sentence telling us what you had for breakfast." "Write a sentence listing the members of your family."
5. Observe to see if the mechanical problem has been eliminated.	5. Observe future writing. Are the students using the skill? If not, provide further direct teaching.

If you follow these guidelines, you will call the children's attention to various punctuation and capitalization items as they encounter them in reading or in dictating charts and stories. This provides readiness for a skill they will need in writing and may enable some children to apply the skill accurately in their own writing. For example, many children are able to begin sentences with capital letters and end them with periods after a teacher has pointed out these mechanics during frequent language experience activities. Some children, however, require additional direct teaching of these skills before they can apply them consistently. When direct teaching is necessary, it should take place in groups, with children who show the same readiness or need for a new or reviewed skill. Table 10–3 shows one method for teaching the separation of words in series with a comma.

Activities

Some children need visual assistance with punctuation and capitalization. Charts that show various writing conventions are helpful. For example, use the colors of traffic signals to mark sentences written on charts. Mark the capital letters at the beginning of sentences, which also signal go, in green; commas, signaling a short pause, in yellow; and periods at the end of sentences, signaling stop, in red.

Let children work with a paragraph written without punctuation, without capitalization, or without both punctuation and capitalization (depending on ability level). As you read the paragraph, ask the children to mark the punctuation according to the verbal signals of your voice.

Upper-elementary children can take dictation from kindergarten and first-grade children. To produce a short, written story that expresses what the younger child means, the older child will have to supply appropriate punctuation and capitalization signals. The older child should then read the selection back to make sure the meaning is what the younger child intended.

Proofreading symbols are often effective with upper elementary students. Ask someone connected with a newspaper to talk to the children and show them proofreading symbols. Children are usually impressed to learn that adult writers also need to proofread and correct their writing before it is published in a paper. Children can also create their own classroom proofreading symbols, or use the standard symbols, which can be found in a dictionary.

Ideas for Teachers from Teachers: Elementary Language Arts, published by the National Council of Teachers of English (1983), describes several activities developed by classroom teachers. For example, you can make punctuation pins from clip-on clothespins. (Paint a punctuation mark on each clothespin.) Print sentences without punctuation on tagboard strips. Ask the children to clamp the correct clothespin markers, in the correct locations, onto the sentences. Another effective activity is based on dialogue created to accompany pictures students bring to class. Each student brings a picture of a character, teams with another student, creates dialogue between the pictured characters, and transcribes the resulting dialogue.

For Your Development

1. Identify a mechanics-of-writing need, such as use of quotation marks or capitalization of proper nouns. Design a small-group instructional activity for appropriate use of that skill.
2. Design a mechanics-of-writing game that reinforces understanding of a punctuation or capitalization rule.
3. Develop a proofreading lesson for use with older elementary children. You may wish to refer to the "Spelling and Proofreading" section in the spelling chapter. Use a similar approach for introducing the proofreading of punctuation or capitalization.

Mainstreaming

Grammar, usage, and mechanics are not ends in themselves. As with handwriting, the major purpose is effective communication. All students need many opportunities to use language in meaningful context. This is especially true for mainstreamed children who have difficulty using syntactic information and generalizing limited grammatical knowledge in a variety of settings. If children demonstrate restricted language ability and vocabulary development, give them many meaningful learning opportunities designed to broaden their language experiences. Table 10–4 presents characteristics of children with learning disabilities that might interfere with learning grammar and suggests techniques for language arts instruction. Table 10–5 presents the same information for children with mental disabilities.

Table 10–4   Mainstreaming and grammar for children with learning disabilities

Characteristics of Children with Learning Disabilities	Teaching Techniques for Language Arts Instruction
1. Deficit in use of grammatical form class and syntactic information (Fay, Trupin, & Townes, 1981; Henderson & Shores, 1982; Johnson, 1993).	1. Have students read aloud materials in which words ending in *ed* and *ing* are underlined. Have the pupils chart errors and identify correct forms necessary to complete sentences (Henderson & Shores, 1982). Provide systematic training in the arrangement of inflectional forms of verbs (Cartelli, 1980). Prepare activities developed around generative-transformational grammar and context (Knott, 1979). Generate transformations of kernel sentences and encourage children to experiment with sentence-pattern variations. Encourage many meaningful oral language activities, such as role-playing, show and tell, puppetry, choral speaking, interviewing, and storytelling (Lerner, 1976). Act out words (Ysseldyke & Algozzine, 1995).
2. Disability in comprehending information signaled by grammatical morphemes (Johnson, 1993; McClure, Kalk, & Keenan, 1980).	2. Emphasize comprehension available through function words, word endings, and word stem changes. Use pictures to help build morphological generalizations (Lerner, 1976; McNaughton, Hughes, & Clark, 1994).
3. Slower speed of lexical access may interfere with comprehension of word meanings and usage (Samuels & Naslund, 1994).	3. Motivate students to read wide and varied sources of materials (Samuels & Naslund, 1994).

Table 10–5   Mainstreaming and grammar for children with mental disabilities

Characteristics of Children with Mental Disabilities	Teaching Techniques for Language Arts Instruction
1. Below-average language ability, restricted vocabulary (Gearheart, Weishahn, & Gearheart, 1992).	1. Provide many opportunities to broaden language experience. Provide structured, concretely oriented experiences consistent with the students' interests and level of language development (Gearheart et al., 1992). Help the children develop sentence sense through easy reading materials, listening activities, and oral readings of their writing (Otto & Smith, 1980). Provide opportunities to improve language clarity by rearranging, deleting, substituting, and adding grammatical elements (Otto & Smith, 1980).
2. Difficulty generalizing and conceptualizing in a variety of settings (Gearheart et al., 1992).	2. Provide many opportunities for functional writing. Diagram letter formats and establish a classroom post office to encourage use of writing and punctuation skills (Cohen & Plaskon, 1980).

SUMMARY

This chapter discusses a three-part definition of grammar: grammar 1, a set of formal patterns; grammar 2, the linguistic science concerned with description, analysis, and formalization of formal language patterns; and grammar 3, the use of language according to language standards for different occasions, audiences, and purposes.

Grammar 2 includes the various systems developed to describe and analyze sentence patterns and to classify words, and it is the grammar taught in most school systems. Traditional grammar is prescriptive; it provides a series of rules for constructing sentences and for classifying parts of speech. In contrast, structural grammar is descriptive; it describes words according to form classes, and describes sentence patterns or positions of words in sentences. Transformational grammar is built on the work of the structuralists but extends grammar into the meaning of language. Whereas structural grammar is concerned primarily with syntax, transformational grammar is concerned primarily with semantics and the generating of sentences. The term *transformational* refers to the division of sentences into kernel sentences and the transforms, or variations, that can be developed from these basic sentences.

Grammar instruction should expand a child's understanding of language; consequently, the best aspects of the newer grammars are often included in instructional programs. Activities using linguistic blocks, cloze sentences, sentence transformations, sentence scrambling, changing word order, sentence expansion, sentence combining, open-response exercises, and cohesive devices help develop an understanding of language and improve spoken and written grammar.

Grammar 3, or usage, refers to appropriate choices of words, phrases, and sentences. Usage deals with attitudes and language standards rather than meaning. Consequently, a level of usage appropriate for one subject and audience might not be appropriate for another. Instead of teaching that a particular form is incorrect, modern usage instruction stresses appropriateness for certain purposes and audiences, and helps children increase their range of usage.

Instruction in usage helps children understand that there is more than one level of usage, although one level may be more appropriate for a specific occasion. Activities such as role-playing help develop this understanding. Inductive approaches help children understand and apply a classroom level of usage. Modern usage instruction helps children move appropriately from one usage situation to another.

The mechanics of writing, including capitalization and punctuation, relate to the understanding of language and grammar. Both capitalization and punctuation are signals that help readers understand written communication.

ADDITIONAL GRAMMAR AND USAGE ACTIVITIES

1. Locate language arts/English textbooks that represent each of the major philosophies of grammar: traditional, structural, and transformational. Identify sentence-combining activities located in each text. Compare the similarities and differences found in the sentence-combining activities. Why might the activities differ according to the philosophy?
2. Locate several language arts/English journals such as *Language Arts, Research in the Teaching of English,* and *College English.* Read any journal articles pertaining to

grammar. What are the issues and concerns? Do these issues and concerns vary according to the audience for the journal?

3. Develop a lesson plan that allows children to experiment with sentence-pattern variations and understand that various sentence patterns are possible and beneficial when writing.
4. Develop a lesson plan that develops ability to expand sentences.
5. Tape-record several examples of children's oral language. Listen for the levels of usage. Are the children able to vary their levels of usage depending on their audience and purpose? What instructional strategies, if any, would you recommend?

BIBLIOGRAPHY

Baele, Ernest R. "The Effect of Primary Reading Programs Emphasizing Language Structure as Related to Meaning upon Children's Written Language Achievement at Third Grade Level." Doctoral Dissertation, University of California, Berkeley, 1968.

Baker, C. L. *English Syntax*. Cambridge, Mass.: MIT Press, 1989.

Baumann, James; and Stevenson, Jennifer. "Teaching Students to Comprehend Anaphoric Relations." In *Understanding and Teaching Cohesion Comprehension*, edited by Judith W. Irwin. Newark, Del.: International Reading Association, 1986.

Beers, Kylene. "Contextualizing Grammar." *Voices from the Middle* 8 (March 2001): 4.

Berger, Joan. "A Systematic Approach to Grammar Instruction." *Voices from the Middle* 8 (March 2001): 43–49.

Breen, Karen; Fader, Ellen; Odean, Kathleen; and Sutherland, Zena. "One Hundred Books that Shaped the Century." *School Library Journal* 46 (January 2000): 50–58.

Cartelli, Lora M. "Reading Comprehension: A Matter of Referents." *Academic Therapy* 15 (March 1980): 421–30.

Chomsky, Noam. *Syntactic Structures*. The Hague: Mouton & Co., 1957.

Christenbury, Leila. "From the Editor." *English Journal* 85 (1996): 11–12.

Cohen, Sandra B.; and Plaskon, Stephen P. *Language Arts for the Mildly Handicapped*. Upper Saddle River, N.J.: Merrill/Prentice Hall, 1980.

Cox, B. E.; Shanahan, T.; and Sulzby, E. "Good and Poor Readers' Use of Cohesion in Writing." *Reading Research Quarterly* 25 (1990): 47–65.

DeHaven, Edna P. *Teaching and Learning the Language Arts*. Boston: Little, Brown, 1983.

Fay, Gayle; Trupin, Eric; and Townes, Brenda D. "The Young Disabled Reader: Acquisition Strategies and Associated Deficits." *Journal of Learning Disabilities* 14 (January 1981): 32–35.

Francis, W. Nelson. "Revolution in Grammar." In *Readings in Applied English Linguistics*, 2nd ed., edited by Harold Allen. New York: Appleton-Century-Crofts, 1964.

Gearheart, Bill R.; Weishahn, Mel; and Gearheart, Carol J. *The Exceptional Student in the Regular Classroom*, 5th ed. Upper Saddle River, N.J.: Merrill/Prentice Hall, 1992.

Goodman, Ralph. "Transformational Grammar." In *An Introductory English Grammar*, edited by Norman Stageburg. New York: Holt, Rinehart & Winston, 1965.

Hartwell, P. "Grammar, Grammars, and the Teaching of Grammar." *College English* 47 (1985):105–27.

Hazlett, James A. *A National Assessment of Educational Progress. Report 8, Writing: National Results*. Washington, D.C.: U.S. Government Printing Office, 1972.

Henderson, Ann J.; and Shores, Richard E. "How Learning Disabled Students' Failure to Attend to Suffixes Affects Their Oral Reading Performance." *Journal of Learning Disabilities* 15 (March 1982): 178–82.

Hill, Julianne. "Writing Careers: Walter Cronkite." *Writer's Digest* 81 (September 2001): 42–43.

Hillocks, George, Jr. *Research on Written Composition: New Directions for Teaching.* Urbana, Ill.: ERIC Clearinghouse on Reading and Communication Skills and the National Conference on Research in English, 1986.

———; and Smith, M. W. "Grammar and Usage." In *Handbook of Research on Teaching the English Language Arts,* edited by J. Flood, J. Jensen, D. Lapp, and J. Squire. New York: Macmillan, 1991, pp. 591–603.

Hirsch, E. D. "Some Principles of Composition from Grade School to Grad School." In *The English Curriculum under Fire: What Are the Real Basics?,* edited by George Hillocks. Urbana, Ill.: National Council of Teachers of English, 1982, pp. 39–52.

Hodges, R. "The Conventions of Writing." In *Handbook of Research on Teaching the English Language Arts,* edited by J. Flood, J. Jensen, D. Lapp, and J. Squire. New York: Macmillan, 1991, pp. 775–86.

Hunt, Kellogg; and O'Donnell, Roy. *An Elementary School Curriculum to Develop Better Writing Skills.* Washington, D.C.: U.S. Department of Health, Education, and Welfare, Bureau of Research, 1970.

Johnson, Doris. "Relationships Between Oral and Written Language." *School Psychology Review* 22 (1993): 595–609.

Kean, John M.; and Personke, Carl. *The Language Arts, Teaching and Learning in the Elementary School.* New York: St. Martin's Press, 1976.

Knott, Gladys P. "Developing Reading Potential in Black Remedial High School Freshmen." *Reading Improvement* 16 (Winter 1979): 262–69.

Krashen, Stephen D. *Writing: Research, Theory, and Applications.* Oxford: Pergamon Press, 1984.

Lamb, Pose. *Linguistics in Proper Perspective,* 2nd ed. Upper Saddle River, N.J.: Merrill/Prentice Hall, 1977.

Lerner, Janet. *Children with Learning Disabilities,* 2nd ed. Boston: Houghton Mifflin, 1976.

Lodge, Helen C.; and Trett, Gerald L. *New Ways in English.* Upper Saddle River, N.J.: Prentice Hall, 1968.

Mackie, B. C. "The Effects of a Sentence-Combining Program on the Reading Comprehension and Written Composition of Fourth-Grade Students." Doctoral Dissertation, Hofstra University, 1982. (University Microfilms No. DA 8207744.)

McClure, Judith; Kalk, Michael; and Keenan, Verne. "Use of Grammatical Morphemes by Beginning Readers." *Journal of Learning Disabilities* 13 (May 1980): 34–49.

McNaughton, David; Hughes, Charles; and Clark, Karen. "Spelling Instruction for Students With Learning Disabilities: Implications for Research and Practice." *Learning Disability Quarterly* 17 (Summer 1994): 169–85.

Mellon, John. *The Basic Sentence Types and Their Simple Transforms.* Culver, Ind.: Culver Military Academy, 1964.

———. *Transformational Sentence Combining: A Method for Enhancing the Development of Syntactic Fluency in English Composition.* Champaign, Ill.: National Conference of Teachers of English, 1969.

Menyuk, Paula. "Linguistics and Teaching the Language Arts." In *Handbook of Research on Teaching the English Language Arts*, edited by J. Flood, J. Jensen, D. Lapp, and J. Squire. New York: Macmillan, 1991, pp. 24–29.

Moe, Alden J.; and Irwin, Judith W. "Cohesion, Coherence, and Comprehension." In *Understanding and Teaching Cohesion*, edited by Judith W. Irwin. Newark, Del.: International Reading Association, 1986.

National Council of Teachers of English. *Ideas for Teachers from Teachers: Elementary Language Arts*. Urbana, Ill.: National Council of Teachers of English, 1983.

National Council of Teachers of English and International Reading Association. *Standards for the English Language Arts*. Urbana, Ill.: National Council of Teachers of English, 1996.

Noden, Harry. "Image Grammar: Painting Images with Grammatical Structures." *Voices from the Middle* 8 (March 2001): 7–16.

O'Donnell, Roy; and Hunt, Kellogg. *Measures for Research and Evaluation in the Language Arts*. Urbana, IL: National Council of Teachers of English, 1975.

O'Hare, Frank. *Sentence Combining: Improving Student Writing Without Formal Grammar Instruction*. Urbana, Ill.: National Council of Teachers of English, 1973.

Otto, Wayne; and Smith, Richard J. *Corrective and Remedial Teaching*. Boston: Houghton Mifflin, 1980.

Pooley, Robert. "Dare Schools Set a Standard in English Usage?" *English Journal* 49 (March 1960): 176–81.

Porter, Jane. "Research Report." *Elementary English* 51 (January 1974): 144–51.

Roberts, Paul. *English Sentences*. New York: Harcourt Brace Jovanovich, 1962.

Samuels, S. Jay; and Naslund, Jan Carol. "Individual Differences in Reading: The Case for Lexical Access." *Reading & Writing Quarterly: Overcoming Learning Difficulties* 10 (1994): 285–96.

Savage, John F. *Effective Communication*. Chicago: Science Research Associates, 1977.

Stewig, John Warren; and Nordberg, Beverly. *Exploring Language Arts in the Elementary Classroom*. Belmont, Calif.: Wadsworth, 1995.

Stoddard, E. P. "The Combined Effect of Creative Thinking and Sentence-Combining Activities on the Writing Ability of Above Average Ability Fifth and Sixth Grade Students." Doctoral Dissertation, University of Connecticut, 1982. *Dissertation Abstracts International* (University Microfilms No. DA 821 3235.)

Stotsky, Sandra L. "Research on Reading/Writing Relationships: A Synthesis and Suggested Directions." *Language Arts* 60 (1983): 627–42.

Strong, William. *Creative Approaches to Sentence Combining*. Urbana, Ill.: National Council of Teachers of English, 1986.

Tiedt, Iris; and Tiedt, Sidney. *Contemporary English in the Elementary School*. Upper Saddle River, N.J.: Prentice-Hall, 1975.

Weaver, Constance. *Teaching Grammar in Context*. Portsmouth, N.H.: Boynton/Cook, 1996.

———; McNally, Carol; and Moerman, Sharon. "To Grammar or Not to Grammar: That Is Not the Question." *Voices from the Middle* 8 (March 2001): 17–33.

Ysseldyke, James; and Algozzine, Bob. *Special Education: A Practical Approach for Teachers*, 3rd ed. Boston: Houghton Mifflin, 1995.

Children's Literature References

Babbitt, Natalie. *Tuck Everlasting.* New York: Farrar, Straus & Giroux, 1975.

Bemelmans, Ludwig. *Madeline.* New York: Viking, 1939.

Blume, Judy. *Are You There, God? It's Me, Margaret.* New York: Bradbury, 1970.

Brown, Margaret Wise. *Goodnight Moon.* Illustrated by Clement Hurd. New York: Harper, 1947.

Bunting, Eve. *I Am the Mummy Heb-Nefert.* Illustrated by David Christiana. San Diego: Harcourt, 1997.

————. *The Man Who Could Call Down Owls.* Illustrated by Charles Mikolaycak. New York: Macmillan, 1984.

————. *The Mother's Day Mice.* Illustrated by Jan Brett. New York: Clarion, 1986.

Cone, Molly. *Come Back, Salmon.* Photographs by Sidnee Wheelwright. San Francisco: Sierra Club, 1992.

Cormier, Robert. *The Chocolate War.* Laureleaf, 1999.

Ehlert, Lois. *Moon Rope: A Peruvian Folktale.* San Diego: Harcourt Brace Jovanovich, 1992.

Fitzhugh, Louise. *Harriet the Spy.* New York: Harper & Row, 1964.

Frank, Anne. *Anne Frank: The Diary of a Young Girl,* edited by Otto H. Frank and Mirjam Pressler. Translated by Susan Massotty. New York: Doubleday, 1995.

Freedman, Russell. *Lincoln: A Photobiography.* New York: Clarion, 1987.

Gág, Wanda. *Millions of Cats.* New York: Coward-McCann, 1928, 1956.

George, Jean Craighead. *Julie of the Wolves.* Illustrated by John Schoenhen. New York: Harper & Row, 1972.

Heide, Florence Parry; and Gilliland, Judith Heide. *The Day of Ahmed's Secret.* Illustrated by Ted Lewin. New York: Lothrop, Lee & Shepard, 1990.

Keats, Ezra Jack. *The Snowy Day.* New York: Viking, 1962.

Kerley, Barbara. *The Dinosaurs of Waterhouse Hawkins.* Illustrated by Brian Selznick. New York: Scholastic, 2001.

Konigsburg, E. L. *From the Mixed-Up Files of Mrs. Basil E. Frankweiler.* New York: Atheneum, 1967.

Lauber, Patricia. *Volcano: The Eruption and Healing of Mount St. Helens.* New York: Bradbury, 1986.

L'Engle, Madeleine. *A Wrinkle in Time.* New York: Farrar, Straus & Giroux, 1962.

Lester, Julius. *John Henry.* Illustrated by Jerry Pinkney. New York: Dial Press, 1994.

Lewis, C. S. *The Lion, the Witch, and the Wardrobe.* Illustrated by Pauline Baynes. New York: Macmillan, 1950.

Lobel, Arnold. *Frog and Toad Are Friends.* New York: Harper & Row, 1970.

Lowry, Lois. *The Giver.* Boston: Houghton Mifflin, 1993.

MacLachlan, Patricia. *Sarah, Plain and Tall.* New York: Harper & Row, 1985.

Milne, A. A. *Winnie-the-Pooh.* Illustrated by Ernest H. Shepard. New York: Dutton, 1926, 1954.

Morpurgo, Michael. *Wombat Goes Walkabout.* Illustrated by Christian Birmingham. Cambridge, Mass: Candlewick, 2000.

O'Dell, Scott. *Island of the Blue Dolphins.* Boston: Houghton Mifflin, 1960.

Paterson, Katherine. *Bridge to Terabithia.* Illustrated by Donna Diamond. New York: Crowell, 1977.

Potter, Beatrix. *The Tale of Peter Rabbit.* New York: Warner, 1902.

Pullman, Philip. *The Golden Compass.* New York: Knopf, 1995.

Rylant, Cynthia. *Henry and Mudge and the Happy Cat.* Illustrated by Sucie Stevenson. New York: Bradbury, 1990.

Say, Allen. *Grandfather's Journey.* Boston: Houghton Mifflin, 1993.

Sendak, Maurice. *Where the Wild Things Are.* New York: Harper & Row, 1963.

Stewart, Sarah. *The Gardener.* Illustrated by David Small. New York: Farrar, Straus & Giroux, 1996.

Seuss, Dr. *The Cat in the Hat.* New York: Random House, 1954.

Wells, Rosemary. *Yoko.* New York: Hyperion, 1998.

White, E. B. *Charlotte's Web.* Illustrated by Garth Williams. New York: Harper & Row, 1952.

Wilder, Laura Ingalls. *Little House in the Big Woods.* New York: Harper & Row, 1932.

Zimmerman, Andrea; and Clemesha, David. *My Dog Toby.* Illustrated by True Kelley. San Diego: Harcourt, 2000.

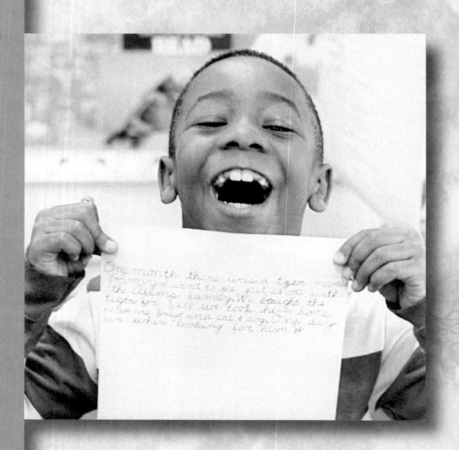

After completing this chapter on handwriting, you will be able to:

1. State some of the issues related to handwriting instruction.
2. Describe some informal means for assessing readiness.
3. Describe some instructional activities to help children see the need for good handwriting and to develop their handwriting skills.
4. Describe some instructional activities that develop fine-motor skills and readiness for letter formations.
5. Develop and demonstrate a lesson that teaches manuscript printing to beginning writers.
6. Evaluate handwriting samples for letter formation, slant, spacing, and line quality.
7. Identify the manuscript errors made most frequently by first-grade students.
8. Demonstrate the formation of manuscript and cursive letters.
9. Develop and demonstrate a lesson that introduces students to cursive writing.
10. Describe and use a technique for collecting handwriting samples under the three conditions of normal, best, and fastest writing.
11. Describe some instructional procedures specific to left-handed writers.
12. Describe a kinesthetic approach for teaching handwriting to students with learning disabilities.

*H*andwriting instruction that emphasizes ornate, consistent penmanship for every student is no longer a part of modern curricula. Modern handwriting instruction, although it does not develop beautiful flourishes, does stress legibility—well-formed letters, consistent slant, and proper spacing of letters and words. Whereas writing was once almost an art form, modern handwriting is viewed as a tool for personal communication. There is now considerable leeway for developing a personal handwriting style, although the writing cannot be so personal that only the writer is able to read it.

Stewig and Nordberg (1995) emphasize the importance of handwriting in today's curriculum: "Today students are increasingly asked to get their thoughts down on paper in all subjects. This surge of interest in written expression has created a new focus on handwriting fluency as a tool. Slow handwriting can affect the quality and content of written expression, a student's learning, and even a student's view of writing itself. Writing must also be legible, a necessity for communicating an idea to others as well as a courtesy to the reader" (p. 301)

In a review of research in handwriting, Hodges (2003) states that "summaries of current practices indicate that handwriting instruction is fairly uniform throughout the United States, typically beginning with manuscript writing in the first grade, with a transition to cursive writing sometime in the third grade" (p. 1057). According to Hodges, direct instruction is common in teaching handwriting. He goes on to state: "What appears to be important in the development of handwriting is the amount of emphasis teachers place on legible, neat writing, and also the presence in the classroom of good handwriting models" (p. 1057).

Summarizing another review of research in the area of handwriting, Farris (1991) emphasizes the importance of including handwriting instruction:

> Without being introduced to and given instruction in the basic handwriting skills such as letter formation, alignment, slant, and size, children are left to discover such skills on their own. As such, they develop inappropriate techniques, and legibility suffers. . . . Teachers in early childhood education should teach handwriting through direct instruction, for it is a basic and important skill for writing. Teachers at both the early and middle childhood levels need to understand handwriting methods and to be able to identify and correct students' problems. The teacher–student conference, a crucial component of whole language instruction, can include direct handwriting instruction just as it serves as a vehicle for improving the content, grammar, and punctuation of a piece of writing. (p. 314)

The influence on teachers' grading may be a very strong motivational source for clear handwriting. Graham, Weintrab, and Berninger (2001) report that "poor penmanship may have a negative influence on teachers' perceptions and the grades they assign" (p. 488). They also report that handwriting difficulties may cause young children to avoid writing and to believe that they cannot write.

Some educators predicted that research and interest in handwriting would decline as the use of computers increased, but Dobbie and Askov (1995) compared research studies in handwriting over several decades and discovered an increase in studies of handwriting. They hypothesize that "maybe interest in handwriting remains as a focus for research because it is usually one of a child's first encounters with literacy" (p. 339).

We should note, however, that many of the studies cited in handwriting articles are older studies. For example, Hodges (2003) has not updated his section on handwriting since his 1991 article on it was published in the first edition of the *Handbook of Research on Teaching the English Language Arts.*

Effective Handwriting Instruction

Naus (2000) offers the following guidelines for effective handwriting instruction:

1. Express the importance of handwriting to the students.
2. Teach handwriting directly in lessons no longer than fifteen minutes.
3. Describe the formation of strokes using clear, consistent language.
4. Insist on good posture.
5. Check that student's feet and desk are firmly on the floor.
6. Make sure that paper is positioned at twenty to thirty-five degrees to the left for right-handers and at thirty to thirty-five degrees to the right for left-handers.
7. Display models of good writing in the room.
8. Emphasize high-quality work rather than large quantities of sloppy writing.
9. Set criteria for acceptable work and teach children to evaluate their writing.
10. Return unacceptable work to the students.
11. Provide immediate feedback when possible.

Handwriting instruction has three phases. First is readiness for handwriting, which is developed at home, in kindergarten, and in early first grade. Second is the formal teaching of manuscript writing, usually beginning in first grade. Third is the formal teaching of cursive writing, beginning about third grade. However, you may need to give special consideration to left-handed writers and mainstreamed writers. In addition, throughout any handwriting instruction, special care should be taken to provide students with opportunities to apply their handwriting skills in meaningful situations. You must also remember that handwriting is a tool—one of the conventions of writing—that leads to meaningful composition and communication.

Writing Readiness

Donoghue (1990) identifies the following six prerequisite skill areas for handwriting: (1) small-muscle development and coordination, (2) eye–hand coordination, (3) ability to hold writing tools properly, (4) ability to form basic strokes, (5) letter perception, and (6) understanding of printed language, including left-to-right progression and language maturity. You can evaluate these readiness skills through simple observation. A child's interest or lack of interest in writing is usually apparent. Does the child ask how to write his or her name or other words? Does the child pretend to be writing?

Informal Assessment

Durkin (1966) found that children who read prior to entering school also show an early interest in learning to print. The learning sequences of these early printers moved from (1) scribbling and drawing to (2) copying objects and letters of the alphabet to (3) asking questions about spelling to (4) reading. It is easy to observe children and assess where they are in this sequence.

This child is working on visual acuity and motor skills.

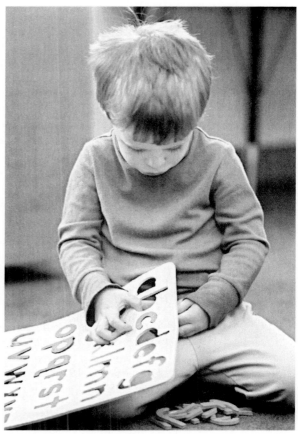

Because both reading and writing progress from left to right, it is logical that understanding this sequence benefits handwriting instruction. Observe each child to see whether the child progresses from left to right when trying to read a book. If you place two dots on a chalkboard or paper, does the child connect the dots in a left-to-right sequence? By observing children in such activities as drawing, bead stringing, paper cutting, and pencil holding, you can learn a great deal about their fine-motor coordination. Observation also permits you to ascertain a child's hand preference.

de Ajuriaguerra and Auzias (1975) recommend looking at handwriting in a framework that includes both language and motor analysis. They believe that in both drawing and scribbling, children first explore paper by using indiscriminate actions; they then show increased purpose and good use of space. Based on de Ajuriaguerra and Auzias's research, Graves (1978) developed the following six questions that can be used to determine children's level of development of the skills necessary for writing and to evaluate how they explore space in artwork, construction, movement, and writing:

1. Is the child consistent in the use of the thumb and forefinger grip? Children who demonstrate a poor grip when using a crayon in artwork will have difficulty controlling a pencil when writing.
2. Does the child show erratic movement in artwork or handwriting? When children first write, the writing stops and starts because they are not familiar with the task. Continued erratic movements suggest underdeveloped fine-motor skills.
3. Does the child change the position of the elbow, affecting the stability of body axis? When children begin to draw or write, they exhibit a great deal of body and elbow motion. Children who do not reduce this motion will have a great deal of difficulty with the fine-motor demands of writing.
4. Does the child change the position of the writing surface in relation to the midline? When children first face paper, they approach it squarely in relation to the body. Gradually, they come to understand the relationship of the position of the paper to the position of the body in writing.
5. Does the child vary the applied strength? In writing, children must suppress large muscles so that small muscles can gain control. Observe changes from light to heavy lines on the paper as well as changes in the body position of the child.
6. How does the child use writing space? Look at how he or she chains letters together. If children do not have good enough fine-motor control, angles will be inconsistent and spaces will be uneven. Children who do not understand the concept of language also show a tendency to run words and sentences together.

Graves believes that any of the preceding factors can contribute to slowness in handwriting and thus affect the quality and content of writing.

For Your Development

1. Observe children in a nursery school or kindergarten. Using informal assessment techniques, describe some of the relevant characteristics of those children you feel are ready for writing and those who may not be ready.
2. Use Graves's (1978) six elements to evaluate children's use of space. Compare samples from children who appear to be ready for writing with samples from those who do not.

Instruction

Early childhood educators contend that the readiness phase in handwriting is as important as the readiness phase in reading. Many activities in nursery school, kindergarten, and early first grade contribute to readiness for handwriting. Early readiness experiences give children opportunities to explore the space provided by paper. As Graves (1978) suggests, at first—at two or three years of age—there is no difference between drawing and writing attempts. Later, children differentiate by drawing pictures and making continuous scribbles across pages to represent writing. When children try to write, they are indicating a need for handwriting. A child who does not feel a need for writing has unusual difficulties with all aspects of writing.

Kindergarten programs that include oral reading and language experience activities, in which children dictate group or individual chart stories, help children see relationships between oral language, printed stories, and handwriting. If children do not understand the concepts of word and sentence, handwriting is meaningless to them. Wordless books provide enjoyable instructional sources for language experience stories. Develop many readiness activities to allow children to see that the purpose for handwriting is composition and communication—not isolated drill.

Moving, drawing, painting, and cutting help develop fine-motor skills. Dances, such as looby-loo and hokey pokey, nurture mastery of left and right. Other activities include drawing cars on a road that goes from left to right and moving small cars and trucks on the road in the classroom or on the playground.

A second group of readiness activities helps children with letter formations. The movements needed to form the manuscript alphabet are primarily circles and lines in vertical, horizontal, or angled positions; therefore, have children practice making these strokes on large paper or on the chalkboard. Kindergarten and first-grade teachers often have children make creative pictures from elements such as those shown in Figure 11–1. One first-grade teacher had those students who demonstrated underdeveloped fine-motor control make delightful stick figures and animals using the basic shapes necessary for formal manuscript writing. Thus, the children experimented with space and line dimensions while enjoying art activity. Tompkins (1980) recommends using basic penmanship strokes to create stories and pictures. She develops activities around the language game "Let's Go on a Bear Hunt," instructions for making jack-o-lanterns, and a snowy day story.

After children have had opportunities to experiment with shapes and lines on unlined paper, teachers often introduce them to the use of lined paper by having them draw the fundamental shapes between the appropriate lines (see Figure 11–2).

FIGURE 11–1 Elements Needed to Make the Manuscript Alphabet

FIGURE 11–2 Fundamental Shapes on Lined Paper

Printing

Printing, also called manuscript writing, is taught to first and second graders in most American schools. Printing rather than cursive writing is considered preferable for beginners because the printing symbols are similar to reading symbols.

Although manuscript writing is taught in most elementary grades, there is some disagreement about what size pencils and what type of paper should be used. According to Askov, Otto, and Askov (1970), research in this area is too scant to permit any conclusions. They cite one research article reporting that children prefer adult pencils to the larger sized beginner pencils. Many educators recommend allowing each child to use whatever pencil size is most comfortable because the larger pencils have not been proven better for beginning writers.

Yardley (1973), a British educator, points out that unlined paper offers a surface free of restrictions when a child's attempts to write are immature. In England, children spend several years working with unlined paper, whereas most American children use paper that progresses from wider to narrower spaces, even for early instruction.

Several instructional programs have been published in the area of handwriting. If your school has approved one of these programs, you should learn the formation of the letters for that program. Children are very observant; they will notice if letters you make are different from those used in the program. Figures 11–3 and 11–4 show manuscript alphabets taught in many schools. The first example is published by Zaner-Bloser, Inc. The second is the D'Nealian handwriting model published by Scott, Foresman. Compare the two examples for letter shapes and strokes.

Writing for personal journals provides an opportunity to practice manuscript in a meaningful context.

FIGURE 11–3   Manuscript Alphabet

Source: Used with permission from *Handwriting: Basic Skills and Application.* Copyright © 1987. Zaner-Bloser, Inc., Columbus, Ohio.

FIGURE 11–4   D'Nealian Manuscript Alphabet

Source: D'Nealian® Handwriting by Donald Thurber. Copyright © 1987 by Scott, Foresman & Co. Reprinted by permission.

For Your Development

Before you proceed with specific instructional techniques for manuscript writing, practice printing the manuscript alphabets shown in Figures 11–3 and 11–4 or the manuscript alphabet used in the schools in your area. Practice the alphabet on paper and a chalkboard until you feel comfortable with it.

Instruction

Readiness activities help children understand the techniques that contribute to legible handwriting. Manuscript writing instruction should involve correct sitting posture, correct letter formation, proper spacing of letters, and uniform slanting of letters. Several language arts authorities stress the role of teachers in helping children analyze a letter before writing it. Furner (1969) recommends a perceptual-motor approach for teaching letter formation. This approach allows children to identify writing position, letter formation, alignment, and spacing of letters before they actually print a letter.

In all early writing activities, remember that writing is a difficult and slow process for many children, so early handwriting practice should not overtire them. Allow children to practice their handwriting through a functional approach as soon as possible. Instead of merely having them copy model sentences, let them write their names and addresses. Let them write diaries, invitations, letters, captions for artwork, weather charts, autobiographies, and so forth. When children are first learning to write, supervise them closely so that they will not reinforce incorrect letter formations. Also, do not waste time repeatedly practicing letter formations they have already mastered.

For Your Plan Book

Lesson Plan

A Handwriting Lesson Using a Letter-Analysis Approach

Teachers should help children analyze a letter by encouraging them to visualize the letter, study its characteristics (beginning stroke, ending stroke, strokes peculiar to the letter, height and width of the letter, and height of various parts of the letter), and check the quality of the strokes. The following lesson plan uses this letter-analysis approach. The objective is to enable the students to analyze and form the manuscript letter *a*. The teaching procedures follow.

Procedures

1. Make lines on the chalkboard similar to the lines on manuscript paper. A musical staff marker with chalk placed in the top, middle, and bottom holders is useful.
2. Ask the children to watch carefully as you make the letter *a*. Ask them: "How am I making the letter *a*?" "What kinds of strokes do you see?" (Circle stroke and straight-line stroke.) You may discuss the fact that the class has practiced these strokes (see Figure 11–5).

FIGURE 11–5   The Letter *a*

3. Emphasize the beginning stroke for the letter *a*. Ask the class to watch as you make the circle portion of the letter. Ask "Where does the circle begin?" (Just below the dotted, or middle, line.) "In what direction does the stroke go?" (The circle goes to the left.) A mark and an arrow will help students visualize this formation (see Figure 11–6).

FIGURE 11–6   Beginning the Letter *a*

4. Have the students watch you make the letter *a* again. This time, ask them to watch the straight-line formation. Ask "Where does the straight line begin?" (The line begins on the dotted, or middle, line.) "Where does the straight line touch the circle?" (On the right side of the circle.) "Where does the straight line end?" (On the bottom line.) (See Figure 11–7.)

FIGURE 11–7   Finishing the Letter *a*

5. Have the students watch again so that they can describe the height of the letter. Ask "How tall is the circle part of the letter?" (The circle is one space high. It touches the middle line and bottom line, but it does not go over either line.) "How tall is the straight-line part of the letter?" (The straight line is one space high. It touches the middle line and the bottom line, but it does not go over either line.) (See Figure 11–8.)

FIGURE 11–8   Size of Letter *a*

6. Ask the children to describe how the letter is formed. Have them write the letter independently, describing the process to themselves.

After introducing the letter *a,* teach other letters in a similar manner.

For Your Development

Develop a lesson plan for teaching one of the letters of the manuscript alphabet. Use your lesson plan with beginning writers or try the lesson plan with a small group of your peers.

Lesson Plan

For Your Plan Book

A Lesson Plan for Developing an Understanding of Early Writing: Hieroglyphs

Objectives

1. To develop an understanding that writing is an important and an ancient skill.
2. To illustrate the importance of writing in early Egypt.
3. To discover the research that accompanied a search for the meaning of the writings in the temples and on the mummy cases found in ancient Egypt.
4. To write a story or captions for drawings using hieroglyphs.

Procedures

1. Collect and discuss illustrations that show hieroglyphs in tombs or on mummy cases.
2. Use maps to show and discuss the location of Egypt.
3. Read Carol Donoughue's *The Mystery of the Hieroglyphs: The Story of the Rosetta Stone and the Race to Decipher Egyptian Hieroglyphs* (1999).

   Use the first chapter, "How the Egyptians Wrote," to introduce hieroglyphs and the importance of the discovery of the Rosetta Stone. Discuss the early writing on papyrus scrolls.

   Read and discuss the second chapter, "How We Know." As you read, stop and discuss the answers to the various questions developed in the chapter. For example, on page 13 the author shows a carving of Rameses II and hieroglyphs found in the Great Temple of Abu Simbel. The text states: "Around the pictures, above them, below them, and sometimes included within the picture, were signs like this: (text shows drawings of hieroglyphs). But what did they mean? If only it were possible to work it out! . . . Would it ever be possible to read what they said? What would you do, if you found something written down in signs which you could not understand? How would you set about working out what the signs meant? What about these signs for instance? Any ideas? Look carefully and see if you notice anything about them" (p. 13). In this second chapter, stress the information on the time line and the pictographs.

   The next few chapters discuss the discovery of the Rosetta Stone and the work of various scholars who have worked on deciphering the meaning of the hieroglyphs carved into the stone. Allow students to speculate about why these scholars considered their task so important.
4. Conclude this lesson, which will probably require several days, by using the final chapter, "Reading Hieroglyphs," to allow students to write a few words, sentences, or even a story in hieroglyphs. Ask them to compare the work that it took them to write in hieroglyphs with the time it takes for them to write in contemporary English.

Lesson Plan

For Your Plan Book

A Lesson Plan for Developing an Understanding About Other Ways of Forming Words: Chinese and Japanese Calligraphy

Objectives

1. To develop an understanding that the art of writing is an ancient skill in China.
2. To discover that the Chinese written characters are like pictures.

3. To read and appreciate books written in English, Chinese, and Japanese.
4. To write a story using calligraphy.

Procedures

1. Share with the students that Chinese writing is very old. According to Joseph Campbell (1976) "the art of writing had been invented c. 3200 B.C." (p. 41). Show students examples of Chinese figures such as those found in John Lewis's *The Chinese Word for Horse and Other Stories* (1980) in which the author states: "Chinese words are like pictures." Another term for this beautiful writing is *calligraphy*.
2. Share and discuss several books that are written in both English and Chinese, including Ed Young's *Mouse Match* (1997), in which the story is written in Chinese on one side of each two-page spread and in English on the facing page, and Ed Young's *The Lost Horse* (1998).
3. Share and discuss several Japanese stories that include both English and Japanese. One example is Arthur A. Levine's *The Boy Who Drew Cats* (1993). After reading and discussing the story, share the characters shown on the final page of the text. Characters are drawn to represent such terms as *cat, child,* and *victory*.
4. Share and discuss the poems and illustrations in Matthew Gollub's *Cool Melons—Turn to Frogs!: The Life and Poems of Issa* (1998). This collection of haiku poetry is especially beautiful. Each poem is translated into English, has an illustration that depicts the poem, and includes Japanese calligraphy on each page.
5. After children have an opportunity to create their own calligraphy, they should discuss the differences between writing English and writing the Chinese and Japanese figures.

Assessing Handwriting

After reviewing strategies for writing and evaluating writing, Hodges (2003) states that the critical criteria for determining handwriting quality are legibility (well-proportioned letters and words) and fluency (rate of writing). He finds that the legibility classification system most commonly used includes letter form, uniformity of slant, letter alignment, quality of line, and spacing between letters and words, all of which may be assessed informally. To check letter formation—the most important factor—Burns and Broman (1983) recommend using a card with a circular hole cut in the center. Move this hole, a little larger than a letter, along the line of writing to expose one letter at a time. Thus, you or a child may identify poorly formed or illegible letters (see Figure 11–9).

You can easily observe letter formation when children use lined paper or when you draw lines across the tops of the letters to see if they are uniform. In the example on the left of Figure 11–10, a second-grade child has formed each letter according to his first-grade

FIGURE 11–9 Cards Allowing Assessment of Individual Letters

FIGURE 11–10 Good and Poor Letter Formation

teaching. In the example on the right, another second-grade child is having considerable difficulty with letter formation.

In both manuscript and cursive writing, the letter slant affects legibility. To evaluate consistency in slant, you or a child can draw straight lines through the letters in words (see Figure 11–11). The lines quickly indicate to the child whether or not the letters are slanted consistently. Posture is the most important factor affecting the slant of handwriting, so observe children while they are writing.

Spacing also affects legibility. Too much spacing between letters can slow the speed of reading. Obviously, if there are no spaces between words, material is hard to read. Some children place their letters so close together that they are difficult to decipher, which can also affect assessment of spelling ability. (See Figure 11–12 for examples of proper spacing and poor spacing.)

When you assess line quality, evaluate the thickness of the lines and their lightness or darkness. For children with well-developed fine-motor skills, the lines will usually reflect consistent pressure. In contrast, for children whose fine-motor skills are not adequately developed, you may notice differences in line quality (see Figure 11–13).

Informal evaluation provides substantial diagnostic information and a basis for planning to meet individual needs. It also provides opportunities for you to correct errors before they become reinforced. Keep folders of writing examples for each child, so that both you and

FIGURE 11–11   Letter Slant

Consistent slant:

Inconsistent slant:

FIGURE 11–12 Spacing

Proper spacing:

the lazy dog

the lazy dog

Poor spacing:

the lazydog

thelazydog

FIGURE 11–13 Noticeable
Differences in Line Quality

the lazy dog

the child are aware of progress. It is helpful to develop a progress chart for each child in order to evaluate the various aspects of handwriting over a period of time. Figure 11–14 illustrates the type of information that you may keep on a progress chart.

As we have mentioned, most children experience some difficulties when first learning to print. It is quite common for beginners to reverse letters, for example, writing *b* instead of *d*. They also commonly omit letters from words or space letters poorly. If these errors are still apparent after a reasonable period of instruction, however, the child probably has a problem that requires special attention. Identifying children who are unable to write with normal legibility and speed is the goal of diagnostic procedures.

Lewis and Lewis (1964) analyzed both the number and types of errors made by first-grade children. Their findings included common errors, letters that are relatively easy to

	Sept.	Jan.	May
Name _____			
Grade _____			
1. Formation of letters:			
a. All correctly formed	_____	_____	_____
b. Incorrect letters	_____	_____	_____
2. Slant of letters:			
a. Consistent slant	_____	_____	_____
b. Irregular slant	_____	_____	_____
c. Too much back slant	_____	_____	_____
3. Posture while writing (hand, body, paper):			
a. Correct	_____	_____	_____
b. Incorrect	_____	_____	_____
4. Spacing within words:			
a. Spaces too wide	_____	_____	_____
b. Letters crowded	_____	_____	_____
c. Spaces irregular	_____	_____	_____
5. Spacing between words:			
a. Spaces too wide	_____	_____	_____
b. Spaces too narrow	_____	_____	_____
c. Spaces irregular	_____	_____	_____
6. Speed of writing:			
a. Appropriate for grade	_____	_____	_____
b. Too slow	_____	_____	_____
c. Too fast	_____	_____	_____
7. Overall appearance of writing:			
a. Neat	_____	_____	_____
b. Poor appearance due to _____	_____	_____	_____

(Place checks, examples, and comments in appropriate spaces.)

FIGURE 11–14   Progress Chart

learn, and letters that are relatively difficult. Some conclusions from this first-grade study follow:

1. Most errors are made in letters that go below the line—*q, g, p, y,* and *j.*
2. Errors are frequent in letters in which curves and vertical lines merge—*J, U, f, h, j, m, n, r,* and *u.*
3. Letters most likely to be reversed are *n, d, q,* and *y.*

4. Errors that are most frequent include improper size, incorrect relationships of parts, and incorrect relationships to lines.
5. Fewest errors are made in the letters *H, O, o, L,* and *l.*

Cursive Writing

As reported by Hodges (2003), most elementary schools require children to change from printing to cursive writing sometime between the end of the second grade and the middle of third grade; however, the transition usually begins in early third grade. Although cursive writing may be more acceptable for some social and business uses, there is no compelling reason to change from printing to cursive writing. Cursive writing, however, is more personal than printing, and usually faster.

Beginning Instruction

Cursive writing is not a new skill that children must memorize in the slow, meticulous way they study printing. By the time children begin cursive writing, they have had several years of practice with printed language and can compare and contrast manuscript and cursive writing. When Furner (1969) introduces her students to cursive writing, she uses two approaches. First, she organizes readiness activities in which she guides the students in recognizing and reading cursive letters. They name the letters, read their own names in cursive writing, and so forth. Next, they examine samples of cursive writing and its formation to compare it with printing.

Cursive writing charts may be used to find the similarities and differences between cursive writing and printing. The cursive alphabets published by Zaner-Bloser and Scott, Foresman are used in most schools (see Figures 11–15 and 11–16). After having the children look

Research has not shown any great advantage in changing from manuscript to cursive writing.

FIGURE 11–15 Cursive Handwriting Alphabet

Source: Used with permission from *Handwriting: Basic Skills and Application.* Copyright © 1987. Zaner-Bloser, Inc., Columbus, Ohio.

FIGURE 11–16 D'Nealian Cursive Alphabet

Source: D'Nealian® *Handwriting* by Donald Thurber. Copyright © 1987 by Scott, Foresman & Co. Reprinted by permission.

at and discuss the cursive alphabet, list printed letters that are similar to those in the cursive alphabet. Also note similarities in direction of strokes, size, and relation to baseline (whether the letters touch or extend below the baseline). The following is a list of some differences to note:

1. The letters are joined in cursive writing, and there are no spaces until the end of a word.

2. Cursive writing has a slant, whereas printing is straight.

3. The letters *f* and *z* go below the baseline in cursive writing, whereas they do not in printing.

4. When a word is written in cursive, the *t* is crossed and the *i* and *j* are dotted after the word is completed, rather than after the letter is completed, as in printing.

5. The position of the paper may be more slanted for cursive writing than for printing.

Continuing Instruction

Burns and Broman (1983) recommend teaching letters and words that have similar strokes at the same time. This procedure progresses from the straight printed to the slanted cursive version of words in the steps shown in Figure 11–17. Lowercase letters that are similar in manuscript and cursive alphabets are *a, d, g, h, i, l, m, n, o, p, q, t, u,* and *y.* Similar capital letters are *B, C, K, L, O, P, R,* and *U.*

Next, teach the letters that are dissimilar, such as *f, k, r, s,* and *z.* Use practical types of writing in instruction. Have the children practice their spelling words or have them write

FIGURE 11–17   Transition from Printing to Cursive Writing

1. manuscript

2. dotted manuscript

3. nonslant cursive

4. cursive slant

letters to each other or to friends or family. At this level, individualize instruction so that each child will have extra practice with the letter formations and combinations that he or she finds difficult.

For Your Development

1. Develop a lesson or series of lessons to demonstrate the transition from manuscript to cursive handwriting. If you are teaching elementary students at the appropriate age, use your lesson plan with them. If you are not teaching, demonstrate your activity to a group of your peers.
2. Investigate the way cursive writing is taught in one of the commercial sets of handwriting materials. Look at suggestions for transition to and development of the cursive alphabet. What skills are stressed? In what order are the letters presented? Are functional practice activities suggested to accompany the instruction? How much time is recommended for handwriting instruction?

Assessing Cursive Handwriting

Handwriting evaluation demands some experience. Consequently, beginning teachers may want to use the *Evaluation Scales for Expressional Growth Through Handwriting* published by the Zaner-Bloser Company in 1969. The scales contain five examples each of manuscript printing for grades one and two. These examples represent high, good, medium, fair, and poor quality. The scales also provide five examples of cursive writing for each grade from three through nine. Looking at the various degrees of legibility may help you evaluate formation, slant, and spacing of letters.

Few standardized tests are available for assessing handwriting. Teachers must rely on either informal sampling procedures or loosely standardized writing scales to evaluate children's handwriting skills. For the evaluation of handwriting of older students, Otto and Smith (1980) recommend gathering handwriting samples under three conditions: (1) usual writing, (2) best writing, and (3) fastest writing. Legibility may be acceptable when a child is able to work slowly and methodically, but it may deteriorate when the child has to write rapidly to keep up with the demands of school assignments. For gathering handwriting samples, Otto and Smith suggest the following procedures:

1. Use a sentence containing most of the letters of the alphabet; for example, "The quick, sly fox jumps over the lazy, brown dog." Write the sentence on the chalkboard (in manuscript or cursive, depending on the grade level) and have the students read it several times to become familiar with it.
2. Ask the students to write the sentence five times. Tell them to write as they normally do. Allow them to write for three minutes. Then, stop the activity.
3. Provide a period of relaxation. Then, tell the students to write the sentence in their very best handwriting. They may take all of the time that they need. Ask them to write the sentence three times, with no time restrictions.
4. Provide a second period of relaxation. Then, tell the students that you want them to write as fast as they are able to write. Allow them three minutes to write the sentence as many times as they can.
5. Compare each child's three writing samples. Use either informal evaluations or an evaluation scale.

You may keep samples of students' handwriting in their portfolios as part of your informal assessment process. Students can also assess changes in their own writing.

For Your Development

Collect samples of handwriting from several children using the procedures for gathering a normal sample, the best sample, and the fastest sample. Evaluate the samples using the informal assessment techniques described. After you have evaluated the samples, place the results on a handwriting analysis chart. (Use the categories on the progress chart shown in Figure 11–14.) Include recommendations for instruction or remediation.

Left-Handed Writers

Teachers today do not try to force left-handed writers to be right-handed writers, as was frequently done in the past. Although left-handed writers are allowed to retain their hand preference, they do require some specific instruction in handwriting. You may wish to use the following procedures when working with left-handed writers:

1. Have the children assume positions that are the *opposite* of those expected of right-handed children, with the added caution that the position should be one that is most comfortable to them.
2. Have the children reverse the position of the paper (it may be less slanted and more toward a straight up-and-down position for left-handers). Have them reverse the direction of the pencil, too. The grip is basically the same as that for right-handed students.
3. Seat left-handed children so the light comes over their left shoulder.
4. Provide much practice writing on the chalkboard. (It is nearly impossible to use the upside-down hand style on the board.)
5. Furnish left-handed children with pencils that have slightly harder lead than those used by right-handers. Harder lead will not smear as easily, giving less reason for twisting the wrist into the upside-down position. The point should not be so sharp that it will dig into the paper.

6. Encourage left-handed children to grasp their writing instrument at least an inch-and-a-half from the point. At this distance, a child can see over or around his or her hand. You can put a rubber band around the pencil at the point where the child should grasp it.
7. If possible, provide children with individual model charts written by a left-handed teacher or community worker.
8. At the primary levels, seat left-handed writers together near the front of the room, where you can give them constant encouragement. After their handwriting habits are formed and no further adjustments are needed, you can discontinue this seating arrangement.
9. Encourage left-handed children to develop a writing slant that is natural and that "feels good."
10. Avoid forcing older left-handed pupils to write a certain way. If an awkward position cannot be easily corrected, it is sometimes best to let the child continue.

Mainstreaming

Mainstreamed children frequently exhibit problems in handwriting as well as in other areas. Martlew (1992) compared children with dyslexia to normal children and found that the handwriting of the dyslexic group was characterized by problems with legibility and poor quality. She recommends that educators "focus on the movement patterns for better formations and words. There needs to be investment in unlearning of inaccurate patterns and the reconstruction of accurate ones. This may be best achieved by encouraging the children to return to writing slowly, consciously adopting structured directions in stroke formation of letters while making sound/grapheme links. It is possible that initial learning in dyslexic children, because it has not been sufficiently structured for their needs, has permitted errors to accumulate to the point where they are resistant to change" (p. 389).

Otto and Smith (1980) also stress the complexity of these handwriting problems. They state that difficulties in handwriting frequently coexist with difficulties in reading and spelling. Both reading and spelling may be influenced by inadequate visual memory, inability or lack of readiness to handle visual symbols, or difficulties with sound–symbol relationships.

Research indicates that a kinesthetic approach to handwriting (one that involves movement of the body and sensations of position) is best for certain students with learning disabilities (Askov, Otto, & Askov, 1970). Students with learning disabilities may require extensive pencil tracing activities and tracing of raised letters with the finger. Birch and Lefford (1967) also imply advantages for adding a tracing component to handwriting instruction for such children. These researchers investigated the ability of five- through eleven-year-olds to draw geometric forms by tracing, connecting dots, and freehand copying. The tracing activity was the easiest for younger children, and it also produced the highest accuracy score. Connecting the dots was the next easiest task, whereas freehand drawing was the most difficult and resulted in the greatest number of errors. Tracing provides a kinesthetic component for handwriting. Add a tracing activity to the beginning analysis approach before requiring children with learning disabilities to form each letter independently.

If adding a kinesthetic activity is still not enough guidance for a student who is having difficulty, Hammill and Bartel (1975) recommend that you teach handwriting with a procedure that encompasses four developmental levels. Reger, Schroeder, and Uschold (1968) also recommend this procedure. In this four-level approach, begin with the first

FIGURE 11–18   Handwriting
Movements

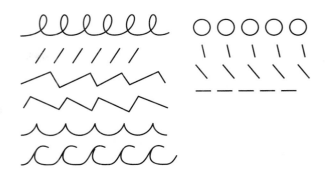

level, and move on to the next level only when the student has mastered the skills at the earlier level.

The first level introduces handwriting movements to the student. Discuss each movement and demonstrate it on the chalkboard. For example, demonstrate the straight-stick movement in manuscript writing and then say "We put the chalk on the board and then go down." Demonstrate the movement on the board; then, have the student make the same movement at the board while looking at your model but not at his or her own hand. The student should say "down" when the movement goes down, or "up" when the movement goes up. Have the student practice the movement, verbalizing the directions, for several days. Then have the student remove the auditory clue and make the movement while looking at the model, but not at the hand. Finally, have the student follow the same procedures with crayon, on newsprint or paper. Figure 11–18 illustrates handwriting movements to demonstrate.

The second level requires the student to repeat the same procedures as level 1, but this time the student looks at the paper as he or she forms the movements. At this level, pay attention to correct posture and the slant of the paper. Make lines on the desk with masking tape to guide paper placement for the student, or line paper with three different colors. You might use the colors of traffic lights, with green at the top, yellow in the center, and red at the bottom. This makes it easy for the child to verbalize directions such as, "Put my pencil on the green line, draw it straight down through the yellow line, and stop on the red line."

During the third-level activities, have the student move on to letter formation at the chalkboard, using the procedures described in level 1 for movements. After the student uses the chalkboard, have him or her go to one-inch lined paper, then to regular lined paper. The sequence for this fourth level follows:

1. Name the letter; for example, "The name of this letter is *b*."
2. Discuss the form of the letter while the child looks at it. "How many shapes are there in *b*?" (A straight stick and a circle or ball.)
3. Make the letter for the student to see. You can use a transparency, and make each part with a different color.
4. Show the student the directions for each movement in the formation of the letter, and discuss the directions.
5. Develop a kinesthetic feel for the letter form by tracing a raised, script letter with a finger. You can make raised letters by placing a few drops of food coloring in a glue dispenser and writing the word in glue on a strip of tagboard. Goodson and Floyd (1974) recommends a kinesthetic method that makes use of a sandpaper board. In this method, 9- by 11-inch pieces of coarse sandpaper are mounted on a piece of board. The student places a sheet of paper over the sandpaper board, and uses a crayon to write the troublesome letter correctly. He or she removes the paper and traces the letter with a finger. Also, you may make alphabets using trays filled with

plaster of Paris. While the plaster is still damp, write the letters with a blunt pencil or stick in cursive or manuscript alphabet. The student can use this tray to trace the letters with a pencil or crayon. Trays are reusable and usually quite inexpensive.

6. Place a model of the letter on each student's paper. (Students with learning problems may have difficulty copying from the chalkboard.) Discuss with the student the letter form and direction. Have the student make the letter while looking at the model instead of at his or her hand.
7. Help each student compare the letter with the model. (Close supervision is necessary.)
8. You or the student may use auditory clues to help with letter formation. If necessary, also hold the student's hand to help with the formation.
9. Have the student write the letter on the chalkboard without looking at the model.
10. Have the student write the letter on paper without a model and without watching his or her hand.
11. Have the student write the letter on paper while watching the paper.

You can use the same procedures to introduce the writing movements in cursive. These begin with chalkboard activities and progress to newsprint and paper. The movements in Figure 11–19 are suggested for levels 1 and 2. As you can see, this is a complicated approach to handwriting instruction, and it is not necessary or desirable to use it with every student in a class. It is designed for those who demonstrate difficulties in learning to write by more conventional approaches. You can use the steps for individual instruction, or for small-group instruction of six or seven pupils. It is too difficult to supervise the movements of larger groups in this detailed approach.

You can also create transparencies. One set might have the manuscript alphabet, with the different parts of letters shown in different colors, such as two-space-high straight lines, as in *b, d, h, k, l,* and *t,* in blue, and complete circles, as in *a, o, b, d, g, q,* in orange, and so forth. Place these transparencies over the student's letters for checking formation.

Regardless of which specialized approach you find effective with specific children, you should remember Lewis and Doorlag's (1995) advice when they state that adaptations to instruction are essential for children with learning disabilities who are experiencing writing problems. These adaptations include providing prompts, giving additional instruction, and allowing extra guided practice. The prompts recommended by Lewis and Doorlag include dotted lines that students may trace to help them with letter formations, directional arrows that show the correct directions to follow in letter formations, color cues on the paper that illustrate where to start and stop each stroke, color-coded baselines and top lines, heavy-lined baselines, and pale vertical lines to suggest formation and spacing of letters.

Table 11–1 presents characteristics that might interfere with handwriting development in children with learning disabilities and suggests teaching techniques for handwriting instruction. Table 11–2 presents the same information for children with mental disabilities. The techniques for language arts instruction result from research and authorities who work with mainstreamed children.

FIGURE 11–19 Some Movements in Cursive Writing

Table 11–1 Mainstreaming and handwriting for children with learning disabilities

Characteristics of Children with Learning Disabilities	Teaching Techniques for Language Arts Instruction
1. Deficits in visual perception, visual-motor integration, and fine-motor skills (Harber, 1979; Lyon & Watson, 1981).	1. Trace on acetate (Spache, 1976). Use four developmental levels suggested by Hammill and Bartel (1975). Use directional arrows, color cues, and numbers to help children trace (Lewis & Doorlag, 1995). Cut with scissors, draw outlines of patterns, and try simple paper folding (Lerner, 1976). Use biofeedback training to help children relax their writing forearm and control forearm tension voluntarily (Carter & Russell, 1980). Provide handwriting readiness activities that encourage development of fine-motor control: coloring, painting, finger painting, chalkboard activities. Use activities that facilitate hand-muscle development (Naus, 2000). Let children with severe motor difficulties use an electric typewriter or word processor (Lerner, 1976; Lewis & Doorlag, 1995).
2. Orientation confusions characterized by rotations and reversals of letters and words (Frith & Vogel, 1980).	2. Add color cues to letter formations (Lewis & Doorlag, 1995). Analyze the situation and try to identify specific bases for children's rotation and reversal errors: a. *Rotation:* Point out that the letter may look better rotated, but it is usually written so it looks upside down. Change to a slanted easel so there is a definite top and bottom. b. *Reversal:* Train children in the importance of left-right orientation of symbols (Frith & Vogel, 1980).

Table 11–2 Mainstreaming and handwriting for children with mental disabilities

Characteristics of Children with Mental Disabilities	Teaching Techniques for Language Arts Instruction
1. Visual discrimination deficits that cause difficulty identifying letters (Adams, Taylor, & Glendenning, 1982).	1. Use positive reinforcement during practice to increase letter discrimination capability (Adams et al., 1982).
2. Tendency to have motor coordination handicaps (Gearheart, Weishahn, & Gearheart, 1992).	2. Provide opportunities for development of motor skills that are prerequisites for writing. Include simplified games and specific motor exercises such as hopscotch, bag throwing, and jumping games to promote eye–hand coordination (Gearheart et al., 1992).

SUMMARY

Modern instruction considers handwriting a tool for personal communication. This viewpoint stresses that handwriting should be taught within the broader context of composition rather than as isolated drill. This chapter stresses readiness for formal handwriting, which includes use of space, interest in handwriting, left-to-right progression, and fine-motor control. Research indicates that the most efficient handwriting instruction utilizes an individualized diagnostic approach, but apparently, few elementary schools actually use such procedures.

The chapter discusses handwriting instruction in terms of readiness, printing (manuscript writing), and cursive writing. Readiness activities that develop a child's understanding of a need and purpose for writing are necessary, as are activities that develop fine-motor skills and readiness for letter formations.

Beginning teachers must become proficient in the manuscript or cursive alphabet taught in area schools. The chapter presents a letter-analysis approach for instruction of printing. It describes evaluative scales and informal means of assessing letter formation, slant, spacing, and line quality. Information on the most frequent types of letter-formation errors is available, although an internalized scale developed through training and experience may eventually help a teacher the most.

The transition to cursive writing usually takes place sometime early in the third grade, although research does not point to any advantage in changing from manuscript to cursive writing and indicates that the time of transition is not very important. The chapter describes an approach that helps children understand the similarities and differences between manuscript and cursive writing.

Few standardized tests are available for assessing handwriting. Consequently, you should gather handwriting samples informally under conditions of normal, best, and fastest writing.

Left-handed writers are no longer required to forgo their hand preference; however, they do need specific instruction in developing their handwriting skills. The chapter includes a set of procedures to follow when working with left-handers.

Since the inception of mainstreaming, regular classroom teachers have been providing instruction for many children who used to be in self-contained special education classes. Research indicates a kinesthetic approach is effective for teaching handwriting to students with learning disabilities. Such an approach begins with teaching the movements of handwriting and extends to teaching the formation of letters.

ADDITIONAL HANDWRITING ACTIVITIES

1. Compile a list of readiness activities appropriate for children who have not developed large-motor and fine-motor coordination.
2. Develop a creative activity that reinforces readiness skills related to basic manuscript strokes.
3. Go to the library and locate language arts curriculum guides published by several school districts. What are the goals for handwriting instruction? What recommendations are included for instructional strategies? How much time is recommended for instruction at various grade levels? Is handwriting taught in isolated drills, or is the subject emphasized during meaningful writing activities?

4. Use ERIC to locate programs designed to improve handwriting capabilities, such as Keller's (2001) "Handwriting Club: Using Sensory Integration Strategies to Improve Handwriting." Describe the program. Do you believe it would be successful? Why or why not? Report your findings to your language arts class.
5. Secure scope and sequence charts from several published handwriting programs. Compare the programs according to expectations at specific levels, pace of instruction, instructional objectives, instructional emphasis, and evaluation.
6. Collect handwriting samples from first-, second-, and third-grade children and analyze them. What developmental changes do the writing samples illustrate?

BIBLIOGRAPHY

Adams, Gary L.; Taylor, Ronald L.; and Glendenning, Nancy J. "Remediation of Letter Reversals." *Perceptual and Motor Skills* 54 (June 1982): 1002.

Askov, Eunice; Otto, Wayne; and Askov, Warren. "A Decade of Research in Handwriting." *Journal of Educational Research* 64 (November 1970): 100–11.

Birch, H. G.; and Lefford, A. "Visual Discrimination, Inter-sensory Integration, and Voluntary Motor Control." *Monographs of the Society for Research in Child Development* 32 (1967): 2.

Burns, Paul C.; and Broman, Betty L. *The Language Arts in Childhood Education,* 5th ed. Chicago: Rand McNally & Co., 1983.

Campbell, Joseph. *Oriental Mythology: The Masks of God.* New York: Penguin, 1976.

Carter, John L.; and Russell, Harold. "Biofeedback and Academic Attainment in LD Children." *Academic Therapy* 15 (March 1980): 483–86.

de Ajuriaguerra, J.; and Auzias, M. "Preconditions for the Development of Writing in the Child." In *Foundations of Language Development,* Vol. 2, edited by Eric and Elizabeth Lenneberg. New York: Academic Press, 1975.

Dobbie, Linda; and Askov, Eunice. "Progress for Handwriting Research in the 1980s and Future Prospects." *Journal of Educational Research* 88 (July/August 1995): 339–51.

Donoghue, M. *The Child and the English Language Arts.* Dubuque, Iowa: Brown, 1990.

Durkin, Dolores. *Children Who Read Early.* New York: Teachers College Press, 1966.

Farris, P. "Views and Other Views: Handwriting Instruction Should Not Become Extinct." *Language Arts* 68 (1991): 312–14.

Frith, Uta; and Vogel, Juliet M. *Some Perceptual Prerequisites for Reading.* Newark, Del.: International Reading Association, 1980.

Furner, Beatrice A. "Recommended Instructional Procedures in a Method Emphasizing the Perceptual-Motor Nature of Learning in Handwriting." *Elementary English* 46 (December 1969): 1021–30.

Gearheart, Bill R.; Weishahn, Mel; and Gearheart, Carol J. *The Exceptional Student in the Regular Classroom,* 5th ed. Upper Saddle River, N.J.: Merrill/Prentice Hall 1992.

Goodson, Roger A.; and Floyd, Barbara J. *Individualizing Instruction in Spelling: A Practical Guide.* Minneapolis: Denison & Co., 1974.

Graham, Steve; Weintrab, Naomi; and Berninger, Virginia. "Which Manuscript Letters Do Primary Children Write Legibly?" *Educational Psychology* 93 (September 2001): 488–97.

Graves, Donald H. "Research Update—Handwriting Is for Writing." *Language Arts* 55 (March 1978): 393–99.

Hammill, Donald D.; and Bartel, Nettie R. *Teaching Children with Learning and Behavioral Problems.* Boston: Allyn & Bacon, 1975.

Harber, Jean R. "Differentiating LD and Normal Children: The Utility of Selected Perceptual and Perceptual-Motor Tests." *Learning Disabled Quarterly* 2 (Spring 1979): 70–75.

Hodges, R. "The Conventions of Writing." In *Handbook of Research on Teaching the English Language Arts,* 2nd ed., edited by J. Flood, J. Jensen, D. Lapp, and J. Squire. Mahwah, N. J.: Lawrence Erlbaum, 2003, pp. 1052–63.

Keller, Melissa. "Handwriting Club: Using Sensory Integration Strategies to Improve Handwriting." *Intervention in School & Clinic* 37 (September 2001): 9–15.

Lerner, Janet W. *Children with Learning Disabilities,* 2nd ed. Boston: Houghton Mifflin, 1976.

Lewis, Edward R.; and Lewis, Hilda P. "Which Manuscript Letters Are Hard for First Graders?" *Elementary English* 41 (December 1964): 855–58.

Lewis, Rena; and Doorlag, Donald. *Teaching Special Students in the Mainstream,* 4th ed. Upper Saddle River, N.J.: Merrill/Prentice Hall, 1995.

Lyon, Reid; and Watson, Bill. "Empirically Derived Subgroups of Learning Disabled Readers: Diagnostic Characteristics." *Journal of Learning Disabilities* 14 (May 1981): 256–61.

Martlew, Margaret. "Handwriting and Spelling: Dyslexic Children's Abilities Compared With Children of the Same Chronological Age and Younger Children of the Same Spelling Level." *British Journal of Educational Psychology* 62 (1992): 375–90.

Naus, Jane M. "Helping Hands: A World of Manipulatives to Boost Handwriting Skills." *Teaching Exceptional Children* 32 (March/April 2000): 64–70.

Otto, Wayne; and Smith, Richard. *Corrective and Remedial Teaching.* Boston: Houghton Mifflin, 1980.

Reger, R.; Schroeder, W.; and Uschold, K. *Special Education: Children with Learning Problems.* New York: Oxford University Press, 1968.

Spache, George. *Investigating the Issues of Reading Disabilities.* Boston: Allyn & Bacon, 1976.

Stewig, John Warren; and Nordberg, Beverly. *Exploring Language Arts in the Elementary School.* Belmont, Calif.: Wadsworth, 1995.

Tompkins, Gail E. "Let's Go on a Bear Hunt! A Fresh Approach to Penmanship Drill." *Language Arts* 57 (October 1980): 782–86.

Yardley, Alice. *Exploration and Language.* New York: Citation Press, 1973.

CHILDREN'S LITERATURE REFERENCES

Donoughue, Carol. *The Mystery of the Hieroglyphs: The Story of the Rosetta Stone and the Race to Decipher Egyptian Hieroglyphs.* New York: Oxford University Press, 1999.

Gollub, Matthew, translated by. *Cool Melons—Turn to Frogs!: The Life and Poems of Issa.* Illustrated by Kazuko G. Stone, calligraphy by Keiko Smith. New York: Lee & Low, 1998.

Levine, Arthur A. *The Boy Who Drew Cats.* Illustrated by Frederic Clement. New York: Dial Press, 1993.

Lewis, John. *The Chinese Word for Horse and Other Stories.* Illustrated by Peter Rigby. New York: Schocken, 1980.

Young, Ed. *The Lost Horse.* San Diego: Harcourt Brace, 1998.

———. *Mouse Match.* San Diego: Harcourt Brace, 1997.

Working with Children Whose First Language Is Not English and Children from Multicultural Backgrounds

After completing this chapter on children whose first language is not English and those from multicultural backgrounds, you will be able to:

1. Describe the differences between a linguistically different and a linguistically deficient concept of language.

2. Understand the problems associated with the use of standardized tests when evaluating children who do not speak standard English.

3. Demonstrate an informal method for evaluating language usage.

4. Describe several factors, such as teacher attitudes and environment, that influence the performance of children whose first language is not English.

5. Describe how to utilize knowledge of the values and learning styles of Latino children for effective education.

6. Describe the educational alternatives suggested by linguists and educators and the rationales for each approach.

7. Demonstrate the teaching of a language experience approach and understand its philosophy, its use with children whose first language is not English, and its integration of writing, oral discussion, and reading.

8. Describe the reasons for developing multicultural education.

9. Develop a multicultural storytelling festival.

10. Develop multicultural units.

11. List criteria for evaluating multicultural literature.

12. Develop a unit that teaches students to authenticate multicultural literature.

*T*he United States and Canada are multicultural nations whose populations include Europeans, Native Americans, African-Americans, Latinos, and Asians. Many of our students come to school with an understanding of a language and a culture that is different from that of the mainstream educational system. The need for cross-cultural understanding that goes beyond the borders of the United States and Canada is emphasized in the following introduction to *The Dictionary of Global Culture*, edited by Kwame Anthony Appiah and Henry Louis Gates, Jr. (1996): "In the year 2000, half the world's people will be Asian, and one eighth will be African; a majority, too, will be non-Christian. And of the world's twenty largest cities, none will be in Europe or the United States. . . . [W]e Americans can no longer afford to be limited to an understanding of culture that begins and ends in the West" (front flap).

The need for cross-cultural understanding and for adaptations in the language arts increases with the demographic shifts that are occurring in the United States. For example, Booth (1998) stresses that the United States is experiencing its second great wave of immigration. The first wave occurred between 1890 and 1920, when immigrants came mostly from European countries such as Germany, Poland, Ireland, Hungary, and Russia. According to Booth, this immigration pattern has now changed: "The overwhelming majority of immigrants come from Asia and Latin America—Mexico, the Central American countries, the Philippines, Korea, and Southeast Asia" (p. 7). Educating the children of these immigrants requires cross-cultural understanding, just as it was needed in the past. According to Hoffman and Pearson (2000), "it is projected that between 2000 and 2020 there will be 47% more Hispanic children aged 5–13 in the United States than are there today" (p. 28). These authors conclude that educators must have knowledge about the cultural and linguistic diversity that is found in the schools.

Reading, writing, and mathematics scores are lower for low-income-family African-American and Latino students. Dropout rates are also related to school achievement. A study by the National School Board Organization (National Public Radio, 1992) reported that dropout rates are 40 percent among Latino students. This is especially alarming because the same study reported that Latino populations have increased in schools by 103 percent. Native American students may be even more at risk than other students. McCarty (1993) concludes that "American Indian students are significantly overrepresented in low-ability, skill-and-drill tracks and, at the same time, experience the highest school dropout rates in the nation" (p. 182).

Educators who are concerned with developing a quality educational system for all students face issues related to linguistically different speech patterns, non-English speech, and cultural diversity. A heightened sensitivity to the needs of all people in American society has led to the realization that language arts programs should heighten self-esteem and create a respect for the individuals, contributions, and the values of all cultures. This chapter considers the selection of literature that presents the values, diversity, and contributions of African-Americans, Native Americans, Latinos, and Asians.

Children Whose First Language Is Not English

The term *dialect* is often used to describe linguistically different speech patterns, although everyone speaks some sort of dialect. The term *dialect* usually means a distinct variety of a language used by a group of people who share interests, values, goals, and communication. Dialects differ from one another in pronunciation, grammar, and vocabulary. The United States contains a variety of regional dialects. One can often tell by listening to people whether they come from New England, the Midwest, the deep South, the Far West, and so forth. Farr (1991) expands the definition of dialect: "[It includes] either a regional variety of a language (e.g., Southern English in the United States) or a social variety of a language (e.g., African-American vernacular English in the United States). Both kinds of varieties, of course, coexist with usually one 'official' or 'national' language of a country (in English-speaking countries, some form of 'standard' English). It is important to point out that standard, national languages often start out as regional dialects themselves, becoming the national standard because of social, economic, and political power of the region in which they are used" (p. 365). Ball and Farr (2003) state, "In general these varieties do not differ greatly from standard English, but instead are closely related to it with different versions of the same rules that govern all varieties of English. As we realign our attitudes concerning language use with the realities of our changing population, these varieties will no longer be viewed as low-status or nonstandard varieties" (p. 436).

Beginning in the 1960s, most American dialect studies began to examine the speech of urban centers, such as New York, Chicago, and Washington, D.C., investigating the influences of social class, urbanization, race, economic levels, and group values. Because the majority of people living in inner cities are black, this type of nonstandard English came to be referred to most commonly as "black English." Yet, the English spoken and taught in most American schools, and recognized by most American teachers, is standard English.

Many studies have focused on the low achievement of inner-city children. In 1969, Cohen reported that 83 percent of disadvantaged African-American children and 45 percent of disadvantaged white children in New York City were one to three years behind grade level in reading by third grade. Eisenberg's (1974) comparative study of metropolitan, commuter county, suburban, and independent schools showed that metropolitan schools had failure rates two-thirds higher than did the commuter county, three times higher than did the suburban schools, and more than fifty times higher than did the independent schools. Although the achievement of African-American students is still lower than the achievement of white students, there has been a steady decline in the achievement differences between blacks and whites. For example, Burton and Jones (1982) analyzed data based on the National Assessment of Educational Progress in reading, writing, mathematics, science, and social studies. They concluded that achievement differences had decreased between 1970 and 1980. An increased understanding of linguistically different speech patterns may account for educational improvements.

Low socioeconomic levels, however, continue to be closely related to poor academic achievement. Chall and Curtis (1991) state that almost every study that relates socioeconomic status to school achievement finds that middle-class children are more advanced than children from low-income families. Following a study of the results reported in various National Assessment of Educational Progress reports, Chall and Curtis conclude: "In the United States, the relationship between socioeconomic status and reading and writing achievement is most clearly demonstrated by the results of the National Assessment of Educational Progress (NAEP). On each of its five assessments of reading, from 1971 to 1986, NAEP's results have shown a large gap between the achievement of disadvantaged urban children and their more advantaged age peers. Moreover, the longer that students are in school, the greater this gap becomes, such that by age 17, low socioeconomic children read below the level achieved by advantaged 13-year-olds" (p. 349).

In searching for reasons why lower class students have academic difficulties, many educators are now focusing on the ways in which various social and ethnic groups use oral and written language, their expectations and environments, and their knowledge about language and writing. In reviewing current attitudes toward the role of socioeconomic status in achievement, Chall and Curtis (1991) identify several class differences that may attribute to lower achievement. For example, many children from low-income families come from ethnic groups whose use of language differs from that practiced in schools. Consequently, some educators attribute low reading and writing achievement to a mismatch between the mainstream style of language used in school instruction and the various styles of language used in the group. Another view focuses on the kind of oral language environment that stimulates literacy development. In this view, children from low-income families do poorly because the kind of oral language environment that stimulates literacy development is not as prevalent in their homes as in the homes of middle-class children. Chall and Curtis argue that children from low-income families may go through the same stages of literacy development as their more advantaged peers, but that the growth in some aspect of low-income children's language or literacy development becomes delayed by conditions at home or experiences in school that affect their later development.

Two quite different theories have been proposed to explain the causes of low achievement by many black inner-city children. In the early 1960s, psychologists discovered that on standardized language tests, these children were unable to reach the standardized norms. Thus, psychologists such as Bereiter and Englemann (1966) and Bernstein (1961) argued that many African-American inner-city children lack a fully developed language system. They argued that black children often come to school with a language system that must be remediated if the children are to progress in school. Intensive language remediation programs such as Englemann's and Osborn's DISTAR reflect this view.

Other educators oppose this theory of a language deficit. In the late 1960s and 1970s, linguists conducted much research pertaining to speakers of black English. They analyzed speech samples under various conditions, studied black dialects, and examined in great detail how those dialects differed from standard English dialects in terms of phonology (speech sounds); morphology (word forming, including inflection, derivation, and compounding); and syntax (the way words are put together to form phrases, clauses, and sentences). Extensive research by Labov (1969, 1970, 1971, 1973) and by Baratz and Shuy (1969) demonstrated that children who speak black English have a system that is fully developed but different from that of standard English. These investigators disagree with the deficit theory, which stresses illogical grammatical structures in black English. In fact, these linguists maintain that black English is just as logical and consistent as standard English. Labov found that structures of black English function in ways similar to the structures in other languages. For example, the use of the double negative to signify negation, which appears in black English, also appears in French and German.

In one study, Baratz (1969) asked black-English-speaking children and standard-English-speaking children to repeat sentences read to them in both standard and nonstandard English. She found that black-English-speaking students had consistent verbal responses. For example, 97 percent of the black-English-speaking children responded in the same way to the sentence "I asked Tom if he wanted to go to the picture that was playing at the Howard." The black-English-speaking children responded with "I aks Tom did he wanna go to the picture that be playing at the Howard." Sixty percent of the black-English-speaking children responded to the sentence "Does Deborah like to play with the girl that sits next to her in school?" by repeating "Do Deborah like to play wif the girl what sit next to her in school?"

The white standard-English-speaking children also followed a definite pattern by translating black English back into standard English when they were asked to repeat sentences. Seventy-eight percent of the standard-English-speaking children repeated the sentence "I aks Tom do he wanna go to the picture that be playing at the Howard" as "I asked Tom if he wanted to go to the picture that was playing at the Howard." Likewise, 68 percent of the standard-English-speaking children repeated the sentence "Do Deborah like to play wif the girl what sit next to her at school?" as "Does Deborah like to play with the girl that sits next to her at school?"

This study not only demonstrated the logic and consistency of speech patterns, according to Baratz (1969), but it also demonstrated that the dialect of black-English-speaking children interferes when these children attempt to use standard English. Problems as to how much interference results and how to provide effective education for speakers of nonstandard English have not as yet been resolved. According to Farr (1991), three positions (mostly politically motivated) relate to teaching students who are not in the language and cultural mainstream: (1) an eradication approach, which attempts to replace certain speech patterns with standard ones; (2) a biloquialism or biadialectism or biculturalism approach, which calls for learning new standard patterns without eliminating the old nonstandard ones or developing negative attitudes toward the nonmainstream cultures and dialects; and (3) an appreciation-of-differences approach that seeks to enlighten mainstream populations about variations in language rather than change any language spoken by various dialect populations. Farr states that debate about these positions has continued for two decades. She concludes that the second, or biloquialism, position is the most reasonable: "Since all speakers, mainstream and nonmainstream alike, shift among more or less formal styles, depending on context, to some degree, this position should be a relatively natural one. It also has the advantage of appearing to be the most reasonable position, presenting a compromise between the two more extreme positions of eradication and appreciation of dialect differences" (p. 366). Farr also maintains that the problems related to teaching standard English and literacy are more complicated than were originally thought.

According to linguist Guy Bailey (personal communication, 1983), many unanswered questions are related to how or if oral language interferes with writing. Bailey states:

> Over the last decade an increasing number of scholars have suggested that students' oral language interferes with their writing: the syntactic structures and coherence devices characteristic of the oral code are used in lieu of those characteristics of the written code. This interference apparently involves both the intrusion of oral styles in writing (for example, failure to include explicit reference and coherence devices in compositions) and the influence of dialect (the absence of tense markers, for instance) or in some cases the student's first language. However, linguists have yet to specify the exact relationships between speech and writing because they lack comparable data from both modes. (p. 1)

Many linguists and educators believe that black English is systematically structured; therefore, it is different and not deficient. But even among those who agree on "different" versus "deficient," there is little agreement on the best educational approach to use to improve the school achievement of black-English-speaking children. Suggested educational alternatives include (1) contrastive analysis of black-English and standard-English sentence structures, (2) language experience approaches, (3) dialect reading and speaking of conventional instructional materials, (4) numerous opportunities for functional and interactive communication, and (5) abundant experiences with written texts. Evidence suggests that such factors as testing bias, teacher attitudes, early identification, parent involvement, early intervention, and long-term intervention programs can influence the achievement of linguistically different children.

Assessment Issues

The results of studies conducted in the 1960s and 1970s resulted in criticism that many commonly used standardized tests are both culturally and linguistically biased in favor of middle-class, standard-English-speaking children. In fact, Bartel, Grill, and Bryen (1973) went so far as to suggest that no standardized tests are appropriate for black-English-speaking children and that use of available tests may result in extreme errors in student placement. These studies also resulted in many nontraditional tests that might be used to acquire language samples.

Nontraditional Tests

Some educators suggest the use of nontraditional forms of assessment to measure cognitive ability and language. Adler (1973) recommends such tests for evaluating linguistically different children. He believes that language tests should consist of analysis of spontaneous speech in naturalistic settings. In fact, the best information about verbal capacity may be obtained by asking children questions that are interesting to them. For this reason, tests should encourage student involvement. For example, the Picture Story Language Test by Myklebust is designed to encourage the telling of a story. When administering any test to a linguistically different child, Adler urges examiners to repeat directions and use practice questions to ascertain whether the child actually understands what is expected. Examiners will probably need to use more oral directions and examples than are provided with the test manual and must be able to understand nonstandard speech.

Mantell (1974) made several suggestions for obtaining language samples and evaluating the language patterns of linguistically different children by nonstandardized methods. One device she recommends is photography of people or places familiar to the children. In this situation, a teacher would ask open-ended questions about the pictures, such as "What is the person in the photograph doing? Why is he doing that? How does the person look? How would he talk about himself? What would the person in the photograph do if . . . ?" Familiar photographs motivate children to talk about something they know and feel comfortable talking about.

A second device for obtaining language samples is what Mantell (1974) calls "The Faceless X." For this informal test, a teacher draws a circular face on a transparency. Students are asked to fill in expressions using eyebrows, mouth, hairstyle, skin color, headdresses, and so forth. The teacher then asks open-ended questions about the face. This activity can also provide insights into attitudes and biases of students.

As a third testing device, Mantell (1974) suggests role-playing in order to analyze a student's ability to alter language according to the requirements of a specific situation. Role-playing situations can be formal or informal. A student who role-plays an interview with the school principal for an article in the school paper or an interview with an employer for a part-time job displays an ability or inability to use more formal language. In contrast, role-playing of an argument between a brother and sister over whose turn it is to do the dinner dishes allows analysis of the student's ability to use casual language. During role-playing situations, ask other students to watch for specific language usage. Note their ability to recognize various usage situations.

Several educators recommend modifying scoring procedures for reading tests so that errors attributable to dialect differences are not counted as reading errors. Hunt (1974) found that black, inner-city third and fourth graders scored significantly higher on the Gray Oral Reading Test when responses reflecting black English variations in language were not counted as errors than they did when the tests were scored according to the directions in the test manual. The Goodman Miscue Analysis also stresses the importance of recognizing dialect differences in reading. It suggests that dialect errors in oral reading not be counted as comparable to errors that change the meaning of the selection. To do this, of course, a teacher must be knowledgeable about the dialect.

Another researcher (Hutchinson, 1972) found that inclusion or deletion of dialect-related items in a word-discrimination test also influenced the grade-level scores of the students taking the test. When dialect-related items were included in the test, 40 percent of the black, inner-city, higher ability third graders scored below grade level; when the dialect-related items were removed, only 2.6 percent of these students scored below grade level. It is important, then, to examine tests for possible unintentional bias before administering them to linguistically different children.

Linguists have provided a great deal of knowledge about the differences between standard English and black English. They recommend that teachers become aware of these differences and utilize their knowledge to more fairly assess the achievement of a black-English-speaking child. Teachers need to become familiar with differences in both pronunciation and syntax. It is very important that teachers distinguish between differences in dialect pronunciation and erroneous interpretations of test material. Only a teacher familiar with the differences between black and standard English can accurately evaluate the language patterns of a black-English-speaking student and establish priorities for effective instruction in oral language, writing, and reading. Tables 12–1 and 12–2 provide guidelines for analysis of the major differences between pronunciation and syntax.

The type of informal testing recommended by many educators requires that teachers understand whatever linguistically different speech patterns the children use. The following resources will also be useful:

- "Major Differences Between Standard English and Black English," in *Reading and the Black English Speaking Child* (Harber & Beatty, 1978), pp. 46–47.
- "Black English: A Descriptive Guide for the Teacher," in *Black Dialects and Reading* (Fryburg, 1974), pp. 190–96.

Table 12–1   Phonological differences between standard English and black English

Feature	Standard English	Black English
Simplification of consonant clusters	test	tes
	past	pas
th sounds		
voiceless *th* in initial position	think	tink
voiced *th* in initial position	the	de
voiceless *th* in medial position	nothing	nofin
th in final position	tooth	toof
r and *l*		
in postvocalic position	sister	sistah
	nickel	nickuh
in final position	Saul	saw
Devoicing of final *b*, *d*, and *g*	cab	cap
	bud	but
	pig	pik
Nasalization		
ing suffix	doing	doin
i and *e* before a nasal	pen	pin
Stress—absence of the first syllable of a multisyllabic word when the first syllable is unstressed	about	'bout
Plural marker	three birds	three bird
	the books	de book
Possessive marker	the boy's hat	de boy hat
Third person singular marker	He works here	He work here
Past tense—simplification of final consonant clusters	passed	pass
	loaned	loan

Informal Assessment: A Portfolio Approach

Many of the informal assessment techniques currently being recommended by educators are useful for teachers of children from multicultural backgrounds. For example, Goodman (1991) recommends using such informal evaluations as portfolios, checklists, inventories, and observations. Particularly useful are individual portfolios in which teachers keep examples of each student's writing, interests, backgrounds, comprehension levels, processes for gaining comprehension, and responses to different types of literature and literacy activities (see Norton, 1992). Pikulski (1989) recommends this approach highly:

> One of the most dynamic assessment concepts currently being discussed in our field is that of a portfolio approach to the assessment of reading and literacy. Since there

Table 12–2   Syntactic differences between standard English and black English

Feature	Standard English	Black English
Linking verb	He is going.	He goin'.
		He is goin'.
Pronomial apposition	That teacher yells at the kids.	Dat teachah, she yell at de kid.
Agreement of subject and third-person singular verb	She runs home.	She run home.
	She has a bike.	She have a bike.
Irregular verb forms	They rode their bikes.	Dey rided der bike.
Future form	I will go home.	I'm a go home.
"If" construction	I asked if he did it.	I aks did he do it.
Indefinite article	I want an apple.	I want a apple.
Negation	I don't have any.	I don't got none.
Pronoun form	We have to do it.	Us got to do it.
Copula (verb "to be")	He is here all the time.	He be here.
Prepositions	Put the cat out of the house.	Put de cat out de house.
	The dress is made of wool.	De dress is made outta wool.

are no tests or test materials that are specifically associated with this approach, it has the potential for placing teachers and students—not tests and test scores—at the very center of the assessment process. (p. 81)

Diverse samples of literacy events, which are collected as students interact with various aspects of the language arts, become what Pikulski refers to as "the fullest, most ecologically valid approach that can be taken to assessment" (p. 81).

When students are considering the development of a portfolio, have them imagine themselves in a profession in which portfolios are popular and extremely useful. For example, have them think of themselves as artists, photographers, or authors who want to demonstrate their talents and breadth of experience. They might ask: "What examples would best show our talents? What examples might show how we have progressed in our chosen fields?" Then, they can think about what might be included in a portfolio of language arts to illustrate their growing understanding of and appreciation for oral language, writing, listening, reading, and literature.

Valencia (1990) provides guidelines for development and management of portfolios, beginning with the selection of large expandable folders to hold samples of work that reflect the goals of the program. She recommends that states, school districts, or individual teachers develop goals for instruction and then decide what information would help to assess those goals. The folders usually include samples of work chosen by the teacher or the student, the teacher's observational notes, the student's self-evaluations, and the progress notes contributed collaboratively by student and teacher. The portfolio could also include results of classroom tests, various written responses, checklists, and audio or video tapes.

The selections should relate closely to the goals and priorities for instruction. For example, by collecting both required evidence and supporting evidence that instructional goals are being achieved, teachers can look systematically at the progress of the students and the effectiveness of the language arts program. Valencia maintains that supporting evidence is especially important because it shows the depth and variety of a student's literacy abilities. In addition to collecting and assessing information in portfolios, Valencia recommends that teachers and students meet every few weeks to discuss progress, add notes, and decide what additional materials should be in the portfolios. At the end of the year, teachers and students can decide which materials will be taken home and which will be kept to show progress into the next year. The portfolios also can be used during conferences with parents and administrators.

For Your Development

1. Review an often-used standardized test. Look at both the pictures and vocabulary. Find items that you feel might be biased because of a child's experience or English usage. Share your findings with your language arts class.
2. If you are teaching children, try one of the nonstandardized testing techniques suggested in this chapter. If you are not teaching at this time, develop a series of pictures and questions or a role-playing strategy, and present the informal techniques to a group of your peers.
3. Begin a portfolio by collecting the works of a student that include various examples of speaking, listening, writing, and reading. Assess changes in the student's ability as shown in portfolio examples over time. Which portfolio examples are the most useful? Why?

Teacher Attitudes

Farr's (1991) review of research associated with dialects, culture, and teaching of English concludes that ethnosensitivity—the understanding that one's views of the world, or ways of using language, are not necessarily shared by others—is the most important principle of effective instruction for students from diverse cultures. Consequently, teachers must have a deep understanding of cultural and linguistic differences, especially among the students in their classrooms. This is especially important if teachers and students are from different cultural and ethnic groups.

The literature and research on teacher attitudes toward children from diverse backgrounds are quite startling. Teachers often not only react negatively toward students who speak nonstandard English but also rate them as lower in class, less intelligent, and less able to achieve academically than their standard-English-speaking peers. For example, in an early study, Crowl and MacGinitie (1974) audiotaped both black and white ninth-grade boys responding with identically worded answers to questions asked in school. Experienced white teachers were then asked to evaluate the appropriateness of the answers. The teachers assigned significantly higher grades to the answers given by the white students than to the identical answers given by the African-American students. Similar attitudes exist among elementary school teachers. Studies in the 1980s found similar results. Watson-Thompson (1985) found that both black and white elementary school teachers expressed negative attitudes toward the use of black English.

There is no doubt that negative teacher attitudes affect the teaching that takes place in classrooms. This author has observed classrooms in which negative and positive attitudes

Interaction with teachers and in small groups is important for students with limited English proficiency.

toward children from diverse backgrounds have been openly displayed. One teacher of mostly African-American, lower-socioeconomic-class children, for example, mentioned that she taught her twenty-five students as one group because testing indicated they were all at a very low level of ability. She implied that one could not expect much from a class made up of mostly students from diverse cultures. In contrast, another teacher divided a similar group of students from diverse cultures into ability groups and taught highly motivating lessons. This teacher felt that the students had a great deal of potential that required exceptional teaching. She not only accepted nonstandard reading renditions from her black-English-speaking students, but also spoke Spanish for the benefit of her Mexican-American students. She encouraged her students to interact with other students during numerous oral and written activities. She praised them as she discussed their work and encouraged them to work cooperatively. The atmosphere in the room was so positive that one could almost feel the learning that was taking place.

Teacher attitudes about linguistically different speech also influence oral reading activities. A popular method of checking oral reading ability is to have a student read a selection to the teacher. In fact, this activity is duplicated millions of times each day in classrooms across the nation. During oral reading activities, teachers are not usually as concerned with correcting errors that do not change meaning as they are with correcting errors that do result in meaning change. However, in a study by Cunningham (1977), 78 percent of the teachers indicated that they would correct dialect errors that did not change meaning, whereas only 27 percent indicated that they would correct nondialect errors that did not change meaning. Consequently, Cunningham recommends that teacher training stress the meaning equivalence between standard and black English and the grammatical nature of black English. If a teacher spends a great deal of reading-instruction time correcting dialect, it is questionable that the children are receiving effective reading instruction.

In a more recent study, Rankin and Parish (1994) assessed both students and teachers to discover the support systems, self-concepts, and level of school adjustment of European American students and minority students. They conclude: "These results suggest that European-American students continue encountering favorable circumstances and consequently manifest academically appropriate behaviors and fairly high self-concepts. Unfortunately, the reverse is the case for the African-American students surveyed in this study, with their Native American and Hispanic-American counterparts falling in between" (p. 254).

It is clear that both teacher and student attitudes are important to the achievement of students. To improve self-image and academic achievement, teachers need to expect more from students, to judge their capabilities independently of race and socioeconomic status, and to understand and respect their dialect and cultural background.

For Your Development

1. Observe an elementary classroom that includes children from diverse backgrounds. Record in writing the questions asked by the teacher, the responses made by the students, and the responses made to the students by the teacher. Analyze the questions and responses. Does the teacher respond differently to children who speak black English as opposed to those who speak standard English?
2. Interview the children's teacher. Ask the teacher to identify which children he or she expects will do well in the class and those who will not. Is there a relationship between the answers and the speech of the children? Discuss your findings in class. If negative attitudes exist, what is the implication for academic achievement? How will you make sure that all children in your classes receive a quality education?

Environmental Factors

How important is the family environment for fostering student achievement? According to Brause and Mayher (1991), "family structures exert a powerful influence on our students' educational goals and their ability to participate in life at school. The size of the gap between the language and values of the school and those at home predicts the level of success the student is likely to achieve in school. Since the family experience has been such an important predictor of school success, it is essential that educators reconceptualize schooling so that all students, regardless of family background, will have not only access to a high-quality education, but be nurtured to succeed in such a setting" (p. 263). Consequently, successful programs bridge the gaps between experience and expectation.

Results of studies conducted in the 1970s through the 1990s all emphasize the importance of environmental factors. An interesting study by Greenberg and Davison (1972) compares the home environments of high-academic-achieving and low-academic-achieving African-American urban-ghetto children. Findings indicate that the high achievers had a more structured home life, more room, and more books than did low achievers. In addition, the parents of the high achievers showed more respect and concern for their children's education, used less punishment, offered more responses, and demonstrated broader social concerns than did the parents of the low-achieving children. Marzano (1991) points out that within any learning situation, the learner is concerned with environmental factors such as safety, order, and general level of comfort. He contends that "learners ask themselves such questions as whether they are safe and relatively comfortable, and whether the setting is orderly. Negative answers to these questions influence students' propensity to learn" (p. 572).

The current emphasis on day-care centers was instituted in response to a need for early stimulation of children. These programs try to provide stimulation that fosters responses through play materials, experiences, and interactions that help small children discover and manipulate auditory, visual, and tactile stimuli in the environment. Many educational authorities recommend both well-run day-care centers and parental education to help overcome environmental deficiencies.

The literature on children from multicultural backgrounds often mentions that African-American, lower-socioeconomic-class children do not feel that they have as many opportunities as middle-class white or black children. It is frequently suggested that the educational environment of these children must build their self-esteem and use instructional materials that show minorities as contributing members of society.

Characteristics of Effective Intervention Programs

The educational environment is of critical concern for lower-socioeconomic-class children who may not have experienced the benefits of homes that foster academic advancement. Early intervention is particularly important for many children from low-income families. Juel (1988) found that children who enter school with little awareness about relationships between words, letters, and sounds experience problems in learning to read. Children who lack this readiness are more apt to become poor readers and writers by fourth grade. Juel contends that if one waits for readiness skills to emerge without intervening, children who are at risk will not succeed. Slavin and Madden (1989) state that the most important element for prevention of student failure is immediate and intensive assistance. They conclude: "Virtually all the programs found to be instructionally effective for students at risk assess student progress frequently and use the results to modify groupings or instructional content to meet students' individual needs" (p. 11).

Kozol (2000) stresses that many low-income, inner-city children also live in areas in which they do not have access to quality reading materials. He states, "Few forms of theft are quite as damaging to inner-city children as the denial of a well-endowed school library" (p. 47). As we consider effective intervention programs, place yourself in two environments: one with an excellent library complete with a skilled librarian, and one with few books and no librarian to help students and teachers. Where would you rather teach?

In exploring the characteristics of effective elementary-school instruction for children considered at risk, Chall, Jacobs, and Baldwin (1990) analyzed the instruction provided for low-income children who were reading at or above grade level. They found the following effective practices: (1) instruction was provided at or above the children's reading levels; (2) direct instruction was given in text comprehension in reading, social studies, science, health, and other content areas; (3) vocabulary was stressed during content-area, reading, and language arts instruction; (4) diverse materials were provided, including a wide range of reading levels; (5) field trips and other activities exposed students to new experiences and helped build background knowledge; (6) homework included workbooks in the early grades and trade books and content-area materials in the later grades; and (7) children's parents were in direct contact with their teachers. In a later study, Chall and Curtis (1991) found that effective instruction was characterized by "a good, strong start in the primary grades, followed in the intermediate and upper elementary grades by structured and challenging instruction in reading, writing, and vocabulary, opportunities for reading stimulating trade books that varied widely, and many opportunities to practice literacy skills" (p. 352). Ball and Farr (2003) report a successful program that uses interactive technology to link at-risk high school students and preservice teachers by building bridges between the students' home communication skills and the academic literacy skills needed in schools.

Bilingual Education and English as a Second Language

Teachers are increasingly concerned with educating the diverse population of students in American schools. Statistics indicate that cities such as Los Angeles, New York, and Houston have high concentrations of children whose native language is not English; moreover, these populations are expected to grow.

Three terms are frequently used in reference to students whose native language is not English. One term, *limited English proficiency,* frequently abbreviated LEP, refers to students from any group who have not as yet mastered English. The other two terms, *bilingual* and *English as a second language* (ESL), are also common in the literature. Allen (1993) describes what a bilingual program involves:

> The school programs designed to assist children who are in the process of acquiring English as their second language have been organized by focusing on the language in which instruction is delivered. Bilingual approaches involve the use of two languages for the instruction of language minority children. Transitional bilingual programs are ones in which children's first language is used as a medium of instruction until they become fluent enough to receive all their instruction in English. ESL is a part of such programs. It is expected that the amount of instruction offered in the child's native language will decrease as the child's ability to use English increases. Almost all bilingual programs in the United States would be identified as transitional programs. (p. 360)

Researchers are beginning to study characteristics of populations other than Mexican-American students. These studies add to our knowledge and improve teaching for specific groups. For example, Lee et al. (1994) tested Chinese children's acquisition of English articles and found that Chinese children's acquisition of the definite article differed from that of children who speak English as a first language and second-language-learning children from other native language origins. In a study of Navajo children, McCarty (1993) reported that "Bilingual students who have the benefit of cumulative, uninterrupted initial literacy experiences in Navajo make the greatest gains on local and national measures of achievement" (p. 191). In a study of instructional preferences of Cree, Inuit, and Mohawk teachers, McAlpine and Taylor (1993) found that the teaching styles of Native American teachers differ in many ways from patterns of teaching found in other teachers. McAlpine and Taylor emphasize the importance of understanding local social and educational factors that influence the preferences of teachers. Consequently, conducting research and understanding instructional preferences are complex areas.

Because considerable research has been done with Mexican-American students, we will focus on this population in the balance of this section. Clearly, there is reason for concern. According to Cortes (1986), about 45 percent of Latino students do not complete high school, with 40 percent dropping out of school before the tenth grade. In a comparative study of achievement, Maestas (1981) examined the effects of rural and urban backgrounds and ethnic differences on the achievement of high-school seniors. He found that Mexican-American achievement, as measured by the Comprehensive Test of Basic Skills and the Iowa Test of Basic Skills, was lower than that of non–Mexican-Americans. Daniels (1987) also reported this finding in a study that analyzed achievement in Los Angeles.

Mexican-American children who have been raised during preschool years in the traditional culture of the Mexican-American community are required upon entering school to adjust to cultural values, language, and teaching styles that differ from anything they have previously experienced. Such children also must continue to function in their culture, so the adjustment problems for Mexican-American children are prodigious.

This student is using two languages in her bilingual program.

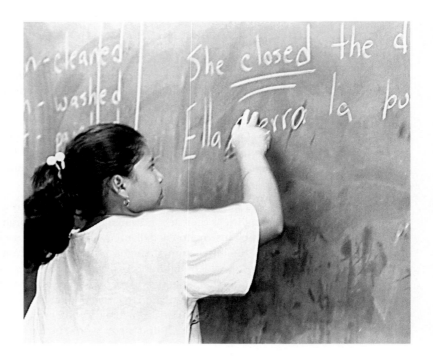

Freedman (1990) maintains that literacy is culturally framed and defined, and that members of diverse cultural groups differ in how they define literacy and what they view as literate behavior. It is important, therefore, to understand how culture shapes the behavior of individuals. Purves and Purves (1986) contend that teachers must investigate the extent to which reading, literature, and writing are valued by the culture. Cultural values and beliefs have deep historical and religious roots. Thus, these authors conclude: "When an individual is transplanted from one culture to another culture, the individual has a great deal both to unlearn and to learn if he or she is to be accepted as a writer in that culture. To some extent, it may be impossible for an individual thoroughly acculturated in one culture to become indistinguishable as a writer from members of another culture" (p. 194).

Critics of the educational system for Mexican-American children maintain that educators have created barriers between the culture of the children and that of the school and have often forced the children to choose between home and school. With the considerable information about the value systems, learning styles, and language of Mexican-Americans that has been gathered since the 1970s, teachers can now effectively improve the learning environment of such children.

Values

Ramírez and Castañeda (1974) identify four major Mexican-American value clusters. First, there are strong family ties in the Mexican-American culture; the needs and interests of the individual are considered secondary to those of the family. Because of these ties, the community and the total ethnic group become an extension of the family. This strong family and community identification contrasts with the stress on a child's separate identity and the development of self-awareness emphasized in most American schools.

Second, interpersonal relationships in Mexican-American communities are characterized by openness, warmth, and commitment to mutual dependence. Emphasis is on development of sensitivity to the feelings and needs of others. Achievements are considered the result of cooperative rather than individual effort. Ramírez and Price-Williams (1974) found that Mexican-American children in Houston scored higher than Anglo-American children on their need to cooperate with other children as well as on their need for sympathetic aid from another person. They also expressed greater need for guidance, direction, and support from authority figures. Consequently, Mexican-American children may achieve better in a cooperative rather than competitive atmosphere. This cultural characteristic of mutual dependence and cooperative achievement contrasts with the individual competition encouraged by American schools.

The third value cluster is role and status definition within the family and the community. Older people hold greater status, and children are expected to model themselves after their parents and other respected members of the community. Mexican-American children may produce higher levels of achievement if teachers take on the role of this status figure and provide a model for the children. The importance of this family and community value is shown in a study by McConnell (1989), who found that the school success of Spanish-speaking migrant children increased when there was interaction between the community and the school. In this program, parents became part of the teaching staff and teachers included people from the ethnic and language group.

The final value cluster is the support and reinforcement of the values provided by the Mexican-Catholic ideology. Emphasis on family ties is reinforced through religious commitment. Individuals are thus encouraged to be respectful of adults and social conventions and to be open to guidance.

Ramírez and Castañeda (1974) contend that development of an understanding of Mexican-American values should be one of the primary concerns of educators, and educators have recently been taking this advice. Many school districts with predominantly Mexican-American populations are providing in-service programs to help make the teachers aware of the cultural characteristics and learning styles of Mexican-American students.

Learning Styles

Children develop their own styles of learning and means of assimilating information about their environments. The values and socialization styles of a culture affect the specific learning styles in children. Cultural values are instrumental in developing preferences for certain types of rewards, and for the type of learning environment that is most rewarding. Schools that recognize these preferences may utilize them in designing educational climates that are rewarding and produce higher achievement.

The motivational styles of Mexican-American children appear to be quite different from the motivational styles of Anglo-Americans. Kagan and Madsen (1971) found that Mexican-American children are more highly motivated in a cooperative setting. In contrast, Anglo-American children are more competitive.

Mexican-American children also show greater desire to interact with others and to belong to a social group (Ramírez & Price-Williams, 1974). Due to their orientation, Mexican-American children may do better when the curriculum has a human content and is closely related to the needs of others as well as to the family and community. Many of these features are found in a successful program described by Quintero and Huerta-Macias (1990) in which children and parents became part of a cooperative, relevant learning environment that included family teams.

Educational Implications for Students with Limited English Proficiency

Students with limited English proficiency face a formidable academic challenge in American classrooms. However, according to Ezer (1990), children can learn to read and write in two languages concurrently if the children have opportunities to interact in supportive environments. Wong-Fillmore's (1986) four-year study of the effects of instructional practices on the learning of English by students from Chinese and Latino backgrounds provides several educational implications. First, the research shows that students vary greatly in their ability to learn a second language. Whereas some students learn in just a few years, most students require from four to six years to achieve the proficiency needed for full participation in school. Furthermore, the research supports certain instructional practices. For example, Latino students gain in both production and comprehension skills if they have opportunities to use the new language while interacting with their peers. In contrast, interacting with peers has little value for Chinese students until they have enough proficiency in the new language to feel confident when using English with their classmates. For the Chinese students, close interactions with teachers and opportunities to use English during teacher-directed instructional activities relate to gains in oral language. Although both Chinese and Latino students gain from high-quality instruction and clear language usage, Latino students (mostly Mexican-Americans) do especially well when the instruction is clearly presented and well organized.

Wong-Fillmore (1986) is especially critical of the quality of much of the instruction. She states:

> I came to realize that what these LEP children generally get in school does not add up to a real education at all. Much of what they are being taught can be described as "basic skills" rather than as "content." Instruction in reading, for example, is mostly focused on developing accuracy in reading rather than on understanding or appreciating textual materials. Writing focuses on accuracy in spelling, punctuation, the niceties of grammar rather than on communicating ideas in written form or on the development of sustained reasoning and the use of evidence in supporting written arguments. (p. 478)

Research by both Cumming and Genishi highlights the importance of encouraging communication within the environment. Cumming (1990) identifies three kinds of thinking strategies that are helpful to students while learning a second language: (1) searching out and assessing appropriate wording, (2) comparing cross-linguistic equivalents, and (3) reasoning about linguistic choices. Genishi (1989) observed a group of second-language learners and drew three conclusions pertaining to children, their teachers, and their learning. First, each child has his or her own approach to learning the second language. Teachers need to accept each child's approach and to encourage all attempts to communicate. Second, classrooms that have a variety of activities and people with many opportunities for oral language are best able to support the second-language learner. Third, effective teachers build on observations related to each child. They encourage oral language by providing a sensitive support system in which children are encouraged to use their new language. They observe when children look confused or interested, respond to nonverbal cues, allow friends to stay together, keep conversations alive, and record signs of children's learning.

Canadian educators provide additional guidelines for effective education. For example, Piper (1986) recommends using traditional stories and fables from various cultural sources (see later section in this chapter) and focusing on awareness of the different languages and different cultural backgrounds. He suggests that teachers compile lists of words that are the same across many languages, write signs in schools in several representative languages, explore emigration patterns of families within the classroom by using maps and family histories, and involve parents in the design and implementation of curricular materials. Sealey (1984) emphasizes that instruction should encourage students to accept and be sensitive to cultural diversity, understand that similar values frequently underlie different customs, have quality contact with people from other cultures, and role-play experiences with other cultures. The literature recommended later in this chapter and the activities that teach children how to identify values in the literature encourage cultural sensitivity.

Several educators have developed principles of effective second-language learning. For example, Early (1990) proposes the following:

1. Learning should build on the previous educational and personal experiences of ESL students, who should be encouraged to honor their cultural identities.
2. Developing proficiency in a language takes many years; it requires that language be used in such areas as learning, socializing, inquiring, imagining, and wondering.
3. Learning should allow for integration of language teaching into various academic content areas so that the ESL students experience continuing cognitive and academic growth.
4. Learning should allow ESL students to be involved with activities or tasks that encourage them to use language interactively across various situations, modes, and text types.
5. Learning should use multimedia approaches, such as drawing, writing, and talking, to make communication clearer and to lower the language barriers for students who are learning subject matter in a second language.
6. Learning and social growth are increased when schools encourage parental participation.

According to Ramírez and Castañeda (1974), authorities on Mexican-American education, teachers should use many nonverbal indications of acceptance, including smiling, touching, allowing children to work next to the teacher, and sharing laughter and other warm experiences. These actions are reminiscent of the close family ties developed in the traditional Mexican-American culture. Teachers should also try to know the children as individuals and relate lesson material to their experiences whenever possible.

The close ties of the traditional Mexican-American family make it appropriate for teachers to work closely and cooperatively with families. Send notes to the family telling them how pleased you are with their child's progress. Notes accompanying excellent examples of student work are especially appropriate. Reward students with frequent reminders of how proud their families will be about their progress. Meet personally with and talk frequently to the families in order to develop a closer relationship.

As noted, researchers suggest that traditional Mexican-American children look up to an authority figure and model themselves after older, revered members of the community. Teachers may provide that model by having children repeat words after them in language instruction or by providing models of how to write, paint, or do other classroom activities. When trying to provide a positive model, show respect for the language of the children by using Spanish frequently during the school day. If the highly respected authority model uses a child's native language, it conveys the message that the language is to be respected. Teachers can also convey respect for the language by teaching Spanish songs and rhymes in addition to addressing Spanish-speaking children and adults in Spanish. Develop respect for the culture by studying famous Mexican-Americans and Mexican holidays and other celebrations.

Educators who use second-language techniques provide guidance for working with Mexican-American children who have limited skills in the English language. Carter's (1982) *Non-Native and Nonstandard Dialect Students: Classroom Practices in Teaching English, 1982–1983* describes approaches in ESL classes. De Félix's (1982) language arts approach is based on the following basic principles: (1) fluency precedes accuracy, (2) students learn concepts and structures when they are ready to use them, (3) teachers should organize successively more challenging tasks, and (4) acquisition of the linguistic function precedes acquisition of the form. The ESL methods in the approach require teachers to slow the pace for students with limited English proficiency, introduce phonics after students have increased their vocabulary, build on children's native language, understand the nature of language strategies, and keep informed of new strategies. De Félix recommends the following five-step approach for working with ESL students:

1. *Develop comprehension:* Use a variety of resources, such as pictures, concrete materials, native language materials, community resources, pantomime, and peer tutors, to help students understand the concepts behind the language to be taught.
2. *Select and analyze for vocabulary, grammar, and linguistic function:* Analyze the materials to be used to help students integrate knowledge. For example, select vocabulary words that can be taught through concrete examples and experiences. When possible, expand this concrete understanding through categories. (If the word is *meat*, teach different kinds of meat or sample foods from different nutritional groups.) Next, select two or three types of sentences found in the lesson and extend the students' use of grammar and the target vocabulary. Construct sentences showing how the vocabulary fits into different sentence patterns. ("I like meat," "I like beef and ham," "Beef and ham are types of meat.") Finally, select linguistic functions to teach through the lesson; for example, phrases that justify actions or identify needs; phrases that direct students' actions; phrases or words that help students interpret materials by recognizing sequences, relationships, and causes; phrases that allow students to hypothesize, anticipate consequences, recognize problems, and predict solutions; experiences, such as puppetry, that allow students to explore language; and experiences, such as songs and games, that encourage students to have fun with language.
3. *Plan activities to meet students' needs:* Plan activities that consider individual needs, such as age, cultural background, and English proficiency.
4. *Present lessons by proceeding from the known to the unknown:* Present new information on the basis of prior knowledge and understanding of concepts to be acquired.
5. *Integrate and reaffirm skills.* Help students integrate concepts into their personal lives and school content areas, and help them reaffirm skills in various contexts.

For Your Development

If you have a bilingual class near your university or college, visit a classroom. Observe the children and describe some of the effective instructional techniques you see. (You may also observe some that are not effective. If this happens, determine why they are not effective.) If you do not have access to bilingual programs, read about an educational program for Mexican-American students. Is the program utilizing knowledge about learning styles as justified in the research?

Instructional Approaches for Children Whose First Language is Not English

In this section we discuss some highly recommended instructional approaches for use with students in ESL classrooms. Many of the approaches discussed in Chapters 2, 4, 5, and 6 are excellent for students from diverse backgrounds. Many of those we will now consider are useful for all populations; others are geared toward a specific group.

Hudelson, Poynor, and Wolf (2003) reviewed results from several elementary school studies and reported the following conclusions about educational implications for bilingual and ESL students:

1. Create an environment that respects the language and literacy development of the child's home and community.
2. Provide many opportunities for both oral and written interactions.
3. Observe children's interactions in activities that reflect the reality of the idiosyncratic nature of literacy development in children.
4. Allow and value the use of the first language in the language and literacy development of the second language.

Many of the approaches recommended for teaching reading to children in ESL classrooms are similar to those recommended for all students. According to Peregoy and Boyle (2001), "Over the past decade, researchers have looked at how people process print when reading in English as a second language. They consistently find that the process is essentially the same whether reading English as the first or second language" (p. 259). Consequently, these authors emphasize such activities as sharing reading with Big Books, reading illustrated stories and poems, using the directed listening–thinking activity to provide scaffolding by modeling how experienced readers make predictions about what they read, Reader's Theater, story and cognitive mapping, writing in literature response journals, and using computers to enhance learning.

Contrastive Analysis

The aim of many educators who try to expand a child's language is improved oral and written communication in the classroom. Some programs stress teaching standard English before children learn to read; other programs teach standard English as an alternative dialect and a useful tool for school and society. This second approach usually teaches standard English usage while maintaining and respecting the original dialect. Thus, students theoretically have a choice: They may use whichever form of language is most useful for the specific occasion. This section looks at a program designed for early primary language expansion and another designed for the middle grades. Many of these programs resulted from extensive research done in the 1970s.

Cullinan, Jaggar, and Strickland (1974) developed a language expansion program for kindergarten through third-grade children attending predominantly black public schools. The teachers in the program were trained to recognize the contrasts between standard English and black English so they could help children perceive the differences between the two forms of language. The program utilized literature selections read to the children daily. After hearing the selections, the children took part in activities that provided opportunities to expand oral language as well as to practice specific patterns of standard English.

The lessons included six different types of language expansion activities. The first activity utilized dramatization and puppetry. Students discussed a story, prepared the scenes to be dramatized, and presented the scenes to the class. The second activity was built on storytelling by the children. Students listened to a story, such as "Curious George," talked about the main character or the parts of the story that they most enjoyed, and then told stories about the character in another situation. (For example, what would happen if George found himself locked in a supermarket overnight?) The third activity used book discussions, stressing various listening comprehension skills as well as clear expression of ideas. In the fourth activity, the children talked about the characters in a story and how the characters felt. They chose specific lines from the stories to illustrate a particular language pattern that needed practice. The students then role-played, using the specific sentence patterns from the story. The fifth activity used even more specific language patterns. Following a story and discussion, a puppet named "Peter Parrot" asked the children to repeat sentences from the story. Children repeated the sentences in unison and individually. The final activity, used after a literature selection, was choral speaking. After a story or poem was read to the children, they were divided into groups to perform the story or poem as a choral-speaking activity.

Mantell (1974) designed a language expansion program built on contrastive analysis (comparing the points of differences between two forms of language) for middle-grade black-English-speaking students. Mantell's program identified the most frequently used grammatical features of black English and then focused specifically on the features that most sharply separate one social group from other social groups. Mantell says it is most important to concentrate on features based on findings by Wolfram (1970). Wolfram plotted features of black English against the following five criteria: (1) sharpness of social stratification, (2) generality of application of the rule, (3) whether the rule is grammatical or phonological, (4) whether the significance is general or regional, and (5) frequency of occurrence of the feature. According to Wolfram, seven syntactic features of black English are important for students to control with respect to social prestige. These features, in the order ranked by Wolfram, include the following categories and examples:

While some students acquire sufficient proficiency in English to become full participants in classroom activities quickly, other students may require four to six years to reach that goal.

1. *s* third-person singular—he go
2. Multiple negation—didn't do nothing
3. *s* possessive—man hat
4. Invariant *be*—he be home
5. Copula absence—he nice
6. *been* auxiliary in active sentence—he been ate the food
7. Existential *it*—it is a whole lot of people

The purpose of Mantell's program is to help middle-school children become aware of the syntactic differences and similarities between black English and standard English, as well as to test the appropriateness of each form of language. Language expansion activities include role-playing and games. Students listen to recorded samples of black English and standard English, and are then asked to isolate the differences on printed copies of the recordings. Students are also asked to collect language samples showing how various people express possession, plurality, time, and negation. Other language expansion activities include providing short sentences as appropriate captions to photographs, storytelling, presenting eyewitness reporting of current or fantasy events for a news commentary, and role-playing. In role-playing activities, a panel of students rates the appropriateness of language.

A final instructional approach in this program uses an incomplete sentence technique. The teacher provides the beginning of a sentence and asks students to complete it; for example, I . . . ; We . . . ; They. . . . This program does not use published materials. Rather, it uses drama, literature, and topics of interest to the students.

For Your Development

Look at an instructional program that stresses expansion of oral language. What do you feel is the basic philosophy of the approach? What are the instructional goals, and how are these goals developed? What do you feel are some strengths or weaknesses of the program?

The Language Experience Approach

The language experience approach is highly recommended because it allows students to use and to expand on their own language and experiences. The approach may be structured to expand literature understanding, oral language development, development of abstract thinking, listening improvement, and written composition.

According to Peregoy and Boyle (2001), "The language-experience approach is one of the most frequently recommended approaches for beginning second language readers. The beauty of this approach is that the student provides the text, through dictation, that serves as the basis for reading instruction. As a result, language-experience reading is tailored to the learner's own interests, background knowledge, and language proficiency. It builds on the linguistic, social, and cultural strengths and interests the student brings to school" (p. 268).

Philosophy. The title "language experience" provides a clue to the nature of the approach. This language-arts-oriented approach includes all of the communication skills—listening, speaking, reading, and writing. It emphasizes that the ideas of children are not only worth expressing, but also worth writing down and reading. This approach stresses a natural flow of language. First, art, literature, and other experiences stimulate oral expression. Then, written expression develops from the oral expression. Children are motivated to read because they see their own language in print. Finally, after reading their own language, children move naturally into reading the published works of others.

Practice.   The language experience approach has been used for many years with linguistically and culturally diverse populations. As early as 1933, some educators advocated the use of this approach with Mexican-American children, whose language was different from that of the school. The students learned to read materials they dictated, so there were no problems with cultural or language interference.

Numerous programs have used language experience approaches with other linguistically or culturally diverse groups. For example, Hall (1965) developed a language experience approach for culturally disadvantaged black children in Washington, D.C. Her students made greater gains in reading readiness, word recognition, and sentence reading than did a group of students taught with traditional basal materials. Calvert (1973) used a language experience approach with middle-school Mexican-American students and found that his students made significant gains in writing, vocabulary, comprehension, and development of positive attitudes toward teachers.

Method.   Language experience stimulates oral language and writing by providing opportunities for discussion, exploration of ideas, and expression of feelings. In turn, language experiences provide the content for group and individual stories composed by children and recorded by teachers. Many teachers introduce students to the language experience approach through a group chart story. This is possible with any age group, but it is frequently a readiness or early-reading activity in kindergarten or first grade.

The motivational experience may be any activity that involves the group and encourages oral language. For example, one teacher brought a baby chick into the classroom. The first graders looked at and listened to the chick, carefully touched it, and fed and watered it. They discussed what they saw, heard, felt, and cared for. An excellent chart story resulted from each child's contributions. A third-grade remedial-reading teacher involved children in making pudding before they wrote an experience story. A seventh/eighth-grade teacher of children with learning disabilities read literature selections to her students. Then she had the class develop chart stories about the main characters. Other motivational materials and activities include trips, films, building projects, pictures, guest speakers, science experiments, puppet shows, music, and poetry. A room that offers a rich environment provides many motivational experiences for the chart story.

After a motivational experience and oral discussion, record the story exactly as each child says it. You may record the story on a large piece of newsprint, on a poster-board chart, or on the chalkboard, from which it is reprinted onto a chart. Whichever means of recording you use, it is essential that children be seated so that they can see each word as it is written in the proper left-to-right sequence. Thus, children see that sentences follow a progressive pattern from the top of the page to the bottom and that sentences begin with capital letters and end with periods. As the children dictate the story, write each word, repeating the word aloud as you write. Following each sentence, read the whole sentence to the group, underlining the word being read with one hand. Ask the child who has dictated the sentence whether the sentence is correct.

After the chart story is complete, read the whole story. Then, have the students reread it with you. If the story does not have a title, have the class discuss an appropriate title. Some students may feel confident enough to try to read the selection individually, whereas other students may read only the sentence they dictated.

For Your Plan Book

Lesson Plan

A Lesson Plan for Developing a Language Experience Chart Story

The objectives of the lesson are to (1) involve the students in a motivational activity that will result in oral discussion and a group-dictated chart story, (2) improve the ability of students to comprehend the sequential order of a selection, and (3) help the students increase the number of sight words they recognize. This lesson was developed with a group of third graders with learning disabilities.

As a motivational activity, begin the discussion by asking the students to tell the group about their favorite desserts. Show a picture of a chocolate pie made from chocolate pudding and a graham cracker crust. Ask the students how many of them have helped make a pie like the one in the picture. Discuss how they think it would be accomplished. Ask them what they think they would need to make the pie in the picture. As they mention various items, remove them from a box and place them on the table (include instant chocolate pudding mix, milk, measuring cup, bowl, egg beater, spoon, and graham cracker crust). Explain to the students that you are not only going to make a pie but also eat the pie and then write a story about the experience in order to share it with the rest of the class and with their parents.

Procedures

1. Lead an oral discussion about desserts, as described in the motivational activity.
2. Place the ingredients and utensils on the table. Clarify terms such as "instant chocolate pudding mix," "glass bowl," "measuring cup," "eggbeater," and "graham cracker crust" as you place each item on the worktable. Label each item so the students can visualize the printed term and associate it with the item.
3. Place the ingredients in the order the students believe is appropriate. Ask them how to verify whether the ingredients are in the proper order. A student may respond that you have to read a recipe. If no one does, tell the students what a recipe is.
4. Read the recipe to the group. As you read each step, have the students check to see if the ingredients and utensils are in the correct order.
5. Orally review the whole sequence, using the concrete items as reminders for the procedure.
6. Make the pie according to the recipe directions. Allow each child to take part in some portion of the pie-making activity.
7. Cut the pie and allow all of the children to have some.
8. Have the students dictate a chart story about the pie-making experience. Print the story on a large chart.

Children dictated the following story as a result of this lesson plan:

We Made a Chocolate Pie

We put chocolate pudding into a glass bowl. We poured milk into the bowl. We beat the milk and pudding with an egg-beater. The pudding got thick. We poured the pudding into a graham cracker crust. We ate the pie. It was good.

Continued

To reinforce this language experience activity:

1. Have students match the labels on the concrete examples with the same terms in the chart story.
2. Cut a duplicate chart story into sentences. Mix the sentences and have the students put them into the correct sequential order.
3. Duplicate the story. During the next class period, have the students read the story, underlining words they know. Test these words in isolation. If the students recognize the words the following day, place the words in the students' word bank.

Individualizing Language Experience.   Teachers often use the language experience approach as an individualized approach, in which each student dictates a story to the teacher. Motivation is also essential for individual stories. A room that is rich with manipulative objects, pictures, animals, and learning centers motivates story dictation. A student's own artwork is often good motivation for language experience. The artwork is highly personal and requires complete involvement on the part of the child. Topics related to the children themselves, such as family, friends, school, and recreation, are frequently preferred by African-American inner-city students.

To develop an individual language experience lesson, let the children take turns dictating individual stories to you or an aide. Record the story on lined paper or on newsprint, or use a primer-size typewriter or large font on the computer. Write the story exactly as the child dictates it. The dictation procedure is similar to the group chart story. As the child dictates the story, read back the words and sentences to the child to make sure that you have properly recorded them and to reinforce the development of the story. It is usually preferable for a beginning story to be only a few sentences long.

After the dictation, have the child read the selection with your help. Have the child underline words that he or she knows in the story. For example, the story in Figure 12–1 was written about a child's drawing of an owl. The girl who dictated the story reread the story with the teacher's help and underlined each word she knew. The underlined words form a beginning for the child's word bank (words that are instantly recognized as sight words). The teacher gradually reduces the number of visible cues in order to help the child recognize the words not underlined. This gradual reduction includes the following steps:

1. Use the total story context to help the child read the story.
2. Point to individual words and ask the child to identify the words.
3. Use a window card to isolate words in the story sequence and ask the child to identify the words.
4. Use a window card to isolate words in the story in a random order and ask the child to identify these words. (You can construct a window card easily: Cut an opening large enough to show a word in a 3- by 5-inch file card [see Figure 12–2]. Move the card across the story and stop at individual words, testing whether a child can identify the words without the help of a total sentence.)

On a small card, print every word that a child still recognizes the second and third day after dictation. The card size should be about ⅜ of an inch by 1 inch. Place these cards in an individual file box labeled with the child's name. Use the cards for frequent review of words, sentence-building activities, word-recognition activities, development of alphabetizing skills, and creative writing.

Most children are motivated to learn more as they see their word banks grow. Children can construct many new sentences with the cards in a word bank. They can also experiment with sentence expansion (see Figure 12–3).

FIGURE 12–1   A Chart Story
Dictated by an Individual Child

This owl <u>sitting</u> under
<u>the</u> moon. <u>He</u> sitting on <u>a</u>
branch. <u>He</u> sleep in <u>the</u>
morning. <u>He</u> hunt at night.

FIGURE 12–2   A Window
Card

You may also use language experience stories and word banks for teaching phonics and structural analysis. Children can find all the words that begin with capital letters or all the words that end with *at*, such as *cat*. They can find all the words that have a certain word ending, such as *ed* in *walked*. After a number of words are in the word bank, the children may discover that they are difficult to find. This occasion provides a good opportunity to introduce alphabetizing. Have the students place small envelopes, one for each letter, inside their word boxes to facilitate the beginning of alphabetical instruction. This is also a logical time to introduce the use of a dictionary. Finally, a word bank provides a readily available source of words for creative writing.

FIGURE 12–3   Sentence
Expansion With Word Cards

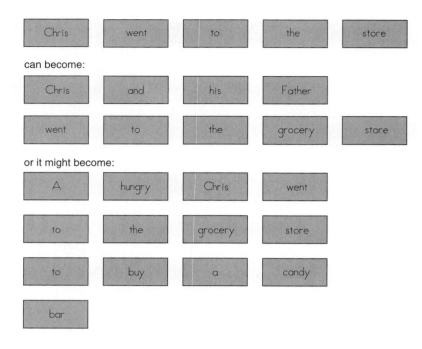

can become:

or it might become:

Lesson Plan

For Your Plan Book

A Language Experience Activity for Children from Linguistically Diverse Backgrounds

The following activity was developed by Nancy Matula during a practicum experience with fifth-grade students, primarily African-American and Mexican-American students. (As you read the activity, try to see how Nancy motivated the students to write and used discussion as part of the experience. When you read about her results, note any examples of black dialect.) This is Nancy's activity described in her own words:

> The language experience activity I used with the fifth-graders dealt with biographies and autobiographies. To begin the activity, I read the students a relatively easy biography about Kit Carson. Following the reading, we discussed the book and talked about the specific type of book. The term *biography* was introduced, and students located the meaning of the word in the dictionary. Next, we discussed several characteristics of a biography. We discussed the fact that every one of us could have a biography written about us.
>
> After the discussion of biographies, I introduced the word *autobiography* to the class. We looked at several autobiographies and discussed the differences and similarities between biography and autobiography. We talked about and listed some of the things that could be included in an autobiography. Such items as birthplace, favorite colors, foods, sports, and pets, among other items, made up our list.
>
> At this point, I explained that we were going to write our own book. Because the book (constructed out of poster board held together by rings) had blank white pages, we needed to fill up the pages. Through discussion, it was suggested that we needed both words and pictures. We took both group pictures and individual pictures. It was decided that the group pictures would decorate the cover of our book and that each page would

contain one student's picture. Beneath each person's picture would be his or her auto-biography. Because we could not write our autobiographies on this same day, I asked the students to continue thinking about what they wanted to include in their autobiographies.

During the following session, we reviewed what could go into our autobiographies. These items were written on the board for further reference. Next, we reviewed writing rules such as beginning sentences with capital letters and ending them with the correct punctuation. The students were off and running (or should I say some were off and walking). Many of the students had difficulty in beginning their writing. They needed assistance with spelling, and a few needed to dictate their stories orally.

Each student completed his or her autobiography and used the story for reading instruction. I also found they were highly motivated to read each other's autobiographies. The book is to be left in the classroom until the end of the school year, because everyone wants to read the whole book. At the end of the school year, each student can remove and keep his page from the book.

The students were extremely excited and happy with this writing experience. We all learned a great deal while writing about a subject we each know better than any other—ourselves.

The following autobiography was written by one fifth-grade boy:

I want to be a singer and a movie star. I have black and white eyes a black pupil, brown hair and afro. My favorite sport is basketball. My favorites singing group is Janet Jackson. My favorites foods is hamburger, frenchfries, hot dog and green, green peas. My favorite music is hotline. My color is black.

Used with permission of Nancy Matula, elementary-school teacher.

For Your Development

1. Choose a motivational activity to foster both discussion and writing. If you are teaching children, develop a language-experience chart story with a group. If you are not teaching, demonstrate your language experience activity with a group of your peers. Include a motivational activity, the writing of a dictated story, and a reinforcement activity.
2. Develop a language experience lesson plan such as one of those found in *Language Arts Activities for Children* (Norton & Norton, 2003).

Multicultural Education

Contemporary education, at both the university and public school levels, is beginning to stress the need for multicultural education. This section focuses on African-Americans, Native Americans, Latinos, and Asians. Lewis and Doorlag (1998) present these reasons for developing multicultural education:

1. Commonalties among people cannot be recognized unless differences are acknowledged.
2. A society that interweaves the best of all of its cultures reflects a truly mosaic image.
3. Multicultural education can restore cultural rights by emphasizing cultural equality and respect.

4. Students can learn basic skills while also learning to respect cultures; multicultural education need not detract from basic education.
5. Multicultural education enhances the self-concepts of all students because it provides a more balanced view of American society.
6. Students must learn to respect others.

Many educators are promoting the need for multicultural education in all aspects of the curriculum. For example, Haukoos and LaBeau (1992) discuss the need for integration of science and culture when developing the curriculum for Native American students. They state that this integration is important because "American Indian cultures do not accept the separation of science from other aspects of their life" (p. 3). Consequently, these educators emphasize the importance of building a school curriculum that reflects the local culture and educational values.

To aid in developing understanding of other cultures, many educators and researchers emphasize the need for high-quality multicultural literature. The selection and use of this literature is especially important because reading and discussing literature is such an important part of the language arts curriculum including oral language, listening, reading, and writing. Hazel Rochman (1993) states the need for multicultural literature very well when she concludes: "The best books break down borders. They surprise us—whether they are set close to home or abroad. They change our view of ourselves; they extend that phrase 'like me' to include what we thought was foreign and strange" (p. 9).

Positive multicultural literature has been used effectively to help readers identify cultural heritages, understand sociological change, respect the values of minority groups, raise aspirations, and expand imagination and creativity. This author has found that multicultural literature and activities related to the literature also improve reading scores and improve attitudes toward African-Americans, Native Americans, and Latinos if the literature and literature-related activities are part of the curriculum and if adults know how to select this literature and develop strategies to accompany the literature (Norton, 1981, 1990, 2001, 2003). In contrast, merely placing the literature in a classroom or a library without subsequent interaction does not change attitudes.

Although we find numerous authorities who identify the need for multicultural literature, the selection of literature that is of both high literary quality and culturally authentic is a formidable task. Universities are beginning to require that students in education, library science, and English take courses that focus on choosing, analyzing, evaluating, and effectively using multicultural literature. Library selection committees, university professors, public school teachers, librarians, and administrators must all become involved in this process of evaluating and choosing multicultural literature.

In addition to the sensitivity required in selecting materials, educators are also emphasizing the moral dimensions that are related to sharing and discussing literature associated with various cultures. Johnston et al. (1998) advise teachers or other adults who work in multicultural settings to "observe classroom events carefully and reflect upon their significance while suppressing the urge to criticize or condemn. The overall message that emerges from our analysis is that what teachers do and say in class does matter—their words and their actions carry great moral weight. Teachers, unavoidably, act as moral agents; how they choose to direct this action is a crucial part of what it means to be a teacher" (p. 180). This is excellent advice for anyone who is selecting, evaluating, and using multicultural literature, especially if the literature reflects cultural values and beliefs that are different from those of the educator.

In this section on multicultural education in the language arts, we consider some of the most effective procedures developed by Norton (2001) and used with elementary and middle-school students and taught in university classes with both undergraduate and graduate students. Some of these activities, such as the multicultural storytelling festival, had large audiences and allowed both elementary children and university students to develop their storytelling skills and present them to an appreciative group. Other activities such as authenticating the historical perspectives and values in books increase both students' understanding of a culture and higher cognitive abilities as they evaluate the authenticity of a book. As students write about their findings, they are increasing their ability to write expository text. Activities such as studying the backgrounds and writings of authors who write about specific cultures may motivate students to research their own culture and to write stories or poems about their own cultures. The chapter concludes with selection criteria for multicultural literature and an annotated bibliography of African-American, Asian, Latino, Middle Eastern, and Native American literature.

Developing a Multicultural Storytelling Festival

This storytelling festival has grown with each year of its existence. It began in a small way as undergraduate university students selected and studied the folklore and oral storytelling styles of various cultures, prepared the stories for retelling, and presented the stories to other university classes and to children in one of the local elementary schools. As the festival expanded, it included bringing in professional storytellers for a two-week residence program during which time the storytellers modeled storytelling to university classes, taught individual students the art of storytelling, helped students prepare stories for elementary children, and presented stories to local schools. The largest festival included tents on the George Bush Library located in College Station, Texas grounds, university students as storytellers, professional storytellers, and busloads of children. Two storytelling guilds have been developed for training in and presenting of storytelling for adults who are interested in becoming storytellers and children who would like to expand their oral language abilities.

To develop a storytelling festival in a school or in a university, you may want to include the following steps:

1. Investigate the values of oral storytelling and how oral storytelling is important in transmitting the folktales, myths, and legends of a culture. Share with students that oral language is important in transmitting cultural information and that oral storytellers keep the cultural past alive. The art of storytelling was so highly valued in some cultures that storytelling competitions were held to encourage the most vivid and entertaining stories. Explain to students that they will be listening to oral storytellers, identifying oral storytelling styles, and creating their own storytelling experiences.

2. Discuss and model storytelling techniques (see storytelling elsewhere in this text). You may ask students to listen to tapes of storytellers from different cultures. Ashley Bryan's tape, *The Dancing Granny and Other African Stories* (1985), is an excellent way to introduce storytelling styles. Ask the students to listen to the tape and then describe this very vivid style. Have them search other sources for descriptions of storytelling styles. They will discover that the style of the traditional African storyteller, still found in many African countries today, can be characterized as a lively mixture of mimicking dialogue, body action, audience participation, and rhythm. Storytellers often mimic the sounds of animals, change their voices to characterize both animal and human characters, develop dialogue, and encourage their listeners to interact with the story. They may also add musical accompaniment with drums or other rhythm and string instruments. See the annotated bibliography for other African stories that are good for storytelling such as Verna Aardema's *Who's in Rabbit's House?* (1977) and Ashley Bryan's *Beat the Story-Drum Pum-Pum* (1980).

3. You may extend the storytelling to other cultures such as Native American with tales such as Paul Goble's *Iktomi and the Berries* (1989) and *Iktomi and the Boulder* (1988), Latino tales such as Harriet Rohmer and Dornminster Wilson's *Mother Scorpion Country* (1987) and Vivien Blackmore's *Why Corn Is Golden: Stories About Plants* (1984), Asian tales such as Anne Laurin's *The Perfect Crane* (1981) and Robert D. San Souci's *The Samurai's Daughter: A Japanese Legend* (1992), and Middle Eastern stories such as Eric Kimmel's *The Tale of Aladdin and the Wonderful Lamp* (1992).

4. Ask storytellers to practice their storytelling, prepare an introduction to the story that emphasizes the culture from which the story originates, and be prepared to present the story to an audience. Monitors and helpers for the storytellers may be asked to consider the introduction to the story, the effectiveness of props or costumes if used, the effectiveness of gestures and eye contact, the overall knowledge of the story, and general comments about the presentation.

5. If presenting the stories to an audience, have a dress rehearsal to allow storytellers to practice their stories in front of a larger audience.

6. Invite other classes or an adult audience to the storytelling festival. The storytellers may include artifacts from the culture, illustrated books that show the culture, and collections of folklore. The illustrated books and collections are very important because these sources may motivate listeners and participants to read additional folklore and conduct their own investigations into the culture.

7. When the multicultural storytelling festival was performed on the grounds of the George Bush Library and Museum it attracted not only children from the surrounding schools but also radio and television stations. Many of my university students indicated that developing and taking part in the multicultural storytelling festival was one of their most valuable educational experiences.

Identifying and Understanding Traditional Values

Multicultural literature can be used to develop many of the language arts goals and objectives such as developing reasoning ability, accepting cultural diversity, and understanding that similar values frequently underlie different customs. Reading, analyzing, and discussing multicultural literature are the best ways to achieve all of these goals. Traditional literature (folktales, myths, and legends) provide excellent sources for exploring the traditional values of a culture. Students gain insights and hone their reasoning abilities as they analyze the values reflected in the stories, compare the values across cultures, consider whether the values are reflected in contemporary literature, and respond to whether the values are important in their lives.

In addition to analyzing the literature for cultural values, the literature should be analyzed to determine if it is authentic for the culture. Folklorists, anthropologists, linguists, and educators use folklore to make discoveries about people who lived in ancient times and in various cultures. Consequently, document authentication is becoming an issue in the selection and evaluation of folklore, whether the folklore is published in highly illustrated single volumes or in anthologies (Norton & Norton, 1998). Hearne (1993) and Stott (1990) are extremely critical of both texts and illustrations in folklore that do not cite the original source or are not culturally authentic.

Allowing students to analyze the literature for values and encouraging them to authenticate the text and illustrations increase the students' cultural knowledge and improve their research and analytical skills. This type of activity can be applied to African, Native American, Latino, and Asian literature. It is especially beneficial with students in middle- and upper-elementary grades. In the following unit, a Native American selection and an excerpt from a contemporary story by a Native American author are compared with respect to the values they reflect. The unit continues with activities that encourage students to authenticate a Native American folktale by comparing the retelling with the original source for the tale and searching for sources that may be used to authenticate text and illustrations.

For Your Plan Book

Lesson Plan

Experiencing Traditional Native American Values and Authenticating Text and Illustrations

Objectives

1. To develop an appreciation for a culture that places importance on oral tradition, respect for nature, understanding between animals and humans, wisdom of the elderly, folklore as a means of passing on cultural and tribal beliefs, and diversity of Native American folktales, cultures, and customs.
2. To listen for and to identify traditional values found in Native American folklore.
3. To compare the traditional values in folklore and contemporary literature.
4. To authenticate the text and illustrations by comparing them with the original source for the text and searching for other examples in informational books.

Sources (Literature)

Tomie de Paola's *The Legend of the Bluebonnet* (1983)

White Deer of Autumn's *Ceremony—In the Circle of Life* (1983)

Barbara Juster Esbensen's *The Great Buffalo Race: How the Buffalo Got Its Hump* (1994)

Sources (Authentication)

Arthur C. Parker's *"The Buffalo's Hump and the Brown Birds"* in *Skunny Wundy: Seneca Indian Tales* (1926)

Bryan Hodgson's "Buffalo: Back Home on the Range," *National Geographic* (1994)

Sam Gill and Irene Sullivan's *Dictionary of Native American Mythology* (1992)

Peter and Jill Furst's *North American Indian Art* (1982) or any other books that include illustrations from earlier time periods in the Seneca culture.

Procedures

1. Discuss ways in which students can identify traditional values found in folklore. For example, they can read the tales to discover answers to the following questions and then analyze what those answers reveal about the values and the beliefs of the people:
   a. What is the problem the characters face?
   b. What do the characters desire?
   c. What actions or values are rewarded or respected?
   d. What actions are punished or not respected?
   e. What rewards are given?
   f. What are the personal characteristics of the heroes or the heroines?
2. Print each question on a chart. Allow room to include several tales. Use the chart to identify the answers to the questions and then to consider what these answers reveal about

Continued

Table 12–A   Folklore analysis

Comparisons	Folklore: *The Legend of the Bluebonnet*	Realistic Fiction: *Ceremony—In the Circle of Life*
What is the problem?	Drought and famine killed the Comanche	Humans are destroying the land
What do the characters desire?	To end drought and famine To save land and people	To comfort and honor Mother Earth To teach humans about Earth
What actions or values are rewarded or respected?	Sacrifice to save land and the tribe Belief in Great Spirit	Honoring and caring for Mother Earth Living in harmony Knowledge, truth, belief
What actions are punished or not respected?	Selfishness Taking from Earth without giving back	Pollution and destruction of the Earth
What rewards are given?	Bluebonnets, as a sign of forgiveness Rain, end of drought Name change	A living pipe, which symbolizes the vision of Earth New strength and knowledge Understanding
What are the personal characteristics of heroes or heroines?	Unselfish love of people and land Respect for the Great Spirit Willingness to sacrifice to gain benefits for all	Love of animals and land Respect for the Star Spirit and ways of the people Desire for knowledge and truth

the beliefs and the values of the people (see Table 12–A). (Use the same chart form for different cultures to help students compare values.)

3. Introduce de Paola's *The Legend of the Bluebonnet.* Ask the students to listen for the answers to the questions printed on the chart.

4. After reading *The Legend of the Bluebonnet* aloud, have students identify the answers and place them on the chart. Discuss the implications for the various answers. How do these answers relate to possible values and beliefs of the people?

5. During another class, introduce White Deer of Autumn's *Ceremony—In the Circle of Life.* Tell the students that this is a contemporary story written by a Native American author who wants to share his vision for the earth and his concerns with Native American children and other children of the world. Ask the students to listen for the answers to the same questions, consider the possible implications of those answers, and compare the values reflected in the two books. Ask them to provide possible reasons for the similarities in values expressed in the two books.

6. During other class periods read other traditional literature from various Native American tribes and other groups. Ask the children to consider what information they learn from these sources. If they select traditional literature from one tribal source they can

read and summarize the values reflected in that literature and then read literature from another tribal source, summarize the values, and compare the values across tribal groups.

7. To introduce the concept of the importance of authenticity in traditional literature, tell students that folklorists, anthropologists, and linguists use folklore to make discoveries about peoples who lived in ancient times and in various cultures. Ask them to consider why it would be important for each of these groups to use authentic literature that really reflects the culture of the people. Explain to the students that retellers of folklore from various cultures have a responsibility to identify the source for the original tale so that readers may evaluate the appropriateness of any changes that may have been made in the tale. Discuss with students why they believe authenticity in text and illustrations is important if they are to make discoveries about the culture.

8. Select an example of folklore that has an author's note that identifies the source and the tribal connection for the tale. Read and discuss the information found in the source note. For example, Barbara Juster Esbensen's *The Great Buffalo Race: How the Buffalo Got Its Hump* includes an author's note that identifies the source for the original tale as the Seneca Indian tribe, which was part of the Iroquois Nation. The source for the tale is identified as "The Buffalo's Hump and the Brown Birds" retold by Arthur C. Parker in his collection *Skunny Wundy: Seneca Indian Tales*. Esbensen identifies the location of the Seneca Indians as New York State, although they fought campaigns that took them to the Mississippi River and beyond. She states: "The patterns and costumes found in the illustrations were inspired by traditional beadwork and clothing found in books on the Iroquois as well as the American Museum of Natural History and the American Indian Museum, Heye Foundation, both in New York" (Note to Reader, unnumbered).

9. Discuss with students how they could use this information to locate sources that would help them authenticate Esbensen's text and illustrations. For example, a search for the original source provides both Parker's background and information about the Seneca. Parker, whose Seneca name is Gawaso Wanneh, was an anthropologist as well as a member of the Seneca tribe. His career in anthropology included experiences at the American Museum of Natural History, the Peabody Museum, and the Rochester Museum of Arts and Sciences. His studies focused on the Iroquois Indians and the League of the Iroquois, a confederation of five tribes or nations: the Mohawks, Oneidas, Onondagas, Cayugas, and Senecas who lived in what is now New York State.

The introduction to Parker's text provides additional information that may be used to authenticate tales about the Senecas. For example, the lands were in a region of forest and lakes in what is now New York state; the people lived in close terms with the animals; clan names, rituals, symbols, and stories reflect the importance of these animals; and different creatures have special traits including the cleverness of fox and raccoon, the easy duping of rabbit, the bravery of bear, the villainous nature of wolf, and the special place for turtle from whose back grew the Tree of Life with Sun at its top.

Students may do a textual comparison of the original "The Buffalo's Hump and the Brown Birds" and Esbensen's retelling. This comparison shows a close similarity in characters, plot, and theme, although the language of the texts is different. In both versions the major conflict is between Old Buffalo and Young Buffalo as they vie for leadership of the buffalo tribe. The members of the buffalo herd are called followers in the original version and tribesmen in the adaptation. The spiritual being is called "The Masterful One" in the original and "Haweniyo, the Great Spirit" in the retelling. Both versions identify trickery as inappropriate behavior in the eyes of the spiritual being. In both versions Old Buffalo and Young Buffalo are punished because of their foolish actions when they

Continued

ignore the rights of the small animals of the fields as the competing herds race westward toward what they believe is rain and green grazing grounds. In both versions it is Brown Buffalo, son of Old Buffalo, who is rewarded because he had the wisdom to stay in the original grazing area and wait for the lush green grasses to return with the rain. Both versions explain why the buffalo has shoulder humps and heavy heads that almost touch the ground so that they will remember to be careful in their dealings with the smaller animals who live or nest on the ground. This care for the smaller animals of the field reflects the close relationship between the Seneca Indians and the animals in the environment.

Additional authentication may focus on locations of the buffalo, the setting in the illustrations, the name of the great spirit, and the patterns and costumes found in the illustrations. In relation to the buffalo, the question arises, "Would buffalo be common in the land of the Seneca, which is the Eastern United States?" A map showing the range of the buffalo, or bison, found in Bryan Hodgson's article "Buffalo: Back Home on the Range," published in *National Geographic,* identifies the bison, circa 1500, as ranging east into what is now the southern portion of New York state. In addition, the Seneca traveled long distances on their war and hunting trips and may have seen the buffalo herds grazing on the prairies. This speculation is especially important for authenticity because Helen K. Davie's illustrations for *The Great Buffalo Race: How the Buffalo Got Its Hump* reflect the prairies with their vast stretches of grass and not the forests and trees of the Seneca homeland.

Instead of the original "The Masterful One," Esbensen's name for the spiritual being is "Haweniyo, the Great Spirit." According to Gill and Sullivan in *Dictionary of Native American Mythology* Hawenniyo (Gill and Sullivan have a different spelling for the name) is the main character in the Seneca origin story of the False Faces and also a Seneca term that later came to be used to refer to the Christian God.

The designs on the costumes in the illustrations are similar to those found in illustrations for designs created out of beads and porcupine-quill-embroidered buckskin found in pictures taken of Seneca artifacts in nonfiction texts such as *North American Indian Art.*

After students have consulted several sources for art and Seneca life, ask them to decide if they believe the text is authentic. What do they believe is authentic and why? What do they believe is not authentic and why?

10. This type of authentication activity may be continued with additional illustrated versions of Native American folklore. It is helpful if the students choose examples in which the authors' notes provide enough information to begin the authentication process.

Developing an Understanding of and Appreciation for Latino Culture Through Folklore

The wide cultural areas for Latino folklore include Mexico, South and Central America, Cuba, and the American Southwest. The folklore incorporates pre-Spanish tales of the Aztecs, Maya, and Incas. The Spaniards colonized the earlier populations, and different groups, such as the Apache and Pueblo Indians, interacted.

Many of the early Aztec and Mayan tales were recorded for European audiences by Spaniards in the sixteenth century. Others were written down by Aztecs who learned to read and write at the Texcoco Seminary. These tales were illustrated in pictographic forms on codices and provide many of the sources used by current folklorists and retellers of the tales.

In this series of lesson plans we use semantic mapping or webbing to identify stories that relate to specific traditional values. Webs such as this one may be developed around Mayan cultural values and Aztec cultural values.

Lesson Plan

For Your Plan Book

A Multicultural Study of Latino Folklore

Objectives

1. To develop understanding and appreciation of the traditional Latino culture through a study of folklore.
2. To read, analyze, and discuss ancient Aztec and Mayan folklore and to identify the values depicted in the folklore.
3. To understand the influence of cultural infusion on the people and their folklore and to read, analyze, and discuss folklore that reflects interaction with other cultures.
4. To analyze the cultural information in illustrations.
5. To respond to the vivid illustrations in highly illustrated versions of folklore.

Sources (Literature)

Books that provide examples of folklore include John Bierhorst's *The Monkey's Haircut and Other Stories Told by the Maya* (1986; twenty-two tales) and *Spirit Child: A Story of the Nativity* (1984; pre-Columbian illustrations accompany an Aztec story), Tomie de Paola's *The Lady of Guadalupe* (1980; a traditional tale with Christian content), Lois Ehlert's *Cuckoo: A Mexican Folktale* (1997; a pourquoi tale written in English and Spanish), Pleasant De Spain's *The Emerald Lizard: Fifteen Latin American Tales to Tell* (1999), Shana Greger's *The Fifth and Final Sun: An Ancient Aztec Myth of the Sun's Origin* (1994), Gerald McDermott's *Musicians of the Sun* (1997; an Aztec myth), and Harriet Rohmer and Dornminster Wilson's *Mother Scorpion Country* (1987; a tale from Central America written in both English and Spanish).

Procedures

1. Introduce the Latino literature unit by reading a quote from Griego y Maestas and Anaya (1980) that emphasizes the complexity of Latino literature and culture. The tales "are a great part of the soul of our culture and they reflect the values of our forefathers.... The stories reflect a history of thirteen centuries of infusing and blending from the Moors and Jews in Spain, to the Orientals in the Philippines, Africans in the Caribbean, and the Indians in America—be they Aztec, Apache or Pueblo" (p. 4). Discuss this quote and its implications with the students. Ask "Would you expect to find influences of other cultures in the folklore? Why or why not?" Tell the students that they will begin their study with the ancient folklore of the Aztec and the Mayan people and then proceed to the folklore that reflects the interaction with other cultures. Through this study they will be able to discover how folklore reflects early beliefs and values and how it infuses other cultures and values.
2. Show the students the locations of the Aztec and Mayan peoples on a map of Mexico and Central America. The titles *Atlas of Ancient America* (Coe, Snow, & Benson, 1986) and *The Maya* (Coe, 1984) include useful maps and information about these cultures.
3. Share and discuss several sources of Mayan folklore. Explain to the students that Bierhorst, in *The Monkey's Haircut and Other Stories Told by the Maya,* identifies several characteristics of Mayan folklore that emphasize cultural characteristics and values. As the students listen to these stories, ask them to identify those characteristics and values. Bierhorst identifies the following: (1) cleverness, as shown by stories that include riddles, puns, double meanings, and tricksters; (2) culture, such as paying a bride service and being godparents; and (3) corn and farming practices. These characteristics and values may

Continued

be placed on a web. As students listen to the stories ask them to place the corresponding stories on the web. They may continue this activity by reading or listening to other Mayan folktales.

4. Additional webs may be developed around Aztec folklore. Continue the practice of identifying the values and the stories that reflect those values. Discuss with the students how folklore reflects the traditional values of the early peoples.

Independent Projects and Other Activities with Latino Folklore

Library research: Ask the students to research the early Aztec or Mayan cultures or one of the cultures that influenced the Latino culture. Ask them to consider which culture had the greatest influence and detail the influence.

Artistic investigations: Investigate the works of Mexican artists who illustrate folktales and other texts.

Creative writing: Ask the students to choose one of the Aesop's fables or another European folktale. Ask them to pretend that they heard this story from one of the early Spaniards who came to their country. Have them adapt the story to reflect their setting, culture, and beliefs.

Develop a multicultural museum: Ask the students to create a museum that shows the important information and artifacts from the traditional culture.

A Multicultural Study of Different Versions of the Same Folktale

Studying variants of the same folktale found in different countries and cultures encourages students to develop understandings of cultural diffusion and common needs and problems. Numerous variants can be selected. For example, the "Cinderella," "Little Red Riding Hood," and "Hansel and Gretel" variants are found in cultures throughout the world. Units also can focus on how folktales change across time. Students can speculate about changes in attitudes, language, and illustrations. These activities encourage understanding of cultural diffusion and how a culture is reflected in the adaptation of a tale.

For Your Plan Book

Lesson Plan

A Multicultural Study of Folktales from Different Cultures: Comparing Different Versions of "Cinderella"

Objectives

1. To read and enjoy variations of the same folktale.
2. To identify common elements within the folktales and to discover how the culture is reflected in the tales.
3. To discover that folktales are an excellent source of information about a culture.
4. To become aware of cultural diffusion.
5. To write a variant of a folktale that reflects students' own culture.

Sources (Literature)

A selection of tales should be chosen for group reading and discussions that reflect the Cinderella motif found in various cultures. Examples include the Brothers Grimm's "Cinderella" (German) in *Household Tales;* Charlotte Huck's *Princess Furball* (British); Charles Perrault's "Cinderella," such as Marcia Brown's *Cinderella* (French); Ann Nolan Clark's *In the Land of Small Dragon* (Vietnamese); Shirley Climo's *The Egyptian Cinderella;* John Steptoe's *Mufaro's Beautiful Daughters: An African Tale;* Lynette Dyer Vuong's *The Brocaded Slipper* (Vietnamese); and Penny Pollock's *The Turkey Girl: A Zuni Cinderella Story.*

Procedures

1. To begin this unit, tell the students that some folktales have common story types found in cultures throughout the world. These folktales are called *variants* because they have basic elements in common, but frequently differ in such areas as settings, names of characters, magical objects, tasks to be completed, and obstacles to be overcome.
2. After students have read or listened to several "Cinderella" stories, ask them to identify the common elements in the different versions, such as those retold in Grimm or Perrault. Remind the students that the common elements should be general such as "The heroine has a lowly position in the family." After students have identified several common elements, begin the study of variants by reading the Brothers Grimm and French versions of "Cinderella" during the same class period. Ask the students to notice the common important elements in these tales. Such a list might include the following:
   a. The heroine has a lowly position in the family.
   b. The heroine is persecuted by stepsisters or other members of the family.
   c. The heroine accomplishes difficult tasks.
   d. The heroine has an opportunity to meet a person who has great worth within the culture.
   e. The heroine is kept from meeting the person of great worth because she lacks clothing to attend a function.
   f. The heroine is helped by a supernatural being.
   g. The heroine is warned to return by a certain time.
   h. The person of great worth is attracted to the heroine.
   i. There is a test for the rightful heroine.
   j. The heroine passes the test and marries the person of great worth.
3. Next, ask the students to identify how each of these common elements is developed in the German and French tales. For example, in both tales the girl's lowly position is caused by the mother's death and the father's remarriage. There are some specific differences, however. For example, the girl in the German version receives her wishes from a bird on the tree near her mother's grave and the girl in the French version receives wishes from a fairy godmother. The endings are also different: The German version ends unhappily for the stepmother and stepsisters, while the French version ends in forgiveness of the stepsisters and their marriage to noblemen.
4. After the students have identified common elements and specific examples across the German and French "Cinderella" tales, ask them to read or listen to variants from other cultures. During this activity they should identify the elements that are similar and those that are different. Why do the elements in the stories change? How are these changes related to the cultures in which the tales were told? They should analyze any illustrations

Continued

for cultural information. For example, Clark's *In the Land of Small Dragon* develops considerable cultural background through the illustrations. The Native American "Cinderella" variant is especially rich with cultural and setting information.

Independent Projects and Other Activities With the Cinderella Unit

Creative writing: Ask the students to pretend they are storytellers who are telling a variant of Cinderella that reflects their own culture, their school, or even their family. They should use the common Cinderella elements, but make the audience understand and picture the new culture.

Written personal response: Ask the students to choose a Cinderella variant and explain why they liked or disliked the plot and the characters.

Artistic response: Ask the students to choose a folktale variant that is not highly illustrated. Through their own illustrations, show the setting and other cultural references. Encourage them to research the area and the culture so they will be as accurate as possible.

Geography insights: Ask the students to point out on a map of the world the locations of the various Cinderella variants. Ask "What does the map reveal about the importance of the Cinderella story?"

Creative drama: As a group project, ask the students to select several Cinderella characters from different cultures. Pretend that the characters are having a conversation. What information would the characters exchange? What questions would they ask each other? What advice would they give? Or, pretend that the more cruel members of the story or the supernatural beings could exchange ideas. What advice would they give?

Oral interviewing and collecting tales: Ask the students to interview people in their community, and ask them which Cinderella tale or tales they remember. Summarize the information to discover which Cinderella variant is the most popular in the community.

A Multicultural Study of Historical Fiction, Biography, and Informational Literature

Historical fiction, biography, and informational books are among the best sources for making discoveries about the values, beliefs, and experiences of people who are members of a culture. Children who read historical fiction gain an understanding of their own heritage. They discover the events that proceeded their own time and made the present possible. Through historical fiction, children begin to visualize the sweep of history. Nonfictional books such as biographies and informational books encourage children to look at the world in new ways, to discover laws of nature and society, and to identify with people either like or different from themselves. Informational books can encourage children to develop critical reading and thinking skills. While reading books written on one subject by different authors, children can compare the books to evaluate the objectivity of the authors and determine their qualifications to write about the subject. Many well-written informational books expand children's vocabularies by introducing new words.

Informational books provide an excellent source for developing literary criticism as students consider the accuracy of the facts, the ability of illustrations to clarify the text, the analytical thinking that should be encouraged, the organization of the book to develop understanding, a style that is interesting to read, and a lack of stereotypes. All of these criteria for evaluation are especially important when reading multicultural books (Norton, 2003).

Lesson Plan

For Your Plan Book

A Multicultural Study of African-American Historical Fiction and Biography

Objectives

1. To analyze the role of African/African-American traditional values in historical fiction and biography.
2. To evaluate the settings, conflicts, characterizations, themes, and authors' style in historical fiction.
3. To authenticate historical fiction and biographies by referring to historical events in informational books.
4. To provide a personal response to the characters and situations developed in historical fiction, biographies, and informational literature.

Sources (Literature)

Strong historical fiction and biographies have been written about overcoming problems associated with slavery and the Civil War and about the fight for civil rights in the 1900s. Teachers can use both periods or focus on one. The following example focuses on overcoming slavery and the Civil War.

Literature of slavery and the Civil War: James and Christopher Collier's *Jump Ship to Freedom* (1981; historical fiction) is the story of a slave who obtains his freedom and that of his mother. Paula Fox's *The Slave Dancer* (1973; historical fiction) is the story of a fife player in 1840 who experiences the slave trade. F. N. Monjo's *The Drinking Gourd* (1970; historical fiction) is a story about the Underground Railroad. Gary Paulsen's *Night John* (1993; historical fiction) develops both the ordeals experienced by the slaves and the hope and perseverance that kept them alive. Biographies set in this time period include Lillie Patterson's *Frederick Douglass: Freedom Fighter* (1965; biography), which presents Douglass's life in slavery and his protests against slavery; Douglas Miller's *Frederick Douglass and the Fight for Freedom* (1988; biography) and Michael McCurdy's *Escape from Slavery: The Boyhood of Frederick Douglass in His Own Words* (1994; biography) are excellent for comparative purposes; and Jeri Ferris's *Go Free or Die: A Story of Harriet Tubman* (1988; biography) is the story of Tubman's experiences during slavery and with the Underground Railroad. Milton Meltzer's *The Black Americans: A History in Their Own Words, 1619–1983* (1984; information) includes writings of many African-American people from different times.

Procedures

1. Prepare the school environment by collecting pictures that show the various stages in African-American history from freedom in Africa to slavery in earlier America to the contributions of contemporary politicians, authors, and musicians. Ask the students to bring to class any examples of music, writing, and art that reflect the African-American culture.
2. Introduce one of the historical fiction books. Explain to older students that authors who write about slavery face special problems. How accurately should historical fiction reflect the attitudes and circumstances of the times? Should authors use terms of the period that are considered insensitive and offensive today? Discuss and get student responses.

Continued

3. Select one of the historical fiction books to share with the group. Students can do this first series of activities around a single book and then read additional selections to independently analyze and then discuss. Review the importance of each of the following literary elements when writing historical fiction: setting, conflict, characterization, theme, language, and authors' styles. Ask students to identify good examples of each of these literary elements. You may also ask them to locate examples that they do not believe are authentic for the time period.

4. After students have read African-American folklore, they can search for evidence of the values and beliefs found in the traditional literature that are similar to those found in the historical fiction and biographies. For example, when they analyze the biography *Go Free or Die: A Story of Harriet Tubman,* they will find the following evidence of values and beliefs that are found in both traditional folklore and in historical fiction:
   a. The themes developed by the author show that freedom is worth risking one's life for and we must help others obtain their freedom.
   b. The values developed by the characters and their actions show that obligations to family and others are important, wit and trickery might be needed to influence the balance of power, responsibility is important, and expressing gratitude is essential.

5. Students will discover that the sources of conflict are person against society as Harriet fights to free African-Americans and combat injustice. When they look to various nonfiction informational sources to identify the historical events, they will discover:
   a. The setting is in America from the mid-1800s to the end of the Civil War.
   b. The story is based on facts about slavery, the Underground Railroad, the 1850 Fugitive Slave Act, and the 1863 Emancipation Proclamation.
   c. They will discover that Tubman freed more than 300 slaves in ten years.

Either in groups or individually, ask the students to read and analyze additional historical fiction and biographies. If this unit is extended into contemporary times, the students should consider any similarities between the themes, values, and conflicts. Ask the students to think about why these themes, values, and person-against-society conflicts might be important in the lives of people today.

Independent Projects and Other Activities to Use with the Multicultural Unit

Creative dramatizations and role-playing: Have students choose a scene and present it as a dramatization, or choose an issue and role-play the various responses that people might have as they take a stance on the issue. Have students choose one of the books and read it as a Reader's Theater presentation.

Dramatic readings: Have students read the poetry of Langston Hughes and prepare several of the poems as dramatic readings to share with the class.

Library research: Ask students to choose one of the African countries from which slaves were sent to America. Compare the country during the time of slavery with the country today.

Personal Responses Through Writing and Art: Ask students to keep a writing journal and to respond to what happens to the characters in the historical fiction of biographical stories. They also can create a collage that expresses their feelings as a historical character faces and overcomes conflict.

Literature expansion: Ask the students to read several works by African-American authors such as Virginia Hamilton, Eloise Greenfield, John Steptoe, Tom Feelings, Ossie Davis, Langston Hughes, Mildred Taylor, or Walter Dean Myers. Have them analyze the types of stories they write, consider how these authors develop a cultural perspective in their works, and respond personally to their works.

Artistic expansion: Ask the students to choose an African-American illustrator such as Leo Dillon, Tom Feelings, Jerry Pinkney, or John Steptoe. Have the students analyze the types of illustrations these artists create and the stories they choose to illustrate. Ask the students to consider how these illustrators develop cultural perspectives in their works and to respond personally to their illustrations.

Evaluation Criteria for Multicultural Literature

1. Are the characters portrayed as individuals instead of as representatives of a group?
2. Does the book transcend stereotypes?
3. Does the book portray physical diversity?
4. Will children be able to recognize the characters in the text and illustrations?
5. Is the culture accurately portrayed?
6. Are social issues and problems depicted frankly, accurately, and without oversimplification?
7. Do nonwhite characters solve their problems without intervention by whites?
8. Are nonwhite characters shown as equals of white characters?
9. Does the author avoid glamorizing or glorifying nonwhite characters?
10. Is the setting authentic?
11. Are the factual and historical details accurate?
12. Does the author accurately describe contemporary settings?
13. Does dialect have a legitimate purpose and does it ring true?
14. Are the illustrations authentic and nonstereotypical?
15. Does the book reflect an awareness of the changing status of females? (Norton, 2003)

SUMMARY

The issues relating to instruction of children with diverse linguistic or cultural backgrounds are complex. Because the majority of children classified as linguistically different have consistently made smaller academic gains than have children who speak standard English, the subject is of great concern to educators. If these children are to compete with speakers of standard English, then teachers must be specifically prepared to understand their different needs and help them to succeed.

This chapter reviewed educational alternatives suggested by linguists and educators. Alternatives include oral language expansion programs, conventional materials read in dialect, and the language experience approach.

Investigators are concerned not only with the interference of black English in instruction with standard English materials but also with the problems of testing children from diverse cultures using tests written in standard English. Some educators suggest that if standardized tests are used, scoring procedures should be modified. For example, oral reading tests should be scored so that mistakes attributable to dialect differences are not counted as reading errors. Other educators recommend the use of nonstandardized tests. This chapter reviewed some informal testing procedures, such as using pictures to elicit oral language samples and role-playing techniques. Teachers cannot provide evaluation unless they are familiar with differences between black English and standard English. In addition to bias within tests, teacher attitudes and environment also influence testing and academic results.

Characteristics of effective intervention programs for children from low-income families are also discussed. The language or literacy development of these children may be delayed by conditions at home. For students in bilingual programs, including English as a second language, recommendations for effective education emphasize interactions among students, teachers, and community, as well as relevant content for the students.

The chapter concludes with recommendations for developing course content relevant for students from diverse linguistic and cultural backgrounds. Teachers should evaluate multicultural literature and balance their educational programs by selecting literature that both recognizes that Americans take pride in their multicultural backgrounds and helps students in their search for identity.

ADDITIONAL MULTICULTURAL EDUCATION ACTIVITIES

1. Informally interview a child who uses black English or listen to conversations on a playground (tape the conversations). Can you identify any of the phonological and syntactic features discussed in this chapter?

2. Read and summarize the findings in three current journal articles that provide information on (a) teaching children from diverse linguistic backgrounds, (b) teaching bilingual classes, and (c) teaching English as a second language.

3. Compare the characteristics of Native Americans in a book published before 1965 (for example, Walter Edmond's *The Matchlock Gun*) with the characteristics of Native Americans in a book published after 1975 (for example, Brent Ashabranner's *Morning Star, Black Sun: The Northern Cheyenne Indians and America's Energy Crisis*). Find quotations that show stereotypic or nonstereotypic characterizations.

4. Read one of the books awarded the Coretta Scott King Award for portraying "people, places, things, and events in a manner sensitive to the true worth and value of things." Read one of the books that the Children's Literature Review Board does not recommend because of stereotypes, unacceptable values, or terms used. For example, David Arkin's *Black and White*, Florine Robinson's *Ed and Ted*, Shirley Burden's *I Wonder Why*, Anco Surany's *Monsieur Jolicoeur's Umbrella*, May Justus's *New Boy in School*, or William Pappas's *No Mules*. Develop a rationale for the recommendations for the King award and for the negative responses for the stereotypic books.

BIBLIOGRAPHY

Adler, Sol. "Data Gathering: The Reliability and Validity of Test Data from Culturally Different Children." *Journal of Learning Disabilities* 6 (August/September 1973): 429–34.

Allen, Adela Artola. "The School Library Media Center and the Promotion of Literature for Hispanic Children." *Library Trends* 41 (Winter 1993): 437–61.

Appiah, Kwame Anthony; and Gates, Henry Louis, Jr., eds. *The Dictionary of Global Culture*. New York: Knopf, 1996.

Ball, Arnetha F.; and Farr, Marcia. "Language Varieties, Culture and Teaching the English Language Arts." In *Handbook of Research on Teaching the English Language Arts*, 2nd ed., edited by James Flood, Diane Lapp, James R. Squire, and Julie M. Jensen. Mahwah, N.J.: Lawrence Erlbaum, 2003, pp. 435–45.

Baratz, Joan C. "A Bi-Dialectical Task for Determining Language Proficiency in Economically Disadvantaged Children." *Child Development* 40 (December 1969): 889–901.

———; and Shuy, Roger. *Teaching Black Children to Read.* Washington, D.C.: Center for Applied Linguistics, 1969.

Bartel, Nettie R.; Grill, Jeffrey, J.; and Bryen, Diane N. "Language Characteristics of Black Children: Implications for Assessment." *Journal of School Psychology* 11 (Winter 1973): 351–64.

Bereiter, Carol; and Engelmann, Siegfried. *Teaching Disadvantaged Children in the Preschool.* Upper Saddle River, N.J.: Prentice Hall, 1966.

Bernstein, B. "Social Structure, Language, and Learning." *Educational Research* 3 (1961): 163–76.

Booth, William. "Diversity and Division: America's New Wave of Immigration Is Changing Its 'Melting Pot' Image." *The Washington Post,* National Weekly Edition, 15 (March 2, 1998): 6–8.

Brause, R.; and Mayher, J. "Our Students." In *Handbook of Research on Teaching the English Language Arts,* edited by J. Flood, J. Jensen, D. Lapp, and J. Squire. New York: Macmillan, 1991, pp. 259–72.

Burton, Nancy W.; and Jones, Lyle V. "Recent Trends in Achievement Levels of Black and White Youth." *Educational Research* (April 1982): 10–14, 17.

Calvert, John D. *An Exploratory Study to Adapt the Language Experience Approach to Remedial Seventh and Tenth Grade Mexican American Students.* Doctoral Dissertation, Arizona State University, 1973.

Carter, Candy, ed. *Non-Native and Nonstandard Dialect Students: Classroom Practices in Teaching English, 1982–1983.* Urbana, Ill.: National Council of Teachers of English, 1982.

Chall, J.; and Curtis, M. "Children at Risk." In *Handbook of Research on Teaching the English Language Arts,* edited by J. Flood, J. Jensen, D. Lapp, and J. Squire. New York: Macmillan, 1991, pp. 349–55.

Chall, J. S.; Jacobs, V. A.; and Baldwin, L. E. *The Reading Crisis: Why Poor Children Fall Behind.* Cambridge, Mass.: Harvard University Press, 1990.

Coe, M. *The Maya,* 3rd ed. New York: Thames and Hudson, 1984.

Coe, M; Snow, D.; and Benson, E. *Atlas of Ancient America.* New York: Facts On File, 1986.

Cohen, S. A. *Teach Them All to Read.* New York: Random House, 1969.

Cortes, C. E. "The Education of Language Minority Students: A Contextual Interaction Model." California State Department of Education. *Beyond Language: Social and Cultural Factors in Schooling Language Minority Students.* Los Angeles, Calif.: California State University Evaluation, Dissemination, and Assessment Center, 1986, pp. 299–343.

Crowl, Thomas K.; and MacGinitie, Walter H. "The Influence of Students' Speech Characteristics on Teachers' Evaluations of Oral Answers." *Journal of Educational Psychology* 66 (June 1974): 304–08.

Cullinan, Bernice E.; Jaggar, Angela M.; and Strickland, Dorothy. "Oral Language Expansion in the Primary Grades." In *Black Dialects and Reading,* edited by Bernice E. Cullinan. Urbana, Ill.: National Council of Teachers of English, 1974.

Cumming, A. "Metalinguistic and Ideational Thinking in Second Language Composing." *Written Communication* 7 (1990): 482–511.

Cunningham, Patricia M. "Teachers' Correction Responses to Black Dialect Miscues Which Are Non-Meaning Changing." *Reading Research Quarterly* 12 (Summer 1977): 637–53.

Daniels, Lee A. "Study Links Academic Skills to Race and Family Income." *New York Times* (October 25, 1987): 15.

de Félix, Judith Walker. "Steps to Second Language Development in the Regular Classroom." In *Non-Native and Nonstandard Dialect Students: Classroom Practices in Teaching English, 1982–1983,* edited by Candy Carter. Urbana, Ill.: National Council of Teachers of English, 1982.

Early, Margaret. "Enabling First and Second Language Learners in the Classroom." *Language Arts* 67 (1990): 567–75.

Eisenberg, Leon. "The Epidemiology of Reading Retardation and a Program for Preventive Intervention." In *The Disabled Reader,* edited by John Money. Baltimore: Johns Hopkins University Press, 1974.

Ezer, H. "Writing Development in a Bilingual First Grader: A Case Study." 1990. *Dissertation Abstracts International* 51: 04A. (University Microfilms No. 90–15,289.)

Farr, M. "Dialects, Culture, and Teaching the English Language Arts." In *Handbook of Research on Teaching the English Language Arts,* edited by J. Flood, J. Jensen, D. Lapp, and J. Squire. New York: Macmillan, 1991, pp. 365–71.

Freedman, B. M. "Literacy and Cultural Identity." *Harvard Educational Review* 60 (1990): 181–204.

Fryburg. "Black English: A Descriptive Guide for the Teacher." In *Black Dialects and Reading,* edited by Bernice E. Cullinan. Urbana, Ill.: National Council of Teachers of English, 1974.

Furst, Peter T.; and Furst, Jill L. *North American Indian Art.* New York: Rizzoli, 1982.

Genishi, C. "Observing the Second Language Learner: An Example of Teachers' Learning." *Language Arts* 66 (1989): 509–15.

Gill, Sam D.; and Sullivan, Irene F. *Dictionary of Native American Mythology.* New York: Oxford University Press, 1992.

Goodman, Y. "Evaluating Language Development: Informal Methods of Evaluation." In *Handbook of Research on Teaching the English Language Arts,* edited by J. Flood, J. Jensen, D. Lapp, and J. Squire. New York: Macmillan, 1991, pp. 502–09.

Greenberg, Judith W.; and Davison, Helen H. "Home Background and School Achievement of Black, Urban Ghetto Children." *American Journal of Orthopsychiatry* 42 (October 1972): 803–10.

Hall, MaryAnne. *The Development of Evaluation of a Language Experience Approach to Reading with First-Grade Culturally Disadvantaged Children.* Doctoral Dissertation, University of Maryland, 1965.

Harber, Jean R.; and Beatty, Jane N. *Reading and the Black English Speaking Child.* Newark, Del.: International Reading Association, 1978.

Haukoos, Gerry; and LaBeau, Dorothy. "Inservice Activity that Emphasizes the Importance of the Culture in Teaching School Science." *Journal of American Indian Education* 32 (October 1992): 1–11.

Hearne, Betsy. "Cite the Source: Reducing Cultural Chaos in Picture Books, Part One." *School Library Journal* 39 (July 1993): 22–27.

Hodgson, Bryan. "Buffalo: Back Home on the Range." *National Geographic* (November 1994).

Hoffman, James; and Pearson, P. David. "Reading Teacher Education in the Next Millennium: What Your Grandmother's Teacher Didn't Know That Your Granddaughter's Teacher Should." *Reading Research Quarterly* 35 (January/February/March 2000): 28–44.

Hudelson, Sarah; Poynor, Leslie; and Wolf, Paula. "Teaching Bilingual and ESL Children and Adolescents." In *Handbook of Research and Teaching the English Language Arts,* 2nd ed., edited by James Flood, Diane Lapp, James R. Squire, and Julie M. Jensen. Mahwah, N.J.: Lawrence Erlbaum, 2003, pp. 421–34.

Hunt, Barbara Carey. "Black Dialect and Third and Fourth Graders' Performance on the Gray Oral Reading Test." *Reading Research Quarterly* 10 (Fall 1974): 103–23.

Hutchinson, June O'Shields. "Reading Tests and Nonstandard Language." *Reading Teacher* 25 (February 1972): 430–37.

Johnston, Bill; Juhasz, Andrea; Marken, James; and Ruiz, Beverly Rolfs. "The ESL Teacher as Moral Agent." *Research in the Teaching of English* 32 (May 1998): 161–81.

Juel, C. "Learning to Read and Write: A Longitudinal Study of 54 Children from First through Fourth Grades." *Journal of Educational Psychology* 80 (1988): 437–47.

Kagan, S.; and Madsen, M. "Cooperation and Competition of Mexican, Mexican American, and Anglo American Children of Two Ages Under Four Instructional Sets." *Developmental Psychology* 5 (1971): 32–39.

Kozol, Jonathan. "An Unequal Education." *School Library Journal* 46 (May 2000): 46.

Labov, William. *Language in the Inner City: Studies in the Black English Vernacular.* Philadelphia: University of Pennsylvania Press, 1973.

———. *The Logic of Non-Standard English.* Washington, D.C.: Georgetown Monograph Series on Language and Linguistics No. 22, 1969.

———. "The Logic of Non-Standard English." In *Language and Poverty,* edited by Frederick Williams. Chicago: Markham Publishing Co., 1971.

———. *Study of Non-Standard English.* Urbana, Ill.: National Council of Teachers of English, 1970.

Lee, Kang; Cameron, Catherine Ann; Linton, Murray J.; and Hunt, Anne K. "Referential Place-Holding in Chinese Children's Acquisition of English Articles." *Applied Psycholinguistics* 15 (March 1994): 29–42.

Lewis, Rena B.; and Doorlag, Donald H. *Teaching Special Students in the Mainstream,* 4th ed. Upper Saddle River, N.J.: Merrill/Prentice Hall, 1998.

Maestas, Leo Carlos. "Ethnicity and High School Student Achievement Across Rural and Urban Districts." *Educational Research Quarterly* (Fall 1981): 33–42.

Mantell, Arlene. "Strategies for Language Expansion in the Middle Grades." In *Black Dialects and Reading,* edited by Bernice E. Cullinan. Urbana, Ill.: National Council of Teachers of English, 1974.

Marzano, R. "Language, the Arts, and Thinking." In *Handbook of Research on Teaching the English Language Arts,* edited by J. Flood, J. Jensen, D. Lapp, and J. Squire. New York: Macmillan, 1991, pp. 559–86.

McAlpine, Lynn; and Taylor, Donald M. "Instructional Preferences of Cree, Inuit, and Mohawk Teachers." *Journal of American Indian Education* 33 (Fall 1993): 1–20.

McCarty, Teresa. "Language, Literacy, and the Image of the Child in American Indian Classrooms." *Language Arts* 70 (March 1993): 182–92.

McConnell, B. "Education as a Cultural Process: The Interaction between Community and Classroom in Fostering Learning." In *Risk Makers, Risk Takers, Risk Breakers: Reducing the Risks for Young Literacy Learners,* edited by J. Allen and J. Mason. Portsmouth, N.H.: Heinemann, 1989, pp. 201–21.

National Public Radio. "Morning Edition." January 9, 1992.

Norton, Donna E. "Changing Attitudes Toward Minorities: Children's Literature Shapes Attitudes." *Review Journal of Philosophy and Social Science* 9 (1984): 97–113.

———. "The Development, Dissemination, and Evaluation of a Multi-Ethnic Curricular Model for Preservice Teachers, Inservice Teachers, and Elementary Children." New Orleans: International Reading Association, National Conference, April 1981.

———. *The Impact of Literature-Based Reading.* Upper Saddle River, N.J.: Merrill/Prentice Hall, 1992.

———. *Multicultural Children's Literature: Through the Eyes of Many Children.* Upper Saddle River, N.J.: Merrill/Prentice Hall, 2001.

———. *Through the Eyes of a Child: An Introduction to Children's Literature.* Upper Saddle River, N.J.: Merrill/Prentice Hall, 2003.

———. "The Rise and Fall of Ethnic Literature." Paper presented at the annual meeting of the National Conference of Teachers of English, Phoenix, Ariz., 1986.

———. "Teaching Multicultural Literature." *The Reading Teacher* 44 (1990): 28–40.

———; and Norton, Saundra E. "Document Authentication of Folklore." *Encyclopedia of Library and Information Science* 61 (1998): 109–21.

———; and Norton, S. E. *Language Arts Activities for Children,* 5th ed. Upper Saddle River, N.J.: Merrill/Prentice Hall, 2003.

Parker, Arthur C. *Skunny Wundy: Seneca Indian Tales.* Chicago: Whitman, 1926.

Peregoy, Susanne F.; and Boyle, Owen F. *Reading, Writing, & Learning in ESL,* 3rd ed. New York: Longman, 2001.

Pikulski, J. J. "The Assessment of Reading: A Time for Change?" *The Reading Teacher* 43 (1989): 80–81.

Piper, David. "Language Growth in the Multiethnic Classroom." *Language Arts* 63 (January 1986): 23–36.

Purves, Alan; and Purves, William. "Viewpoints: Cultures, Text Models, and the Activity of Writing." *Research in the Teaching of English* 20 (May 1986): 174–97.

Quintero, E.; and Huerta-Macias, A. "All in the Family: Bilingualism and Biliteracy." *The Reading Teacher* 44 (1990): 306–12.

Ramírez III, Manuel; and Castañeda, Alfredo. *Cultural Democracy, Bicognitive Development, and Education.* New York: Academic Press, 1974.

Ramírez III, Manuel; and Price-Williams, D. R. "Cognitive Styles of Children of Three Ethnic Groups in the United States." *Journal of Cross-Cultural Psychology* 5 (1974): 212–19.

———. *The Relationship of Culture to Educational Attainment.* Houston, Tex.: Center for Research in Social Change and Economic Development, Rice University, 1971.

Rankin, Charles; and Parish, Thomas. "Discerning the Multicultural Hierarchies of the '90's: Who's On First?" *Reading Improvement* 31 (Winter 1994): 253–54.

Rochman, Hazel. *Against Borders: Promoting Books for a Multicultural World.* Chicago: American Library Association, 1993.

Sealey, D. Bruce. "Measuring the Multicultural Quotient of a School." *TESL Canada Journal/Revue TESL Du Canada* 1 (March 1984): 21–28.

Slavin, R. E.; and Madden, N. A. "What Works for Students at Risk: A Research Synthesis." *Educational Leadership* 64 (1989): 4–13.

Stott, Jon. "In Search of Sedna: Children's Versions of a Major Inuit Myth." *Children's Literature Quarterly* 15 (Winter 1990): 199–201.

Valencia, S. "A Portfolio Approach to Classroom Reading Assessment: The Whys, Whats, and Hows." *The Reading Teacher* 43 (1990): 420–22.

Watson-Thompson, O. B. "An Investigation of Elementary School Teachers' Attitudes toward the Use of Black English in West Alabama." 1985. *Dissertation Abstracts International* 46: 11A. (University Microfilms No. DA 8600778.)

Wolfram, Walt. "Sociolinguistic Implications for Educational Sequencing." In *Teaching Standard English in the Inner City,* edited by Ralph Fasold and Roger W. Shuy. Washington, D.C.: Center for Applied Linguistics, 1970.

Wong-Fillmore, Lily. "Research Currents: Equity or Excellence? *Language Arts* 63 (September 1986): 474–81.

ANNOTATED MULTICULTURAL CHILDREN'S LITERATURE REFERENCES

The following books are examples of literature that meet the multicultural criteria listed in this chapter. The books include an interest level designated by age (I:5–8) and a readability level designated by grade (R:3).

African-American Literature

Traditional Tales

Aardema, Verna, retold by. *Anansi Does the Impossible: An Ashanti Tale.* Illustrated by Lisa Desimini. New York: Simon & Schuster, 1997 (I:5–8). Anansi and his wife outsmart the Sky God.

————. *Bringing the Rain to Kapiti Plain: A Nandi Tale.* Illustrated by Beatriz Vidal. New York: Dial Press, 1981 (I:5–8). A cumulative tale from Kenya tells how a herdsman pierces a cloud with his arrow and brings rain to the parched land.

————. *Misoso: Once Upon a Time Tales from Africa.* Illustrated by Reynold Ruffins. New York: Alfred A. Knopf, 1994 (I:6–10, R:5). This is a collection of twelve African folktales.

————. *What's So Funny, Ketu? A Nuer Tale.* Illustrated by Marc Brown. New York: Dial Press, 1982 (I:5–8, R:6). The repetitive language and African words adds authenticity.

————. *Who's in Rabbit's House?* Illustrated by Leo and Diane Dillon. New York: Dial Press, 1977 (I:7+, R:3). A Masai folktale is illustrated as a play performed by villagers wearing masks.

Bryan, Ashley. *Beat the Story-Drum, Pum-Pum.* New York: Atheneum, 1980 (I:7+, R:6). This text includes five Nigerian folktales.

Bryan, Ashley. *The Dancing Granny and Other African Stories.* New York: Caedom, 1985. (I: all). The tape includes four folktales.

Daly, Nicki. *Why the Sun & Moon Live in the Sky.* New York: Lothrop, Lee & Shepard, 1995 (I:5+, R:4). A Nigerian folktale.

Echewa, T. Obinkaram. *The Magic Tree: A Folktale from Nigeria.* Illustrated by E. B. Lewis. New York: Morrow, 1999 (I:5–8). A special tree helps an orphan boy.

Faulkner, William. *The Days When the Animals Talked.* Chicago: Follett, 1977. An excellent adult reference that includes African-American folktales and interpretations about how they developed.

Gatti, Anne, retold by. *Tales from the African Plains.* Illustrated by Gregory Alexander. New York: Dutton, 1995 (I:all). This is a collection of 12 folktales from Kenya.

Grifalconi, Ann. *The Village of Round and Square Houses.* Boston: Little, Brown, 1986 (I:4–9, R:6). This is a folktale from Cameroon.

Hamilton, Virginia, retold by. *The Girl Who Spun Gold.* Illustrated by Leo and Diane Dillon, New York: Scholastic, 2000 (I:4–8). A West Indies version of "Rumpelstiltskin."

———. *The People Could Fly: American Black Folktales.* Illustrated by Leo and Diane Dillon. New York: Alfred A. Knopf, 1985 (I:9+, R:6). This book contains animal, fanciful, supernatural, and slave tales.

Harris, Joel Chandler. *Jump Again! More Adventures of Brer Rabbit.* Adapted by Van Dyke Parks, illustrated by Barry Moser. San Diego: Harcourt Brace Jovanovich, 1987 (I:8+, R:6). Five stories appear in this illustrated version.

Hooks, William H. *The Ballad of Belle Dorcas.* Illustrated by Brian Pinkney. New York: Alfred A. Knopf, 1990 (I:8+, R:4). This folktale has a theme about love and freedom.

Kituku, Vincent Muli Wa, retold by. *East African Folktales.* Little Rock: August House, 1997 (I:8+). Each of the 18 tales ends with a moral.

Knutson, Barbara, retold by. *How the Guinea Fowl Got Her Spots.* Minneapolis: Carolrhoda, 1990 (I:all, R:4). This Swahili folktale is about friendship.

Lester, Julius. *John Henry.* Illustrated by Jerry Pinkney. New York: Dial Press, 1994 (I:all, R:4). This is a retelling of the legend of the powerful man who beat the steam drill with his sledgehammer.

———. *The Tales of Uncle Remus: The Adventures of Brer Rabbit.* Illustrated by Jerry Pinkney. New York: Dial Press, 1987 (I:8+, R:5). This is a new retelling of the Joel Chandler Harris tales.

Martin, Francesca. *Clever Tortoise: A Traditional African Tale.* New York: Candlewick, 2000 (I:5–8). Rhythmic language and Kiswahiti words tell a story about brains overcoming brawn.

McDermott, Gerald. *Zomo the Rabbit: A Trickster Tale from West Africa.* San Diego: Harcourt Brace Jovanovich, 1992 (I:all). Zomo, the trickster, discovers the true meaning of wisdom.

Shepard, Aaron. *Master Man: A Tall Tale of Nigeria.* Illustrated by David Wisniewski. New York: HarperCollins, 2001 (I:all). This folktale is from the Hausa.

Walker, Barbara, retold by. *The Dancing Palm Tree and Other Nigerian Folktales.* Illustrated by Helen Siegel. Lubbock, Tex.: Texas Tech University Press, 1990 (I:all, R:5). The text includes eleven Nigerian folktales.

Poetry and Songs

Brown, Marcia. *Shadow* (from the French of Blaise Cendrars). New York: Charles Scribner's Sons, 1982 (I:8+). Poetry and collage paintings evoke the image of African storytellers and shamans.

Bryan, Ashley. *All Night, All Day: A Child's First Book of African American Spirituals.* New York: Atheneum, 1991 (I:3–8).

———. *I'm Going to Sing: Black American Spirituals, Volume Two.* New York: Atheneum, 1982 (I:all). Words and music are complemented by woodcuts.

———. *Walk Together Children: Black American Spirituals.* New York: Atheneum, 1974 (I:all). This book includes twenty-four spirituals.

Davis, Ossie. *Langston: A Play.* New York: Delacorte Press, 1982 (I:10+). Langston Hughes's poetry is used as part of the dialogue in a play about the famous poet.

Gershwin, George; Howard, Du Bose; Heyward, Dorothy; and Gershwin, Ira. *Summertime, From Porgy and Bess.* New York: Simon & Schuster, 1999 (I:all). Based on words from the folk opera.

Hughes, Langston. *The Dream Keeper and Other Poems.* Illustrated by Brian Pinkney. New York: Alfred A. Knopf, 1994 (I:8+). This is a newly illustrated edition of poems first published in 1932.

Contemporary Realistic Fiction

Greene, Bette. *Phillip Hall Likes Me. I Reckon Maybe.* Illustrated by Charles Lilly. New York: Dial Press, 1974 (I:10+, R:4). A humorous book about a girl's first crush is set in the Arkansas mountains.

Greenfield, Eloise. *Sister.* Illustrated by Moneta Barnett. New York: Thomas Y. Crowell Co., 1974 (I:8–12, R:5). A thirteen-year-old reviews the memories written in her book.

Hamilton, Virginia. *The House of Dies Drear.* Illustrated by Eros Keith. New York: Macmillan, 1968 (I:10+, R:4). This contemporary suspenseful story is about a family living in a home that was on the Underground Railroad.

———. *M. C. Higgins, the Great.* New York: Macmillan, 1974 (I:10+, R:4). A boy dreams of leaving his home and the spoil heap that threatens his security; instead, he builds a wall to protect his home.

———. *The Planet of Junior Brown.* New York: Macmillan, 1971 (I:10+, R:6). Three outcasts create their own world in a secret basement room.

———. *Zeely.* Illustrated by Symeon Shimin. New York: Macmillan, 1967 (I:8–12, R:4). A girl discovers Zeely's identity and also discovers her own.

Kurtz, Jane. *Faraway Home.* Illustrated by E. B. Lewis. San Diego: Harcourt, 2000 (I:5–8). A father tells his daughter about his Ethiopian homeland.

Mathis, Sharon Bell. *The Hundred Penny Box.* Illustrated by Diane Dillon. New York: Viking Press, 1975 (I:6–9, R:3). A penny represents each of the years in the life of a 100-year-old woman.

Mollel, Tololwa M. *My Rows and Piles of Coins.* Illustrated by E. B. Lewis. New York: Clarion, 1999 (I:6–9). Set in Tanzania, a boy works and saves money for a bicycle.

Myers, Walter Dean. *The Mouse Rap.* New York: Harper & Row, 1990 (I:10+, R:5). A boy describes his summer in Harlem.

Quintana, Anton. *The Baboon King.* Translated by John Nieuwenhuizen. New York: Walker, 1999 (I:10+). An African boy survives in the wilderness.

Steptoe, Joe. *Stevie.* New York: Harper & Row, 1969 (I:3–7, R:3). A boy is jealous at first but then discovers the importance of friendship.

Historical Fiction

Collier, James; and Collier, Christopher. *Jump Ship to Freedom.* New York: Delacorte Press, 1981 (I:10+, R:7). A slave obtains his freedom and the freedom of his mother.

Curtis, Christopher Paul. *Bud, Not Buddy.* New York: Delacorte, 1999 (I:10+). Set during the Depression, a ten-year-old boy searches for his father.

Curtis, Gavin. *The Bat Boy & His Violin.* Illustrated by E. B. Lewis. New York: Simon & Schuster, 1998 (I:5–9). Set during the African-American baseball league.

Fox, Paula. *The Slave Dancer.* Illustrated by Eros Keith. New York: Bradbury, 1973 (I:12t, R:7). A fife player experiences the slave trade.

Grimes, Nikki. *Jazmin's Notebook.* New York: Dial Press, 1998 (I:10+). Set in Harlem of the 1960s, the book is written in diary format.

Lowery, Linda. *Aunt Clara Brown: Official Pioneer.* Illustrated by Janice Lee Porter. Minneapolis: Carolrhoda, 1999 (I:7–9). A freed slave becomes a Colorado pioneer.

McGill, Alice. *Molly Bannaky.* Illustrated by Chris K. Soentpiet. Boston: Houghton Mifflin, 1999 (I:8+). A freed indentured servant marries a freed slave.

Monjo, F. N. *The Drinking Gourd.* Illustrated by Fred Brenner. New York: Harper & Row, 1970 (I:7–9, R:2). An "I can read" history book tells about a family on the Underground Railroad.

Paulsen, Gary. *Night John.* New York: Delacorte, 1993 (I:10t, R:4). A slave teaches children to read.

Polacco, Patricia. *Pink and Say.* New York: Philomel, 1994 (I:9+, R:5). In a Civil War story, two soldiers, a white boy and an African-American boy, learn about courage, family, and slavery.

Siegelson, Kim L. *In the Time of the Drums.* Illustrated by Brian Pinkney. New York: Hyperion, 1999 (I:7+). An African-American slave boy watches his grandmother lead an insurrection of slaves.

Taulbert, Clifton L. *Little Cliff and the Porch People.* Illustrated by E. B. Lewis. New York: Dial Press, 1999. Set in the Mississippi Delta of the 1950s.

Taylor, Mildred. *The Gold Cadillac.* Illustrated by Michael Hays. New York: Dial Press, 1987 (I:8–10, R:3). An African-American family encounters racial prejudice when they attempt to drive an expensive car into the segregated South.

———. *Let the Circle Be Unbroken.* New York: Dial Press, 1981 (I:10+, R:6). The author continues the story of the family in *Roll of Thunder, Hear My Cry.*

———. *Roll of Thunder, Hear My Cry.* Illustrated by Jerry Pickney. New York: Dial Press, 1976 (I:10+, R:6). A Mississippi family in 1933 experiences night riders and humiliating experiences but retains their independence.

Nonfiction

Adoff, Arnold. *Malcolm X.* New York: Thomas Y. Crowell Co., 1970 (I:7–12, R:5). This biography of a black leader highlights the changes that took place in his life.

Bray, Rosemary L. *Martin Luther King.* Illustrated by Malcah Zeldis. New York: Greenwillow, 1995 (I:7–11, R:4). A highly illustrated biography of the African-American leader.

Bridges, Ruby. *Through My Eyes.* New York: Scholastic, 1999 (I: all). The author tells about her experiences during integration.

Burns, Khepha; and Miles, William. *Black Stars in Orbit: NASA's African American Astronauts.* San Diego: Harcourt Brace Jovanovich, 1995 (I:10+, R:6). The text provides a history of African-American pilots and covers pilots, scientists, and physicians who worked for NASA.

Ferris, Jeri. *Go Free or Die: A Story of Harriet Tubman.* Minneapolis: Carolrhoda, 1988 (I:7t, R:4). The biography describes Tubman's experiences during slavery.

Hamilton, Virginia. *Anthony Burns: The Defeat and Triumph of a Fugitive Slave.* New York: Alfred A. Knopf, 1988 (I:10+, R:6). This is a biography of the escaped slave whose trial caused riots in Boston.

Lasky, Kathryn. *Vision of Beauty: The Story of Sarah Breedlove Walker.* Illustrated by Nneka Bennett. New York: Candlewick, 2000 (I:8–10). A biography about an African-American businesswoman in the cosmetics industry.

Lazo, Caroline. *Arthur Ashe.* Minneapolis: Lerner, 1999 (I:8+). The biography traces the career of the tennis champion.

McCurdy, Michael, edited by. *Escape from Slavery: The Boyhood of Frederick Douglass in His Own Words.* New York: Knopf, 1994 (I:9+). This autobiography presents Douglass's original language.

McKee, Tim. *No More Strangers Now: Young Voices from a New South Africa.* Photographs by Anne Blackshaw. New York: Dorling Kindersley, 1998 (I:10+). Personal narratives describe experiences.

Meltzer, Milton. *The Black Americans: A History in Their Own Words, 1619–1983.* New York: Crowell 1984 (I:10t R:6). Short writings provide a political and social history.

Meltzer, Milton, edited by. *Frederick Douglass: In His Own Words.* Illustrated by Stephen Alcorn. San Diego: Harcourt Brace Jovanovich, 1995 (I:10+). This is a collection of speeches given by Frederick Douglass.

————. *There Comes a Time: The Struggle for Civil Rights.* New York: Random House, 2001 (I:10+). A survey of the Civil Rights movement.

Miller, Douglas. *Frederick Douglass and the Right for Freedom.* New York: Facts on File, 1988.

Patterson, Lillie. *Frederick Douglass: Freedom Fighter.* Champaign, Ill.: Garrard, 1965 (I:6–9, R:3). This is a biography of a great African-American leader.

Pinkney, Andrea Davis. *Alvin Ailey.* New York: Hyperion, 1993 (I:6–8, R:4). This is a biography of a pioneer in American dance.

————. *Let It Shine: Stories of Black Women Freedom Fighters.* Illustrated by Stephen Alcorn. San Diego: Harcourt, 2000 (I:8+). Short biographies of women who worked for equal rights.

Schraff, Anne. *Ralph Bunch: Winner of the Nobel Peace Prize.* Springfield, N.J.: Enslow, 1999 (I:8+). A biography of the diplomat who risked his life for peace.

Venezia, Mike. *Jacob Lawrence.* Dansbury, Conn.: Children's Press, 1999 (I:all). A heavily illustrated biography about the artist.

Asian-American Literature

Traditional Tales

Asian Cultural Center for UNESCO. *Folk Tales from Asia for Children Everywhere,* Book Three. Weatherhill, 1976 (I:8–12, R:6). This is a collection of folktales from many Asian nations.

Conger, David. *Many Lands, Many Stories: Asian Folktales for Children.* Illustrated by Ruth Ra. Tutle, 1987 (I:8+, R:5). Fifteen folktales are identified by their countries of origin.

Demi. *The Empty Pot.* New York: Henry Holt, 1990 (I:5–9, R:4). This tale develops the importance of honesty.

————. *The Stonecutter.* New York: Crown, 1995 (I:4–8, R:4). This Chinese tale is similar to "The Fisherman and His Wife."

Ginsburg, Mirra, ed. *The Chinese Mirror.* Illustrated by Margot Zemach. San Diego: Harcourt Brace Jovanovich, 1988 (I:5–8, R:4). A mirror causes confusion in a Korean folktale.

Hamanaka, Sheila, retold by. *Screen of Frogs.* New York: Orchard, 1993 (I:5–10, R:5). A Japanese folktale in which a man is rewarded for saving the land for the frogs.

Laurin, Anne. *The Perfect Crane.* Illustrated by Charles Mikolaycak. New York: Harper & Row, 1981 (I:5–9, R:6). A Japanese folktale tells about friendship between a magician and the crane he creates from paper.

Lee, Jeanne M. *Legend of the Milky Way.* New York: Holt, Rinehart & Winston, 1982 (I:5–8, R:4). A Chinese folktale tells about the origin of the Milky Way.

Louie, Ai-Lang. *Yeh Shen: A Cinderella Story from China.* Illustrated by Ed Young. New York: Philomel, 1982 (I:7–9, R:6). This is a Chinese variation of the "Cinderella" story.

Mahy, Margaret. *The Seven Chinese Brothers.* Illustrated by Jean and Mou-sien Tseng. New York: Scholastic, 1990 (I:5–8, R:5). These brothers show unusual qualities.

Paterson, Katherine. *The Tale of the Mandarin Ducks.* Illustrated by Leo and Diane Dillon. New York: Dutton, 1990 (I:7–10, R:5). Compassion is rewarded in this Japanese folktale.

San Souci, Robert D. *The Samurai's Daughter: A Japanese Legend.* Illustrated by Stephen T. Johnson. New York: Dial, 1992 (I:5–8, R:5). The heroine slays a sea monster.

Stamm, Claus. *Three Strong Women.* Illustrated by Jean and Mou-sien Tseng. New York: Viking, 1990 (I:6+, R:5). A wrestler is trained by three women in this Japanese folktale.

Yagawa, Sumiko. *The Crane Wife.* Illustrated by Suekicki Akaba. New York: William Morrow & Co., 1981 (I:7–10, R:6). A wife returns to her animal form when her husband breaks his promise.

Yep, Laurence. *The Rainbow People.* Illustrated by David Wiesner. New York: Harper & Row, 1989 (I:8+, R:5). This text includes Chinese folktales collected from Asian-Americans.

Young, Ed, translated by. *Lon Po Po: A Red-Riding Hood Story from China.* New York: Philomel, 1989 (I:all, R:5). The girls outwit the wolf in this version of the tale.

Contemporary and Historical Literature

Carlson, Lori M., edited by. *American Eyes: New Asian-American Short Stories for Young Adults.* New York: Holt, 1994 (I:12+, R:6). This is a collection of stories in which Asian-Americans search for their identity.

Friedman, Ina R. *How My Parents Learned to Eat.* Illustrated by Allen Say. Boston: Houghton Mifflin, 1984 (I:6–8, R:3). This humorous story tells about trying to eat with chopsticks or with knives and forks.

Garland, Sherry. *The Lotus Seed.* Illustrated by Tatsuro Kluchi. San Diego: Harcourt Brace Jovanovich, 1993 (I:5–8, R:4). A Vietnamese woman brings an important lotus seed with her when she and her family resettle in America.

Look, Lenore. *Henry's First-Moon Birthday.* Illustrated by Yumi Heo. New York: Simon & Schuster, 2001 (I:4–8). A Chinese-American family prepares for a one-month birthday.

Lord, Bette Bao. *In the Year of the Boar and Jackie Robinson.* Illustrated by Marc Simont. New York: Harper & Row, 1984 (I:8–10, R:4). Developing a love for baseball helps a Chinese girl make friends in America.

Nhuong, Huynh Quang. *The Land I Lost: Adventures of a Boy in Vietnam.* Illustrated by Vo-Dinh Mai. New York: Harper & Row, 1982 (I:8–12, R:6). The author tells about his boyhood experiences.

Partridge, Elizabeth. *Oranges on Golden Mountain.* Illustrated by Aki Sogabe. New York: Dutton, 2001 (I:5–9). A picture book set in nineteenth-century California.

Salisbury, Graham. *Under the Blood-Red Sun.* New York: Delacorte, 1994 (I:10+, R:5). Set in Hawaii during World War II, this historical novel focuses on the dilemma of Japanese who live on the island.

Say, Allen. *Grandfather's Journey.* Boston: Houghton Mifflin, 1993 (I:all). The illustrations and text convey the story of the immigration of a Japanese American.

———. *Tea with Milk.* Boston: Houghton Mifflin, 1999 (I:7+). A Japanese-American girl overcomes homesickness for America when she returns to Japan.

———. *Tree of Cranes.* Boston: Houghton Mifflin, 1991 (I:5–8, R:4). A Japanese boy's mother shares her California Christmas with her son.

Stanley, Jerry. *I Am an American: A True Story of Japanese Internment.* New York: Crown, 1994 (I:10+, R:6). In a photo essay, the text chronicles the experiences of Japanese-Americans during World War II.

Uchida, Yoshiko. *Invisible Thread.* Messner, 1995 (I:10+, R:6). A Japanese-American tells her own experiences in this autobiography.

———. *Journey Home.* Illustrated by Charles Robinson. New York: Atheneum, 1978 (I:10+, R:5). In a sequel to *Journey to Topaz,* Yuki and her parents return to California after World War II.

Wallace, Ian. *Chin Chiang and the Dragon's Dance.* New York: Atheneum, 1984 (I:6–9, R:6). A young boy dreams of dancing on the first day of the Year of the Dragon.

Yep, Laurence. *Child of the Owl.* New York: Harper & Row, 1977 (I:10+, R:7). A Chinese American girl learns about her heritage when she lives with her grandmother.

———. *Dragon's Gate.* New York: HarperCollins, 1993 (I:10+, R:6). This historical novel is set in 1867 at the time Chinese workers were working to build the transcontinental railroad.

———. *Dragonwings.* New York: Harper & Row, 1975 (I:10+, R:6). This historical book is set in San Francisco, 1903.

Yin, *Coolies.* Illustrated by Chris Soentpiet. New York: Philomel: 2001 (I:5–9). This picture book focuses on nineteenth-century Chinese immigrants.

Latino Literature

Traditional Tales

Bierhorst, John. *Doctor Coyote.* Illustrated by Wendy Watson. New York: Macmillan, 1987 (I:all). This fable is from the Indians of Mexico.

———. *The Monkey's Haircut and Other Stories Told by the Maya.* Illustrated by Robert Andrew Parker. New York: Morrow, 1986 (I:8+, R:6). The book contains twenty-two tales.

————. *Spirit Child: A Story of the Nativity.* Illustrated by Barbara Cooney. New York: William Morrow & Co., 1984 (I:8–12, R:6). Pre-Columbian style illustrations accompany an Aztec story.

Blackmore, Vivien. *Why Corn Is Golden: Stories About Plants.* Illustrated by Susana Martinez-Ostos. Boston: Little, Brown, 1984 (I:all, R:5). This book includes folktales about corn.

de Paola, Tomie. *The Lady of Guadalupe.* New York: Holiday, 1980 (I:8+, R:6). This Mexican tale is about the patron saint of Mexico who appeared to an Indian in 1531.

De Spain, Pleasant. *The Dancing Turtle: A Folktale from Brazil.* Illustrated by David Boston. Little Rock: August House, 1998 (I:5–8). An animal uses its wits.

De Spain, Pleasant. *The Emerald Lizard: Fifteen Latin American Tales to Tell.* Illustrated by Don Bell. Little Rock: August House, 1999 (I:10+). A large collection of tales.

Dorson, Mercedes; and Wilmot, Jeanne. *Tales from the Rain Forest: Myths and Legends from the Amazonian Indians of Brazil.* Ecco, 1997 (I:8+). A collection of folktales.

Ehlert, Lois. *Moon Rope.* San Diego: Harcourt Brace Jovanovich, 1992 (I:all). This Peruvian tale is about two animals that try to reach the moon.

Fine, Edith Hope. *Under the Lemon Moon.* Illustrated by Rene King Moreno. New York: Lee & Low, 1999 (I:5–8). A girl summons La Anciana, the Old One, to heal her lemon tree.

Greger, C. Shana, retold by. *The Fifth and Final Sun: An Ancient Aztec Myth of the Sun's Origin.* Boston: Houghton Mifflin, 1994 (I:8+). A myth about the creation of the sun.

Griego y Maestas, Jose; and Anaya, Rudolfo A. *Cuentos: Tales from the Hispanic Southwest.* Illustrated by Jaime Valdez. Museum of New Mexico, 1980 (I:9+, R:5). This is a collection of tales.

Hinojosa, Francisco, adapted by. *The Old Lady Who Ate People.* Illustrated by Leonel Maciel. Boston: Little, Brown, 1984 (I:all, R:6). These four frightening tales are from Mexico.

Lattimore, Deborah. *The Flame of Peace: A Tale of the Aztecs.* New York: Harper & Row, 1987 (I:all, R:6). This story is based on Aztec mythology.

McDermott, Gerald. *Musicians of the Sun.* New York: Simon & Schuster, 1997 (I:all). An Aztec myth.

Rohmer, Harriet; Octavio, Chow; and Viduare, Morris. *The Invisible Hunters.* Illustrated by Joe Sam. Chicago: Children's Press, 1987 (I:all, R:5). This is a tale about European traders.

Rohmer, Harriet; and Wilson, Dornminister. *Mother Scorpion Country.* Illustrated by Virginia Steams. Chicago: Children's Press, 1987 (I:all, R:5). A Central American tale written in both English and Spanish.

Van Laan, Nancy. *The Magic Bean Tree: A Legend from Argentina.* Illustrated by Beatriz Vidal. Boston: Houghton Mifflin, 1998 (I:all). A young boy is rewarded with carob beans.

Volkmer, Jane Anne, retold by. *Song of Chirimia—A Guatemalan Folktale.* Minneapolis: Carolrhoda, 1990 (I:6–10, R:5). A Mayan folktale in English and Spanish tells how a man tries to win the hand of a Mayan princess.

Contemporary and Historical Literature

Anaya, Rudolfo. *Farolitos for Akuelo.* Illustrated by Edward Gonzales. New York: Hyperion, 1998 (I:5–9). A young girl places farolitos at the grave of her grandfather.

Cherry, Lynne; and Plotkin, Mark J. *The Shaman's Apprentice: A Tale of the Amazon Rain Forest.* San Diego: Harcourt Brace, 1998 (I:6–8). A boy learns the importance of the shaman's wisdom.

Ets, Marie Hall; and Labastida, Aurora. *Nine Days to Christmas, A Story of Mexico.* New York: Viking Press, 1959 (I:5–8, R:3). The book has lovely illustrations of a girl preparing for a Mexican Christmas holiday.

Krumgold, Joseph. *And Now Miguel.* Illustrated by Jean Charlot. New York: Thomas Y. Crowell Co., 1953 (I:10+, R:3). Miguel, a member of a proud sheep-raising family, wishes to go with the sheepherders to the Sangre de Cristo Mountains.

Mohr, Nicholasa. *Felita.* Illustrated by Ray Cruz. New York: Dial Press, 1979 (I:9–12, R:2). A family tries to adjust to a new neighborhood.

O'Dell, Scott. *The Captive.* Boston: Houghton Mifflin, 1977 (I:10+, R:6). A Spanish seminarian witnesses the exploitation of the Mayas during the 1500s.

————. *Carlota.* Boston: Houghton Mifflin, 1977 (I:9+, R:4). A girl fights beside her father in California during the Mexican War.

————. *The Feathered Serpent.* Boston: Houghton Mifflin, 1981 (I:10+, R:6). The seminarian in *The Captive* witnesses the arrival of Cortés.

Politi, Leo. *The Nicest Gift.* New York: Charles Scribner's Sons, 1973 (I:5–8, R:6). There are many Spanish words in the text and illustrations from the barrio in East Los Angeles.

————. *Song of the Swallows.* New York: Charles Scribner's Sons, 1949 (I:5–8, R:4). Illustrations of Spanish architecture appear in a story set in Capistrano.

Soto, Gary. *Baseball in April and Other Stories.* San Diego: Harcourt Brace Jovanovich, 1990 (I:11+, R:6). This is a collection of stories about Mexican-American youth in California.

————. *Neighborhood Odes.* San Diego: Harcourt Brace Jovanovich, 1992 (I:all). This collection of poems is about an Hispanic neighborhood.

————. *Taking Sides.* San Diego: Harcourt Brace Jovanovich, 1991 (I:10+, R:6). A boy faces problems of loyalty as his new basketball team meets the old team from the barrio.

————. *Too Many Tamales.* Illustrated by Ed Martinez. New York: Putman, 1993 (I:6–8, R:4). This family story is set during Christmas Eve.

Taha, Karen T. *A Gift for Tia Rosa.* Illustrated by Dee deRosa. Minneapolis: Dillon, 1986 (I:5–8, R:3). A young girl faces a neighbor's death and learns about love.

Nonfiction

Ancona, George; and Diaz, Jorge Ancona. *Pablo Remembers: The Fiesta of the Day of the Dead.* New York: Lothrop, Lee & Shepard, 1993 (I:5–8, R:4). Through colored photographs and text, the authors present a photo essay about a family preparing for All Hallows Eve, All Saints Day, and All Souls Day. A Spanish edition is available.

Brimner, Larry Dane. *A Migrant Family.* Minneapolis: Lerner, 1992 (I:all). The text and photographs describe the life of Mexican-American migrant workers in California.

Brown, Tricia. *Hello, Amigos!* Photographs by Fran Ortiz. New York: Holt, Rinehart & Winston, 1986 (I:6–9). This photographic essay is about a Mexican-American boy who lives in San Francisco.

Cozzen, Judy, ed. *Kids Explore America's Hispanic Heritage.* Santa Fe, N.M.: John Muir, 1992 (I:all). This is a report of a school project.

Fritz, Jean, et al. *The World in 1492*. Illustrated by Stefano Vitale. New York: Holt, 1992 (I:8+). The section, "The Americas in 1492," written by Jamake Highwater, includes information about the Aztecs and Incas.

Mann, Elizabeth. *Machu Picchu*. New York: Mikaya/Firefly, 2000 (I:9+). The text introduces and discusses the Incas.

Middle Eastern Literature

Traditional Literature

Ben-Ezer, Ehud. *Hosni the Dreamer: An Arabian Tale*. Illustrated by Uri Shuleviz. New York: Farrar, Straus & Giroux, 1997 (I:6–8). The author identifies the story as based on an old Arabian folktale.

Bushnaq, Enea, edited by. *Arab Folktales*. New York: Pantheon, 1986 (I:12+). This is a large collection of Arabic folklore.

Cashford, Jules, retold by. *The Myth of Isis and Osiris*. Cambridge, Mass.: Barefoot Books, 1995 (I:all). An Egyptian myth based on the cycle of life, death, and rebirth.

Climo, Shirley. *The Egyption Cinderella*. Illustrated by Ruth Heller. New York: HarperCollins, 1989 (I:7–12). A variant on the classic tale.

———. *The Persian Cinderella*. Illustrated by Ruth Heller. New York: HarperCollins, 1999 (I:7–12). A variant from the Middle East.

Hickox, Rebecca. *The Golden Sandal: A Middle Eastern Cinderella Story*. Illustrated by Will Hillenbrand. New York: Holiday, 1998 (I:5–8). A tale from Iraq.

Kherdian, David, retold by. *Feathers and Tails*. Illustrated by Nonny Hogrogian. New York: Philomel, 1992 (I:5–9). This collection includes a Sufi fable.

Kimmel, Eric A., adapted by. *Rimonah of the Flashing Sword: A North African Tale*. Illustrated by Omar Rayyan. New York: Holiday House, 1992 (I:6–9). An Egyptian version of the "Snow White" tale.

———, adapted by. *The Tale of Aladdin and the Wonderful Lamp: A Story from the Arabian Nights*. Illustrated by Ju-Hong Chen. New York: Holiday, 1992 (I:6–9). Retold from the Arabian Nights.

Maugham, W. Somerset. *Appointment*. Adapted by Alan Benjamin. Illustrated by Roger Essley. New York: Simon & Schuster, 1993 (I:all). A servant cannot escape a fateful death.

Zeman, Ludmila, retold and illustrated by. *Sindbad: From the Tales of the Thousand and One Nights*. Toronto: Tundra Books, 1999 (I:all). A beautifully illustrated book that reflects the art of Persian miniatures.

Poetry

Gordon, Ruth, selected by. *Under All Silences: The Many Shades of Love*. New York: Harper & Row, 1987 (I:9+). The anthology includes several Egyptian and Persian poems.

Ichikawa, Satomi. *Here a Little Child I Stand: Poems of Prayer and Praise for Children*. New York: Philomel, 1985 (I:all). The collection includes an Islamic prayer to Allah.

Nye, Naomi Shihab, selected by. *This Same Sky: A Collection of Poems from Around the World*. New York: Four Winds, 1992 (I:9+). The anthology includes poetry from Saudi Arabia, Kuwait, Pakistan, Iraq, and Lebanon.

———, selected by. *The Space Between Our Footsteps: Poems and Paintings from the Middle East*. New York: Simon & Schuster, 1998 (I:all). An anthology of poems and paintings.

Contemporary and Historical Literature

Alexander, Sue. *Nadia the Willful.* Illustrated by Lloyd Blood. New York: Pantheon, 1983 (I:7–10). A Bedouin girl teaches her father about the importance of remembering a lost son.

Dalokay, Vadat. *Sister Shako and Kolo the Goat: Memories of My Childhood in Turkey.* Translated by Guner Ener. New York: Lothrop, Lee & Shepard, 1994 (I:10+). The former mayor of Ankara recalls his childhood.

Fletcher, Susan. *Shadow Spinner.* New York: Atheneum, 1998 (I:10+). The story is set in ancient Persia during the time of Shahrazad.

Heide, Florence Parry; and Gilliland, Judith Heide. *The Day of Ahmed's Secret.* Illustrated by Ted Lewis. New York: Lothrop, Lee & Shepard, 1990 (I:6–9). A picture storybook set in Cairo.

————; and Gilliland, Judith Heide. *Sami and the Time of Troubles.* Illustrated by Ted Lewin. New York: Clarion, 1992 (I:6–9). A Lebanese boy and his family live in a basement shelter.

Hicyilmaz, Gaye. *Against the Storm.* Boston: Little, Brown, 1992 (I:10+). A boy learns about survival in Ankara.

Schami, Rafik. *A Hand Full of Stars.* Translated by Rika Lesser. New York: Dutton, 1990 (I:12+). A boy in Damascus becomes involved with an underground newspaper.

Staples, Suzanne Fisher. *Haveli.* New York: Random House, 1993 (I:12+). This is a sequel to *Shabanu: Daughter of the Wind.*

————. *Shabanu: Daughter of the Wind.* New York: Knopf, 1989 (I:12+). A girl in Pakistan asserts her independence.

Nonfiction

Crosher, Judith. *Ancient Egypt.* New York: Viking, 1993 (I:9+). A highly illustrated book presents the history of ancient Egypt and its people.

Ferber, Elizabeth. *Yasir Arafat: The Battle for Peace in Palestine.* Brookfield, Conn.: Millbrook, 1995 (I:12+). This is a biography about the Palestinian leader.

Gordon, Matthew S. *Islam: World Religions.* New York: Facts on File, 1991 (I:10+). This informational book provides an overview of Islam.

Haslam, Andrew; and Parsons, Alexandra. *Ancient Egypt.* Minnetonka, MN: Thomas Learning, 1995 (I:9+). This informational text includes directions for making models related to ancient Egyptian civilization.

Hermes, Jules. *The Color of Morocco.* Minneapolis: Carolrhoda, 1995 (I:8+). Full-color photographs and text describe the homes, work, and ways of life of children and their families.

Honeyman, Susannah. *Saudi Arabia.* Littleton, Colo.: Raintree/Steck-Vaughn, 1995 (I:8+). This informational book provides an introduction to the land, climate, daily life, and culture of Saudi Arabia.

Husain, Shahrukh. *Mecca.* New York: Dillon, 1993 (I:8+). Color photographs and text present important aspects of this religious city of the Muslims.

King, John. *Conflict in the Middle East.* New York: New Discovery Books, 1993 (I:9+). This informational book discusses the causes of conflict in the countries of the Middle East.

Lasky, Kathryn. *The Librarian Who Measured the Earth.* Illustrated by Kevin Hawkes. Boston: Little, Brown, 1994 (I:9+). This is an illustrated biography about the chief librarian in Alexandria.

Macdonald, Fiona. *A 16th Century Mosque.* Illustrated by Mark Bergin. New York: Peter Bedrick, 1994 (I:all). Detailed illustrations show the mosques built in Istanbul.

Wormser, Richard. *American Islam: Growing Up Muslim in America.* New York: Walker, 1994 (I:12+). The book describes the lives of American teens who follow the Islamic religion.

Native American Literature

Traditional Literature

Baker, Olaf. *Where the Buffaloes Begin.* Illustrated by Stephen Gammell. New York: Warne, 1981 (I:8+, R:7). A Prairie Indian legend tells about the lake in which buffaloes are created and how the buffaloes help a boy who believes.

Baylor, Byrd. *And It Is Still That Way: Legends Told by Arizona Indian Children.* New York: Charles Scribner's Sons, 1976 (I:all, R:3). This is a collection of tales told by children.

Begay, Shonto. *Ma'ii and Cousin Horned Toad: A Traditional Navajo Story.* New York: Scholastic, 1992 (I:5–8, R:5). In a pourquoi tale, Horned Toad plays tricks on Ma'ii, the coyote, until the coyote promises to leave him alone.

Bierhorst, John, retold by. *The People with Five Fingers: A Native Californian Creation Tale.* Illustrated by Robert Andrew Parker. Tarrytown, N.Y.: Marshall Cavendish, 2000 (I:all). Coyote and other animals create the world.

Caduto, Michael J.; and Joseph Bruchac. *Keepers of the Animals: Native American Stories and Wildlife Activities for Children.* Illustrated by John Kahionhes Fadden. Golden, Colo.: Fulcrum, 1991 (I:all). The text includes folklore about animals and suggested activities to accompany the titles.

———. *Keepers of the Earth: Native American Stories and Environmental Activities for Children.* Illustrated by John Kahionhes Fadden and Carol Wood. Golden, Colo.: Fulcrum, 1989 (I:all). The text includes folklore about the earth and suggested activities to accompany the tales.

Cohn, Amy L., compiled by. *From Sea to Shining Sea: A Treasury of American Folklore and Folk Songs.* New York: Scholastic, 1993 (I:all). This collection progresses from Native American folklore to folklore of more contemporary times.

de Paola, Tomie. *The Legend of the Bluebonnet.* New York: Putnam, 1983 (I:all, R:6). In a Comanche tale, unselfish actions are rewarded.

Esbensen, Barbara Juster. *The Great Buffalo Race: How the Buffalo Got Its Hump.* Illustrated by Helen K. Davie. Boston: Little, Brown, 1994 (I:all, R:5). A Seneca Indian tale.

Goble, Paul. *Beyond the Ridge.* New York: Bradbury, 1989 (I:all, R:5). An elderly Indian woman from the Great Plains experiences death and goes to the afterlife.

———. *Buffalo Woman.* New York: Bradbury, 1984 (I:all, R:6). A bond between animals and humans is developed in a tale from the Great Plains.

———. *The Girl Who Loved Wild Horses.* Scarsdale, N.Y.: Bradbury, 1978 (I:6–10, R:5). An American Indian girl, who loves wild horses, joins them in a flight during a storm.

———. *Iktomi and the Boulder: A Plains Indian Story.* New York: Orchard, 1988 (I:4–10, R:4). This trickster tale is good for choral arrangements.

———. *Iktomi and the Berries.* New York: Watts, 1989.

Highwater, Jamake. *Anpao: An American Indian Odyssey.* Illustrated by Fritz Scholder. Philadelphia: J. B. Lippincott Co., 1977 (I:12+, R:5). A Native American travels across the history of traditional tales in order to search for his destiny.

Rodanas, Kristina. *Dance of the Sacred Circle: A Native American Tale*. Boston: Little, Brown, 1994 (I:all). This is a Blackfoot myth.

Spencer, Paula Underwood. *Who Speaks for Wolf*. Illustrated by Frank Howell. Austin, Tex.: Tribe of Two Press, 1983 (I:all). This Native American learning story emphasizes the need to consider animals.

Van Laan, Nancy, retold by. *Buffalo Dance: A Blackfoot Legend*. Illustrated by Beatriz Vidal. Boston: Little, Brown, 1993 (I:7+, R:4). This is a story about respect between humans and animals.

Vogel, Carole G. *Legends of Landforms: Native American Lore and the Geology of the Land*. Brookfield, Conn.: Millbrook, 1999 (I:10+). Includes fourteen tales about various landforms.

Poetry and Songs

Baylor, Byrd. *The Desert Is Theirs*. Illustrated by Peter Parnall. New York: Charles Scribner's Sons, 1975 (I:all). The poetic form captures the life of the Papago Indians.

————. *Hawk, I'm Your Brother*. Illustrated by Peter Parnall. New York: Charles Scribner's Sons, 1976 (I:all). A young boy longs to glide through the air like a hawk.

Bierhorst, John. *A Cry from the Earth: Music of the North American Indians*. New York: Four Winds, 1979 (I:all). This is a collection of Native American songs.

Field, Edward. *Magic Words*. Illustrated by Stefano Vitale. San Diego: Harcourt Brace, 1998 (I:all). These poems are based on Inuit folklore.

Philip, Neil, edited by. *Songs Are Thoughts: Poems of the Inuit*. Illustrated by Maryclare Foa. New York: Orchard, 1995 (I:all). Both illustrations and text provide an introduction to the Inuit way of life and emphasize the importance of sung poetry.

Smithsonian. *When the Rain Sings: Poems by Young Native Americans*. New York: Simon & Schuster, 1999 (I:all). A collection of poems from different tribes.

Sneve, Virginia Driving Hawk, selected by. *Dancing Teepees: Poems of American Indian Youth*. Illustrated by Stephen Gammell. New York: Holiday, 1989 (I:all). This is a collection of ancient and contemporary poems.

Wood, Nancy, edited by. *The Serpent's Tongue: Prose, Poetry, and the Art of the New Mexico Pueblos*. New York: Dutton, 1997 (I:8+). A large collection of poetry and tales.

Contemporary and Historical Literature

Dorris, Michael. *Morning Girl*. New York: Hyperion, 1992 (I:8+, R:5). This book is set in the Bahamas in 1492.

Erdrich, Louise. *The Birchbark House*. New York: Hyperion, 1999 (I:8+). Set in 1847 on an island in Lake Superior, a seven-year-old Ojibwa girl lives through summer and winter.

George, Jean Craighead. *Julie*. New York: HarperCollins, 1994 (I:10+, R:6). In a sequel to *Julie of the Wolves*, George develops a survival story that emphasizes the survival of the Eskimo culture.

————. *The Talking Earth*. New York: Harper & Row, 1983 (I:10+, R:6). An Indian girl tries to discover her heritage.

————. *Water Sky*. New York: Harper & Row, 1987 (I:10+, R:6). A boy discovers his Eskimo heritage.

Hudson, Jan. *Sweetgrass*. Edmonton: Tree Frog, 1984 (I:10+, R:4). A Blackfoot girl grows up during the winter of a smallpox epidemic in 1837.

Kroll, Virginia. *The Seasons and Someone.* Illustrated by Tatsuro Kiuchi. San Diego: Harcourt Brace Jovanovich, 1994 (I:4–8). A young Eskimo girl describes the seasons in her Arctic environment.

Martin, Bill; and Archambault, John. *Knots on a Counting Rope.* Illustrated by Ted Rand. New York: Holt, Rinehart & Winston, 1987 (I:7+). This is a rhythmic tale of a blind Native American boy who rides in a horse race.

Miles, Miska. *Annie and the Old One.* Illustrated by Peter Parnall. Boston: Little, Brown, 1971 (I:6–8, R:3). Annie's love for her grandmother causes her to interfere with the completion of a rug she associates with the probable death of her grandmother.

O'Dell, Scott. *Black Star, Bright Dawn.* Boston: Houghton Mifflin, 1988 (I:8+, R:6). An Eskimo girl enters the Iditarod Trail Sled Dog Race in Alaska.

———. *Sing Down the Moon.* Boston: Houghton Mifflin, 1970 (I:10+, R:6). The 1864 forced march of the Navajo is told through the viewpoint of a young girl.

———; and Elizabeth Hall. *Thunder Rolling in the Mountains.* Boston: Houghton Mifflin, 1992 (I:10+, R:6). This historical novel is told through the point of view of Chief Joseph's daughter.

Paulsen, Gary. *Dogsong.* New York: Bradbury, 1988 (I:10+, R:6). An Eskimo boy journeys 1,400 miles by dogsled as he crosses the ice.

Sneve, Virginia Driving Hawk. *High Elk's Treasure.* Illustrated by Oren Lyons. New York: Holiday, 1972 (I:8–12, R:6). A dream beginning in 1876 is renewed in the late 1970s.

White Deer of Autumn. *Ceremony—In the Circle of Life.* Illustrations by Daniel San Souci. Milwaukee: Raintree, 1983 (I:all). A contemporary boy learns about his heritage and the importance of living in harmony with nature.

Yolen, Jane. *Encounter.* Illustrated by David Shannon. San Diego: Harcourt Brace Jovanovich, 1992 (I:6–10, R:5). This is a hypothetical story of a Taino boy who tells about the landing of Columbus.

Nonfiction

Ancona, George. *Powwow.* San Diego: Harcourt Brace Jovanovich, 1993 (I:all). Photographs and text explain the Crow Fair in Montana.

Brown, Tricia. *Children of the Midnight Sun: Young Native Voices of Alaska.* Photographs by Roy Corral. Anchorage: Alaska Northwest, 1998 (I:8+). The author focuses on the daily lives of children.

Cooper, Michael L. *Indian School: Teaching the White Man's Way.* New York: Clarion, 1999 (I: 9+). A history of Native American boarding schools beginning in the late 1870s.

Ekoomiak, Normee. *Arctic Memories.* New York: Henry Holt, 1990 (I:all). The text is written in both Inuktitut and English.

Finley, Carol. *Art of the Far North: Inuit Sculpture, Drawing and Printmaking.* Minneapolis: Lerner, 1998 (I:8+). This is a brief history of the Inuit people and the culture associated with their art.

Fradin, Dennis Brindell. *Hiawatha: Messenger of Peace.* New York: Macmillan, 1992 (I:10+, R:5). This is a biography of the Native American leader who brought together warring Iroquois tribes in a constitutional relationship.

Freedman, Russell. *Buffalo Hunt.* New York: Holiday, 1988 (I:8+, R:6). Illustrations and text show the importance of the buffalo to Great Plains Indians.

————. *Indian Chiefs.* New York: Holiday, 1987 (I:8+, R:7). These are biographies of six native American chiefs; photographs add authenticity.

Fritz, Jean. *The Double Life of Pocahontas.* Illustrated by Ed Young. New York: Putnam, 1983 (I:8–10, R:7). A biography of Pocahontas focuses on her involvement with two cultures.

————; et al. *The World in 1492.* Illustrated by Stefano Vitale. New York: Holt, 1992 (I:8+). The section "The Americas in 1492" is written by Jamake Highwater and includes Native Americans of North America.

Hoyt-Goldsmith, Diane. *Buffalo Days.* Photographs by Lawrence Migdale. New York: Holiday, 1997 (I:8+). A photographic essay describes life on the Crow reservation in Montana.

Lawlor, Laurie. *Shadow Catcher: The Life and Work of Edward S. Curtis.* New York: Walker, 1994 (I:all). The text is illustrated with photographs by Edward Curtis, the man who spent thirty years documenting the Indian cultures of North America.

Left Hand Bull, Jacqueline; and Haldane, Suzanne. *Lakota Hoop Dance.* New York: Dutton, 1999 (I:all). The book follows the activities of the dancers.

Littlechild, George. *This Land Is My Land.* Chicago: Children's Press, 1993 (I:all, R:4). The author, a member of the Plains Cree Nation of Canada, shares his feelings about his history and his peoples' way of life.

Martin, Albert. *Sitting Bull and His World.* New York: Dutton, 2000 (I:10+). A biography of the Lakota Sioux chief.

Morrison, Dorothy Nafus. *Chief Sarah: Sarah Winnemucca's Fight for Indian Rights.* New York: Atheneum, 1980 (I:10+, R:6). Sarah Winnemucca was a leader of the Paiute people.

Library and Reference Skills

After completing this chapter about library and reference skills, you will be able to:

1. Describe the composition of print and nonprint items recommended for school libraries.
2. Describe several methods for acquiring minimal-cost materials for classrooms or school libraries.
3. Evaluate a student's use of library skills.
4. Describe the library skills taught in the primary, intermediate, and upper-elementary grades.
5. Develop a learning activity for teaching reference skills in the primary, intermediate, and upper-elementary grades.
6. Describe how literature could be used to introduce technology in the classroom.
7. Describe how to publish book reviews on the Internet.
8. Bring specialists into the classroom through the Internet.
9. Develop a lesson that teaches students the harm of plagiarism.

*A*s we enter new and remodeled libraries and media centers in the twenty-first century, we notice changes from the libraries of the previous decades. In a review of "Six Trends in Library Design," Harrington (2001) points out some of the new or changing features in libraries that may influence how libraries are used or how teachers and librarians approach the teaching of library and reference skills. As you read about these trends try to evaluate your own library. Are these new features found in your library? If they are, how do these features influence the teaching of library and reference skills?

First, libraries are becoming more "self-guided" so that patrons can easily follow the layout of the spaces and locate the various collections. Second, library design is becoming flexible so that integration of technology and various space requirements can be more easily met. The walls and shelves may be movable so that floor space can change to meet the needs of library programming. For example, imagine a storyteller who presents a program to a large group of children. New libraries may be capable of meeting this changing space need by moving a few walls. Third, library design is making use of the natural environment's sunlight and landscaping to enhance the building and provide an aesthetic quality.

Fourth, because libraries in many public school districts are suffering cutbacks in funding resulting in fewer librarians, library services, and resources, increased cooperation is being seen among public, school, and college libraries. This is especially true in California where, to receive state support from the bond act, "public libraries must cooperate with local schools, either by building joint facilities or by working together to create family literacy centers, computer centers, homework centers, career centers or other mutually beneficial programs" (Harrington, 2001, p. 13).

Fifth, we are seeing renewed interest in aesthetics with such features as an increased use of glass to join inside and outside spaces, to integrate art into the library, to include artistic displays such as fountains, or to provide spaces for special collections. Sixth, libraries are being customized to meet the needs of local communities. Many of these libraries are "responding to educational curricula, using collaborative learning by including group study rooms as well as writing centers, multimedia labs, and production studios" (Harrington,

2001, p. 14). New libraries may include computer training centers and electronic classrooms where students work with librarians to learn research strategies. If a library with these new features is available in your community, how does it change the community and school use of the library? Are there any new library and reference skills that need to be taught?

Many of us will not have opportunities to work in the ideal libraries of the twenty-first century. In a library survey, "How Does Your Library Measure Up?," Miller and Shontz (1999) report both good and bad results. Although 75 percent of library media centers have access to the Internet, the number of hours spent by librarians in formal and informal planning with teachers has declined by 20 percent since the mid-1990s.

In this chapter we explore the library and the reference skills that should be included in a language arts program. We consider the resources that should be in the library, library skills essential to students, and issues that relate to the increasing use of and availability of websites. Unfortunately, we also need to consider two rapidly increasing concerns of educators at all levels: (1) How do we teach children to evaluate the accuracy of websites? (2) How do we prevent the rapid increase of plagiarism that often results from the use of websites when conducting research?

Access to Books

How important is the access to books within a library? Kozol (2000) states that "Few forms of theft are quite as damaging to inner-city children as the denial of a well-endowed school library" (p. 48). He expands on the importance of books to inner-city children because "[b]ooks in beautiful school libraries developed with the artfulness of skilled librarians remain the clearest window to a world of noncommercial satisfactions and enticements that most children in poor neighborhoods will ever know" (p. 48). Inner-city neighborhoods do not need to be places where children are deprived of books. In "The Best Little Library in Texas," Margolis (2001) describes how a branch library and a school worked together to develop an outstanding library program. Consequently, the Terrazas Branch Library was the first winner of the Giant Step Award in 2001 presented by the *School Library Journal*. The award presents a $10,000 prize to the public or school library that provides the most improvement in services to children. As you read Margolis's article, notice how it is possible to answer Kozol's concerns and have an effective library program in an inner-city neighborhood.

For Your Development

Those interested in improving school or public libraries will find recommendations in the descriptions of two libraries that have won the Giant Step Award presented by the *School Library Journal* to the public or school library that has greatly improved its services to children.

1. Read and analyze Rick Margolis's description of "The Best Little Library in Texas" (2001). With your class discuss the characteristics of this library and how the improvements could be applied to any library.
2. Read and analyze Virginia A. Walter's "Lindbergh Takes Off" (2002). This article is about the second winner of the Giant Step Award. Discuss the characteristics of this library and how the improvements could be applied to any library. You may also consider the list of Giant Step Runners-Up. If any of these libraries are near you, visit the libraries, view the changes, and interview the librarians and teachers who made a difference in these libraries.

The school library and media center are becoming increasingly important in schools that emphasize literature-based instruction. In *Becoming a Nation of Readers: The Report of the Commission on Reading,* Anderson, Hiebert, Scott, and Wilkinson (1985) emphasize that quality books, the nature of instruction, and opportunities for meaningful practice are all essential factors in improving literacy in our schools. They conclude that ready access to books is extremely important.

This access to books is important at all levels. For example, Cullinan, Greene, and Jaggar (1990) describe an innovative program in the New York Public Library to teach librarians how children become literate, to develop collections of materials for young children, and to provide services for young children and their caretakers. The librarians study research on language learning, early literacy learning, and child development. They develop criteria for selecting print and nonprint materials and explore ways to work with both children and parents.

The library literacy program for young children is shaped around three aspects of practice developed in New Zealand and Australia: reading to, reading with, and reading by children. The librarians read to children, so that the children learn book language and discover story patterns, story conventions, and concepts about their world. Reading with children, also called shared reading or lap reading, occurs with an individual child or a small group of children. Now, the children see the print and take part in the storytelling and reading process. Reading by children emphasizes independent practice. Children select such materials as board books, picture books, and easy-to-read books and are praised for their early attempts at reading. In this program, librarians learn to interact with children during reading. Cullinan, Greene, and Jaggar conclude: "There is no one right way to read a book with a child. The key is to keep reading aloud embedded in a social and cultural context and to keep children involved and interested" (p. 754). The program also shows the benefits of developing relationships between librarians, early childhood educators, and parents.

Interrelationships between teachers, librarians, and libraries become increasingly important as teachers integrate more literature into their reading programs. Dales (1990) describes new visions for access to information: "[Librarians can] view themselves more as teachers, and teachers can view libraries as their own classrooms. Both need to see each other as team-teachers" (p. 734). Hiebert, Mervar, and Person (1990) point out that guidance in classrooms and libraries is crucial for both students and teachers in selecting and sharing books. They found that children who are involved in literature-based programs are more apt to give elaborate reasons for their selections and indicate specific books, illustrators, or authors when they go to the library than children in textbook-based classrooms. The latter require more guidance in book selection from librarians.

Lamme and Ledbetter (1990) describe library media centers in which children frequent the library before, during, and after school as they search for books to read during sustained silent reading. They look for specific genres of books, books by particular authors or illustrators, and books recommended by other students. In this same center, teachers in the media production room bind their students' writing, publish newsletters to keep parents involved and informed, and read and discuss articles. The teachers help students select good books and find resources that relate to their classroom studies.

Allington and Cunningham (2002) recommend that effective classroom libraries for primary grades should have between 700 and 750 books. They include recommendations by the American Library Association that maintain that the minimum standard for an elementary school library is about 20 books per child. This means that a school with 500 students needs a library of between 10,000 to 12,000 books plus other media and software. Allington and Cunningham also conclude that these numbers may be too small for schools that stress literature-based curriculum or thematic units.

Media Center Resources

School libraries no longer contain only books. If you visit a well-developed library, you will find children using encyclopedias, dictionaries, newspapers, magazines, films, filmstrips, and recordings. To provide adequately for a full range of learning possibilities and activities, a library must contain materials covering varied reading levels and subjects.

Research shows that children who have access to a well-staffed, well-stocked school library read more books and have higher verbal test scores. They read more than twice as many books and a greater variety than do children who have access only to a classroom library or a centralized, school-district library. Both a school library and a classroom library are essential for easy and frequent access to materials. Lamme and Ledbetter (1990) identify the following resources that characterize an effective school library:

1. *Materials that relate to thematic studies*—anthologies of poetry and humor; indices to poetry and songs by topic; and files of community volunteers and guest speakers categorized according to topics of study
2. *Materials that relate to authors*—information files about individual authors and illustrators and filmstrips and videos featuring particular authors and illustrators
3. *Materials that relate to literature*—lists of books by genre, including ideas for student involvement, and literature sets that may be checked out by teachers
4. *Materials that relate to activities to accompany stories*—collections of stories that are good for storytelling; collections of flannelboard patterns; information on how to make puppets and perform puppet skits; tape recordings of good storytellings; and packaged story-hour ideas, with book titles and matching flannelboard sets or filmstrips.

If you are teaching in a school that does not yet have an outstanding library and you want to augment your classroom library, there are a number of creative ways to do this at minimal cost. In one school, for example, a program was initiated to teach communication and language arts skills to fifth- and sixth-grade students of lower reading ability. The teachers needed motivating reading materials in the classrooms and recreational reading materials that students could keep. The teachers used two methods to acquire the paperback books many of the students preferred. First, they sent a letter to parents of children in the school district explaining the new educational program. They asked the parents to donate children's books, especially paperbacks, so that other children could enjoy them. The response was excellent. They set up an attractive book corner and had enough books left over to start a paperback reading center in the school library as well. The students could use the books in the classroom or check them out. The teachers also established a paperback book exchange. Students who found books they especially wanted to keep had only to bring in other paperback books to trade.

The teachers used several methods to augment the reference materials in the classroom. The letter asking for paperbacks also asked for donations of periodicals, such as *National Geographic, Smithsonian, Life Magazine,* hobby magazines, *Popular Science, Popular Mechanics,* sports magazines, and so forth. The periodicals served as reading materials for special interests and provided materials for a picture-information file. The students compiled the file, and thus learned such library skills as classifying materials, alphabetizing, and developing a card index.

As a final means for collecting additional reference information, the students wrote for free or inexpensive materials. This activity required them to use their letter-writing skills. When the materials arrived, the students had to file them for easy retrieval, thus reinforcing their library skills. If the materials contained advertising, the children critically evaluated it for bias and propaganda techniques.

Criteria for Evaluating Materials

Spiegel (1990) provides the following criteria for evaluating resources for developing reference and study skills:

1. Does the material have content validity? Does it develop activities or lessons that focus students' attention on performing some research or real study? After completing the activity, will the students be able to identify the process used to complete the task?
2. Does the material have transfer potential? Are the skills and strategies practiced with the specific material of value when using other materials, in other settings, and for real purposes?
3. Does the material include adequate reinforcement? Do students get enough, but not too much, practice in the target skill or strategy?
4. Does the material contain clear and complete directions? Do the directions enable the students to use the materials independently? Are sufficient examples given? Is the language at an appropriate level?
5. Is the material adaptable and flexible so that it is appealing to and appropriate for many types of learners?
6. Is the material free from any content bias? For example, are minority groups, including females, represented in the examples?

Library Skills

Library skills are essential for locating information. They also help students develop positive attitudes toward research, stimulate their interest in functional and recreational reading, and increase their knowledge about how libraries can enrich their lives.

Children need to know where to find and how to use different types of books.

Reference skills become more important in intermediate grades.

Instruction in library skills cannot be left to incidental learning. Usually, a librarian and classroom teacher teach these skills cooperatively. Certain skills are taught as early as kindergarten, when teachers introduce children to the proper care of books—how to hold a book, how to turn pages, how to use a bookmark, how to put a book back on the shelf, how to put a book down on a desk or a table, and how to care for a book when taking it home. Kindergarten teachers also introduce children to school and classroom libraries. Teachers and librarians should cooperatively teach children where to find the picture books, easy-to-read books, and other materials. Students also need to learn how to check out books and return them.

During the primary grades, children learn to find specific types of materials, to refer to books by author and title, and to use some of the reference materials. Introduce skills such as alphabetizing; using an index; using a table of contents; and categorizing items according to subject, title, or author. Acquaint children with picture dictionaries, primary school dictionaries, thesauruses, and encyclopedias.

In the intermediate and upper-elementary grades, teach library skills more formally, so that children become competent in locating books on the shelves from information in card catalogs and online resources, preparing new books for shelves, and creating bulletin boards and displays of colorful books.

For Your Development

1. Visit an elementary school library. What print and nonprint materials are included? Observe what learning activities are going on in the library. Are the activities vital extensions of the classroom?

2. Interview a school librarian. Find out what instructional tasks he or she performs. What does the librarian feel is the most important aspect of the job? How does this librarian cooperate with classroom teachers?

Evaluation of Library Skills

Formal instruction in library skills does not usually begin until the intermediate grades, although the readiness skills are taught in the primary grades. Evaluate attainment of these skills by observing students as they use the library and its various print and nonprint reference materials. Instead of using paper-and-pencil tests, use checklists to evaluate a student's skills, and discuss learning activities that are prerequisites for assignments requiring library skills.

The Primary Grades.   This is the time to develop positive attitudes toward books, teach the children where to find and how to use specific types of books, and introduce other prerequisites for using a library to its fullest. Table 13–1 illustrates the library skills you might evaluate for primary-grade children.

Table 13–1   Checklist of library skills—primary grades

Skill	Evaluation		
	Yes	*Sometimes*	*No*
1. Care of books—Is able to			
a. hold book correctly	_____	_____	_____
b. turn pages correctly	_____	_____	_____
c. care for book when taking it home	_____	_____	_____
2. Library orientation—Is able to			
a. find specific types of books and other media in the library	_____	_____	_____
b. refer to books by author and title	_____	_____	_____
c. check out books	_____	_____	_____
3. Miscellaneous skills—Is able to			
a. manage the classroom library	_____	_____	_____
b. make simple author-card for classroom library	_____	_____	_____
c. make simple title-card for classroom library	_____	_____	_____
d. make simple subject-card for classroom library	_____	_____	_____
e. alphabetize a short list of words by first letter	_____	_____	_____
f. use a primary picture dictionary	_____	_____	_____
g. make and use a class telephone directory	_____	_____	_____
h. use a class-made encyclopedia	_____	_____	_____

Table 13–2   Checklist of library skills—intermediate grades

Skill	Yes	Evaluation Sometimes	No
1. Library orientation—Is able to			
a. find specific books and media	_____	_____	_____
b. check out materials independently	_____	_____	_____
2. Library use—Is able to			
a. understand and demonstrate appropriate uses for library at different times	_____	_____	_____
b. use librarian for appropriate reasons	_____	_____	_____
c. explain how books are arranged	_____	_____	_____
d. select materials at an appropriate level of difficulty	_____	_____	_____
3. Dictionary skills—Is able to			
a. alphabetize words according to 2nd, 3rd, and 4th letters	_____	_____	_____
b. use guide words	_____	_____	_____
c. locate correct meaning for a word from multiple definitions	_____	_____	_____
d. locate synonyms and antonyms	_____	_____	_____
4. Other reference materials—Is able to			
a. use a children's encyclopedia	_____	_____	_____
b. use a telephone directory	_____	_____	_____
c. understand importance of various reference materials	_____	_____	_____
d. use card catalog or computer to find books on shelves	_____	_____	_____
5. Parts of a book—Is able to			
a. use the table of contents and the index to find information in a reference book	_____	_____	_____
b. refer to the copyright date, and use it to evaluate information	_____	_____	_____

The Intermediate Grades.   Instruction in library skills becomes more formal in the intermediate grades. Consequently, there are more opportunities to evaluate a student's attainment of certain skills. Table 13–2 indicates the skills to evaluate in the intermediate grades.

The Upper-Elementary Grades and Middle School.   As the various subject areas begin to demand greater involvement with library references, upper-elementary and middle-school children must be able to find and use library materials efficiently and effectively. You should review their skills every year, so that the students feel comfortable and secure in their library searches. Especially crucial times for teaching and diagnosing library skills are when

Table 13–3 Checklist of library skills—upper elementary or middle school

Skill	Evaluation Yes	Sometimes	No
1. Dictionary usage—Is able to			
a. alphabetize words by 5th or 6th letters, if necessary	_____	_____	_____
b. use guide words	_____	_____	_____
c. find spellings for phonetically regular words	_____	_____	_____
d. find spellings for phonetically irregular words	_____	_____	_____
e. find the correct meaning from multiple meanings	_____	_____	_____
f. find synonyms and antonyms	_____	_____	_____
g. use pronunciation symbols to find correct pronunciation	_____	_____	_____
2. Library orientation—Is able to			
a. locate specific items in the library (e.g., check-out desk, card catalog, computer)	_____	_____	_____
b. locate different categories of books	_____	_____	_____
3. Card catalogs and/or online resources—Are able to			
a. demonstrate how and when to refer to a subject card	_____	_____	_____
b. demonstrate how and when to refer to an author card	_____	_____	_____
c. demonstrate how and when to refer to a title card	_____	_____	_____
d. understand the need to use, and uses of a cross-reference card	_____	_____	_____
4. Classification systems—Is able to			
a. use the Dewey decimal or Library of Congress classification system	_____	_____	_____
b. locate books by call numbers	_____	_____	_____
5. Encyclopedia—Is able to			
a. find and use the index of an encyclopedia to locate related articles on a subject	_____	_____	_____
b. use the cross reference in an encyclopedia	_____	_____	_____
c. use guide words in an encyclopedia	_____	_____	_____
d. check copyright date of an encyclopedia	_____	_____	_____
e. choose an encyclopedia on an appropriate level of reading difficulty	_____	_____	_____
f. use more than one encyclopedia to compare information	_____	_____	_____

Skill	Evaluation		
	Yes	Sometimes	No
6. Other tools—Is able to			
a. understand the purposes for, and use:			
other reference materials	_____	_____	_____
biographical dictionaries	_____	_____	_____
atlases	_____	_____	_____
almanacs	_____	_____	_____
specialized encyclopedias	_____	_____	_____
(e.g., science and social studies)			
7. Finding information in periodicals—Is able to			
a. understand that periodicals can provide the most recent information on a subject	_____	_____	_____
b. identify subject headings that might provide references	_____	_____	_____
c. use the *Reader's Guide to Periodical Literature*	_____	_____	_____
d. understand abbreviations in the *Reader's Guide*	_____	_____	_____
e. find the correct periodicals after locating references in the *Reader's Guide*	_____	_____	_____

students proceed from elementary to middle school (at the end of fifth grade) or when they proceed from elementary to junior high school (at the end of sixth grade). The students not only change schools but change from a self-contained teaching environment to one in which classes are completely departmentalized. Teacher expectations may also be different. Elementary teachers usually provide considerable guidance in library searches, but this is not necessarily the case with middle-school content-area teachers. In middle schools, any language arts skills, including library skills, are usually the responsibility of the language arts, or English, teacher. Often, however, students lack the skills they need to do reports in the content areas, so a major instructional shift is required. Introduce students to an appropriate skill before and at the time it is needed. Do not assume that students have mastered adequate library skills before coming to class. Table 13–3 indicates library skills to evaluate for upper-elementary or middle-school students.

For Your Development

1. If you are now teaching students, use the appropriate checklist (Tables 13–1, 13–2, or 13–3) to evaluate a student's library skills. What skills have reached the level of independence? What skills require further instruction?
2. Look at language arts textbooks used in elementary or middle schools. Choose a specific series and grade level and design a checklist of library skills to correspond with that series.

For Your Plan Book

Lesson Plan

A Unit for Teaching Library Skills (Upper-Elementary Grades and Middle School)

An effective way to supplement initial orientation visits to a library is to prepare a series of classroom tape presentations. Use the tapes to:

1. Introduce students to library facilities at the beginning of the year.
2. Reinforce the location of materials and facilitate their use when they are needed.
3. Introduce the library to students who transfer into class later in the year.
4. Organize an effective learning center on library skills.
5. Provide reinforcement and additional study for students who need more time to assimilate the necessary information.

In addition, make the tapes to fit the available library facilities and to present necessary information in a sequence the teachers and librarians consider most appropriate.

Lesson One: Introduction to the Library

Overview

Lead the students on a walking tour of the library that includes:

1. The location and a brief explanation of the most important physical facilities
2. A discussion of the rationale behind the usual behavior expected in libraries
3. An outline of regulations specific to the library the students will use.

Activities

To encourage students to reinforce the introductory information they have received from the tape, include some application activities. Put these activities on the tape or put them on cards and incorporate them into a learning center.

1. Draw a sketch of our school library, locating the following:
   a. Circulation desk
   b. Card catalog and/or computers
   c. Shelves
      (1) Fiction
      (2) Nonfiction
      (3) References
      (4) Periodicals
      (5) Audiovisual materials and CD-ROMs
2. Using your own materials and imagination, make a bookmark suitable for use in any book.
3. Using your own materials and imagination, make a cartoon or drawing that shows an important library regulation or encourages use of the library. You may use pictures cut from magazines and other periodicals. This cartoon or drawing can be notebook size.
4. Using your own materials and imagination, make a poster suitable for display in the library or a classroom illustrating a library regulation or encouraging use of the library.

Continued

5. Interview one of the librarians to find out what librarians do besides checking out books, and how someone prepares to become a librarian. Here are some questions you might ask (you can probably think of others):
   a. Who chooses books for the library and how are they chosen?
   b. What steps does the librarian go through to get a book on the shelf?
   c. What other tasks does a librarian do?
   d. How does a librarian learn what to do?
   e. What are the advantages and disadvantages of being a librarian?

Lesson Two: Arrangement of Books in the Library

Overview

This lesson is designed to:

1. Enable students to become proficient in locating books of fiction and biography.
2. Introduce students to the general arrangement of nonfiction books.
3. Introduce students to library classification systems.

Outline

By following this general outline, you can provide your students with the necessary information to become proficient in finding books in the library.

  I. Books of fiction
    A. General information
      1. Definition of fiction
      2. Distinction between full-length books of fiction and story collections
      3. Symbols often used on the spine to indicate a book of fiction and those often used to indicate a story collection
    B. How fiction books are arranged on shelves
      1. Alphabetically by author's name
      2. Alphabetically by title when several books are available by the same author (*a, an,* and *the* are disregarded in alphabetizing)
    C. How to use the card catalog and/or computers to locate a book of fiction
      1. Use of the title card to find the author
      2. Use of the subject index to select a book of interest

  II. Biography and autobiography
    A. General information
      1. Definitions of biography and autobiography
      2. Distinction between individual biographies and collective biographies
    B. How biographies are arranged on shelves
      1. Biographies and autobiographies
      2. Collective biography
    C. How to use the card catalog and/or computers to locate a biography

  III. Nonfiction books
    A. Distinction between fiction and nonfiction
      1. Definition of nonfiction
      2. Contrast with fiction. Often, teachers falsely assume that students have a clear concept of the distinction between fiction and nonfiction. Actually, many students have translated these two terms into "false" and "true." As a result, their concept of fiction is limited to books of fantasy, while their concept of nonfic-

tion includes all books about "real life." To have a common reference base, use popular television shows as examples to explore your students' concept of these two terms.

  3. Examples of nonfiction books

IV. Library classification systems

  A. Rationales behind library classification systems
    1. Need for order to provide easy access
    2. Desire to organize knowledge

  B. Two major classification systems used
    1. Library of Congress: formerly used with large libraries, such as universities, but now becoming popular in public libraries
    2. Dewey decimal system: still the most popular in school libraries

  C. General divisions of the Dewey decimal system. Avoid any temptation to get too detailed here. Students are to be users of a library, not librarians. However, many students are fascinated by learning what the numbers mean. You may wish to include an explanation of the interrelationship of the broad classifications of the Dewey system, as well as prepare a handout for the students.

Activities

1. Put the following books of fiction in the order they would appear on the shelf. Put author's name first.

The Call of the Wild—London	*Mary Poppins Comes Back—Travers*
The Witch of Blackbird Pond—Speare	*And Now Miguel—Krumgold*
The Bronze Bow—Speare	*It's Like This, Cat—Neville*
The Secret Garden—Burnett	*Mary Poppins—Travers*
The Voyages of Dr. Dolittle—Lofting	*The Big Road—Clarke*
Charlotte's Web—White	

2. Find the answers to these questions about our school library and write them on notebook paper.
   a. How are fiction books marked?
   b. How are biographies marked?
   c. How are collective biographies marked?
   d. How are story collections marked?

3. On the plan of our library you made for Lesson One, locate the biography shelves. Using the card catalog and/or computers find a title and its author, and mark whether biography or autobiography, for the following:
   a. a president of the United States
   b. a sports figure
   c. a famous woman

4. Survey the biography shelves in the library to locate:
   a. three books about one famous person.
   b. a collective biography that contains an article on that person.
   c. any three biographies.
   List the title and author of each book and write a short identification of the subject of each book. Arrange your list in the order these should be found on the shelves.

5. Making the Dewey system work for you:
   a. Make a chart of the ten main classifications. List two types of books you would find in that category.

Continued

Example: 000–009 General works: encyclopedias, dictionaries

   b. Using your chart, give the general numbers (for example, 500) for the following types of books:

     (1) American history   (5) How to build a house
     (2) Basketball   (6) Teenage problems
     (3) Poetry   (7) Greek gods
     (4) Chemistry

   c. Give the general numbers (for example, 500) of sections where you would expect to find the following titles:

John Paul Jones   *Stars for Sam*
Alligators and Crocodiles   *Pioneer Art in America*
History of South America   *Poems Every Child Should Know*
The Yellow Fairy Book   *Myths of Greece and Rome*
Mathematics Made Easy   *America Sings*

6. Use the card catalog to find a biography or autobiography of each of the following persons, and list the titles and authors of the books. Look through the book to answer these questions:
   a. Approximately when did this person live?
   b. What nation claims this person?
   c. What was this person's main occupation?

Louisa May Alcott   Richard Byrd
Hans Christian Andersen   Cleopatra
Louis Armstrong   Coronado
John James Audubon   Bob Cousy
Benedict Arnold   Althea Gibson
Johann Sebastian Bach   G. Marconi
P. T. Barnum   Jim Thorpe
Clara Barton

7. Make a set of posters illustrating the classifications of the Dewey decimal system.

Used with permission of Mary Russell, an English professor who teaches courses in English and language arts methods.

Reference Skills

Why is it so important for students to develop effective reference skills? Think for a moment about the last time you were required to write a factual report or research paper. Where did you look for information? What sources did you use? Did you read an entire reference book? How did you know where to find what you needed? How did you pull together ideas from various sources to write your final report? As a college student, the task was probably fairly easy for you. The first time you had to write a report, however, you probably found the assignment anything but easy. You may have been confused about where to locate information or what to do with the reference books after you finally found them.

To use a library successfully, students must know which references to use and where they are located. There are also prerequisite skills for using dictionaries, encyclopedias, and card catalogs. Have you ever watched children grope through a dictionary when they do not have sufficient skills in alphabetizing? Alphabetizing is equally important for locating information in encyclopedias and card catalogs. Furthermore, to find information in encyclopedias, card catalogs, and reader's guides, students must be able to identify categories under which to look. Whereas formal dictionary, encyclopedia, and card-catalog instruction may not begin until about fourth grade, readiness for these sophisticated skills begins earlier.

The Primary Grades

Even first-grade children can use the easy picture dictionaries published for them. In these dictionaries, a picture is used to define each word entry. Introduce these books when children are discussing the meaning of a new word in a reading class or during early writing activities to help them see how to use a dictionary to find the proper spelling of a word. The pictures and words are alphabetized, so you can also introduce the concept of alphabetizing.

Language Experience Word Banks.   Word cards, normally used in the primary grades, may be used to develop alphabetizing skills. A word card contains a word that a child should know. A collection of word cards forms a word bank for individualized instruction. As the number of word cards increases, the children experience more difficulty in locating specific words for their writing activities. Therefore, the need for an efficient way of grouping word cards becomes apparent. First, alphabetize the word cards according to the first letters, then according to the second and third letters (Figure 13–1).

Class-Made Picture Dictionaries.   Another activity that allows children to practice alphabetizing skills is constructing individual and class picture dictionaries. Picture dictionaries can center around specific categories, such as animals or famous people. Have the children start with one page for each letter (for example, *ant, bee, cat*) and later add pages that require alphabetical arrangement according to second letter (for example, *ladybug, lion, lobster, lynx*) and third letter (for example, *ladybug, lamb*). They can draw the accompanying pictures or cut them from newspapers and magazines. Real photographs also add interest to picture dictionaries.

Class Telephone Books.   The telephone directory is another source that requires understanding of alphabetical order. Have the students examine real telephone directories to see how they are organized. Then, have them assemble a class telephone directory that contains the same kind of information.

FIGURE 13–1   Alphabetized Word Cards

Manipulative Objects.   Alphabet blocks allow children to practice putting the letters in sequential order. Children can also string wooden beads with printed letters in alphabetical order. To make an inexpensive alphabet tray, fill an old cookie sheet with damp sand or plaster of paris. Carve the letters into the sand or plaster of paris with a blunt object, such as a tongue depressor. Let the students use the tray to trace the letters with their fingers as they recite the alphabet.

Encyclopedias.   Primary-grade children are not too young to be introduced to encyclopedias. Show them how to develop their own encyclopedia by creating a picture file and arranging subject words in alphabetical order. Have them list categories, such as animals, cities, families, farms, holidays, houses, seasons, transportation, and weather, on dividers. Then, have them place pictures and other information under the appropriate subject. As the encyclopedia gets larger, materials will fall into more than one category. The need for an index will then become apparent.

Card Catalogs.   To use a card catalog or computerized card catalog effectively, children must eventually understand three classifications: title, author, and subject. Primary children can begin to understand the card catalog by constructing a simple catalog for the books in their classroom library. Class discussion will lead to several suggestions for arranging the books, and usually someone will mention alphabetical order by author's name or by title. Children should first concentrate on one kind of classification, and put the necessary information for each book on a 3- by 5-inch index card, then arrange the finished cards by alphabetical order in a file box. Whichever method they begin with, children soon realize that more than one arrangement of categorizing and filing can be useful. If the library is using a computer system for cataloging, students will require instruction in the use of the computer.

An Integrated Approach.   Keel (1985) identifies the following practices to improve the instruction of library media skills:

1. Teach children only the skills they need, at the time they need them.
2. Make instruction specific, simple, practical, brief, and entertaining.
3. Involve as many senses as possible in the presentation.
4. Lead children to discover conclusions for themselves.
5. Give them opportunities to use new skills as soon as possible.
6. Give each child praise, encouragement, and guidance. (p. 51)

Keel teaches library skills lessons that coincide with the beginning of various social studies units. To meet a multimedia goal and involve as many senses as possible, she uses filmstrips, pictures, charts, posters, transparencies, tape recordings, records, and slides. For example, when introducing the reference skills for a third-grade study of Mexico, she uses Mexican folk music and a narrated slide presentation showing children how to locate the subject heading "Mexico," where to find books about Mexico in the library, and how to find books most useful in answering specific questions about Mexico. Later, she teaches children how to find and use other materials about Mexico, such as those found in filmstrips, picture files, vertical files, and recordings.

The Intermediate Grades

Formal instruction in reference skills usually begins about fourth grade. At this point, children have developed enough reading skills to use easy-to-read dictionaries and encyclopedias. Some children are already quite proficient, whereas others require considerable formal instruction.

Alphabetizing.   Intermediate-grade teachers should have children progress from simple to more demanding alphabetizing skills in order to discover which students still require assistance in alphabetizing. Have the students begin by alphabetizing a list of words by initial letters: *frog, count, vine, round, light, antler, water, peace.* Students who have difficulty with this task may need to work on the readiness activities suggested for primary grades, especially the alphabet tray and other manipulative devices.

Next, ask students to alphabetize a list of words according to second letters: *after, avenue, apple, air, able, amount, acrobat, attic.* Then, have them alphabetize according to the third letter of a word: *dew, death, deck, detail, debate, defend, design, delight.* Finally, have them alphabetize according to the fourth letter of a word: *stress, strong, stray, struggle, stride.* Similar lessons can require students to alphabetize given different levels of difficulty. Use envelopes filled with word cards of different combinations for alphabetizing according to first letter, second letter, and so forth, for individualized instruction and additional practice.

Dictionaries.   To find words quickly in a dictionary, a student must understand the function of and be able to use guide words. Even when students know how to alphabetize, they often ignore the guide words at the top of dictionary pages. Approach this understanding inductively. For example, have the students open their dictionaries to a specific page and ask them to examine it carefully to see how it is organized. After they have discovered the organization, have them look at the tops of the pages to see what is printed at the left and the right sides of each. Next, have them try to decide how the two words at the top of the page were chosen. They will usually deduce quickly that the word on the left is the first word on the page and the word on the right is the last word on the page. Then, have them look at other pages to see if this generalization is true for all pages and also for other dictionaries. Tell the students that these words are called *guide words.* Guide words help dictionary users locate a word quickly because all words on the page must come after the left-hand guide word and before the right-hand guide word.

You may use a skeleton dictionary to focus attention on guide words. The skeleton dictionary lessons come after an introduction to a dictionary and demonstration of its organization. A skeleton dictionary consists of several pages containing only guide words and page numbers; the pages should correspond to a classroom dictionary used for instruction. Figure 13–2 is an example of a skeleton dictionary page. Students should compare the skeleton pages with the real dictionary and then indicate where certain words would appear in the skeleton dictionary, explain why they would be on a certain page, and verify the location with the real dictionary. Finally, from another list of words, the students should locate the guide words that appear on the page containing a specific word and verify that the word is actually on that page.

Another dictionary skill that needs practice is locating the correct definition for a word from the multiple definitions presented. Some students have a tendency to read only the first definition after a word and ignore the remaining information. One student interpreted the sentence "John will fast all day Friday" as "John will be held firmly to some object all day Friday, because fast means to fasten firmly." This problem results from dictionary practice in which students find the meanings of words presented in isolation. To stress multiple meanings, list several sentences using the same word with different meanings:

1. The clock is *fast;* it shows 5:00.
2. The boat was tied *fast* to the dock.
3. The Olympic runner was very *fast.*
4. It was a holy day, so the monk had to *fast.*

FIGURE 13–2 A Skeleton
Dictionary Page

| ground | 318 | guard |

Are these words on this dictionary page: *grumble, green, guess, gruff, gypsy, great, growl*? Why or why not?

Ask for a definition of the word *fast*. Then, discuss with the students whether that definition makes sense in each sentence. Next, ask the students to look up *fast* in the dictionary, notice how many meanings are given, and find the correct definition as it applies to each sentence.

Dictionary races give children practice in finding words. For a dictionary race, write a sentence on the board with one word underlined. Allot points to each team that finds a word first, gives the correct guide words on the page, gives the correct meaning, pronounces the word correctly, gives the correct part of speech, and gives correct synonyms and antonyms.

Encyclopedias. In the intermediate grades, children begin using an encyclopedia for reference. The encyclopedias available in libraries are written for different levels of ability. Thus, it will be helpful to both teacher and students to know what reading level each encyclopedia requires. The following encyclopedias are identified according to different ability groups:

1. Upper elementary (fourth grade and higher): *Britannica Junior* (Chicago: Encyclopedia Britannica); *The World Book Encyclopedia* (Chicago: Field Enterprises Educational Corp.).
2. Upper elementary and middle school: *Compton's Encyclopedia* (Chicago: F. E. Compton & Co.).
3. Middle school and high school: *Collier's Encyclopedia* (New York: Crowell Collier & Macmillan); *Encyclopedia International* (New York: Grolier).
4. High school, college, and adult: *Encyclopedia Americana* (New York: Americana Corp.); *The Encyclopedia Britannica* (Chicago: Encyclopedia Britannica).

Card Catalogs.   If intermediate-grade children have made classroom card catalogs, they already understand the function of author, title, and subject cards. Some intermediate children may have been using a library card catalog since early primary grades, whereas other children have no understanding of the system.

There are three things to teach intermediate-grade children about a card catalog: (1) the abbreviations used on the cards (for example, © *1997* means *copyright, 1997; 127 pp. illus.* means the book has 127 pages and contains illustrations); (2) cross-reference cards direct users to other sources of information; and (3) call numbers indicate where to find a book in the library. Instruction in these three areas may take only a few lessons for some children, but it is extremely important that all children digest the information thoroughly, regardless of how long it takes. One fourth-grade teacher, for example, introduces her students to the card catalog by having them put on a play about the card catalog, adapted from a play printed in *Instructor* (Tompkins, 1971). The play introduces Charlie Catalog, Art Author, Terry Title, Sam Subject, Dewey Decimal, Ruthie Reference, Dottie Dictionary, Al Atlas, Amy Almanac, and Ed Encyclopedia.

After presenting the play, the students make an author card, a title card, and a subject card for the same book. Next, they use the card catalog in the library to search for answers to questions such as the following:

Who is the author of _____?

What books has _____ written?

How many pages does the book _____ have?

What books might help us find out more information about Mars?

This teacher gives the children many opportunities to use the card catalog and guides them while they use the references.

The Upper-Elementary Grades and Middle School

In the upper-elementary grades and in middle school, review and refine reference skills through instruction requiring students to use encyclopedias, card catalogs, and computerized card catalogs, and other references designed for specific content areas.

Further Reference Instruction

Once you have introduced your students to the library, you may want to encourage them to use the library facilities to find information. Two of the most useful tools are the card catalog and computerized card catalog. The following activities and exercises may prove helpful in designing instruction on the card and computerized card catalog.

1. On manila folders or cardboard notebook covers, prepare sample author, title, and subject cards that contain only essential information, so the students can learn the location of the information they will use.

2. Prepare exercises that will give students practice in interpreting the information on cards. For example, using a sample subject card, have them answer the following questions:

What is the title?

What is the call number?

Who is the author?

When was the book published?

Where was it published?

Who published it?

How many pages?

What does *illus.* mean?

What kind of card is this one?

Under what letter of the alphabet would this card be filed?

Then, from the information on the sample subject card, have them prepare sample author and title cards.

For Your Development

Develop an instructional lesson plan to teach a reference skill at the primary, intermediate, upper-elementary, or middle-school level. If you are now teaching, present the lesson to a group of children. If you are not teaching, present the lesson to a group of your peers.

The Technology Revolution and the Language Arts

What do we know about the effectiveness of technology to improve instructional content in the language arts? The *Report of the National Reading Panel* (2000) found few studies that related to reading and computer technology. The panel concluded: "Computer technology is different from other areas the NRP analyzed. It cannot be studied independently of instructional content and is not an instructional method in itself" (p. 17). The panel used limited findings to conclude that the seven studies that added speech to computer-presented text suggested that this may be a promising use of technology in relation to reading. The panel stated "the use of computers as word processors may be very useful given that reading instruction is most effective when combined with writing instruction. Striking in its absence is research on the incorporation of Internet applications to reading instruction. . . . In sum, the panel is encouraged by the reported success in the use of technology for reading instruction, but relatively few specific instructional applications can be gleaned from the research. Many questions need to be answered" (p. 18).

Although the NRP found no research supporting Internet applications, language arts teachers cannot ignore the Internet. In studies sited by Minkel (April 2002a), various forms of media are very influential in children's lives. For example, most children watch television for three to five hours every day and at least 60 percent of families with children have Internet access at home. Minkel's concern is that "few young people receive training in media literacy—in how to evaluate what they are looking at for bias and accuracy" (p. 31). To overcome concerns related to the use of the Internet, Minkel maintains that students need to be taught about the meaning of intellectual property and plagiarism.

Introducing Technology through Literature

Books that focus on authors who develop stories related to computer technology provide interesting motivation for computer-related vocabulary and understanding. For example, in Susan Cooper's *The Boggart* (1993), two young people inherit a Scottish castle and a mischievous spirit that comes with it. After the children accidentally transport the Boggart back to Canada with them, they must use computer technology to help the Boggart return to Scotland.

Using Cooper's book, you may ask students to discover and discuss the vocabulary words associated with technology that appear throughout the book such as the following: *keyboard, computer screen, megahertz, computer workstation, thirty-four-inch color monitor, hard drive, bit, computer games, virus, antivirus program, into-loop, lapsing into computalk, the computer will crash, voice synthesis, copy a file,* and *transferring files.*

To involve students even more with technology and this book, ask them to search on the Internet for images and information about ancient Scotland, the Scottish highlands, Scottish castles, and ghosts or legends of Scotland. They could work alone, in pairs, or in small groups. For example, to get them started with a search, students could do a country search for Scotland under United Kingdom at http://www.yahooligans.com. Another useful site that provides information on ancient and modern Scotland is BBC Online (http:www.bbc.co.uk/history/scottishhistory). A related BBC site (http://www.bbc.co.uk/history/forkids) is aimed at younger students. It offers a "walk through time" with a chronological time line of Scottish history for children ages seven to nine. Castles of Britain (http://www.castles-of-Britain.com) has pictures of castles, a listing of "castle ghosts" of Scotland, and a "Castle Learning Center," which presents information about everyday life in medieval Scotland including what it was like to live in a castle. Students could compare and contrast medieval life in a castle with the modern experiences of the family that inherits the castle. They could also compare and contrast medieval life in a castle with their own lives at home.

Other books that could be used to introduce technology through literature include Elizabeth Levy's *The Creepy Computer Mystery* (1996) and Seymour Simon's *Einstein Anderson, Science Detective: The On-Line Spaceman and Other Stories* (1997).

Writing and Publishing Book Reviews on the Internet

Another way to relate literature to technology, to improve critical reading skills, and to respond to the writing of other students is to write a book review that will be published on a website. You may begin by discussing with students some of the different components of a good review.

Students are less intimidated than adults in reviewing, evaluating, and utilizing multimedia resources.

First, the review should summarize the plot of the story in a few sentences: What was the story about, who were the main characters, what did the main characters do in the story, and who was your favorite character and why? Second, the review may relate to a personal experience: Could you relate to any of the characters? Have you ever done the same things that the characters have done or felt the same way? Third, the review might include your opinion about the book: Did you like the book, what was your favorite part, what was your least favorite part, and what would you change? Fourth, the review might include a recommendation: Would you recommend this book to another person and who would like this book?

You should ask students to read their reviews to the class and to make any necessary revisions in the reviews. Now you could have students read examples of reviews written by other children. Book reviews written by children and published on the Internet can be found at sites such as these:

Education Place (http://www.eduplace.com/kids/rdg/chall.html)

Kids Bookshelf (http://www.kidsbookshelf.com/kidserv.asp)

Read Write Now (http://yahooligans.com/school_bell/language_arts/book_reviews)

Spaghetti Book Club (http://www.spaghettibookclub.org/index.shtml)

World of Reading (http://www.worldreading.org)

Students may submit their reviews to an Internet site that publishes reviews written by children. They may also read reviews written by other students about the same book. They can write a response to these reviews. Did they agree with the review? What did they disagree with in the review? What is missing in the review? What is the strength of the review? What would make the review stronger?

Bringing Specialists into the Classroom through the Internet

Articles such as McLaughlin's "Mentors Log On to Help Students Make the Grade" (1997) stress how classes can bring field experts into the classroom via the Internet. Field specialists from universities, businesses, government, or other schools can serve as electronic mentors to students who want to explore specific topics of study. There are several ways to contact field experts. For example, useful lists of e-mail addresses for subject area experts can be found at Ask an Expert (http://www.askanexpert.com/askanexpert). You can also post a request for participation on the Internet or write or call individuals to request their participation.

The Electronic Emissary Project (http://emissary.ots.utexas.edu/emissary/index.html) is an online matching service that helps teachers locate experts in different disciplines who use the Internet and who are willing to engage in electronic exchanges with teachers and students. This service also helps volunteer experts, teachers, and students to structure a mentoring project and share what they learn with other students through e-mail. Other useful sites include Community Learning Network (http://www.cln.org), Ask A+ Locator (http://www.vrd.org/locator), and Ask Eric (http://ericir.syr.edu). Another excellent source for websites is the *School Library Journal*. Each month the journal includes recommendations for effective websites.

A virtual field trip to the White House in Washington, D.C., and research associated with the White House is available through the White House website (http://www.whitehouse.gov). The White House website includes press releases and presidential speeches as well as history and information about past presidents and first ladies. It is basically user friendly for students in upper elementary and middle school. The White House for Kids website (http://www.whitehouse.gov/kids/presidentsday) has been specifically designed for younger children and can be accessed from within the main White House website. The White House for Kids website includes a newspaper addressed to children. It also provides a virtual tour of the White House and links to information about U.S. history, the presidency, the first family, and children and pets who have lived there. Older students may explore "America's Timeline to Freedom" presented on the White House website. The site includes such subjects as: Lydia the Unlikely Spy, the Underground Railroad, the Statue of Liberty, the beginning of the March of Dimes, and the Berlin airlift.

A primary source for historical documents is the Library of Congress On-line (http://www.loc.gov). The special collection "American Memory" is particularly interesting because it includes documents, motion pictures, photographs, and sound recordings that trace different aspects of the American experience. One of the virtual exhibits in American Memory is called "Words and Deeds in American History: Selected Documents Celebrating the Manuscript Division's First 100 Years." This exhibit contains original works that have been copied and transferred into digitized images. (Lesson plans designed to develop complete directions for using these and other Internet sources are found in *Language Arts Activities for Children,* Norton & Norton, 2003.)

For Your Development

The April 2002 edition of *School Library Journal* includes an annotated bibliography of notable videos, recordings, software, and websites evaluated and selected by the Association for Library Service to Children. Page 63 presents websites entitled "ASPCA's Animalland," "Building Big," "The Children's Museum of Indianapolis Fun On-line Page," "Cool Science for Curious Kids," "Coolmath.com," "Lemony Snicket," "Secrets of the Lost Empires: Medieval Siege," "Soda Constructor," and "Ways of Knowing Trail." With a group of your peers select and view several of these websites. Why do you believe that they were selected as "notable" by the Association for Library Service to Children? With your class, develop a set of guidelines for excellent websites.

Issues Connected with Using and Teaching through Websites

Two issues are currently making the use of websites without teacher instruction hazardous to young learners: How authentic and reliable is the information on the websites and how can teachers help reduce the increasing use of online plagiarism?

The ability to evaluate materials on the Internet is of particular importance when teachers are preparing students to use inquiry-based learning. This type of learning according to Owens, Hester, and Teale (2002) requires that "[s]tudents select a topic of interest to research; they formulate questions about the topic; gather, sift, and synthesize information; and finally do something with it. The last component is often the most difficult aspect for many students, but it is what distinguishes inquiry-based projects from typical school research projects. . . . When inquiry-based learning is used well, students engage in 'What does this mean, and how can I use this information?' (p. 617). They conclude that to use this type of teaching "[s]tudents must learn how to judge the accuracy and legitimacy of their sources in ways they may not have used in the past" (p. 623).

"Gullible's Travels" is the title of an article in which Block (2002) argues that students must be taught to "guard against misinformation, disinformation, and spin on the net" (p. 12). Block cites research that shows that 76 percent of regular Internet users believe they can obtain everything that they need to know from the Internet and that 51 percent believe that the most accurate information is found on the Internet. Block concludes that "librarians and teachers must train students in the skills of discernment when it comes to the Internet" (p. 12).

She lists a number of questions that students should ask themselves about various websites: Am I being manipulated? What are the site developers trying to sell me or to make me believe? Does the information of the site make sense when I compare it with what I know about the topic? Can I verify the statistics and the other information on the website through other published sources? Block includes a list of sixteen sites that teachers may use to help students become more skeptical about Internet content and to show them the need to verify information found on the web. A few of these sites include the following:

CDC Health-Related Hoaxes and Rumors (http://www.cdc.gov/hoax_rumors.htm)

Statistical Resources on the Web (http://www.lib.umich.edu/govdocs/stats.html)

The Virtual Chase: Groups That Alert the Public to Internet Fraud, Fanaticism, and Bad Information (http://www.virtualchase.com/quality/alert.html)

How important is plagiarism? How much damage does it do to an understanding of and the development of students who will hopefully develop a respect for scholarship? This issue of plagiarism is one of the greatest issues for both university classes and public schools. In a recent special presentation on plagiarism on National Public Radio's "All Things Considered" (2002), one of the panelists cited the major culprit in plagiarism as the Internet and said "The most Internet cheating results from cutting and pasting."

Walter Minkel, the technology editor of *School Library Journal* (April 2002b), cites an increased permissiveness among a cut-and-paste generation of students and their parents who do not understand that it is wrong to copy. To develop his points, Minkel quotes a Pew Internet & American Life Project that finds that 94 percent of students with access to the web use it for research and 71 percent of these students use it for their main information for school projects. Minkel concludes, "But the Web has turned out to be a double-edged sword: while providing swift access to sought-after information, it has made cheating irresistibly easy and more pervasive" (p. 51). Numerous studies show that students are not adverse to plagiarizing from Internet sites when they write their papers.

To overcome plagiarism, teachers need to define plagiarism for students and show them how to recognize it and how to credit works of others correctly. Students need to understand that when they plagiarize they are not learning the useful research skills that they will need throughout their education. Students must understand that plagiarism at many universities will result in expulsion. In other situations plagiarism results in law suits.

As we all know, it is not always difficult to identify plagiarism in the work of our students. When their papers are written at a level, either linguistically or contextual, that is above their usual work, we question the authenticity of the paper. Teachers are discovering that with the advent of the Internet they have to change their assignments. Minkel states (April 2002b), "Educators need to give students assignments that require traditional sources of research that do not revolve around the Web. Students should also be required to list their references" (p. 53). Beginning with early elementary classes, assignments should be designed that discourage copying and pasting.

Several websites are available that can help teachers combat plagiarism. For example, "Plagiarism: What It Is and How to Recognize and Avoid It" (http://www.indiana.edu/~wts/wts/plagiarism.html) is from the Indiana University's Tutorial Service. This site recommends that students put quotations around everything that comes from a text and check paraphrases against the original text to make sure that they are not plagiarizing.

For Your Development

Develop a lesson plan in which you teach students to understand plagiarism.

1. Include a definition for plagiarism such as the following: *Plagiarism is the failure to give credit to another person's writing or ideas.* Stress that these ideas and words are part of a person's intellectual property. Discuss with students how they would feel if someone stole their ideas and claimed the ideas belonged to them.
2. Discuss with students how plagiarism actually hurts the students by not teaching them how to use research skills and to develop their own ideas.
3. Share examples with students to show them how easy it may be for the teacher to identify papers that have been plagiarized.
4. Teach students how to cite websites as part of their references.
5. Share with students that many schools ask students to sign a "Code of Honor" that refers to not cheating or plagiarizing. Ask the students to develop such a Code of Honor for their class.
6. You may ask students to review websites that are designed to recognize and to combat plagiarism. You might use the following examples:
   The New Plagiarism: Seven Antidotes to Prevent Highway Robbery in an Electronic Age (http://www.fno.org/May98/cov98may.html) Noodletools (http://www.noodletools.com)
   Plagiarism Stoppers: A Teacher's Guide (http://www.ncusd203.org/central/where/plagiarism_stoppers.html)
7. Ask the students to develop their own guide for recognizing and combating plagiarism.

For Your Development

Evaluate the websites recommended earlier in the text for elementary education. Is Walter Minkel (January, 2001) correct when he states that the vast number of these sites that are targeted for K–3 are not "developmentally appropriate for kids under third grade, and are not really appropriate for whole classrooms of kids until fourth grade?" (p. 41).

1. You can evaluate several of the sites discussed by Minkel such as Charlotte-Mecklenburg County Library's "Storyplace" (http://www.storyplace.org) that he considers appropriate for children under grade 3 because the site requires little adult assistance. Why do you believe that Minkel recommends this site for younger children?
2. You can compare the "storyplace" site with the ones found on sites such as the History/Social Sciences section of SCORE (Schools of California Online Resources for Education), which he believes are too difficult for students under third grade. One such site that he mentions is "Kid's Window—Learn About Japan" (http://www.jwindow.net/category/kids.html) that is recommended for first graders. Why do you believe that Minkel believes that this site is too difficult for younger children?
3. Develop a list of websites that could be used at the lower-elementary, middle-elementary, and upper-elementary levels. What is your criteria for placing each website in each developmental area?

SUMMARY

School libraries no longer house only books. They have become media centers emphasizing both nonprint and print media. Access to a good school library increases both the number and variety of books students read. Methods for acquiring free or inexpensive materials for classrooms include (1) asking parents for donations of used children's books, (2) paperback book exchanges, (3) requesting donations of used reference periodicals, and (4) writing letters to request free or inexpensive materials.

Library skills are essential for finding materials efficiently. Such skills are necessary for the development of independent study skills, positive attitudes toward investigation, interest in functional and recreational reading, and knowledge about libraries that will last a lifetime. Do not leave library skills to incidental learning.

Students need to know which references to use, where the references are located, and how to use them efficiently. Instruction in the primary grades emphasizes readiness and prerequisite skills, such as alphabetizing, class-made picture dictionaries, class telephone directories, manipulative objects, learning centers, encyclopedias, and computerized card catalogs. Formal instruction in reference skills usually begins in the intermediate grades and includes dictionary skills, such as alphabetizing; using guide words; locating correct definitions for multiple definitions; determining pronunciation; and finding synonyms, antonyms, and parts of speech. Students are also taught to use encyclopedias, computerized card catalogs, and other library references. The upper-elementary and middle-school grades review and refine these skills.

An important portion of this chapter focused on technology and the language arts. The chapter discussed introducing technology through literature, writing and publishing book reviews on the Internet, bringing specialists into the classroom through the Internet, and issues connected with using and teaching through websites.

ADDITIONAL LIBRARY AND REFERENCE SKILLS ACTIVITIES

1. Visit several school, public, and/or university libraries. Interview the librarians. What reference skills do the librarians believe students and adults require?
2. Look at an elementary language arts scope and sequence. What library and reference skills are included? At what grade levels is instruction recommended?
3. Look at several journals such as *Book List* and *School Library Journal* that review literature. If possible, find references to nonprint media. Compile a current list of recommended nonprint media and share it with your language arts class.
4. Interview a media center specialist at your university. What changes does the specialist believe will occur during the next ten years? How will these changes affect the language arts program?
5. Select several dictionaries or encyclopedias designed to be used with early elementary grades, middle-elementary grades, and upper-elementary grades. Compare the readability levels, content, and illustrations.
6. Conduct a debate on the usefulness of computers in the elementary classrooms. Several sources that stress various viewpoints include Clifford Stoll's "Who Needs Computers?" (2001). A quote from his article could be the focus for the debate: "From an educational perspective, computers often do kids more harm than good, says a leading

critic. In fact, a great school doesn't need them" (p. 46). Another article might include Walter Minkel's "Pew Study Shows Students Prefer Web to Library" (2001).

7. Read an article that discusses planning and directing a school library program such as "The New & Improved School Library: How One District Planned for the Future" (Johnson, 1995). If possible, discuss the information with a school librarian. Share your responses with your language arts class.

BIBLIOGRAPHY

Allington, Richard; and Cunningham, Patricia M. *Schools That Work: Where All Children Read and Write,* 2nd edition. Boston: Allyn & Bacon, 2002.

Anderson, R.; Hiebert, E.; Scott, J.; and Wilkinson, I. *Becoming a Nation of Readers: The Report of the Commission on Reading.* Washington, D.C.: National Institute of Education, 1985.

"Association for Library Service to Children's 2002 Notable Videos, Recording, Software & Web Sites for Children." *School Library Journal* 48 (April 2002): 58–63.

Block, Marylaine. "Gullible's Travels." *School Library Journal Net Connect* (Spring 2002): 12–14.

Cullinan, B.; Greene, E.; and Jaggar, A. "Books, Babies, and Libraries: The Librarian's Role in Literacy Development." *Language Arts* 67 (1990): 750–55.

Dales, B. "Trusting Relations between Teachers and Librarians." *Language Arts* 67 (1990): 732–34.

Harrington, Drew. "Six Trends in Library Design." *School Library Journal Supplement: 2002 Buyer's Guide and Web Site Directory* (December 2001): 12–14.

Hiebert, E.; Mervar, K.; and Person, D. "Research Directions: Children's Selection of Trade Books in Libraries and Classrooms." *Language Arts* 67 (1990): 758–63.

Johnson, Doug. "The New & Improved School Library: How One District Planned for the Future." *School Library Journal* 41 (June 1995): 36–39.

Keel, Helen. "Library Skills." In *Instruction in School Library Media Center Use (K–12),* edited by Thomas L. Hart. Chicago: American Library Association, 1985.

Kozol, Jonathan. "An Unequal Education." *School Library Journal* 45 (May 2000): 46–49.

Lamme, L.; and Ledbetter, L. "Libraries: The Heart of Whole Language." *Language Arts* 67 (1990): 735–41.

Margolis, Rick. "The Best Little Library in Texas." *School Library Journal* 47 (January 2001): 54–58.

McLaughlin, Abraham T. "Mentors Log on to Help Students Make the Grade." *Christian Science Monitor* (May 22, 1997): 1.

Miller, Marilyn; and Shontz, Marilyn. "How Does Your Library Measure Up?" *School Library Journal* 45 (October 1999): 50–59.

Minkel, Walter. "Media Literacy—Part of the Curriculum?" *School Library Journal* 48 (April 2002a): 31.

_____. "Not So Elementary." *School Library Journal* 47 (January 2001): 41.

_____. "Pew Study Shows Students Prefer Web to Library." *School Library Journal* 47 (October 2001): 26.

_____. "Web of Deceit." *School Library Journal* 48 (April 2002b): 50–53.

National Public Radio. "All Things Considered." May 21, 2002.

Norton, Donna E.; and Norton, Saundra E. *Language Arts Activities for Children,* 5th ed. Upper Saddle River, N.J.: Merrill/Prentice Hall, 2003.

Owens, Roxanne; Hester, Jennifer L.; and Teale, William H. "Where Do You Want to Go Today? Inquiry-Based Learning and Technology Integration." *The Reading Teacher* 55 (April 2002): 616–25.

Report of the National Reading Panel. Washington, D.C.: National Institute of Child Health and Human Development, December 2000.

Spiegel, D. L. "Content Bias in Reference and Study Skills." *The Reading Teacher* 44 (1990): 64–66.

Stoll, Clifford. "Who Needs Computers?" *School Library Journal* 47 (October 2001): 46–49.

Tompkins, Sister Mary Denis. "A Friend in Need." *Instructor* 81 (November 1971): 90–91.

Walter, Virginia A. "Lindbergh Takes Off." *School Library Journal* 48 (January 2002): 46–49.

CHILDREN'S LITERATURE REFERENCES

Cooper, Susan. *The Boggart.* New York: Macmillan, 1993.

Levy, Elizabeth. *The Creepy Computer Mystery.* New York: Scholastic, 1996.

Simon, Seymour. *Einstein Anderson, Science Detective: The On-Line Spaceman and Other Stories.* New York: Morrow, 1997.

Name Index

Subject Index